Contents

Introduction for the student

People, Communication and Organisations in this new edition represents a fourth major revision and reworking of a text first published some twelve years ago.

In undertaking the research for each of its four new editions, I have been impressed – and sometimes astonished – at the sheer pace of change and advance in the world of organisational communication systems which support people's interpersonal relationships and networks at work.

New developments in telecommunications are now occurring in *yearly cycles*, instead of the thirty-year cycles of Marconi's time, some ninety years ago. Everyone working in business and the public service is nowadays having to accept and master new skills and new office equipment technologies, as each new cycle of invention extends the boundaries of communication and information systems.

This new edition of *People, Communication and Organisations* has therefore been entirely reviewed and most extensively revised so that you have available to you help and guidance on the latest communication practices, systems, office electronic equipment, and organisational customs. However, you must determine – from the very outset – to keep abreast of your field of study, not only during the period of your course, but throughout your career! Only in this way will you hold on to job security and promotion prospects by maintaining and developing your marketable skills in an ever-changing business world. And always remember, the computer has not yet been designed which is as complex, fascinating, versatile and demanding as – people in organisations!

Good luck, and good studying!

Desmond W Evans

Acknowledgements

The author gratefully acknowledges the help, advice and support – including permission to reproduce copyright material – supplied by the people and organisations listed below. Without their generous interest and assistance, the illustrative concept of this textbook could not have been attained.

Aldus Europe Limited
British Telecom
IBM United Kingdom Limited
Muirfax Systems Limited
Torus Systems Limited

The author and publishers have made every effort to trace ownership of all copyright material and to obtain permission from the owners of the copyright.

In particular, the author wishes to acknowledge his indebtedness to Macdonald & Evans and their authors, for permission to access the following texts as references and for permission to use charts and diagrams taken from them:

Administration in Business 2nd Edition, Josephine Shaw, 1984
Quantitative Approaches in Business Studies, 2nd Edition, Clare Morris, 1989
Data Processing 5th Edition, R G Anderson, 1984
Organisation and Methods 2nd Edition R G Anderson, 1980
Pocket Guide to Programming John Shelley, 1982

The author wishes to thank the following for permission to reprint material:

Chichester College of Technology, Board of Governors
Oxford University Press
Penguin Books Limited
West Sussex County Council
Scientific American
McGraw-Hill Inc.
G Langley
Hoover Limited
The Plessey Company plc
The Coca-Cola Company, Atlanta GA
BBC Radio Light Entertainment
Chichester District Council
Pitman Publishing
Waterlow Business Supplies
GEC Plessey Telecommunications Limited
Mar-Com Systems Limited
Informix Software Limited
Compsoft plc

Microsoft Corporation USA
SPSS (UK) Limited
Ferranti GTE Limited
Lake Publishing Company
Methuen and Co., Publishers
Western Riverside Waste Authority
Centaur Limited
Michael Joseph Limited
John Offord (Publications) Limited
Fretwell-Downing Data Systems Limited
Select Offices Chichester
C H Longley (Rinnai UK)
British Telecom International
The Chartered Institute of Bankers
Professor Alec Rodger
NFER Publishing Company
Chichester & District Angling Society
US Bureau of Labour Statistics
Dr Peter Zorkoczy
Invalid Children's Aid Association
Ron Grant Advisory Teacher Reading
Warner-Lambert (UK) Limited
WordStar International Inc
Charmian Goodson ⎤
Eileen Spooner ⎟ for their advice during the
Kathie Cotton ⎟ production of the text
Allun Clark ⎦
Students of the BTEC National Certificate and RSA HIDAP courses at Chichester College of Technology
Derek Attewell, Photographer, Chichester

Finally, the author would like to thank Pitman Publishing for facilitating the inclusion of extracts taken from the author's previous publications:

People & Communication
*All In A Day's Work**
Communication at Work
Secretarial Procedures in the Electronic Office

*Produced in collaboration with Ron Dauber, and to whom thanks are also due.

The production of a text – from initial idea to distributed printed copy – is dependent upon a publishing team, including publishers, editors, designers, printers, administrative, distribution and sales staff. The author gratefully acknowledges the expert advice, support and suggestions of Pitman Publishing's team, without whom this text could not have been produced as envisaged.

Men and women in business

Throughout the text, I have referred to 'managers', 'administrators', office staff and so on. For the sake of a simple syntax, I have sometimes employed a generic 'he' to cover both male and female managers, accountants, etc. Of course, both women and men today fill important posts throughout organisations, and, so, for 'he' please read on occasion 'he/she', or 'she/he'.

How to study effectively

Photo Sally & Richard Greenhill

Overview

Unit 1 provides you with information and guidelines on:

- How to study effectively and to organise your weekly pattern of work efficiently.
- How to design and equip your personal study location.
- How to take good notes and to organise and store the study materials you will acquire during your course.
- Where to find helpful sources of study material.
- How to use your library and its cataloguing system to best effect.
- What potentially useful reference texts and journals exist to aid your studies.
- How to extract the 'meat' of a textbook as economically as possible.

Introduction

By the time you set about pursuing this topic, you will have almost certainly 'studied' for a number of assessments or examinations, since by the term 'study' we may simply mean 'follow a course at school or college'. At the end of such a course may have loomed public examinations – sat in examination halls and preceded perhaps by classwork or homework, which will have contributed to the overall result.

For the teachers and examiners involved in such examinations there occurs an annual bout of depression which is the result of seeing bright and able students fail in the examinations and assessments they take, as a result of an inability to study effectively. Some students regrettably never master the vital skills of effective studying, whether full-time students doing nothing else, or part-time, mature students returning to college after a period at work.

Why should this be so, given that almost all students want to learn and to absorb the skills and expertise being imparted? There is no single, simple answer, but almost certainly the root cause lies in their inability to organise:

1 their time
2 their environment or location for study
3 their learning resources
4 a systematic and coherent approach
5 the records and notes they keep for future reference.

In order that you in particular, and as an individual in your class group, make a good start in this important area, this Topic has been included at the outset in the text so that it may influence all that follows. Even if you fancy yourself as a 'pretty useful studier' it will do you no harm to read through this section − you may pick up some further useful tips!

Organising your time

There is a well-known proverb which goes:

If you want something done in a hurry − ask a busy person!

Behind this seeming contradiction lies the fact that busy people − managers, teachers, government officials − have to make prompt decisions and are used to regulating their working day very closely.

Thus, for example, they will buy in one minute the postcard which takes the holiday-maker half an hour to choose!

One of the best ways of organising your time is to make out a timetable of your waking hours for the whole week and then to fill in those times taken up with: eating, travelling, lectures, socialising or relaxing.

The time which is left is then clearly seen as available for personal study and will include such times as:

● private study periods between lectures
● 'twilight' times between 4.00 pm and 6.00 pm
● time while travelling on bus or train (not ideal)
● time after tea or supper
● time during week-ends

and if you are a skylark who can rise cheerfully at 6.00 pm in the mornings, time before breakfast!

Clearly, the more time you have entered in your timetable for socialising and relaxing, the less there will be for study and so from the outset you must decide where your priorities lie. Similarly, if you have to pursue a part-time job in order to help finance your studies, then you must be particularly disciplined in maintaining your study times. An ex-

Study timetable of Frances Jones

	Monday	Tuesday	Wednesday	Thursday	Friday	Saturday	Sunday
7.00 am 8.00 am		GETTING UP, BREAKFAST					GETTING UP + BREAKFAST
8.00 am 9.00 am		AND TRAVEL					
9.00 am 10.00 am	LECTURE	LECTURE	LECTURE	LECTURE	LECTURE	PART-TIME JOB	STUDY TIME:
10.00 am 11.00 am	LECTURE	PRIVATE STUDY: WRITE UP NOTES	LECTURE	PRIVATE STUDY: ASSIGNMENTS	PRIVATE STUDY: LIBRARY		ASSIGNMENT PRODUCTION
11.00 am 12.00 am	PRIVATE STUDY LIBRARY	LECTURE	PRIVATE STUDY LIBRARY	PRIVATE STUDY: ASSIGNMENTS	LECTURE		
12.00 am 1.00 pm	LECTURE	LUNCH	LECTURE	LECTURE	LECTURE		
1.00 pm 2.00 pm	LUNCH	PRIVATE STUDY: ASSIGNMENTS	LUNCH	LUNCH	LUNCH		LUNCH
2.00 pm 3.00 pm	LECTURE	PRIVATE STUDY ASSIGNMENTS	LECTURE	LECTURE	PRIVATE STUDY: WRITE UP NOTES		
3.00 pm 4.00 pm	LECTURE	LECTURE	LECTURE	LECTURE	LECTURE		STUDY TIME
4.00 pm 5.00 pm	TRAVEL +	BADMINTON IN GYM	PRIVATE STUDY LIBRARY	LECTURE	TRAVEL+		FLEXIBLE USE
5.00 pm 6.00 pm	TEA			TRAVEL+	TEA	FREE	
6.00 pm 7.00 pm	STUDY TIME	TRAVEL +	FREE	TEA	FREE		
7.00 pm 8.00 pm	READING	TEA		STUDY TIME WRITE UP NOTES			
8.00 pm 9.00 pm	FREE	FREE	FREE	FREE	FREE	FREE	

Once you have devised and agreed with your Course Tutor a realistic and sensible weekly private study timetable − make sure you stick to it.

ample indicating the sort of timetable which may be devised is shown on page 2.

Having produced your own timetable, it is not just a matter of putting in some study time where the blanks occur, but of analysing critically the pattern of your living week and of assessing where and how you can best accommodate your private study time.

A perfectly fair question in this context is: How much study time is enough? There are unfortunately no simple or easy answers since much depends on your own ability, skills, experience and time availability. However, as a rule of thumb guide, a full-time student should be prepared to commit some 12–15 hours per week to studying and assignment production, while a part-time student ought to devote some 6–8 hours to study outside of, and in addition to, classroom lectures.

In organising your own weekly study times on your timetable, you should adopt the following guidelines:

Make sure you have three main types of time:

a) for writing up your notes at the end of each day – Mondays to Fridays
b) for accessing reference books in your school, college or public library, and for carrying out research
c) for extended *uninterrupted* periods to produce assignments.

Clearly, the different study tasks involved in these three types of time needed will involve you in ensuring that different locations are available. Obviously, you will need to tailor your reference checking times to those times and days in the week when your campus and local libraries are open. On the other hand you can write up your notes at home in the early evenings while lectures are still fresh in your mind. Lastly, you will need to ensure that your location for assignment production is one which is attractive to work in but free from interruptions.

The illustrated timetable opposite provides a model which takes all these factors into account.

While on the subject of time in relation to study, it is well worth keeping the following advice firmly in mind:

Individuals have different biological clocks and while some people are 'skylarks' others are 'owls'. Having made this observation, however, it should be remembered that most people work in a higher mental gear in the mornings than in the afternoons, and that mental work in the evenings, quite naturally, after the efforts of the day, takes place at the lowest level of mental energy. This being broadly the case, it is a mistake to think that brilliant work is going to be begun at ten or eleven pm and continue into the early hours of the morning! Always remember that these special hours are reserved for those who either cannot or do not wish to study *at much more effective times.*

Shorter periods of study are generally more effec-

tive than longer ones. In other words, it is usually better to work hard and without interruption for one or two hours than to stick doggedly at studying for periods of two to four hours without a break. It pays to organise study times so that they are not all bunched up, say, from 9.00 am to 3.00 pm on Sundays with the rest of the week free. When we come to consider how our memories work, we shall see how the brain needs time to digest information and how 'overstudying' in periods which are too long causes 'mental indigestion'!

In our consideration of time as the most precious study resource, it is important to plan in an organised way how to ration it out evenly between the various study subjects or units which go to make up a complete course of study. In the study timetable of Frances Jones, there are four possible slots for assignment production, totalling nine available hours, and eight slots totalling nine-and-a-half hours for other kinds of study such as reading, notes, revision etc.

In evolving an effective pattern of study which can be maintained conscientiously over one or two academic years, it is important:

1 to have available more study slots than are needed. This allows for flexibility within the week, so that the unexpected invitation to a disco or party may be allowed for, and
2 to have available a variety of study slots within any given week in which to put current study activities, like the assignment due for the coming Monday or the need to re-read a chapter on consumer law which proved thorny. In this way weeks which include a great deal of writing may be just as readily coped with as those with a lighter load.

Keeping a balance

The presence of some 18½ available hours of personal study time in Frances' timetable does not mean that she will be studying for all those hours, but that they are available to use in a flexible weekly study plan which may extend to some 12–15 hours of study in all.

Also, by making out such a weekly timetable structured around meal-times, lecture-times, travelling times and socialising times, Frances will ensure that she keeps to a regular pattern of study which is also flexible. The development of regular study times within the week is essential if work is to be handed in on time and if she is to avoid the trap of falling behind with handing in work, since this can rapidly lead to her demotivation with the course altogether.

Thus in any given week, Frances Jones knows where she can devote three or, if needed, four study slots to produce written assignments, two of which – since they take place in school/college time – also provide access to the library and course teaching staff.

By the same token, Frances has at her disposal eight slots to divide between, say, the six units of study she is pursuing, for:

- follow-up further reading
- reference-checking in the library
- re-reading and writing up of notes
- researching information for assignments
- discussing a group assignment with fellow students.

Further, by keeping the Sunday afternoon period flexible, Frances can spend some time thinking about what needs to be reinforced or followed up from the past week, and what particular unit or topic studies should be planned for what study slots in the coming week.

Finally, in your use of time and overall study planning, it is essential that you have from each of your subject lecturers two central schedules of information:

1 the course syllabus or outline of aims and objectives to be met, and
2 the broad diary sequence of when what sort of assignments are going to be set throughout the academic year. This diary may be modified as the course progresses, to take into account unforeseen situations such as, for example, the teaching of report writing taking longer than anticipated.

Nevertheless, with these two study aids, you will be able to plan your general study strategy both in termly and monthly time-spans.

Though much of these observations about the effective use of time may seem – and indeed are – simple and straightforward, it is always a source of dismay for teachers that some otherwise able students find it so difficult to design and then stick to such a weekly plan. So take the above advice to heart and do not let yourself become the sort of student who always seems disorganised and short of time!

Organising your study environment

Having taken practical steps to make study time properly available outside the classroom, the next important step towards effective study methods is to consider carefully the location where the 'pearls of wisdom' are to be cultured!

Broadly speaking, these are the following places where it is likely that you will study:

- in your own study/bedroom or 'den'
- on the dining-table in the dining room or through-lounge
- on the bus or train travelling to and from school or college
- in your school/college/public library
- at your friend's house
- at work during the lunch period.

Certainly there are other locations where studying is possible but probably difficult and one of the first cardinal rules for finding and then using regularly productive study areas is to be honest with yourself about the effectiveness of some of the places you have used to study with little to show for it. For example, the above checklist includes some ideal study situations and others which may be far from suitable.

Certainly the best of study environments outside school or college is your own personal bedroom/study to which you can retire knowing that you will be left alone to get on with it. Not all students are so fortunate, however, and may well have to share a room with a brother or sister. In this case, an alternative location may be needed.

One student in this situation found an ideal solution in doing most of his studying in the college library each day, after lectures and before going home. In this way squabbles and upsets at home were avoided.

While the expanse of the dining-room table may be ideal across which to spread books and files, this site is no good at all if your studying has to compete with the family's TV entertainment. Even a budding Sir Isaac Newton would have found it difficult to resist the temptations of the latest pop or rock show or first TV showing of a searing and passionate Hollywood film. So unless you can commandeer the dining-room or lounge for yourself alone, avoid it – family leisure time and your studying will not mix.

While we have all seen young school pupils feverishly copying maths homework from a friend's exercise book while travelling on the bus into school, this is to be viewed rather as the study location of the desperate rather than the organised student. Firstly, reading and writing on a bus journey may well make you feel sick and secondly, the bustle of the journey in peak commuting times is likely to distract you constantly. However, some students who have long train journeys daily in rural shires may well be able to do some useful light reading in this time.

The use of the library as a study centre is going to be essential during your course but you must make sure you learn to get the best out of it by becoming fully confident in using the filing systems under which titles and authors are recorded, and the Dewey Decimal System by which knowledge is classified – see page 11. Similarly, it will pay handsome dividends if you take the trouble to win the confidence and good-will of the librarian and staff, as opposed to their wrath for being a constant loud chatterer!

This point leads on to a central one in terms of library study:

Do avoid becoming one of a small clique of three or four students who use the library (if they are allowed to get away with it) as a gossip-shop. Hours can drift by during the week's private study periods in *sotto voce* discussions of boyfriends, girlfriends, favourite groups, summer holidays and the like without a book being opened or an assignment begun!

Try to find a place away from any such nuisances and determine to make the best use of the library's facilities and your private study time.

Going to a friend's house for the evening to do some joint studying can certainly help to make a difficult patch more bearable in a demanding unit or topic, but only if some worthwhile work gets done. It's no good at all kidding yourself that you are busily engaged in earnest study if all you are really doing is idly leafing through notes or textbooks to the blasting decibels of your friend's favourite tapes or CDs. What is worth while, though, in this particular context is to test each other's recall of factual data which has to be remembered or to try out your approach to an 'open-ended' problem on a sympathetic ear. At all events, you must be the honest evaluator of such a study routine.

If you are studying and working full-time then you may find it possible to make legitimate use of your place of work, but keep in mind that studying in the firm's time (other than via day-release) is cheating and could land you in trouble, and that your break times are needed for just that – a break. However, you may well be able to manage a little reading over lunch-times or, by arrangement, stay on after normal finishing time to make good use of a quiet environment.

Designing your own study location

While you will be unable to make drastic structural alterations to your study location, there is a great deal you can do cheaply and quickly to ensure that it is a place where:

- you will feel comfortable and want to be;
- your study resources – files, books, photocopies, disks, etc. are methodically classified and stored for easy retrieval;
- your fixtures and fittings are up to the job of supplying a good reading light, proper sitting support and sufficient heating with circulating fresh air.

> **Remember!**
>
> During your course of study you will be spending many hours in your study location, so it will pay to design and equip it with care and thought! The following checklist highlights the chief areas for you to consider.

Study location design checklist

1 Lighting Whenever possible strong natural light is best. Try to avoid positioning your desk/table so that you are studying in your own shadow. For reading, pearl-finished lightbulbs of at least 100 watts are recommended; adjustable table lamps are ideal since they illuminate the desk area while avoiding eye-strain from dazzling direct light.

2 Heating For most students, heating comes free, courtesy of Mum's and Dad's chequebooks! But this is no reason for you to study in a Gobi Desert environment of 30°+C! Indeed, overheating your room will dull your brain and make you sleepy. Try to stick to a temperature of about 20–22°C. If you are paying for your own heating, remember in winter to put on several layers of clothing and to keep your head warm. You don't have to be designer dressed to study well!

3 Noise Some students appear to have mastered the knack of absorbing complicated printed arguments as their eardrums are being pulped by 120 plus decibels of pop music! However, more ordinary mortals need quiet – even hushed silence – in which to study seriously. Yet others feel a sense of loneliness and isolation without some music playing in the background. Whatever your own particular preferences, seek to eliminate distracting noise by using curtains, covers and draught excluders around doors and windows, and do not convince yourself that meaningful study is taking place when you are really only enjoying your latest tape or CD disk.

4 Interruptions There are moments in every student's life when any kind of interruption is better than the required reading or assignment production in hand. But seek to arrange your self-study timetable so that you are guaranteed at least two-hour stretches of uninterrupted study at a time. Tactfully let parents, friends and younger brothers or sisters know that you really are incommunicado. Once interrupted, your flow of ideas and points may not easily return and, the thread of your concentration broken, you may not feel that you want to resume that day.

5 Your desk and chair Your study desk and chair (with good lighting) are crucial to effective studying. Make sure that the height of your desk or table allows you to write and use a keyboard comfortably, without causing your shoulder muscles to cramp and strain. Also, ensure that your desk/table's surface area is large enough to take several open books and files. It is irritating to have to keep lifting aside one opened book to get at another. In this context, a table-top lectern for holding the pages of books and papers in place for easy reading is very useful.

Try to obtain an adjustable typist's-type chair (to give you a suitable table height) and to provide good posture support. At all events, do not use a chair which is too low for your table and in which your body frame slumps.

Study resources management

A simple and logical system for storing acquired study materials – notes, photocopies, magazines, floppy/hard disks, books, etc – is absolutely essential to your success and deserves careful thought and planning at the outset. The following tips will help you to set up your own system.

Shelving

Erect sufficient shelving with at least lever-arch file vertical spacing between shelves. An inexpensive set of shelves can be set up using blockboard planks and housebrick spacers.

Install your books in alphabetical sequence of author's surname and always put your books back in the same slot on your shelves. This way, they are always promptly to hand. You may wish to use this sequence within the individual Unit areas of your studies, by grouping texts, etc. under People In Organisations and Finance, etc.

Boxfiles and ringbinders

Invest in a set of A4 boxfiles/capacious ringbinders. There is no point in laboriously taking notes, making press-cuttings and taking photocopies if, a few months later, they are effectively lost for ever because you did not store them properly. Use dividers and labels to organise such material logically – say by sub-divisions of each course unit of study.

Computer files

If you are lucky enough to possess your own PC, then make sure you maintain good computer-file naming procedures. A file called XJCT.1BN does nothing to aid the memory while another entitled PIOMTGS.1 immediately conveys the first established People in Organisations file on Meetings.

Computer database records

Also, the time taken to set up and maintain a database which classifies your study material as you obtain it and tells you what it is and where you are storing it is invaluable when it comes to assignment production and revision. Your database should include details of title, author, date of publication, source (if part of a larger text), summary of content, and location within your study location. Your computerised database is best set up to group data within course units and their sub-divisions.

Two self-study survival tips

1 If you do allow yourself to be persuaded to lend your books, notes or other materials to fellow students, make sure you have your name in them and make a note of who borrowed what and when they promised its return. Do not be shy of demanding your material back. You don't have to be inconvenienced because you did someone a good turn.

2 Never carry weeks or months of notes and accumulated study resources to and from your school/college each day. Always transfer such precious material to your study files each day or so. Strong students have broken down and cried at the loss of a year's notes left on the bus, train or classroom desk!

And remember, effective study is made up of 5% inspiration and 95% effective organisation and productive use of time!

Organising your notes and handouts

Some ill-advised students are so neglectful when it comes to taking, revising and storing notes that what they end up with is so scanty that it scarcely needs any organising! The conscientious student soon realises, however, the value of such memory-joggers and guidance aids during a long and demanding course of study.

It pays, therefore, to give careful thought to the most effective way of organising these important study resources.

There are several ways in which your study materials – notes, handouts, photocopies, newspaper cuttings, etc, can be systematically filed and indexed, so you know where to put your hand on even a single piece of A4 paper promptly and reliably.

One simple method to adopt is to store your index in a card index filing system under subject or unit headings. An individual card may look like this:

Unit: People in organisations

Major topic: Meetings
Sub topic: Format and content of
                    Chairman's agenda.
Resources: 1. Notes 25.1.19XX
                    2. Specimen of Agenda
                    3. Handout on Content
                    Approach
Location: PIO Boxfile or PIOMTG.1 as
                    computer disk filename

Other sources of
information: 'People, communication and
                    organisations' D. W. Evans,
                    Pitman Second Edition
                    (1990)
                    'Meetings' L. Hall, M & E
                    Handbooks, Macdonald &
                    Evans (1987)

At the outset of your studies you may think setting up such a filing system or database is a chore and scarcely worth the trouble, but as your study material builds up, and as you begin to produce assignments in which the content of various units is integrated, you will soon reap the benefit of your own means of quickly accessing useful information.

Indeed, nothing is more infuriating in the later stages of your studies than to have only a vague recollection of a super chapter or article you could use but cannot locate, or to have taken the trouble to produce equally super notes that you put away somewhere and cannot lay hands on just when you could use them to good effect!

As an alternative to the card-index system you may wish to consider putting your materials index on to a computerised database using one of the commercially available packages. This is an ideal way of organising your sources of information if you have access to a computer at home.

Golden rule: Start right, stay right!

Not even an Einstein can carry in his or her head all the information collected during a period of one or two years' study!

So you must determine, right from the start, to acquire, store and review from time to time your notes and other study aids – conscientiously!

Using study materials effectively

As the diagram opposite illustrates, there are nowadays many sources of information about people working in organisations and how they communicate, which may be used as helpful sources of

Range of possible study aids

1   Pen and file paper produced notes

2   Handwritten or text processed assignments

3   Duplicated handouts

4   Tape-recorded audio observations

5   Cuttings from newspapers, periodicals, magazines

6   Library books, newspapers, journals and audio-visual aids

7   Single photocopies of pages of books, magazines, journals

8   Video tapes of TV documentaries or features

9   Copies of photographs, drawings, graphs, charts, etc and collected specimens of forms and documents used in organisations

10   Educational computer software packages

11   Free handouts at exhibitions, displays, and public sector information offices

12   Class/group computer databases of researched information available for general use during year

IF YOU CAST A WIDE AND IMAGINATIVE NET, THERE IS A WIDE RANGE OF STUDY AIDS AND MATERIAL AVAILABLE TO YOU, MUCH OF IT INEXPENSIVE OR FREE!

study information in addition to and complementing textbooks like this one.

As part of your regular study routine, you should make sure that you include the following good practices in your daily and weekly studies.

- **Read and 'skim-read' the business sections of a good daily and Sunday newspaper**. Cut out relevant articles for future reference. Remember that newspaper articles are up-to-the-minute, brief, and mostly straightforwardly written.
- **Make a habit of checking in advance in television and radio programme** magazines such as Radio Times and TV Times to see what helpful programmes are shortly to be broadcast. Make arrangements to view or listen, and to record by audio or video means, any programme which looks likely to be particularly helpful. But in doing so always ensure you conform to copyright laws!
- **Photocopy any useful diagrams, articles, charts etc from books or magazines in your library**. (It is useful to keep a supply of coins by you for this purpose for your library's photocopier.) By and large copyright is not infringed by the taking of a single photocopy of material for study/research purposes. If in doubt, check with your librarian first.
- **Always be on the look-out for good specimens of actual documents in use** – circular letters, agendas, invoices, balance sheets published by public companies etc. You can check out by this means how successful organisations view their printed communications and compare them with others to obtain an informed view of current practices. Also, such a collection will provide you with practical help on the design of forms and documents and how to present information with visual effect.
- There are now a number of software packages available in schools and colleges which will provide invaluable assistance in helping the student to acquire both useful study skills and marketable career skills. These are packages such as the spreadsheet, database and file assistant.

In this context, it will pay handsome dividends – whether or not you pursue them as part of your course – to acquire keyboarding skills and the ability to operate a personal computer (PC). The chances are that you are already some way along this path, but if not, now is the time to get started!

How to take effective notes

As we have seen, a wide range of potentially useful audio-visual study material is available. Nevertheless, the textbook and specialist book still remain a central source of study data and information.

Similarly, though current courses of study involve the student in active learning situations – role-play, project, business-game and so on, nevertheless, there are times when it is necessary to take notes in class of an oral presentation of information.

The advantages of securing coherent notes for future revision have already been aired and this section aims to provide practical help in both the oral and written situation.

Taking notes of an oral presentation

Taking notes of what someone is saying as he or she says it is a demanding task. Practice is required and, as the proverb goes, makes perfect. The following pointers will help you to develop such skills promptly, provided you make a determined effort.

1 Make sure you arrive for your class on time. Miss the beginning of an oral presentation and you may never catch up and grasp the gist!
2 Arrive for the lecture organised. This means having a reserve pen or ball-point, sufficient note-paper and any other helpful 'tools' such as a ruler and eraser. This advice may seem extremely basic but teachers and students are always being asked to lend out just such items.
3 Make sure you sit where you can obtain a good view of the black/white board or OHP screen.
4 Listen to what is being said actively and with concentration. Try to avoid 'switching off' or allowing your attention to wander.
5 Seek to establish the structure in which the teacher is presenting the information.

It may be that the lecture follows what is called an expositional pattern (that is, it sets about imparting information in a logical sequence) from the delivery of generalisations and principles or theories to the citing of examples or illustrations to support an initial, general view. Such a structure usually centres upon factual information. In your notes, therefore, you will need to ensure that you set down in sufficient detail the general principles or major points and the main examples.

Remember that teachers tend to repeat their points and that their presentations often follow this structure:

Tell 'em what you're going to tell 'em.
Tell 'em.
Tell 'em what you've told 'em!

- This being the case, the good teacher will give you plenty of opportunities to grasp the most important points.

Another kind of structure used in oral presentations is the one called 'argumentative'. In this sense the label means the presenting of both sides of an argument, case, or discussion. This being so, the sort of structure likely to be followed is:

Model: how to take effective notes

To illustrate the suggested approach to taking notes and to itemise important factors, the preceding section has been set out below in note form

HOW TO TAKE EFFECTIVE NOTES 12.9.19XX

Source: People, Communication and
Organisations   D.W. Evans, Pitman
                   ISBN. 0273 03269 0

Effective notes to be taken in two contexts:
  Orally delivered lectures/presentations
  Summaries of written word: texts
  magazines etc.

1.0 Taking Notes In An Oral Situation

  1.1 Make sure arrive on time - or
  risk failing to grasp opening points.

  1.2 Arrive organised - with reserve
  pens and all needed 'equipment.'

  1.3 Ensure seat gives good view
  of board or OHP.

  1.4 Always listen actively - avoid
  'switching off.'

  1.5 Seek to spot early likely
     structure of lectures:

      1.5.1 Expositional
      logical structure,
      from general to particular,
      often factual main points
      with illustrations.

      1.5.2 Argumentative
      presents two-sided case -
      pros and cons thus:

        - intro main issues
        - pros points
        - cons points
        - summary both sides.
        - come down on one side.

  1.6 Teachers usually repeat information
     to aid students to absorb points via:
       tell 'em: intro
       tell 'em: main delivery
       tell 'em: repeat summary

Checklist of Points of Note

Always title notes in capital letters.

Always date your notes and record their source fully – you may wish to find original in the future.

Notice statement on the two major contexts.

Note the use of initial capitals and underlining for section headings.

It helps to number sections and points for easy absorption of information.

The points made are abbreviated from full, grammatical English, but not so much that their meaning is lost.

Note the way that the notes are indented across the page to aid visual impact and show the relationship of major points to sub-points.

Notice underlining of important sub-point headings.

Don't be afraid to put notes into your own words. Include an example if it makes a good point or aids understanding.

a) Introduction of major issue or issues.
b) The arguments for – the pros.
c) The arguments against – the cons.
d) A brief summary of the pros and cons – major points.
e) A decision on which case is stronger or more logical or more justified – the outcome or conclusion.

6 Never remain a passive listener! If you fail to grasp a point during the oral delivery in an informal classroom situation ask your teacher to go over it again – there is absolutely no point in making copious notes about something you don't understand!

Also, if the teacher is going too fast (or too slow) tell him or her in polite terms that this is so. All teachers have a vested interest in your success, so they will not mind your helping them to help you.

7 Inevitably in an oral presentation the speaker will sometimes repeat points, digress into an anecdote or provide information that is 'padding' or trivial. Seek to 'edit' such information out of your notes as you take them so that you only record the most important points a single time.

8 Remember to make a note of any important questions and explanatory answers which may add further information to your notes at the end of the presentation.

9 Always go through your notes of an oral presentation within twenty-four hours so that, once you have digested the lecture, you can correct, revise, add to or delete information in your notes and make them a fully coherent set of notes which are going to be of some value to you in one or two year's time. Otherwise you may find that your initial note-taking work has been a waste of time!

How to find out

Your library and your study resources

Having spent some time on examining how to study effectively, it is now necessary to consider in some detail the ways of getting the best out of your library and the textbooks and other study aids you will wish to use, or borrow, for study use.

Using your library to best effect

Obviously, if the library in question is your school library which you have inhabited since transferring to secondary school, then you will already know a great deal about it. However, you may be new to a college library and, in any case, a 'refresher' examination of library organisation will do no harm!

At the outset, it is important to realise that there are various kinds of knowledge available to the serious student and that a library is a centre or treasure-house for all sorts of knowledge – factual, philosophical, religious, imaginative and so on. This being so, it is necessary to understand that you do not need, nor do you have the time to learn by heart, everything you will encounter during your studies. You must therefore acquire the skill of finding quickly the precise location in your library of the sort of information you need, and learn to make value judgements along these lines:

What information

1 is important enough to make careful notes of for future use?
2 do you need to be aware of via browsing and skim-reading?
3 do you need to be aware of and know the location of in case of future detailed need?

If you regularly employ these three yardsticks, you will soon become proficient in using your library's reference section during the production of an assignment, in searching its non-fiction shelves expertly with an informed understanding of the Dewey Decimal System, and in checking out regularly in its newspaper and journals section for useful articles or extracts. Most libraries, however they are organised geographically, incorporate the following sections or divisions:

Fiction An area set aside for fictional novels and stories.

Non-fiction An area in which the universal body of knowledge is set out according to a carefully devised classification system. In most UK libraries the Dewey Decimal System is employed. (See below.)

Reference section An area which contains the year-books, dictionaries, directories and books of specialised reference of interest to public service officials, engineers, linguists, musicians and so on. These books are not usually allowed to leave the library.

Newspapers and journals Many libraries take out subscriptions for daily and Sunday newspapers, magazines, journals and newsletters etc, spanning a wide range of specialist interest. For example – *The Economist* for those interested in business, politics and the economy. *Computing* for those involved in computer use and so on. A brief list is set out below.

New additions Librarians are always keen to advise their clientèle of new additions to the library stock and it is well worth keeping an eye on this area for an up-to-the-minute book on a topic central to your studies.

Catalogue and index section This is the place where the library keeps its index of all the books, reference texts and other study materials it holds. Some libraries still employ card-index systems in wooden cabinets for this purpose and others use more extensively a computerised system for recording: the works an author has produced, the extent of the library's stock on a particular subject, helpful information such as date of publication, Dewey Decimal and ISBN references and so on. Make sure with your teacher's and librarian's help that you learn to use the cataloguing system in your library as quickly as possible if you are not entirely expert as yet.

Computer information databases Many libraries today also provide rooms or booths having microcomputers and viewdata facilities to scan the databases of Prestel, TTNS and Campus 2000 and so on. Make sure you know how to take advantage of such equipment.

The Dewey Decimal System

The father of the modern library indexing system was Melvil Dewey (1851–1931). He was an American and invented the 'Dewey Decimal System' while working at a training library in Albany in 1876.

Dewey's system is based on dividing all human knowledge into ten broad categories. Each category

---

Dewey book classification outline

000	**General Works**		630	Agriculture
030	Encyclopaedias		635	Gardening
070	Journalism		640	Household Management
100	**Philosophy**		641.5	Cookery
150	Psychology		650	Business Practices
			658	Management
200	**Religion**		660	Chemical Technology
220–280	Christianity		670–680	Manufacturing
290	Non-Christian Religions		690	Building
300	**Social Sciences**		**700**	**The Arts**
310	Statistics		710	The Landscape, Town Planning
320	Political Science		720	Architecture
330	Economics		730	Sculpture, Metalwork
340	Law		740	Drawing
350	Public Administration		745	Decorative Arts
355–359	Armed Forces		745.5	Handicrafts
360	Social Services		746.44	Embroidery
370	Education		750	Painting
380	Commerce		760	Graphic Arts
385	Railways		770	Photography
390	Customs, Folklore		780	Music
391	Costume		790	Recreations
400	**Language**		792	The Theatre
420	English Language		793–799	Sports and Games
430	Germanic Languages		**800**	**Literature**
440	French		810	American Literature
450	Italian		820	English Literature
460	Spanish		830–890	Other Literatures
470	Latin		See 400–490	Languages
480	Greek		**900**	**Geography, History**
490	Other Languages		910	Geography, Travel
500	**Science**		913	Ancient World, Archaeology
510	Mathematics		914	European Geography and Travel
520	Astronomy		915–919	Other Continents
530	Physics		See 930–990	History
540	Chemistry		929	Genealogy
550	Earth Sciences		930	Ancient History
551.5	Meteorology		940	History, Europe
560	Paleontology		950	Asia
570	Life Sciences		960	Africa
580	Botanical Sciences		970	North America
590	Zoological Sciences		980	South America
600	**Technology**		990	Australasia
610	Medicine		998	The Polar Regions
620	Engineering		B	Biography and Autobiography

is identified by a three-digit code number coming before a decimal point:

000.	general books	600.	technology
100.	philosophy	700.	the arts
200.	religion	800.	literature
300.	social sciences	900.	geography, history
400.	language	B	biography,
500.	science		autobiography

Within each section of one hundred points, the broad area of, say, languages is sub-divided into a series of specialist areas. Thus books on the English language are to be found in the 420s. Alternatively, in the applied science section, books on business English applications are in the 651 section. Further degrees of specialisation are indicated by the use of numbers behind the decimal point:

651.74 English for business students
651.77 committees
651.78 report writing

while a further area of specialisation is introduced at a slightly later point: Computers in the Office, Pitman 658.054.

In this way, the Dewey Decimal System is able to expand to include modern technologies like micro-electronics or newly devised shorthand systems.

Libraries using the Dewey system display their books in consecutive order, starting with the 000s and ending with the 900s. In most libraries, books which are not lent out, but retained for reference are kept in a separate area, but indexed in the same way.

It should be noted that the Dewey system is not international. The Americans have now replaced it with their Library of Congress system which uses a series of numbers and letters to break down knowledge in a similar way. In Great Britain, however, the Dewey Decimal System is widely used, save in some universities.

Once you have mastered the logic behind Dewey's system, it will now take you only a minute or two to locate the section you need. The table on page 11 will show you how the ten categories are further broken down.

The catalogue system

It is difficult to generalise about library cataloguing systems, since many libraries employ different variations on the Dewey or Library of Congress theme.

Most libraries now employ a form of computer-based cataloguing, and organise the records of the books they stock under the main headings of:

author or **subject**

Under the author section, the authors are listed alphabetically and each book is listed below its author. Under the subject section, books are indexed according to where they come in the Dewey or Library of Congress coding.

Some libraries record this information on cards filed in labelled boxes, others hold the information in large ring-binders of modified computer print-out.

Golden rule

If, at any time, you are unable to find what you want quickly – ask the librarian! No one knows his or her library better, and he or she will prove a helpful information source.

It is important, when one's work relies upon sources of information, to build up a checklist of useful reference books. Of course the nature and scope of such a checklist will depend on the type of job – the solicitor will need to know where to find information relating to law in all its aspects, the production manager will need to know where to check on established rules for manufacturing different types of product. The office administrator will need to know about postal and telecommunications services, directories of organisations and companies, specialist dictionaries and business reference books.

The following list is intended for such an office worker. It is by no means exhaustive, but will provide a basis from which to build:

Dictionaries
Oxford Shorter English Dictionary
English Pronouncing Dictionary
The Pergamon Dictionary of Perfect Spelling
Cassell's New Spelling Dictionary
Dictionary of Acronyms and Abbreviations
A Dictionary of Modern English Usage
Fontana Dictionary of Modern Thought
Oxford Dictionary of Quotations
Pitman Dictionary of Shorthand

Use of English
The Complete Plain Words
Roget's Thesaurus
ABC of English Usage
Usage and Abusage
The King's English

Directories
Directory of British Associations
Kelly's Business Directory
Kelly's Directory of Manufacturers and Merchants
Current British Directories Yearbook
Guide to Current British Periodicals
UK Trade Names

Yearbooks
British Standards Yearbook
The Post Office Guide
Whitaker's Almanac

The Municipal Yearbook
Social Sciences Yearbook
BBC, ITV Handbooks
Various Trades' Handbooks e.g. Engineering

Business reference books
ABC Railway Guide
Who's Who
International Who's Who
Who Owns Whom
Kompass
Chambers World Gazeteer
Times Atlas of the World
Titles and Forms of Address
How to Find Out About Secretarial Practice
Basic Medical Vocabulary
Businessman's Guide
The Retail Directory
The Secretary's Yearbook
Business Terms, Phrases and Abbreviations
British Exports
Europages: The European Business Directory

Encyclopaedias
Encyclopaedia Britannica
Larousse Illustrated International Encyclopaedia
DTI Guide to Single EEC Market

Hotels and restaurants
Egon Ronay's Lucas Guide Yearbook
AA Guide to Hotels and Restaurants in Great Britain and
    Ireland
The Good Food Guide
RAC Hotel Guide

Newspapers
The Times
The Independent
The Financial Times
The Guardian
The Daily Telegraph
The International Herald Tribune

Periodicals
Business Systems and Equipment
Office Magazine
Network
Communicate
Economist
New Statesman
Banking World
Caterer and Hotelkeeper
Computer News
Desk-top Publishing Today
PC User
Which Computer?

Using study texts effectively and economically

Having made it your early business to explore the geography of your library and its various stocks of study resources – including any IT resources – it is now necessary to become proficient in the skills of extracting the information you need from a variety of books quickly and economically. For example, you certainly will not have the time to read each and every useful book you encounter from cover to cover, and it would indeed be senseless even to try! This being so, it is helpful to know what information you can glean from the format of a text to help in saving precious time and effort.

In developing a useful approach to this aspect, always consider, before settling down to read a text, the following questions:

- What do I need this book's information for?
    – detailed study, background reading, awareness, skim-reading etc.
- Do I need to absorb all the information it provides, or only some of it?
    – a particular chapter or section, a helpful appendix, a useful diagram, chart or graph.
- At what level is the text pitched and is it suitable for my purposes?
    – 13-year-olds, BTEC National level students, university students or PhD postgraduates.
- How up-to-date is the information in the text?
    – only months old, one year, two years or ten years.
- How much does it matter that the information is not right up-to-date?
- totally, fairly, not much, not at all.
- How long will it take to extract the information in the text and is it worth the effort?
    – well worth it, worth it, not worth it (find a shorter and more readily assimilated text).

Posing such questions while leafing through a text and sampling extracts of it will help you to get best value for your time and effort, always allowing for the range and age of books available to you.

To find the answers to the sort of questions posed above, it helps to be familiar with the customary layout or sequence of non-fiction texts:

Title page
Publication details
Table of contents
List of illustrations
Sequence of chapters or sections
Preface
Acknowledgements
Chapter summaries
Footnotes
Appendices
Bibliography
Questions/assignments and answers
Index

As you can see from the above checklist, there is more to the structure of a textbook than meets the eye! Below you will find some illustrations of these components to help you to become familiar with them; most readers — as opposed to students — tend to make straight for the chapters.

Parts of the textbook explained

The title page

As a conscientious student you are soon likely to develop a permanent crick in your neck from trying to read the titles of library books from their upright spines as they range along library shelves! But it pays to make a thorough search via titles and authors' names. If you got on well with a particular author check in your library's cataloguing system to see what else he or she may have written.

Publication details

Make sure you have checked the date of the book's publication and make a note of its Dewey Decimal Number and ISBN number so that you can locate it again quickly.

Look for reprint and subsequent editions details. A book which is frequently reprinted and revised indicates that it has proved very popular and this may well mean that it is well written and worthwhile.

Preface

Take the trouble to read the book's preface or prefaces — these will very often give you a quick insight into the author's or editor's attitude to the subject or his basic approach to it and this will help you to decide whether to invest some of your time in reading it or looking elsewhere. The preface also provides an outline in many books of the structure of the text.

Acknowledgements

Here the author publicly thanks the owners of the copyright of books, magazines, newspapers etc from which extracts have been printed in the book.

Consequently, the information provided in an acknowledgement section may help you to identify other books and sources of information helpful to your studies.

Table of contents

Always take the trouble to scan the book's table of contents carefully. It forms in effect the bare skeleton of the book's 'body', and you should think carefully about whether you need to read and make notes on all the book, or only on one or two of its chapters. In this way it is often possible to save time by going straight to what is directly and immediately relevant to your needs, and then perhaps doing the same in other books so as to obtain, say, two or three experts' views on interview techniques or staff appraisal before you make your own mind up. Such a technique of study will ensure that you acquire balanced views and arguments or approaches reinforced by the unanimity of several specialists.

List of illustrations

In some books a list of illustrations or diagrams is provided. It is well worth checking through it and turning to likely sources of relevant information with a view to making a photocopy. The Chinese have a proverb:

A picture is worth ten thousand words!

Thus the retention of a chart, map, diagram or illustration in your study notes may well prove invaluable later in your course.

Sequence of chapters or sections

Some books are constructed in a careful sequence and this makes it difficult to read a middle chapter without having any knowledge of preceding ones. In this situation you should 'skim-read' what comes before and after the chapter you wish to read and make notes so as to get the feel of the author's overall approach. (See below for skim-reading guidelines.)

Some authors go to the trouble of including chapter summaries at the start of each chapter, and these are a boon for the student who can thus obtain a quick outline of the content so as to judge whether it is relevant or useful.

If there are no such chapter summaries in evidence, adopt the technique of reading the first and last paragraphs of a chapter before committing yourself to reading all of it. In this way you will often obtain a shrewd notion of its content by means of the main points made in an introduction to the chapter and the major aspects chosen as part of its closing and summarising chapter.

Footnotes

Authors include footnotes as a means of providing additional information or explanation of a particular point or as a means of indicating further sources of information. It is worth reading them — even if they are sometimes set in fine print!

Appendices

The appendix — usually placed near the end of the book — is often a very helpful source of information. The function of the appendix is to act as a location or storage point in the book of particular data which has a relevance to all or part of the book's subject-matter. For example, a book on retailing may include as an appendix salient extracts of various consumer and trades description laws. Alternatively, an appendix might comprise a list of useful addresses. Often the appendix lends itself to photocopying as a means of follow-up reference or source of detailed information on a matter of background relevance.

Bibliography

The word bibliography stems from Latin and Greek and means 'a list of books'. Authors who have made reference to books in their own text very often list them in alphabetical order of author's surname or clustered under topic headings. A bibliography is of great help to the student as a short cut to other useful texts which has been compiled in a list by the author as part of his or her service to the reader and thus is always worth consulting!

Questions/assignments and answers

Some texts include (at the back) a section of questions or assignments to undertake, and may also provide answers. It may be that as a formal part of your course you are requested to undertake some of these to gain practice and to try out new-found skills. If you should come across such a section in a book you locate in your library, it is well worth browsing through them, and sometimes making notes of the major assignment topics, since, when you think about it, the book's author has identified these topics as sufficiently important to include in the assessment section − so they must be worth noting!

Another value of such a section is that it provides you − if answers are also included − with an opportunity to undertake some self-testing during your course.

Index

The inclusion of an index in a text is particularly helpful to the discerning student. It provides an opportunity to glean relevant information quickly and without having to read or scan a series of chapters.

As the example below illustrates, an index is compiled alphabetically in subject order with page numbers supplied after the entry.

The supply of an individual page number usually means that the topic is referred to on that page but perhaps only in passing, by name. The reference which implies a number of pages:

217−229

means that the topic is handled and discussed throughout the pages cited: in the above example,

in 13 pages. Thus there will clearly be some extended data in this part of the book worth checking.

CCITT   (International Telegraph and Telephone
            Consultative Committee), 138
CCTV (Closed Circuit Television), 183
chairman, in organisation, 8
chart, organisational, 5
cheque,
    crossed, 244−5
    Euro-, 247
    open, 244−5
    traveller's, 246
cheque book 244,
    components of, 244
cheque guarantee cards, 248
CIM (computer input microform), 61, 81
circulation list, 181

Indexes also provide cross-references:

bits, see Computer binary digits

here the reference to 'bits' of information in computer form are shown as being dealt with under the index heading 'Computer binary digits'. The entry for this subject in the index supplies the page references.

As you can see, the index provides a direct short-cut to detailed information which would otherwise be 'buried' in thousands of words of text. A good practice, therefore, when researching information for an assignment, is to make sure you consult the indexes of the books you locate. This regular study habit will save you hours of time during your course and almost certainly result in your finding a wide range of useful data.

Summary

The above checklist of book components has, all being well, shown that there is more than meets the eye to extracting information from library texts. If you use the guidelines suggested regularly and conscientiously, you will soon become accomplished in locating and extracting helpful information quickly and simply.

Developing reading skills

It must seem rather strange to come upon the above title of a topic on reading when you have almost certainly read thousands upon thousands of words in your life so far! Nevertheless, it is important at the outset of an extended course of study to reconsider the ways − rather than way − that reading may be undertaken.

It is therefore helpful to consider the ways in which we all read, depending upon the cir-

Example of publication data

PITMAN PUBLISHING
128 Long Acre, London WC2E 9AN

A Division of Longman Group UK Limited

©Desmond W Evans 1986, 1990

First published in Great Britain 1986
Second edition 1990

British Library Cataloguing in Publication Data
Evans, Desmond W.
   People, communication & organisations.—2nd. ed.
   1. Communication skills
   I. Title
   302.2
ISBN 0-273-03269-0

Typset by Avocet Robinson, Buckingham
Printed in Great Britain

1. Before you do anything:

Check carefully when it was first written and whether you are looking at a recent edition.

If you think you will want to use it again make a note of its ISBN number and its Dewey decimal classification.

It may be that the text is not sufficiently up-to-date — if so, proceed no further!

Contents

2. Go next to the book's Table of Contents. Study now the structure of the book in this helpful 'skeletal' outline to see if you need to refer to all of it or only one or two sections. In this way you can save yourself much time!

3. While you are studying the contents section, skim through it to see what other chapters or parts could be worth noting (in your notebook!) for a future topic, of your course.

Example of an index

Index

4. Before delving into chapters check (usually at the back of the book) if there is an index. If so, this can take you directly to the particular area you wish to research.

Notice that single page references usually are quite restricted while those hyphenated deal with a topic at length.

Also, a good index provides helpful cross-references, or explanations.

---

cumstances in which the reading takes place, and to incorporate such approaches consciously in study reading routines.

Examples

1 Very quick reading of an important letter to get to the essential message as quickly as possible – as in a letter about a recent interview for a job or place at college or university.

In this circumstance, the non-essential, 'leading-up' and congratulating or 'letting down lightly' parts of the letter are initially glossed over in a first reading and only taken in more carefully at a second reading, because only the essential message is initially important.

2 Scanning paragraphs quickly with the eye being used almost like a satellite camera which only stops when a key word or phrase is spotted.

This sort of reading is done when, for example, a student is leafing through a magazine or journal of articles to check whether there is one worth stopping to consider in a slower more detailed way.

Such a 'skim-reading' technique is very helpful to 'pre-digest' possibly useful information, but it must be made clear that it is not a substitute for careful, painstaking reading.

3 Reading for clear understanding and remembering is a much slower business. People like accountants, lawyers, doctors and professors, whose daily lives require the reading of long, specialist and often complex documents will read the same piece perhaps three times:

First: fairly quickly to get the gist of it.
Second: slowly to absorb the meaning fully.
Third: fairly quickly to get the feel of the structure and logical sequence and to summarise mentally the main points.

4 Reading for note-taking combines the approaches suggested in 2 and 3 above. In addition, it requires pauses at paragraph intervals to allow information to be digested and then noted. Thus the technique of reading a passage or chapter may be summarised as follows:

- first skim-read the whole piece to get the feel of its approach and in so doing let key words and phrases 'hit' your eye and consciousness
- then read the first and last paragraphs to check introductory issues and summarising closing points
- it may be necessary to read the whole chapter first at a steady pace before attempting to make notes of it
- next read the passage a paragraph or 12–15 lines at a time
- make your notes of this paragraph or section in your own words, seizing upon major points, names, dates and other essential factual data
- continue this practice until you complete the chapter
- lastly, re-read your notes to make sure you have

omitted nothing of importance, while the chapter is fresh in your mind. Also check that your notes make sense and will also make sense in six months' time!

'Unit 1: How to study effectively' has outlined a number of tips, guidelines and useful practices to assist you in swiftly settling into a happy and pro-

ductive routine. Of course, every student is different and will naturally develop habits and routines in step with his or her life-style and general approach to learning. The advice set out in this Unit results from much teaching and studying experience and should provide you with a helpful start to your studies in general. In the following Summary of Main points are set out 12 golden study rules which you should always keep in mind.

Summary of main points

1   At the very outset of your studies, make time to analyse the pattern of your lectures and private study at college and at home so as to devise a regular yet flexible study programme to which you can commit yourself and stick to.

2   Avoid starting to study late in the evening or when you are tired. You must have an alert and sharp mind to study effectively.

3   It is better to study in a series of 3–4 1 hour periods with 15–30 minute breaks in between than to attempt to 'slog' without a pause or break through study stints of 3–4 unbroken hours.

4   Take time before your studies start in earnest to design and equip your home study location comfortably and efficiently.

5   Always ensure that your main body of notes are kept safe at home, secure from loss.

6   It pays to develop your own study materials catalogue and location index, so take the trouble to devise a database or index system so as to be able to find quickly what you filed months previously and so as to provide a memory-jogging index of what study data you have amassed.

7   Always be on the look-out for useful study material from the wide range of audio-visual sources around you.

8   Take proper care with developing note-taking skills and make a regular routine of writing up your notes clearly while they are still fresh in your mind, in order that they will provide you with useful data you will be able to understand months later.

9   Ensure that you develop an expert knowledge of how your local libraries' cataloguing systems work, including the Dewey system. Learn how to use the libraries' available resources to the utmost and make friends with the librarians – they are a precious source of help.

10   Make the time to build up your own checklist of where to find useful sources of information, such as the library location of, say, *The Economist* or *Communicate* journals, or the Campus 2000 networked database and relevant reference texts.

11   Revise your approach to reading techniques; practice skim-reading and accessing a text's table of contents, index, chapter summaries and headings to obtain a quick idea of its potential usefulness.

12   Remember always: success in studying is a mix of 90 per cent self-organisation and self-discipline and 10 per cent intuition and 'top-of-the-head inspiration'.

Self assessment questions

1 Are you satisfied that you have devised an effective personal weekly study timetable? Do you know when and where all your lectures are due to take place and who is giving them?

2 Have you set up a congenial, effective self-study location?

3 Are you happy with your system for cataloguing and storing your acquired study materials?

4 Do you feel confident about using the cataloguing and referencing systems of your college/school/public libraries?

5 Have you made time to check out and list the potentially useful reference books, magazines and journals held in your local libraries?

6 Have you purchased or ordered the course textbooks and study materials you need?

7 In short, are you satisfied that you are properly 'kitted out' to make a strong and effective start to your course of study? If not, re-read Unit 1 and make a checklist of omissions and weaknesses for instant remedial action!

Activities and assignments

Quick review quiz

1 What factors should be considered in drawing up a weekly personal study timetable?

2 What facilities exist in your locality to aid your self-study programme?

3 How long is an ideal period of private study? What are the best times to study?

4 List the factors you would take into account in setting up your study location and describe elements of good practice for each.

5 Make a checklist of techniques for taking effective notes.

6 List the range of available media from which study materials may be assembled.

7 What techniques would you employ to extract study material effectively and economically from a textbook?

8 Explain how each of the following works:

a) the Dewey Decimal Library Classification System
b) the index of a textbook
c) the technique of skim-reading

9 Identify a set of self-study 'distractors' and how these should be overcome.

10 Explain how you would set up an effective system in your study area for cataloguing and storing your acquired study materials.

11 Make a list of the techniques students should employ to produce top quality assignments.

Research and report back assignments

1 Draw up your personal Weekly Study Timetable. When you have discussed it with your Course Tutor, highlight clearly:

a) Lectures
b) College private study times
c) Home study sessions
d) Social activity breaks

Keep a copy in your travelling ring-binder and another over your desk at home.

2 In groups of three to four, design a classifying and indexing system for the books you purchase and the study materials you acquire which shows easily and clearly essential reference information and location of each item. Design your system to work either on a computer database software application package or in a card-index reference system.

3 Browse around the reference sections of your college/school and local public libraries to see what is available. Make a checklist of the texts, journals, directories, dictionaries, computer databases, audio and video cassettes, etc. relevant to your study programme and where to find them. Remember: it is essential to note each item's catalogue number. Check particularly those newspapers, magazines and journals which are subscribed to, since these will naturally provide you with information which is bang up-to-date!

4 Having carried out your research, give a 5–10 minute illustrated talk to your group on one of the following:

a) How the Dewey Decimal system works.
b) What information related to your course is available on Prestel, and how this invaluable viewdata information bank may be accessed.
c) What computer-based information is available in your local libraries.

5 In groups of three or four, design a suitable database record, employing appropriate fields for interrogation which your class can use to store information acquired during the course for general class access. After each group has presented its design, choose the best one and install it on a database application package for use on the class personal computer.

Part of your initial research should be to secure a demonstration of available college/school database software from a DP/IT teacher.

Decide upon a shared class procedure for ensuring that useful incoming data is installed in the database at frequent intervals.

6 Check with your librarian to see what potentially useful BBC/ITV/Satellite TV programme series (especially educational ones) are in the offing. Make arrangements for suitable radio or TV programmes to be recorded for your class's information database. Draw up a class rota to ensure that a continuous watch for good material is kept for forthcoming broadcast programmes, etc, and that transmission times are posted in your base room.

7 Obtain a copy of the course aims/objectives/competences for each study unit or module for your course. Post a copy in your study area, since you can't study effectively without a study map.

Memorise the major groupings of study topics so

you always have an eye open for relevant material in the books and journals you encounter.

8 If you do not already possess them, take expert advice, and then buy a good English Language Dictionary, English Language Thesaurus, and glossaries of Business and Management Terms and Information Technology/Data Processing Terms. These handy study aids will start your lifelong personal reference library – essential for the professional!

9 If these programmes are not included in your course, enrol for them as either part-time day or evening classes now:

a) an intensive course in computer keyboarding
b) a course in a good word processing system

You are bound to need these vital skills in your first job, and they will prove extremely helpful in your studies.

10 When you have 9a and 9b under your belt, make sure you learn as soon as possible how to drive good spreadsheet and database software packages.

Work experience and simulation assignments

1 First undertake your fact-finding, then write an account of the ways in which the organisation to which you are attached manages its reference and information sources.

To start your fact-finding: you may need to consider British Standards and manufacturing, names and addresses of potential customers for marketing, price lists and product specifications, records of designs and drawings, activities of competitors and so on.

2 After having carried out your research, write an entry for your attachment organisations's training manual (of about 500 words) entitled:

'How your local reference library and in-house reference unit can help you in your job.'

3 Assume that you are currently attached to the office of the Personnel Manager of Sentinel Pensions Limited, a company specialising in life assurance and pensions services. The Personnel Manager is concerned about the effect that the current downturn in teenagers emerging from local schools and colleges is having on the expansion plans of Sentinel. And so he gives you this briefing:

'I'd like you to do some research and find out as much as you can about the demographic trends regarding school and college leavers and the availability of mature returners to work in our county. Hopefully you will be able to produce some graphs and visuals as well as a factsheet to give me a briefing on the current situation. This will be invaluable in helping to gauge where we should direct our recruiting efforts and subsequent training inputs, etc.'

Use your initiative to obtain the information requested and present it as interestingly as possible.

4 Having carried out your research, draw up a checklist of up-to-date information and reference sources for use by the staff who work in the department or unit to which you are attached. In an accompanying paper, supply your reasons for including each item you selected. For example, the *Municipal Year Book* is invaluable in local government, and *Kompass* in sales and marketing.

Case study

'You can't afford to be wrong'

The following interview recently took place between Frances Barker, a marketing manager, and David Jackson, an educational researcher:

DAVID JACKSON   Let's turn to sources of information. When you were following your business education course did you make much use of your college library?

FRANCES BARKER   Well, not enough – initially! When I first started at the college, I used to walk past the library and feel somehow 'put off' by the rows and rows of books. I suppose it looked a bit intimidating. We were all given an induction and the library staff were very helpful, but even so, I just didn't make the effort to get to grips with the way it was organised and then, of course, I felt I didn't want to have to ask basic questions about where to find books.

DAVID JACKSON   Did your failure to use the library have any adverse effects?

FRANCES BARKER   Oh, yes! It wasn't long before my work suffered. Both the teaching staff and I knew that I wasn't doing any proper research for assignments or checking up on half-remembered facts and so on.

DAVID JACKSON   Well, Frances, what caused you to change your attitude towards using the library?

FRANCES BARKER   Oh, I almost blush to tell you even now! I was brought up with a jolt when I was asked to produce a programme introducing a distinguished speaker invited to the college to give a talk to students in my department. Well, I thought I knew how he spelled his name and also, I'd somehow missed the fact that he'd been knighted in a New Year's Honours List. He really was an eminent person in the business field, with a string of letters after his name – all of which I could have checked and included in the programme, which in the event was duplicated in something of a rush. Well, you can imagine my embarrassment! People were definitely not amused, and I just wanted to hide! From that day on I vowed I would become expertly acquainted with the library and its information and reference services. It was a salutary lesson, and one which has stood me in good stead in my own management career.

DAVID JACKSON   Did you find that being familiar with library services helped you in your job?

FRANCES BARKER   Absolutely! You see, in my view there are basically two types of knowledge – firstly, simply knowing a thing for sure, and secondly, knowing how and where to look up and find out about something when you're not sure or simply don't know. In my present job. I work for a senior marketing manager with contacts and associations in all sorts of fields – local government, the civil service, manufacturing companies and overseas organisations. I never know what he'll want to find out about next – it could be exporting regulations to Brazil or the name and address of the Chief Executive of the Berkshire County Council. And in such matters – I found out early – you can't afford to be wrong!

   Also, my principal's interested in what is absolutely new on the market and on what our competitors are doing, so I often have to refer to the specialist trade journals and magazines – which incidentally are taken by my local public library!

DAVID JACKSON   What about the librarians themselves, do you use their expertise?

FRANCES BARKER   Very much so. In fact, I'm frequently on the telephone asking for some rather obscure piece of information and they're most helpful, and their expertise saves me an awful lot of time. And even when they don't have the book or journal I need, they'll obtain it for me. In fact I don't think I could do my particular job without the help they provide.

DAVID JACKSON   Thank you, Frances, that's been a most interesting account. It's funny, isn't it, how sometimes an isolated incident can cause people to change an attitude completely. And in your case, I'm sure it was all to the good.

Assignments and discussion topics

1 Read the above case study concerning the experiences of a former student and in a group discussion, consider the following questions:

a) What is it about libraries which some students find so off-putting and daunting?
   Is it that some students fail to take the trouble to find out what a help a library can be sufficiently early in their courses and then don't like to 'lose face' by showing they feel intimidated and embarrassed by not knowing how to locate a book or use the cataloguing system?

b) Do some students use their sense of discomfort at being in a library as an excuse for underlying laziness?

c) What do you think could be done in your school or college to encourage students to make more effective use of the library?

2 In pairs of groups of 3–4 students, carry out a careful survey of the range of services and resources which your library offers and produce a leaflet or brochure including suitable diagrams and illustrations which would appeal to other student groups within your centre. Your aim in producing

this leaflet should be to encourage doubtful library users to overcome any hesitations in using the library's facilities to the full.

Your leaflet should not include more than 250–300 words in total.

3 Arrange for two of your class students to meet with your librarian to discuss:

a) how your class could receive a copy of the regularly published list of new acquisitions for posting in your base room,

b) when it would be convenient for your librarian or deputy to provide your class with a tour of the library and to give an introductory briefing on how it works and what resources it possesses.

2

The communication process

Photograph by courtesy of British Telecom

Overview

Unit 2 provides you with information and guidelines on:

- The theory of communication and the stages of the communication process when a sender and receiver interact to send and receive a message.
- The major causes and remedies of breakdowns in communication in an organisation.
- The major communication media and routes in current use and the pros and cons of each.
- How communications are routed throughout organisations – vertically, laterally, diagonally, etc.
- How Information Technology has enabled organisations to introduce computerised management information systems (CMIS) and how they work.
- The major communication activities and preoccupations of the manager and secretary,
- The impact of IT upon communication styles and practices in organisations and how their cultures are affected.

Introduction

'I've always believed in calling a spade a spade . . .'
'I don't believe in beating about the bush . . .'
'Always speak my mind . . .'
'I fancy I'm pretty clear-minded . . .'

'Communication? No problem – it's the other people round here . . .'

It's a fact of life that we all consider ourselves to be good communicators. After all, by the time we start work we've been at it for at least sixteen years, and we manage to get what we want. Or do we? Part of our self-esteem, that image of ourselves which acts as a kind of defence-mechanism in the face of the bruisings of this world, requires that we see ourselves as straight-talking, level-headed, able, honest, and above all, effective communicators.

Yet how often do we fail to see ourselves as others see us?

'Trouble with Harry, he always calls a spade a shovel . . .'

'Like a bull in a china shop at the last meeting . . .'

'Every time she opens her mouth, she puts her foot in it . . .'

'Janet's all right, she just has a talent for rubbing people up the wrong way . . .'

'He's all right as long as it's only the computer he's talking to!'

All too often there is a difference between what we say and what we think we have said, and between how we feel we have handled people and how they think they have been treated. When such 'gaps' occur between the intent and the action often it is stated that there has been 'a breakdown in communication'. Sometimes the breakdown is allowed to become so serious that the gap becomes a chasm – relatives in families ceasing to speak to one another, managements and trade unions refusing to meet and governments recalling ambassadors when relations between states reach a low ebb.

In fact, whenever people communicate, either as individuals or within groups, problems inevitably occur – instructions may be impossible to carry out, offence is taken at a particular remark, a directive is ambiguously phrased, or people's attitudes are coloured by jealousy, resentment or frustration.

During the past fifty years, industrial, commercial and public service organisations have grown prodigiously to meet the needs of advanced technological societies. Sometimes as many as 10 000 people work on one site, or one company employs more than 50 000 people. Multinational companies send electronic messages on facsimile transmitters around the world at the press of a button. Clearly, good communications are essential to the efficient operation of any organisation, and vital to the fulfilment of all those who commit their working lives to it.

For this reason, management specialists and behavioural scientists have devoted much thought and energy over recent years to analysing the problems caused by bad communication practices, and to creating good communication climates, and systems.

As a result of the current structure of societies and economies, most of us will spend our working lives in an organisation – for many of us it will be a large one. If we are to understand our working environment it is essential that we become good communicators with effective social skills.

Theory and process

Ever since the 1930s, management and communication specialists have sought to explain the complex processes of human communication with the help of models. Two such American researchers, C Shannon and W Weaver devised a model identifying the key processes of communication to explain their work in telephone and radio telecommunications in the late 1930s.

Basically, the Shannon and Weaver model illustrates a one-way system, since they were interested in how an electrical signal was transmitted along a wire or radio wave and what happened to it during transmission. Their concept of noise allowed for the distortion and interference of static upon the message's signal which might prevent its clear reception. Today, the concept of 'noise' in human communication models refers to anything interfering between the transmission and reception of the message. For example, an urgent memorandum might lie undetected upon an executive's desk if blanked out by a canopy of white paper documents. Or the distraction of a noisy office might prevent a manager from grasping the crucial points of an orally delivered report.

Other communication theorists have emphasised the importance of the two-way nature of communication in which the success of the process depends heavily upon the sender receiving feedback. Naturally, the sender needs frequent reassurance that his points are being received and understood – hence the regular confirmations we all make over the telephone to assure our contact that we are still paying attention: 'Yes, of course . . . no, no . . . Absolutely!', etc.

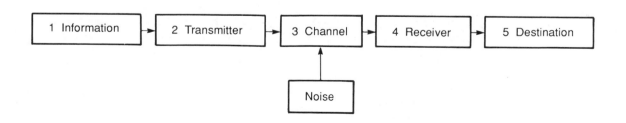

(From Fiske, John, *Introduction to Communication Studies*, Methuen & Co.)

Without such feedback, the speaker wavers, soon thinking he may be talking into an empty void! By the same token, the sender of a written letter needs to obtain prompt confirmation that its message is being dealt with – 'Thank you for your letter of 14 June 19-- which is currently receiving our attention . . .'. Similarly, fax transmitters issue instant confirmations that the faxed message has been successfully received somewhere around the globe.

The following circular model of the communication process serves as a general purpose one in which six stages are identified, three involving the sender, and three the receiver. At each stage, key actions are highlighted, together with illustrations of what can go wrong, and thus impair the process.

Self assessment questions

1 How much thought have you given to your own techniques of communication as a student in terms of quality and effectiveness? Review your personal performance: orally in class; as a working member of a class group; in written assignments; interacting with teaching staff and local employers; interpreting correctly body language signals from others etc.

2 Are you clear about the ways in which noise and distractors in the transmission phase of the communication process can distort the clear reception of the message? Make up a short list of examples and check them out with fellow students and your teacher.

Theory and process of communication

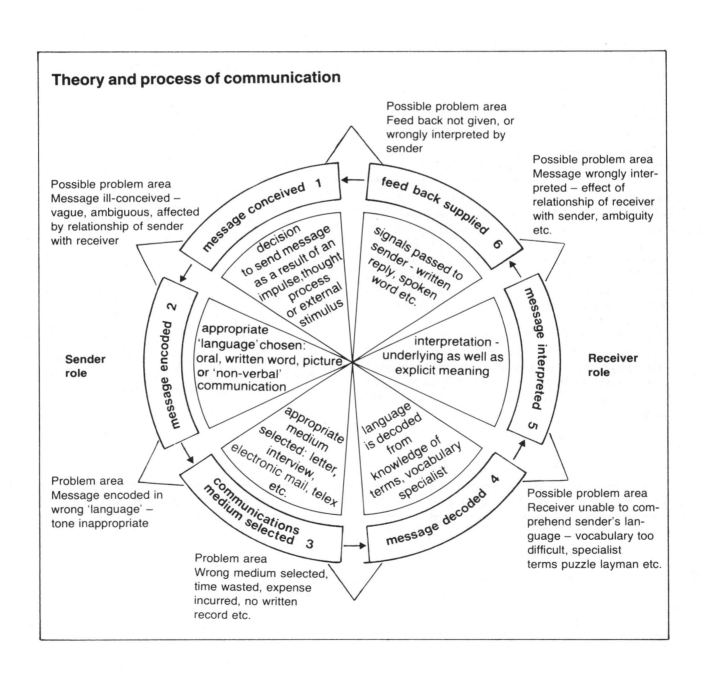

Key factors in successful communication

Stage

1 Conceiving the message

As the homespun philosopher so rightly advised: 'Think before putting mouth in gear!' Consider the best means of getting your message across and remember that timing is important. Study your recipient(s) carefully and pitch your message to suit their particular needs.

2 Encoding the message

Choose the medium (or media mix) in which to encode your message thoughtfully. Graphics and pictures have immediacy and can be emotive; words and numbers convey detail but may be dull; the spoken word is fast but may leave no record. So think before leaping into print or reaching for your phone and decide beforehand what specific outcomes you need from your communication.

3 Selecting the communication channel

The Information Technology revolution in electronic office equipment has made an array of telecommunication channels available – computerised telephones, mobile phones and pagers, fax, electronic mail, etc. alongside their traditional paper-based counterparts. All embrace a trade-off between speed, cost, simultaneous receipt of message, confidentiality and so on. So make sure you have made an intelligent decision on channel selection before despatching your message. And always remember electronic mail memos zapped out in anger cannot be retrieved!

4 Decoding the message

The spate of messages arriving in offices has grown enormously in the past ten years. Thoughtful systems are therefore necessary today to ensure that important incoming messages are given the priority they deserve, that all messages are routed promptly and that time is taken to absorb their meaning. This implies that the receiver is equipped to understand, perhaps, abstruse and technical jargon or speaks the EEC language used, or shares the sender's business culture and outlook. Furthermore, the receiver is duty bound to ensure that he is not acting as a block to the message as a result of hostility towards its sender, or from destructive rivalry, etc.

5 Interpreting the message

As a result of the subtle and, indeed, sometimes devious relationships which exist between human beings, the explicit or overt meaning of a received message may conceal a hidden meaning – of a message to be read 'between the lines' –

'Sorry about old Jonesy. Not a bad bloke really. Still, I daresay they'll be looking for someone with real DP experience to head up Computer Services now!'

In such ways, superficial feelings are phrased – consciously or unconsciously – to reveal underlying ones. And people often communicate in a kind of code which is meant to exclude others not part of an inner circle. It is always important therefore for the message receiver to devote sufficient time and reflection to ensuring that incoming messages are interpreted correctly.

6 Feedback

Unless the message's sender is provided with prompt and unambiguous feedback, then the communication process is likely to be frustrated. The receiver, then, however busy, must take immediate steps to provide feedback. In person-to-person oral communication, this is not generally a problem; with written messages, self-discipline and courtesy are needed to ensure that a customer's letter of complaint, say, is immediately acknowledged pending investigation, or that a sales order is directly actioned and a confirming advice note raised.

Talking points

1 Do you think that communication models help to explain the process or that they tend to over-simplify it?
2 In what ways has the widespread introduction of electronic office equipment affected communication processes? Are the changes made for the better, or worse in your view?
3 'The theory's all very well in principle, but in practice you just don't have time to indulge in all this prior thinking and decision-making stuff!'

Routes of communication

In developed organisations, communications flow down, up and across, from board-room to shop-floor and back, between departmental managers or between sales assistants. They also move diagonally between different levels of different departments:

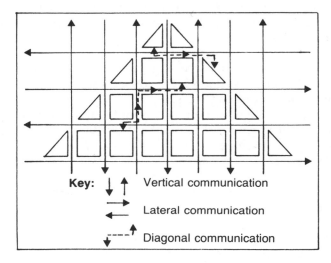

Key:
↓ ↑ Vertical communication
→ ← Lateral communication
╌╌→ Diagonal communication

Vertical communication

This term is used to describe the principal channel for routing directives, instructions and policies from top decision makers down through the organisation to the people who, at various levels, will implement them.

Correspondingly, the term describes those upward channels through which flow ideas, suggestions, criticisms and queries from the retail branch, factory floor or middle management.

To an organisation, an upward communication flow is just as important as a downward one. When downward communication becomes an avalanche and upward communication a tremble, then, sooner or later, an organisation will suffer from poor morale, low productivity and potentially explosive frustration in its employees.

The downward flow of communication is most frequently channelled through an organisation's 'line of authority', from manager to subordinate in a 'reports to' relationship.

Lateral communication

The most frequent and routine communication occurs between people who operate at the same or similar levels. For example, sales assistants behind a counter may share an on-going dialogue as part of the daily serving of customers. Similarly, clerical staff in a large county council office need to interact constantly in the course of their business. Lateral communication occurs at all levels of an organisation and is generally marked by the increased frankness and ease with which groups at similar levels – peer groups – communicate. The reason is that they are less affected or inhibited by the 'chain-of-command' situation which employees tend to experience when communicating with superiors.

Sometimes, however, lateral communication between peer groups may be adversely affected by attitudes of rivalry or jealousy. At other times remote geographical location prevents frequent communication. For this reason, among others, the relatively lonely sales representative is brought to meet his fellow representatives at the Annual Sales Conference.

Diagonal communication

Frequently tasks arise in organisations which span departments. In this situation there may be no obvious line of authority through which a middle-manager, for example may 'require' a service or a job to be performed. He may be dealing with a colleague more senior to him in another department, and if the colleague is junior to him, he or she still will not report to him, and may therefore feel under less of an obligation.

Diagonal communication, therefore relies heavily on reservoirs of cooperation and good-will which the proficient communicator will have been careful to nurture by way of the friendly greeting or brief chat to this and that colleague on his journeys through the company's offices.

Summary

One of the most demanding tasks in any organisation lies in keeping all communication routes as open as possible. They are the veins and arteries carrying the organisation's life-blood.

The routes or channels along which communication flows may be classified in another way:

formal	grapevine
informal	bypassing

Formal

This description is applied to those communications which are routed through what have been called 'official channels'. For instance, a written memorandum from a managing director to his departmental heads to call a meeting, or a written report from a regional manager to his sales manager are termed 'formal communications'.

This route, understandably, is used to disseminate an organisation's directives and instructions for execution, since it is reinforced by the authority of those executives who act as 'staging-posts' in relaying such requirements.

Informal

A surprising amount of communicating is done in organisations informally even when it is official. That is to say that much information is passed on by word of mouth among interested colleagues who have received it from various sources – briefings, memoranda, visits, reports and so on. Spontaneous gatherings around a desk may spark off the exchange of such informal information. Informal meetings act in the same way. Usually, however, even when staff communicate informally there is an underlying presence of line authority in that they may share a restricted access to certain types of information, and unwritten rules exist to ensure that it does not leave a particular set of people.

Grapevine

Every organisation has its grapevine. The term describes the interleaving branches of a totally unofficial communication system which has been constructed informally and which is constantly changing.

Users and distributors of grapevine sources of information find their material in the form of confidential letters left unattended on desks, accidental, careless remarks, loud voices coming from behind closed doors or sudden changes in established routines and practices. The basis of the grapevine is gossip and rumour. It is often the cause of misplaced resentments or unfounded fears. It flourishes more particularly in organisations in which communication channels are more closed than open. And it is not entirely unknown for senior managers to use the grapevine from time time as a means of disseminating a message they choose not to endorse openly. Like the real grapevine, it is extremely hardy, and flourishes on many different types of soil. Unlike the real grape, however, its fruit is seldom sweet!

Bypassing

Sometimes the urgency or importance of a communication requires that its sender, perhaps a managing director or sales manager, chooses a route which bypasses any intermediate management or supervisory stages. For example, the managing director may wish to send an individual letter to all company employees regarding rumours of a proposed merger, or a sales manager may wish to relay direct to all sales staff details of a new bonus scheme.

Most middle managers are mindful of their authority, which is sometimes uneasy in between top management and junior staff. Too frequent bypassing of them in the communication process tends to lead to resentment. This route, therefore, is used judiciously.

Self assessment question

In order to clarify your understanding of communication routes in organisations, analyse with a fellow-student the routes employed in the college or school in which you are studying and compare your findings with the theory.

Talking points

1 'If people concerned themselves less with communicating and more with doing some actual work, we might get something done round here!'

2 'You're either a born communicator – 'gift of the gab' and all that – or you're not!'

3 'The trouble is, once you get everybody chipping in their two-penn'orth, you get further away from a decision, not nearer.'

4 'You either believe in all that communication mumbo-jumbo or you don't. Either way, I don't think it makes any difference.'

5 'As far as I can see, a lot of the communication thing goes on without people being aware of it. If that's the case, it doesn't seem to matter whether you develop these techniques or not.'

6 'I can't see how communication techniques affect me. You see, in my job I'm asked to do something and I do it. Simple as that.'

7 'It's all right, I suppose, if you're a manager, but if you're at people's beck and call like me, you don't get much chance to be a whatdoyoucallit, "communicator chappie".'

8 'All this new technology just gets in the way of good, old-fashioned plain speaking!'

Management information and communication systems

During the past twenty or so years, organisations around the developed world have invested billions of pounds in installing management information systems (MIS), usually coordinated by computers. A single mainframe computer (perhaps linked to others and carefully backed up) holds all company data, which is constantly being updated and revised and to which all staff have various degrees of access, depending on their status and clearance.

Such computer-based information systems are also having a significant impact upon organisational communication. Because of the sophistication of communication systems and the growing emphasis upon top-quality presentation of information – both within the organisation and outside it, new posts have been devised to meet changed organisational needs and practices. For example, in many organisations, the former secretary/PA is now a Support Services Officer. Erstwhile assistant office managers have taken on new duties as Communication Officers or Information Services Managers.

Part of the role of such support service personnel is to monitor the ways in which communication takes place within the organisation and with its external contacts and clients, so as to ensure that inefficient approaches are dropped and more efficient and cost-effective ones substituted.

For example, changing company activities may require new communication structures in which a cumbersome hierarchy of line management is replaced by a series of small and fast-moving project teams – see diagram below.

Talking point

In terms of interpersonal communication in the workplace, is IT going to help or hinder over the next decade?

The media of communication

The electronic revolution, following its mechanical predecessor has brought profound changes to the way that organisations communicate. The 'communications explosion' is still resounding through the final decade of the twentieth century. The developments in telecommunications, computers and information technology have revolutionised the business world. Executives speak of 'drowning in a sea of bumf', the shrill sound of telephone bells punctuates some offices incessantly and computer print-out has the capacity to paper the walls of many an office tower block! The world of Victorian copperplate, hand-written invoicing already seems centuries old.

Traditional and flexible sales department structures

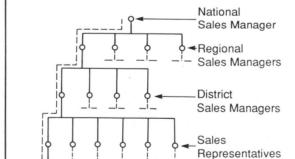

MODEL 1 Traditional structure

National Sales Manager
Regional Sales Managers
District Sales Managers
Sales Representatives
CUSTOMERS

– – – Line management and stepped communication route to Sales Representatives selling ALL product lines

NOTE THE CRUCIAL ROLE OF NETWORKED COMPUTERISED INFORMATION SYSTEMS UNDERPINNING MODEL 2

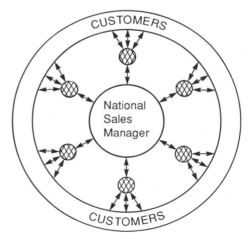

MODEL 2 Flexible structure

National Sales Manager

The National Sales Office coordinates and services product sales forces

CUSTOMERS

National Sales Manager

CUSTOMERS

Semi-autonomous *Product* sales forces with national brief to sell *one* product line or small group of related products

The sheer range of communications media, their sophistication and the technology which makes instant communicating possible, place heavy demands upon those who communicate within organisations. The manager must control and direct the flow of communication which he generates and receives; the secretary must become proficient in the use of a wide range of business systems and pieces of business equipment; he or she needs to have mastered often very complex record storage and retrieval systems. The diagram above illustrates the broad extent of the manager's and secretary's business activities and the range of communications media available, together with some of the communicating 'tools'. Every employee within an organisation is making constant value-judgements about what to communicate, how to do it, what medium to choose, and 'what tool' or equipment to employ. Moreover, being successful in one's job means mastering the media and equipment rather than allowing them to master you!

Talking point:

Behind every good communicator stands a competent and versatile technician

Communication: the functions, the media, the tools

The manager

reads
speaks
listens
drafts

informs
explains
persuades

decides
delegates
consults
proposes
suggests
organises

classifies
analyses
evaluates

selects
summarises

appraises
assesses

plans
thinks

Written communication
word processed –
letters, memoranda, reports
minutes, mail-merged circulars,
minutes;
Email messages etc.
faxed and telexed documents,
wide area networked Email

Oral communication
conversations, interviews,
meetings, conferences, presentations,
seminars, briefings,

telephone/mobile phone-calls,
audio and tele-conferencing,
voice-mail/answerphone messaging,
audio-dictation etc etc.

Non-verbal communication
facial, hand, body gestures and
positioning; expression, movement,
stance etc.

Communication tools
voice, face, body, PC computer terminal,
fax, telex, video tv, audio cassette,
computerised telephone system, laptop
computer and modem, viewfoils, slides
videofilm, desk-top publishing system,
colour and mono photocopier, microform
systems, graphics software, posters,
bulletins, public address, electronic
mailboxes etc.

The secretary

reads
speaks
listens

takes shorthand
transcribes
types
word processes
and prints documents
produced from desk-top
organising integrated
software
maintains electronic
diary and meetings
scheduling systems

proof-reads
edits

disseminates
filters

informs
explains
consults

processes data
files data
extracts and
disseminates data
classifies
evaluates

confirms
arranges
assists

Talking point

How do you see the communication process in organisations evolving over the next decade as a result of comprehensive IT uptake?

Talking point

What potential dangers and pitfalls do you detect in organisational reliance upon computerised information processing systems and networks?

Advantages and disadvantages of principal communications media

	Advantages	*Disadvantages*
Written communication		
Letter Memorandum Report Abstract Minutes Article Press release etc.	**Provides written record** and evidence of despatch and receipt; capable of relaying complex ideas; provides analysis, evaluation and summary; disseminates information to dispersed receivers; can confirm, interpret and clarify oral communications; forms basis of contract or agreement.	**Can take time to produce, can be expensive;** communication tends to be more formal and distant; can cause problems of interpretation; instant feedback is not possible; once despatched, difficult to modify message; does not allow for exchange of opinion, views or attitudes except over period of time.
Oral communication		
Face-to-face conversation Interview Meeting Oral briefing Public address Oral presentation Telephone call Conference Training session etc.	**Direct medium of communication;** advantages of physical proximity and, usually, both sight and sound of sender and receiver; allows for instant interchange of opinion, views, attitudes – instantaneous feedback; easier to convince or persuade; allows for contribution and participation from all present.	More difficult to hold ground in face of opposition; **more difficult to control when a number of people take part;** lack of time to think things out – quality of decision-making may be inferior; often no written record of what has been said; sometimes disputes result over what was agreed.
Visual communication		
Non-verbal communication – expression, gesture, posture Diagram Chart Table Graph Photograph Film slide Film Video tape Model Mock-up etc.	**Reinforces oral communication;** provides additional visual stimulus; simplifies written or spoken word; quantifies – provides ideas in number form; provides simulations of situations; illustrates techniques and procedures; provides visual record.	**May be difficult to interpret** without reinforcing written or spoken word; requires additional skills of comprehension and interpretation; can be costly and expensive in time to produce; may be costly to disseminate or distribute; storage may be more expensive; does not always allow time for evaluation.

Computerised telecommunications

	Advantages	*Disadvantages*
Local/wide area networks Fax Telex Packet switching Teleconferencing Computer conferencing/ networking	**Speed of transmission:** WAN messages, London to Sydney, Australia in 11 seconds. **Versatility:** Fax can transmit text, number, graphics, artwork and photographs all on one side of A4 if need be. Tele-and computer conferencing provide interpersonal exchanges visually and via VDU screens. **Accuracy:** Instantaneous message-reading and checking of electronic circuits operating between sending and receiving equipment during the transmission of high-speed 'bits' of the message in packet-switching of computer data ensure the message is accurately received in remote locations. **Feedback/instantaneous exchange:** Computerised telecommunications allow for a virtually simultaneous exchange of information and responses.	**Volume of transmitted data:** The volume of telecommunicated information is increasing at such a rate that business personnel are unable to absorb it within relevant time limits. **Costs:** Telecommunicated messages have billing premiums placed upon them to pay for the enormous development and hardware investments made nationally and internationally. However, the cost of fax, telex and communications modems etc is falling rapidly in an expanding market. **Legal implications:** Words printed on paper at source still have a legal currency that a faxed message does not (but which telex does!). **Instant delivery:** The almost instantaneous delivery of LAN/WAN Email messages etc can cause upsets if messages are composed in anger or are 'half-baked' and then despatched irretrievably.

Talking point:

Effective communication is usually the result of a careful selection of the appropriate medium, or combination of media available

---

The communication process and information technology

As the information technology 'explosion' continues to expand in office communications, it is still worth remembering that human beings have to rely on the same old five senses with which to communicate – however sophisticated IT hardware and software may be. Nevertheless, the widespread – indeed all-embracing – impact of IT upon organisations and office systems has changed fundamentally the ways in which office personnel communicate.

In a nutshell, computerised telecommunications have created a truly global village in terms of the immediacy within which people across continents can share conversations, televised pictures, interactive software on VDUs, maps, circuits, graphics and the like.

The process of decision-making has also become much faster, thanks to instant access to vast databanks of information held in huge mainframe computer memory banks. One downside effect of this trend, however, is that managers and support staff have much less time in which to absorb and respond to large inputs of information transmitted across the world. For example, the agent of the Hudson Bay or East India Company in the eighteenth century would wait months for an instruction to arrive by sailing ship, and the owners a similar period for a response. Today, fax, Email, telex, teleconferencing and telephone link-ups enable complex policy and strategy decisions to be shared and thrashed out within the hour or day, literally across the five continents!

Looking to the future, the very nature of people's jobs, their working locations and cultures, are likely to change radically as a result of the IT revolution. Already the term 'telemuting' has been coined to describe the growing pattern of working from home, linked to the office by modem and computer terminal. The rapidly expanding take-up of local and wide area network (LAN/WAN) messaging systems along with allied fax/telex/viewdata communications modems as personal computer add-ons enables a manager or secretary to establish worldwide communication links without even the need to move from his or her desk-top computer terminal!

At the same time, the amount of face-to-face oral communication, across the office desk or around the meetings table, may decline in the face of computer-based video, telephone or computer screen hook-ups, and the value of vital face-to-face contact may yield to electronic wizardry which both distances and impersonalises.

So rapid has the introduction of IT-based office technologies proved, that many managers in middle age have settled for coping with rather than managing a semi-computerised office information system. It is therefore vital that tomorrow's managers and office support staff still in vocational education and training make the time, not only to master the mechanics of IT technology, but also to determine the extent to which they are prepared to interact with it. As with all technologies, IT is already proving an excellent slave, but could yet become a bad master!

Self assessment question

Review your own opinions and views about the applications of IT in organisations. How committed are you to attaining an early competence in using computer applications, say, in your own studies? Have you started to acquire keyboarding skills yet? Have you managed to obtain a self-study floppy disk to aid this vital skill? Have you started to word-process your assignments yet? Can you yet use database and spreadsheet packages? Have you set up yet a filing system to store magazine clippings and photocopies on the latest applications of IT in offices? If your answer is 'no' to some of the above questions, then devise your personal action plan and get stuck in now!

Talking point

'Information is power!' Do you think that IT in organisations is more or less likely to provide better access to information for managers and support staff throughout the organisational hierarchy? If you had to devise a policy for controlling the distribution of information in a largish company, what would be your first thoughts and approaches?

IT has created 'The global village'

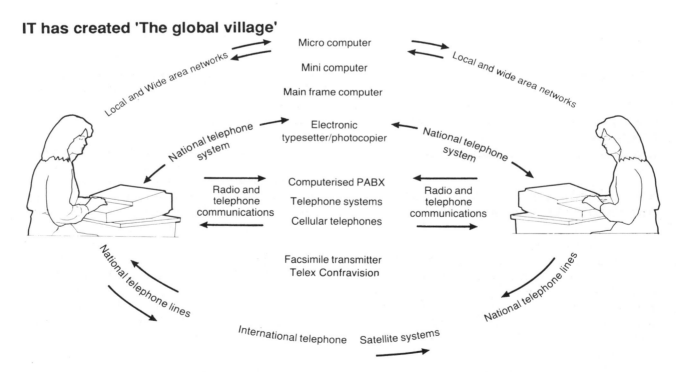

"The new electronic interdependence recreates the world in the image of the global village".
The Gutenberg Galaxy, Marshall McLuhan

Summary of main points

1 Shannon and Weaver's communication model identified five main phases – information: transmitter: channel (with noise aspect): receiver: destination The Unit's all-purpose model comprises six stages: message conception: encoding: selection of medium for transmission: interpretation: feedback.

2 Communication within organisations tends to follow these routes: vertical (up and down line management structures): lateral (across tiers in the hierarchy – among peer groups): diagonally (outside the normal line management structure, eg, between departments): bypassing (skipping over and around established hierarchic lines of management): grapevine (moving by informal word-of-mouth around the organisation).

3 Many national and multinational organisations now coordinate their information needs through management information systems (housed in a central mainframe computer) in which a *single* body of data is constantly updated and modified in the light of organisational activities and events.

4 The major media of communication in current use include: computer-based telecommunications: fax, Email, telex, viewdata; print-outs of text or VDU screen displays; oral communication; non-verbal communication; visuals and graphics – viewfoils, charts, films, videos, cctv; microfilm, desktop publishing, photographs etc.

5 Factors to be taken into account when selecting a medium for transmitting a message include: speed, costs, simultaneous delivery, confidentiality, accuracy, immediacy, feedback needs, legal requirements, degree of complexity of message.

6 Aspects of Information Technology affecting organisational communication trends include: working from home (telemuting): replacement of face-to-face communication by Email, fax and telephone (depersonalisation): information overload from 'global village effect': need for new generation managers to control IT in organisations – so it does not subvert face-to-face communication.

Talking points

In the 1960s, a communication expert, Marshall McLuhan wrote: 'The medium is the message'. What he meant was that people's lives and outlooks were deeply influenced by the ways in which the mass media – TV, film, newspaper and radio – handled and presented information and entertainment. For example, frequent televising of violent events is said to make viewers more indifferent to them.

Do you think that office employees' outlooks and attitudes are likely to be affected in a similar ways through prolonged daily interactions with PC terminals?

Is face-to-face communication likely to be adversely affected by comprehensive IT take-up, or is the danger being over-emphasised?

Do you think that people in organisations are likely to be dominated by computerised systems over the next decade, or is a breed of manager likely to emerge capable of exercising control over the information explosion now occurring?

Do you think that the widespread uptake of computerised communication and information systems in organisations is likely to change their structures and the work patterns of their employees significantly? If so, in what ways?

Activities and assignments

Discussion assignments

Discuss the following extracts from conversations:

'I've never been so insulted in my life! All I wanted was to try the set on approval and I was informed over the phone that this was entirely possible. When I arrived your assistant asked me for a deposit against possible damage – anyone would think I was a hi-fi vandal!'

'Listen here, Smith, just because you won the Affordale contract you think you're the bee's-knees round here! Let me tell you, some of us in this office were winning contracts when you were still in nappies! So don't come so condescending with us – we won't wear it!'

'Well, you see, I'm new here . . .'

'I don't know, it's all very frustrating. Sales are up in the air because of the extra paperwork. Accounts are complaining about the costs. Marketing are determined to push it through at all costs. And Personnel maintain we can't staff if. Still, I daresay it will sort itself out . . .'

'Don't ask me, I only work here!'

'The trouble with Jonesy is, he ain't got the nerve to sort out the late-comers – too many of his golden boys among 'em. But I'm telling you, this place don't get started properly until half-past nine in the morning – and he calls 'isself a manager!'

'No, sorry. You're the sixth person to ask for the blue one this week. Trouble is, we don't get much call for the blue ones . . .'

'I've had just about enough! This is the fifth week running that they've messed up my pay-slip. They ought to bury that wretched computer down the deepest coal-mine. They must know when the thing's gone wrong! Look, answer my phone for me will you? I'm going over to wages to sort this out right now!'

'Nothing to do with me, chum. Try Servicing . . .'

'It's no good. Harry, you've just got to take the bull by the horns, or there'll be no factory. If you'd grasped the nettle six months ago it might have been easier. As it is, you'll have to handle it the best way you can. But it's got to be done!'

'You're wasting your time. Take it from me. Just keep your head down, wait for pay-day and keep your nose clean. I mean, if your idea was any good, they'd have thought it up years ago, now wouldn't they?'

'I don't care who you are! There's nothing in my contract says I have to put up with your carry on!'

'Can't you read the notice? It says ''No refunds on sales goods''. I mean, if they didn't mean it, they wouldn't have put it there, now would they?'

'Look, Jenkins, when I want advice from you I'll ask for it. OK?'

'No, I didn't get it sorted out. He just waffled on about spirals and escalations or something. They always tie you up with words. Anyway, I'm going to be looking for something else now . . .'

'Yes Mr Theobald. Of course Mr Theobald. No, no. . . . it was nothing really. It was just that . . . No, I know. I realise you're busy . . . Yes, I know I can see you any time . . . No. Sorry to have troubled you'. (Puts down 'phone.)

Quick review quiz

1 What advantages are there in devising communication models to explain the theory of the process?

2 List the six major stages in a two-way communication process.

3 Identify at each of the stages you list in Question 2 major types of problems or pitfalls which may occur.

4 Draw up a checklist of the principal media in which a message may be communicated today.

5 Outline briefly the advantages and disadvantages of using each of the media you identify in Question 4 above.

6 Explain the importance of feedback in the communication cycle.

7 Make out two checklists of the main communication activities of a) a manager and b) a secretary.

8 Explain briefly how IT is affecting the communication activities of people in organisations.

9 What is meant by the acronyms MIS and CMIS?

10 Explain: unified information database real-time environment.

11 Describe the major ways in which IT is influencing the communication process at work and summarise possible dangers.

Assignment case studies

A high price to pay!

Dick had worked in the Office Administration Department of the head office of Buy-rite Supermarkets Ltd for the past ten years. He'd started off as a junior clerk and was now responsible to the Senior Administrative Officer, who herself reported to the Assistant Office Manager.

Dick was fairly conscientious and tended to keep himself to himself. He prided himself on a faultless record in producing the weekly schedules of selling prices which were distributed to each branch manager, and displayed a certain touchiness if anyone strayed into what he considered his 'patch' or questioned his performance.

He liked to recall to his fellow-clerks in the pub the occasion when he'd 'put one over' Miss Jameson, the Senior Administrative Officer, when she had queried the price of butter on the schedules:

'Forgot clean about the head office bulk purchase discount she had,' Dick would say, 'came over all hoighty-toighty. When I told her she should do her homework first. Still, what d'you expect from a woman? Think they know it all. Still, I soon put her right!'

The other clerks would smile politely but kept their own counsel.

About six months ago, as the company's business had grown, it was decided that Dick should be given a junior assistant to help generally and to learn the job.

'I don't need any help Mr Richards,' Dick had said to the Office Administration Manager. 'That'll be the day when I'm not on top of my job!'

Nevertheless, John was appointed as Dick's assistant, and Dick was asked to bring the youngster along and show him the ropes. John was rather quiet and rather self-conscious about a stammer he would develop when nervous.

'Here you are,' Dick had said to John on his first day, giving him a bulky computer print-out, 'when you've memorised these prices you can come and find me. Carry 'em all in my head I do. Never been caught out yet!'

Some weeks later, Dick was overheard shouting at John:

'Come on! Spit it out, you daft beggar! Why didn't you remember that two-pence off? I told you about that yesterday – It's too late now, all the schedules have been duplicated. You m-m-m-might well be sorry! Here, give 'em me!'

Later that morning, Dick was called into Mr Richards' office and confronted with the fact that a complaint had been made about his treatment of John.

. . . 'That's a lie!' said Dick. 'In any case, people have got to learn from their mistakes. Anyway, who's complained! Come on, you tell me! I don't see why I should have to justify myself for some anonymous Johnny. Was it the lad?'

The Office Administration Manager indicated that John had said nothing and that he wasn't prepared to divulge his sources:
'But I will say this; this is the second complaint I've received and called you in over in the last two months. If there is another instance I shall further implement the provisions of the company's disciplinary procedure.'

To which Dick replied:

'Well, you know what you can do with your procedure! Keep your job! I don't have to work in some kind of police-state outfit!'

And with that he stormed out.

Assignment

What was the nature of Dick's shortcomings? Were they entirely his fault? Did Mr Richards handle the interview correctly? Could the outcome have been avoided? Make a written analysis of the case study outlining problems and causes. Alternatively, analyse the case study in syndicate groups and discuss your findings in your full group.

Research and report back assignments

Your teacher may ask you (singly, in pairs or as a small group) to research into the following topics and to report back orally, or by means of a written report or factsheet, or by giving an AVA (audio-visual aids) supported presentation to your class. Remember to secure overall authorisation from your teacher before contacting people outside your college or school and arranging visits etc. Make sure you store class reports, etc. in a computerised filing system for later reference etc. And, most important, make sure you respect confidential information – as professionals always do.

1 Arrange to interview *one* of the following local people in order to find out what their major communication activities are and how they structure and perform them:

a) the sales manager of a local manufacturing company

b) the secretary of a local general practitioner (GP) or departmental manager

c) a solicitor

d) a sales assistant in a local departmental store

c) an accountant in a business with more than 50 employees

d a local government officer in a housing, social services, treasury or education department

2 When you have been assigned your contact in Question 1 above, prepare a set of interview questions including:

a) In what ways do you most frequently communicate? Why?

b) What sort of breakdowns in communication do you typically experience?

c) How do you set about putting them right?

d) Has the introduction of information technology made much difference to your job?

e) What advice about communicating well would you give to a young person starting a full-time job in your kind of career sector?

3 When you have carried out your researches into the above Assignments, in pairs report back on your findings to your group. Then, devise an insert for a new employee's induction manual which provides advice on how to communicate effectively in an organisation during the first weeks of appointment, using the information you obtained from your interviews.

4 Arrange to interview a retail store branch manager and sales assistants within the following general topic areas:

a) What communication skills are needed in jobs which involve extended and direct contact with customers?

b) How do you handle customer complaints?

5 Make an appointment to interview a departmental manager in a company or local authority department (of an organisation of 50 plus employees) and find out how he or she communicates and receives communications within the vertical/lateral/diagonal and informal (grapevine etc) routes of the organisation.

Try to obtain 'for instances' of good practice, company policy, difficulties and pitfalls etc. And remember when reporting back not to inadvertently betray any confidences or 'off-the-record' remarks which could cause embarrassment etc.

6 In pairs, arrange to visit a local large, medium and small organisation using computers and electronic office equipment and find out how communication practices have been affected by the introduction of IT. Report back to your class through an oral AVA-supported presentation.

7 Having carried out the researches associated with Questions 1–6, in groups of 3–4 draw up a code of practice aimed at promoting effective and ethical communication practices for employees in organisations – a kind of Communicators' Charter. Compare the code your group drew up with the others produced. Consider whether you could (or indeed should) conduct your working life in accordance with the best code your class produced.

Work experience and simulation assignments

1 Design a chart to show clearly how information and communications flow around the organisation to which you are attached. Indicate also the major ways in which it communicates with its external contacts and networks.

2 Within your attachment organisation, carry out a survey on what communications media are used for what types of message. Find out what staff regard as the advantages and disadvantages of each medium. Choose an appropriate method to convey your findings to your attachment supervisor and fellow students.

3 Find out how departmental personnel in the department you are working in ask for work to be done or information to be made available from staff in other departments. Use your findings to write a paragraph in the New Staff Induction Manual which highlights good practice and explains 'how to get things done' amicably.

4 Arrange to shadow one of the following members of staff, and, over the course of the working day,

make a log of the different types of communication dealt with, the media used and the reasons for using them as well as any useful tips on effective communication practices:

a) a departmental manager or deputy
b) a personal secretary
c) a sales representative
d) a clerical officer
e) a works foreman

5 During your attachment, keep a diary of noteworthy occurrences about the way that the communication processes of the staff you work with are affected by the fact that they are at work, in an organisation. For example.

How are customers spoken to or written to?
How do senior/junior staff communicate with each other?
Are staff more or less formal than you expected?
How do people communicate so as to get tasks done by due dates etc.?

As part of your post-attachment debriefing with your group, give a suitably anonymous oral report to your group on your findings. Seek to define what factors determine communication processes in organisations.

Case study

Clean sweep at Colorama

Kathy Wilkins joined the head office of Colorama plc on the first of September 19-- as the company's new Office Administration Manager. Colorama are a national company which manufactures a wide range of wallpaper and interior decoration fabrics. There are four factories strategically dispersed across the UK and a head office located in Walsall. Currently Colorama employs some 2000 employees, 120 of whom work at head office.

The major role of the Office Administration Department is to provide a support service – in-house printing, stationery supplies, office equipment purchasing, contract management for cleaning etc. company tenders coordination and so on.

Kathy Wilkins was appointed as the result of her unremitting hard work and personal commitment to the job. She had come from a smaller company and been doing a similar job. She was considered hard but fair. Her former company – and former colleagues – had benefited from her drive and determination. Colorama was in a much bigger league, however. During the DIY boom of the 1960s, the company had ridden on the crest of the home improvement wave and acquired three of its four factories between 1965 and 1969. A favourite watchword of the MD's was 'What we lack in whizzkids we make up for in continuity!'

During the past two years, though, sales had proved disappointing and Colorama's image was fast becoming staid and 'old-hat', as younger and more aggressive companies ate into Colorama's markets – in no small part as the result of having installed fast and cost-effective computerised management information and communications systems.

Kathy saw her central role as helping the company to catch up with its rivals in this regard. About four months after her appointment, she sent this Email memo through the Office Administration's newly installed local area network (LAN) communications system to all Departmental staff:

| Unclassified | Page 1 | 12 January 19-- |

From: Katherine Wilkins

To: All Departmental Staff

Subject: Use of LAN Office Communications System

You will recall that at my first Staff Meeting in September of last year, I informed the Department of my dissatisfaction at the poor performance I perceived on arrival. I told you all then that a fundamental change in attitude and performance was needed and that a new computerised communications network would be installed as a company pilot scheme to improve our administrative procedures and systems.

To this end, a great deal of effort was put into installing a LAN system against the clock. Colorama has also invested significant finance in securing LAN training for all Departmental staff since November.

I am therefore appalled to see in my daily movements around the Department that the LAN system is being scarcely used at all. I detect a widespread apathy regarding the use of the Email system – apart from offensive and sexist messages being sent. And I see little or no use of the electronic diary and desk-top management features. What I do see is the same old wasteful use of photocopying practices and the same time-consuming practice of typing out and filing of endless paper memos and reports.

Clearly my policies and instructions are being flouted. You are therefore reminded of the obligations implicit in your conditions of service concerning adherence to company policies and routines and to supply a degree of commitment related to your remuneration. Unless I detect an immediate improvement from each member of staff, I shall take firm and immediate steps to rectify matters.

KATHERINE WILKINS
Office Administration Manager
11:23 All Group C 12/01/9-

Within three hours of Kathy Wilkins having sent out her Email memo on the LAN network, she was called into the MD's office. A stormy interview ensued. She was told there was no room at Colorama for any Catherine The Greats. Kathy's answer was that she considered her memorandum fully justified and had a right to get the fullest support from top management regarding its requirements needed to overcome what she identified as 'Colorama's cosy and cushy complacency'. If her resignation was required it was immediately available.

Case Study Questions

Either: Discuss the following questions as a class
Or:　　Provide individual written answers for each one

1　Did Kathy go wrong in her approach to what she saw as the response to the installation of the LAN network?

2　If Kathy's Email memo goes wrong, where does it and how does it?

3　In Kathy's place, what would you have done to resolve the situation?

4　How would you have handled the interview with the MD?

5　If you think that the memorandum is less than appropriate, rewrite it as you think it should be.

6　Did she choose the right medium in which to send the message?

Communication process: case study

'Name of Jackie Sumthin' '

*Scene: The Staff Cafeteria of Europlex Pumps Ltd.
Time: 1.00 pm*

'Afternoon, Hazel.'
　'Oh, hello Arthur, Come and sit down. How's the world treating you these days?'
'Not very often! Too busy trying to cope with Our Leader's new customer credit software. Got green numbers before me eyes, not spots, I don't mind telling you!'
'Well, I can't say I'm surprised. Right new broom your Mr Blenkinsop. In fact, a little bird told me he's going to introduce, what do they call it, a fully integrated accounts package – right through the Accounts Department! It'll do all the postings to

ledgers, number crunching, auditing the lot! Reckon a good few jobs'll go. What do you think?'
'First I've heard of it', grumbled Arthur. 'Anyway, who told you about it?'
　'Never you mind. And another thing.' Hazel leant across the Formica-topped table to get closer to Arthur's ear, 'I shouldn't really tell you this, but, well you know the new girl just started in the Sales Ledger Section – name of Jackie Sumthin – well, apparently she used to work at Allbright's. You know where Mr Blenkinsop came from. Word is they knew each other *very well*!
'Geddaway!'
'I'm telling you! And, from what I hear, she's on the inside track for the new supervisor's job in your section. You could soon be reporting to her!'
Not if I can help it, thought Arthur, who also had set his heart on the same post. 'Well, who'd've thought, eh? Thanks for the tip, Hazel. Gotta go, more little green numbers beckon and that.'
'Don't you breathe a word, Arthur, promise!'
'Never on your life! Wild horses, an' that!'

*　*　*　*

' 'Scuse me Mr Blenkinsop,' said Arthur, stepping into his Accounts Manager's office a few days later. 'Wonder if you'd mind looking over these sales ledger print-outs for me. Nothing but 'garbage in . . .' lately. Can't understand it. Always used to go like clockwork . . . I believe that new girl's doin' the data inputting. Name of Jackie Sumthin . . .'

Case study questions

1　Given the flavour of the above case study and its implications, what can the management of organisations do to counter baseless and sometimes highly damaging grapevine rumour and gossip?

2　If you were Mr Blenkinsop, how would you deal with the matter that Arthur has just drawn to your attention?

3　What do you think prompts employees like Hazel and Arthur to indulge in the sort of conversation of the case study?

4　Assuming that a sharp-eared friend of Jackie's overheard Hazel and Arthur's conversation and told her all about, what do you think she should do about it?

5　What should be the entry in your group's Communication Code Of Ethics regarding organisational grapevines? Write a suitable paragraph in not more than 100 words.

3

Organisations: their structures and functions

Overview

Unit 3 provides you with information and guidelines on:

- How private and public sector organisations are structured with examples of typical structures in both sectors.
- What factors determine the structures and shapes which organisations develop – size, geographical location, nature of work, type of customer, etc.
- How the communication process evolves and develops as organisations grow.
- What is understood by line, staff and functional relationships connecting people in organisations.
- Who are the key people in private and public sector organisations and what they do – from shareholder to machine operator and junior clerk, and from county councillor to junior local government officer.
- What characterises the work of typical company departments – Marketing, R&D, Computer Services, Sales, Personnel, etc.

Introduction

The term 'organisation' covers a multitude of industrial, commercial, service industry and public service activities. Indeed, the word is an abstract label for any group of people who come together and interact with one another in order to achieve a set of predetermined ends or aims.

In our very complex society there are organisa-
tions, for example, which recover the natural minerals we need and turn them over to other organisations to serve as fuels or raw materials for manufacture into something else. Then there are the distributive and retailing organisations which take over the finished manufactured goods and take them to where they can be sold and then sell them to many different kinds of customer. In addition, organisations like insurance companies, banks and

solicitors provide valuable services to the productive and retailing industries by supplying sources of finance, financial security, the underwriting or financial cover of risk-taking, and legal advice and representation.

Such organisations, which act in the sector of the economy which aims to buy and sell so as to make a profit are called **private sector organisations**.

The essential aim of private sector companies is to make a profit while keeping and increasing their customers and − of recent years − while contributing positively to community life and the environment.

There are, of course, millions of people employed in the United Kingdom who work for the **public sector organisations**, those which are financed out of central or local government taxes and which provide a very extensive range of services such as:

Government Departments like Defence, Employment, Health and Social Services, etc
The Inland Revenue Service
Customs and Excise
Immigration
Public utilities such as British Rail and the National Coal Board.
Her Majesty's Prisons and Detention Centres
Job centres, libraries, schools, colleges, etc.

Public sector organisations aim to serve the local and national populace cost-effectively while also improving each citizen's quality of life. In fact there are many national networks in the public sector which coordinate the activities of tending the sick, coping with unemployment, providing a transport service and so on. Such national organisations are responsible for carrying out the bills or laws enacted by successive British governments and may be considered as a kind of infrastructure of government − a series of interlocking meshes or cogs which carry out much of the work of central government.

At a more regional and local level of public service there are the county, district, borough, city and parish councils, which, with varying degrees of authority and power, implement the authorised instructions of both central government and local elected councils. Such organisations have traditionally been concerned with the management of various functions and activities:

● running primary and secondary education
● maintaining roads and thoroughfares
● running county police forces
● providing a fire service
● providing a housing service

and many other kinds of provision.

There are clearly, then very many different types of organisation, or groups of people at work today in the UK, which have been structured to serve a host of different purposes, from the greengrocer's shop in the precinct shopping centre employing two or three people, to the national utility like British Rail, employing tens of thousands of people from Holyhead to Dover and from Penzance to Aberdeen!

As a result of such contrasting factors such as size, geographic location and nature of activity, profit-making or public service-giving, organisations take on very different shapes and structures. Moreover, they are not designed with particular people put into certain places at various ranks or levels within the organisation where they remain for ever, but are constantly changing and evolving as they anticipate events in the economy and society, and react to them. In this way, organisations are said to be dynamic.

Organisational structures

Thus the structure of any organisation is very much the product of 'what it was, what it is and what it would like to be'. That is to say that structures are not static but constantly evolving.

In industry and commerce, organisations are continually alert to the 'needs of the market-place'. The development of a new technology or manufacturing process may have far-reaching consequences for a manufacturing company. Changes in the purchasing behaviour of consumers may radically alter the pattern of trading of a retailing organisation − for example shopping malls, hypermarkets and fast-food cafés have mushroomed over recent years. In the public sector changes in society are mirrored in, say, the restructuring of local government, the integration of some central government departments, and the privatisation of public corporations.

The forms which commercial organisations take depend very much upon the scope of their activities. For example, some companies carry out the entire process of manufacturing goods, marketing them, and distributing them to their own retail outlets:

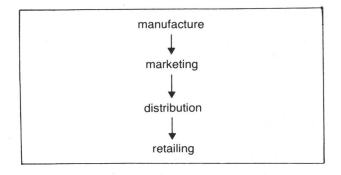

Example of a vertically integrated structure.

When the whole operation is undertaken within one company, it is said to be 'vertically integrated'.

Other companies specialise in one activity only −

manufacturing or distribution or retailing. In such instances a company either makes for others to distribute and retail, acts as a distributing 'middleman', or buys in for retailing goods which a distributor or wholesaler has purchased from a manufacturer. The advantages of vertical integration stem from extensive control and the potential for greater profits, whereas the specialist is able to concentrate expertise and experience within a specific part of the trading area.

Such differences of approach affect the shape of a company's organisational structure. A manufacturing company may look like this:

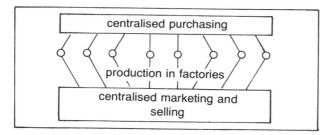

A retailing company may be structured differently.

Thus the manufacturer may not need a dispersed sales force and the retailer concentrates on direct selling to the consumer. In this way, different communication needs are established, ranging from maintaining good shop-floor industrial relations to keeping retail customers satisfied.

Organisations tend, therefore, to become 'product intensive' or 'people intensive'; that is to say that the constraints imposed upon them come from making things, where assembly-line flow, quality-control and the meeting of deadlines and output targets are crucial, or from dealing with people, servicing their needs, where selling techniques, customer satisfaction and understanding consumer behaviour are central to the activity.

Of course, whether the organisation concentrates on manufacturing or sells to consumers in the High Street, it will need to care about people's needs, about its own employees and its customers.

Franchises

A good example of a 'flat' organisational structure is the franchised operation, in which a centralised company provides a range of promotional and supportive services to dispersed semi-independent outlets.

What factors affect the way an organisation is structured?

Private sector organisations

The main factors which are likely to affect the way an organisation is built or structured are:

- its **size**: 1 or 100 or 1000 or 10 000 employees?
- its location: in one office block? ten supermarkets within a region? fifteen factories spread across the country?
- its **nature**: mining? growing? manufacturing? distributing? retailing? providing a professional service?
- its **clientèle**: three or four international companies? twenty to thirty major distributors or factors? two to three hundred retailing companies? ten thousand mail-order customers? two million High Street shoppers?
- its **past shape**, its **current structure**, its **future needs**: the structure a company had as a family business may not suit the chain store which bought it out; to grow or even to survive, a company may need to change shape by acquiring different businesses or by transforming the traditional nature of its activities i.e. by diversifying its range of products or acquiring a varied range of companies to spread its risk of failure – not all companies will do badly simultaneously.

Public sector organisations

The structural characteristics which private sector organisations experience are largely mirrored in the public sector – the number of employees, the location of the organisation's buildings, what sort of activities it carries out, etc, will have a similar effect upon the structure or shape. These are additional factors in the public sector, however:

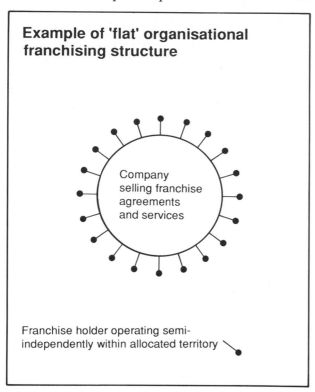

Example of 'flat' organisational franchising structure

Company selling franchise agreements and services

Franchise holder operating semi-independently within allocated territory

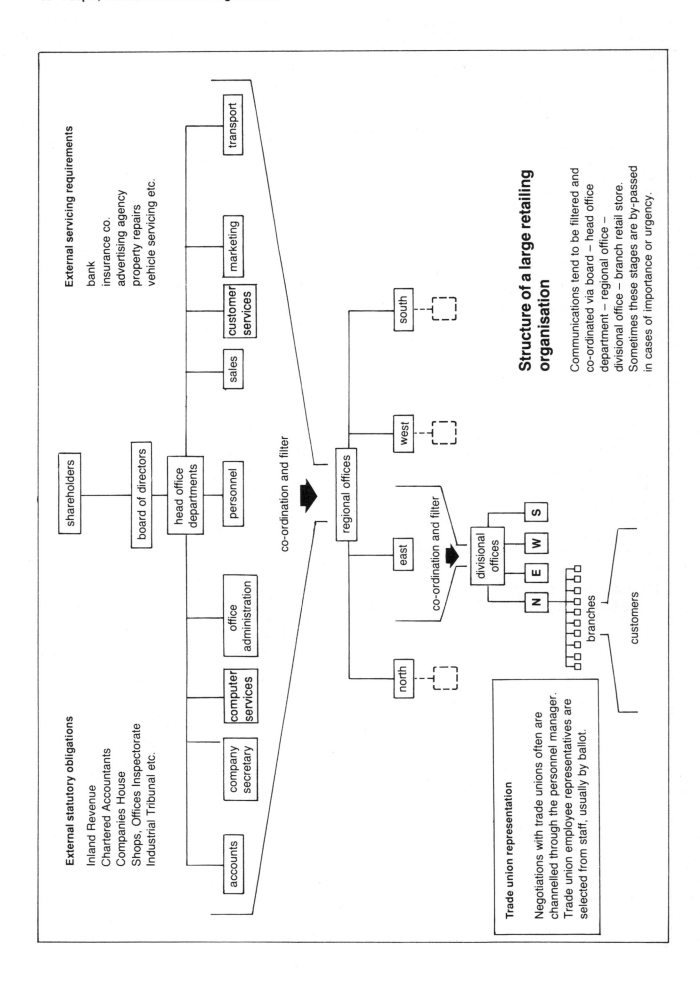

External servicing requirements

bank
insurance co.
advertising agency
property repairs
vehicle servicing etc.

External statutory obligations

Inland Revenue
Chartered Accountants
Companies House
Shops, Offices Inspectorate
Industrial Tribunal etc.

shareholders

board of directors

head office departments

personnel

accounts

company secretary

computer services

office administration

sales

customer services

marketing

transport

co-ordination and filter

regional offices

north

east

west

south

co-ordination and filter

divisional offices

N E W S

branches

customers

Structure of a large retailing organisation

Communications tend to be filtered and co-ordinated via board – head office department – regional office – divisional office – branch retail store. Sometimes these stages are by-passed in cases of importance or urgency.

Trade union representation

Negotiations with trade unions often are channelled through the personnel manager. Trade union employee representatives are selected from staff, usually by ballot.

- the **extent of the duties and obligations imposed** upon it by government and statute, which the public authority must carry out;
- the **boundaries of its authority**: national, regional, county, district, borough, parish;
- the amount of income it has to spend either supplied by central government or via local rates;
- the impact of government policies, for example, to reduce public spending. (Note a recession in the economy may have a similar effect on the size of private companies.)
- whether the organisation or part of it is in **direct contact with the public or not**. (Note that there is some similarity between the manufacturing and retailing private sector factors, where activities are either machine intensive or people intensive.)
- **changes in technology**. For example, county councils during the past twenty years have developed sophisticated Computer Services Departments. (As indeed have private organisations.)
- **changes in society's expectations**. Citizens expect to be told more about local and central government activities so more meetings are open to the public and more councils now have public relations units and officers.
- **increasing complexity of the work** to be carried out. Many County Councils now have senior Policy and Resources Committees to help Chief Executives in making policy decisions.

Hierarchies

Apart from the structures which are determined by an organisation's general activities – whether in the private or public sector, whether selling goods or services – most organisations are internally structured.

Perhaps the most significant aspect of organising people into groups which have specific aims and functions is that either intentionally or unconsciously a 'pecking-order' is established. Few groups operate successfully without leaders and followers. Organisations are no exception. When organisations are composed of 'layers' or gradings of personnel they are termed hierarchies. A popular way of expressing this concept is the organisational pyramid.

The structuring of organisations into hierarchies is in many ways inevitable – although some organisations are evolving other structures, such as the franchise system (see diagram on p. 43). The need for important decisions to be made by people with expertise and experience, in consultation very often with those affected, together with the need to provide a person with sufficient authority to execute a decision, results in the 'pyramid effect'; by this means a small number of senior managers or officials are given the responsibility of directing an organisation's activities. It should be pointed out,

however, that they are also, by dint of office, made accountable for its success or failure!

Specialist divisions

As the example on page 44 shows, the other source of the pyramid effect in organisations is the division of the total operation into specialist departments, all of which are answerable to a more senior co-ordinator.

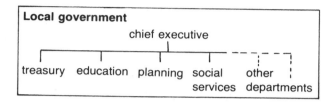

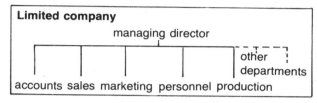

Each department will have its own pyramid structure of head, senior, middle and junior staff, and career hopes and expectations will cause employees to seek to climb the pyramid.

There are problems in communication, administration and effectiveness – which are attributable to the size and the complicated grading of authority in some hierarchic structures. To avoid such complications many organisations deliberately limit size and grant extensive independence to departments.

A structure evolves

First, it is necessary to examine how communication paths and systems are established in organisations. For a model, let us consider the story of Fred Parkins, greengrocer. Fred started out by selling fruit and vegetables in a small shop he rented. Though he had other worries, his communication paths were straightforward, in that he dealt directly with everybody:

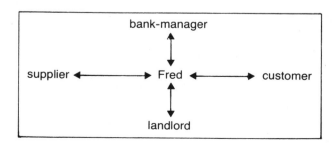

Organisational structure of West Sussex County Council

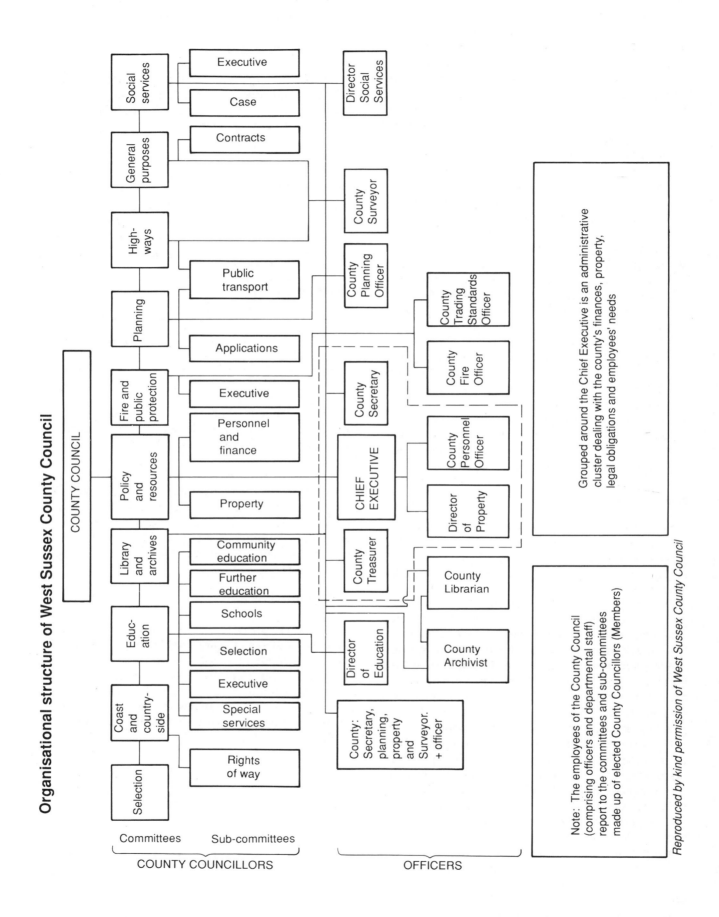

Grouped around the Chief Executive is an administrative cluster dealing with the county's finances, property, legal obligations and employees' needs

Note: The employees of the County Council (comprising officers and departmental staff) report to the committees and sub-committees made up of elected County Councillors (Members)

COUNTY COUNCIL

Committees   Sub-committees

COUNTY COUNCILLORS

OFFICERS

Social services — Executive, Case — Director Social Services

General purposes — Contracts

High-ways — County Surveyor

Planning — Public transport, Applications — County Planning Officer

Fire and public protection — Executive — County Trading Standards Officer, County Fire Officer

Policy and resources — Personnel and finance, Property — County Secretary, CHIEF EXECUTIVE, County Personnel Officer, Director of Property

Library and archives — Community education — County Treasurer, County Librarian

Education — Further education, Schools, Selection, Executive, Special services — Director of Education, County Archivist

Coast and country-side — Rights of way

Selection

County: Secretary, planning, property and Surveyor. + officer

Reproduced by kind permission of West Sussex County Council

As a result of his hard work and enthusiasm, Fred's business prospered – he took on Harry, a sales assistant. This one act transformed Fred's communication system. He had become an employer, and soon found that he was no longer able to see to the needs of each customer personally – frequently he had to delegate, and communicate his requirements to Harry.

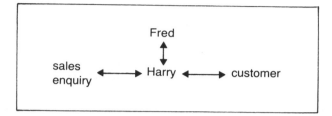

And Harry now first handled some of the sales enquiries. Clearly, Fred's business success now very much depended upon Harry as well, and it became important for both to communicate effectively.

Fred's business prospered further, and he decided to open another shop. Harry was put in to manage it, and Fred, meanwhile, had trained another assistant, Jack, to manage the founding shop. His organisational structure looked like this:

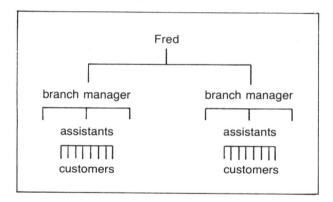

Part of the price of Fred's success was that he could no longer manage all the administration himself. He found it necessary in the end to appoint a number of administrative personnel. His organisation had become more complex.

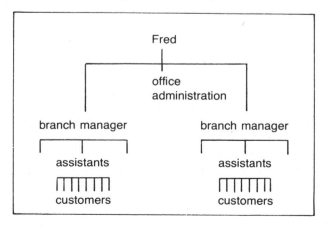

Fred found that he had generated a number of new problems with his extra business:

● In some ways he felt he had 'lost control' and missed serving his customers.
● He did not always get to know about customers' complaints until events had taken a serious turn.
● His two branch managers did not always like it if any of the assistants approached him directly about problems.
● Relations were not always good between the shop and office staffs.
● There was a certain amount of unproductive rivalry between the branch managers – for example when one branch was re-fitted.
● His instructions had a way of becoming distorted and misinterpreted by the time they reached the assistants.

In other words, Fred, in building up his organisation, encountered many of the communication problems common to most organisations. His problems stemmed from his having to learn to achieve his aims and objectives through his employees and overcoming many of the problems which occur when people work in groups which are structured as hierarchies.

Self assessment questions

Do you think you now have a clear understanding of the reasons for organisations adopting particular shapes and structures to aid them in meeting their defined aims? Do you think you could readily accept a situation in which you are expected to follow instructions given to you by someone who is your superior? If not, will your views affect the kind of career you carve out for yourself? Do you see yourself, for instance, 'Starting up on your own'?

Organisational functions

So far we have seen how the structure of an organisation varies according to its size, dispersal of its parts, and the scope and nature of its activities and that external constraints or economic conditions will have distinct effects upon the way the organisation is built up. Also, the term 'hierarchy' has been used to describe the pyramidic steps or levels of an organisation – rather like the steps up an Aztec pyramid. The reasons for such a stepped hierarchy have been suggested as stemming from the need for the control and authority of certain functions to be placed within the hands of fewer people as the staffing within the hierarchy becomes more senior: via section heads, heads of departments and directors. Bear in mind, however, that other forms of organisational structure do exist; i.e. the workers' cooperative, run on more democratic lines; the franchising arrangement where a central organisation sells its product or name to individual and almost totally independent operators, who enjoy much more freedom than does the traditional departmental head; or the subsidiary company within a group of companies, controlled by a 'holding company'.

Indeed, management teams in both the private and public sectors over recent years have introduced cross-department' task forces, think-tanks, quality-circle brainstorming groups, etc to overcome some of the 'downside' effect of the pyramidic structure such as departmentalism, tram-line thinking, bureaucratic growth, and so on.

We have also seen how communication and organisational problems may grow as the small sole trader or small partnership type of organisation evolves into a larger limited or public company, where the top decision-makers are five or six steps removed from their customers or members of the public.

What has not yet been fully made clear is that the single most important factor in the structuring and allocation of functions within organisations arises from the perceived need to delegate authority and responsibility from the most senior member of the organisation downwards, as the organisation expands in terms of personnel and the establishment of multiple sites, branches or offices. Hence the creation of specialist divisions and departments in organisations as a means of making possible the undertaking of a myriad of tasks large and small, and of ensuring that the clearly allocated responsibility for success and achievement is not lost beneath a tangle of job responsibilities and overlapping involvements.

In order to clarify to all concerned in an organisation how it is structured, and who has what functions, government departments, limited companies and councils devise often very complicated organisational charts to depict visually the interrelationships of departments, sections and units.

The functions of people in organisations

The line relationship in organisations

As we have just seen, the development of Fred's business has led to the establishment of an 'organisational hierarchy' – people in specialist posts at various levels of responsibility and authority within the organisation. Some of these act as supervisors and managers and have a responsibility for the work of others and for ensuring that through other people as well as from their own hard work, the organisation's policies and objectives are met.

In the retail organisation whose organisational chart on page 44 we are examining, these functions

have been identified at the following levels or grades of staff:

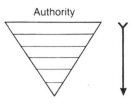

1   Directors
2   Heads of Department
3   Regional Managers
4   Divisional (or Area) Managers
5   Branch Managers
6   Sales Assistants

There is evident in this list of job designations a clear line of authority, from director to sales assistant, and as this is a selling organisation, the 'line of authority' is traceable through the six grades or levels of staff. People who have such a relationship through the direct giving and acceptance of instructions to do with the job of selling, as illustrated in the organisational chart under discussion, or with manufacturing goods in a factory are said to belong to the 'line management' or 'line function' of the organisation:

Line management function

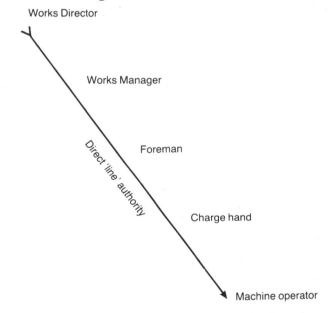

The staff relationship in organisations

As well as a line function in organisations there is also a relationship between people, termed a 'staff relationship'. For example, a senior manager in a retail or manufacturing company will often have a senior assistant known as an administrative secretary or personal assistant. This assistant will report to, say, the Sales Manager and carry out his instructions and requests, but the assistant does not have a 'line relationship' with the regional or divisional personnel reporting to the sales manager. The assistant, when relaying an instruction on the telephone, will therefore often explain that his or her authority is directly derived from the boss:

'Mr. Jenkins has asked me to remind you that your sales report must reach him by Tuesday morning's first post at the latest.'

Thus a staff relationship within an organisation lies outside of the line relationship. Another example would be of the management consultant appointed by the managing director of a company as a specialist to examine current efficiency within the company. His authority stems from the MD and he reports solely to the MD. Consequently, the consultant would not be able to instruct a departmental head, although in practice it would be customary in such circumstances for the departmental head to offer his full cooperation.

Line and staff relationships

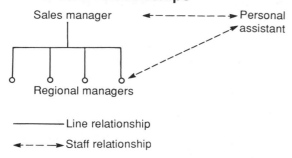

Line relationship
Staff relationship

Functional responsibilities

In larger organisations there are activities which spread across the entire operation. A nationwide organisation may employ people to act as company inspectors or to work in a personnel department which reports to the managing director directly. Such staff are given responsibilities and authorities which span several different departments of the company. These responsibilities are termed functional.

The three 'people' relationships

Thus three relationships have been identified:

LINE   STAFF   FUNCTIONAL

Within each, people will respond in a different way. For instance, a person within a department is duty bound (within reason) to accept the 'line' instructions of his immediate superior or more senior manager, but will not react too kindly to being given instructions from the head of another department. A person in a staff position will normally advise people rather than instruct them and the person in the functional role will take pains to keep line heads fully informed and avoid 'ruffling feathers' by acting with too heavy a hand. The member of staff, for

instance, with a company-wide role on office safety (Health and Safety At Work) will report any defects to a departmental head for putting right, or report back to the MD directly for a general instruction to be sent from the MD's office in the case of an important matter.

Furthermore, the establishment of an organisational hierarchy embracing line, functional and staff relationships will inevitably cause more complexity and protocols in the ways in which people communicate with each other. As we have already discovered in the process of expansion in Fred's business, his 'line' deputies – the branch managers – soon came to resent it if he went over their heads or bypassed them in order to instruct more junior staff directly. Similarly, it would be a rash head of department who tried to give orders to the staff of a different department. So you can see that in order to fit into the people network of a large organisation, a new employee needs to know about these relationships and to respect the patterns of behaviour through which the organisation functions.

Self assessment question

How far do you go along with the given reasons for organisational hierarchies and layers of 'reports to' lines of management? As a manager in training, what personal communication skills do you think you need to develop so as to be able to work effectively in a line management structure?

Key people in organisations

Private sector organisations

The shareholder

- private and public limited companies are financed by money (capital) from people buying shares in the company
- shareholders may be individual members of the public, organisations like trade unions or other companies with cash to invest
- public company shares may be purchased by anyone through a stock exchange, whereas private company shares can only be bought from the shareholder, and are usually held by the company's directors
- shareholders attend annual general meetings and extraordinary general meetings of the company
- they have legal rights of access to information
- they vote to elect the directors
- they may acquire sufficient shares to control or take over the company

The chairman

- bestrides the top of the organisational pyramid
- is elected by the board of directors
- chairs meetings of the board of directors
- may have executive status or may leave day-to-day running of the company to the managing director

The directors

- decide on important matters at board meetings
- have legal obligations and responsibilities under the Companies Act 1985
- may exert influence on company activities by having extensive shareholdings in the company
- the board of directors presents its annual report to the shareholders for approval at the end of each trading year

The managing director

- the executive head of most organisations, with authority over all the staff
- is a member of the board of directors

The company secretary

- responsible to the managing director and board to ensure all the company's affairs are conducted according to legal requirements
- services and attends meetings of the board of directors
- attends to all correspondence involving shareholders and the calling of shareholders' meetings
- is usually responsible for fire, health and safety regulations, company contracts, trade mark registrations, etc
- acts as legal advisor to the company

The departmental manager

- is responsible to the managing director for the work of one department in the organisation
- directs the work carried out by the members of staff in the department
- ensures targets are met, eg projected (budgetted) annual sales turnover is achieved at the desired level of gross profit (profit before tax)
- is provided by the company with the human, equipment and financial resources to reach the pre-set targets

The section supervisor

- is responsible to the head of department for the work of a section or unit in the department (eg a large accounts department may have sections for the sales ledger, purchase ledger, nominal ledger, payroll, credit control, etc.)

- reviews work in progress with the head of department to ensure targets are met
- is responsible for section staff

The shop steward

- is responsible for trade union matters within the section/organisation
- represents the trade union members in negotiations with management
- is responsible to area branch secretary and trade unions' officers

Public sector organisations

County councillor/District councillor

- is elected by those registered to vote in each local area
- usually a member of a political party
- makes decisions in full council meetings or in committees
- is responsible for setting budgets and carrying out legally imposed duties

Local government officer

- full-time official who carries out the policies of the elected members under the direction of a chief executive
- officials are divided into departments and sections covering specific areas of the work

The chairman of a public corporation

- is responsible to a central government department for the administration of a public corporation; the central government department will be headed by a Permanent Secretary responsible to a Minister – a senior Government Member of Parliament
- duties resemble those of a company chairman.

Talking point

'Organisations are not bricks and mortar or plant and equipment, or even neat little diagrams on paper. They are people!' Is this an over-simplified view of organisations?

The work of departments in business organisations

Although you will naturally be preoccupied with the work of your own department, it is important right from the start to appreciate that the success of any business enterprise depends entirely on the

Key people in the local government public sector organisation

Central government agencies:
Whitehall departments and
Regional Administrators

Local pressure groups:
e g Chamber of Commerce,
civic heritage and
environmental groups

Business
and
personal
taxpayers as
financers

Elected members
County, District and
Parish Councillors
County and District
Chief Executives
Departmental heads
Graded Officer posts
Clerical posts

Local
inhabitants
and
businesses
as users

External services:
e g newspaper advertising,
contract cleaners,
management consultants,
equipment and consumables

Related interest groups:
e g voluntary
organisations and
charities, educational
and leisure groups

cooperation between departments which are interdependent. Furthermore, you will undoubtedly be in daily contact with many colleagues in other departments and so it is important for you to gain a thorough knowledge of what they do and what preoccupies them.

Research and development department

- designs and tests new products
- improves and updates existing products
- researches into new areas of interest
- analyses and tests competing products
- works with the production department to develop prototypes (initial models) and construct the equipment to manufacture new products
- helps to ensure that new products comply with legal requirements, British Standards and safety laws

Production department

- manufactures the company's range of products
- monitors factors like wastage and costs of bought-in parts so as to maintain profit margins
- designs tools to help make products and buys in the necessary plant and equipment
- writes or buys in computer programs which control much of the set routines of production-line manufacturing
- controls and coordinates the rate and quantity of manufacture so as to meet given orders within pre-set deadlines – plans its activities in advance
- monitors trends in production techniques internationally so as to remain competitive

Accounts department

- is responsible for overall financial aspects of the organisation's activities
- records and monitors all areas of financial activity: sales, purchases, running costs (heat, light, payroll, etc), manufacturing costs, dividends issued etc and checks these against annual budgets.
- supplies timely information aimed at ensuring that the organisation works at a profit, ie that sales revenue is not exceeded by cost of sales; provides financial reports for senior management on a regular basis
- produces information for shareholders at regular intervals – in the form of financial reports including balance sheets and profit and loss accounts
- maintains financial information required by law, such as the details of income upon which tax must be paid

Marketing department

- ensures that the organisation remains competitive by providing information about what products and services the market wants and what sort of prices it will pay
- maintains a market research function to explore new markets and new product opportunities; monitors the success/failure of its own products and competing products
- works with R & D and production departments in the design of attractive and 'sellable' new products, as well as the updating and improving of existing ones

The work of company departments

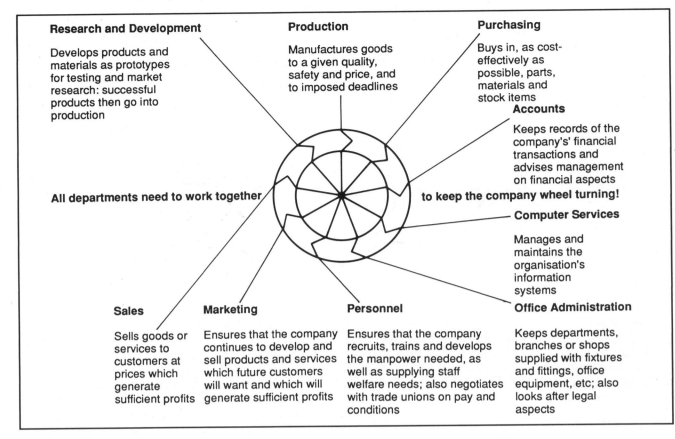

Research and Development

Develops products and materials as prototypes for testing and market research: successful products then go into production

All departments need to work together

Production

Manufactures goods to a given quality, safety and price, and to imposed deadlines

Purchasing

Buys in, as cost-effectively as possible, parts, materials and stock items

Accounts

Keeps records of the company's' financial transactions and advises management on financial aspects

to keep the company wheel turning!

Computer Services

Manages and maintains the organisation's information systems

Sales

Sells goods or services to customers at prices which generate sufficient profits

Marketing

Ensures that the company continues to develop and sell products and services which future customers will want and which will generate sufficient profits

Personnel

Ensures that the company recruits, trains and develops the manpower needed, as well as supplying staff welfare needs; also negotiates with trade unions on pay and conditions

Office Administration

Keeps departments, branches or shops supplied with fixtures and fittings, office equipment, etc; also looks after legal aspects

- designs and develops advertising materials and campaigns aimed at increasing sales
- monitors local and national trends in consumer demand or industrial marketing needs
- provides advice on the termination of existing products and the introduction of new ones at appropriate intervals; in large companies, maintains computerised models of markets and uses them to predict what will sell

Sales department

- prepares an annual sales plan which breaks down how many of what type of product will be sold at what profit in the year; divides the plan up into regions, districts and branches, or sales representatives' territories
- supplies point-of-sale material and advice to customers to help sell products
- monitors discreetly the sales of competing products in customers' outlets
- supplies market intelligence to the marketing department on current sales activities; sales representatives provide weekly sales reports to senior sales department personnel
- aims to secure new business with new customers and to increase sales with existing customers on a given target basis

Personnel department

- ensures that the organisation has the human resources needed to achieve its aims
- coordinates employee selection, promotion and termination; supervises appraisal schemes
- provides a staff training and development service
- maintains the organisation's employee records, including pension, sickness benefit and superannuation payments
- supervises industrial negotiations on pay and conditions of work with trade unions and associations
- provides a confidential employee counselling service and runs welfare and social activities in many instances
- monitors personnel activities in competing companies so as to avoid key staff being lured away by increased offers on pay and fringe benefits, etc

Office administration department

- provides a service for other departments in areas such as centralised purchasing of stationery and office supplies, and advice on what equipment to purchase for office use
- coordinates the internal or external design and printing of forms and schedules

- oversees a centralised reprographics service for bulk photocopying/printing for other departments
- provides word processing/desk-top publishing/ text production services, if required
- maintains the organisation's insurance requirements
- monitors any leasing arrangements
- where an organisation has dispersed branches or retail outlets, supervises their administration with the help of branch inspectors

Computer services department

- acquires and maintains company computing equipment
- secures or creates computer software needed by all departments: in larger organisations many computer functions are supplied via custom-designed software
- maintains computer records of organisational information and archived data: large companies have a single database of information which is constantly extended and updated and accessible according to security clearance: back-up duplicate records are essential!
- coordinates and supports national and international computer-based communications on behalf of staff
- maintains a watching brief on new developments in information technology to ensure competitiveness and efficiency
- may run staff training schemes for new staff in various computer/data-processing functions
- installs new/updated versions of software as they are released; ensures hardware is able to match growth in company's activities and increased use by staff

Transport department

- coordinates the organisation's transport needs, from directors', managers' and sales representatives' cars to acquisition and maintenance of fleets of lorries and/or vans
- keeps service records and renews insurances, vehicle registrations etc
- designs cost-effective delivery routes via computer for delivery fleets
- negotiates purchases and leasings with car/HGV dealers
- provides training as needed

Note: Some business organisations have separate purchasing departments and training departments, while some amalgamate marketing and sales. They may also have a press or public relations office to promote their company image and publicise the company's products in a general way, perhaps by sponsorship of a sports event. Generally, the larger the organisation, the more specialised departments it is likely to create. Remember that the number of departments and the work they do depends directly upon the nature of the organisation's activities, its size and the degree to which it can afford to employ specialist as opposed to generalist employees and managers.

Integrating the departmental activities

Though it is helpful for organisations to divide their activities into separate departments in order to encourage specialist skills to develop, it is essential that senior management and heads of department work as a team and ensure that they actively promote a system of communication within the organisation and outside it which works to pull the enterprise together as a single unit of activity.

And indeed, in larger organisations, this is easier said than done. There are a number of communication problems which arise when organisations grow and have to divide the range of their activities into manageable sections, as we have already come to realise. The following checklist reviews some problems already identified and also includes further problem areas which departmental structures tend to create:

1 The basic problem of size It is so much easier to get a message across to 10 people rather than 10 000 without it becoming distorted in the process.

2 The problem of geographic dispersal of staff and buildings It is difficult to relate to other people as part of one big team if you never meet them or get to know them in any way.

3 The problem of relating to people who are engaged in some other set of activities For example, it may be difficult for sales staff to understand the accounts staff's preoccupation with regular and detailed returns of a financial nature such as expenses or petrol receipts. Again, if a member of staff's only contact with another department's personnel arises from mistakes occurring in his or her monthly pay, it may be difficult for that person to sympathise with the problems they may be experiencing with a new payroll software package.

4 The problem of inter-departmental rivalry Because of the separated nature of departments there arises a tendency for staff to identify strongly with their own department and its head (with whom they communicate closely) and to see only their own activities as supremely important and those of other departments either as inefficient, poor by comparison or even a drag upon their own efforts:

If only Personnel had the wit to select the right staff, we wouldn't be in this sales target mess!
or: You've got to be an accountant to get on here!

or: The trouble with the sales reps is they think the whole company revolves around satisfying their whims and fancies – never did an honest day's work in their lives!

While such comments are made and resentments or jealousies allowed to flourish, the corporate or total company effort is being constantly undermined.

5 The problem of specialisation and concentration upon a part of the whole organisational operation

If organisations are to flourish, it is inevitable that the vast range of activities within them – across seven or eight different departments – will be broken down into small sets of tasks such as managing the despatch of mail, ordering company stationery, filing customer records, updating price lists etc, etc. Yet this very approach of dividing tasks into smaller areas with restricted levels of responsibility can result in the staff concerned becoming very 'blinkered' and limited in their understanding of what the firm is doing as a whole, with little interest in anything happening outside their own particular corner:

Sorry, can't help you. I just look after the transport records.

Who? Never heard of him! Can't work in this office!

Look, if you've found a mistake in the adding up, that's Accounts' problem! They don't come round here helping us out!

Charlie! There's a bloke on the phone says he's enquiring about some order that's adrift . . .

Oh, tell 'im we're Packing, and he's got the wrong extension – and come and give me a hand instead of 'anging about on that blinkin' phone all day!

6 The problem of the hierarchic structure of organisations

By their very nature, organisations shaped like pyramids will have fewer people being promoted as the grades of job become more senior – ten company directors may oversee the work of a company of twenty thousand personnel. There may arise therefore, among some staff, a sense of having been unjustly passed over in the promotion stakes or a feeling that, given the chance, the machine operator could do a better job than the foreman, or the section head than the departmental manager. Thus there needs to be a constant effort upon the part of managers and supervisors in organisations to minimise as far as possible these counterproductive feelings and attitudes by means of good communication practices, fair opportunities for advancement and what is known as leadership from the front, where the boss earns the respect of his staff by his or her example and extra effort and know-how.

7 The problem of complexity of the communications process

As organisations grow, they tend to become more bureaucratic and unwieldy in the processes they design to acquire, store and distribute information. Like parliament, sometimes new rules and regulations are invented without older ones being cancelled, so that employees become so bogged down in, for instance, filling in endless returns for the higher tiers of management that sales suffer and customers are put off.

8 The problem of rapid changes in technology

While Information Technology (IT) has brought many blessings, including the eradication of some monotonous and repetitive clerical tasks, it has meant that people right up the organisational ladder have had to acquire new skills and specialisms at a time in their working lives when grasping new concepts and techniques can cause unease and worry about loss of face in front of younger staff educated in the new technology at school, college, polytechnic or university.

Communication practices and integration

The above checklist of problem areas serves to illustrate some of the daily communication and human relations difficulties which organisations may have to overcome in order to achieve success. For example, the customer on the telephone who has been routed to the wrong extension is not going to make allowances for the fact that he is talking to a junior packer and not a skilled sales receptionist. He regards the company as a single entity and himself as a customer of all of it!

The talking points on page 57 will help you to concentrate upon identifying the kind of activities which would help to prevent communication problems like those illustrated above from arising, or to find a solution to such problems once they have become apparent.

Self assessment questions

1 How confident are you – at the end of Unit 3 – that you possess a good working knowledge of the functions of the major private and public sector departments in organisations? What practical self-directed study steps do you need to take to strengthen this area?

2 Units 1, 2 and 3 have dealt with the themes of getting organised for study, communication theory and processes and organisational structures and functions; having checked your notes and handouts, and reviewed your own achievements and progress to date, are you happy to move directly into Unit 4, or are there some weak areas (may be due to sickness absence) you should go over again – now!

Summary of main points

1 Underpinning all the activities of private sector organisations is the need to earn profits while meeting national and economic needs; while public sector organisations do not have the same kind of profit motive, they do seek to give value for money as a public duty, since almost all their income derives from taxpayers' money.

2 The factors which shape and influence the ways in which organisations are structured are: the nature of their work, their size, their location, the kinds of customer they serve, the kinds of task their employees perform and the extent to which they use IT.

3 Organisational growth and development inevitably leads to the delegation of tasks and this promotes the development of task-specific specialisms. As departmentalised work grows, the need to establish lines of communication in clearly defined patterns and networks is crucial to the success of the enterprise.

4 As a result of 3 above, those organisations structured in hierarchies tend to develop line, staff and functional interpersonal relationships within which to organise the work to be done. Organisational tasks are effected down the line chain of command; staff personnel work outside the line and generally provide assistance and support to senior executives; functional employees carry out organisation-wide activities like supplying computer and personnel services.

5 The key people in organisations are:
  Private Sector: shareholders; company chairman, managing director and directors; company secretary; departmental heads, section supervisors; trade union/association employee representatives – and, of course, customers!
  Public Sector: central government members of parliament working in committees and ministries, senior civil servants and regional administrators; county, district and borough councillors; local government senior executives, departmental heads and officers – and the general public they serve.

6 Typical departments within private sector organisations are: research and development, production, accounts, marketing, sales, personnel and training, office administration, computer services, customer services and transport/distribution.
  County and district council departments include: policy and resources, social services, treasury, highways, planning, highways, fire and public protection, education, library and archives; amenities and recreation, environmental health, housing services, personnel, finance and general purposes.

7 Major problem areas in securing effective communication in large organisations include: sheer size of organisation, dispersed and separated centres of activity, destructive inter-departmental and unit rivalry, the 'blinker' effect of specialising within small groups, the growth of bureaucratic practices and procedures, the growth of complexity in all functions, the problems attaching to continuous change – technological, task-related, new product-related etc, the problems of managing effectively the work of a large labour force in, often, dispersed locations.

Activities and assignments _____

Quick review quiz

1 What are the essential differences between the aims of private and public sector organisations?

2 Identify the factors which shape the structures of organisations. Give examples of three contrasting structures and account for their differences.

3 What is meant by the term 'vertically integrated'?

4 What is a franchise?

5 List the major types of department typically found in private sector large companies – in the manufacturing, distribution and retailing and service sectors.

6 List the departments typically found in:

  a) a county council and *b*) a district council

7 Explain briefly the kinds of communication problems which may arise as a sole trader business expands, and what actions are necessary to overcome them.

8 Explain clearly the difference between 'line', 'staff' and 'functional' relationships in an organisation.

9 Describe some of the main changes in the structure of departments arising from the widespread introduction of IT.

10 Describe the major responsibilities of *one* of the 'people in organisations' from *a*), *b*), *c* and *d*) and *one* from *e*), *f*) and *g*).

a) a company director
b) a company secretary
c) a departmental head
d) a shop steward or trade union representative
e) a county councillor
f) a county treasurer
g) a local government worker in a department of your choice

and outline briefly their major communication requirements.

11 What principal communication problems arise from an organisation's having grown very large?

12 What key roles for key people can you devise which would promote the development of an effective communication system in the organisations of the 1990s? Where would you slot them into the existing structures of, say, a private or public sector company employing more than 100 employees?

Research and report back assignments

1 Having carried out your research, design an organisational chart for one of the following:

a) the college in which you are studying
b) the school in which you are studying
c) the organisation in which you are working or undertaking work experience.

Devise a suitable means for illustrating clearly in your chart any line, staff or functional relationships you discover. By means of audio-visual presentations compare and contrast the charts produced by your group.

2 In pairs, arrange to interview a manager in either a private or public sector local organisation. Ask him or her to outline some of the major demands and problems encountered in maintaining communication and relationships within a hierarchic organisation like those outlined in Unit 3. Provide an oral report for your class of about ten minutes' duration of your findings.

3 First carry out your research and then write an article of about 500 words which provides a clear account of the facilities and services available to citizens in your district which provide information.

4 Choose one of the following agencies in your locality and then arrange to visit your nearest branch and, in groups of three, undertake the assignment detailed below:

a) a Job Centre
b) a Citizen's Advice Bureau
c) a Trade Union Branch Office
d) a Public Library
e) a Police Station

Find out how it is organised and structured. Establish what kinds of communications resources are available and for what they are used. Interview a senior member of staff in order to find out what communication networks and relationships the organisation maintains and how it links with and liaises with other internal and external organisations/departments.

  Produce a report of your findings of about 500 words for copying to other members of your class.

5 In groups of two or three, arrange to visit a local organisation in each of the following sectors:

a) a manufacturer
b) a retailer
c) a clearing bank or building society branch or solicitor's offices.

Your aim is to find out in particular how and why their structures and communications activities differ, and, from discussions with staff, to ascertain what they see as the major communication activities they pursue and what kind of external organisations, agencies and institutions they work with.

Write an account of some 500 words detailing your findings, and in particular, highlighting what you found to be the communicating and external relations differences between each firm which stem from the contrasting work they do.

6 In pairs, arrange to interview one of the following:

a) a public relations officer
b) the information officer of a county council
c) the principal or headteacher of a college or school

Find out how they maintain in your locality 'a good image' for the organisation they represent, and what communications media they employ. In an oral report back to your group, relate your findings and then discuss the value of an organisation having a good corporate image and the means of getting the image across to the general public.

7 In groups of three or four devise a questionnaire to be completed by local consumers interviewed in your High Street. Your questionnaire should seek to establish what local people expect from the retail firms they use in terms of:

a) information about how retail organisations are shaped to meet their needs
b) what product information they require
c) what information they expect about how the organisation is changing to meet future needs
d) what staffing structures and facilities may be needed to improve shopping convenience
e) what after sales services they expect etc.

From an analysis of your questionnaires, discuss the place of the customer in organisational structures and functions.

8 Having, as a class, undertaken the research and report back activities outlined above, consider in general discussion the following topics:

a) What constraints are placed upon what may be seen as 'normal and natural behaviour' by having to work within a hierarchy?
b) Were there any common threads among the communication problems and preoccupations you discovered in the people you interviewed? What were they? Why do you think they were common to all?
c) Did you discover any essential differences of approach to work and communication needs and activities between private and public sector personnel?

d) From your experiences, can you agree that the way an organisation is structured affects the way in which it communicates and its staff interrelate?
e) Did you discover any tensions arising from organisations on the one hand seeking to integrate all they do and on the other from their having set up separate departments and units through which to do it?
f) What problems, if any, do customers experience in obtaining information from and communicating with organisations?

Talking points

In a group of about five or six students, choose one or more of the following topics and spend about 10 to 15 minutes discussing each and noting the main conclusions reached. Then, in turn, compare your conclusions with those of the other groups by electing a spokesman to summarise your discussion:

1 In what ways could communications among employees in a large organisation be supported and strengthened?

2 Supposing that you had to improve communications between distant factories and offices, all belonging to one firm, what suggestions could you make to aid the communications process? Is there a role for IT telecommunications here?

3 How could communications between separate departments be improved in order to create better morale and a total sense of putting the customer first?

4 Is any organisational structure other than the pyramidic hierarchy a practical proposition in private sector companies?

5 What causes rivalry among people? Can it be minimised by changing communications processes? If so, how would you seek to achieve co-operative working relationships among people?

6 What is meant in the sense used in the above checklist by the term bureaucracy? How does the increase in rules and regulations affect communication practices in your view? What would happen in a large company without any rules and regulations governing work routines?

7 Why is it that older and senior staff sometimes feel uneasy about new practices and technologies? Where would you start, for example, in introducing a new system of information handling – like a LAN- linked set of desk-top computers in a traditionally-minded organisation – at the top, in the middle or at the bottom and why?

You may wish to consult parents, relatives or working friends before starting these discussions, and you should bring to bear as appropriate any personal experiences arising from a full or part-time job you may have.

Case study

Hopgood Sports Limited

Jack Hopgood's problems can be summed up in one word – success!

Four years ago, following a modest pools win, he started up on his own, as a retailer of sports and camping equipment. He rented a shop in Westleigh High Street, which, to begin with, he ran on his own. Within a year, Hopgood Sports Limited was in full swing. Jack had taken on two full-time assistants – Les Green, aged 36, and Beryl White, aged 48. Les soon proved an enthusiastic salesman, becoming Jack's 'right-hand man', while Beryl, a placid but conscientious employee, took on much of the book-keeping and office work.

Two years ago, Jack felt the time was right to open a second shop and he chose premises in the Rosegreen Shopping Precinct, a busy shopping centre in an affluent Westleigh suburb. For some time, Jack travelled between his two branches, since he felt that Harry Pritchard, aged 22, was insufficiently experienced to manage at Rosegreen on his own. Besides, Jack just loved to sell and talk to his customers! About eighteen months ago, the turnover at Rosegreen justified the appointment of a junior sales assistant. Jack appointed Carol Brooks, aged 17. Also, Saturday was always busy and so two part-time staff helped out – Linda Warren at the High Street branch, and Bernard Lincoln at Rosegreen.

With an eye to the changing patterns of consumer purchasing, Jack saw his chance to open a Camping and barbeque shop on the site of a busy self-service petrol station on the London Road, just north of Westleigh. He arranged with the owners to pay rent and a percentage of the profit in return for the floor-space on which the camping shop was situated. The current arrangement is that the petrol station staff take the money for the camping and barbeque goods, which Jack keeps stocked up in self-service merchandisers opposite the petrol sales till. Jack is not very happy with the level of sales, however, and is convinced that they would increase dramatically if someone in his own employ were put in to sell the products full-time, particularly as the more expensive items are not selling and the petrol station personnel lack the required sales expertise.

'Behind every successful man stands a woman!' In Jack's case, it is definitely Mrs Elsa Hopgood, who handles all the account customer sales, processes the ordering of stock and attends to much of the increasing business administration of Hopgood Sports Limited. Recently, however, her enthusiasm seemed distinctly wilted:

'I don't know, Jack, I can't see the point of our having such a successful business if it means we both have to work a twenty-five hour day! You seem to spend your time tearing about all over the place and our 'Book At Bedtime' is usually this month's accounts! Take it from me, you're heading for a breakdown or something if you don't sort out the business! You can't tell me we can't afford some extra help. Anyway, look at the business opportunities we miss because no one can ever get hold of you – you're always on the way to somewhere else! And another thing! They might just as well not have invented computers as far as you're concerned! Surely we could benefit from some of these small business packages I've read about. You've just got to learn that you can't go on for ever doing it all on your own – you want to do more thinking and proper administrating instead of just buzzing around in circles. Besides, I want a holiday next month in Florida! The one you promised me two years ago!'

Never a woman to waste her breath, Elsa Hopgood's pointed comments caused Jack to do his first real thinking about Hopgood Sports since he had established the three outlets.

'She's right – as usual,' mused Jack. 'Now how could I organise things properly! Not only for the present, but also to allow for future expansion over the next five to ten years . . .'

Assignments

1 In the light of Jack's current business situation, what should he do to follow up Elsa's advice? In small discussion groups, make out a checklist of actions needed and put them into an order of priority. Then compare your checklist with those drawn up by other groups.

2 What do you consider to be the advantages and disadvantages of a small trader owning a cluster of some three or four retail shops in separate locations in a large town, as against his owning a single, larger store centrally located. What current shopping trends and environmental factors would have to be taken into account in making a decision as to maintaining several small shops or changing to a single larger store?

3 How could the introduction of IT help Jack's business?

Follow-up assignments

4 Find out what facilities exist within your district to aid small businessmen and women in setting up a business and ensuring its survival.

5 Having given some thought to the problems encountered by a small, growing business, interview a local retailer and try to find out what makes up his or her current preoccupations. Find out what factors enable a small business to keep going in the light of fierce competition from national chainstores.

6 Find out how small business proprietors in your locality are using computers and for what kinds of task and report back to your group.

Case study

All change

Bettadecor is a large national company in the home furnishing retail and distribution markets. The company has over 150 branches throughout the country linked by divisional and regional offices. Its head office is in London and its national marketing headquarters are based in Bristol. The company has recently computerised its sales and accounts systems from a newly-established computer centre in St Albans. The growth of Bettadecor has been swift and is the talk of city financiers.

(*Scene inside the Hightown retail store*)
'Been waiting long?'
'About ten or fifteen minutes – everyone seems to be dashing about . . . but . . . three of 'em in there, are all engrossed in something or other . . . Well, I dunno. I think I'll call back . . .'

(*The Divisional Office of the western district of the Southern Region*)
'Could you put me through to the Regional Manager's Office, please. Hullo! Miss Davidson? Ah. Jack Griffin here . . . I was wondering whether you got my order for the new Peterson wallpaper range . . . Yes I know you sent out a questionnaire . . . Well I sent in an order about two weeks ago, asking for 300 extra rolls in about 30 patterns under the special arrangement . . . only I'm being badgered for them. Oh, there's a new special order form. How many copies? You're kidding! My office has just had one of the company's new fax machines installed. Why can't you accept our orders on it?'

(*Bettadecor's Head Office. The Transport Manager meets the Assistant Accounts Manager in the corridor*)
'How's tricks, Harry?'
'Don't ask! I've just done an exercise on town and country mileage. Could help to cut servicing costs. But you'd never believe the trouble I've been

having getting the returns in from the branches. They must need cushions or something – sit on things so long!'
'Yeah, you don't need to tell me. Between ourselves, this computer's new integrated accounts software is giving me grey hairs – we sent a processing manual to every branch, but the mistakes! It's not as if the new computerised system is very different from the old paper-based one. Dave Pritchard's tearing his hair out at St Albans. . . .'

(*Sales Manager's Office at the Quarterly Regional Managers' Sales Meeting. The Sales Manager is speaking.*)
'Frankly, it's extremely disturbing. The company seems to have lost all impetus. The figures for the second quarter are simply not good enough: But before anyone starts blaming the computer, there are some questions I'd like answers to about the new order processing scheme to speed special orders. . . .'

(*The Manager's Office of the Newtown retail branch*)
'Fred, flip the closed sign on the door, will you. And come in here and give me a dig out with these sales analysis returns. They've been on the phone from Divisional Office. Jack Griffin's been on the warpath. Wants 'em yesterday, or, preferably, the day before!'

Assignments

1 What do you see as Bettadecor's fundamental problem? How is it manifested? What could be done to improve matters? Can you draw any conclusions about problems which beset large companies as opposed to small ones?
2 Write an analysis of the kinds of problem which Bettadecor are experiencing and what could be done to improve matters. Alternatively, discuss the case-study in syndicate groups and discuss your findings in a full group analysis session.

4

Working in organisations 1

Overview

Unit 4 provides you with information and guidelines on:

- The central components of a personal code of ethics to support your working life.
- A checklist of the characteristic features and qualities of successful managers and administrators.
- The typical traits and characteristics of groups, in both a social and organisational context and the main requirements and expectations of group working.
- The factors which affect and influence interpersonal relationships at work and examples of stresses and conflicts with their underlying causes.
- A table of communication styles with examples to illustrate how, when and why to use different communication tones and registers.
- Central communication features of the communicating manager, secretary and support assistant.

'Start right, stay right!'

This well-known engineering watchword applies just as much to starting out in full-time employment as it does to, say, setting up an engineering process to shape a piece of metal or to ensure a trouble-free production run. We have already discovered that work organisations have developed procedures – some backed by legislation, and others adopted as sets of social behaviour – which control and affect quite radically how staff interact within an organisation and with those people external to it, like customers and government officials. Starting a first

full-time job in an organisation can be very bewildering, not only because of a host of new faces and personalities to get to know, but also because of the stresses caused by wanting to do well yet not knowing what is expected, nor how much is enough.

Furthermore, since organisations are made up of employees all in competition for advancement and promotion, it is not always easy to obtain helpful advice or to be told kindly how or when one is going wrong from more experienced peer group colleagues.

It is therefore important – right from the start – to have given careful thought to those factors which will contribute to a personally happy and upright working life:

- Honesty
- Integrity
- Personal ethics and morality
- Work rate
- Punctuality
- Self-starting skills
- Social skills
- Cheerfulness
- Ability to work with others in a team
- Ability to respect confidences
- Willingness to share information
- Respecting the contributions of others

Towards a personal code of ethics

In the last decade of the twentieth century, a high value has been placed upon material acquisitions and ethics in business have sometimes been forgotten – even by the most senior of directors and managers.It has been found necessary, for example, to legislate against insider dealing by stockbrokers and market makers capitalising upon illegal use of privileged information. By the same token, many millions of pounds worth of materials and products are lost each year by companies as a result of employees pilfering office consumables or manufactured products, which they deem to be 'perks' and part of their overall pay package.

It is sometimes better, therefore, not to learn by the example of others, but to have a considered personal code of ethics and morality within which to feel comfortable and which you can defend. Consider, for example these situations to which you could be exposed very early on in your first job:

- You are working on late in the office, and, through a glass partition you see a senior colleague with long service taking some money from the petty cash box held in the departmental secretary's desk drawer. Looking around furtively, your colleague pockets the money and replaces the box and slips out of the office.

What action would you take?

- Part of your job is to maintain the sales records for your region's sales force who work to preset targets each month and gain bonuses for meeting them. You are a friend of one such sales representative who rings you up just before month end saying: Could you push my sales turnover figure up a bit – I'm in a bit of a financial jam this month and I need the bonus – I promise you it'll all come right by the end of the next month, I've got some really good orders in the offing!'

What action would you take?

- Your manager is just about to leave for the day. You know he's got a date with one of his assistants and that their association is the talk of the department. He says, 'Oh, give my wife a call, will you. Tell her I've got a supper engagement with Crawshaw (an important customer). Should be home by eleven.'

What do you do?

- You've noticed your supervisor taking longer and longer 'wet lunches' and suspect she may have an incipient drink problem. You have already covered for her absences when senior management ring up and ask for her well after lunch-time. Today the MD phones and says he needs her directly in his office, as you spot her returning looking the worse for wear.

How would you tackle such a situation?

As the above scenarios illustrate, working within an organisation can place daily pressures and stresses upon individuals at all levels in areas which are sometimes hard to assess in simple black and white terms. The following questions are intended for a group discussion upon the area of personal ethics and morality as an employee:

Group talking points

1 Is there a difference between 'grassing on' or 'shopping' a colleague and reporting him or her to a superior for a breach of company regulations? Where would you draw the line?

2 Traditionally, secretaries and PAs are very loyal to their managers and sometimes have to cover up for their oversights and sins of omission etc. How would you define the limits of upward and downward loyalty between senior and subordinate staff, and between employees who are also friends?

3 'A good day's pay deserves a good day's work!' How would you react to a situation in which peer group colleagues are lazily coasting through the day while you are working hard to get the job done because you are conscientious?

4 You check your computerised payslip before pocketing it and discover that it is for some £200 too much! A gift from the gods, or a call to your accounts payroll clerk?

5 You fall out with a popular colleague over a dispute about who was supposed to complete an important sales order before an urgent deadline. You are fairly new. She is very popular in the office. Your colleagues take her side and 'send you to Coventry'. What do you do? Do you involve your manager?

6 'Working in an organisation's no different from being in the army – it's only wrong if you get found out!'
Give your views on this comment.

Self-starting skills

Considering that each new intake of employees, say, trainee managers, starts with a large firm on an equal footing and with exactly the same opportunities for advancement, why is it that after a few months some are shining and others are floundering? Given that all have met the essential qualification and entry requirements, the reasons must lie within their individual characteristics and work styles. And success for many new appointees lies in their ability to organise themselves – especially when working under pressure. The following section examines those factors which combine and are predominant in a self-starter. Measure yourself against the checklist below and identify which areas you will need to work at to transform weaknesses into strengths!

The Self-Starter's Strong Points!

● Makes a point of arriving at work in good time and being punctual for appointments.
● Maintains an orderly desk-top, where telephone message pads, addresses, telephone numbers, working papers, reference data and directories etc are always readily to hand.
● Keeps up-to-date a memory-jogging list of active jobs – tasks which have to be progress-chased or completed within set dates, either on his VDU or as a paper checklist. Checks and amends this list at least daily! Chivvies staff for due feedback and output accordingly.
● Ensures that appointments, meetings, deadlines, memory-joggers are recorded in an electronic or paper diary to which assistants or secretaries have access. Remembers to keep secretarial/support staff advised of freshly made commitments!
● Does not forget to carry out/follow up requests from the manager.
● Makes careful notes of any due deadlines of work assigned and devises a detailed plan of what needs to be done by when if the deadline is to be met. Gives support staff enough time to complete tasks delegated to them well before deadline falls due.
● Checks the progress of a time-constrained task on a regular basis and at predetermined dates which support staff know about in advance. Makes sure that backsliding support staff meet deadlines and provides help if needed.
● Knows how to find out where the organisation's information resources are kept.
● Ensures that his or her work is backed up by a reliable management records/filing system. Takes trouble to remain fully acquainted with the location of files in case of late working etc.
● Keeps a constant eye upon security and confidentiality, Does not leave sensitive material on the desk for visitors and night cleaners to read and disseminate.
● Knows how to keep secrets and shared confidences.
● Is always alert for useful information – from colleagues, clients, competitors, neighbours, etc and makes sure senior staff are informed of potentially important items.
● Replies to letters, Email notes, phone calls, faxes, etc promptly sends copies to interested colleagues. Lists arising tasks in jobs checklist.
● Makes a point of nurturing relationships with colleagues and contacts who are in a position to provide help in emergencies, such as the reprographics assistant or office caretaker.
● Checks out with his or her manager any matter relating to an assigned task which is unclear or becoming problematical. Advises the manager early of any likely problems or tricky matters in the offing – does not 'drop the boss in it'!
● Is willing to share ideas rather than acting as an information hoarder and blocker.
● Does not duck a difficult decision. Involves colleagues and support staff in the decision-making process as part of an open-management approach to the work of the group. Has strength of will to stick to a decision – but also the nobler ability to admit to it when wrong.

While the above checklist is by no means exhaustive, it does illustrate some of the major skills and qualities which successful executives develop as they move up the career ladder and assume more responsibility for managing the work of others.

Group assignment

In groups of three or four, consider the following collection of attributes which a successful executive could be expected to possess. Allocate each item with a score of 1–5, where 5 signifies most important and 1 least. Then compare your scores with those of the other groups in your class and discuss the reasons which supported your rating of each attribute.

Able to meet deadlines
Respects confidences
Always punctual
Stands by decisions
Always open to suggestions
Does not hoard information
Does not pass the buck
Able to identify key priorities
Organises time effectively
Knows how to delegate

'Any chance of joining your group?'

The attributes of a group

Identity	It is identifiable by its members and (usually) by those outside it
Norms of behaviour	It requires its members to conform to established norms or patterns of outlook, attitude and behaviour
Purpose	It has aims and objectives either clearly defined or intuitively understood which direct its activities
Hierarchy	It evolves either formally or informally a leadership and 'pecking-order' or hierarchy which its members accept
Exclusivity	It has the power to grant or deny admission and also to expel anyone from membership
Solidarity	It demands loyalty of its members and is capable of experiencing internal conflict while displaying an external front
Capacity for change	Its life may be either long or short. It may form, disintegrate and re-form depending upon external circumstances and stimuli.

Belonging to a group

What makes a group? Certainly it is quite different from a random collection of individuals waiting for a bus or train. Firstly, a group has an identity which its members recognise. This identity may be formally acknowledged, as in a committee or working-party, or it may be totally informal, as in a children's gang or a set of commuters using the same train compartment daily. The establishment of a group identity leads anyone to being an 'insider' or an 'outsider' as far as the group is concerned.

The next aspect affecting the creation and composition of groups is that all human beings share the need to belong to one group or another. Very few people survive long periods of isolation. Indeed, long periods of solitary confinement have been proved to be positively injurious. Similarly, few actively seek the life of the hermit or recluse.

Belonging to a group involves an individual in accepting and being accepted. The whole purpose of some groups seems to lie in maintaining a jealously guarded exclusivity and in setting often very extensive formal or informal entry 'exams'. What the individual has to demonstrate is that he or she accepts and is willing to comply with the 'norms' of the group – that is to say the established outlooks, attitudes and behaviour patterns which the group displays. For example, it would be a reckless probationary golfer who never replaced divots, frequently picked up other golfers' balls, cheated on his scorecard and always wore his spiked shoes in the teak-floored club lounge! It is only by clearly demonstrating similar ideas and behaviour that an individual becomes accepted by a group.

In society groups exist in many forms. The basic, indeed fundamental group is, of course, the family. Extensions to this group are formed through relatives and close family friends.

Yet further, separate groups are readily identified in the local sports or social club, residents' association or parent-teacher association etc.

As well as possessing a discernible identity and norms of behaviour, groups also exist to achieve aims and objectives, whether commercial cultural, sporting or community centred. Such groups will evolve, either formally or informally, procedures for choosing leaders and will also establish 'pecking-orders' which derive not only from official status, but also from length of membership, degree of assertiveness or demonstrated expertise. Most cricketers, for example, defer to the club's fast bowler or move aside to allow the 'Father of the House' to reach the bar.

It is interesting to note that within any group of reasonable size sub-groups will also exist or come together temporarily. Within a music society, for example, there may lurk a secret, hard-core nucleus wishing to oust Gilbert and Sullivan to put Mozart on the throne! Such a group may only be identified when the future programme comes up for discussion and they form a solid caucus at a meeting. Once the purpose has been achieved, however, such a group may disperse as quickly as it was formed.

Talking point

'The best working group is a committee of one!' Is this an autocratic management view, or is there some truth in its implied criticism of the quality of work undertaken by working groups like committees?

Groups in organisations

Companies strive to establish a corporate identity among their employees and to build a corporate image through advertising and publicity to make themselves readily and pleasingly identifable to the general public. Both private and public service organisations encourage staff to feel more involved and committed by circulating house journals, newspapers and magazines and by staging social and sports events. Also, in many organisations there is tremendous loyalty and a will to survive in members facing external competition and adverse circumstances.

If it is true that work-centred organisations embody characteristics shared by most groups, how are they to be identified? Firstly, it should be pointed out that, although an organisation as a whole may have a recognisable identity and character, the whole is, in fact, made up of many smaller groups, and, within them, sub-groups. As we have discovered, organisations are divided into specialist divisions, which themselves may take on the characteristics of a distinctly identifiable group – 'the marketing wallahs', 'those whizz-kids from R & D', 'the Scrooge brigade in accounts'. Indeed, groups are often formed as a kind of self-defence and means of survival in the face of other groups. In addition, within any specialist or departmental group there will form sub-groups of people who associate together for a variety of reasons – shared activities, outlooks, physical proximity, common goals and so on. The following represent some of the reasons why groups are formed within work organisations:

1 It is difficult as an individual to feel a part of a large organisation.
2 People need to have a sense of belonging and to feel that they make a meaningful and accepted contribution somewhere.
3 People are drawn together by striving to achieve common goals and objectives.

4 People often form groups by reason of daily proximity and shared work-places.
5 Common expertise may be the basis of a group as may also be common outlooks and interests.
6 Positions in similar grades may also form a group characteristic.
7 People may wish to join a group because its activities make it look desirable.

Some groups within organisations are created and then develop extremely tight-knit relationships as the result of a formal activity. For example, a committee may be set up to make an investigation or develop a product. Though its members may not, initially, know one another very well, being drawn from different departments and levels, nevertheless, if the work is protracted, and if the members become thoroughly committed to the group's defined goals – especially if the committee faces external criticism – then very often it will become distinctly recognisable as a group. Other groups, however, are formed quite informally, springing from likings which A and B and C may have for one another. Such groups are often found within departments, but may also span them.

Working as an effective group member

People who become successful and effective members of working groups, whether in the form of committees, task forces or quality circles, tend to possess the following characteristics:

● The ability to cooperate and share in decision-making
● A willingness to listen to and accept other people's ideas and suggestions
● The capacity to modify their own ideas so as to fall in with evolving proposals and decisions
● A preparedness to undertake within preset deadlines tasks which form only a part of a greater design or project under the direction of a group leader and to see praise and recognition go to the group rather than to the individual
● A willingness to come up with ideas which could be 'shot down' rather than merely coast along as the group's 'sleeper', and so to do a fair share of the group's tasks
● An inclination to support other group members and the group's work rather than to undermine it
● A willingness to accept responsibility as a group member for the outcomes of the group's activities

Relationships at work

The employee, whether as part of a group or as an individual, will create, maintain and develop a number of different relationships at work with those

Relationships affecting and influencing the employee

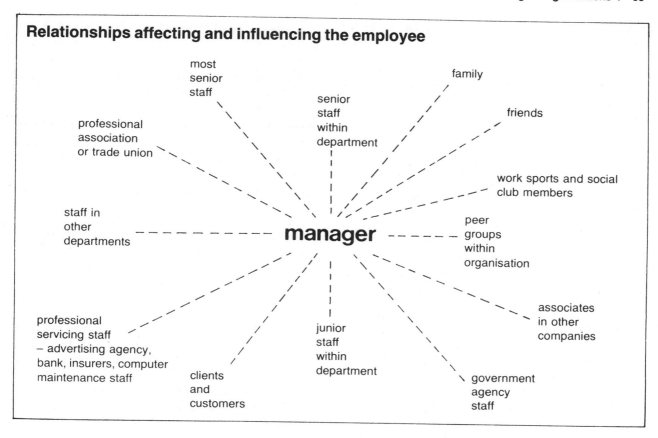

people with whom he has contact. The nature and extent of such relationships obviously depend a great deal upon the employee's job and position in the organisation's hierarchy. The diagram above indicates the wide range of relationships which, in this case, a manager may have with people both inside and outside his company.

Talking point

Should an employee consciously modify his or her communication tone and style when interacting with a superior – or a subordinate? Or does it happen anyway?

What the employee communicates and how he communicates is very much influenced by the nature of the relationship between sender and receiver. Indeed, the success or failure of communication depends upon both sender and receiver perceiving that a relationship exists and that it places constraints upon the communication process. We regard the polite handling of a difficult customer by a sales assistant as 'professional'; we admire the way a resourceful secretary handles her boss, who may be under pressure; we applaud the manager who executes an unpopular directive without alienating his subordinates. Each in his or her way has seen a relationship and has used communicating skills to overcome a problem without transgressing

the protocols, etiquettes or conventions which undoubtedly characterise the relationship.

Conflicts

When communication goes wrong the fault may lie in any one of a number of different areas:

1 The communication process may break down in any one of the six main stages.
2 The wrong communications medium may have been chosen.
3 The route for communication may have been disrupted by 'interference' of one kind or another.
4 The context or background of a situation may have been misread.
5 Arising more particularly from 1 above, the relationship between sender and receiver may create a conflict in one or other or both.

This last area may cause deep-seated problems. One main reason for such conflict is that all members of an organisation embody within themselves a number of different obligations and responsibilities which come to the fore at different times, depending upon which particular duty they are discharging and with whom they are relating, whether to a group or an individual.

Jim Harper's problems

Take Jim Harper, for example. Jim works as senior clerk in the production department of a large manufacturing company. He is also the representative of an office staff trade union. For some years he has been actively involved in the works sports and social club and has recently been elected its chairman. He is also a husband and father. As the diagram below illustrates, all these duties or 'roles' overlap and together go to 'make up' Jim both at work and at home.

The various roles of Jim Harper

In some parts of each of his roles there is no problem – Jim is able to carry out his duties without feeling tension or conflict. But there are also areas which overlap, where aspects of one role and the relationships it creates with other people impinge upon another role with accompanying difficulties. Imagine, then, how Jim would feel in the following situations:

1 He has been asked to work late on the night he promised to take his family to the cinema – a treat they had all been looking forward to.
2 His trade union is in general dispute with employers over a pay settlement.
3 His departmental manager is appointed to the works sports and social committee saying, 'Don't worry about me, Jim, just treat me as another committee member'.
4 As trade union representative he is given confidential information to the effect that the company is likely to require the sports field for the expansion of the works.

The conflicts which are bound up in such situations are not easily resolved and membership of any organisation, in whatever capacity, is likely to involve the employee in similar, difficult circumstances. Resolving such problems requires much communication expertise and reserves of goodwill and mutual sympathy on both sides of a relationship.

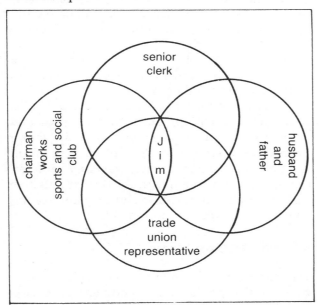

Effective communication, then, is totally bound up with an understanding of how people behave in groups or as individuals and also with an appreciation of the ways in which relationships – managing director/senior clerk, foreman/operative, secretary/principal – affect the process of communication. For example, the managing director, because of his power and status may only get to hear what his staff think he wants to hear; the departmental group which represents the older, long-service staff may express resentment at the changes being energetically introduced by a newly-appointed young manager; the machine operator may have a disagreement with the foreman in fuller and franker terms than he would with the production manager.

Thus communication tends to be coloured by a number of factors based on group attitudes and person-to-person relationships:

1 Communication with a superior tends to be more formal or guarded than with an equal: 'I'd better be careful what I say here.'
2 Communication with a subordinate tends also to be formal and restrained: 'I don't wish to lose my authority by becoming too familiar.'
3 Communication with an equal tends to be fuller, franker and less restrained: 'What I tell Charlie will not affect my position.'
4 Informal groups may not always communicate directly, but 'let their feelings be known' in various ways.
5 People expect other people to communicate in ways associated with their position and mutual relationship: 'The boss don't stand for no nonsense,' or, 'Janet? Oh, yes, always polite. I'd be sorry to lose her.'

Styles of communication

Directing
Instructing
Requiring

If the objectives of an organisation are to be achieved then orders and directives need to be sent down the authority line which are clearly expressed. The authority of the sender backs up the 'requiring' message which the subordinate is expected to accept.

Accepting
Undertaking
Executing
Effecting

Accepting and undertaking – doing – are central to the subordinate's role. In fact the directing/accepting relationship is the linchpin of organisational communication since it lies at the heart of the contract between the employee and the employer. Acceptance of employee status requires self-discipline and if the receiver cannot accept and undertake courteously phrased instructions he or she is probably in the wrong job!

Requesting
Suggesting
Proposing

Nevertheless, some directives are more tentatively phrased – especially when the receiver's active goodwill is central to the task. Requesting also characterises those liaising relationships between departments, while suggesting and proposing typify the manner of communicating up the authority line.

Informing
Clarifying
Confirming

A great deal of communication in organisations takes the form of passing information up, across and down. Since there is no attempt to secure action from the receiver the communicating style is much more neutral than in directing or requesting.

Persuading
Exhorting
Explaining
Reassuring

Despite the existence of lines of authority and the manager/subordinate relationship, people still need to be led rather than driven. Active cooperation is crucial to effective performance and very many communications need to be persuasive – employees may need encouragement to sell more, to accept changes or to be reassured over developments.

Motivating
Involving
Encouragement

Underlying *all* communication is the need for the sender to motivate the receiver to action or sympathetic understanding. If the receivers of messages are to want to carry them out, then the senders' communicating style must be motivating, involving and encouraging.

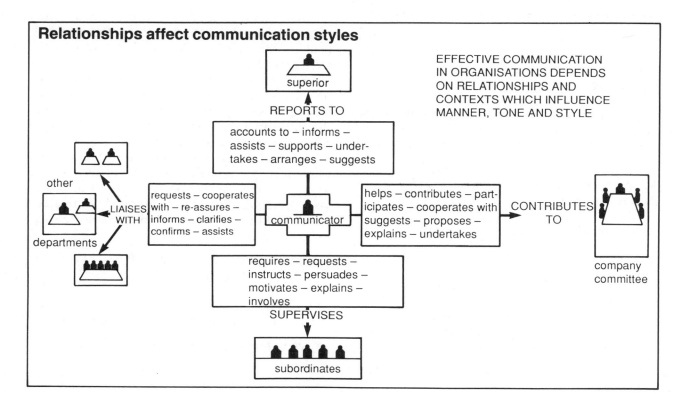

Relationships affect communication styles

EFFECTIVE COMMUNICATION IN ORGANISATIONS DEPENDS ON RELATIONSHIPS AND CONTEXTS WHICH INFLUENCE MANNER, TONE AND STYLE

superior

REPORTS TO

accounts to – informs – assists – supports – undertakes – arranges – suggests

other departments

LIAISES WITH

requests – cooperates with – re-assures – informs – clarifies – confirms – assists

communicator

helps – contributes – participates – cooperates with suggests – proposes – explains – undertakes

CONTRIBUTES TO

company committee

requires – requests – instructs – persuades – motivates – explains – involves

SUPERVISES

subordinates

Helping
Assisting
Cooperating
Contributing

In many relationships where the communicator makes a contribution to a group activity – meeting, task-force or working party – then the communicating style needs to display a willingness to help, contribute and cooperate. In this way a team-spirit will be built up without which little will happen. Also, the communicator must be willing to accept criticisms and modifications to his or her contributions.

Questioning
Disagreeing
Criticising

Perhaps the most difficult task facing the communicator is coping with expressing disagreements or criticisms. Organisations with any common sense accept the need for disagreement and criticism in the decision-making process, yet it is an area needing tact, discretion, restraint and above all timing – no one likes being dressed down in public before colleagues. Also, disagreeing while keeping on good terms is an art to be studied which pays handsome dividends!

Reminder

Before embarking upon a communicating process think carefully about your aims, the relationship, the context and prevailing attitudes. Then select thoughtfully the most appropriate manner and style in which to express the message.

Examples

'If production deadlines are to be met and the imposition of penalty-clauses avoided, it is essential that the above causes of delay are dealt with quickly.'

(extract from managing director's memorandum to production manager)

'Come on, Charlie, this ain't a sit-in!

(foreman to operator after tea-break)

'I think your idea of introducing the mobile tea-trolley for tea-breaks by the machines would certainly secure increased productivity. The trouble is, mid-morning and afternoon tea-breaks have become traditional in the eyes of the men. . . .'

(production manager to organisation and methods officer at a meeting)

'It is therefore recommended that a working party be set up to investigate the feasibility of introducing a local area network to link our range of electronic office equipment.'

(extract from an investigatory report from data processing manager to board of directors)

'So I was wondering, Jack, if we could possibly borrow your slide-projector for the Bristol presentation.'

(assistant sales manager to training officer over the 'phone)

'This one's a tricky one, John, so I decided to ask you to handle it.'

(extract from briefing of a personal assistant by the marketing manager)

'I very much regret the trouble you have been caused and assure you that the defect is being given urgent attention at the company's Birmingham works. The machine will be delivered to you no later than . . .'

(extract from regional sales manager's letter to a customer)

'I appreciate that Mr Jenkins – it's just that no one appears to be controlling the flow of work and the girls are being pressured late in the afternoon and left with little to do in the mornings . . .'

(extract from a secretarial supervisor's conversation with office manager about the recent introduction of a word processing pool)

'I know – and you know – that the company, and indeed the country, have been going through a difficult trading period. Equally, I know that the strength of Allied Products lies in its ability to meet a challenge. It hasn't been easy, and I can give you no guarantee that it will get better at all quickly. What I do know is that if anyone is going to lead the company into a better tomorrow, it is you, its sales representatives. And so my closing message to you all is: the company is proud of what you have done during a difficult year and will back you all to the hilt in the coming months; but it will only be your determination and continued enthusiasm which will turn the corner during the next year. I know I can rely on you!'

(conclusion of managing director's address to the Annual Sales Conference of Allied Products)

'If it will help, I don't mind staying on to type the letter – Monday's my stay-at-home night anyway.'

(secretary to manager late Monday afternoon)

The communicating manager

The role of the manager in any organisation involves the acceptance of many responsibilities. It also places a number of constraints upon the person who manages, whatever his or her title or designation. Certainly the manager needs to be a good communicator, since communicating lies at the heart of what the manager is doing, achieving given objectives through other people. The following table indicates some of the principal managerial qualities; they all direct or influence what the manager says, writes or does and the manner in which it is done and add up to what is an asset in any organisation – the communicating manager:

As an executor of tasks

decision-making
problem-solving
accountability
authority
initiative
anticipation
effectiveness

That the manager often acts under pressure to achieve objectives imposed from above is not always fully appreciated by his subordinates. Such accountability imposes strains, tensions and conflicts reflected in daily inter-personal communication. Helping the manager – who usually is only too aware of his problems – is a duty of the subordinate. In such ways teams are built and climates established essential to enjoying life at work.

As a leader

delegating
motivating
developing
involving
counselling
reconciling
healing

It is, however, the manager's responsibility to provide the lead and impetus in building a team based on cooperation and goodwill. This involves trust on both sides. The communicating manager needs to make constant efforts to be aware of the expectations, needs and anxieties of his team. Indeed, as much time may be needed to develop and hold the team together as in achieving tasks, since the latter is wholly dependent upon the former.

As a subordinate

integrity
loyalty
discretion
tact
diplomacy
self-discipline

The manager is also, usually, a subordinate. Much of his effectiveness relies on the development of personal qualities, reflected in communication practices, which result in his being trusted. Access to confidential or privileged information assumes qualities of tact, discretion and integrity – and the total subordinate role requires a high degree of self-discipline.

As an information source

informing
disseminating
listening
relaying
interpreting

If his team is to perform effectively, then the manager needs to keep sources and routes of information as open as possible, allowing for obvious needs such as security and confidentiality. He will need to develop skills in ascertaining what his team needs to know in order to perform and then to supply that need.

As a contributor to the organisation's development

thinking
planning
proposing
suggesting
querying
disagreeing

The manager is also a contributor to his organisation's development. If he is to be of benefit, then he needs to put his experience and expertise to use by thinking about what he is doing, putting forward suggestions and proposals, criticising constructively and using instances of disagreement to re-appraise what he is doing as well as to cause others to think about what they are doing.

The communicating secretary

The secretary's role has been significantly enlarged in recent years, partly as a development of information technology, and partly as the result of the changing economic and social climates regarding women at work. Nowadays, the secretarial post is much more frequently a route to executive responsibility. In any case, secretaries have always been linchpins or sheet-anchors in many an organisation. Many discharge responsibilities out of all proportion to their designations as assistants to senior managers, and are, in effect, executives in their own right. Moreover, the scope of the secretary's role is enormous, embracing not only the routine duties of dictation, typewriting or filing, but also coping with unexpected potential disasters, using initiative and resourcefulness and often, extreme delicacy and discretion. Good secretaries are treasured by managers in all organisations, since their price is truly 'above rubies'! Perhaps the best definition of the secretary's role is as the hub of a communications wheel around which a manager, staff — in fact a whole department — may revolve.

As a subordinate

loyalty
integrity
discretion
tact
cooperation

The secretary is often, literally, 'at the right hand' of his or her principal, acting in coordination with and as an extension of the manager. In addition to qualities like those already outlined in the manager as subordinate, the secretary needs to be particularly aware of the need for personal loyalty.

As a supervisor

delegating
checking
maintaining standards
helping
developing

Very often the secretary acts as a supervisor to junior staff, and is, consequently, in a similar position in many ways to the manager. The secretary will need to set high standards by personal example, yet be accessible to staff, many of whom may be young, diffident and inexperienced, and so also has a responsibility to enrich and develop the staff in her charge.

As an executor of tasks

accuracy
precision
editing
efficiency

Much of the secretary's work lies in written and oral communication, in producing as finished products the manager's messages. Such work entails painstaking care, and may include the discreet editing of rough drafts.

As an assistant

ability to cope
initiative
resourcefulness
perceptiveness
helpfulness

In addition to the routine range of secretarial duties, the secretary is very often given, or assumes the role of assistant or confidant(e) to his or her principal. In fact very many management functions are, in reality, carried out by a team of two. Thus taking an interest and being committed may soon lead to a creative and fulfilling assistant's role.

As receptionist and 'filter'

charm
intelligence
poise
grooming
perception
alertness

Most secretaries have an involvement in reception work. In this role they may be understudies for an absent principal and may form a lasting first impression on a visitor or client. Also, alertness and perceptiveness may prove invaluable in relaying information or attitudes regarding customers or competitors who visit or telephone. Also, the secretary needs to be resourceful in deciding what she can deal with and what needs the principal's attention.

The assistant/support staff role

The nature and scope of administrative jobs has changed over the past decade as a result of the widespread introduction of computers. In many organisations, the job title of secretary is being replaced by more meaningful alternatives like Information Assistant, Support Services Assistant, Assistant Manager and so on. It is now likely that your own career route will commence with a job role which includes much of what many secretaries do and so the above Communicating Secretary checklist will be directly relevant to you in your first post.

Talking point:

A major cause of communication failure occurs when the receiver considers the manner, tone or style of the sender's message inappropriate . . . He can't talk to me like that!' . . . 'Cheeky young puppy' . . . 'I can never take him seriously' . . . 'if only he'd come out and tell you what he really wants' . . .

Self assessment question

How good are you at: giving instructions, accepting orders, persuading others, motivating other people, disagreeing and questioning without rancour or aggression? Identify those aspects you need to work on and make time to practise the associated communication skills!

Conclusion

Nowadays people acknowledge much more readily the central part which good communication techniques can play in overcoming the problems which occur when objectives are to be achieved by people working in tiered structures or hierarchies.

This is not to say that all problems related to work are easily overcome – newspapers provide evidence to the contrary every day. Nevertheless, systems and processes are being improved. In many organisations employees are consulted and involved far more extensively than in the past. In the area of industrial relations, managements and unions have developed sophisticated 'negotiating machinery' and government agencies have been created to arbitrate where necessary. Further, a workers 'social contract' of employment rights is now part of the EC's programme of legislation.

Talking point

In industrial relations situations which lead up to strikes being called, it is often said that the positions of management and trade union(s) involved have 'polarised'. How does this development illustrate the attributes of working groups? What communication approaches are available to resolve such conflicts?

The improvements in education during the last 100 years have resulted in individuals being more aware and articulate, with the result that, both as managers and as subordinates, they have more insight and perception of 'the other fellow's point of view'. More recently, the study of human behaviour and human relations has revealed much more of the psychology involved in human communication processes – of 'what makes people tick'.

In addition, organisations in recent years have been casting a much more critical eye over their systems and structures. Management specialists and consulting industrial psychologists are able to demonstrate the problems deriving from a line of authority which is too long or the problems arising from groups which are too big or from doing work which is unsatisfying. There is now a greater appreciation of the fact that people like, on the whole, to work in small, closely-knit groups; there is also more understanding of the need for people to be given the initiative to solve problems or to effect manufacturing processes in their own way.

For this reason many organisations are now more loosely controlled from the centre and more independence is given to subordinate parts. The trends of the future, resulting from the findings of the communication and behavioural sciences, may well be away from the giant corporations and back to smaller, locally based manufacturing or servicing units.

Also, the installation of sophisticated computer-based information systems to facilitate local, national and international communications is enabling far greater inter-communication between personnel in the middle-lower tiers of organisations. This is resulting (along with the introduction of unified databases) in the middle-ranking employees having access to far more information than formerly.

One thing is certain, however. Whenever people, even in comparatively small numbers, are put together in a working environment, human nature will ensure that problems ensue! Overcoming the problems of human interaction in the world of work is, in effect, what business communication is all about.

This unit aimed to set out some of the main theories and principles which underpin good communication techniques and group working practices and to indicate some of the problems which only developed social skills and positive human relations attitudes will overcome.

All really worthwhile skills not only take time to learn, but also need daily practice to maintain. Communication is no exception.

The chances are that you already are, or shortly will be working in an organisation. Whether you love it or hate it, whether you become fulfilled or frustrated in your working life, will depend very much on how well you manage to put good communication skills into daily practice. Doing so requires self-discipline and dedication and the benefit of experience – plus the counsel of those who 'have been around' if you are wise enough to seek it.

But the effort is worth it – especially if you consider that you will probably spend some 80 000 hours of your life at work!

Talking point

How do 'us and them' situations tend to arise in organisations? What tactics could be adopted by all parties concerned to avoid such situations?

Checklist of available support services

The following checklist indicates the major areas of support which exist in organisations to aid the work of personnel. Note, some of the services may be set up in cross-company centralised units, while others may be limited to individual departments.

Centralised records: holding data in electronic/ microform or paper systems
Technical library: acting as information source and disseminating abstracts
Reprographics centre: providing black/white and colour photocopying, slide and OHP foil produc-

tion; desk-top publishing unit for the creation of brochures, leaflets, circular letters, in-house newspapers; collating and binding services
Text processing unit: providing word processor and audio transcriptions of letters, reports, schedules, etc for groups of managers
First line maintenance: technical support for office machinery and equipment which goes down
Computer services: giving 'cradle-to-grave' support for all computer-based activities
Centralised purchasing: a service which monitors best prices and back-up and organises the acquisition of all goods and services, eg contract cleaning, for the organisation
Personnel: part of this function may be to provide recruitment, training and counselling services for all departments/personnel
Medical welfare: larger organisations employ resident doctors/nursing staff in case of emergency and to supply preventative screening, creche, etc.

Assignment

Select *one* of the above services and investigate the range and scope of provision which is typically provided. Find out what local organisations have and then give an oral presentation of your findings (of about 10–15 minutes) to your group.

Talking point

While some working groups are consciously created by organisational managers to achieve set goals and objectives, others are created quite informally and spontaneously among subsets of employees. Of the latter, some may prove quite anti-establishment, arising as a result of poor management. What could a new management team do to secure the cooperation of unofficial and 'concealed' work groups!

Summary of main points _____

1   Developing a successful and worthwhile career requires the individual to evolve a personal code of ethics encompassing standards of honesty, integrity, work rate, trustworthiness, loyalty, conscientiousness and respect for others.

2   Success as a 'self-starter' in an administrative/management post demands skills and abilities such as: punctuality and good time-keeping, disciplined desk-top organisation, regular updating and prioritising of jobs in hand, effective diary and appointments logging, good management records systems, meeting of deadlines, effective security, open management communication approaches, effective and consistent decision-making skills, ongoing consultation and involvement of colleagues/support staff.

3   Group attributes include: common/shared identity, accepted norms of behaviour, agreed goals, accepted 'pecking order', exclusivity, solidarity and capacity to change.

4   Working as a member of an organisation group requires: cooperation and sharing in decision-making, listening and modifying outlooks and ideas, working to deadlines under supervision, forgoing personal praise, active participation, loyalty, collective responsibility.

5   Sets of roles carried out by an employee may result in conflicts and tensions arising from: conflicts of loyalty, role reversal with a superior, conflicts between family and work demands, conflicts between strongly held personal views and imposed job requirements.

6   Communication styles in organisations vary according to the context of the message and will span: directing/instructing, complying with/accepting, requesting/asking, informing, persuading/ exhorting, motivating/encouraging, helping/supporting, questioning/disagreeing with.

7   The communicating manager assumes roles as: an executor of tasks, as a leader of personnel, as an intermediary between senior and junior staff, as an information source and as a contributor to the organisation's development.

8   Secretarial support services staff assume roles as: subordinates, superiors, executors of tasks, aiding assistants, receptionists and 'filters' and trouble-shooters.

Activities and assignments _____

Quick review quiz

1 Draw up a list of the qualities you think most important in an individual's personal code of ethics at work.

2 Identify the characteristics you consider most important in a self-starter at work.

3 Define the principal attributes of a group, and explain why they are central features of any group.

4 Outline the main qualities needed in an effective group member within a working context.

5 List a typical set of people with whom a manager may be expected to have professional relationships in and outside of the organisation.

6 Identify four typical causes of role conflict in organisations.

7 List as many styles of communication as you can recall in which *a*) a manager and *b*) a secretary/support assistant may be expected to become proficient.

8 Explain why and how different scenarios at work require differing communication styles. Give examples to support your answer.

Research and report back assignments

1 Find out what the British Institute of Management's Code of Practice and the Management Charter Initiative (MCI) have to say about a manager's ethical responsibilities.

2 Review the ways in which your class has worked since the start of your course and, in not more than 100 words, draw up a definition which you consider applicable to your class as a group. Compare your definition with those produced by your fellow-students.

3 In pairs, interview a selection of your teaching staff and neighbourhood contacts working in organisations and ask them to supply you with examples of role conflicts they have experienced. In a suitably anonymous way, share your findings with your group and see if you have established any common threads.

4 First, ensure you understand what is meant by 'peer group pressure'. Then carry out your research into industrial relations problems which have hit the news – nationally or locally – and give a presentation to your class on how peer group pressure has affected the problem and its solution. *Hint*: many strikes involve peer group pressure upon both management and trade unions.

5 In groups of three or four, collect a set of documents – letters, leaflets, memos, official notices, advertisements, bulletins, etc which contain what you think are good examples of various communication styles at work. Incorporate them into a collage/wall poster for your base room as specimens of good practice.

6 Conduct a straw poll among your teachers and contacts working in organisations to find out what communication practices and shortcomings they find most irritating and annoying. Make out a checklist of your findings and compare them with the lists your fellow students have compiled. Check for similarities and correspondences and determine to avoid them in your own career!

Work experience and simulation assignments

1 Find out what kinds of working groups are in action in the organisation to which you are attached. Arrange to interview leaders/members of two or three groups and establish:

- Why they were set up
- What their goals/objectives are
- How they organise themselves
- How they relate to other organisational units/ groups
- What problems they encounter and how they handle them

2 Arrange to sit in on a group meeting as an observer. Make notes on:

Contribution rates – the frequency with which each member contributes to the discussion; consider the roles and personalities of the major contributors and the impact they had on the group meeting; consider why those who said little did so.

Decision-making process – watch and listen carefully and then make notes on how decisions were reached on the basis of:

- assertive members making points strongly
- an evolving rational argument
- points based on emotional/subjective argument
- interruptions and contradictions
- chairman's interventions
- consensus or majority view
- the impact of facts and figures calmly presented
- supportive or opposing interventions

3 With your supervisor's help, find out what the following group-based specialist terms and functions stand for:

- Quality Circles
- Buzz Group
- Brainstorming
- Group Norms
- Group Dynamics
- Group Maintenance Techniques

Select one of the above terms and explain what it stands for to your class, supplying helpful examples.

4 Find out how new members of staff are inducted into the organisation to which you are attached and report back on your findings to your group.

5 Find out how the organisation's personnel arm works to help staff who may find themselves at odds with the group/unit/department in which they work. For example, consider how sexual harassment and personality clashes are handled. Again, report back to your group – respecting confidences in you usual way.

Case Study

Fitting in

It was Gary Hammond's first job. The memory was still bright of the day some three weeks ago when he'd rushed into the kitchen at home to tell his Mum he'd got the job at Goldsmiths, a company which distributed books and magazines nationwide from a large warehouse complex.

'I got it!' he'd yelled excitedly, 'Trainee Manager in the Despatch Department – start Monday!' That evening there were celebrations in the Hammond household and Gary was bursting to start work after his recent success in his BTEC National Diploma in Distribution.

'Well, done lad,' his Dad had said, gruffly. 'They're a good firm and you'll have no trouble fitting in there, I'm sure. Have to mind your ps and qs, though I'll be bound, until you know the ropes.'

* * *

Gary waited until it was morning tea-break time. Then, quietly, he slipped out of the Distribution Department's open-plan office and knocked hesitantly at the office door of Mrs Grenfell, the Despatch Department Manager.

'Come in,' said Mrs Grenfell. 'Oh, it's you, Gary. Hope it's nothing too complicated, I've got to go out in a few minutes.'

'Oh, well. I could come back later . . . .' Mrs Grenfell paused, picking up the crestfallen look on Gary's face and the twitching of a muscle in his right cheek.

'Just a moment Gary.' She picked up the phone asked her secretary to reschedule her appointment for an hour later. 'Sit down, I've got the feeling that there's something on your mind that needs sorting out.'

'How did you know?' asked Gary, surprised and now feeling embarrassed, wishing he'd gone to the staff canteen for his tea-break.

'Intuition and experience!' replied Mrs Grenfell. 'I've seen your kind of look before and know that something's bothering you. Come on, out with it,

while I pour you a cup of tea.' Gary's muscle began to twitch faster, and his jaw flexed as he ground his back teeth.

'Well, ah, I've decided to give in my notice!' Having managed to articulate what had been on his mind for the past week, he felt a little less nervous, although beads of perspiration began to form on his forehead.

'You what?' gasped Mrs Grenfell, whose intuition and experience had not prepared her for this bombshell, 'But you've only just arrived! I thought you were settling in nicely and Jack (Gary's immediate supervisor) has been saying how hard you've been working. What's brought all this on?'

A long and difficult pause ensued. Gary coloured and then, taking a deep breath, gave out a torrent of words.

'I just don't know where I am! I just don't know why I'm doing what I'm doing. Every time I allocate a pallet for a consignment of books someone tells me it's the wrong pallet, or it's in the wrong place, and if I move it, someone else tells me that it was OK where I first put it! I don't know how to work the computer properly to check the delivery schedules and every time I ask, people are always too busy. They just say, "Oh, don't worry, you'll soon pick it up" – but I'm not!'

Mrs Grenfell's mouth edges had dropped at this unsuspected outburst. Quietly she interposed and asked, 'And how are you getting on with Jo, Alan and Bridget (Gary's co-workers) in the office?'

'Well, all right I suppose, but they keep geeing me up about my qualifications and taking the mickey. I don't think it exactly made their day when I arrived, though I'm sure I don't know why. I've done my best to fit in with them.'

'What makes you think you're not fitting in with them?'

'Oh, I dunno. I always have to start a conversation. They'll never volunteer anything. I have to ask constantly about the least thing – where does this go, what's this form for, where do I go to find out about that. Makes me feel really small! And they're always having a go at me for working too hard. Too hard – I hardly know yet what I'm doing!'

'What about Jack, how are you getting on with him?'

'Jack's OK. He's the only one I think who has accepted me. Trouble is, he just doesn't seem to have the time to answer my questions and so on. His desk seems like the battlements of a castle – with Jack's bowed head just visible in between!'

'Well, at least your sense of humour's not entirely disappeared,' said Mrs Grenfell, smiling encouragingly. 'Is that all of it – off your chest I mean?'

'Gary looked down, feeling like a kid who'd rushed in to his mum to complain about being picked on by the street gang. 'I shouldn't have come. It just seemed to get on top of me. I'll let you get on, I'm sure it'll sort itself out . . . .'

'Sit down, please Gary. You see, it won't sort itself out, just like that. And you needn't feel bad about coming to see me. In fact you've done me a very good turn.'

'How d'you mean?' asked Gary, wondering what she was driving at.

'Well, your coming to see me has brought matters to a head. I've been meaning to look into the way in which Goldsmiths handles the appointment of people like you – and we certainly need prospective managers who've studied distribution. I want you to promise to say nothing about your resignation thoughts or this interview to anyone for the time being. And I'd like you to come and see me at 11.00 am tomorrow. And please don't worry. You *will* fit in here at Goldsmiths – but I've got some earnest thinking and planning to do.'

Gary got up and left, as Mrs Grenfell turned to a filing cabinet to lift out a folder entitled Induction Procedures. Walking slowly back to the office, his mind raced as he wondered whether he'd done the right thing at all. Yet Mrs Grenfell had seemed to understand how he felt . . . .

Questions

1 In your view, should Gary have gone to see Mrs Grenfell in the first place?

2 How do you rate Mrs Grenfell's handling of the situation which unfolds? What do you see as her strengths and weaknesses as a manager?

3 Did Goldsmiths fail Gary in his first three weeks' work there? If so, how?

4 Mrs Grenfell promised Gary that she would be directly looking into the problems of which his predicament was a symptom. If you were Mrs Grenfell, what actions would you take to rectify matters – for Gary, and generally?

5 What part does Non Verbal Communication (NVC) [see Unit 8] play in the interview between Gary and Mrs Grenfell? What lessons may be learned in this context about oral communication skills?

6 How do you rate Gary as a 'self-starter'? What do you see as his weaknesses?

In groups of three or four, having considered the above Questions, make out a checklist of the sort of information and support which a new trainee manager should be given on starting a first job.

Then, draw up a set of practices and procedures which you think Goldsmiths should introduce in their revised induction programme for new management trainees.

5

Information technology 1: hardware and systems

Overview

- How Information Technology works within the systems information processing model.
- The development of IT from dedicated, stand-alone word-processors to a network of interconnected electronic office equipment.
- An overview of the uses of various types of software packages in different departments.
- How local and wide area networks (LANs and WANs) have transformed office communications.
- How fax, telex, viewdata (Prestel) systems work on networks.
- How the range of office reprographics equipment — printers and photocopiers work, and what they can do to present office documentation to best effect.

Introduction – defining Information Technology

The term Information Technology was first widely employed in 1981 to describe the equipment and systems which were being introduced in both private and public sectors to create, store and distribute information. Since then the term has been abbreviated to 'IT'.

Underpinning the definition of IT lies a model which provides a helpful explanation of the way in which computers process information, since it was the computer – in its mainframe, mini and personal, or PC, forms – which made the revolution in office electronic technology possible. The systems model defining the computer-centred processing of information is shown on page 78.

Information Technology's rapid growth within office-based information systems has led to a renewed interest in the systems concept for processing information. Essentially, the systems approach (see Unit 11) in terms of electronic equipment and its use for handling information may be divided into five distinct phases: 1 Input, 2 Processing, 3 Storage, 4 Output, 5 Feedback. The cycle within the system begins with the putting of data into the system (often a computerised network) by, for example, composing a letter on a terminal's keyboard using a word processor. The keyed-in data is then processed electronically into a layout on the monitor screen. It may then be stored on disk for subsequent recall, or it may be 'outputted' immediately in the form of a print-out on company notepaper. Once despatched, essential feedback will be needed as to the action or information the letter requested (see also Unit 2).

Follow-up assignment

What other examples of input, process and output phases can you think of?

The input phase

As the diagram illustrates, incoming information in the input phase arrives or is created in a variety of media: fax or telex messages, viewdata pages, telephone calls, video teleconferencing pictures and monitor screened computer programs, not to mention the stubborn mountain of paper documents.

Input information is frequently fed into computers as digitised data which may have been beamed across continents by satellites or sped along telephone companies' fibre-optic networks in the

form of electronic mail, either from within a multi-storey office block, nationally or globally.

Process And Storage Phases

However it starts out, such information, if it is to be used in a computer-based system, has to be transferred into a medium capable of being processed or stored electronically. For example, it is common practice nowadays for incoming correspondence printed on paper to be read by a scanner – a piece of equipment which converts it into a digitised format – so it may be stored as a computer file just like those created on floppy or hard disks. As a result, an Email message can be sent to all staff likely to need to read the letter in its electronic form, alerting them to its arrival and providing a file name for accessing it.

Other kinds of information, however, need to be processed before storing. For instance, a secretary may first transcribe a manager's draft report by shorthand and then create a first draft using a desktop terminal and a word processing package. Once created, this draft may be delivered to its originator either as a hard copy print-out or Emailed file for any alterations or corrections. As often as is needed, successive drafts may be processed by the secretary who only needs to alter those words or paragraphs which have been changed. Long gone are the days when typewriter technology required the rekeying of the whole report each time!

Information processing function in the office

STORAGE MEDIA

Media of incoming information

Media of outgoing information

Optical disc
Microfiche
Photocopies
OHP transparencies
Slides
Video-tape
Audio-tape
Film

Floppy/hard computer disk
Databases on computer
Manual – paper filing
Card index, forms

Information storage systems

Input → Information processing → Output

Feedback messages

Examples of the input phase:
- Incoming electronic mail item
- Incoming fax message
- Selected Prestel page
- Memo being dictated
- Incoming telephone call
- Viewing of video-tape
- Discussion at a meeting
- Incoming letter or invoice

Examples of the output phase
- Fax message dispatched to Hong Kong
- Email (electronic mail) message calling meeting sent to staff computer terminals
- Advice note sent with consignment of goods to customer
- Confirmation of an order sent by sales rep to sales office via British Telecom Gold Email Service
- Dictated, typed letter mailed to client via Post Office service

Oral, written & non-verbal:
Queries, confirmations
Requests for further information
Returned assignments and responses
No feedback received = follow-up needed

Examples of the process phase:
- Keying an appointment into an electronic diary
- Entering fresh figures on to a spreadsheet
- Producing a staff holiday rota for visual display
- Revising a report via word processing
- Arranging the time, date and location of a meeting for dissemination via electronic mail

All kinds of information is received via various media, dealt with and processed into appropriate forms of message for onward distribution. Copies, records and back-up files are stored in a wide range of paper and media, as archived data or for future reference.

The output phase

Once the information has been processed satisfactorily – whether in the form of text, number, graphics or programming language – it may need to be distributed in an output phase. The above diagram illustrates some of the main media which may be employed to distribute information. Currently, the explosion of telecommunications technology is resulting in messages criss-crossing the world as various kinds of high-speed, digitised, radio signals using satellites, telephone cables, laser-based networks or radio waves. Within more traditional communication networks, output often takes the form of a print-out, delivered by hand or by post, of the computer processed message in the form of, say, letter mailshots, memoranda, batch-produced invoices and statements for goods sold on account and so on.

Of recent years, great strides have been made using IT to distribute graphic images, photographs and videoed live meetings which enable executives to 'meet' without leaving their offices, which may be spread throughout Europe. Also, intercommunicating computers allow engineers and scientists located, say, in London and Sydney simultaneously to examine and modify on their respective monitors an electronic circuit, construction blueprint or company organisational chart!

The feedback phase

As we have already learned in Unit 2, which dealt with the communication process, no exchange of information is complete without feedback having been sought and supplied. Nor are computerised systems any different. An electronic message mailed to San Francisco in 11 seconds may still prove ineffectual if its urgently required response is not forthcoming.

In the design of computerised information systems, thoughtful systems analysts and programmers have often included built-in feedback devices, such as the visual tag which is displayed on the sender's monitor screen as soon as a one of his Email message recipients has 'opened his mail' and read the message. So no longer can the recipient say he didn't know, or wasn't told! Also in such Local Area Network (LAN) software, confirmations are screened automatically to the effect that a message has been successfully distributed or that incoming mail has arrived.

Living with IT

The speed at which IT systems and technologies have been taken up by business and public service organisations is truly astonishing. The first commercial microprocessor or silicon chip – the minaturised bundle of electronic circuitry on which IT depends – was marketed in the United States by the Intel Corporation in 1971 and each one cost over $100. Today their equivalents are produced by the billion and cost pennies. Thus vast economies of scale arising from worldwide demand for computers have led to remarkable reductions in prices while performance and reliability have improved dramatically. In today's business community even the humblest sole trader employs a PC to keep his books and records.

It is for this reason that every student of business and communication needs to become fully expert in IT and to grasp the fundamental changes that are being wrought in organisations in the areas of information management and processing, job roles, organisational cultures, management techniques, communication practices and industrial relations.

The rest of this Unit examines the various types of IT equipment currently in use in organisations and explains how they employed. You must keep in mind always that because of the pace of IT developments, manufacturers are constantly bringing new equipment and improved software packages to the market. This being so, it is most important that you make it a regular practice to browse through office equipment and communication systems magazines in your library (see page 13) to keep abreast of such developments. Remember that even newly acquired marketable skills are not that marketable after one or two years of study if they are not kept bang up-to-date!

Talking point

What dangers exist for both manager and secretary to be aware of in this era of almost instant message despatch and delivery – around the world and at all organisational levels! What approaches could a manager and secretary devise to guard against them?

Talking point

'A by-product of IT take-up in large organisations such as supermarket chains, High Street multiples and service industry consortia is that the smaller trader will go to the wall, and consumer choice be limited to what "the big boys" decide to supply.'

Group assignment

In groups of three or four, select one of the applications packages listed on page 82. Arrange to research it thoroughly and then give an AVA-supported presentation, with handouts, to your class as a 'state of the art' briefing on the subject.

IT and office equipment systems

From dedicated word processors to total convergence

As the diagram (page 81) illustrates, it has taken office equipment technologists some 120 years to develop text and information processing equipment culminating in today's highly efficient networks and intercommunicating computers.

Significantly, the qwerty keyboard is still used as a principal means of inputting information into highly sophisticated computer systems, although the touch screen and mouse (devices for amending, assembling or arranging data displayed on a VDU screen) should not be overlooked.

Self assessment question

Are you happy with the concepts of the systems information processing model? Test its validity against some information cycles and procedures with which you are familiar in the department in which you study and/or work.

The problem of the paper culture

For many centuries paper has been the principal medium for the recording of written information. Indeed, one could say that the administration of the industrial revolution in the nineteenth century relied upon the availability of cheap paper. As a consequence, many generations of office workers were accustomed to the medium and felt comfortable and secure with their foolscap, A4 and A5 bond and bank sheets of paper. The use of paper-based records involved the maintenance of filing systems which occupied valuable space, although the employment of microfiche (a film-based filing system) proved to be a valuable space-saving method for certain applications where the extra cost could be justified, for example, in the storage of bibliographical data.

In the early 1970s 'the paperless office' was a catchphrase of electronic office equipment suppliers, but, as the office paper mountain continued to grow in spite of the introduction of new computerised techniques, this premature slogan was quietly modified into 'the less paper office'.

The advent of the dedicated word processor

Not long after, however, a piece of office equipment was marketed which was destined to change radically the ways in which offices and the people who worked in them operated, and which made the prospect of the paperless office much more likely.

Hitherto, personal computers small enough to sit on desk tops had tended to be home computers used by enthusiasts. Alert marketing experts perceived a vast international demand for a piece of equipment capable of displaying and manipulating text and other data input from a keyboard. They saw how the computer's word processing software progam was able to add, delete, modify and move text around solely on the operator's screen until a satisfactory version was created. This version could then be sent to a waiting printer for rapid print-out and subsequent delivery to, say, a manager for perusal and amendment.

Talking point

What cultural/social problems do you envisage in personal intercommunication as the paperless office becomes a reality? What would you see as a balanced approach to paper/electronic technologies in organisations?

The particular beauty of this technological leap forward was that the entire text – perhaps comprising some 10–20 A4-equivalent pages – could be safely saved and stored on what was the forerunner of the floppy disk, a set of 'mag-cards' which looked like audio-tape in the form of luggage labels and which were inserted into the word processor's central processing unit (CPU).

Never again would the copy typist have laboriously to re-type an entire report several times until the manager was happy with it. All that was needed was simply to alter those specific words and sections which had been changed.

It is worth dwelling on this moment of IT evolution, for the arrival of the stand-alone word processor in offices really did herald a fundamental change in the whole approach to information processing and office administration, and from it was born a movement which by degrees took data/information processing out of the hands of data processing departments (sometimes staffed by 'high priests' who jealously guarded their computing expertise) and put it into the hands of office personnel at the sharp end of sales, marketing, accounts and personnel departments etc.

The stand-alone personal computer

So successful was the introduction of the dedicated WP unit, that manufacturers in the latter 1970s scrambled to develop desk-top computers which could handle a variety of word processing, spreadsheet work, database creation and graphics design.

Of course, the hardware of the desk-top PC was only as good as the software that specialist houses were marketing and making more user-friendly to non-expert users.

The evolution of IT communication systems in the office

1870s – 1970s
The stand-alone typewriter was the office workhorse – from mechanical manual to electric, to electronic and electronic with memory

1970s – 1980s
The dedicated, stand-alone wordprocessing personal computer was introduced (Could only perform WP tasks with 'built-in' software)

1980s – 1990s
'Connectivity' or 'convergence' evolved: local and wide area networks (LANs and WANs) interlink computers, printers, fax, telex, viewdata, copiers, etc.

1990s – on
Open Systems Connection introduced internationally – protocols are developed to enable computers of different manufacture, using different operating systems, to communicate with each other

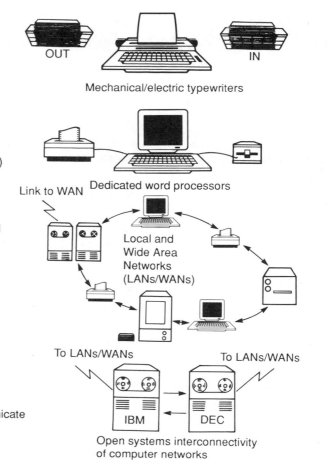

Mechanical/electric typewriters

Dedicated word processors

Link to WAN

Local and Wide Area Networks (LANs/WANs)

To LANs/WANs   To LANs/WANs

IBM   DEC

Open systems interconnectivity of computer networks

During this hectic period, computer manufacturers worked hard to design disk storage systems capable of meeting the demands for bigger memories and faster file-retrieval times.

Also, electronics engineers were successful in their efforts to design low-cost monitors capable of screening colour images and compositions. Indeed the arrival of colour monitors at affordable prices made the PC irresistible in the eyes of status-conscious managers, and certainly assisted the regular WP and DP users to absorb more quickly the components of a complex line graph or database record.

Talking point

'Given the choice, nine out of ten office staff would rather revert to paper and ball-point, than interact with your average desk-top terminal!' How far would you agree with this viewpoint? Why do some people have a fundamental unease about IT at work?

The impact of electronic filing

By the beginning of the 1980s, market-leading organisations had installed stand-alone PCs in every department capable of supporting the kind of information systems approach we considered on pages 77–8 in which data was input, processed, stored and output by electronic means.

Those progressive managers who grasped the nettle and installed PCs on their own, as well as their secretaries' desks, quickly found that they could set up their own personal databases of, say, customers' particulars, product sales statistics or notes about jobs in hand. Having this technology at their fingertips enabled them to call up this information quickly and without assistance.

Such managers also discovered that they could key in straightforward memoranda and messages and obtain instant print-outs, thus preserving total confidentiality or enabling the secretary or PA to work on an urgent report without interruption.

Both managers and secretaries quickly realised the benefits of electronic file storage systems as the following chart illustrates:

Typical files created and stored electronically

Department	Application software package	Type of file
Sales	Database	List of account customer particulars and purchasing limits
	Spreadsheet	Records of salesforce, actual to target sales
		Sales representatives' expenses
	Word processing	Sets of mailmerged sales circular letters – easily updated
R & D/Production/Marketing	Project management	Introduction of a new product – from prototype to launch
Marketing	Graphics and modelling software	Analysis of market penetration/client types/market share, etc
	Desk-top publishing	Advertising copy – display ads, leaflets, brochures, etc
Personnel	Database	All employee records
	Database	Training/staff development notes
		Promotion/pay increase records
Accounts	Spreadsheet	Management accounting reports and ratios
	Integrated accounts package	All ledgers – sales, purchasing, nominal, etc plus payroll
Transport	Database	Fleet servicing records
	Tailor-made	Optimum journeys and routes to distribute goods
All departments		
All staff	Unified database	Specifically designed data files relevant to the organisation's work
Manager/PA – secretary	Local area network operating software	Email messages, notes to self, diary, appointments and meetings schedulers, etc
	Integrated modular management package (allows data to be merged from one application to another)	Letters, reports, tables, calculations, graphs and charts, database records, etc
Created by technicians and secretaries for managers	Desk-top publishing	News sheets, bulletins, invitations, reports, etc
PA/secretary	Word processing	Letters, memos, reports, minutes, abstracts, press releases, price-lists, etc

Note: The above chart indicates the extent to which business/public service application software packages have mushroomed since the original dedicated WP software of the mid 1970s. As the section on convergence which follows indicates, the arrival of computer networks meant that such files could also be shared amongst the different users on the network.

Talking point

What advantages can you identify which the electronic file possesses compared with its paper counterpart? Keep a checklist of your conclusions for future reference.

Computer storage

One letter (or character) of text requires one byte of storage.

1000 bytes = 1 kilobyte (written as 'kb').

1000 kb of data = 1 megabyte (written as 'mb').

1000 mb of data = 1 gigabyte (written as 'gb').

Floppy disk storage capacity is normally measured in kb.

Note:

- An average A4 page of printed typescript contains approximately 2 500 letters and therefore requires about 2.5 kb of computer storage capacity.
- A typical 5.25-inch floppy disk is capable of holding 0.5mb of memory, or some 200 A4 pages of typed text.
- A typical hard (Winchester) disk holds some 30mb of memory, or about 12 000 A4 typed sheets.
- A typical 5.25-inch optical disk can store some 500mb of data, or 250 000 sheets of A4 typed text.

Mainframe computer

Desk-top portable computer

Self assessment questions

Can you now:

a) format a floppy disk,
b) create files on both hard and floppy disks,
c) devise file names and call up files successfully,
d) carry out housekeeping functions on file directories,
e) copy files and transfer them from one disk to another?

Convergence and interactivity arrive!

While improvements in disk technologies allowed more information to be stored more cost-effectively and be retrieved more swiftly, office staff either had to move physically to fetch floppy disks containing the files that they needed to access, or similarly to move to a desk-top PC incorporating a hard disk containing the files that they wanted to work with.

By the same token, it was common for just a single printer to be available in offices, which meant that only one member of staff at a time could have access to the machine to obtain print-outs of files and this caused inconvenience and delay for the other members of staff wishing to use the printer. Once more, resourceful computer engineers tackled the task of bringing the facilities of computers, printers, fax machines, telex, intelligent photocopiers and the like to each and every member of staff with a desk-top terminal to hand.

Local and wide area networks (LANs and WANs)

This challenge was largely solved with the introduction of local area networks, which initially were restricted to a campus or office complex of some 100 metres radius, and extended later by the development of wide area networks which allowed, say, all the users in a multi-storey office block to communicate individually and directly with their contacts and clients internationally.

LANs within office complexes usually consist of:

File servers – 'memory boxes' which hold the operating software, applications packages and files that users create.

Delivery circuits – cables interconnecting each item of equipment on the network in a kind of ring.

Individual terminals/support equipment (eg printers, fax, etc) – Each LAN user possesses a PC and is able to transmit and receive messages from other users, to access files on the file server, and to communicate with remote fax, printing, Prestel, telephone or telex services.

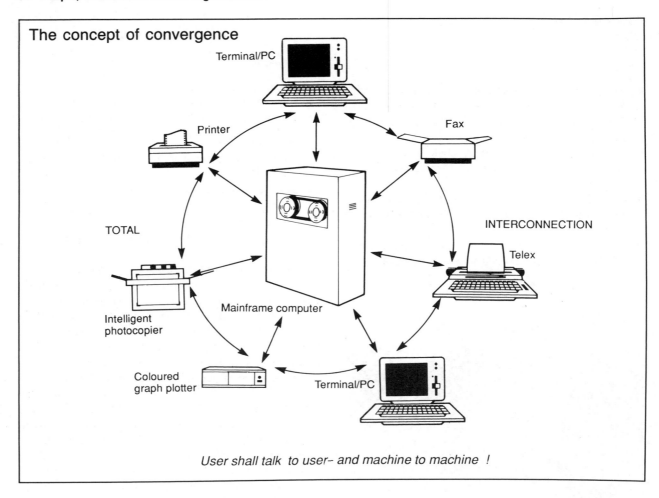

The concept of convergence

Terminal/PC

Printer

Fax

TOTAL

INTERCONNECTION

Telex

Intelligent photocopier

Mainframe computer

Coloured graph plotter

Terminal/PC

User shall talk to user- and machine to machine !

LANs and WANs: agents of a communications revolution in offices

Some 15 years after the arrival of the first stand-alone WP equipment, the development of LAN/WAN networks transformed office administration and working practices.

The technology underpinning such networks allowed messages or files to be created and then to be transferred around the network until being delivered at the electronic address of the intended recipient(s). Each message was carried along by a kind of electronic conveyor belt which was ever ready to pick up and deliver electronic messages. In the same way, the facilities provided by equipment like fax, telex and laser printers could be made accessible to the user at each workstation on the network.

Moreover, the inclusion of a desk-top PC within a LAN/WAN network in no way prevented it from acting alone as an independent workstation, allowing its user to work quite confidentially with any one of the network's installed software applications.

Networked offices are no longer characterised by the 'waltzes and rhumbas' of their forerunners, where staff had constantly to move around each other to gain access to the various machines in dif-ferent locations! And instant access to electronic software and files is at last making a dent in office paper mountains.

Instead of time-consuming paper memos having to be created, photocopied and distributed by hand, the LAN/WAN's electronic mail service enables staff at all levels to create messages and to send them in an instant. They can be sent either to an individual recipient, or to predetermined groups like section heads, working groups such as payroll clerks or district managers.

And even if this were not enough, the network's software provides confirmation of the date and time when a message was despatched and when it was first read by its recipients. Read files and messages can then be erased, stored electronically, or transferred into paper print-outs at will.

Talking point

What are the implications of the extensive developments in IT of the past decade for education and training? How should IT staff development be handled in firms with personnel departments?

How a Local Area Network enables people and their equipment to intercommunicate

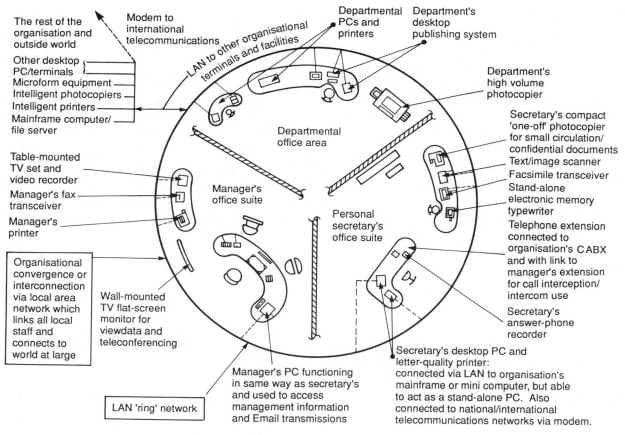

The rest of the organisation and outside world

Modem to international telecommunications

LAN to other organisational terminals and facilities

Departmental PCs and printers

Department's desktop publishing system

Other desktop PC/terminals
Microform equipment
Intelligent photocopiers
Intelligent printers
Mainframe computer/ file server

Departmental office area

Department's high volume photocopier

Table-mounted TV set and video recorder

Manager's fax transceiver

Manager's printer

Manager's office suite

Personal secretary's office suite

Secretary's compact 'one-off' photocopier for small circulation/ confidential documents
Text/image scanner
Facsimile transceiver
Stand-alone electronic memory typewriter
Telephone extension connected to organisation's CABX and with link to manager's extension for call interception/ intercom use

Organisational convergence or interconnection via local area network which links all local staff and connects to world at large

Wall-mounted TV flat-screen monitor for viewdata and teleconferencing

Secretary's answer-phone recorder

LAN 'ring' network

Manager's PC functioning in same way as secretary's and used to access management information and Email transmissions

Secretary's desktop PC and letter-quality printer: connected via LAN to organisation's mainframe or mini computer, but able to act as a stand-alone PC. Also connected to national/international telecommunications networks via modem.

LAN network 'Tapestry' – the home screen

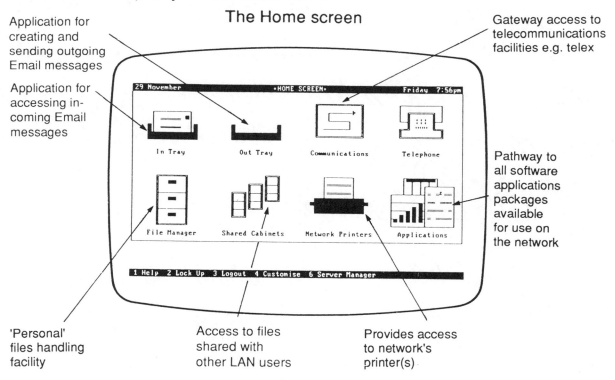

The Home screen

Application for creating and sending outgoing Email messages

Application for accessing incoming Email messages

Gateway access to telecommunications facilities e.g. telex

Pathway to all software applications packages available for use on the network

'Personal' files handling facility

Access to files shared with other LAN users

Provides access to network's printer(s)

The tapestry user accesses the home screen directly after logging on.
The network's facilities all begin here.

LAN installed in a multi-storey head office linked to a remotely located branch office

The manager station

One PC acts as a manager station holding details of the shared resources and authorised network users of the other PCs connected to it. Storing this information centrally permits changes to be made at a single location and accurate presentation of available resources.

Network domains

A system of domain management is necessary if more than about 50–100 stations are involved in order to control the network effectively. Each domain is a portion of the total network representing a single department or a floor of a large building. Each domain has its own manager station.

Internetworking

The use of packet switched data networks based on the international X25 standard provides an ideal basis for internetwork links for companies based on multiple sites.

Major attractions of a LAN

The attractions of a LAN for larger offices – say spread over many floors of a multi-storey building – are as follows:

- ease of intercommunication between users
- speed of message/data transmission and feedback confirmation of receipt,
- very high standards of user security – even during the shared access of software packages,
- availability of secure personal filing 'cabinets' within hard disk storage system,
- organisational savings – only *one*-printer or scanner needed for extended cluster user groups on network,
- instant access to a worldwide network of telecommunications services and to other LANs via modem interfaces – hence links to wide area networks (WANs),
- access to international computer databases via gateways in, for example, Prestel's viewdata service,
- access to up-to-the minute and real-time computerised data and records stored on the organisation's central mainframe computer,
- capability of each PC terminal to act as a stand-alone desktop computer using floppies or built-in hard disk drive,
- user-friendliness: icon menus and window over-lays enable the user to consult several application packages at a time on the VDU and to transfer work from one package/file to another.

As a result of increased international cooperation, standards for WAN designs have been agreed by major authorities to ensure problem-free transmission across the world.

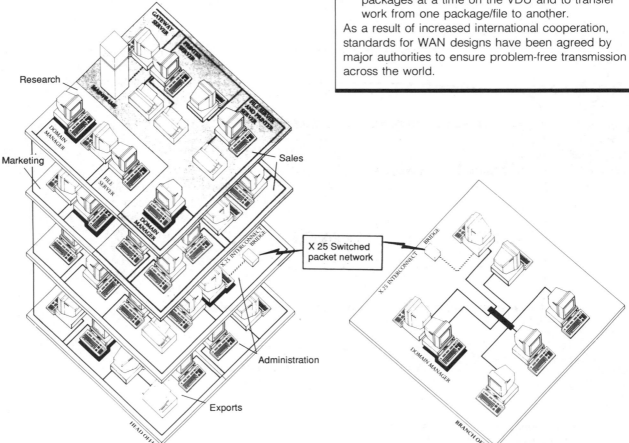

Short glossary of computer terms

bits and bytes terms for units of information storage; a bit is either a 0 or 1 and is the smallest unit a computer handles, representing the presence or absence of an electrical impulse: a byte is the number of 'bits' – typically 7 to 8 – joined together to signify a letter, number or symbol. Note also kilo-, mega- and giga-byte measurements (1 thousand, 1 million and 1 billion bytes respectively).

bug the term given to a fault or overlooked error in operating or application software which causes the program to fail or to block the user's commands. The term 'virus' is also now used to describe rogue programs which irresponsible computer hackers implant into software in the public domain which (if imported) can erase entire sets of files and destroy large parts of an organisation's data if left undetected.

central processing unit the 'brains' of the computer, holding all its operating systems, programs and stored files, usually abbreviated to CPU.

configuration the label for the items of equipment – CPU, VDU, printer, disk drive, etc which make up a computing facility.

floppy disks these are flexible magnetic recording disks held in protective envelopes in 8-inch and 5.25-inch diameters; they record data on a series of circular tracks in specific sectors on both sides of the disk – hence their label 'dual density, double-sided'. Now more powerful 3.5-inch counterparts housed in stronger plastic containers are replacing the original floppies.

hard disk drive (Winchester disk drive) a protected 'drum' located within the computer on which data is stored semi-permanently, including loaded application software packages.

mainframe largest capacity computers used to run total organisational requirements, including databases and information processing and international communications.

microcomputer/PC smallest in the range, originally designed for individual use but now often linked to LAN/WAN networks.

monitor the TV-like screen upon which data is displayed, either in monochrome or colour. *Note:* the term pixel is used to describe the density of dots per square centimetre on a colour screen – the more pixels, the higher the quality of the colour picture. This is especially important in graphics and DTP work.

optical disks these are metal-based and protectively coated. Data is written to and read from the disk by a laser beam: characterised by very high storage capacities – typically 500 megabytes of memory, or some 250 000 typed pages of A4! For the moment, optical disks have a capacity to be written on only once, but read many times – hence the term 'worm'.

peripheral blanket term to describe any piece of IT equipment interconnected with a central computer or network.

port a socket in a computer for connecting a printer, LAN cable, fax or telex facility.

programming language computers are designed to interpret instructions written in a variety of languages which have been created to meet specific needs like scientific calculations, business applications, or high-volume work: current languages in use include: BASIC, FORTRAN, PASCAL, COBOL'C', etc.

random access memory (RAM) a series of memory locations whose contents can be modified.

read only memory (ROM) a series of memory locations whose contents the user cannot erase or modify. Typically used for storing the instructions/programs which comprise the computer's built-in operating system.

supermini/minicomputer middle of the range computer, but the most powerful are able to support 20+ networked terminals.

terminal label for a VDU/keyboard set attached to a remote computer. Note: 'dumb terminal' indicates that it cannot work independently of this central computer.

Specialist IT jargon terms

Use the above short glossary as a start for your own collection; IT jargon simply *has to be absorbed* if you are to succeed in your studies!

'You'll soon fit in, Blenkinsop. As you can see, DP is pretty straightforward here'

Interconnectivity – fax, telex and viewdata systems

So far, we have considered the central role of the networked computer in information processing. It is now important that we examine the range of telecommunications and electronic office equipment which is now linked to computers by LAN/WAN systems, and which extends them.

A natural grouping occurs in those appliances which enable messages to be sent out of offices to local, national and international locations – fax, telex, two-way viewdata and video/audio conferencing systems.

Merlinfax (© British Telecommunications plc)

Facsimile transmission – Fax

While universally known as fax (or telefax in the EEC), the full name for this messaging medium explains its function, since a facsimile is an exact and faithful reproduction of text, photographs or graphic images.

Essentially, a facsimile transceiver works as follows. It accepts printed paper documents and passes them over an electronic scanner which encodes every least printed item – text, numbers, logos, photographs, etc – into electronic signals. Either immediately, or after a timed interval (to secure cheaper transmission rates) the transceiver will transmit the set of signals representing the letter, leaflet or diagram to the fax address entered as part of the transmission process. The address, of course, is that of another fax machine located almost anywhere in the world served by telephone lines, cables or radio/satellite networks.

The receiving fax machine decodes the set of signals back into precisely the same pattern of text or images of the original and prints it out onto a specially treated paper which is loaded in a roll in-to the machine and guillotined into an appropriate size.

Delayed transmission

In order to save costs or avoid busy peak transmission times, most fax systems allow the user to 'stack' a number of messages for onward transmission until a predetermined transmission time – say overnight UK time. At the appropriate moment a timer is activated to set the transmission sequences into operation. This function is usually set up at the end of the office day when no further messages are to be sent by normal means.

Status reports

A very useful feature of fax transmission is the intermittent (say after 50 transmissions) issuing of a status report which lists the number of calls made, their date, time and transmission duration, their destination and the number of pages transmitted. This provides a means of monitoring the fax bills when they arrive.

While much younger than telex, fax seems destined to oust its less flexible predecessor. Fax is particularly user-friendly and simple to operate. Fax addresses are, in effect, telephone numbers which employ STD prefixes and individual machine numbers. For example, dialling up 01-240-5771 would connect you with Pitman Publishing directly!

Today's fax machines are highly sophisticated. They can store as many as 100 abbreviated addresses send multiple copies out to, say, account customers; ensure confidentiality by requiring a keyed in password at the receiving end for a designated recipient to access an incoming fax; send batches of fax overnight and during low-cost periods; receive incoming faxes automatically and stack them for collection; monitor all transmitted faxes and provide regular status reports and costs to date, etc. While the quality of print-out hitherto has been only adequate, the latest fax equipment can be connected to laser and ink-jet printers.

As a trainee manager, you should take the trouble early in your studies to become thoroughly conversant with fax technology and operating systems. Undoubtedly fax will figure in your working life from day one. Fax equipment is becoming cheaper and one telephone company already guarantees a connection to anywhere in the world within two minutes! Indeed, so popular has fax become that mobile lap-top versions are proving highly successful, and indispensable to globe-trotting executives.

Talking point

Is IT taking us down the 'scenic route' to Big Brotherdom?

Three routes for fax transmissions *(Reproduced by kind permission of Muirfax Systems Ltd)*

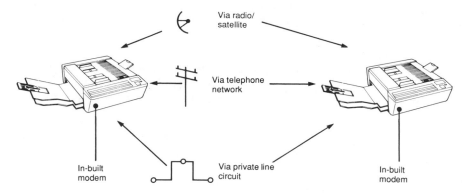

Via radio/satellite

Via telephone network

Via private line circuit

In-built modem

In-built modem

Telex

The telex system preceded facsimile transmission and it is not unusual, therefore, that it should embody features which are similar in many ways to those of fax. For example, message receivers are contacted over the telephone wire and a 'ready to receive' confirmation known as an 'answerback code' is confirmed by the receiving teleprinter – both fax and telex machines employ a kind of 'handshake' system to tell one another that they are ready to communicate. Also, telex employs many fax-type facilities such as retrying busy numbers, logging and reporting on calls and sending telexes to multiple recipients.

As by now you will have come to expect, the advent of IT gave a large boost to telex communications systems and current telex equipment resembles a desktop PC, rather than the outsize, heavy typewriter appearance of earlier teleprinters. Indeed, the user may either opt for a dedicated telex terminal or may incorporate a telex facility into a networked computer terminal. For the present, a major advantage of the telex system lies in the large number of telex terminal/system owners throughout the world. Nevertheless, the advent of fax has brought about fierce competition and telex is unlikely to continue for much longer in its present form.

Telex operations

By employing electronic text preparation and editing techniques, telex messages may be prepared, edited and checked prior to transmission by means of VDU or LCD display and microprocessor memory systems. Using features very much like those of fax transceivers, such messages may be kept on electronic file until a later transmission time and then despatched automatically. Having prepared the text of the telex, the user makes contact with the recipient by typing the telex number, obtaining a confirmatory answerback code response and providing sender identification (ie the user's own answerback code). The telex may then be despatched. Once the message has been delivered, the telex system immediately resumes a message acceptance mode, ready to receive incoming telexes, and will provide a series of print-out message status reports.

Specimen telex message

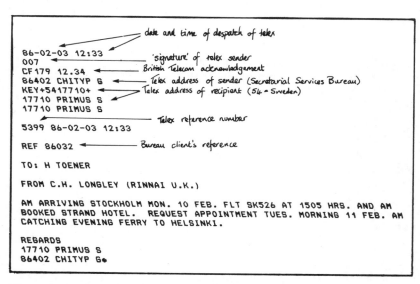

```
                              date and time of despatch of telex
86-02-03 12:33
007                  'signature' of telex sender
CF179 12.34   ←      British Telecom acknowledgement
86402 CHITYP G  ←    Telex address of sender (Secretarial Services Bureau)
KEY+5417710+  ←      Telex address of recipient (54 = Sweden)
17710 PRIMUS S
17710 PRIMUS S
                     Telex reference number
5399 86-02-03 12:33

REF 86032  ←         Bureau client's reference

TO: H TOENER

FROM C.H. LONGLEY (RINNAI U.K.)

AM ARRIVING STOCKHOLM MON. 10 FEB. FLT SK526 AT 1505 HRS. AND AM
BOOKED STRAND HOTEL.  REQUEST APPOINTMENT TUES. MORNING 11 FEB. AM
CATCHING EVENING FERRY TO HELSINKI.

REGARDS
17710 PRIMUS S
86402 CHITYP G+
```

This message was despatched by a Secretarial Services Bureau on behalf of a client.
Reproduced by kind permission of Select Office Services, Chichester and Mr C H Longley (Rinnai UK)

Viewdata and videotex

You will be forgiven for experiencing some confusion about the labels which the experts have given to various telecommunications systems. We have to learn to distinguish between telex, teletex and teletext and also have viewdata and videotex to unravel!

Actually, there is no problem here for they are both terms which are used to describe the same system. British Telecom employ viewdata to describe its Prestel service, while videotex is the internationally agreed term to label the interactive services based on a central computer, telephone transmission lines, modem, and a monitor and keyboard capable of accepting colour graphics and text.

How does videotex work?

The UK viewdata system widely in use is BT's Prestel service. At its heart are ten regionally located computers which contain a large database of information on all sorts of topics. Some of this information is provided by government and public bodies – such as data on university and polytechnic courses – and some is provided by private companies such as hotel brochures or car-hire offers.

Each Prestel user needs a monitor adapted to accept Prestel transmissions, a computer and keyboard to relay instructions and a modem with call-up facilities to link the computer terminal to the appropriate Prestel computer. Indeed, any desk-top PC may be adapted to accept Prestel.

Prestel is accessed by keying in a customer identity number and password. Once connected, costs are incurred by the minute for the duration of on-line connection.

Prestel information is viewed and interrogated as a series of screen colour pages of information made more interesting by the inclusion of graphic diagrams and design. Private and public organisations (Information Providers) pay Prestel a fee for having a page of data included in the Prestel database. Each page is given a unique number which is used to locate and display it on the user's screen. The Information Provider may update, modify or withdraw a given page by arrangement with Prestel.

At the present time there are some 360 000 pages of information available for scrutiny and the database is divided into the following sectors:

Agriculture ● Banking ● Education ● Finance-Citiservice ● Insurance ● Microcomputing ● (including a hobbyists network) ● Teleshopping ● Travel.

Prestel advertisers of interest to the trainee manager include:

air travel ● advertising rates (Press) ● bank services ● British Telecom services ● business equipment ● car hire ● cleaning services ● computer services ● employment agencies ● ferry services ● financial advice ● hotel booking ● insurance ● entertainment ● office services ● shopping services ● teleshopping ● tourist information ● What's On, etc.

Technically, the Prestel database is termed a branching or hierarchic database. The user starts at an initial menu or index listing the major sectors and then proceeds along the chosen one, branching off at will. For example, Business Information can take the user on to advertising or money markets or statistics and so on. Alternatively, a simple command will transport the user into an entirely different sector. Prestel pages are generally accessed by keying in a desired number once this is known, and the Prestel Directory lists keywords and numbers in blue and page numbers in black.

Perhaps the most important feature of Prestel for managers and secretaries is its interactivity. The user may locate, for example, a page which lists hotels in Birmingham and there and then effect an instant booking. Or a check may be made what shows are on in London and tickets for a musical purchased for some visiting foreign clients. Prestel also offers such time-saving interactive facilities in banking, travel arrangements, hotel reservations, office services bureaux and so on.

A further useful feature of Prestel lies in its ability to connect the user – at a fee – to private computerised databases of information via 'gateways' – a simple term used to describe the sophisticated electronic network which links two remote computers to the user. Thus a manager in Edinburgh can browse through the menus of a United States university's database on, say, American taxation laws or registered patents on inventions!

BT also offer private versions of Prestel to larger organisations entirely for their own use. The travel industry, for example, uses a videotex system connecting tour operators with travel agents so as to reserve flight seats and hotels at the time of enquiry

(subject to confirmation and deposit). City financiers also use viewdata systems to relay up-to-the-minute share prices to dealers.

Additional Prestel features include: an electronic mail system called Mailbox, which has recently been extended to link in with BT's Telecom Gold service; Closed User Groups services which link specific users privately; a means of accessing BT's telex service, and the facility of communicating with other databases through BT's gateway services.

Mailbox on Prestel does not directly link with Telecom Gold. However, various combined subscriptions offer the user a gateway link to Telecom Gold.

What does Prestel cost to use?

Given the speed, range of data, interactivity features and user-friendliness of Prestel, its costs are very reasonable to the public user. The connection charges to a Prestel computer are priced at *local call rates* and using Prestel at cheap rate times improves value for money, as does the taking of a page of data as a print-out instead of reading it while on line to Prestel. All Prestel users also pay a quarterly standing charge and a time charge which acts as a further tariff on top of the telephone charge. This charge is not levied after 6.00 pm Mondays to Fridays, nor from 1.00 pm on Saturdays until 8.00 am Mondays. Some frames or pages of information display a number which indicates an extra charge payable levied by the information provider.

Schools and colleges have a special flat annual rate which includes an amount for time charges.

Viewdata videotex and the future

Prestel originally got off to a slow start and some telecommunications experts consider that the service should have been concentrated on the business user rather than the man in the street. That the technology offers a marvellous opportunity to bring the information in reference books, research documents, encycolopaedias, timetables, catalogues, etc, swiftly and easily to the office executive and secretary is beyond doubt. That its two-way communications system offers tremendous savings in time and effort for making bookings and confirming travel arrangements and so on is also not in dispute. It remains to be seen how BT will develop Prestel so as to make its database less dependent upon the commercial interests of some information providers and more comprehensive as a public information service.

One of the trends is to offer users a combination of Prestel databases with links to Telecom Gold electronic mail and Gold databases, such as Profile which carries full text of quality newspapers.

IT and telephone communications

No office information system has been transformed so quickly and so extensively as the telephone communications network during the past decade. Switchboards, handsets, distribution cables and satellites have all been radically redesigned and improved as a result of microchip and fibre-optic technology sweeping through the world of telecommunications.

Today, fibre-optic telephone-line technology has made possible the introduction of the Integrated Services Digital Network (ISDN) which carries not only thousands of telephone conversations simultaneously along a single, slim cable, but also digitised computer data at high speeds, Prestel and privately leased viewdata transmissions, fax, telex and videoconferencing hook-ups. Thanks to the development of modems and multiplexers, business people at home and abroad can link into such telephone networks and access their terminals to view their mail or to send home Email messages and so on.

ISDN has also made possible the development of computerised 'System X' public telephone exchanges in the UK (Public Switched Telephone Exchanges or PSTN) which are providing enhanced services under BT's 'Star' scheme such as:

- call warning signals,
- abbreviated call coding of up to 27 numbers,
- repeat last call,
- charging advice,
- call diversion,
- 3-way calling,
- and call barring.

Also, the growing use of 'smart' plastic cards with resident microprocessor memories (up to the equivalent of some 400 A4 pages!) will be able to provide telephone users with such handy communication props as:

- accessing ex-directory numbers pre-programmed on to the card,
- automatic dialling of selected abbreviated numbers,
- access to organisational voice-mail message banks,
- multiway telephone hook-ups,
- credit payment for long distance/international phone calls.

Mobile phones

On the mobile phone front, UK telephone companies have launched the truly portable pocket phone (see BT's Phonepoint and Mercury's Call-point systems) which link into nationwide telepoint relay networks housed in pubs, shops, restaurants or even bus stops. Rental costs are coming down for such phones and the era of fully mobile and portable telephones has arrived.

Furthermore, two-way video phones are being test-marketed as an added communications device housed in the ubiquitous desk-top terminal and the TV-wristwatch-phone is now technically quite feasible and likely to be introduced by the end of the 1990s!

Mobile phone (Courtesy of British Telecom)

IT and organisational telephone systems

Within organisational complexes and multi-storey offices the pace of change has also been impressive. Powerful switchboards and networks are now installed which are capable of coordinating 200–500 extensions and of controlling the flow of hundreds of local/international calls simultaneously. Small to medium-sized organisations can nowadays install CABX networks whose electronics occupy no more space than a wall-hung fire-extinguisher and whose operating console is no larger than a ring binder! Yet such equipment can handle with ease the needs of 30–100 distributed extensions.

Talking point

In what ways do you think offices will evolve further in terms of IT installations and systems over the next ten years?

Computerised key systems

For partnerships, GPs' surgeries and small businesses the tried and tested key system

telephone network has been updated and refined. Such a system typically comes in a 6–12 handset network in which any one extension can accept and re-route incoming calls, and where a master phone coordinates the system, monitoring active calls visually and fulfilling the switchboard role. Modestly priced, key systems now possess many of the sophisticated features of their more powerful CABX counterparts.

Computerised Automatic Branch Exchanges (CABX)

The abbreviation CABX acts as a useful shorthand to describe the current branch exchanges which have superseded PBX/PABX (Private Branch Exchange/Private Automatic Branch Exchange) systems installed in organisations, emphasising as it does the radical impact of computerisation.

At the heart of CABX networks is their *programmability*. Each and every connected handset may be variously programmed to provide services under a centralised control, such as a direct outside line, access to local call-making only or restriction to internal interconnection. Also, extensions can be identified within existing departmental or central unit cost-centre groups so that telephone use can be monitored and arising costs charged back to each individual cost-centre.

As far as the individual user is concerned, the microchip in the phone system has provided an impressive array of support features – provided he or she knows how to use them! For example:

- Incoming calls can be readily diverted to another handset.
- Incoming calls can be held while a confidential enquiry is made on behalf of the caller with an associate on the network.
- Pre-scheduled telephone meetings are easy to set up.
- A colleague's extension can be programmed to connect to another user's the moment the phone is put down (call back when busy) or he returns to the office and first uses the phone – without the user having to cradle his phone in his cricked neck all the while!
- CABX systems can be simply programmed to ensure that incoming calls are routed around the network so as to follow an executive's movements.
- other programs exist to seek out alternative staff who work in a team if a desired contact is out (group hunt).

Indeed, the features of today's CABX systems are highly imaginative and have done much to help office personnel organise their time much more cost-effectively. The following chart illustrates some of a contemporary CABX network's major features:

Major typical features of a large CABX system

This table is based upon the Ferranti GTE OMNI System and is kindly made available by Ferranti GTE Ltd

Some of OMNI's system features

Administration message recording – to provide usage reports
Dictation access – providing a link to dictation services
Group hunting – seeking out any one of a working team's extensions available to take an in-coming call by trying each in turn
Intercom groups – linking users via intercom speakers
Music on hold – playing a soothing tune over the phone while a caller is waiting to be connected
Paging and code calling access – ability to activate pagers used by roving staff
Standby power – facility to keep system going in event of power failure
Call barring – ability to restrict the range of connections availability on any extension

Some attendant features

Automatic recall re-dial – system keeps trying to connect to a busy number
Break in – facility to break into an active conversation in case of urgency
Call waiting – provision to alert extension user of another call awaiting attention
Camp on busy – ability to wait, having dialled a number until it becomes available and then to ring dialler's extension having effected the connection
Conference – linking of several extension users so all can converse with each other over the phone – system can also include outside callers

Some extension features

Abbreviated dialling – often used numbers are given a short 1/2 digit code to save time
Boss – secretary – direct interconnection
Call forwarding follow me – instruction for incoming calls to be routed from a customary extension to others near to a roving staff member
Call hold – facility to keep line open to caller while specific staff member located
Direct inward dialling – facility to enable incoming calls to be routed directly to selected extension by adding its number to normal organisation's number
Direct outward dialling – facility to access PSTN directly
Do not disturb – cuts phone off while meeting etc. taking place; avoids irritating interruptions
Extension to extension calling – for direct in-house phone calls

Reception area of TSB (Courtesy of Plessey)

Self assessment questions

1 Can you operate a PC or terminal competently now?

2 Are you now able to use the extensive options of a laser/ink-jet printer competently in designing document layout and typography?

3 Have you yet tried your hand at the following applications software packages?

    a) word processing
    b) spreadsheet
    c) database
    d) integrated information management

4 Have you yet arranged to see each of the following in action?

    a) fax
    b) telex
    c) Prestel
    d) microform/computer system

5 Have you managed to send and receive electronic messages – Email – on a local area network and seen the scope of such a system at first hand?

6 Have you yet seen in action or used a CABX telephone system?

7 Have you started your own glossary of IT terms and phrases yet?

If the answer to any of the above is, 'Well, not yet . . .' then now is the time to consolidate and deepen what you have learned in Unit 5, since every aspect in Questions 1–7 will almost certainly affect your job and career!

GPT iSDX System Architecture

Diagram of an 'all-in' ISDN Telecommunications system

This diagram of Plessey's GPT ISDX System Architecture provides a 'see-at-a-glance' explanation of the Integrated Services Digital Network which will dominate office communications in the 1990s.

ISDN can distribute not only telephone conversations but also fax, telex, viewdata, electronic mail and digitised inter-computer packet switching. As the Plessey diagram shows, *all* an organisation's messaging in-house, local, national and international, can now be distributed at high speed and high volume thanks to ISDN technology.

Examples of British Telecom telephone services to business

Audio conferencing
Providing regional/national/international telephone hook-ups for meetings etc.

Call cost indication
Informing user of the cost of a telephone call just completed.

Citicall
Information service on stocks and shares.

Yellow Pages
1.4 million listed business services in district directories; available in paper or electronic database.

Credit authorisation
Acceptance of credit payment for phone calls, etc.

Pay card sales
Sale of units of phone call time via a plastic card: many public phone boxes accept this form of payment and erase time used from the inserted card (cards sold in units of 10, 40 and 200).

Freefone service
Businesses accept sales enquiries by phone and pay for the incoming calls – up to a preset time limit.

Mobile radiophone and car/train phone service
Mobile, cordless telephones connected by radio to BT telephone network; equipment is sold by Cellnet and Vodaphone for national use via BT's Cellnet system to route messages over more than short local distances.

Ship's telephone service
Long-established passenger phone service routed via radio signals and/or satellite.

Star services
Eight services provided by System X exchanges: call waiting warning signal; abbreviated call coding, up to 27 numbers' repeat last call; charge advice; call diversion; 3-way calling; call barring.

Telephone credit cards (national and international)
Internationally placed calls are accepted and placed by the operator upon the citing of your credit number; especially useful for sales representatives.

Radio paging

Individuals are 'bleeped' anywhere in UK by radio signal and asked to get into telephone contact
Note: some pagers only emit certain tones, others will communicate short messages on an LCD strip.

Data sources: British Telecom and *The Telecom User's Handbook*: and Telecommunications Press.

Office reprographics

Note: desk-top publishing is treated in detail in Unit 11.

Just as IT has brought about enormous advances in local and worldwide communications, so it has also transformed the ways in which data can be represented in print. The generic term 'office reprographics', is widely used to cover aspects such as printing, photocopying, collating and binding, as well as film-slide, OHP, microform, desk-top publishing and video reproduction techniques.

So important has the area of information presentation become, that no manager in training can afford to remain unaware of what IT-based office reprographics can do to provide strong visual appeal and high acceptance features. This section will therefore emphasise how principal office reprographic equipment works and how it will help your created data to communicate effectively.

Electronic printers

The dot matrix printer

The universal impact of desk-top computing would have counted for little over the past 15 years, were it not for the parallel development of extremely reliable electronic printers – the hard-copy workhorses of the IT revolution.

Carrying the standard was the original dot matrix printer which printed letters on the page by means of eight needles which 'dotted' ink through a ribbon in the form of numbers or characters upon instructions from the user's PC:

```
THE DOT MATRIX PRINTER CREATES
CHARACTERS FROM DOTS
```

Eight-pin dot-matrix printers have now been superseded by 24-pin (or 'wire') counterparts, since the fundamental shortcoming of the 8-pin was that it could not produce letter quality print. A typical 24-dot printer operates at some 400 characters per second (cps) in draft mode and some 50–60 cps in letter quality mode. The introduction of insertable colour ribbon cartridges permits documents to carry multiple colours, though the process is rather laborious. The continuing attraction of the dot-matrix lies in its low cost and reliability, especially for draft quality in-house working documents.

Daisywheel printers

The term 'daisywheel' derives from the nature of the printing technology employed, in which each letter or character to be used is located at the end of a series of radiating spokes set in a kind of miniature cartwheel. Emulating the action of a typewriter, each character print-head is 'hammered' at high speed on to the loaded paper as the daisywheel moves back and forth. The daisywheel printer was popular between 1975 and 1985 because of its print quality, but changing founts (typefaces) was cumbersome, and the daisywheel could not print graphs or charts etc. This technology has now been superseded by ink-jet and laser printing.

Ink-jet and laser printers

The widespread demand for better quality and more versatile printing in the 1980s quickly led to more sophisticated printers being developed, namely the ink-jet and laser printer.

Briefly, an ink-jet printer literally sprays the print of each character at high speed on to those parts of the page which have been electrostatically treated to carry the text. A special fast-drying ink is used to avoid smudging, which was a disadvantage of some early models.

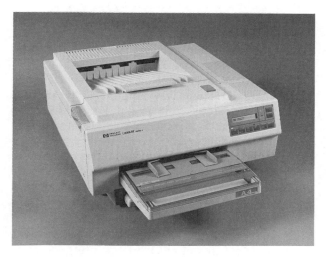

Laserjet printer (Courtesy of Hewlett Packard)

Ink-jet printers can produce text at the rate of some 100 cps at near letter quality (NLQ) and current models provide high standard letter-quality print. Like the dot-matrix printer the ink-jet can accept both fanfold and cut-sheet paper and embodies both tractor- and sheet-fed features. Moreover, it possesses a variety of important text presentation features such as:

* emboldening
* underscoring
* double-spacing
* proportional spacing

- double height and width characters
- italics
- variable fount options

Typical speeds are: 200cps draft quality and 75 cps NLQ.

Undoubtedly the most sophisticated of electronic printers is the laser. Simply, laser printing technology uses a beam of light to create lines of text (or graphics or photographic images) on a drum which passes over the sheet of paper which will receive them. The paper, having been specially treated, accepts toner on to those parts which will carry the printed material. The 'unique selling benefit' of the laser printer lies in its extremely high resolution of some 90 000 dots per square inch! Such an inking density supplies very high letter quality printing.Furthermore, the laser is thus able to provide the resolution and clarity needed for graphics printing in desk-top publishing, especially where images are enlarged or reduced to fit a required format on a printed page, and where half-tones are essential for reproducing photographs.

If this were not enough, laser printers are able to store 70 plus different founts or typefaces in their memories and to print them out in a wide range of printer's point sizes (sizes of print ranging from minuscule to newspaper banner headlines). Many laser printers can also accept specialised founts installed on insertable electronic cards, and are thus extremely versatile. And they possess high printing speeds. Some professional laser printers can run at 200 A4 pages per minute. Typical office lasers print out at 10–12 A4 pages per minute.

As a result of laser printing technology (allied to sophisticated DTP software), organisations are now able to produce their own very attractive documents, of a high standard and visual appeal in house. As a result, in larger organisations information printed by ink-duplicators, bandas or outmoded dot-matrix printers has a very low acceptance and credibility factor. IT printing technology has transformed document presentation expectations among senior managers and directors in particular. This is why you must now set about mastering the scope and features of electronic printing, so as to be in a position to ensure that your documents maximise their appeal and impact!

Photocopiers

Office administrators tend to take the whole process of photocopying for granted, as something that is conveniently carried out by clerical assistants instantly upon demand! As long as sufficient copies of an acceptable quality arrive in time they are content. Such administrators, however, may well be responsible for unnecessarily high copying costs. They may also fail to get the best out of what is, today, an extremely versatile and sophisticated office equipment technology.

The Minolta EP 870 photocopier

At present there are some 200 photocopying machines on the market, ranging from single-sheet feed desk-top machines for single copies and very small runs, to copying giants known as systems copiers, housed in printing departments which can churn out thousands of photocopies each day. The following section highlights the main types of photocopier you are likely to encounter at work, and lists their principal features.

All managers and administrators are inevitably judged by the quality of the written communication they distribute. It therefore makes sense to acquire a thorough understanding of what current photocopying technology can do (as outlined below) to convey your messages promptly, clearly and attractively.

Low volume desk-top copiers

The low volume desk-top copier works slowly, but is reliable and cheap to buy. It is designed to handle occasional copying needs such as making a copy of an incoming letter three to four times to circulate to section heads, or to copy internal memos, notices or bulletins a few at a time.

Such copiers operate at approximately 8–15 copies per minute (cpm) and will only copy on one side of the paper at a time – to copy the reverse of a sheet requires reinsertion. The low volume desk-top copier generally incorporates these features:

- hand-feeding of single sheets (a laborious process)
- light-dark adjustment to compensate for good/ poor originals
- toner level indicator – to warn when toner is becoming used up
- paper jam indicator
- simple trays to hold paper passing through the copier before and after the process.

The mid-range or departmental copier

Such copiers are becoming increasingly popular since they occupy little space – not much more than a desk-top yet provide a very much larger range of features, while the cost of the modest single sheet copier is a few hundred pounds, the middle range copier (sometimes referred to a departmental copier) will cost anything from £1500–£10 000. As with all office equipment, the buyer tends to get what he pays for. The following checklist illustrates some typical features of the mid range copier:

- Able to copy from A6 postcard and A5 to A3 paper sizes.
- Automatic enlargement and reduction.
- Automatic document feed – for copying sets of different originals.
- Bypass feed to do a quick single-sheet copy in the middle of a long job.
- Automatic exposure control – to adapt to originals of varying quality.
- At least a 10-copy stacking bin which automatically collates copies into sets of reports, minutes, etc.
- User control system – either a security lock or insertable type of credit card which meters copies made.
- At least two automatic paper feed trays (A4 and A3) Note: some models automatically activate the appropriate paper 'cassette' tray according to the size of original.
- Capacity to hold at least 1 ream (500 sheets of copy paper) – many will hold 200 sheets or more.
- Automatic enlargement and reduction features – both by predetermined ratios (according to paper sizes A5, A4, A3, etc, or by percentage – from, say 50% to 150% of original by single percentage steps – sometimes referred to as 'zoom magnification'.
- Emergency override switch to halt the photo-copying process in the event of a mistake or machine fault.

Such is the pressure of competition to sell photocopiers – a market leader sold over half a million worldwide last year – that even the above range of features in the middle tier of copiers is being increased by such sophisticated facilities like:

- **Editing board and stylus** – rather like a computer's monitor and light-pen, this additional equipment enables the user to edit existing originals on a screen electronically and to blank out unwanted portions (image overlay), to join together part of different originals without tell-tale lines showing and to adjust margins for right or left hand sheets in a bound document.
- **Automatic double-sided copying** (sometimes called duplexing) – a feature which prints simultaneously on both sides of the paper from two originals placed side-by-side (tandem copying).
- **Colour printing** – the incorporation of red, blue, sepia, etc, colours one to a single sheet (not to be confused with full-colour copiers which can reproduce colour photographs) at the touch of a button.
- **Copying of three-dimensional objects**, such as jewellery for insurance purposes and bound books without showing dark areas where light has been let in.
- **Automatic electrical power saving mode** operated when the machine is not in active use (to save electricity and costs).

Given the present pace of copier design development, such features and facilities are being extended and improved virtually every month as a new or upgraded model is introduced. Therefore the effective trainee manager will take steps to become fully proficient on the equipment his or her organisation employs and keep an eye on incoming sales leaflets and office equipment magazines to stay up to date and *au fait*. Local exhibitions of office equipment, which are sometimes mounted in hotels, are very useful in this respect.

The systems photocopier

The systems photocopier or print-room model will copy at speeds of 40–200 cpm and handle an output of millions of sheets per year. Such copiers will carry out all the above applications and will also:

- accept the continuous fan-fold paper for computer data copying,
- adjust to various specialist modes for, say, converting colour photo originals to black and white with good clarity,
- collate, staple/bind extensively paged documents and insert coloured chapter pages and front/back covers,
- conduct complex enlargement, reduction and automatic document reversal operations,
- handle a wide range of paper sizes – A5 to poster size from automatic feeder trays and effect runs up to 9999 copies long without stopping.

Colour copiers

Recently a wide range of full-colour photocopiers have been marketed which bring exciting design and presentation within the reach of the office manager in medium-size to large organisations.

Such machines can reproduce colour photographs and paper copies of original photographs with remarkable faithfulness, and one market leader's model can provide up to 64 tones of each major colour! Such machines operate on the laser principle and are revolutionising the quality of in-house document and quick-response sales brochure standards. Such copiers work at about 5 cpm.

Photocopying costs

The factors which go to make up photocopying costs are very similar to those for electronic printers. Most office administration managers circulate offices with regularly updated costs per sheet according to machine used, paper size, type of copying and volume etc.

Photocopying paper varies widely in cost and care should be taken to select copying paper which can accept print on both sides, will not cause jams, for example, because it is too light in weight, and which is problem-free from insert to collation state for ream after ream.

In terms of recurring photocopying costs, it is worth remembering that, while the photocopier with more automatic facilities may cost more to buy or lease, it will undoubtedly save money each month in saved personnel time – compare the time taken to hand-feed single sheets with a fully automated feeding and collating operation which may be left unattended.

Photocopiers and the future

The next phase in photocopier development is already under way with one leading Japanese manufacturer marketing a copier which is also a fax and telex transceiver and scanner! Such multifunctioning equipment is only made possible by the extensive use of reliable microprocessors and clean design.

In addition, copier manufacturers will undoubtedly want to develop further the editor board and stylus operation which resembles the kind of page creating and modifying ability fast becoming popular with users of desk-top publishing equipment (see Unit 11).

We can certainly expect to see a rapid introduction of 'intelligent photocopiers' in offices with LAN networks so that text may be originated at an individual's desk and networked to the office copier for automatic duplication according to copy commands which the user keys in at the end of the text and which instruct the copier accordingly, much like existing computer print commands. Equinox, for instance, is a new electronic system for combining the function of photocopier, word processor, laser printer, fax, modem and document scanner, with a desk-top publishing system, and is also IBM compatible.

Summary of main points

1   Information Technology is the generic term used to describe the processing of information using microprocessor-based electronic equipment; IT applications generally conform to the systems approach to managing information.

2   The introduction of the dedicated, stand-alone word processing unit in the early 1970s transformed techniques of text processing and led to electronic filing and information storage systems being introduced into offices.

3   The development of the desk-top personal computer using word processing, spreadsheet, database, desk-top information management and allied applications software heralded a new era in office communication practices. Desk-top PCs radically affected the work roles of managers, secretaries and clerical support staff alike.

4   The arrival of local and wide area networks into offices in the mid-1980s enabled dispersed office personnel to communicate with each other and with clients by electronic mail both locally and internationally. The connection of large numbers of PC terminals to powerful mainframe and mini computers allowed organisations to develop single unified information databases which supported constantly updated data available to staff in remote locations. Wide area networks made possible computer-based, two-way communication across continents within seconds.

5   The addition of fax, telex and viewdata communications systems to LAN/WAN systems further improved desk-top access to colleagues and clients across the world in a fast, flexible and secure environment.

6   Computerised Automatic Branch Exchange (CABX) telephone systems have introduced many time-saving and helpful features like 'call back when busy', telephone conferencing, group hunt etc.

7   The impact of IT upon office reprographics – particularly the development of laser printers and desk-top publishing led to far higher expectations of document presentation standards by senior managers with knock-on effects upon middle-management and support staff.

8   Photocopier technology in the 1980s advanced swiftly, with the introduction of versatile, high-speed departmental and systems copiers and the advent of faithful colour and three-dimensional copying.

Activities and assignments _____

Quick review quiz

1 List five different ways in which information is inputted into a computer.

2 Explain briefly what is meant by the term 'electronic filing'; what are paper-based, electronic filing and microform records management systems best used for?

3 What is the difference between:
 a) a floppy disk,
 b) a hard disk,
 c) an optical disk?
Give examples of typical uses of each.

4 List five different ways in which information created on a computer may be disseminated.

5 Draw up a checklist of the principal features which a CABX telephone system offers an extension user.

6 What is meant by each of the following terms?
 a) dedicated,
 b) stand-alone,
 c) dumb terminal,
 d) convergence,
 e) bits and bytes,
 f) kilo-, mega- and giga-bytes,
 g) electronic mail,
 h) wide area network,
 i) dot-matrix,
 j) draft mode
 k) fount
 l) systems photocopier,
 m) pull-down menu,
 n) photo-typesetting,
 o) scanner,
 p) bypass feed,
 q) editing board.

7 Explain simply how a local area network system works and how it makes intercommunication among users more effective.

8 How does an office administrator benefit from having electronic equipment set up in a networked system supporting fax, telex, viewdata and communication modems?

9 Write out the following abbreviations/acronyms in full:
 a) ROM
 b) RAM
 c) CRT
 d) OSI
 e) CADCAM
 f) LAN and WAN
 g) LASER
 h) COBOL
 i) NLQ
 j) CPS
 k) DTP
 l) WORM
 m) CABX

10 Make a list of the features you would expect to find in a middle-of-the-range departmental photocopier.

Research and report back assignments

1 First carry out your research in student pairs, then give an oral presentation to your group (of about 10 minutes) supported by AVA on *one* of the following:

 a) computer-based electronic file storage and management systems
 b) microform information management systems
 c) how Prestel's hierarchic branching database works
 d) how a CABX telephone system works

2 Find out what the main features are of *one* of the following and how it is typically used in organisations:

 a) optical disk drive,
 b) interactive television,
 c) scanner with optical character recognition (OCR),
 d) video-conferencing CCTV system,
 e) radiopager,
 f) packet-switching digital transmission terminal,
 g) modem kit with laptop computer.

3 In pairs, arrange to interview a manager and/or secretary who regularly uses one of the following applications software packages. Find out what its main features are, and how it helps its user in the work he/she does.

PA/Secretary:	professional word processing package
Accountant:	integrated accounts package spreadsheet
Manager/Secretary:	integrated information management package database package graphics package

4 By arrangement, in groups of two or three, visit a local organisation which has a LAN/WAN system installed, so as to see it taken through its paces and, all being well, for you to try out. Also, obtain and peruse some current dealers' sales literature listing the specifications and features of popular network software.

Having fully briefed yourselves, write an illustrated account of what such networks can do for an organisation.

5 Find out how much it costs to send an electronic message of not more than 100 words via a WAN system from your locality to Vancouver Canada. Brief your group generally on the costing basis for WAN telecommunications.

6 Find out what services British Telecom and Mercury provide for multinational organisations to exchange large volume, digitised, computer data. Brief your group on your findings orally and then with a duplicated factsheet.

7 In pairs, arrange to visit a local organisation with a fax and/or telex facility; observe the fax/telex messaging process in action and seek to obtain non-confidential print-outs for your base-room bulletin board as specimens. Also, find out what information is included in the BT fax directory, as part of your assignment.

8 Choose *one* of the following telecommunications services and in about 250–300 words compose a summarised explanation of how its services are priced and how a user could operate it most cost-effectively:

a) facsimile transmission,
b) telex,
c) BT Gold Email Service,
d) Prestel,
e) packet-switched data transmission,
f) BT's Teleconferencing Service.

9 The head of department of the school or college in which you are studying has been given a windfall of £8,000 from capital funds. After conferring, he has decided to spend it on acquiring one of the following pieces of electronic office equipment. But before committing the money, he has asked you (in groups of three or four) to find out what uses the piece of equipment would be put to, and hence what features would be a) essential and b) useful.

a) a departmental photocopier,
b) a desk-top publishing unit,
c) a three-terminal demonstration LAN system for the Training Office.

Choose *one* of the above, and, having researched into potential applications and your own departmental needs, and having obtained sales literature about 2–3 models in the price-range, write a report for your head of department. Set out your findings and make recommendations appropriately (see Unit 6, The Report). When your class has produced reports on each of the three items listed above, make sure you obtain a photocopy of the reports on the equipment you did not research yourself.

10 First, carry out your research in pairs, then compose an entry in an induction manual of a medium-sized company for new trainee managers which outlines company policy on the use of *one* of the following, and how to ensure that it is used economically and cost-effectively:

a) the departmental photocopier,
b) the networked fax service,

c) Prestel and allied gatewayed databases,
d) the department's telex facility,
e) the company's desk-top publishing unit,
f) a key system telephone network.

11 First carry out your research, and then write an article of about 350–400 words for your firm's house journal entitled:

'How fax can help generate sales!'

or,

What a laser printer can do to improve the image and impact of your department's documentation!

12 In pairs, research the state of the art mobile phones and pagers and give a 10-minute illustrated presentation to your group.

13 When you have fully briefed yourself, write a memorandum for the Departmental Heads of your 2,000 employee-strong company manufacturing pop records, compact disks and tapes (sold both at home and overseas) entitled:

'How Prestel can help you help the company!'

Note: Your Computer Services Department has just added Prestel to the company's LAN/WAN system.

NB Consider also which other personnel might benefit from informational copies of your memo.

Work experience and simulation assignments

1 Under suitable supervision, arrange to send/receive an international fax and/or telex message. If possible, keep a copy of your transmitted message and set it on a sheet of A3 with arrowed explanations of what each entry stands for to act as a model for your group on return to study.

2 Having secured the approval of your supervisor, arrange to interview LAN users in your attachment organisation and then produce a checklist of principal applications of the LAN and how it aids productivity/efficiency etc. If possible, arrange to send and receive an international WAN message and retain print-outs.

3 Find out what reprographics applications your attachment organisation uses DTP for and bring back (with permission) specimen documents for your class to examine, produced by various equipment.

4 With approval, carry out a survey of the various methods and media employed in your attachment organisation to store information. Make careful

notes and then brief your group on the major strengths and weaknesses each storage medium possesses and identify the optimum uses to which each should be put.

5 Find out what software is used in your organisation's Accounts or Treasury Department and seek to see it in action. Write an account of the assistance it provides in about 350 words for your attachment supervisor to vet before duplicating it as a class informational handout

6 With permission, carry out a 'compare and contrast' survey of the electronic printers your organisation uses. Obtain copies of print-outs to bring back to your class for comparison of quality and displayed features.

7 Having secured authorisation, arrange to interview key personnel in various departments and units who have to provide photocopying services and control costs. Take notes of typical paper and toner costs and leasing/purchasing costs of equipment, etc and what a side of A4 will cost to photocopy in varying print runs using different ranges of equipment. Design a table to illustrate your findings to your group and provide a commentary of helpful guidelines on the cost-effective use of photocopying.

Case study

'Open all hours!'

Arun and Lata Patel's lives had been 'open all hours', ever since they first bought their business – a minimarket in a suburban shopping precinct – some five years ago. Then, the 150 houses on the Westbury Park development had been only half completed and business had been slow and hard to build. Thanks to the Patels' relentless hard work and willingness to rise at the crack of dawn and retire well after midnight, the minimarket had prospered, as the Westbury suburb of Grafton, a busy industrial town, had rapidly expanded. The store, called the Minimax Grocers & Newsagents, was in the middle of five shops in a parade lying back from a busy through-route to the A6. The Patels, with their 16-year-old daughter, Sonal and 10-year-old son, Naresh occupied a flat over the store.

Minimax had started out as a run-of-the-mill general stores, specialising in those small order items which local shoppers had forgotten to buy at the supermarket or did not want to make a special journey for. With a bus-stop into town just opposite, and room for parking out front, Arun quickly realised, however, that there was ample scope for selling newspapers, magazines and sweets, etc. Before much longer, he was employing six newspaper delivery youngsters. They also picked up orders for home-delivered groceries, which Arun delivered mid-mornings around the adjacent estates in his elderly but trusty van. The delivery side of the business expanded rapidly to a point where Arun had to stop taking on new customers – much against his will.

About a year ago, with the completion of the up-market Westbury Park development, customers who had acquired a taste for exotic micro-oven ready meals, gave Arun and Lata the idea of making room for another open freezer which would stock the spicy and different dishes which innovative food manufacturers were marketing under Chinese, Indian, Mexican and Indonesian brand names.

By this time, the Patels badly needed more helping hands. As luck would have it, two of Arun's nephews moved into the district looking for work in Grafton's textile industry. Both in their early twenties, they were just the trustworthy help that the shop urgently needed. Nor did they need much persuading, when Arun outlined his longer term plans for acquiring additional outlets. Ramesh, the elder brother took over the newsagency and confectionery side, while his brother Raj delivered the grocery orders and with his easy humour and persuasive ways quickly extended business.

Soon after, an incredible stroke of luck occurred – the butcher's shop next door came on to the market. The sitting tenant had been content to provide a mediocre service, and as a consequence could not afford the new lease's increased rents. Arun was quick to see his chance and had clinched the deal before the local estate agent had even displayed the particulars in his front window!

This time it was Mrs Patel who had her say. 'You know,' she had said, 'what Westbury needs is a really good fast-food takeaway!' Always with an eye to market trends, she had overheard snippets of conversation among teenagers and young married couples about the nearest fast-food outlet some two miles away which had a good reputation for ample portions and really tasty dishes. 'If they'll drive over there, they'll walk in here,' she observed shrewdly. 'We could also fit in a few tables for people who want to eat here, too,' she added. After meeting some demanding requirements, Arun obtained planning permission for the change of use and early in November, the grand opening of Arun's 'Tandoori Takeaway' took place, with Mrs Patel in charge!

* * *

Some eight weeks earlier, Sonal had started a two-year BTEC National Diploma course in Business and Finance at Grafton College of Technology. From day one, with business in her bones, she had never looked back. She seemed to devour the course material – especially those parts dealing with business information processing.

She had a natural flair with software and had achieved a Grade A in her Business Information Studies GCSE.

One evening, having just finished an assignment, she poked her head round her father's upstairs office in the flat. He was almost buried under paper! It bulged out of cardboard wallets, ring-binders and box files; it was festooned around the walls, suspended from rows of bull-dog clips, it littered his desk and window sills. Advice notes, invoices, handwritten orders, catalogues, price-lists, special offers and bank statements! It seemed as though Arun had kept every single piece of paper since the first day's trading. Sonal scooped up a handful and let it drop back on to the desk.

'Stop that you silly girl!' shouted Arun. 'Now look what you've done. I'd just sorted those invoices into sequence!'

'Daddy, look at you! You're drowning in a sea of bumf!'

'What do you mean, bumf – I know exactly where everything is kept – or did until you interfered – now go away and let me finish!'

'Not until you make me a promise you'll keep.' Sonal paused dramatically, for she well knew she was the apple of her father's eye.

'Certainly not! What promise?'

'That first thing tomorrow you go down to Computerama and get fixed up with a decent PC set-up and some suitable software – before you go down for the third time and all your past flashes before your eyes! I don't know how you've managed up till now, but with the new shop and the deliveries expanding, soon you won't need to stop for sleep – you won't have time!'

* * *

For several days Sonal's words echoed around Arun's brain like an advertising jingle that wouldn't go away. Eventually he brought the matter up with Lata. 'I think she's probably right. You should move with the times,' Lata responded. 'How can you even think of new outlets when you're drowning in the paper from just two!'

Outnumbered and out-argued, Arun was waiting the next morning outside the front door as they opened up Computerama for business!

Assignments

Talking points

1 Is Sonal right to think that computerising the Patels' business would help? What factors do you think would affect the success or failure of installing a PC, printer and software packages!

2 What aspects of the family business would installing a computerised system most assist?

3 What other IT-based office equipment/systems would it be realistic for Arun to install to aid profitability and service?

4 Assuming that Arun's plans are successful and within two more years he has promoted his two nephews as branch managers of two more Minimax stores, how would this growth affect an existing computerised administration system in the Patel business? Should Arun take future expansion into account in planning to introduce computing applications? If so, how?

Activities

1 Arun asks his daughter to carry out a survey of current computer configurations and specifications in order to benefit from her advice and expertise. In pairs, undertake Sonal's project and then produce a suitable report with recommendations on your findings which Arun can follow and base his decision upon. You should note that the Patels' current annual turnover is £250 000 and that any purchases must lie within a realistic ceiling – whether acquired from profit, a bank loan or leased.

2 Next, explore your local market for best prices of the software application packages which you think Arun should install. Produce a schedule displaying your findings and justify your reasons for the 'best buys' you identify.

6 Business letters

Overview

Unit 6 provides you with information and guidelines on:

● Current conventions and practices in paper-based letter layouts, including blocked and centred styles and open/closed punctuation systems.
● Clear explanations of the functions of the letterhead, logo and typescript components with examples and specimen letters.
● Explanations of the uses of different types of letter – complaint, adjustment, mailmerged sales, accounts collection, disciplinary, etc, with examples and models.
● Guidelines on devising suitable structures and styles in letter composition.
● Helpful 'do and don't' tips on letter composition.

Introduction

The death of the paper-based letter in organisations, has been exaggerated by the protagonists of IT. While the next millenium is very likely to see the demise of 'Postman Pat' and a boom time for home Email, for the present, business and public service letters (albeit created on IT systems) are still going to be circulated in their annual billions across the world.

Some significant reasons for letters continuing to be printed on paper are of course cultural and historical. Furthermore, UK law and international law still have some way to go in accepting electronically created and preserved data as legal evidence. For the moment, telexes are legally binding but not faxes. And so, in many commercial and industrial transactions, while much initial work will be undertaken using fax, telex or Email, confirmatory and contractual letters on paper will continue to be despatched, received and stored in conventional cabinets and safes as tangible proofs of agreements and positions.

Another important feature of the letter printed upon paper is its visual impact and effect on its recipient. Sophisticated advertising agency art designers spend much time and effort today on creating memorable corporate images, logos and livery for their clients. A central – indeed key feature – of such corporate graphics resides in the letterhead and logo (and indeed in the coloured inks and parchment papers). These combine to announce what an organisation is and what it does through the crisply folded letters which directors, managers, proprietors and public service officials alike receive daily.

Thus the letter produced on paper still has a central role in the sales, marketing, public relations and contractual activities of organisations. In fact, in every situation where it is important not only to inform or persuade but also to maintain an image of reliability, innovation, expertise or reassurance. For the above reasons, it is essential that you master the conventions and processes which underpin attractive and effective paper-based letter production.

Format

The letterhead

The letterhead is basically the printed part of the letter sheet. Its design is extremely important, and skilled graphics designers take great pains to produce a format of letters and colours displaying the trading-name, logo, address and other legally required components of a company or institution, which will create an appropriate image of that concern for the letter's recipient.

Company letterhead legal requirements

The example below of Pitman's letterhead and logo provides a good illustration (the original is printed in red and blue coloured inks) of a clean and crisp image clearly set out for respondents to read and refer to.

However, it is useful to note the checklist below of legal requirements which letterheads are obliged to display legibly to meet the 1948 Companies Act (Sec 201) and the European Communities Act 1972, Chap 68, Sec 9 Para 7:

- The company's trading name,
- Its status as a limited company if appropriate,
- A list of its directors if founded after 23 November 1916,
- The registered office address, number and location of registration – eg England, Scotland or West Germany, etc.

The nationality of directors who are not EC nationals must also be shown, eg F Herzberg (USA).

Letter logos

Ever since Roman times, shopkeepers have advertised their location, products and services with the help of symbols – bushes, barber-poles, inn signs, etc – which quickly caught the eyes of the passers-by. Similarly, for the past two hundred years, manufacturers, retailers and service providers have devised often witty and engaging trademarks to act as memory joggers which reinforce customer loyalty and promote familiarity.

The logo – the graphic symbol on the letterhead – is very often the same as the trademark used on product packaging, delivery lorries, newspaper

Pitman Publishing

128 Long Acre
London WC2E 9AN

Telephone 01-379 7383

Telex 261367
Pitman G

Cables Ipandsons
London WC2

Fax 01-240 5771
Pitman Ldn

Pitman Publishing Division of Longman Group UK Limited Registered Office 5 Bentinck Street London W1M 5RN Registered number 872828 England

Examples of memorable logos

---

advertisements and the like. Indeed, many such trademarks or logos have become universally recognised symbols, like the Coca Cola company's distinctive script, the American vacuum cleaner manufacturer Hoover's simple yet timeless emblem, the faithful dog listening to 'His Master's Voice, and the imaginative radio-wave which instantly convveys Plessey's electronics manufacturing interests:

Thus the incorporation of the trademark as a logo on letterheads provides a widely distributed medium through which to sustain a company's corporate image and identity.

Fully blocked/blocked layout style

Letter layout

It is important to note that there are no absolute rules governing letter layout, although leading examining boards like the Royal Society of Arts and London Chamber of Commerce and Industry promote consistency and good practice in their secretarial and business administration examinations.

New technology more than anything else has modified letter layout practice over the past ten or so years. The advent of the typewriter carriage with automatic return (to the left-hand margin) and the subsequent introduction of wrap-round text in word processing software (in which text is automatically justified to the right-hand margin and continued from the preset left-hand margin) led very quickly to a letter layout style termed fully blocked or, simply, blocked style. The essential characteristic of blocked layout is that all the typescript entries down the letter notepaper start from the same left-hand margin:

An alternative layout (but one less often seen today) is that of the **semi-blocked** or **centred style**. Here, while typescript entries like the recipient's address and the main body of the letter are set to the left-hand margin, paragraph openings are indented and entries such as the letter's subject-heading and complimentary close are centred across an imaginary centre-line for visual appeal and effect:

Centred/semi-blocked layout style

Open and closed punctuation

Just as office equipment technology encouraged the
development of the fully blocked layout, so the
drive for text processing productivity brought about
open punctuation. This convention omits virtually
all punctuation marks (but not apostrophes) from
those typescript entries outside the body of the letter. In this way, some 30–50 keystroke depressions
may be saved in keying in the typescript of a typical
letter. Thus a letter combining a fully-blocked layout
with open punctuation achieves elegance with
economy.

Closed punctuation is a survivor of a preceding
convention in which commas and full-stops marked line ends and the ends of abbreviations such as:
J. Wilson, Esq., M.Sc., F.B.I.M. for entries outside
the body of the letter and on envelopes. Both the
use of 'Esq' and the peppering of interspersed dots
and commas are fast becoming obsolete in letter
punctuation conventions.

Post Office preferred address layout on envelopes

```
                                              [20p stamp]
          Miss Caroline Williams M Ed B Sc IQPS
          Information Officer
          Skyline Holidays Ltd
          121 – 130 Grove Crescent
          LONDON
          WC 2D  4AJ
```

Note: this name and address is set out in open punctuation format and the recipient's name and address
in the letter will look just the same. Indeed, many
firms use window envelopes to display addresses
on suitably folded letters to save repetitious typing.
The *Post Office Guide* lists those postal addresses
where a county entry is not needed in the address
because of the size of the town or city.

Paper and envelopes

You should be aware of the international
agreements which have been accepted in many
countries to standardise paper sizes. The following
table lists the principal sizes in use in the UK, of
which A4 and A5 are commonly used for letters and
memoranda:

Standard international paper sizes

Size	Millimetres Deep	Millimetres Wide	Application
A7	74	105	visiting/business card
A6	148	105	postcard
A5	148	210	short memo
A4	297	210	letter long memo report
A3	297	420	tables graphics accounts data
A2	594	420	notices bulletins
A1	594	841	posters
A0	1189	841	advertise-ments

By the same token, the Post Office in its annually
published Post Office Guide (an essential information source for all office administrators) indicates its
'Post Office Preferred' envelope sizes:

Standardised envelope sizes

A4 sheet folded 3 times:	DL	220mm × 110mm
A4 sheet folded twice:	C5	229mm × 162mm
A4 sheet unfolded:	C4	324mm × 229mm
A5 sheet folded once:	C6	144mm × 162mm
A5 sheet unfolded:	C5	229mm × 162mm

Typescript components checklist

Letter references commonly author's and text processor's initials and electronic or paper file reference

```
Our ref:  DWE/AJ  Pitlet.24
```

Date set in sequence day, month, year:

```
22 June 19--
```

Status of letter eg

```
Personal, Confidential
```

Name and address of recipient name, organisation, street, town, county, post-code

Attention leader eg
```
For the attention of Miss D Jones
```

Salutation eg

```
Dear Sir,  Dear Madam,  Dear Mr Smith
```

Subject-heading eg

```
Launch of Actovol Cereal Nutrient
```

Note: set variously as initial capitals, block capitals, with or without emboldening etc.

Body of letter taking the form of blocked or indented paragraphs with, perhaps, centred tables; separated by double spacing

Subscription or complimentary close eg:

```
Yours faithfully,  Yours sincerely,

With best wishes,
```

Signature space for handwritten signature

Author's name and job designation set in typescript beneath signature eg:

Alison K Spearing

```
Alison K Spearing
Personnel Manager
```

Enclosure reference typically:

```
enc  encs  Enc  Encs  enclosure

Enclosures
```

Note: some solicitors affix red stars to catch the eye and sometimes a typescript solidus/or dashes - - - are set in the left-hand margin to mark the reference to the enclosure eg

```
/or . . application form for you . . .
```

Copy/copies sent reference typically:

```
copy to, circulation:
```

Continuation sheet details So as to ensure subsequent sheets of notepaper can be linked back to the first sheet, continuation sheets display at their head: recipient's name, page number and date:

```
D Jones        2        12 May 199–
```

Notes

1 'Your ref' is the reference shown on the *incoming* letter being replied to as 'Our ref'; 'Our ref' on the letter being created identifies its author, producer and file reference.

2 Avoid the North American practice of sequencing the date as: July 4 199-

3 The recipient of a letter may be variously referred to as follows:

● by personal name and job title:
  Mr John Brown
  Sales Manager
● by presumed designation when not clearly known:
  The Secretary, The Sales Manager, The Accounts Director
● by department or unit:
  The X-Ray Department
  The Transport Department
● by name of the organisation alone:
  Wholesome Foods Limited

Clearly, letters addressed to named individuals in specified departments will arrive more swiftly and be dealt with much faster.

Note: in each of the above cases, the rest of the postal address – name of department, name of organisation, street number and name, town/city, county and post code – will follow (see examples on pages 110, 116 and 117 ideally set out in not more than five lines of text.

Talking point

Why does the business letter on paper remain such a popular communication medium, given its production costs (approx £15 each) and the time taken to deliver it?

Styles of address

The currently accepted styles of address in common use are:

for female recipients: Miss Ms Mrs Dr Lady Dame Baroness
for male recipients: Mr Dr Sir Lord Baron
for partnerships: Messrs, Mesdames
Note these usages:

Dear Sir Richard
Dear Lord Walderton
Dear Lady Massingham
Dear Baronness Wargrave
Messrs Smith & Jones . . . Dear Sirs

Should a female letter-writer not provide a detail of her married status under her signature – Jean Cartwright – it is acceptable either to write to her as Mrs or Ms – Dear Ms Cartwright. Again, if the writer does not show male/female status – D P Williams, Accounts Manager – then write back to Mr D P Williams.

Whenever in doubt about correct forms and titles of address, consult a handy reference like: *Black's Titles and Forms of Address*. Make sure you have a copy accessible to you in your job.

Handling people's letters and qualifications

As medical doctors or PhD graduates may have spent upwards of eight years acquiring their qualifications, it is not surprising that such people like to see them used correctly in the correspondence they receive. As the psychologist says, 'Nothing is more important to an individual than his or her name!' You should always ensure, therefore, that the letters you send out pay due attention to this important aspect. There is a running order for letters after people's names:

1 orders and decorations
2 degrees and diplomas
3 memberships of professional bodies

eg James Grey Esq OM DFC MSc FRSA

Higher degrees precede lower degrees:
M Sc B Ed, Also, both medical and other doctorates awarded are acknowledged either as:

Dear Dr Phillips
or as
James Phillips Esq MD (if medical)
or as
James Phillips Esq Ph D

Note: the inclusion of Esq as illustrated above is fast becoming obsolete; it is still not good practice, however, to use Mr or Dr followed by the name and then abbreviated qualifications.

In the case of female letter recipients, it is common practice to retain the Miss Ms or Mrs before the name and qualifications string:

Miss G Simpson MA Dip Ed ARCM

The following table illustrates the conventions which link together salutations and subscriptions in letters. Note the *small* f and s of faithfully and sincerely. Also, many letter-writers today write to associates and colleagues in a much more informal register than hitherto, so make a note of usages like: My Dear Jack . . . With kind regards and, Dear Sue. . . . With best wishes.

Table of linked salutations and complimentary closes in use

Salutation	Complimentary close
Dear Sir, Dear Madam, Dear Sirs,	Yours faithfully,
Dear Mr Green, Dear Miss Sharp, Dear Mrs Howes, Dear Dr Ivors, Dear Lord Chilgrove, Dear Sir Richard, Dear Lady Hatton,	Yours sincerely,
Dear Jim, Dear Jenny,	Sincerely, Kind regards,
My Dear Susan, My Dear Harry,	Affectionately, Best wishes.

Note that 'Yours truly' as an alternative to 'Yours faithfully' is no longer used.

The salutations and complimentary closes other than, 'Dear Sir, . . . Yours faithfully,' or 'Dear Mr Green. . . . Yours sincerely,' are becoming less bound by conventions as contemporary letter-writers give their letters a more personal stamp.

Letters with Personal, Private & Confidential and Confidential status

Envelopes marked 'Personal' or 'For the personal attention of' should only be opened by the specified recipient. By arrangement, managers and executives may permit their PAs or personal secretaries to open all mail marked 'Private & Confidential' or simply 'Confidential'. However, strict instructions should be issued to mailroom personnel, and insisted upon, that incoming mail showing any of the above status labels must be sent on to the departmental secretary *unopened*!

1   ▓▓ **Pitman Publishing**

3   128 Long Acre
London WC2E 9AN

2

Telephone 01-379 7383

Telex 261367
Pitman G

5   Cables Ipandsons
London WC2

6   Fax 01-240 5771
Pitman Ldn

7   CONFIDENTIAL

8   Your ref   JG/PD

9   Our ref   AG/NL/ 4

10   15 April 19--

11   Mr J Green
Appletrees
Windmill Lane
Peppard Common
READING
Berks
RG24 3PC

12   Dear Mr Green

13   PROPOSED TEXTBOOK ON SECRETARIAL ADMINISTRATION

14   Following upon our telephone conversation of Tuesday last, I am pleased to
confirm that our Project Committee met yesterday, and that your proposal was
fully considered. As a result, Mrs Jean Simpson, Publisher, Secretarial Studies
Division, wishes me to offer you a contract to publish your text early next year.

May I take this opportunity to offer my personal congratulations with the sincere
hope that your first textbook will prove a resounding success. I should also
like to assure you that your manuscript will receive my careful attention in the
coming months, so please do not hesitate to let me know if I may help in any way.

--- 15   I enclose a copy of our standard Agreement form for your information and shall
contact you shortly to arrange a convenient date to finalise contract details.

16   Yours sincerely

17   *Ann Grant*

18   Ann Grant
Editor Secretarial Studies Division

19   enc.

20   Pitman Publishing. Division of Longman Group UK Limited Registered Office 5 Bentinck Street London W1M 5RN Registered number 872828 England

Format of the fully blocked letter

1   Company logo and trading name. Five company addresses:

   2   Postal address, including postcode
   3   Telephone number
   4   Telex address
   5   Cable address
   6   Fax number and address

7   Prominently placed letter status indicator.

8   Your reference is that of the letter's recipient, John Green (JG) and his assistant, Pat Dawson (PD).

9   Our reference is that of the letter's sender – here Ann Grant as the writer (AG), and Nicola Lawson, secretary (NL). The number 4 indicates this is the fourth letter written to John Green and is a helpful filing reference.

10   Date: expressed as day (number), month (word) and year (number) and *never* as 15/4/19-

11   Recipient's full postal address: note town in capital letters and postcode on its own line (whenever practicable).

12   Salutation: Here the less formal 'Dear Mr . . . Yours sincerely' is used, as opposed to its formal counterpart 'Dear Sir . . . Yours faithfully'.

7–12   This letter's layout conforms to the conventions of blocked format and open punctuation; in blocked format all lines commence from the pre-set left-hand margin as all punctuation (outside the body of the letter) is omitted.

13   Subject heading prominently displayed in capitals with good space around it; subject headings should convey briefly the letter's theme or subject.

14   Body of the letter: note that points are made succinctly in brief paragraphs and that the chosen style is informal without becoming over-friendly or familiar.

15   Eye-catching enclosure symbol: note that *** and / are also sometimes employed.

16   Appropriate subscription for 'Dear Mr, Mrs, Ms or Miss, etc'.

17   Sufficient space allotted for writer's signature.

18   Typescript confirmation of writer's name and job title (Note: some female letter-writers include Mrs, Ms or Miss after their names).

19   Further confirmation of an enclosure included; see also 'encs', 'enclosure', etc.

20   All business letters must include the address where the company is registered and its registration number to comply with the Companies Acts.

Self assessment question

If you had to, could you draft a legally acceptable letterhead for a new company or partnership! Are you able to vet the production of letters because you are fully proficient in current conventions of layout and style?

Common categories of letter

Area	Letter classification	Explanation of use
General	Enquiry	to seek information, confirmation
	Acknowledgement, Information	to provide information, confirmation
	Complaint	to seek redress of a deficiency
	Adjustment	to rectify a complaint
Financial	Collection 1, 2, 3	to obtain settlement of a debt
	Letter of credit	to authorise an advance of credit
	Financial standing	to check credit-worthiness
Sales, Advertising	Sales letter	to sell goods or services
	Follow-up sales letter	to remind of sales offers
	Unsolicited sales letter	to advertise goods or services
Orders, Estimates	Order	to place an order for goods etc
	Confirmation of order	to confirm a submitted order
	Estimate	to submit a projected price
	Tender	to submit a contractual price
Appointments	Application	to apply for a post
	Resignation	to confirm resignation from a post
	Reference enquiry	to seek confidential particulars
	Reference reply	to provide confidential particulars
Circulars	Circular to personnel	to reach a group, organisation
	Circular to customers	or company customer in one despatch
Special category	Letter requiring especial tact	to convey delicate information etc tactfully
Legal	Solicitor's letter	to secure outstanding debts or to warn of impending proceedings so as to obtain out-of-court settlements
Personnel	Disciplinary	to provide a legally required written warning as part of disciplinary procedure
	Recruitment	mailmerged standard letters confirming application receipt, interview calling, rejection, etc
Network maintenance	Congratulating condoling, etc	keeping 'lines open' to contacts and clients with personal responses to happy/unhappy events

Standard letters and word processing

Although advances in word processing techniques and software design have undoubtedly aided the purveyors of junk mail, such advances have also proved a boon to managers in all walks of private and public sector life. For example, multiple copies of master documents can be created in the form of standard letters to which particularised data, held on non-document or data word processor files, can be added. A good example is a reminder letter con-cerning an unpaid account, the body of which can be produced as a standard form of wording to which items such as the client's name, address and details of the outstanding account can be added.

Solicitors, for example, now store standard paragraphs relating to wills and testaments on WP software and merely ask for 'para 124 here' or 'para 96 here' as they draw up a will to meet a specific client's requirements.

Thus the form or standard letter created through WP software now has a central role to play in routine letter production.

Content

Structuring the message

1 The opening paragraph – puts the message into a context

The function of the opening paragraph is to put the detailed message into a clearly defined context, either by initiating an action, by responding to a received stimulus or by introducing the next stage in a sequence or exchange of letters. This may be achieved by:

1 Acknowledging the date, receipt and subject of any received correspondence
2 Supplying the reason for the letter being written
3 Providing essential names, dates, locations or other data to put the message into context.

2 The middle paragraph(s) – develops detailed message

In the middle paragraph(s) the detailed data which comprises the letter's message is logically, briefly and clearly set down. For example, the precise nature of a complaint may be described, the benefits of goods for sale listed, the sequence of payment requests repeated or the essence of bad news gently imparted.

In complex letters, several middle paragraphs may in turn, deal with one principal aspect of an involved message. This will make it easier for the reader to grasp.

To aid impact, some data may be displayed in tabular form, perhaps as a table of discounts, schedule of prices benefits, list of selling points or specification of building materials.

3 The closing paragraph – states action needed

In addition to providing a résumé of the main points of a complex letter's message, the essential function of the closing paragraph is to state simply and clearly what action the writer needs from the recipient.

The time and effort needed to send a letter require that it promotes an active desire in its recipient to act upon its message, whether by paying a bill, ordering some perfume or meeting a rates demand.

Since the action statement is the entire reason for writing letters other than informational ones, the requirement or request for action appears virtually at the letter's end, thus remaining uppermost in the recipient's mind, followed only by a courteous closing statement.

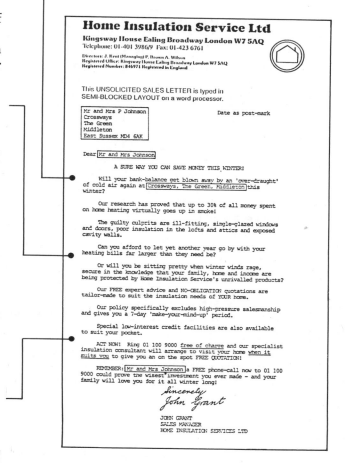

Talking point

Have 'junk-mail' unsolicited letters now gone beyond the pale, given the widespread sale of consumer profiling lists or are they still legitimate sales promotion tools of value to the consumer?

Analyses of structures

Letter of complaint

```
┌─────────────────────────┐
│ SALUTATION              │
└─────────────────────────┘
            ▼
┌─────────────────────────┐
│ SUBJECT – HEADING       │
└─────────────────────────┘
            ▼
┌─────────────────────────┐
│ REASON FOR LETTER:      │
│ CONTEXT:                │
│ date, location,         │
│ invoice, model,         │
│ personnel               │
└─────────────────────────┘
            ▼
┌─────────────────────────┐
│ DESCRIPTION OF:         │
│ nature, extent of       │
│ damage, or defect:      │
│ detail of defective     │
│ parts                   │
└─────────────────────────┘
            ▼
┌─────────────────────────┐
│ IMPLICATIONS OF:        │
│ time lost, custom lost, │
│ inconvenience, work     │
│ delayed                 │
└─────────────────────────┘
            ▼
┌─────────────────────────┐
│ INDICATION OF:          │
│ action needed to        │
│ remedy complaint:       │
│ replacement             │
│ reimbursement           │
│ time-limit              │
└─────────────────────────┘
```

tone: polite but firm throughout

1 Opening paragraph

who	regret
why	at
what	incon-
when	venience
where	caused

2 Middle paragraph(s)

precise	result
nature	of
of	check on
complaint	complaint

3 Middle paragraph(s)

ensuing	action
incon-	taken
venience	to
caused	remedy

4 Closing paragraph

action	apology
needed	and hope
to	goodwill
put	is
right	retained

Letter of adjustment

```
┌─────────────────────────┐
│ SALUTATION              │
└─────────────────────────┘
            ▼
┌─────────────────────────┐
│ SUBJECT – HEADING       │
└─────────────────────────┘
            ▼
┌─────────────────────────┐
│ STATEMENT OF REGRET     │
│ letter is acknow-       │
│ leged and confirm-      │
│ ation given that        │
│ complaint is            │
│ understood              │
└─────────────────────────┘
            ▼
┌─────────────────────────┐
│ CAUSE OF DEFECT:        │
│ explanation given       │
│ after investigation     │
│ of why 'x' went         │
│ wrong                   │
└─────────────────────────┘
            ▼
┌─────────────────────────┐
│ ACTION TO BE TAKEN      │
│ explanation of          │
│ action to be taken      │
│ to 'adjust' com-        │
│ plaint                  │
└─────────────────────────┘
            ▼
┌─────────────────────────┐
│ APOLOGY                 │
│ RESTATEMENT:            │
│ together with           │
│ hope expressed          │
│ that goodwill           │
│ will be retained        │
└─────────────────────────┘
```

tone: conciliatory and helpful

Remember!

When writing a letter of complaint, remember that the recipient must receive clear details of the transaction and a careful explanation of the faults complained of. He must also be informed of what action is expected to put the matter right and any deadline required. Correspondingly, the adjustment letter must, while expressing regret at the inconvenience caused, take pains to explain *why* things went wrong and what is *speedily* being done to put them right, especially since the customer's goodwill is the linchpin of commerce.

Tactful letters

Perhaps the most difficult of all letters to write are those whose messages must either affect the reader adversely, or which require great tact or delicacy, so as not to offend the recipient − particularly when the writer hopes to prompt action in spite of difficult or unwelcome circumstances. Many managers or officials find themselves all too frequently having to impart bad news, having to say 'no' gracefully, or to communicate an unpopular directive.

The diagram below illustrates how a four-paragraph structure could be employed to break bad news to a recipient − perhaps of failure in a promotion application, or a transfer to a different position with less authority, or the closing-down of a branch-manager's store because of falling turnover. The permutations are numerous.

Although the letter-writer's aim is basically to convey the bad news clearly and unambiguously, he or she has an equal obligation not to wound the recipient's feelings by insensitivity, indifference or terseness. As the diagram illustrates, the letter must be carefully structured to cushion the impact of the bad news, which can neither be baldly stated in the first paragraph, nor 'tacked on' to the closing paragraph almost as an after-thought.

The context and circumstances surrounding the bad news are used carefully to prepare the reader for what is to come. Similarly, once the bad news has been imparted (towards the end of the second paragraph in the diagram), the writer must take pains to ensure that some positive factors are found, with which the reader may identify and so not be left feeling entirely overlooked, discarded, incompetent or passed over.

The most difficult task is to avoid any sentiments which may be interpreted as being insincere. And, as may be readily imagined such letters require careful drafting and scrutiny before despatch.

Now turn to page 126 and study the model letter which aims to convey disappointing news tactfully.

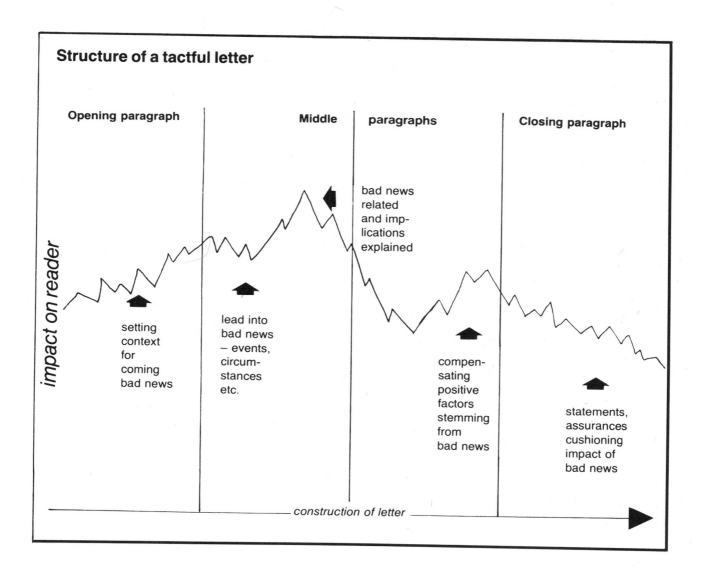

Structure of a tactful letter

Opening paragraph — Middle paragraphs — Closing paragraph

impact on reader

setting context for coming bad news

lead into bad news − events, circumstances etc.

bad news related and implications explained

compensating positive factors stemming from bad news

statements, assurances cushioning impact of bad news

construction of letter

Model letters: complaint and adjustment

1 Letter of complaint

> This letter has been set out in the centred style using open punctuation.

South London Garages Limited

121 WIMBLEDON ROAD LONDON SE1 5GT
HMF and Porsche Authorised Dealers
High Quality & Trusted Service!

Tel: 01-567-8901/4 Telex: 456901 Solondgar Fax: 01-345-6677

Our ref: BS/GJ/HMFUK.78   Your ref:

25 March 199–

For the urgent attention of:

Mr P Goodwright
UK Sales Director
Hessische Motor Fabriken (UK) Ltd
HMF House
110–112 Ipswich Road
PETERBOROUGH
Cambs   P16 9HK

Dear Mr Goodwright

NON–DELIVERY OF ORDER KX4592: FIVE HMF TURBO TOURERS MK II

On 12 January 199– my company placed a telexed order
(5466 90–12–01 12.15) with you for five HMF Turbo Tourer
Mark II saloons, specifying three Moonlight Silver and
two Stardust White models. The telex included details of
required delivery dates arising from firm orders from
long-standing, repeat-purchasing customers.

Your telex reply (ref: 7856 90–12–01 2.46) confirmed
our order and indicated that there would be no problems in
meeting the specified delivery dates – all now gone by –
nor in supplying the colours our customers requested.

I am therefore extremely concerned that the commitments
which South London Garages Limited has given to valued
customers cannot be met because of your inability to deliver
the five HMF Mark IIs as promised.

At present my sales staff are under a great deal of
pressure from the customers involved, who are now threatening
to cancel their orders worth a total of £126,450:00.

My company simply cannot afford to lose such valuable
business, and I am therefore asking you to intervene in this
matter personally so as to ensure a satisfactory outcome for
my customers as a matter of extreme urgency.

I look forward to hearing from you at your earliest
opportunity.

Yours sincerely

Brian Smith

Brian Smith
Sales Manager

copy to Gordon Watson General Manager

Format of a fully blocked letter with open punctuation

2 Letter of adjustment

Hessische Motor Fabriken UK Limited

HMF House 110 – 112 Ipswich Road
Peterborough Cambridgeshire P16 9HK

Tel: 0733 29634   Telex: 313123 HMF UK
Fax: 0733 827169
HMF UK Ltd A subsidiary of MMF Aktiengesellschaft
Bundesrepublik Deutschland. Registered in England 963472
Registered Office: HMFAG 241 Knightsbridge, London W3 4AJ

Your ref   BS/GJ/HMF UK. 78

Our ref   PG/ATY/SLGL/192

28 March 199–

Brian Smith Esq
Sales Manager
South London Garages Limited
121 Wimbledon Road
LONDON
SE1 5TG

Dear Mr Smith

YOUR ORDER KX4592 FOR FIVE HMF TURBO TOURERS MARK II

I was very concerned to receive your letter of 25 March 199–
in which you complain about the non-delivery of your order
KX4592, 12 January 199–, for five HMF Turbo Tourer Mark II
motor-cars.

As I explained in my telephone conversation with you yesterday,
these vehicles are (very unfortunately) still on board the SS
Hamburg at Milford Haven docks and we have not been able to secure
them because of the current unofficial industrial dispute which
our transport contractors are experiencing between their drivers
and the port's cargo handlers.

I fully appreciate how frustrating this must be for you, having
already closed firm sales for the Tourers and that your customers
are putting you and your staff under pressure for delivery.

It may assist you to know that I have located one Mark II (colour
Velvet black) at our Watford depot and three Mark Is in the
Midlands (Pine green, Pewter grey and Aubergine).

In view of our inability to supply for the time being your order as
placed, I should be pleased to offer you an additional 7.5% discount
on the supply of the Mark Is. If you would like to take advantage
of these substitutes, please telephone me directly and I shall arrange
for you to have the motor-cars by the beginning of next week.

May I finally give you my sincere assurance that HMF is doing all it
can to secure the release of the cargo at Milford Haven and offer my
sincere apologies for the inconvenience you are experiencing. As soon
as the situation improves I shall contact you at once.

Yours sincerely

P Goodwright

P Goodwright
UK Sales Director

'Appleblossom'
South Downs Way
Burleys
Hampshire
PO23 4QR

Tel: 0705–496843

Dear Sir,

I should like to apply for the post of personal assistant to your Export Sales Manager recently advertised in 'The Daily Sentinel', and have pleasure in enclosing my completed application form and a copy of my curriculum vitae.

The advertised post particularly appeals to me, since my own career aspirations and education have been specifically directed for the last two years towards an office administrative appointment in the field of export sales.

In the sixth form at Redbrook High School I specialised in Advanced-level German, French and English and proceeded in September 199- to Redbrook College of Technology, where I embarked upon a bilingual secretarial course leading to the Institute of Export's Diploma in Export Studies.

The course includes intensive commercial language studies (I am specialising in German), communication, office administration and export studies with particular emphasis on E.E.C. procedures and documentation. In addition, The Diploma course provides shorthand, word processing and E.E.C. telecommunications components, including work in the special foreign language.

I anticipate achieving a good pass in the June Diploma examination and attaining shorthand and typewriting speeds of 100/50 wpm, having already secured passes at 80/40 wpm.

During my full-time education, I have travelled extensively in the Federal Republic of Germany and in France, and have become familiar with the customs and outlooks of both countries. In August 199- I gained a valuable insight into German business methods during a month's exchange visit to a Handelsschule in Frankfurt-am-Main.

Assisting my father for the past two years in his own company has afforded me an opportunity to use my own initiative and to obtain helpful work experience in areas such as sales documentation, customer relations and the use of data processing in a sales context.

If called, I should be pleased to attend for an interview at any time convenient to you.

My course at Redbrook College of Technology finishes on 30th June 199- and I should be available to commence a full-time appointment from the beginning of July onwards.

Yours faithfully
Jane Simmonds (Miss)

(Note: It is usual for letters of application such as the one above to be handwritten)

The post Jane Simmonds applied for:

FINOSA FABRICS LTD require a PERSONAL
ASSISTANT to the EXPORT SALES MANAGER
(EUROPE)

A knowledge of two EEC foreign languages is
required and experience of export sales procedures
is an advantage. The successful candidate will
work on his or her own initiative and be able to
handle incoming telephone, fax and telex
messages and documentation from French or
German agents. He or she must also be prepared
to travel abroad.

The company provides excellent conditions of
service, including five weeks paid holiday per
annum subsidised insurance and restaurant
facilities. Salary negotiable according to age and
experience.
Apply in writing to: The Personnel Manager, Finosa
Fabrics Ltd, 4 York Way, London WC2B 6AK

Applications to be received by 30 May 19—

Model letter of application

Commentary

Jane Simmond's letter of application begins by
acknowledging the source of the advertisement,
makes a formal application statement and refers to
relevant enclosures.

In her second paragraph, Jane endeavours to
establish a close link between her own career
aspirations and vocational education and the
essential nature of the advertised post.

Jane goes on to draw particular attention to those
aspects of her more recent education which she
considers have equipped her with a sound
preparation for the post.

In case her prospective employers may be unfamiliar
with them, Jane outlines the relevant course
components of the Diploma, emphasising those
parts which would be most likely to interest her
potential principal.

Jane endeavours to display self-confidence without
immodesty, and evidence of existing achievement.
Since she lacks full-time work-experience, Jane
makes the best of her travels and knowledge of the
countries relating to the advertisement. She also includes mention of a course of study which has provided relevant insights.

Realising that her lack of work-experience could
prove a stumbling-block, Jane emphasises the practical work-experience she has had, and highlights
aspects of it which she hopes will be relevant to her
application.

Availability for interview is made as easy as
possible.

Since she needs the job, Jane displays a willingness
to start just as soon as possible after the end of her
course, thus demonstrating her 'earnestness of
intent'.

Assignments

1 In syndicate groups, study Jane Simmonds' letter from the point of view of Finosa's Personnel
Manager and consider the following questions:

Has Jane's letter succeeded in arousing your interest? If so, why? If not, why not? Does Jane's letter succeed in meeting the aims suggested in the
commentary? Do you have any criticisms to make
of Jane's letter in terms of the information supplied,
its structure, its tone and style? Could it be improved upon? Does it adequately match the requirements implied in the advertisement?

2 Draft letters from Finosa to:

a) call Jane Simmonds to attend an interview
b) inform Jane Simmonds of her failure to obtain the
     post after interview
c) offer Jane Simmonds the post after interview

In groups of two or three consider whether the
above letters could be created as mailmergeable
standard letters, and if so, how.

3 As Jane Simmonds, assume that, while awaiting
news from Finosa after interview, you have been
offered, and accepted a post with another company
as a result of an earlier application. Write a letter
to Finosa appropriate to the situation.

Talking point

Should letters of job application still be
hand-written?

Style

Language

Essential to conveying the letter's message effectively is the form of language used – the style in which
the letter is written.
   Immediately any written form of communication
is employed problems occur which are much more
easily overcome in, say, face-to-face oral communication. The transmission, assimilation and
feedback cycle of the oral conversation are supported and reinforced by a range of non-verbal communication signals such as the smile, nod, gesture

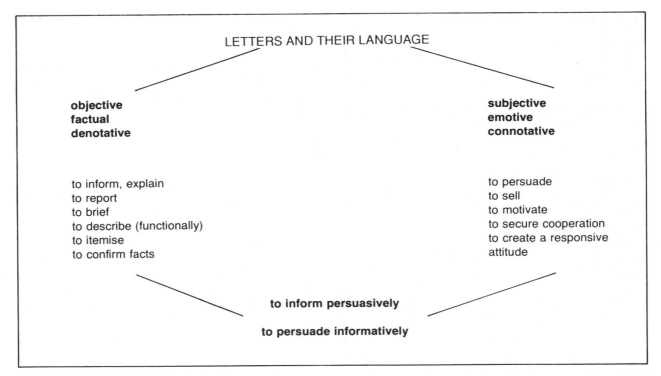

LETTERS AND THEIR LANGUAGE

objective
factual
denotative

subjective
emotive
connotative

to inform, explain
to report
to brief
to describe (functionally)
to itemise
to confirm facts

to persuade
to sell
to motivate
to secure cooperation
to create a responsive
attitude

to inform persuasively

to persuade informatively

or posture. In oral communication offence caused by misunderstanding over inappropriate tone or ambiguity is much less likely to occur and much easier to put right. Correspondingly the permanence of the letter as a written record and the absence of the supportive effect of non-verbal communication mean that special care must be given to the way in which the letter's message is expressed. The construction of the message, the 'what', should be carefully organised in the letter's structure, and in the same way, the 'how', the choice of words expressing the message, should be just as carefully chosen so that the letter's basic aim is reinforced and the desired action from the recipient thereby generated.

Some letters are written principally to convey information, while others are active selling 'weapons' in the armoury of the advertising manager, and seek to persuade. Yet others may seek to inform and persuade simultaneously.

Simply put, style may be defined as 'the most effective words in the most appropriate order', and the letter-writer must be continually checking to ensure that the words he or she is using are creating the right effect, whether it be to inform objectively, or to sell subjectively:

The emulsion paint embodies a vinyl additive which improves both its covering capacity and durability.

Wondacover! Its warm and satiny vinyl finish makes it go on great! And then go on and on and on!

The Latin, Saxon, Norse and French roots of English have rendered it extremely rich when it comes to finding alternatives or synonyms to express an idea or sentiment, and, in *The King's English*, H W and

F G Fowler have synthesised three proverbial guidelines which the letter-writer would do well to follow:

1 Prefer the short word to the long
2 Prefer the Saxon word to the Romance (Latinate)
3 Prefer the single word to the circumlocution.

When the letter-writer poses the question, 'What action do I wish to generate!' he is thinking of the effect of his words on his recipient. His style will also be affected, however, by the 'strength dimension' of the letter's context and the relationship between writer and recipient, where the writer may be:

directing
requiring
requesting
asking a favour
seeking help
in dire need of
'baling out'.

The recipient

As well as developing a style in a letter appropriate to its aim, the letter-writer must also keep firmly in mind the kind of person for whom the letter is intended:

- How old is the recipient?
- What sort of education?
- What kind of business background?
- What professional interests?
- What tastes, preferences, leisure interests?
- What prejudices, *bêtes-noires*?

The response of the recipient is bound to be affected by a wide range of factors which have moulded his or her life and experiences — either a wealth of practical experience, or a lengthy higher education, a specialism in a narrow field, or a succession of varied appointments, either a metropolitan, sophisticated life-style or a traditional, rural background.

To remain indifferent to the recipient's personality is to run the risk of communication breakdown, perhaps by using terminology and syntax which the reader does not understand, or to cause unpremeditated offence by tactlessness or by an insensitive reference. Whatever the cause, failure to write specifically for the letter's recipient may cause him or her to ignore the letter's message and to refuse to act upon it.

Use this plan and your letters will always 'IMPRESS'!

I DEA	– Decide upon the principal aim(s) of the letter
M ETHOD	– Structure the letter's main points in a plan
P ARAGRAPHS	– Follow the opening, middle and closing scheme
R ECIPIENT	– Remember who will receive the letter
E MPHASIS	– Guide the letter's progress to its action statement
S TYLE	– Employ a style appropriate to the letter's aim(s)
S AFETY	– Check the letter for errors or omissions before despatch

---

Above all, keep thinking!

. . . 'Ah, take a letter, please, Miss Smith . . . Bombay Animal Supplies Ltd, etc . . . Dear Mr Singh comma subject-heading Order No. 8692 . . . Letter begins . . . Further to my order of 21st August 19— comma please supply comma in addition comma three elephants open bracket Indian close bracket comma two tigers open bracket striped close bracket comma three cobras with hoods if possible and two mongooses . . . er no, mongeese . . . No, start again . . . and one mongoose. Letter ends Yours etc . . . P.S. Please send another mongoose.' . . .

Style Examples

Don't

In view of the recent increase in postal rates and because of rising labour costs, a surcharge of 10% will be levied to cover the cost of postage and packing.

Although the holiday which you request is now fully booked, the latter holiday to which you refer is still on offer, together with Holidays 164 and 169 in our Sunny Days brochure, although the former is more expensive than the latter.

I trust this information will help you to make your choice.

The aerial to which you refer is no longer available from stock, since the radio was withdrawn six years ago. I suggest you try local stockists.

We are unable to deliver the goods you ordered before mid-July.

. . . but do

Keep it brief but polite

A 10% surcharge is, regrettably, payable on orders under £5.50 to cover postage and packing.

Keep it clear and simple

I regret to inform you that Holiday 161 is fully booked. You referred, however, to Holiday 179, which is still on offer, and I also strongly recommend Holidays 164 and 169 in our Sunny Days brochure. Of the three holidays, number 164 is more expensive, but features additional attractions . . .

Be helpful

The radio, model XL49, was withdrawn from our product range six years ago. I have located a spare aerial at our Oxford service depot, however, and have made arrangements for it to be posted to you c.o.d.

Be positive

The goods you ordered will be delivered by 16 July 199- at the latest.

Don't

. . . but do

Be persuasive

Our new range of wall-coverings are advantageously priced. We also supply on request our merchandiser free-of-charge.

Not only will our new range of wall-coverings give you a much better deal, the free-of-charge merchandiser ensures they sell themselves!

Avoid officialese

The extent of community charge for which residents are eligible is dependent upon the level of earnings in gainful employment.

The amount of community charge to which you are entitled depends on how much you earn.

Be tactful

I regret that I shall be unable to keep our appointment on 21 March 19—, as I have to see one of our larger account customers.

I am sorry to have to ask you if we may postpone our appointment for 21 March 19—, as a matter has arisen requiring my personal attention.

Remember the recipient

Dear Sir,

You application for a reduced-fare omnibus pass is awaiting process pending receipt of a photostat birth-certificate in compliance with public transport departmental regulation 46, our letter 16 June 19— ref. AT/TG refers.

Dear Sir,

I should be grateful if you would kindly send a photocopy of your birth certificate as soon as possible to enable us to send your reduced-fare pass by return of post.

Avoid clichés

We acknowledge receipt of yours of 15 January 19— re our new upholstery fabrics catalogue.

Thank you for your letter of 15 January 19—, in which you request our new upholstery fabrics catalogue.

Be courteous

I am obliged to inform you that your claim against warranty in respect of your hair-dryer cannot be met, since accidental damage lies outside the terms of the conditions laid down.

On receipt of £12.50 the company is prepared, without prejudice, to undertake the repair of your hairdryer, although it accepts no responsibility to ensure that such repairs are efficacious.

I am sorry to inform you that your claim against warranty for a replacement hair-dryer cannot be met, since upon inspection, it was discovered that the appliance had, apparently, suffered from accidental damage.

The company would, however, be most happy to undertake the repair of your hair-dryer at a nominal charge of £12.50. As I feel sure you will appreciate, however, such repairs do not carry our guarantee.

Avoid over-familiarity

Dear Sir,

Sorry we haven't been round yet to fix your TV. The van has been on the blink since Monday, and the service engineer is off with 'flu.

As you can imagine, things have been a bit tricky lately, but we hope to send someone round before Saturday.

Sorry about the waiting.

Yours truly,

Dear Sir,

Please accept my apologies for the delay in repairing your television set.

Our service engineer is ill with influenza, and the service van has suffered repeated breakdowns, now traced to an electrical fault.

Nevertheless I am very hopeful that a service engineer will be able to call before Saturday.

I hope the delay will not prove too inconvenient.

Yours faithfully,

Don't

. . . but do

Avoid irrelevance

Dear Sir,

I am writing to complain about the way I was treated by your counter-clerk last Thursday, when I came in to enquire about a tax rebate, to which I feel I am entitled, since I have been off work for the past three weeks, as a result of an industrial accident, which was occasioned by the negligence of a colleague, although I do not hold him personally responsible . . .

Dear Sir,

I wish to complain about the way I was treated by your counter-clerk when I came in on Thursday 14 April 19— to enquire about a tax rebate.

After a long, but admittedly unavoidable wait, I was curtly informed that . . .

Don't blame other people

Dear Mr Green,

I am sorry to have to advise you of the delay in delivery of your personal Ariel 2000 lap-top computer by next Wednesday as promised.

Unfortunately the Sales Department have lost your original order and efforts to find it at the company's Computer Centre have so far failed. . .

Dear Mr Green,

I am sorry to have to advise you of the delay in delivery of your Ariel 2000 lap-top computer by next Wednesday as promised.

Unfortunately there is a temporary delay in supply, but I am following up your order personally and will contact you as soon as possible . . .

Letter writing approach check-list

Don't

Allow a letter to become formless.

Lapse into long-windedness.

Allow the letter to become obscure or ambiguous.

Let the message become irrelevant or trivial.

Opt for jargon, officialese or deliberate complexity.

Ramble or 'butterfly' around the message.

Adopt a tone which is aloof, hostile, over-familiar, condescending or mixed with slang expressions.

Talk down to the letter's recipient or baffle him or her with inappropriate language.

Be vague or ineffectual, or overlook the action to be generated by the letter.

Ever allow a letter to degenerate into rudeness, sarcasm, offensiveness or tactlessness.

Allow the language to become stale, cliché-ridden or hypocritical.

Settle for a half-hearted or indifferent approach.

Allow a letter to be despatched which contains careless errors either in its composition or in the typescript.

Forget that a letter provides a written record – don't commit to paper what you may later regret having written.

Do

Keep the basic aims firmly in mind.

Plan the letter's points before starting to write or dictate.

Aim for brevity.

Ensure that ideas are clearly expressed.

Keep to the relevant points.

Prefer the simple to the complex.

Check that the message is logically structured.

Adopt a tone appropriate to the letter's aim.

Remember who will be receiving the letter and adopt the appropriate vocabulary, syntax etc.

Be positive.

Write a clear action statement or request.

Take care at all times to ensure that the letter is courteous and tactful.

Take trouble to keep the language fresh and sincere.

Use your powers of persuasion when it matters.

Check carefully for careless mechanical errors –
  spelling,
  punctuation,
  usage.

Remember that every letter is an ambassador.

Model letter: unsolicited sales circular

This unsolicited sales letter is typed in semi-blocked layout on a word processor

Home Insulation Service Ltd

Kingsway House Ealing Broadway London W7 5AQ

Telephone: 01-401 3986/9 Fax: 01-423 6761

Directors: J. Kent (Managing) P. Brown A. Wilson
Registered Office: Kingsway House Ealing Broadway London W7 5AQ
Registered Number: 846971 Registered in England

Mr and Mrs P Johnson
Crossways
The Green
Middleton
East Sussex MD4 6AK

Date as post-mark

Dear Mr and Mrs Johnson

       A SURE WAY YOU CAN SAVE MONEY THIS WINTER!

    Will your bank-balance get blown away by an 'over-draught' of cold air again at Crossways, The Green, Middleton this winter?

    Our research has proved that up to 30% of all money spent on home heating virtually goes up in smoke!

    The guilty culprits are ill-fitting, single-glazed windows and doors, poor insulation in the lofts and attics and exposed cavity walls.

    Can you afford to let yet another year go by with your heating bills far larger than they need be?

    Or will you be sitting pretty when winter winds rage, secure in the knowledge that your family, home and income are being protected by Home Insulation Service's unrivalled products?

    Our FREE expert advice and NO-OBLIGATION quotations are tailor-made to suit the insulation needs of YOUR home.

    Our policy specifically excludes high-pressure salesmanship and gives you a 7-day 'make-your-mind-up' period.

    Special low-interest credit facilities are also available to suit your pocket.

    ACT NOW! Ring 01 100 9000 free of charge and our specialist insulation consultant will arrange to visit your home when it suits you to give you an on the spot FREE QUOTATION!

    REMEMBER: Mr and Mrs Johnson a FREE phone-call now to 01 100 9000 could prove the wisest investment you ever made - and your family will love you for it all winter long!

            Sincerely
            John Grant

            JOHN GRANT
            SALES MANAGER
            HOME INSULATION SERVICES LTD

The entries shown in boxes are inserted by means of mailmerging WP techniques to personalise sales circulars.

Model letter: final collection letter

LANCASHIRE TYRE DISTRIBUTORS LTD

42 Warrington Road, Liverpool LW4 9RT
Telephone: 051-423 6934/5/6

Telex: 349764
Telegrams: Lancstyre L'pool

Registered Office:
42 Warrington Road,
Liverpool LW4 9RT
Registered No. 468973
Registered in England

Directors
A. Rowe (Managing)
F. Piercey
T. Rowlands
S. Wainwright

Ref: SGS/JB/ATC 16

14 May 19--

H. R. Baxter,
Proprietor,
Ajax Tyre Centre,
Stretford,
MANCHESTER.   MS14 3RF

Dear Sir,

OVERDUE ACCOUNT: £1492.43

In spite of the copy statement and reminders sent to
you on 3 April, 21 April and 7 May 19--, your account for
February 19-- totalling £1492.43 remains outstanding;
enclosed please find a final statement.

As previously stated, the period of credit extended to
your company was agreed as one calendar month from receipt
of statement.

Unless the above overdue account is settled in full
within seven days, I shall be compelled to instruct my
company's solicitors to undertake the necessary legal action
to recover the debt.

Yours faithfully,

S. G. Simmonds
Accounts Manager

enc.

This COLLECTION LETTER, the last of a series of three, is displayed in CENTRED
LAYOUT with CLOSED PUNCTUATION, as a mailmerged standard letter.

☐ Items which are inserted via word processing into a standard form letter of
collection according to the state of the individual customer's overdue account

```
                                                  46 Park Road
                                                  Hightown
                                                  Midshire  HT12 5MS


        12 September 199-


        Miss P Johnson
        Honorary Secretary
        Hightown Drama Club
        HIGHTOWN
        Midshire  HT4 2MS


        Dear Miss Johnson
```

(1) Thank you for your letter of 10 September 199- inviting me to act as stage manager for the Club's forthcoming production of 'South Pacific'.

(2) In your letter, you mention that rehearsals will take place on Wednesday and Friday evenings between 7 00 pm and 10 30 pm, and that the three weeks commencing 5 December 199- would be taken up with a week's rehearsals and a fortnight's production of the play.

(3) As you may be aware, I took a number of GCSE examinations last June and, unfortunately, failed the mathematics examination. As this particular subject is important to me, I have enrolled at Hightown College of Technology in an evening class on a Wednesday evening, leading to a resit examination at the end of November.

(4) Much as I would wish to accept your kind offer to act as stage manager, I feel I must decline, as I should not be able to carry out the responsibilities of the position as I would wish, and as the standards of the Club require.

(5) I should like to take this opportunity, however, of wishing the Club every success in the venture and shall certainly support it by helping with publicity and ticket sales.

Please let me know whom I should contact to help with the publicity.

(6) I look forward to hearing from you.

```
        Yours sincerely


        John Chandler

        John Chandler
```

Model letter saying 'No' nicely

Commentary

1 John Chandler puts his letter into a clear context by citing the prompt for his letter.

2 He leads into the detail of rehearsal times and dates as a 'soft' prelude to paragraph 3.

3 John emphasises his commitment to resitting his GCSE exams.

4 After a gentle build-up, John clearly but politely declines the invitation to act as stage manager, having supplied a valid reason.

5 He does not forget to wish the venture well nor to offer less demanding support.

6 He closes his letter on a positive note.

Talking point

In what ways is IT in offices likely to change letter writing and handling in the next ten years?

Summary of main points

1   The letterhead and logo play an important part in conveying an organisation's image; letterheads must also display legally required information about a company's registration and directors.

2   Most frequently used letter format styles are the fully blocked – all typescript entries start from the left-hand margin; and the centred or semi-blocked – some entries are centred on the notepaper.

3   Open punctuation discards virtually all punctuation marks outside the body of the letter; closed punctuation, characterised by line-end commas and full-stops is becoming obsolete.

4   Letter paper is manufactured to internationally agreed standards with A4 and A5 most commonly employed in the UK.

5   The Post Office's annually published *Post Office Guide* is a most helpful compendium of information about postal matters.

6   Conventions of styles of address for letter recipients and for opening and closing letters exist which must be carefully followed.

7   Many letters are produced in common categories – debt collection, complaint/adjustment, dicsiplinary, etc which follow accepted conventions of structure and style.

8   Most letters can be produced by following a simple three-point structure plan for devising beginning, middle and ending paragraphs.

9. An appreciation of the personality and role functions of the letter's recipient is essential for arriving at a suitable tone and style.

10   The IMPRESS plan is a useful aide-mémoire for letter production: Idea, Method, Paragraphs, Recipient, Emphasis, Style, Safety.

Activities and assignments _____

Quick review quiz

1 Make a checklist of the components of the printed letterhead.

2 Explain the role of trademarks and logos in corporate image-making and the business letter.

3 What components are required by law to be displayed on letterheads! Why?

4 Explain the main layout characteristics of:

a) fully blocked/blocked letter layout style
b) semi-blocked/centred letter layout style

5 Explain the difference between open and closed punctuation as used in letter production.

6 Set down your own home address according to Post Office preferred envelope addressing stipulations.

7 List the principal typescript components of the business letter.

8 Set down two acceptable ways of indicating an enclosure accompanying a letter, and that copies of it have been circulated.

9 Explain how 'Our' and 'Your' letter references are typically compiled and why they are included in letters.

10 What are the components of a continuation sheet reference?

11 List the various ways in which the intended recipient of a letter may be identified in the recipient's address.

12 Write down the salutation for Mr Rodney Charlton, who has just been knighted.

13 How do you address a business partnership whose partners are Gary Dixon and Gail Webb?

14 What is the running order sequence for letters after someone's name? Set the following down in the correct order:

Dip Tech Williams Joan OBE Mrs Ph D FRS B Sc

15 What subscriptions follow:

Dear Lady Wotherspoon
Dear Sirs
Dear Dr Brown
Dear Madam?

16 What action should be taken with correspondence arriving in envelopes marked: 'Personal', 'Private & Confidential' and 'Confidential'?

17 How has the widespread adoption of word processing software affected letter authoring and production and techniques during recent years? Give some examples.

18 Explain how a business letter is typically structured into three main parts.

19 Explain the structures which you would create in the following letters:

a) letter of complaint
b) letter of adjustment
c) letter imparting bad/disappointing news
d) unsolicited sales letter

20 What features would you look for in a good job application letter?

21 What characteristics of a letter's intended recipient have a bearing on the letter's style and tone?

22 List ten major style traps to be avoided in effective letter writing.

Case Study

Excelsior – for people on the move!

Mr Harold Langstone, Office Administration Manager of Tuffa Tools Limited, 14–16 Fordingley Road, Westport, Midshire WP12 5AG, is due to retire in four weeks' time.

As his assistant, you organised a 'whip-round' in the company's head office to purchase a suitable retirement gift for him. He has dropped broad hints that an overnight bag would be especially welcome, as he intends to spend the early months of his retirement visiting friends and relatives.

Accordingly, you bought an Excelsior Model XD overnight bag from Bags Galore, 32 High Street, Westport, Midshire WP3 2FD on March 2nd 19—. It cost £34.95 and was fully guaranteed for two years. When showing it to your office colleagues, the zip fastener jammed shut, and defied all efforts to ease it. On returning with the bag to Bags Galore, you were told by the shop assistant who had served you that they were unable to replace it, as it was the last one they had in stock and was referred to for the first time in your hearing as 'an obsolete model'.

The assistant suggested that you write to Excelsior Limited, Longmoor Road, Stoke-on-Trent, Staffordshire. Though sympathetic, the assistant informed you that she could not refund your money, but that you could expect Excelsior to supply an alternative bag through Bags Galore.

Preliminary assignment

Find out the legal position regarding your purchase of the overnight bag and what your legal rights are.

Main assignment

As a result of your investigations in the Preliminary Assignment, compose a letter using a simulated Tuffa Tools letterhead to the manager of the Bags Galore Westport branch outlining your experience and indicating how you would like the matter to be resolved.

As the manager of Bags Galore, write a letter answering the one received in the Main Assignment, indicating the action you are taking to adjust the complaint.

Follow-up assignments

1 Imagine that your principal has recently heard about a new lightweight lap-top computer marketed by 'Electronic Business Equipment Ltd', Queensway House, Great Russell Street, London WC1 3AQ, which embodies modem and printer ports together with fanfold and cutsheet feeds.

Write a letter to enquire about the availability, performance and cost of this machine. Provide a suitable letter-heading. Note that your company prefers to use the open punctuation blocked letter format.

2 Assume that you are Mr Peter Jones, Sales Manager of 'Electronic Business Equipment Ltd'. Write a letter which embodies an appropriate letterhead replying to the letter outlined in Question 1 above, providing a suitable recipient's address. Bear in mind that you have published a brochure advertising the Travelmate Lap-top Computer referred to above. Also, demand has greatly exceeded supply, and at present, there is a six weeks' waiting period for delivery. Your company has a nationwide sales force, and demonstration machines are available. Use the centred open punctuation format.

3 Your company recently purchased a beverage dispensing machine from Semperflo Beverages Ltd of Highdown Industrial Estate, Birmingham BS3 4RA. Since its installation it has repeatedly broken down, and your company has no alternative means of providing for coffee-breaks etc.

Write a letter of complaint with a suitable letterhead and preferred layout style.

4 As Sales Manager of Semperflo, you learned upon investigating the complaint outlined in Question 3 that the defect was caused by faulty installation by subcontractors whose services you no longer employ.

Write an appropriate letter of adjustment, with letter-heading, to redress the complaint, providing recipient details as necessary.

5 Write a final letter of collection to R J Hill Esq, BSc, Econ, ACMA, Accounts Manager of Maxi-Markets Ltd, whose head-office is at 14–18 Richmond Way, Edinburgh E14 6ST.

Maxi-Markets are a chain of retail supermarkets. Your company has been supplying their Newcastle branch with a range of delicatessen sausages. Your company is owed £436.13 in respect of purchases invoiced for the month of September 19—. Your letters are neither being acknowledged nor replied to.

Provide your letter with a suitable letter-heading and adopt an appropriate format and style.

6 Your company sells a range of double glazing units which are sold on a mail order basis.

Recently your company decided to adopt a change in policy by offering householders an opportunity to inspect your products by being ferried to local sales sites where they can inspect constructed sample windows.

Draft an unsolicited sales letter, embodying an appropriate letterhead, which actively promotes these points:

Your policy is to keep prices down by 'cutting out the middle man'.

Sales representatives are well-trained and able to demonstrate your products.

By returning in the envelope provided a detachable slip, customers can specify a date and time for representatives to call to collect them.

Design your letter so as to suit a WP mailmerge production using electoral roll names and addresses. You are making a special offer of a window-cleaning kit to all customers who reply within an appointed time.

You may add any additional supportive material. It may be helpful to collect and discuss a range of unsolicited sales letters before attempting this question.

7 Your company has employed Mr Fred Jenkins for the past 17 years. During that period, Mr Jenkins, who is well-liked in the company, has had a variety of jobs mostly of a handyman, storeman nature. Currently he is in charge of your mail-room, but recently his disability occasioned by injuries sustained during military service has worsened. His doctors have advised him that he should give up his job or run the risk of a severe deterioration in his health. He has a small disability pension, but is 58 years old, and male personnel in your company are not entitled to a pension until aged 65.

Mr Jenkins could be kept on in a part-time capacity if his health improved. Ex-gratia payments are at the managing director's discretion.

As personal assistant to the managing director, you have been asked by him to draft a suitable letter to Mr Jenkins, who is at home following a set-back. You have been told to use your discretion and submit the draft when the managing director returns from a visit.

8 Assume you are personal assistant to Mr Brian Smith, Sales Manager of South London Garages Ltd, a company with a chain of garages specialising in car sales and servicing, motor-accessory retailing, petrol trade and retail sales, and general parts and body-repair sales to the trade.

In six weeks' time your branch at Midchester is to be relocated at 8–16 Bedford Road, Midchester, Bucks ME12 2BG. Telephone: Midchester 4631/2.

The new premises afford the following advantages:

Showrooms for 15 new cars
Sales area for 50 used cars
Ample customer parking
A diagnostic centre
Large body repair shop

10 self-service petrol pumps
8 while-you-wait tyre, battery and exhaust fitting bays
A motor-accessory supermarket.

Write a circular letter:

a) to trade customers
b) to account customers

to advise them of the forthcoming relocation. You may add any additional material you consider justifiable.

Choose a format you think appropriate, supplying a letterhead and logo.

9 First re-read the letters on pages 116 and 117 concerning the delivery problems surrounding the five HMF Mk II Tourers. Assume now that you are Brian Smith's sales assistant. He has just received the letter from HMF's Peter Goodwright. In the same post an irate letter arrived from Brigadier Harold Warnscombe MC MSc of Long Acres, Blossom Crescent, Wimbledon SW4 6WS. In it he advises Brian Smith that, unless he receives his Moonlight Silver HMF Tourer within the next seven days, he can consider the order cancelled.

Brian Smith asks you to draft a suitable letter to Brigadier Warnscombe using your initiative in the circumstances, but to let him approve the draft prior to its despatch.

Having considered the situation carefully, compose a draft which you think most likely to prove successful.

10 Write a letter in support of your application for the post which you hope to obtain either at the end of your studies, or as your next appointment. Assume that your letter is accompanied by a completed form of application and a copy of your *curriculum vitae*.

Such letters are customarily hand-written.

11 General Pensions plc have just advertised in your local paper for temporary office assistants to help out during the summer vacation period. The pay is good and there are prospects of an eventual full-time post. They are looking for college/sixth form students who are computer literate, with good number and written English skills. You need some cash urgently for your own summer break. Write a suitable letter of application for one of the temporary posts.

12 Design a letter of collection to be sent to any library user who has books long overdue indicating the fines already accumulated and the action to be taken if the books are not returned in 7 days. Underline those parts of the letter which the word processing operator would need to insert individually in each letter.

Case studies

Gayglo burns fingers

In order to promote a new range of eye make-up, Gayglo Cosmetics Ltd recently placed a series of advertisements in women's magazines to offer a free mascara kit (brush, mascara disc and mirror in a plastic wallet) to all women ordering the new pack of Gayglo eye-liners, cost £6.50. The total cost value of the mascara kit was 75p on the basis of an order for 12,000 kits. Gayglo had anticipated a demand for some 12,000 kits and had budgeted some £9000 for the whole promotional venture. To Gayglo's consternation, however, more than 30,000 replies were projected on the basis of the initial level of demand. As the advertisements had already been published, there was no way of reducing the demand. To meet the demand for an additional 18,000 kits would mean that a loss would be incurred on the first production run of the eye-liners, since in making the original offer, Gayglo had banked on establishing repeat-purchases of the eye-liners. The company's directors reached a conclusion that their only solution was to refund the postage to the disappointed customers for their mascara kit orders, and to send out a form letter explaining the situation as tactfully as possible as orders came in.

In such circumstances should Gayglo have absorbed the cost of the additional kits to maintain its favourable public image?

Given the directors' decision, what should the form letter aim to do?

Could any mitigating factors be introduced? Draft an appropriate letter, either singly or in syndicate groups, which you think most suitable. Then discuss and justify your draft.

Trouble bubbles at the Cauldron

Recently production at the Cauldron Engineering Ltd's factory has been declining dramatically. The root of the trouble is a long history of industrial disputes. Both management and factory-workers have been to blame for the deteriorating relations which have left both sectors mutually hostile. Yesterday the board of directors held a meeting after unproductive consultations with the unions involved to try to find a peace formula. It was decided to send out a circular letter to all company personnel outlining the gravity of the situation. Unless a solution is made to work, large-scale redundancies seem inevitable, as the factory is losing money. The basis of the management offer is that, provided production is increased by 15% within four weeks and at least maintained at that level, the company would re-introduce overtime working, re-negotiate productivity bonus payments and make substantial investments in re-tooling, which is much needed.

What would be the letter's main aims? What tone should it adopt?

Draft an appropriate letter, either singly or in syndicate groups and then evaluate each version.

All in a good cause

You and three close friends in your class were very moved when you recently visited a local charity-run drug rehabilitation centre where you met people of your own age, as well as older addicts who were coming off hard drug addiction and beginning to make a fresh start to their lives. You were all impressed by their determination to overcome their addiction and to resume a worthwhile and normal life under their own control.

As a result, you decide to seek permission to mount a charity pop concert (or disco) at your school/college in order to raise funds for the centre's work. As part of the necessary planning and preparation, you need to compose the following letters:

1 A letter to the Principal/Headteacher of your college/school to seek permission to organise the charity event. Being a busy person, the principal/headteacher will want to be given a clear idea of what is involved – who, where, when, costs, break-even point on ticket sales, safety precautions, security, teaching/caretaking support, etc – in order to be able to make an informed decision.

2 A circular letter to local retailers, wholesale firms, banks and leading industrial companies seeking financial support in the shape of:

a) prizes for a Giant Raffle,
b) purchase of advertising space in your forthcoming pop concert programme (or disco newsletter),
c) donations to sponsor the running costs of the concert/disco or the purchase of equipment for the centre,
d) a letter of enquiry to your local pop group agent to find out what the fees would be to provide a suitable band (or disco outfit).

In groups of three or four, organise the authoring and production of the above series of letters and compare the strengths and weaknesses of your set with the others produced in your class.

Food for thought
Consider as a class undertaking a local charity project like that of the above case study for real, and not just as a simulation, carrying out all the administration and document creation yourselves as a by-product of helping some people in need.

Multi letter-writing assignment

Leisure Press Limited

Situation

The sales of *Home Hobbies*, a monthly magazine aimed at 'do-it-yourself' home improvers have slumped badly in recent months.

The magazine is written, printed and marketed by Leisure Press Ltd, 42 Regency Crescent, London SW1 4TD.

Home Hobbies is produced monthly and marketed by direct subscription to householders responding to unsolicited sales letters followed up by tele-sales calls from the company's representatives.

At present the 64-page magazine costs £18.50 per year and is supported by a wide range of advertising. The peak circulation nine months ago was 84 000 copies per issue.

The managing director is of the opinion that what is needed is some 'young blood and fresh ideas'.

Assignments

1 For the past two years Leisure Press Limited has used the services of the Grafix Advertising Agency. The Home Hobbies account is being managed by Mr Peter Cos, senior accounts manager. His address is:
Grafix Advertising Ltd
Grafix House
22 Hampstead Park Road
London
SW1 4TD

As assistant sales manager of Leisure Press, you have been requested to draft a letter for the sales manager, Mr John Lloyd's signature, expressing your dissatisfaction with the current unsolicited sales letter used to promote the sales of *Home Hobbies* to householders.

You would like Grafix to submit for your approval two specimen unsolicited sales letters, one for young, married house-owners, and another for established householders. You will need to outline your ideas clearly.

2 The management of Grafix takes the letter from Leisure Press (Home Hobbies Dept) very seriously, and the managing director calls a meeting to see if a 'brain-storming' session will come up with some new ideas for the unsolicited sales letters. Your group should simulate the meeting (syndicate groups may be used), produce two suitable drafts, and set them out with a suitable covering letter to Mr Lloyd.

3 For the past two years, you have been a regular subscriber to Home Hobbies. Unfortunately, for the past six months delivery of your copies has been late and two copies never arrived. On another occasion, an 'enclosed' free gift of a tape-measure was not included.

Write a letter of complaint to the sales manager of the Home Hobbies Department at the London address, outlining your complaint and what you would like done to remedy it.

4 As sales manager of Home Hobbies Department of the Leisure Press Ltd compose an answer to a letter you have received from the customer making the above complaint. The problem has arisen because of staff turnover in your despatch section. Conditions of service have now been improved.

5 Compose an appropriate letter of application in response to the following:

ASSISTANT SALES MANAGER required by LEISURE PRESS LIMITED for *Home Hobbies* Magazine Dept.

Energetic, well-educated young person with business administration ability needed to assist sales manager of successful magazine. Top conditions and excellent salary for right applicant. Drive and ideas more important than experience. Suit college/school leaver.

Apply in writing to:
The Personnel Manager
Leisure Press Limited
42 Regency Crescent
London
SW1 4TE

The above letters should include letterheads and may be composed either by individuals or by syndicate groups. The assignment should conclude with a group evaluation and analysis session.

Case study

Launching tasties at Savoury Snax

You work in the advertising unit of Savoury Snax Limited's marketing department. The company is to launch a new product in two month's time – a potato-based chip, coated with Chinese Chicken Tika, Hungarian Goulash or Mexican Taco flavourings.

Currently, Savoury's customers – freehouse pubs, newsagents, clubs, leisure centres, grocery chains, etc – are structured in three tiers or groupings, depending upon the levels of discount they are given, which in turn relies upon their turnover and order sizes and their ability to break their own bulk to minimise your distribution costs.

In order to support the launch of the new snack, to be called 'Tasties', Savoury will give away the following:

- initial orders over 50 000 packets: a stacking hi-fi stereo system with CD play: value £250.00
- initial orders over 25 000 packets: a stereo mains/battery driven portable radio: value £120.00
- initial orders over 15 000 packets: a ladies hair-care curling and drying kit: value £75.00 or gentleman's electric razor/toothbrush travelling kit: value £75.00

Further, the launch is to be supported by four free sales promotion merchandising point-of-sale packs, which have been designed specifically to meet the needs of each of the following types of outlet:

a) grocery/general store
b) public house/club
c) leisure/sports centre
d) newsagent/confectioner

Thus an especially designed pack is available for each of Savoury's type of customer entitled:

a) Take Away Some Tasties Today!
b) Enjoy Some Tasties With Your Drink!
c) Build Back Your Energy With Tasties!
d) There's Always Time For A Pack Of Tasties!

Finally, Savoury will be delivering first consignments as follows:

Retail outlets: week commencing 10 April 199-
Clubs/leisure centres: week commencing 24 April 199-

Savoury is suggesting a sales price for individual packs of 19p and for family six-packs of 99p.

The Tasties will be available from one of six regional distribution depots – you have details of each depot manager, telephone numbers and addresses etc.

Assignments

1 In pairs, design a suitable letterhead and logo for Savoury Snax Limited, whose head office and registered office are at: Savoury Snax House, 136–142 Bolton Road, Stretford Park Industrial Estate, Manchester M 14 3ED. You should devise suitable telecommunications numbers and addresses, and seek to convey an image appropriate to a snack-food enterprise.

2 Compose a customer sales/briefing letter for production on word processing software which will:

a) promote Tasties suitably for *each* of the four categories of Savoury's customers,
b) prove suitable for mailmerging from master and non-document source files which incorporate the data shown above.
   Indicate in your mailmerged mailshot draft the spaces for displaying the interchangeable items of data you select, and what information is to go into what spaces,
c) promote the appropriate free gift offers associated with the launch,
d) provide clear details on how orders may be placed in order to qualify for the free gift promotion.

Note: Your mailmerge master must be capable of being sent to a large, medium or small customer in each of the A-D client groups, addressed and directed to the owner/manager personally.

On completion, compare your draft letter with those produced by your classmates, and decide together what constitutes the key data to be imparted by the letter, and what data should be inserted for each, different type of customer.

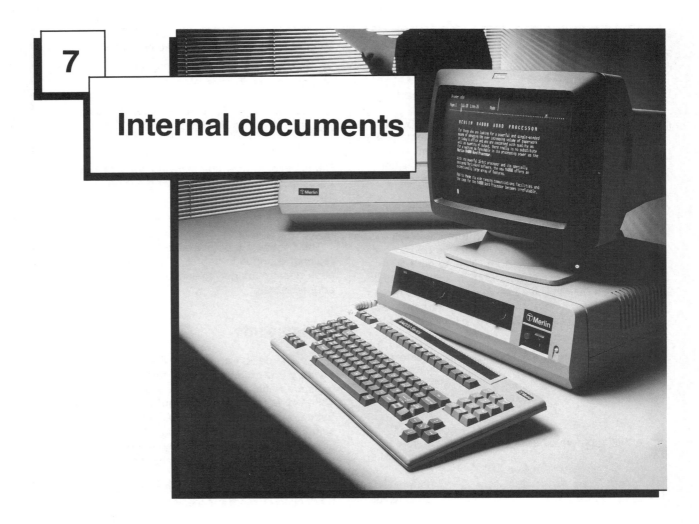

7

Internal documents

Overview

Unit 7 provides you with information and guidelines on:

- Current conventions and practices for composing and routing memoranda (see Unit 11 for LAN networked Email memoranda treatment).
- Guidelines on devising suitable structures and styles in memoranda composition with examples and models.
- Tips on effective memoranda handling.
- How to design effective notices.
- Current conventions and practices for composing formal and informal reports with examples and specimens of each major type.
- Explanation of report referencing systems and schematic layout techniques.
- Guidelines on structuring reports and creating suitable styles.
- How to produce effective summaries, precis and abstracts.
- How to devise factsheets with appeal and impact.
- How to create effective and attractive forms.

The memorandum

Components

The memorandum carries out functions very similar to those of the letter, save that it is restricted to internal organisational use. Thus many of the tips and guidelines you have picked up in studying the format, presentation and structure of the letter may be applied to the memorandum. There remain, however, a number of features of effective memorandum creation and distribution to be mastered.

Internal document routes

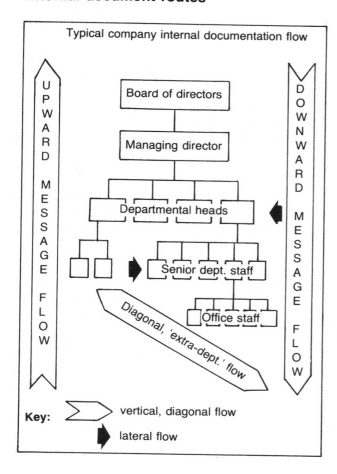

Typical company internal documentation flow

UPWARD MESSAGE FLOW

DOWNWARD MESSAGE FLOW

Board of directors

Managing director

Departmental heads

Senior dept. staff

Office staff

Diagonal, 'extra-dept.' flow

Key: vertical, diagonal flow

lateral flow

Pre-printed components

Just as the letter contains a number of pre-printed letterhead items, so the memorandum is generally printed either in A4 or A5 single sheets or in pads with the following components in general use: memorandum (heading), to, from, subject, date and reference.

The order and location of such components varies according to preferred house style but sufficient space is allocated for the identity of the memorandum's recipient(s) and author to be inserted, as well as the date and a subject title for the memorandum. A memorandum with the 'memohead' components entered in typescript is shown on page 136.

Typescript components

Just as there are conventions regarding forms of address in letters, so there are in memoranda. Again, these vary according to custom and practice in different organisations and the degree of formality of the memorandum:

Addressing the recipient

It is common practice to address a memorandum's recipient by his or her job title only, such as manag-

ing director or south east regional manager or assistant personnel officer. Sometimes authors include the person's name as well: John Brown, Managing Director. But this approach can become too long, given the limited space in which to type in a memohead. Some memos are sent to 'Susan Williams, Accounts Department', where the recipient has no obvious title, but is one of, say, eight accounts clerks.

Many memos are sent to groups or teams of staff – 'To All sales representatives' or 'To Production Department Personnel'.

Author's styles of title

The same approach is used for the insertion of the author's job title – perhaps with name – 'From Public Relations Manager' or 'From Jean Robinson, Marketing Manager'.

The date and subject-heading

The conventions of entering the date on a memorandum are just the same as those for the letter, and so also for the memorandum's subject-heading, with the proviso that it is always a help to provide a reference if appropriate, eg 'SUBJECT OFFICE EQUIPMENT REQUISITION: ORDER NO HA14362'. This allows the recipient to cross-check quickly to an original requisition order. Similarly the author/text creator reference is useful in a subject-heading: 'Subject Resignation of Miss Carol Peters (HJK/AWC 3 June 199-). It is always good practice in letter and memorandum subject-headings to keep them short, while communicating clearly and accurately their content.

Enclosure, copy, circulation

For showing enclosures, copies, circulation, continuation sheets and references, the same conventions apply as for the letter and will vary according to the house style preferred. An important point to note in copying a memorandum is that *all* interested parties must be given action or information copies. Executives feel they have lost face if left 'out of the picture' (however accidentally), having been omitted from a copy list.

The body of the memorandum

A fully-blocked or indented paragraph format may be employed (but consistently) and the same guidelines about paragraph titles appearing either blocked or centred, with initial capital letters and underscoring, etc, will apply.

Here, a useful guideline is to keep paragraphs

short and to aid the reader with 'summarising headings' if the memorandum's message is long and wide-ranging. (Some reports may be set out on A4 memorandum paper with continuation sheets and incorporate a suitable report format.)

How to handle memoranda effectively

There are a number of good reasons why memos are created and distributed within organisations:

Written records

They provide a written record — to act as a memory-jogger on a person's desk, to be stored for future reference, or to convey information which needs to be absorbed and returned to at intervals.

Communication aids

They help (through the copying system) to keep team members or interested staff informed of decisions and developments.

They also act as devices through which to issue instructions simultaneously to groups of often widely separated personnel.

Feedback channels

They provide feedback to managers by confirming, for example, sales for the month of July, the acquisition of a major new client or the success of a programme of staff development.

Memorandum checklist of components

A4 memorandum

```
              COURIER TRAVEL LIMITED
                     Memorandum

STRICTLY CONFIDENTIAL

To    Personnel Manager            Ref   CW/VF

From  Home Sales Director          Date  24 October 19--


Subject  Miss Kay Parkinson, Sales Department

Miss Parkinson has been employed by Courier Travel for just over three
years, during which time she has proved a loyal and conscientious
employee.  For the past two months she has been reporting to Jim
Weaver, our Adventure Holiday Coordinator.

From the outset, there has been a regrettable clash of personalities
which I have been unable to resolve.  Today Miss Parkinson requested a
personal interview with me to express her unhappiness with the current
situation, and I promised I would do all I could to put matters right.

I should therefore be grateful if you would kindly arrange to see Miss
Parkinson as a matter of urgency in order to explore the possibility
of a departmental transfer or other opportunity from which she and the
company might benefit.

Also, I should be grateful if you would find an early opportunity to
discuss with Jim Weaver how he is finding his new post, as I am
beginning to think that the problem with Kay Parkinson may be
symptomatic of difficulties he is experiencing but not admitting to.

I enclose a copy of the appraisal recently carried out for Kay
Parkinson, and you will see that the agreed summary shows her in a
very good light.  I should be most sorry if the company were to lose
her services.

enc


cc Marketing Director
```

1 Memohead components: from, to, date, reference, subject,

   Check names, job titles and references are correct

2 Ensure subject heading is sufficiently clear and detailed

3 Memorandum body (keep A5 messages short and avoid going too far down A5 sheets)

4 Check before despatch for manager's 'OK to issue' initials

5 Remember enclosure references

6 Ensure all who are supposed to receive them are sent copies. Check if any blind copy is required and indicate who received it on manager's retained file copy as 'bcc'

7 Do not forget continuation sheet reference on A4 memorandum if a second page is required

How to structure effective letters and memoranda

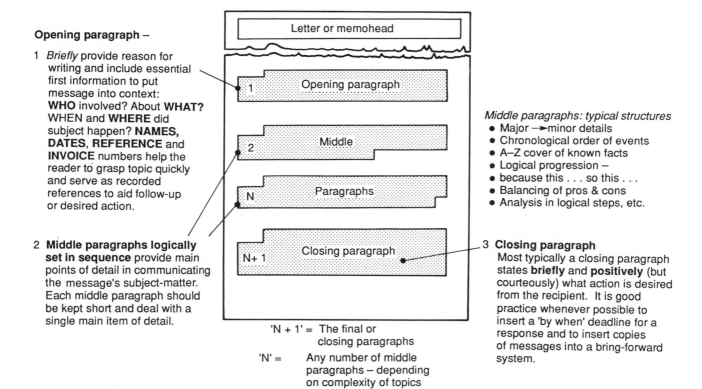

Opening paragraph –

1 *Briefly* provide reason for writing and include essential first information to put message into context: **WHO** involved? About **WHAT**? **WHEN** and **WHERE** did subject happen? **NAMES, DATES, REFERENCE** and **INVOICE** numbers help the reader to grasp topic quickly and serve as recorded references to aid follow-up or desired action.

2 **Middle paragraphs logically set in sequence** provide main points of detail in communicating the message's subject-matter. Each middle paragraph should be kept short and deal with a single main item of detail.

Middle paragraphs: typical structures
- Major →minor details
- Chronological order of events
- A–Z cover of known facts
- Logical progression –
- because this . . . so this . . .
- Balancing of pros & cons
- Analysis in logical steps, etc.

3 **Closing paragraph**
Most typically a closing paragraph states **briefly** and **positively** (but courteously) what action is desired from the recipient. It is good practice whenever possible to insert a 'by when' deadline for a response and to insert copies of messages into a bring-forward system.

'N + 1' = The final or closing paragraphs

'N' = Any number of middle paragraphs – depending on complexity of topics

---

> **A word to the wise**
> *Always remember* – the memorandum, once in print and despatched, (like the letter) cannot be retrieved for second thoughts, because it should not be as curt, impatient, grudging or sarcastic, etc. So be on your guard against sending out memoranda that you may later regret having sent!

Tips on effective memorandum handling

As you can see, the memorandum is a very important item in the organisation's communication toolbox. As an effective administrator, you should therefore absorb these tips into your daily memorandum-handling routines:

- **Despatch the memorandum promptly.** Just because memos are an internal form of communication does not mean that they are never urgent.

- **Always provide current and correct names and job titles of recipients and room/office locations** – a sloppy approach here may cause a vital message to become lost or delayed. If you work in an organisation which produces internal personnel directories at regular intervals, make sure you receive your copy and make the time to scan it for changes.

- **Adopt a helpful filing method.** For example, some organisations employ various coloured copy papers where a given colour will convey:
  For action, For information only, Departmental file copy.
  Also, where you are likely to want to follow up and progress-chase a despatched memorandum, make sure you include it in your bring forward system *well before a given deadline* and don't always wait to be asked to do so.

- **Avoid leaving copy memoranda for filing in a growing stack of papers.** You may have to refer to a particular memorandum urgently, if for example, your manager phones you to discuss its contents.

- **Always ensure draft memoranda are so labelled and clearly dated and numbered,** eg Draft 3 and that your office's staff are all working on current drafts.

- **Never despatch a sensitive memorandum without first giving yourself a chance to see it in print after an elapsed interval.** Its content may have been dictated in a fit of impatience or frustration and second thoughts are often the best ones. Many managers – and their secretaries – have got on by knowing which memoranda were exercises in venting frustration, etc, and best consigned to the shredder! In this area some secretaries and managers operate a system where the manager initials each memorandum before despatch as part of the post-signing routine. If file copies also display such initialling, then there is no room for doubt as to whether the manager wished the memorandum to go out.

- **Make sure support staff know if a given memorandum is to be designated confidential or personal**. And use envelopes accordingly. Never deliver such memoranda as open versions for all to read.

- **Message as notice or individual memorandum to group?** Decide which is more appropriate before drafting.

- **Provide dated deadlines for required actions and responses**. Avoid including action requests in a memorandum like:

'Please let me have your completed returns *as soon as possible*:
or 'I shall be pleased to receive your response *in due course*'

For some staff such indefinite action requests tend to be translated as 'mañana' and we all know 'tomorrow never comes!'

Memoranda and electronic mail

Increasingly memos are being created in the medium of electronic mail messages which are instantly despatched to the workstations of intended recipients.

The normal trend in offices is for such messages to be keyed in very much like the spoken word:

'OKI DOKI! I'll check into it and come back to you in a jiff!'

Such electronic mail 'notes' tend to be very short-lived and are wiped off a networking system after a few days or a month as a matter of custom. Sometimes, however, electronic mail messages are important and are kept on electronic file for a considerable time.

It is therefore important for the effective administrator to be conscious all the time of the status of various Email messages and to adopt a suitable style and tone. Also, where paper memos are in use, much more time is available to reconsider a memo and to destroy it unsent. The speed of electronic mail delivery – and its potential for instant reading and wide distribution – make it vital to avoid sending ill-considered or aggressive Email notes or messages!

Specimen Email memo sent to Mr Smith over a LAN office system (IBM's PROFS)

```
Unclassified              Page 1              7 April 19--


FROM :    ALISON GEORGE

TO:       M R SMITH

SUBJECT:  MANAGEMENT SUPPORT MEETING


Following the meeting on 5 April 19XX, although your area has no specific
actions due, I should be grateful if you would continue to attend the
meetings for a further two months until we are sure problems will not
recur.

Thank you.


ALISON GEORGE
Communications Officer
D.220  26/32 extn 721-4943
HVTVM2(AGEORGE)

AG:JS
```

Note: Entries are keyed in against displayed 'prompts'.

(Reproduced by kind permission of IBM (UK) Ltd)

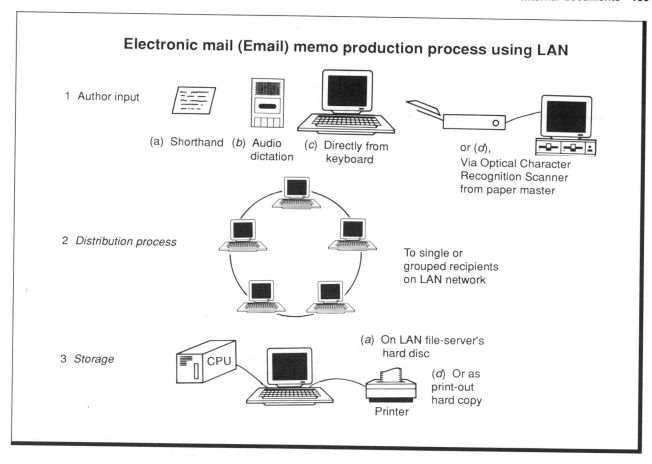

Electronic mail (Email) memo production process using LAN

1 Author input

(a) Shorthand (b) Audio dictation (c) Directly from keyboard or (d), Via Optical Character Recognition Scanner from paper master

2 *Distribution process*

To single or grouped recipients on LAN network

3 *Storage*

CPU

(a) On LAN file-server's hard disc

(d) Or as print-out hard copy

Printer

Advantages of emailing memos

- High speed despatch-receipt cycle
- Direct input from keyboard
- Virtually instant despatch/receipt monitoring of arrival and opening
- Simultaneous distribution to pre-selected groups
- Instant response possible
- Reports, factsheets, disk files etc can be appended to Email memos
- Excellent security from access restrictions
- Ideal for split-site communication

Talking point

Does the 'paper memo' possess any advantages over its Email Counterpart?

Written confirmation

Perhaps the most important single aspect of the memorandum's application lies in its provision of a *written* record (for retention, future reference, circulation etc.) of previously conducted oral communications – conversation, telephone calls, meetings, informal corridor encounters and so on.

It is therefore essential that the content of the memorandum in such circumstances is factual accurate, unambiguous, devoid of inference or 'sideswipes' and fair to quoted third parties.

Memoranda and style

The dictates of context

The style of memoranda varies enormously. Directives, for example, from a managing director or chief executive may be couched in formal, depersonalised terms and delivered with all the crisp authority of a laser printer. On the other hand, hasty, handwritten messages produced on a 'memo-pad' and passed to a colleague's desk may be written in a much more personalised and familiar language.

Copy to: The Reader – for future action. 'Memos and all other documents should always bear dates and initials. One of my colleagues once spent a twelve-hour night working on an undated document which turned out not to be the current draft. Why he was not convicted of mayhem remains a mystery.'

Robert Townsend, *Up the Organisation*

Talking point

In what circumstances should the spoken word be preferred to a written memo or report, and vice versa?

Factors affecting style

The style of the language in which the memorandum is couched depends very much upon the following:

1 The context of the message – a crisis, congratulation, reprimand, routine order etc.

2 The status, personality or background of the recipient – high/low position in organisation, higher education, practical background etc.

3 The nature of the message – factual, informational, congratulatory, persuasive, soliciting, requiring etc.

4 The urgency or priority of any action needed – crisis, routine re-stocking order, need for liaison or cooperation, instructions for all staff etc.

Appropriateness

In such varying situations the mechanics of the style will be different:

1 Syntax – sentence length may be longer or shorter, may include or exclude subordinate clauses or phrases.
2 Vocabulary – the choice of words will vary enormously: some may be complex technical or specialist words or phrases, others may be deliberately factual, devoid of emotive overtones (in an explosive situation), still others may be engaging and familiar in a persuasive role.
3 Tone and nuance – the shades of meaning, or connotations given to the messages's component parts will differ, depending on whether the message is factual or persuasive, the situation is 'fraught' or routine, the recipient responsive or obstructive.

Reaching the recipient

The style of the memorandum is also very much dependent upon the kind of recipient:

1 Fellow specialist 'in the know' – understands specialist, 'jargon' terminology.
2 Peer group – colleague(s) among whom is an unconstrained familiarity and directness.
3 Junior personnel – where the difference in authority, experience and 'reports-to' situation affects the way in which a communication is made.

4 Range of staff within hierarchy extending from senior to junior levels, where age, experience, background require a 'consensus' style approach avoiding obscurity, condescension or a patronising tone.

Talking point

How important are tone and style in memoranda? Why is it that the style of Email memos tends to be more colloquial and informal than paper memos?

Message situations

The choice of either subjective or objective language or a mixture of both will also be decided by the nature of the memorandum:

1 Informing – where the message may confirm a revised discount, call a meeting or raise an order.
2 Directing – where action requirements are 'passed down the line' (persuasion may also be needed here to secure active cooperation).
3 Requesting – where there is no 'line-control' and colleagues may need 'wooing' for their help.
4 Motivating – where senior management needs, perhaps, to boost morale, exhort or persuade in engaging, motivating terms.
5 Suggesting – where junior executives attempt to 'sell' an idea to busy, sceptical seniors.
6 Confiding – where closely-working executives exchange highly personalised information informally and directly.

One last word – please!

No reference to style would be complete without mention of a simple, short word which matters so much when the cooperation of colleagues is sought: 'Please'. It pays ample dividends to remember that courtesy – even to long standing colleagues – is *always* important:

'Would you please ensure that I receive your report by the 21 March 19—.'

Talking point

Electronic messaging is expanding in organisations at a fast rate. Are there any communication pitfalls in switching exclusively to electronic messaging in your view?

Models for analysis

Jim Grainger is a good salesman – he could sell ice to eskimos – but when it comes to routine admin, Jim is a laggard! Despite exhortations at a recent Area Sales meeting, he still isn't submitting his weekly reports on time.

Which of the following alternatives do you think his Area Sales Manager should send to Jim to motivate him to meet his Monday deadline? What criticisms can you make of the memoranda you reject? Or are they all inappropriate?

A

Further to the Area Sales Meeting of 13th May 199-, you are reminded of my reference to punctuality in despatching weekly sales reports, especially now that you have access to the Company's Local Area Network. This reference was occasioned by the need for the efficient compilation of Area Sales figures, Head Office statistics and Company Bonus Scheme returns.

I note, however, that I am still not receiving your returns Emailed by 10.00 am on Mondays. Unless your performance improves, I shall be compelled to take the matter further.

B

At our last Area Sales Meeting on 13th May 199-, I stressed the need for all sales representatives' weekly sales reports to reach me by mid-morning on Mondays.

You will recall that I emphasised the importance of using our Local Area Network to send in weekly reports on time, not only to allow me to appraise the area sales situation, but also for our Head Office to produce national sales turnover statistics and monthly bonuses.

I should, therefore, be grateful if you would ensure that your weekly sales report is Emailed to my office in time for me to deal with The Area Sales Report without delay.

C

At our last Area Sales Meeting on 13th May 199-, I mentioned how important it was for your weekly sales report to reach me via the Local Area Network early on Mondays. My own sales picture, company sales figures and the monthly bonuses all rely on my receiving sales representatives' reports in good time.

Your own territory is playing an important part at the moment in our area sales recovery programme, and for this reason I am relying on you to send me those figures by 10.00 am on Mondays, so that I can finalise my own report to Head Office.

I know you won't want to hold up my report unnecessarily, and I set too much store by your ability and enthusiasm to feel that I need to remind you again.

D

I'm concerned about not receiving your weekly sales report on time. You remember I raised the problem at our last Area Sales Meeting on 13th May 199-, and told everyone how important it was to send in their reports to me on the LAN as soon as possible on Mondays.

Well, I don't seem to be receiving yours until Tuesday or Wednesday, and so I'm held up in sending my own report to Head Office, giving our own situation and supplying information for our overall sales and bonus scheme.

It would certainly help me on a Monday, if I had your figures along with everyone else's. I know I can rely on you to rally round,

Keep up the good work!

Talking point

What do you think Robert Townsend is driving at in his book *Up The Organisation* when he refers to 'memo warfare'? What actions and attitudes should be adopted to avoid it?

Designing an effective notice

While the letter and memorandum tend to receive more attention in examining internal communications within organisations, the importance of the notice is not to be undervalued. As part of a staff noticeboard, it has an important part to play in interpersonal communication. All too often, however, it happens that no one is delegated to keep the noticeboard tidy and up-to-date, with the result that notices in some firms are seen to be frayed, yellowing, pinned haphazardly on top of others so that their entire credibility suffers and staff ignore them. Given an efficient treatment, however, the internal notice can provide an inexpensive and prompt means of disseminating certain types of information, usually that which affects significant proportions of staff, which is not confidential and which does not need to guarantee notice and assimilation by everyone.

Notices may take on a range of formats, from the extra copy of an A5 memorandum affixed to the noticeboard to an especially printed version on coloured paper including an element of graphics design.

Essential features

Whatever the intention of the notice, its designer should keep the following production guidelines firmly in mind:

- Make sure the paper size is large enough for the message but not so large as to swamp the noticeboard. People will have to read the text from a distance of 2–3 feet and will not bother with tiny, cramped wording.
- Give it a sufficiently bold and clear set of headings to arrest the attention of its intended recipients:
  ATTENTION ALL SQUASH LOVERS!
  and to convey its title:
  JOIN OUR NEW AEROBICS CLUB NOW!
- Keep the text of the notice short, sharp and to the point, avoiding long-winded constructions and lengthy words – the art is to impart the message as quickly, clearly and simply as possible.

```
                    ATTENTION ALL OPERA BUFFS


            EVENING PERFORMANCE OF DON GIOVANNI BY W A MOZART
                      FESTIVAL THEATRE KENT OPERA
                      7.30 P.M. THURSDAY 14 JUNE 19--


        An amazing group discount deal has been struck with the Festival Theatre management
for the single performance of Mozart's Don Giovanni being performed by the excellent
touring company of Kent Opera.  This is a traditional production in beautiful costumes with
classic sets.

        The performance starts at 7.30 p.m. prompt and is scheduled to finish at about
10.45 p.m.  Afficionados will recall the splendid review this production received in last
Sunday's 'Despatch'.

        Tickets cost £6.50 each and are available from:

            Maureen Connolly
            Accounts Department
            Ext:   234

        SUPPLIES ARE LIMITED SO DON'T MISS YOUR CHANCE TO ENJOY THIS
                   MARVELLOUS PRODUCTION


Sue Jones, Social Club Secretary                              28 May 19--

    Authorised:   K. Jones
                  Communications Officer

    Display from:  28 May to 14 June
```

- Make sure the notice indicates clearly what the recipients should do if any action is needed and who – name, job title and telephone extension – the contact person is to obtain forms or further details from.
- The notice should be 'topped and tailed' with the date of its composition, the name and designation of its author and, as appropriate, the signature of the person authorising its display.

Note that in some organisations each notice is given a display life period entered on it: 'Display from 1 June 19-- to 14 June 19--.' Then the person maintaining the board knows when to get rid of outdated notices.

The example on page 142 illustrates these main points.

The report

The commission and production of reports plays a crucial part in achieving the goals which organisations set themselves. The more important decisions become, whether about people, finance or production, the more it is likely that specialist reports will be required by decision-makers to ensure that the process of decision-making is informed, impartial and considered.

The popular concept of a report is of a long, schematically set-down document, full of 'paras' and 'sub-paras', punctuated by references such as 'B4 (iii) d', and it is true that some complex reports do require a logical referencing system. The format and methods of reporting are, however, many and varied, both spoken and written, and produced in a number of different contexts.

The range of reporting may be illustrated by the following two examples:

Situation one

Susan Spicer, personal assistant to the Sales Manager, Mr Jones, has just emerged from a meeting on administering a new bonus scheme. By chance, she encounters her principal, the Sales Manager.

'How did the meeting go, Susan?' she is asked. What follows will be an orally communicated report which synthesises the main features of the meeting as Susan saw them.

As the example on page 144 illustrates, Susan displays the care and attention which she devoted to her role of substitute at the meeting.

She follows the order of the items discussed at the meeting and dispenses with those parts which she does not think sufficiently important – so she is having to use her judgement as she goes along, selecting only the main and relevant points as she sees them in the context of Mr Jones' and the sales department's needs and interests. Susan also structures her oral report to proceed from the most important to the least important – she realises that Mr Jones is a busy man and has no time for trivia. In addition, she is particularly careful to ensure that Mr Jones is made aware of action which is shortly expected of him, particularly since the instructions come from a representative of top management, Mr Jackson. Lastly, Susan checks that no further action is expected from her, so that she may dispose of the meeting, as it were, in her mental checklist of 'matters outstanding', and move on to the next job.

Classification and context

1 Regular and routine reports
equipment maintenance report
sales report
progress report
safety inspection report
production report etc.

2 Occasional reports
accident report
disciplinary report
status report etc.

3 Especially commissioned reports
investigatory report
market-research report
staff report (personnel)
market forecasting report
product diversification report
policy-changing report etc.

Logic not magic!

There is nothing magical about the ability to deliver effective oral reports. The secret is to listen alertly as a participator in all office business, to make careful notes, to develop a clear memory, and to practise delivering information in a fluent, organised and logical sequence.

Talking point

'I don't know why people make so much fuss about writing reports. When you've submitted them people either don't read them at all, or they simply ignore the recommendations in favour of their own prejudices!' What steps should senior managers take to avoid this kind of criticism?

Example of an oral report

Susan Spicer, giving an oral report of a departmental managers' meeting she attended in place of her boss, Mr Jones, Sales Manager.

'As you requested, Mr Jones, I sat in on yesterday's meeting for you, which Mr Jackson (Deputy Managing Director) chaired. Only the production manager couldn't attend.

'Matters were very much routine until Item 5 on the Agenda – "Proposal to form a Training Department." Mr Jackson set out the background which you know about. One important development has taken place, though, that affects us directly. It seems that the budget won't stretch to building a new training centre, so we're likely to be asked to give up our storage rooms on the ground floor. However, the main point was that all the departmental heads are in favour – Mrs West submitted a summary of production's views. Mr Jackson asked the Personnel Manager to submit a detailed scheme for discussion at the next meeting. Heads were asked to submit suggestions to Mr Jackson by next Wednesday.

'There wasn't anything else particularly important, except that the introduction of the staff holiday rota arrangements were given the go-ahead.

'Under Any Other Business, Mrs Davidson complained about the poor response to the forthcoming Social Club Dance, so I've asked Julie to do her best to sell some more tickets.

'I think that was about it. Is there anything you'd like me to follow up?'

How Susan structured her oral report:

Clear beginning At the outset, Susan confirms those present and who chaired the meeting.

Development of essential and relevant points in the middle Aware of the scope of Mr Jones' interest, Susan skips over some early items of no relevance to the sales department – her report selects the particularly relevant points.

Confirmation of action Mr Jones must take himself She anticipates those areas in which her boss must make a response and provides the key details, and deadlines.

Descent to more minor points Susan also confirms that action may now be taken on the rota system.

Confirmation of conclusion and request for further instructions arising from the meeting Nearing the end of her report, which has gone through the same sequence as the meeting's business items, Susan relays details of action she has taken on her own initiative. She closes by asking if there is anything further she should do arising from the meeting.

Situation two

Later the same day, Susan is called into the Sales Manager's office:

'I'm worried about the steady fall in sales turnover at our Bournemouth branch, Susan. You'd better have a thorough look at the situation, get down there and let me have a report on what's gone wrong and how we put it right. Oh, and I'll need it by next Wednesday. I'll write to put the Regional Sales Manager in the picture.'

Such orally communicated instructions, or 'terms of reference' define the limits within which Susan may act, and are usually confirmed in a memorandum. Having collected and classified the information, Susan will present it to the Sales Manager as a written report to assist her principal in making a decision – whether to close the branch, redeploy staff or institute a hard-hitting advertising campaign.

In addition to the orally-delivered or detailed, investigatory reports, there are numerous routine reports the formats of which are designed to allow information to be inserted into boxes following questions or to permit a tick or cross to show a 'satisfactory/unsatisfactory' message. Such 'check-list' reporting systems save time and simplify routine reporting procedures.

Format

The format of written reports varies considerably. Some may run to hundreds of pages, such as those produced by Royal Commissions, others may be quite short and set-out on an A4 memorandum sheet. Some may be produced as a succession of paragraphs of continuous prose, while others may be displayed under a series of headings and sub-headings with lists, tables and diagrams.

The table on page 145 indicates some of the principal contexts and forms in which reporting takes place.

The choice of format for a report is most important. Therefore, before producing his report the report-writer should decide carefully which layout will best relay his message.

In some circumstances the powers of persuasion and emphasis of a direct oral report may outweigh the advantages of producing a written document – particularly when a time-factor is an over-riding consideration. Similarly, when more than one recipient is concerned, a report may best be delivered orally at a meeting, where the information may easily be verified, confirmed, questioned and examined.

Talking point

The production of an extended report is often dubbed 'the most demanding task a manager is expected to fulfil'. Why do you think this should be so?

Reporting applications

Messages in letters or memoranda

Oral briefings or reporting back

Minutes of meetings

Routine 'check-list' reports

Progress reports – architects' site meetings

Annual reports to shareholders

Profiles of candidates for interview

Sales reports

Newspaper reports/news releases

Technical reports

Balance sheets for annual audit

Statistics in various visual formats

In many situations, however, the sheer wealth and complexity of report data require that it be transmitted in a written form, so that recipients keep a record for reference, and have repeated access to it and so assimilate it more easily. Moreover, in the context of the meeting, it is common practice to circulate reports in advance to allow participants to arrive at the meeting prepared to discuss a report's contents on an informal basis.

The following check-list provides a guide to the components which, in various combinations, form the parts which go to make up the whole of a range of different report formats:

**Investigative Reports:
Components check-list**

1 Title
2 Author
3 Identity of report's commissioner
4 Date
5 Reference
6 Contents, pagination
7 Status e.g. Confidential
8 Background/history/introduction/terms of reference
9 Method/procedure/*modus operandi*
10 Information/findings/data input
11 Conclusions/synopsis/synthesis
12 Recommendations/suggestions for action
13 Footnotes
14 Appendices
15 Index
16 Circulation list

Types of report

1 The extended formal report

This format is used for high-level, extensive reports by central or local government and large companies.

Layout

Sectionalised with schematic organisation and referencing.
Format key: extended report (see Component check-list)

Structure of above-listed components

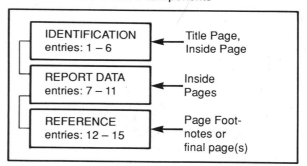

Principal components

1 Title page
2 Contents, pagination
3 Synopsis of findings
4 Terms of reference
5 Procedure
6 Sectionalised findings
7 Conclusions
8 Recommendations
9 Appendices
10 Bibliography

Note: where a reporting committee cannot agree, some members may submit a 'Minority Report'.

2 The short formal report

This format is used in formal reporting situations (mostly internally directed) where middle or senior management reports to senior or top management.

Layout

Sectionalised with schematic organisation and referencing.

Principal components

1 Title page or heading
2 Terms of reference
3 Procedure or identification of task
4 Findings
5 Conclusions
6 Recommendations (where required)
7 Appendices (if appropriate)

Note: This format should be reserved for situations where the context, nature and complexity of the data warrant a formalised report.

3 The short informal report

The short, informal format is used when the information is of a lower status and less complex than that of the 'short formal report'. It is frequently used in 'subordinate reporting to departmental head' situations. (See model on page 150).

Layout

Usually three-part and less elaborately schematic in its organisation.

Principal components

1 (variously styled) background
                     introduction
                     situation etc.
2 (variously styled) information
                     findings etc.
3 (variously styled) conclusions
                     action required etc.

Note: Any recommendations required are usually included in the final, 'conclusions' section.

4 The memorandum report

The memorandum format is used for internal reporting, especially within and between departments. Its format is extremely flexible, since the 'title' information is contained in the memorandum heading and the space of the sheet below 'Subject' may be employed in a variety of ways to display the content of the report.

Layout

Heading as for memorandum. May be sectionalised with headings and include tabulated information.

Principal components

No pre-determined components – the format of the memorandum report may be structured to suit the nature of the data.

Display techniques

DOUBLE HEIGHT/WIDTH CAPITALS

used for report titles, and major section headings

EMBOLDENED CAPITAL LETTERS

used for section and sub-section headings

Emboldened Initial Capitals

Used for entries of lower value than those above, for contrast and to indicate subordinate points

Initial Capitals With or Without Underscore

Indicative of restricted printing facilities, obsolescent

Decimal Point Referencing Systems eg.
                1.0, 2.0 3.0 etc
                1.1, 1.2., 1.3,
                1.1.1, 1.1.2. 1.1.3 etc

Note 1: the mixture of Roman Capital letters and numbers – eg C.III (iv) or with Arabic numbers A.1 (a) is fast becoming obsolete, the more elegant decimal point system being preferred

Note 2: The introduction of on-line laser printers has transformed the way in which reports are designed and printed for presentation, since they not only offer emboldening and double height/width features, but also multiple founts and printers' point size facilities and thus provide a powerful report presentation and display tool.

The decimal point referencing system

In the Civil Service and Local Government a decimal point referencing system is frequently employed, which utilises a system of numbered sections: 1. 2. 3. 4. etc. to introduce major sections of the report. Successive sub-sections within a major section are referenced: 1.1, 1.2, 1.3, etc. and subordinate points or paragraphs within each sub-sections are referenced by the addition of a further full stop and number: 1.2.1, 1.2.2, 1.2.3, 1.2.4, etc.

In the references illustrated immediately above,

the points being referred to would be the first, second, third and fourth points of the second subsection of the first major section. This system has the advantages of using only one 'code', the Arabic numeral system and full-stops, and is economic to display.

Use of space and indentation

Apart from considerations of logically discriminating between major and minor sections or points, the use of space − either by centring titles, or leaving lines blank above and below a section heading − is extremely important in enabling the reader's eye to travel more easily down the page and to take in the impact of the report more readily. Long paragraphs of continuous prose are extremely difficult to digest, particularly when the information they contain is specialised or technical. The use of progressive indentation, similarly helps to convey the report's information quickly.

The impact of word processing and laser printing on report production and display

The effect that word processing software has had upon the production and presentation of reports has been enormous. What was once a laborious chore for text producers − creating sometimes many drafts of a top-level report − has been replaced with a WP/printing technology which includes these significant features:

- on-screen editing of modified words/phrases
- relocation of paragraphs/sections/unit at will
- simple introduction of contrasting type founts
- sophisticated selection of display features such as enlarging/emboldening text, reverse printing, access to international and scientific alphabets and symbols, pagination, footnote positioning, spell-checking and correction, use of macros − 'files' which hold names, phrases for quick repetition in text, etc.

Moreover, the introduction of LAN/WAN networks now enables the report producer to zap it in draft form to the manager's terminal for perusal and editing and to recover it − in electronic form − when ready.

Also, the connection of the report producing WP terminal to an on-line laser printer and OCR scanner also permits the inclusion of eye-catching graphics and photographic material in the report as well as the extensive textual display facilities referred to above.

As a manager/office administrator in training, it is now essential that you become fully conversant with WP and laser printer-driven techniques of report production and presentation.

Content

All reports are prefaced with certain information which is displayed either on a title page (in the extended, formal report) or as a series of headings (in the memorandum or short, informal reports):

1 The subject of the report, displayed as its title
2 The identity of the report's recipients
3 The identity of the report's author
4 The date at completion
5 A reference (optional)
6 A circulation list
7 An indication of priority or confidentiality as required.

Structure of the short formal report

The structure of this report is divided into four or five sections (depending on whether recommendations have been asked for in the 'Terms of Reference'). The report is set down schematically as the following diagram broadly illustrates:

```
1.0  TERMS OF REFERENCE

2.0  PROCEDURES

3.0  FINDINGS

     3.1  Main Section Heading
     3.2  Main Section Heading
     3.3  Main Section Heading

          3.3.1  First Sub-Heading of Section 3.3
          3.3.2  Second Sub-Heading of Section 3.3
                 etc.

4.0  CONCLUSIONS

5.0  RECOMMENDATIONS

     5.1  First Main Recommendation
     5.2  Second Main Recommendation etc.
```

Note: the decimal point referencing system illustrated above is also used to indicate series of numbered (single phrase or sentence) points, as well as section headings during the flow of the report (see the model short formal report on pages 153−4); also, as points become more subordinate, they are progressively indented across the page to show this relationship.

1.0 TERMS OF REFERENCE
In this first section of the report, the author details the scope of the report, or its 'parameters', within which he may investigate. Sometimes the report's commissioner asks for recommendations; at other times they are made by the recipient(s) of the report.

2.0 PROCEDURE

Having outlined the report's scope, the writer identifies the means he or she adopted to collect its data:

by scrutinising documents,
by interviewing personnel,
by visiting branches,
by observation,
by examination, analysis etc.

3.0 FINDINGS

Here the detailed information which has been collected is sifted for relative importance and relevance and classified under appropriate headings, usually in descending order of importance, where the most important comes first.

4.0 CONCLUSIONS

In this section a résumé or synopsis of the principal findings is written, and is particularly helpful to those who may not wish to read the entire report.

5.0 RECOMMENDATIONS

Having classified the detailed information of the report and summarised its main conclusions, the writer's last duty, if required, is to identify the means by which a problem may be solved or a deficiency remedied, so that decisions may be made or advice acted upon.

Structure of the short informal report

The content of this report falls into three principal sections, equating to a 'beginning, middle and end', and may be used in a variety of situations where the subject of the report is neither too long nor complex. Its sections may be variously titled but the three sections may be considered as follows:

1 Background outlined
2 Problem/situation analysed
3 Problem/situation resolved

The content of each section is detailed in the three boxes below.

---

1 First section – headed:

Background or
Introduction or
Situation etc.

This opening section puts the report into a context and briefly outlines the essential background information needed to make the detailed information which follows in the middle section intelligible to the reader.

For example, if the report were entitled, 'Report on the Prevention of Wasteful Use of Stationery', the first section might well indicate a situation in which waste of stationery had been detected and a dramatic increase in stationery costs delivered. This section would also indicate who had commissioned the report, its author and any further details corresponding to the 'Terms Of Reference' section of the Short Formal Report.

---

2 Middle section – headed

Information or
Findings or
Analysis of problems etc.
This section displays systematically the detailed information which has been collected by similar methods to those identified in the 'Procedure' section of the Short Formal Report.

The detailed information of this middle section may be organised as a series of continuous prose paragraphs beneath sub-headings, which may also contain numbered lists or tabulated information. Generally the input of this section is not sufficiently complex to justify a highly schematised, indented layout.

---

3 Final section – headed

Conclusions or
Action required or
Resolution etc.
In this last section the main points of the report are summarised as conclusions and any actions required, recommendations or means of resolving a problem outlined. Thus the 'Conclusions' and 'Recommendations' sections of the Short Formal Report are combined.

The final section may be set out as a single continuous prose paragraph (or as a series of paragraphs), or may itemise its main points in a numbered list of sentences or phrases.

Structure of the memorandum report

If the subject may be treated analytically, the structure of the Memorandum Report will correspond to that of the Short Informal Report. Indeed, the A4 memorandum sheet, and continuation sheet(s) if needed, may be used for the Short Informal Report.

Additionally, the structure of the Memorandum Report is extremely flexible, and by employing the various display techniques available in typescript, it may be used for a range of internal reporting situations.

Detailed information in the form of charts, graphs and tables is often placed at the end of a report as an appendix.

Illustrated below are the section headings for a candidate profile in a job application situation:

1 Personal details
2 Education
3 Qualifications
4 Experience
5 Personality/disposition
6 Interests
7 Circumstances

Each section will be displayed in whatever manner is easiest for the reader to absorb.

Style

The style of report-writing should be factual and objective. In the case of investigatory and analytical reports, the decisions to be made and actions to be taken should be based on information and recommendations devoid of self-interest or bias.

The author of the report should not allow prejudices or emotional responses to intrude into the presentation of the Findings, Information or Recommendations sections of the report. Even when opinions are presented, these should be supplied in an *informed* and balanced way.

In practice, however, it is difficult for the report-writer to avoid influencing his or her report by subjective value-judgements, whether made consciously or subconsciously. Indeed, it is often the case that the member of personnel assigned to investigate and to report upon a situation is chosen on the basis of possessing a sound reputation in matters which require judgment. Subjectivity or bias may be exercised, not only in the style in which the report is written, but also in the *selection* of points or topics to be included and in the omission of other material which may be deemed irrelevant or too trivial to warrant attention.

Some reports may be couched in entirely denotative language, devoid of rhetoric or persuasion. Frequently, however, the report writer is seeking not only to inform but also to persuade. Therefore, the report writer must always be on his guard to avoid subjectivity creeping in.

Most experienced senior executives, usually the recipients of reports, have a developed sense for detecting unfairness, biased selection or partiality in a report, the effect of which is usually to detract from the reputation of the writer. It is therefore extremely important when choosing the style of writing of a report to check continually, both in the organisation of the data and the use of language, for signs of inappropriate subjectivity or partiality.

Impersonal constructions

One important convention employed particularly in the writing of formal reports is the use of impersonal constructions to convey information. The use of 'I' or 'we' and their respective cases is avoided. Instead, ideas are expressed, not with a first, but with a *third* person subject. Instead of writing: 'I found that . . .' constructions are preferred such as: 'It was evident that . . .' or, 'The statistics revealed that . . .'.

The underlying reason for preferring such impersonal constructions lies in the exclusion of any subjectivity associated with 'I', 'my', 'mine' and 'we', 'us', 'our', 'ours'.

Both before drafting a report and during composition, it is helpful to keep in mind a check-list of guide-lines or yard-sticks to ensure that the end product accords with the intentions or aims which are to be met:

Style check-list

1 What is the principal aim of the report — to inform by presenting a body of facts, to persuade by supplying a distillation of opinions, or both?

2 What sort of people are the report's recipients? Are they specialists who will understand specialised or technical language, or laymen for whom facts must be presented simply?

3 What is the context of the report? Does it require the use of formal language, or may points be made informally and familiarly?

4 What sort of language will be appropriate? Should the report be couched in objective terms, using impersonal constructions and the passive voice? Should its vocabulary deliberately seek to avoid connotative, emotive meanings? Should technical and jargon words be avoided, or may they be employed? Should sentences be kept short and simple, or may they contain provisos and modifying ideas?

5 How should the data be organised? Are the themes of the major sections all relevant and important? Is the material of each section connected and related to its heading? Does the complexity of the report's data require the use of a detailed schematic format?

6 Do the recommendations or suggestions given derive from the Findings rather than from personal bias?

7 Have presentation techniques been used to best effect to display information clearly and in a logical sequence so as to help the reader to digest the data easily and grasp the connection between various sections and points?

Model of a short informal report

CONFIDENTIAL

FOR: Mrs K Pearson, Office Manager

FROM: Christine Fellows, Personal Assistant

Ref: CF/AB

12 August 199–

REPORT ON THE PREVENTION OF WASTEFUL USE OF STATIONERY AND REPROGRAPHIC
SERVICES ①

1.0   INTRODUCTION ②

On Tuesday 28 July, you asked me to investigate the current wasteful use
of stationery in the department and <u>to suggest ways</u> in which it might be ③
used more economically in future. My report was to be submitted to you
by Friday 14 August 199–.

2.0   INFORMATION ④

2.1   <u>Stationery Use Investigated</u> ⑤

The range of departmental stationery investigated comprised: headed
letter and memoranda notepaper, fanfold, tractor-fed printer paper,
cut-sheet printer and photocopying paper, fax paper and the range of
envelopes in use.

2.2   <u>Stationery Associated with Correspondence/Internal Mail</u>

The suspected increase in wasteful practices was confirmed upon   ⑥
investigation. <u>I spoke to executive staff</u> who confirmed that, despite
our extensive use of WP drafting, a significant proportion of
ostensible final copies were being returned because of errors still
present.

<u>Observation and discussion</u> with secretarial staff confirmed that
clerical and executive staff in particular are using printed
stationery and unused envelopes on occasion as message pads.

Regarding envelopes, white ones are being used where manilla would
serve, and much non-confidential internal mail is being sent in
sealed envelopes. No member of staff appears to be re-using envelopes.
Also, despite the introduction of the LAN, staff are still distributing
paper-based memoranda and attached copy files when multiple distribution
could be achieved through the network with commensurate cost-saving on
photocopying.

2.3   <u>Photocopying Practices</u>

The departmental copier is in need of servicing and staff are wasting
extensive amounts of copy paper as a result of a fault which creases
the paper.

Furthermore, departmental staff continue to use our three single-   ⑦
sheet copiers for batch copying instead of the much cheaper departmental and company systems copiers, despite regular requests not to
do so.

2.4   <u>Increase in Stationery Costs</u>

I analysed the cost of departmental stationery, comparing this year's
second quarter with the first, and this year's consumption to date
against last year's.

The stationery bill for the second quarter of this <u>year is 30% higher</u> ⑧
than for the first quarter (Jan–March: £621.50 April–June: £807.95).

Allowing for increases in price, the department's stationery bill for this year to date against an equivalent period last year is some 18% higher — £1731.01 compared with £1419.42 last year. This increase does not appear to be justified by an equivalent increase in the output of the department. <u>Moreover, the rate of increase is rising</u>. (9)

3.0 CONCLUSIONS (10)

The investigations I have made <u>do justify the concern</u> expressed about excessive waste of office stationery and reprographic services and its impact on departmental running costs.

The increase in careless use of stationery is <u>not confined to one section</u> (11) but is to be found, in different forms throughout the department. If action is not taken immediately <u>the department is unlikely to keep within</u> (11) <u>its administration budget</u>.

I should therefore like to recommend the following measures for your consideration:

3.1 <u>A meeting with senior secretarial staff</u> should be called to discuss the (12) gravity of the problem and to obtain their cooperation in improving both managerial and secretarial performance. A refresher course could be mounted by the training department.

3.2 <u>Control of stationery issue</u> should be tightened; sections should be (12) required to account quarterly for stationery if this proves practicable in principle.

3.3 Consideration should be given to centralising <u>all</u> reprographics work carried out in the department so as to ensure that cost—effective approaches are optimised.

3.4 <u>Departmental policy on LAN Emailing</u> procedures and <u>message routing</u> (12) should be revised and all staff notified.

[Note: the underscorings in the report are only there to draw your attention to the circled points 1—12 explained in the commentary below; they form no part of the report's layout]

Reference heads section

The report is clearly headed with the appropriate information for despatch and filing.

Note the use of the CONFIDENTIAL classification resulting from the nature of the report's information, since some staff are clearly open to criticism.

A report's title[1] should always indicate briefly yet clearly what it is about.

Introduction section

This section[2] establishes concisely: 'What? Who? When? Why?

Note that from the outset it is clear that the report will include recommendations for action[3].

Information section

The INFORMATION section[4] could be made up simply of continuous prose paragraphs, but the in-

clusion of sub-headings[5] helps to break down the information into more easily digested sections, which emphasise the particular areas of investigation Christine Fellows thought important.

Note that the first sub-section identifies and defines the range of stationery to be investigated. In so doing, an effort has been made to break down the range into logical groupings.

Much of the report's information relies on Christine's observations and discussions with staff[6] and, in the report, takes the form of assertions. Mrs Pearson would need to rely on Christine's judgement — it is important, therefore, that in reports [7], investigators are just and fair, and as far as possible, support their assertions[8] by quoting facts, figures or clearly evident practices. This reassures the report's reader that the report is based on fact, rather than opinion or purely personal views.

To this end, Christine has taken the trouble to examine the department's spending on stationery over the past 18 months. Her factual financial evidence is hard to ignore, and has the effect of emphasising the need for urgent action.[9]

Conclusions section

In the short informal report, the CONCLUSIONS section[10] provides a summary of the main factors[11] which arise from the INFORMATION section, and also relays to the reader any suggestions or recommendations[12] which may have been asked for.

Note: In more complex reports, these two aspects, of summarising the findings of a report and then of specifying recommendations are in two separate sections.

In terms of the report's visual impact on the reader, it might have been helpful for Christine to have headed each recommendation with a suitable 'label':

3.1   Secretarial staff

A meeting with senior . . .

Such display techniques are a matter of personal judgment, since there are, in fact, no hard and fast rules governing report format; it is a matter of using most effectively the display facilities of the typewriter and setting out information in a logical and clear manner.

Model of memorandum report

MIDSHIRE COUNCIL
Memorandum

CONFIDENTIAL

To: Director of Education   **Ref**: HJK/RT   DE 156

From: Personnel Services Manager   **Date**: 12th August 199-

Subject: Appointment of Personal Assistant to Director of Education
          Candidate Profile: Miss Sara Harris

PERSONAL DETAILS

Full Name:	Sara Jane Harris	Date of Birth: 22nd April 199-
Age 24:	Status: Single	Nationality: British
Address:	14 Highmoor Drive, Midtown, Midshire, ME12 4TG	

ATTAINMENTS

Secondary School: September 199- to July 199- Waverley College.
                  'A'-levels: English Lit A, History B, Sociology B.
University: October 199- to June 199- Cumbria University.
                  Graduated B.A. Hons in English Literature,
                  Second Class.
Post-graduate: September 199- to June 199- Midtown College of F.E.
                  R.S.A. Higher Diploma in Business Administration,
                  Distinction.

GENERAL INTELLIGENCE

Miss Harris's academic record evidences a lively intelligence and her success in higher education courses suggests an ability to deal with problems conceptually and analytically. Reports from Cumbria University and Midtown College of F.E. confirm initiative and resourcefulness in problem-solving situations, and a genuine interest in education matters.

SPECIAL APTITUDES

During her post-graduate course, Miss Harris did particularly well in shorthand, typewriting and word processing and gained a distinction in her R.S.A. Higher Diploma.

While studying at Cumbria University, Miss Harris served on the Students'
Union Education Committee and published a paper entitled, 'The Future
of Higher Education - Open Access For All!'

INTERESTS

An accomplished violinist, Miss Harris is Honorary Secretary of the
Midtown Orchestral Society. She also enjoys sailing and is interested
in industrial archeology.

DISPOSITION

Reports indicate a tendency towards impatience with viewpoints commonly
identified with the 'establishment' but also reveal a willingness to
modify a point of view when faced with a superior argument. Miss
Harris's personality has been variously described as 'forceful' and
'dynamic' and she is generally held to possess a cheerful, outgoing
personality and a good sense of humour. She has been universally
described as a young woman of integrity and loyalty.

CIRCUMSTANCES

Since completing her course at Midtown College of F.E., Miss Harris
has been staying with her parents and would be immediately available
for employment if successful in her application.

Signed...*HJK*.......................

Specimen short formal report

CONFIDENTIAL

FOR: P J Kirkbride, Managing Director   REF: HTD/SC/FWH 4

FROM: H T Dickens, Chairman, Flexible
       Working Hours Working Party   DATE: 14 February 199-

REPORT ON THE PROPOSAL TO INTRODUCE A FLEXIBLE WORKING HOURS SYSTEM IN HEAD OFFICE

1.0 TERMS OF REFERENCE

On 7 January 199- the Managing Director instructed a specially set up working party to
investigate the practicality of introducing a system of flexible working hours in all
head office departments, and to make appropriate recommendations. The report was to be
submitted to him by 21 February 199- for the consideration of the Board of Directors.

2.0 PROCEDURE

In order to obtain relevant information and opinion, the following procedures were
adopted by the working party to acquire the information in the report:

2.1 Current office administration literature was reviewed. (Appendix 1 Bibliography
     refers.)
2.2 A number of companies were visited which have adopted flexible working hours
     systems and the views of a wide range of staff were canvassed.
2.3 Current departmental working loads and practices were observed and evaluated.
2.4 Soundings of likely staff responses were obtained from departmental managers and
     senior staff.
2.5 The cost of introducing a flexible working hours system was considered.

3.0 FINDINGS

3.1 Principles of the Flexible Working Hours System

The essence of a flexible working hours system consists of establishing two
distinct bands of working hours within a weekly or monthly cycle and of ensuring
that staff work an agreed total of hours in the cycle.

3.1.1 Core Time Band

During this period (say 10 15 am to 3 45 pm) <u>all</u> staff are present at work, allowing for lunch-time arrangements.

3.1.2 Flexi-time Band

Periods at the beginning and end of the day (say 7 45 am to 10 15 am and 3 45 pm to 6 15 pm) are worked at the discretion of individual staff members in whole or part, allowing for essential departmental staff manning requirements.

3.1.3 Credit/Debit Hour Banking

According to previously agreed limits and procedures, staff may take time off if a credit of hours has built up, or make time up, having created a debit to be made good. Most companies require that the agreed weekly hours total (in the case of head office staff 37½ hours per week) is reached but not exceeded, though some firms adopt a more flexible approach, which permits some time to be credited/debited in a longer cycle.

3.1.4 Recording Hours Worked

In all systems, it is essential that logs or time-sheet records are kept and agreed by employee and supervisor for pay and staff administration reasons.

3.2 <u>Discussions with Departmental Managers</u>

Most departmental managers were in favour of introducing a flexible working hours system, anticipating an improvement in both productivity and staff morale. The Sales Manager saw advantages in his office being open longer during the day to deal with customer calls and visits. Also, most felt the introduction would be timely, given the current demographic downturn in the 16-19 age range and our need to recruit more 'mature women returners'. Reservations were expressed by both the office administration and accounts managers arising from the likelihood of increased workloads to administer the system.

3.3 <u>Sounding of Staff Opinion</u>

Discreet enquiries were made via senior staff regarding the likely response of staff at more junior levels.

3.3.1 Summary of Favourable Responses

Secretarial staff in particular would welcome the means of tailoring their work and attendance to fit in with their principals' presences and absences. Many staff would enjoy working when they felt at their personal 'peaks'. Over 35% of female staff are mothers with children of school age and would probably welcome the opportunity to fit their work around family responsibilities and according to seasonal daylight hours. Weekday shopping opportunities would be improved and travelling in peak rush-hour times avoided.

3.3.2 Summary of Unfavourable Responses

Few staff at junior levels intimated an unfavourable response but more senior staff were concerned about key personnel not being available when needed for consultation etc. Older staff seemed less enthusiastic and any introduction of flexible working hours would need to be carefully planned and full consultation carried out.

3.4 <u>Cost of Introducing a Flexible Working Hours System</u>

The increase in costs of heating, lighting and administration of the system would be offset to some degree by a decline in overtime worked and the cost of employing temporary staff to cover for staff absences, which may be expected to reduce. (Appendix 3 provides a detailed estimate of the cost of introducing and running a flexible working hours system.)

```
4.0  CONCLUSIONS
```

In the working party's view, the advantages of introducing a flexible working hours system outweigh the disadvantages. Head office service to both customers and field sales staff would improve; staff morale and productivity are also likely to rise. Administrative costs do not appear unacceptable and senior staff have the necessary expertise to make the system work. Of necessity, the working party's view was broad rather than detailed and the introduction of any flexible working hours systems should allow for the particular needs and problems of individual head office departments to be taken into account as far as possible.

```
5.0  RECOMMENDATIONS
```

As a result of its investigations, the working party recommends that the Board of Directors gives active consideration to the following:

5.1 That the introduction of a flexible working hours system be accepted in principle by the Board and staff consultations begin as soon as possible with a view to establishing a time-table for implementing the change.

5.2 That all departmental managers be requested to provide a detailed appraisal of their needs in moving over to a flexible working hours system and of any problems they anticipate.

5.3 That a training programme be devised by personnel and training departments to familiarise staff with new working procedures and practices.

5.4 That a code of practice be compiled for inclusion in the company handbook.

5.5 That arrangements be made to inform both field sales staff and customers at the appropriate time of the advantages to them of the introduction in head office of flexible working hours.

Summaries and factsheets

Today the term 'information overload' has become something of a cliché because it is used so often. Yet, with networked computers, print-outs by the metre, fax, telex, viewdata, and CABX telephone systems − not to mention mobile phones, audio- and videoconferencing − it is true that managers and support staff are becoming ever more submerged in information of all kinds. Moreover, the pace of today's business world makes great demands on office staff to supply all kinds of information speedily. Nowadays the firms which survive are those geared up to obtain, sift and act upon information arriving from all quarters all the time and in high volumes. As a result, expertise that can promptly deliver the following is at a premium:

● oral summaries of meetings and events,
● written summaries, briefings, presentations, abstracts, factsheets, bulletins, and so on from information culled from all kinds of source.

The time of senior managers and company directors is always highly expensive, and so they naturally appreciate those assistants who can convey key facts and opinions clearly and succinctly, and present them so that they are easily absorbed and understood.

The following section provides you with a simple and clear procedure for summarising written information. Make sure you go through it carefully, since once embarked on your full-time career, you may rest assured that a day will not pass without your being asked to provide some form of oral or written summary.

The essential skills

All those who produce information in such circumstances need to acquire summarising skills broadly identified as:

● comprehension
● classification
● analysis
● evaluation
● selection

Essentially, they will exercise their powers of discrimination in deciding which parts of a given piece of material need to be extracted and relayed in a particular format to meet the needs of a third party.

Indeed, one of the most valuable assets of the executive, personal assistant or secretary is the ability to relay the essence of a 'message' which will involve meeting the following objectives in whole or part:

1 Ability to comprehend a range of information, data or opinion
2 Ability to identify salient points for a particular purpose
3 Skill in analysing and evaluating material to distinguish the essential from the trivial
4 Practice in working objectively so that personal attitudes do not influence selection processes
5 Skill in using language to convey the tone or attitudes of the original
6 Familiarity with business practice to ensure that appropriate formats are used when reproducing data

Self assessment questions

1 Can you write fluently in an impersonal, objective style? Can you work happily in the passive voice of main verbs?

2 How articulate and fluent are your oral reports?

Applications of summarising techniques

- Relaying to a principal the outcome of a meeting.
- As chairman, summing up a discussion at a meeting.
- Passing a message, either orally or on a message pad.
- Designing an advertisement for a job.
- Delivering the chairman's report at a company's annual general meeting
- Producing a sales report.
- Writing a letter or memorandum conveying information or a point of view.
- Relaying instructions from above to subordinates.
- Editing a press-release for inclusion in a newspaper.
- Writing an article for inclusion in a house magazine.
- Drafting a notice or circular.
- Using the telephone – particularly over a long distance!
- Interviewing a candidate for an appointment.
- Giving a briefing to a group, working party or taskforce.
- Getting across a point of view or suggestion.
- Despatching a telegram or telex message.

Many oral and writing situations arise daily requiring summarising techniques.

Though the summarising process is present in so many communications channels, nevertheless there are a number of documents produced frequently in an organisation which require differing summarising techniques:

Documents needing specific summarising techniques

Précis	a faithful, selective miniature reproduction
Summary	selective reproduction of *required* data
Abstract	selective data from long article, paper
Abridgement	shortened version of a book, thesis etc.
Précis of documents, correspondence	summary of a series of related documents
Minutes	summary of decisions (background) of a meeting
Conclusions, synopsis sections of the formal, extended reports	summary of main points of 'Findings' section (or Synopsis), introductory essence of report
Fax, Email, Telex, messages	abbreviated message reduced to essentials
Press release	submission to newspaper of newsworthy item

(For a more detailed examination of minutes see 'Meetings' in Unit 12.)

Self assessment question

Are you sure you can confidently distinguish between situations which require either an extended formal, or short informal report? Have you mastered the intricacies of report structures and formats to your own satisfaction?

Précis or abstract

Note the difference: The précis seeks to reduce a passage to about a third, and aims to retain both its major features and attitudes in a faithful, miniature reproduction. The **summary** selects points to meet a specific brief or requirement and is therefore selective of the passage's material, extracting only those points relevant to a desired purpose. The **abstract** is also selective, reducing a much longer article or passage far more extensively, but again, its length is determined by the *specifically directed* requirements of its recipient.

Principles of summarising

Stage one

Check that you understand clearly the requirement or brief – which may only involve *part* of the item for summarising, and also what the end document is to be used for.

Stage two

Read the item or source documents *thoroughly*, since you cannot summarise what you do not fully grasp. Read for:

a) The general drift or meaning
b) For the meaning of individual words or phrases
c) For the structure of the item and the development of its ideas or arguments.

Stage three

Give the item a title conveying the essence of the summary. This will act as a yard-stick against which to measure points for importance and relevance.

Stage four

Select the principal points, keeping the 'terms of reference' of Stage One in mind. A useful technique is to identify the 'key topics' of paragraphs as a starting point.

Stage five

Check your list of points against the original in case something has been overlooked. Check your points against your title for relevance.

Stage six

Establish which format is appropriate for the sum-marising version – schematic layout or paragraphed continuous prose.

Stage seven

Compose a rough draft leaving room for subsequent refinements and using your own words to convey the sense rather than copying phrases or sentences; remember that you need not find alternatives for specialist terms like 'inflation' or 'wage-freeze' etc.

Stage eight

If you are limited to a specific number of words, it is wise to aim to exceed this limit in a rough draft by some 10–15 words in the context of a passage of 300 words to be reduced to some 110, since it is easier to prune further than to insert extra points into a rough draft.

Stage nine

Check the rough draft to ensure that the points are linked in connected sentences that read smoothly and where the progression is logical and intelligible. Then polish into a final version by improving vocabulary, syntax, tone etc. Ensure that the final version has been checked for transcription errors of spelling, punctuation etc.

Stage ten

Add the details of the item's sources, the author's name and status, as well as your own. The summary may be passed to its recipient by means of a covering memorandum. All such work should bear a completion date, to indicate that it is current work.

The acid test

The acid test of all summarising work is that its recipient can clearly understand it without ever having seen the original!

Self assessment question
Do you feel confident yet in composing memoranda which communicate instructions or aim to rectify shortcomings and deficiencies among staff?

Talking point
'It's a fallacy to believe that reports can ever be objective!' Do you agree?

When summarising . . .

Don't

Skimp the reading stages – the original *must* be clearly understood

Include items in your points list which are trivial, repetitious, and, broadly, illustrations or examples

Abbreviate your points list too dramatically or allow yourself to be verbose

Allow your own personal views to obtrude into the summary

Forget that it takes at least twice as many words on average to expand a points list into continuous prose

Try to 'borrow' phrases or sentences from the original – they won't fit into your smaller version comfortably – and you may use them wrongly

Allow your rough or final version to suffer from 'over-compression', where the meaning is lost in a kind of shorthand language

Allow your summary to look like a list of unconnected and hence meaningless statements

Overlook the fact that the recipient may never see the original. Your version must stand on its own two feet and not rely on a reading of the original to render it intelligible

Forget that the context dictates the format of the final version – a schematic layout may be essential for quick reference in a meeting

. . . but do

Check your brief carefully before starting

Check unfamiliar words

Convey fairly the author's own attitudes and outlooks

Measure your points list against relevance and importance to theme

Cross-check against passage and chosen title

Convey the sense rather than the wording of the original

Think of reducing the original to its basic 'skeletal' form

Keep essential illustrations short – use collective nouns when possible

Bear in mind that authors tend to repeat main points several times and 'say it only once'

Make a draft before attempting a final version

Ensure that your tone and style are appropriate either to the author's approach or the recipient's needs – e g factual or persuasive

Ensure that the rough draft to final version stage is free from mechanical errors – spelling, punctuation, syntax

Choose an appropriate format

Précis of documentation or correspondence

Sometimes it is necessary to produce a summary of an exchange of letters or of a number of related documents. Such techniques involve selecting only the most essential points and connecting them as follows:

1 Specifying the context, authors' names and designations and organisations in a title section.
2 Proceeding chronologically showing dates and authors and the essential point of each document or letter.

The abstract

In compiling an abstract, it is extremely important to act only upon the requirement of your briefing – do not produce a précis when the recipient has asked for a particular aspect to be synthesised from points dispersed in the original. Follow the method shown on page 157. Remember that you will need to be far more stringent in excluding non-essential material, and that a schematic presentation may be needed for the abstract to be used in a discussion or meeting. Lastly, always cite the source, authorship and date of the original, together with your name, status and the completion date.

How to produce an effective factsheet

All the guidelines on creating coherent and readable summaries may be applied in essence to factsheet production.

However, a factsheet is never produced in a vacuum, but is requested in order to meet a specific need, which may be to brief an executive who has never travelled before to a particular foreign country and who needs to know quickly and simply the key facts about its climate, politics, economy, social, cultural and religious life, established business links and so on.

The following guidelines will enable you to produce helpful and effective factsheets:

● Always ensure that your source reference

material is as up-to-date as you can get. No one wants to look silly by using outdated data with clients or senior colleagues.

- Before starting, decide what the most essential topics are to be imparted to the recipient. Don't waste time on the irrelevant and trivial.
- No one wants to read a factsheet like a murder novel, so put your key topics in **a running order which starts with the most important** (unless a chronological or historical sequence is needed).
- Display key facts and figures in **emboldened or similar eye-catching style** to aid their retention.
- Use **plenty of white space and schematic layout techniques** to give your data instant visual appeal.
- Above all, **keep your factsheets short**. No busy executive is going to have time to absorb a factsheet that thinks it's a long formal report!

A GOOD FACTSHEET IS CLEAR, STRAIGHTFORWARD AND EASY TO DIGEST

THE DEVELOPMENT OF THE OFFICE

1 **HISTORICAL BACKGROUND**

1.1 **2600 BC Ancient Egypt:** early form of office – site managers' supervision of pyramid construction.

1.2 **750 BC – 500 AD Ancient Greek and Roman Civilisations:** development of offices to administer government and trade and transcribe written orders etc to far-flung governors.

1.3 **500 AD – 1000 AD Dark Ages in Europe:** offices situated in abbeys and monasteries to aid manuscript transcribing and management of farms and lands etc.

1.4 **1000 – 1485 Medieval Feudal System:** offices employed by Norman barons and abbots (and their successors) to administer taxes and work of tied peasants.

1.5 **1485 – 1800 Expansion of National/International Trade:** the modern office has its roots in the counting houses of 16th century merchants and the blossoming of international trade via merchant trading companies using sailing ships.

2 **DEVELOPMENT OF THE MODERN OFFICE**

2.1 **Influencing Factors**

The following factors influenced the development of the modern office in the 19th century:

2.1.1 Increase in world trade following the Industrial Revolution.

2.1.2 The invention of shorthand (1837) by Sir Isaac Pitman.

2.1.3 The improvement in general literacy as a result of Victorian educational reforms.

2.1.4 The invention of telegraphy (also 1837) by Samuel Morse and of the typewriter (Scholes 1868 and Remington 1874).

2.2 **Activities of the Early 20th Century Office**

Creating attractive and effective forms

To many managers and support staff, especially those who work in large bureaucratic organisations, dealing with endless batches of forms can seem at times like a recurrent nightmare!

And despite the impact of IT, the pre-printed form seems to be livelier and reproducing more of its kind than ever. The reasons for the ongoing widespread use of forms in organisations may be summarised as follows:

- They are invaluable for collecting data in **standardised** procedures.
- They ensure that **all the information needed** must be provided by the form-filler.
- They **sequence the data in a preferred priority**.
- They provide **handy sources of reference** and can act as **computer data input sources**.
- They ensure a **uniformity and consistency of approach** in dispersed government, bank or insurance branches, etc.
- Clerical **staff can be readily trained to vet** accurate completion of forms.
- New forms may be **readily designed to meet new or revised policies** and procedures.

If forms are so helpful and useful, then why do so many people's hearts fall on having to complete them? The answer lies almost entirely in a lack of forethought and inadequate skill among the legions of form designers, who on occasion require form-fillers to recite their autobiographies within spaces no bigger than postage stamps! Or who devise gobbledegook completion instructions, or who require information which is deemed irrelevant or highly personal by the completer!

While the above comments are perhaps a little exaggerated, as a future office administrator or manager, you should take them to heart and ensure that *your* created forms will be a joy for all to use. To get you started along the way of effective form design, the tips set out below highlight the major features you will need to practise and refine:

Tips on effective form design

1 Take time to consider in detail:

Why is the information needed?
When is it needed? In what time cycle?
Who needs it? And *from whom*?
How would the information be best presented?

2 Then, make up a checklist of all the parts and pieces of information needed, eg:

full name, address, telephone/fax/BT Gold/telex numbers, age, date of birth, sex, nationality, personnel reference number, payroll number, qualifications, education, work experience, full driving licence, disabilities, health record, etc.

3 Next, consider how the form might best be structured:

Should it move down chronologically like a history from old to current time?

Should the most important parts come first? What *are* the most important parts?

What items in the initial checklist are trivial and not really needed? What items are crucial in the eventual collating and comparing which will happen when the completed forms are gathered in?

Seek to put your checklist of items into a running order or sequence which you will reproduce in designing the form.

4 Then draw a mock-up of the form in rough – either in longhand, on your typewriter or database software.

Always ensure your boxes or lined spaces into which responses will be inserted are large enough for the response required.

Check that your questions or instructions are: *short, simple, clear and unambiguous*.

Make sure you have not omitted any important question or data requirement and that your instructions on what must be done with the completed form are clear.

5 Produce a test model of the form. Try it out on close colleagues first. Ask them to criticise it constructively. Make any necessary amendments.

6 Print the form for use and check the first users' responses:

Did they understand what was needed?
Were any parts left uncompleted?
If so, why?

Acid test: Did the form produce the data needed – in the form expected, within the required deadlines, in a manner which permitted analysis and summary, from all those issued with it?

7 Lastly: Don't forget to monitor your forms from time to time. Events sometimes overtake regular routines, so always ask:

'Is this form *really* needed?'

If it isn't, ditch it! You will gain much valuable time and many friends!

Talking point

'Devising endless forms for people to complete is like stacking and restacking the deckchairs on the Titanic – it spells imminent death by bureacracy for the organisation concerned!'

Examples of pre-printed forms in common office use

Job application • interview notes record • personnel records • accident report • lateness record • sickness self-certification • sickness absence • job appraisal • performance evaluation report • holiday request form • holiday rota schedule • suggestions form • memorandum NCR forms • message forms • expenses claim forms • sales report forms • petty cash vouchers • purchase requisition forms • stock requisition forms • delivery notes • invoices • statements of account

Computerised databases and form-filling

Software designers now market a wide range of database application packages, from simple name and address labelling to highly sophisticated relational databases capable of holding thousands of records and millions of fields, so help is at hand for those who create, and complete, forms under pressure.

Already, insurance, banking or account-seeking customers, as well as medical patients, holiday-makers or investors are finding helpful assistants who key in data into such databases (or, with confidential data, do it themselves) in much more user-friendly circumstances. The software involved is especially designed to avoid lengthy sentencing in favour of simple space-bar or return-key responses to questions displayed on the monitor. For example, many insurance brokers are now able to identify in a few seconds which companies best suit individual customers' needs.

Talking point

'Lots of people talk a lot, but very few can deliver a good oral report!' What makes good oral reporting so difficult? What steps would you advise to improve this vital skill?

Summary of main points

The memorandum

1 Commonsense conventions exist for devising memohead formats, indicating sender, recipient, date and subject.

2 The memorandum is simply 'an internal letter' routed within organisations and so techniques of letter structuring also apply.

3 The paper-based memorandum is now being superseded by its electronic Email LAN networked counterpart which does away with expensive photocopying and paper-based filing needs.

4 Studying and allowing for the personality traits and positions of memo recipients is also important for effective internal organisational communication.

The notice

5 Effective notices are essentially: short and to the point, composed in sufficiently large typescript/DTP typography, eye-catching and clear about any actions required of their readers; out-of-date notices should be promptly discarded!

The report

6 Reports are composed to meet either standardised, routine reporting needs – eg, on the condition of a piece of equipment – or as the result of a call for an analytical investigation.

7 Reports may be requested in the form of oral briefings or presentations (with AVA support) or in written form, in four major types: extended formal report, short formal report, memorandum report or short informal report.

8 Investigatory reports are characterised by a fully referenced *structure* and schematic layout; currently the decimal point referencing system with progressive indentation is popular.

9 Techniques of desk-top publishing and laser printing have had a radical impact on report display and presentation.

10 Typically, an extended report comprises: Terms of Reference, Procedure, Findings, Conclusions, Recommendations, Bibliography and Appendices sections; a short informal report condenses these to: Introduction, Information, Conclusions (or similar) section headings.

11 An effective report style should be factual, objective and disinterested, avoiding the personal and subjective views of the writer (unless these are specifically requested in terms of reference).

12 Summarising skills are needed daily at work, in oral, written and graphics media; a basic distinction exists between the précis and summarising of an item – the former providing a faithful miniature reproduction and the latter a selective résumé.

13 Summaries may take the form of a précis, abstracts, abridgements, précis of correspondence, briefings and factsheets, etc; the type of summary produced will depend entirely upon the instructions of the requesting manager.

14 The technique of summarising can be accomplished in some ten steps which follow a sequence of comprehending the original, reducing it to its basic skeletal structure, omitting trivial repetitious and extraneous material and bringing the selected material together in clear, connected prose or schematic presentation.

15 Factsheets are schematically set out facts and figures brought together in a logical sequence to act as an informational and briefing tool. Like good notices they should be brief, eye-catching, with up-to-date material and clear structure.

16 Forms meet a number of administrative needs, especially where data has to be standardised and sequenced prior to processing.

17 Techniques of effective form design include: careful analysis of the information needs to be supplied, itemising of the data required in sufficient detail before the design phase, trials of a prototype form and accompanying instructions, rehearsal of the analysis of data provided prior to printing and distribution of the final version.

Activities and assignments

Quick review quiz

1 List the typical components of both paper and Email memoranda.

2 Why is it good practice for a manager to initial a memorandum prior to despatch?

3 Describe the standard way in which a memorandum is structured.

4 Provide a set of brief guidelines on effective memorandum handling.

5 What are the main advantages of creating and sending Emailed memos in comparison with their paper counterparts?

6 What dangers do you see in an over-reliance on paper/electronic memo messaging?

7 List the factors which influence good memorandum-writing style.

8 Outline 5–6 commonly occurring communication situations in organisations which the memorandum in either paper or Email form is well suited to support.

9 Describe briefly the main features of effective notice design.

10 Distinguish between the four main types of report dealt with in Unit 7.

11 Set down in correct order the main sections of an extended formal report and explain the function of each.

12 Explain the difference between a routine and an investigative report and supply examples of the use of each.

13 What features characterise effective oral reporting?

14 When is an oral report more appropriate than a written one?

15 Distinguish between situations which call either for an extended formal or a short informal report.

16 Explain clearly how the decimal point referencing system works.

17 Describe the features of WP applicaions software and laser printers which promote appealing report production and presentation.

18 Explain the different functions of the Conclusions and Recommendations report sections.

19 What style features should a good report embody?

20 Give 7–10 examples of summary techniques used in business.

21 When are précis of correspondence likely to be needed?

22 List the ten main stages of producing a written summary.

23 Explain the major techniques of effective fact-sheet production.

24 What constitutes good form design practice? What features of bad form design are to be avoided?

25 How are databases being used to replace some form-filling chores?

Document production assignments

The memorandum

1 Recently there have been several instances in your company when confidential information about your products and activities has been secured by rival firms. As a result, your office administration manager has asked you to draft a memorandum to all office staff reminding them of the need for maintaining security and confidentiality at all times, and outlining the procedures they should follow when using both paper and electronic production media.

2 A fire-drill in your offices last week revealed a number of alarming inadequacies. Many members of staff behaved quite indifferently; others seemed to have no idea of what they should do, while one or two simply did nothing at all, saying that they were 'far too busy'. As a consequence, you have been detailed to draft a memorandum to all staff aimed at emphasising the possible dangers in remaining indifferent to company regulations in case of fire and at securing an improved response.

3 Your recently introduced LAN network has been plagued by installation bugs and breakdowns. As a result, morale in your department is at rock bottom regarding the whole process of moving over to networking from familiar paper files and documents. However, your directors are committed to computer-managed information systems and telecommunications and so have asked you to draft a memorandum to all departmental staff aimed at improving morale. To this end, you have been authorised to inform staff that more money is go-

ing to be put into staff training and that the firm commissioned to install the LAN have been 'fired' in favour of an alternative. The departing on-site installation supervisor, however, grumbled that 'the kit's OK, if people trouble to use it properly!'

Compose a suitable memorandum, and compare yours with others produced by your group.

4 After deliberating on ways to overcome persistent late-coming on the part of the factory and office staff, your managing director decided three weeks ago, in the spirit of industrial democracy, to introduce clocking-on and off for *all* company staff, himself included! Your departmental office staff did not particularly welcome such an innovation, and feelings since have been running high, and the MD has relented. You have therefore been requested to draft a memorandum to departmental staff aimed at improving the situation and securing cooperation while reiterating the need for punctuality in all staff.

5 Write a critical evaluation of the four alternative memoranda on page 141 and justify which version you consider as being likely to secure the punctual submission of Jim Grainger's sales reports.

6 Analyse the memorandum on page 136 from the point of view of the style in which it has been composed and comment on the ways in which the choice of words and syntax is likely to contribute to the effectiveness of the memoranda.

7 Assume that you are a departmental head at Kaybond Ltd, and that your staff have indicated that they are not keen to work under the proposed flexible working hours system. (See model report on pages 153–4.)

Write a memorandum to S Kilbride, managing director, outlining the staff's response to and misgivings about the proposal and stating clearly what you consider to be the best next step.

The report

8 You work as a trainee manager in the Gifts Department of a large department store. Three days ago, one of the sales assistants was involved in a difficult situation with a customer who wished to make an account purchase but who did not have her account credit card with her. Following company regulations, the assistant declined to give credit, whereupon the customer became abusive. You witnessed the scene and have been called in by the departmental manager to report on what you saw.

Deliver your oral report. (Note this assignment may be carried out in a role-playing situation.)

9 Britahomes plc, a company which manufactures a wide range of paints and varnishes for interior and exterior home decoration hit a bad patch over the past twelve months. They lost sales to competitors whose marketing and sales promotion were superior. As a result, profits have slumped and there is no prospect of a dividend being announced at the company's forthcoming annual shareholders' meeting. Further, a hostile take-over is on the cards by a long-standing competitor, Bettadecor, with a successful sales record but an aging product range.

A ray of hope emerged earlier this week in the Research and Development Department of Britahomes, where you work as Assistant Product Liaison Officer. Your industrial chemists have at last cracked the formula needed to revolutionise paint production. They have developed a highly effective additive which does away with the need to paint primer and undercoats on to household and garden surfaces prior to a top coat. Their formula works with gloss, matt, silk and emulsion paints and looks set to turn Britahomes around – given some patience on the part of shareholders, as product development is expected to take some six months before the paints are in the shops.

As a result of your close involvement and communication skills, the MD has asked you to carry out the following assignments:

a) Compose a draft of that part of the Britahomes Annual Report which publicises the development of the formula – to be marketed as 'Wuncoat X23' – and defends Britahomes vis-à-vis its competitors and recent performance.

b) A confidential memorandum to all Britahome sales personnel to boost morale and explain the selling features of Wuncoat X23 paint additive.

c) The recommendations section of a short, informal report listing how your team considers the additive could best be marketed and promoted over the next 12 months.

10 Last week a row broke out among the office personnel in your department over the drawing up of the annual summer holiday staff rota.

In past years it has been the practice to approach senior and long-service staff first and to follow an informal and delicate 'pecking order'.

Two weeks ago, however, the senior clerical officer, over-worked and under pressure at the time, delegated the job to a relatively new and inexperienced subordinate. Unaware of the customary procedure, he compiled a list on a 'first come, first served' basis, and then circulated the list without any consultation.

Several members of staff took exception to the way in which the rota had been drawn up and a row occurred which had the effect of polarising attitudes between senior and junior, older and younger departmental personnel.

In order to retrieve the situation and to improve departmental staff relations, your office **manager** has informed staff that he is currently 'looking into the matter', and has asked you, his deputy, to investigate the situation and to produce a written report for him, establishing what went wrong and why, and suggesting how the current problem may best be resolved and how an equitable procedure may best be established for the future.

Write a suitable report, adding any additional authenticating material you consider appropriate.

11 The head of the department in which you are studying is currently reviewing the ways in which the department's courses are marketed. At this time there is a distinct downturn in the number of teenagers applying for courses because of the drop in overall numbers of 16–19-year-olds – a direct result of a fall in the birthrate. As a consequence, competition among the educational institutions offering post-16 education and training has sharpened. Also, local employers are becoming concerned about the problems of securing suitably qualified people – especially in the office administration sector.

As part of his marketing review, the HOD has asked you (a group of three or four students) to research carefully into the following areas:

a) to find out why students joined your own particular course, and also the other full-time courses which were on offer to your year,
b) to establish clearly how they came to hear about the courses offered by the department,
c) to find out how effective in the eyes of the department's customers the department's marketing/informational leaflets and prospectuses were in aiding student's decision-making; and to ascertain whether they could be improved and if so, in what ways,
d) to seek feedback on the department's application and enrolment procedures and to check whether they could be simplified or speeded up,
e) to find out how students in their first year have reacted to their courses of study and the general departmental and college/school environment so as to establish whether it met their expectations, and if not, how it could be improved.

The HOD has suggested that you devise a suitable questionnaire and sample representative groups of students in the department. Having secured your raw data, he then wishes you to compile a short, informal report, with recommendations, and including any numerical tables/percentages, etc for his attention. He needs your report within three weeks, in time for a departmental heads of section meeting.

The summary, abstract and factsheet

12 You work as Assistant Information Officer for Westchester District Council. Part of your current duties is to edit the Council's monthly newsletter.

At the moment, your boss is having a drive on improving the staff's consciousness about document presentation in an IT context. You showed her the section in Unit 11 about desk-top publishing. As a result, she now wants you to produce a précis of the piece entitled 'How Desk-top Publishing Works' on pages 272–5 Space constraints mean that you have to keep your précis down to no more than 375 words.

13 Your manager, who is responsible for the office administration of a medium-sized head office whose staff include some 35 PAs, secretaries and text production assistants, feels that the firm's image is suffering as a result of letters being produced with out-of-date and time-wasting layout conventions.

In order for staff who deal with correspondence to be given an update on currently accepted conventions and cost-effective practices, he has asked you to produce a suitable abstract from the Letter section of Unit 6 for their assistance (see pages 106–12).

14 Also, he wants you to compose a suitable factsheet – using The Letter section and your own research initiative entitled:

'How To Get The Best From The Post Office's Letter Post Services'

This factsheet is intended for circulation among managers and secretarial support staff alike.

> ### Self assessment question
>
> Have you fully mastered the techniques of summarising and have you practised them sufficiently?

Research and report back assignments

1 Working in pairs, collect a set of *one* of the following types of document. Devise a suitable presentation sequence and demonstrate to your class what you see as their strengths or weaknesses along with any other noteworthy points:

a) A set of what you see as successful (or unsuccessful) letterheads.
b) A set of typescript letter components which you consider well laid out and/or containing successful structures and tones/styles.
c) A set of well-designed memoranda-heads and (if you can secure some) examples of memo structures and styles.
d) A set of different kinds of report -eg annual company report, investigative report, accident/inspection report forms etc which supply examples of current design and instances of effective structure and style.

e) Examples of well designed and structured factsheets.

f) Examples of good form design, which are user-friendly and meeting their intended purpose.

Having selected the best specimens in the documents identified in *a*) to *f*) above, display them in a wall-mounted exhibition in your baseroom.

2 Arrange to talk to local managers and their secretaries and find out what they consider to be the skills needed to produce effective letters and memoranda.

Either report your findings orally to your group, or present them in appropriate summary form.

3 In groups of two or three, arrange to interview a manager and his/her team who have recently undertaken a project which culminated in the production of a report. Find out how they set about interpreting their terms of reference, and what procedures they adopted to secure their findings data.

Give your group a suitable oral report on what you discovered.

4 In pairs, seek out a local organisation which produces reports on a regular basis and find out what techniques they use to print and present them, using what equipment.

Summarise your findings as a hand-out for your group.

5 Find out what regulations local firms adopt to coordinate the production, display and removal of notices and bulletins. Produce your findings as a factsheet for distributing to your group.

Self assessment question

Have you yet designed a factsheet and a form which you felt met your given brief fully?

Work experience and simulation assignments

1 With the help of your supervisor, obtain sight of (and samples as permitted) of what your supervisor thinks are good examples of letter production in a range of the organisation's activities.

With permission, retain copies for your file and to show classmates.

2 Carry out a survey of how letters are produced in your attachment organisation and using what equipment. Report back orally to your group, explaining clearly software and equipment applications, as well as procedures adopted as 'house-style'.

3 Find out how the use of a LAN network may be changing patterns of memoranda messaging and summarise your findings for group distribution.

4 Interview your supervisor and organisation managers to find out what part oral and written reporting plays in their work. Deliver an oral account of your findings to your group.

5 Interview a series of different departmental managers and secretaries and ask them to provide you with their tips on designing and handling forms. Summarise your findings in a suitable set of points for your group to examine.

6 Design a factsheet about what your attachment organisation does. Your factsheet is intended to brief your work experience attachment successor.

7 With permission, carry out an investigation into the ways in which your attachment organisation recruits staff and how they are planning to meet future manpower needs. Compose a suitable report, including any recommendations on how systems and procedures may need to be changed. Submit your report to your supervisor.

Case study

'Ariel calling!'

You work as Deputy Office Administration Manager of Ariel Courier Services Limited, a company operating in greater London and the South East, specialising in high-speed delivery services of letters, packages, sealed document pouches etc. At present the company employs some 65 people in its head office and four regional offices, most of whom supervise the collection and distribution of packages, and some 105 couriers operating with motor-cycles and delivery vans, supported by 12 vehicle-servicing personnel operating from two mobile workshops.

Originally Ariel Courier Services Limited was set up 'on a wing and a prayer' by Johnnie and Liz Barker, currently Chairman and Managing Director. As a result of various industrial problems in the public mail delivery sector, Ariel's cash flow has rocketed in the past two months. The Barkers see this a heaven-sent opportunity to invest in a really efficient management information system, allied to some really up-to-the-minute mobile telecommunications equipment and systems. In fact the essence of their business is to push information as fast as possible around the organisation about pick-ups, drops, routes, overriding priorities etc. They also need to have a really good system for processing orders and transactions and billing customers promptly.

Yesterday, Johnnie Barker came into your office and rattled off the following instructions:

'Look, I'm sorry Gail's off sick (your boss), but this just can't wait! I want you to drop everything – and delegate the rest – so as to concentrate on producing a really top-notch report for me, Liz and the Board, which investigates the best way we can equip the company to maximise efficient and effective communications – including the four regional offices in Reading, Guildford, Ealing and Ashford. Oh, and not forgetting the 'flying tigers' of our vehicle servicing mob! I reckon we've got top-whack, absolute max £85 k (£85,000) to put a really good basic system in, capable of expansion as we can afford it and the market warrants. So I want you to get your skates on with your team – you can put Gail in the picture as you go along – and come up with your very best shot with detailed recommendations that the Board and I can work to!'

Assignments

1 In a group of three or four, hold a meeting (as the Deputy Office Administration Manager's task force) to decide how to go about meeting Johnnie Barker's briefing, and to agree on the most practical and time-effective means of conducting the project, bearing in mind that your report has to be with the Board in precisely four weeks' time!

2 In groups of three or four, research and then produce, in extended formal report form, the report which Johnnie Barker has requested. Bear in mind that Ariel's finances are limited, so you have to go for essentials and for a system capable of expansion.

3 Having selected the best report from those produced, as a class, role-play a meeting of Ariel's Board of Directors and the Office Administration Team which has been called to provide an oral briefing (with, say, AVA) to explain and enlarge upon the thrust of the report's recommendations. After the oral presentation, the board have to agree on how it will implement the report.

4 Observers of the role-play should take notes of the proceedings as source material for producing narrative minutes (see Unit 12).

5 As Johnnie Barker, compose a memorandum to the Office Administration group which responds to their report and indicates what action is to be taken.

Case study

The Bournemouth problem

'I'm getting seriously concerned about the slide in sales at Bournemouth, and from what I hear, there's also a staff problem there. I think the time has come to get to the heart of the matter. I want you to have a good look at the picture as we have it here at Head Office, and then get down there and find out what's gone wrong. Let me have a report by Wednesday week, in time for my meeting with Mr Green (the regional manager for the Southern Region). Oh, and you'd better let me have your own views on how the matter can best be put right. Now, about this draft advertisement . . .'

It was with these words that Harold Grafton, managing director of Countrywide Food Stores Ltd, briefed his personal assistant on the need for an investigatory report into the slump in sales at the Bournemouth branch.

After having carefully researched the relevant documentation at head office – sales statistics, personnel files, marketing reports and the like, and having visited the Bournemouth branch, Harold Grafton's P.A. uncovered the following information:

After a steady increase during the last five years, sales have dropped by 31% during the past nine months.

Company advertising and sales promotion has recently been criticised by a number of branch managers and divisional managers.

Customer relations at Bournemouth suffered for two months as a result of a faulty cash-register which has now been repaired.

Branch stocks are replaced by a system of drawing from a regional warehouse to ensure fresh stocks, quick turnover and avoidance of shortages.

A rival company opened six months ago a branch some three-quarters of a mile away, which has been engaging in price-cutting and extensive sales-promotion.

Mrs Harris, the branch manager, was appointed 12 months ago. Her background was sales assistant, assistant branch manager and temporary branch manager at three of your company's branches in Lincoln, Harrogate and Warrington.

A memorandum from the Central Southern Divisional Manager drew attention four months ago to the increasing demands of head office regarding the completion of a host of returns issued by various head office departments to all branches.

Telephone and customer serving techniques leave much to be desired at the Bournemouth branch.

The fixtures and fittings of the branch are old and were put in as a 'temporary' measure some three years ago.

Basically, office administration, merchandising and branch appearance are satisfactory if unremarkable.

An urban redevelopment plan is at present responsible for the demolition of 500 houses about half a mile from the branch as part of an urban renewal and rehousing scheme.

Marketing Department wrote a eulogistic report about the business potential of the area when a decision to purchase was being made three years ago.

Company branches at Poole and Christchurch are eclipsing the Bournemouth branch's turnover.

Assignment

As Harold Grafton's personal assistant, draft a suitable report according to his brief above, incorporating whatever aspects of the above information you consider relevant, and adding any appropriate, additional material you wish.

Case study

The Sherbury Leisure Centre

For several months public unrest has been growing in the town of Sherbury, county town of Wealdshire, about the lack of leisure amenities and facilities in the town, particularly for young people. A recent police report revealed that cases of vandalism had risen by 32% in the last 12 months, and teenage arrests for drunk and disorderly behaviour by 24%. Social workers have also expressed their concern about the mounting incidence of teenage alcoholism, and teenage gangs roaming the town centre and housing estates, bred as they see it, from boredom deriving from little or nothing to do in the evenings. The town's two youth clubs are oversubscribed, and there have been incidents when older teenagers have attempted to disrupt youth club activities when denied entrance.

During the past six weeks the local weekly newspaper, *The Sherbury Chronicle* has been campaigning for improvements in leisure facilities, with hardhitting editorials under headlines such as, 'Council Fuddy-duddies Forget Their Youth'. The paper has also carried a lively correspondence on the subject. Readers' views have ranged from the sympathetic to the condemnatory – 'Sherbury's years of indifference towards the needs of the young are now bearing a bitter fruit,' and, 'In my youth people were too tired from a hard day's work to worry about whether they could play ping-pong or not. As a ratepayer I fail to see why I should subsidise the indolent by forking out for some white elephant Leisure Palace!'

Some town councillors have been actively canvassing for a Leisure Centre to be built to provide what they consider as sorely lacking amenities. At a recent council meeting, Councillor James Hillingdon referred to 'the shocking state of affairs that exists when a town of this size should have nothing to offer its young people in the evening but violent films from its one cinema and alcoholic beverages from its ten central public houses.'

Local sports clubs and associations have been making representations to councillors and to County Hall officials. Some sports enthusiasts are travelling thirty miles or more to find the amenities they seek. The existing facilities are predominantly those for outdoor sports on recreation park pitches or for a few indoor sports such as judo in the small and over-crowded Community Hall at the western end of the town. The activities which have been suggested for inclusion in any future Leisure Centre include squash, badminton, basketball, tennis, swimming, aerobics, karate, volleyball, ten-pin bowling, snooker and billiards, gymnastics and for older members, yoga, relaxation classes and keep-fit courses, together with a club-room for darts, dominoes and other 'less strenuous pursuits'.

A rough projection has put the cost of building a Leisure Centre at £4.2m, for a centre suitable for existing needs. Two sites have been identified as suitable. The first is at the end of the Charles Bowley Memorial Recreation Park, in the town's southern suburb, and the second is a central site which would require the centre to be built as a multi-storey building.

Councillors think that some increase in Community Charges will be inevitable, but could be significantly offset by running the Centre commercially. Local sports and social clubs have offered to get together to mount a series of sponsored events to help finance the sports equipment needed in the Centre.

Assignment

As a result of the mounting pressure to provide a Leisure Centre, Sherbury's Chief Executive has decided to form a working-party made up of representatives of the Planning, Architect's and Education departments, including the Youth and Community Officer, the Sports Advisory Office and coopted representatives from local sports clubs and associations. He has asked this working-party to investigate the need for a Leisure Centre, to make projections as to its likely building and maintenance costs, suggestions as to its location having regard to parking and transport considerations, proposals as to the kind of activities it should house and the kind of rooms or halls it should contain. Lastly he wishes the working party to make recommendations which could be submitted to the Council. As secretary to the working party you have been asked to draft the report.

8

Oral and non-verbal communication

Photograph courtesy of Warner-Lambert (UK) Ltd.

Overview

Unit 8 provides you with information and guidelines on:

- The role of oral and non-verbal communication in organisations.
- An evaluation of speaking and listening skills.
- How to structure oral messages and adopt effective speaking styles.
- How to interpret non-verbal communication signals – NVC – kinesics, proxemics, paralinguistics, etc.
- How to use personal NVC signals – expression, gesture, posture, etc to best effect.
- Techniques of face-to-face communication.
- Guidelines for developing effective telephoning techniques.
- Oral aspects of meetings and developing effective speaking skills.

Introduction

'Considering the amount of oral communication that goes on in all organisations, it never ceases to surprise me how few people can converse well. And, given the importance of oral and non-verbal communication, how little time is devoted to it in in-house training and staff development.'

The above comments made by a senior management consultant highlight both the central importance of good oral communication skills at work and also how they are undervalued in general. Perhaps the underlying reason is that we all consider ourselves pretty good at oral communicating, having survived satisfactorily into adult life! There is, however, a world of difference between possessing survival skills and demonstrating a sure-footed mastery of the many work-place activities dominated by oral, and non-verbal communication, such as:

- Client/colleague reception
- Telephoning
- Taking part in meetings

- Interviewing and appraising
- Giving a presentation
- Briefing and demonstrating
- Addressing and public speaking
- Motivating or disciplining
- Selling and persuading
- Training and developing staff

Each of the above commonly occurring activities requires differing specialist skills. For example, a hard-pressed company director may have to think very quickly on his feet in order to answer a shareholder's pointed question convincingly at an annual general meeting. Again, a skilled chairman may need to pull out all his oral communication skill stops in order to prevent a crucial meeting breaking down into divisive recriminations and abuse. And the much under-valued sales representative may need to summon up reserves of telephone selling expertise in order to calm a customer upset about the non-delivery of an urgently needed order.

There is, then, little doubt about the need for *all* intending managers and their support staff to become expert in oral communication. Furthermore, this particular set of skills can be improved beyond expectation – even by those people hampered by shyness or self-effacing personalities.

Non-verbal communication (NVC)

Whether we are aware of it or not, we are continuously giving off body language signals whenever we communicate face-to-face or through video/CCTV media, with other people. Body language may be simply divided into expression, gesture and body positioning (posture) signalling. We all know from an early age how to read the signs of anger, anxiety, happiness or irritation in someone's face and gesture. We can also quickly gauge whether someone is sitting or standing in a relaxed, alert, nervous or nonchalant way. Furthermore, as we grow up we learn a host of unwritten rules about the proximity or distance that people like to establish with their contacts, ranging from a close embrace to the cross-desk interview or military inspection.

In the heat of the moment, or because our minds are preoccupied, we often forget at work to remain alert for NVC or body language signals, but they are often vital clues to suppressed or unconscious communication and as such are valuable in providing feedback or responses during the oral communication process.

Unit 8 examines the fields of oral and non-verbal communication in detail and supplies you with a series of guidelines and tips to aid your own development. But in order to improve, you must be prepared to take a good look at yourself in an un-tinted 'communication mirror', and be prepared to remedy careless speech habits, unsuspected NVC

signals you give off, or unhelpful attitudes and outlooks. Your ego may take the odd knock in group work role-play and simulation, but if you look upon your study period as a cricketer looks upon a session in the nets, then you will quickly realise the value of realistic trial-goes before the real thing.

Talking point

Effective oral communication techniques tend to be overlooked because people are loath to admit – even to themselves – that they are less than expert in any aspect.

The building bricks of oral communication

As with many other subjects, oral communication may be divided into two basic components – the what and the how. The 'what' or content of an oral message requires skill in marshalling thoughts and ideas in a structured and sequenced order that listeners can easily follow and absorb. The 'how' or tone of the message – the way of communicating it by intonation, expression, emphasis and register – serve to help and promote its successful delivery. Thus successful oral communication is a happy blend of message organisation and delivery skills.

Consider, for example, these comments which we typically make in response to observing people communicating orally at work, or contemplating their own gaffes or 'boo-boos':

'I could have bitten my tongue off!'
'Every time Bert opens his mouth, he puts his foot in it!'
'I stood there wishing the earth could swallow me up!'
'The trouble with Helen is that she ought to think before she puts her mouth in gear!'
'You can always rely on Harry to pooh-pooh a new idea . . .'
'His trouble? I'll tell you what his trouble is – he just never ever listens!'
or,
'Better let Jackie handle the press, she's got the gift of the gab'
'Mike could do the commentary, he's pretty quick on his feet.'
'Let Charlie go, he could sell ice-cream to Eskimos!'
'I think Anne should chair the meeting, she's got a clear head and is good at handling arguments.'

Whether to praise or blame, we are all quick to assess other people's performances and then to slot them into pigeon-holes as good, bad or indifferent communicators. It therefore matters a great deal in career and advancement terms that your oral skills promote positive responses in others. Rightly or wrongly, for example, it is a known fact that the people who get their way in meetings are those who can speak boldly and who have the self-confidence to dominate the proceedings without becoming boorish.

Talking point

The way a person speaks is a highly personal matter. People are best left to 'sort things out' for themselves.

Checklist of speaking and listening skills

The following checklist identifies the skills of combining the what and how of oral communication, both as a speaker and a listener:

1 As a speaker

Creating the message

In order to create a well-structured oral message the speaker should:

- decide first and foremost the context of the oral communication and what outcomes are desired,
- establish which are the key points to get across and what running order would best link them together in a beginning (to introduce the topic), a middle (to develop main points and arguments), and an end (to emphasise actions needed to be taken by the recipient or general follow-up required),
- select in advance the salient facts and figures which will support the argument/position taken,
- decide before embarking on what the delivery style of the message should be: rational/objective, exhorting/enthusing, convincing/persuading, analysing/evaluating, etc since this will fundamentally influence the 'how' of the message's delivery,

(*Note*: whenever possible you should make the time – say before a phone-call – to jot down your key points and desired outcomes in advance, to ensure you get across *all* your message, especially when dealing with a strong personality.)

- once embarked on delivering the message, the speaker should monitor constantly the feedback he receives – whether by watching and hearing or just hearing – and be prepared to modify the message's delivery in the light of misunderstanding, impatience, hostile reaction, etc especially in the cut-and-thrust of two-way dialogue,
- lastly, the speaker should know when he has said enough – that the message has been suc-

cessfully transmitted – and then stop on a positive note.

Styling the message

The extent of the orally delivered message's acceptance in face-to-face communication depends very much on:

- facial signals emitting: friendliness, conviction, warmth, sincerity, even-handedness, rapport.
- gesture signals communicating: determination, solidarity with the audience/listener, emphasis, conviction, tolerance.
- stance signals conveying: ease and relaxation, respect for a formal situation, authority, physical presence.

In enunciating the words of the oral message, a person's speech habits – clipped starts and endings, umming and erring, speaking into his shoes, gabbling, uttering boring monotones etc – will radically affect the message's acceptance. Important speech features to master are:

accent, pronunciation, enuciation/articulation, intonation, emphasis and projection

- **Accent**: today regional accents are perfectly acceptable, provided that people in other regions can follow them and are not foxed by local dialect words.
- **Pronunciation**: no one likes to hear speech marred by ugly or affected habits: ' 'Ere! Gissanuvverotdog wujja!' or, 'Hellair! Waive come dine for Arscot, but Jimmie's gorn orf this mornin, for a quick rind of goaf!'
- **Enunciation/articulation**: good oral communication – especially over poor telephone-lines or in large halls – depends on vowels being well-rounded and not swallowed, and consonants not being slurred or clipped:

'Sumfin's appnd to innerupt the eggsekitiv decision-makin' process an conserkwenly a returnawork tommora is definally outadaquestion!'

- **Intonation/emphasis**: nothing causes listeners to switch off faster than the ponderous utterance of drab monotone and the even thud of dull cadences. Experienced speakers know when to emphasise key words and phrases and when to lift, and drop the voice to provide contrast and colour to their message, or by phrasing, when to make telling pauses or add enlivening pace, etc.
- **Projection**: inexperienced and unsure speakers tend to mumble as if to escape responsibility for their utterances! Effective speakers adopt erect stances and head positions which allow the free and unconstricted escape of air from the lungs and mouth, which are essential to clear delivery – especially in large rooms and halls; their vocal chords are also practised in creating resonant

sounds which can carry without harshness or shouting.

2 As a listener

A failure to develop effective listening skills is a vulnerable weak-spot in most people. Most of us constantly feed our ego needs by wanting to dominate conversations as speakers, and by planning what we are going to say next, instead of listening properly to the other person.

Yet at the heart of all effective management and leadership is the ability to keep constantly in touch with staff's views and attitudes and to possess an attuned listening ear for evidence of upsets, disagreements, ideas and suggestions and the like. Acquiring good listening skills like those set out below is *vital* if you are to become a good oral communicator:

- Keeping concentration upon what is being said, and avoiding distractions and mind-wandering which result in blank patches which can last from seconds to minutes.
- Repeating key words and phrases in the mind to help retain and recall them – especially important names, dates, facts and figures, etc.
- Keeping a close eye (and ear) on the speaker's face, gesture and posture (as well as voice patterns) so as to pick up those aspects which he or she considers important or is in disagreement with; checking whether NVC signals agree or conflict with what is being said.
- Staying alert for pauses or falls in the speaker's speech rhythms, which signal opportunities for responding, interposing or putting follow-up questions.
- Being ready to ask a question or provide a remark which causes the speaker to explain or amplify a point to aid the listener's understanding of the message.
- Providing regular feedback responses which indicate that the message is still being received and understood: 'Quite', 'You're right', 'I quite agree' etc or is being queried or disagreed with: 'No, I think you're wrong there', 'What makes you think that?' 'I don't think I would go that far . . .', etc.

- Monitoring and controlling personal NVC signals: such as those which provide the speaker with positive feedback and help establish rapport and provide encouragement; nipping in the bud signs of boredom or indifference or concealing anger, resentment or irritation, etc unless these are intended for the speaker to pick up.
- Listening especially attentively for points and sections of personal importance or relevance; ensuring that actions and personal follow-up requests are fully and clearly understood before the speaker rings off, departs or a meeting is closed.
- Ensuring that written or tape-recorded notes are made clearly and in sufficient detail for future reference and follow-up work.

Oral communication assignments

1 Check the clarity of your accent and delivery by tape-recording the following sentences by yourself:

Blue Skies Tours mean fine, warm days!

Mining underground often requires working in confined spaces.

Tempered steel displays both strength and elasticity.

Strict adherence to company regulations is essential.

Advertising is quickly becoming an integral part of people's lives.

Picking grapes is a popular choice for a working holiday.

Baking bricks is a back-breaking business!

Play back your recording and check that:
the open vowels are really open,
-ed, -ing endings are not clipped,
'h's' have not been omitted,
's' and 'z' sounds are clear,
syllables have not been slurred,
consonants are clearly sounded.

2 Study the following extracts from three different work situations. Consider how you would use intonation, emphasis, pauses and voice-levels to make them as effective as possible when spoken. Then

record them on to tape and submit your version for evaluation by your group:

'I wanted to speak to you about a personal matter as you know I have been with the company now for eighteen months as far as I know my work has always been satisfactory and I feel that I have been a conscientious employee I should therefore like to ask you for an increase in my salary.'

'I have called you in to discuss a most serious matter with you during the past three weeks I have received a number of complaints from customers upset by your apparent rudeness while serving them I propose to outline the circumstances of each complaint from the customer's point of view and then to ask you for your own account of what allegedly took place.'

'Charlie we're in trouble Johnson's have just phoned a large order in but they must have it by tomorrow morning I told them I couldn't promise anything until I'd spoken to you is there any chance of your fitting in another production run I'd certainly appreciate it if you could use your influence.'

3 The following passage is the closing section of a managing director's address to his Annual Sales Conference. Study it carefully and then record it on to tape for play-back analysis. Your aim should be to fire the sales representatives with enthusiasm during a difficult period:

'I know – and you know – that the company, and indeed the country, have been going through a difficult trading period. Equally, I know that the strength of Allied Products lies in its ability to meet a challenge. It hasn't been easy, and I can give you no guarantee that it will get better at all quickly. What I do know is that if anyone is going to lead the company into a better tomorrow, it is you, its sales representatives. And so my closing message to you all is; the company is proud of what you have done during a difficult year and will back you all to the hilt in the coming months; but it will only be your determination and enthusiasm which will turn the corner during the next year. I know I can rely on you!'

Check the recorded versions for the following:
audibility–clarity
delivery–pace, emphasis
commitment–sincerity
ability to enthuse
Where any version may be considered to have fallen short, try to decide the reasons for its lack of success.

4 As a means of gaining practice in using the spoken word effectively, form pairs in your student group and make a recording on audio or video equipment of one of the following situations. When the recordings have been made, play them back to the group for comment and discussion of such factors as: clarity, fluency, persuasiveness, rapport, effectiveness, etc.

Before attempting the recording, the pairs of students should make notes of their aims and objectives and of their roles or attitudes in the situation. Also, a few 'trial goes' may be needed.

a) Choose a piece of office or school equipment which you know well and, as a salesperson, seek to sell it to a prospective customer who has to think carefully before spending money on office equipment.

b) Sally Jones, audio-typist, is normally conscientious. Recently, however, her work has become untidy and marred by messy erasures. Her supervisor decides the time has come to tackle her on the subject!

c) Recently, the wholesaling chain of Office Supplies Limited went over to a computerised system for rendering accounts to its credit customers. Jim/Jane Harris, a customer of long standing, keeps getting demands to pay an account of £243.22 which he/she paid several months ago. Peter/Petra Ford is the sales representative of Office Supplies who has to take the brunt of the complaint when making a call on Jim's/Jane's store.

Talking point

Too much consideration of oral communication techniques destroys natural, unselfconscious rapport between people.

Non-verbal communication

Non-verbal communication (NVC) is a fascinating area of study. It concerns the many ways in which people communicate in face-to-face situations, either as a means of reinforcing or of replacing the spoken word. Sometimes people employ non-verbal communication techniques consciously, at other times the process is carried out unconsciously. In many instances, the response is involuntary. A sudden shock, for instance, may result in someone draining in facial colour, opening his or her eyes wide and becoming slack-jawed.

Non-verbal communication may be divided into three main areas, with rather technical labels for readily observable activities or responses:

Kinesics

Facial expressions

Smiles, frowns, narrowed eyes transmitting friendliness, anger or disbelief etc.

Gestures

Pointing fingers, 'thumbs up' sign, shakes of the head, transmitting an emphasising focus, congratulations or disagreements etc.

Movements

Quick pacing up and down, finger-drumming, leisurely strolling, transmitting impatience, boredom or relaxation.

Proxemics

Physical contact

Shaking hands, prodding with the forefinger, clapping on the back, transmitting greetings, insistence or friendship.

Positioning

Keeping a respectful distance, looking over someone's shoulder, sitting close to someone, transmitting awareness of differing status, a close working relationship or relaxed mutual trust.

Posture

Standing straight and erect, lounging, sitting hunched up, leaning forward, spreading oneself in a chair, transmitting alertness and care, self-confidence (or even over-confidence), nervousness or ease.

Non-verbal communication assignment

What NVC signals are the above people transmitting?

Photos centre left and lower right Sally & Richard Greenhill

Para-linguistics

Feedback sounds of surprise or agreement of annoyance or impatience –
'uh-uh, 'whew!', 'oops!', 'tsk', 'tut-tut' etc.

A heightened awareness of what people are 'saying' non-verbally greatly assists the manager or secretary to read a situation and to act – perhaps to head off a personality clash or to calm an irate customer.

NVC and effective communication

Working successfully in an organisation requires that staff develop human relations skills by becoming more aware of how other people are reacting or feeling. Specifically, it requires the ability to 'read' a situation quickly and correctly. Though information and attitudes may be readily conveyed by means of the spoken word, the constraints of courtesy and staff relationships may result in the spoken message masking how someone is really feeling or relating. At other times, a correct interpretation of NVC signals may allow the interpreter to act positively.

For example, the sales representative who recognises that the nods, smiles and approaching movements of the prospective customer mean that he or she is won over, is able to proceed confidently to close the sale. Equally, the secretary who correctly interprets her principal's frowns and toe-tapping as he or she reads a report, may rightly decide to postpone until a more favourable moment her request for a salary increase! Moreover, the receptionist who recognises annoyance in the hurried approaching steps of a member of staff who bursts into the office, eyes narrowed, chin jutting forward and mouth down-drawn, will have the common sense to ensure that her opening words are calming:

'I'm very sorry, Ms Jones is out at the moment. Is there anything I may do to help meantime?'

rather than exacerbating:

'Ms Jones is out. I'm afraid you'll have to call back.'

Thus the ability to recognise NVC signals and to modify responses in their light is essential to the maintenance and promotion of good human relations within an organisation as well as being a valuable tool in helping the manager, secretary or clerk to achieve objectives involving direct personal contact with others.

Talking point

Studying the way people communicate non-verbally is rather like hitting them below the belt.

Expression, gesture and movements

Facial expression

The human face is capable of conveying a wide range of expression and emotion. Various parts of the face are used to convey signals:

A range of responses	Facial components
ACCEPTANCE REJECTION ENJOYMENT DISLIKE FRIENDSHIP HOSTILITY INTEREST DISINTEREST ANGER LOVE SYMPATHY JEALOUSY ASSURANCE NERVOUSNESS AGREEMENT DISAGREEMENT ATTENTION BOREDOM ACCEPTANCE DISBELIEF SURPRISE FEAR IMPATIENCE FRUSTRATION ENVY EMPATHY EASE DISCOMFORT ALERTNESS STUPOR PAIN PLEASURE ECSTASY TORMENT SATISFACTION DISPLEASURE	Forehead – upward and downward frowns Eyebrows – raising or knitting, furrowing Eyelids – opening, closing, narrowing Eye pupils – dilating Eyes – upwards, downwards gazing, holding or avoiding eye contact Nose – wrinkling, flaring nostrils Facial muscles – drawn up or down, for grinning, teeth clenching Lips – smiling, pursing, drawn in Mouth – wide open, drawn in, half-open Tongue – licking lips, moving around inside cheeks, sucking teeth Jaw/Chin – thrust forward, hanging down Head – thrown back, inclined to one side, hanging down, chin drawn in, inclined upwards

Though the above check-list of responses may not, perhaps, be manifested in every office or factory, it does indicate the incredible range of emotions and feelings visible in the human facial expression!

Assignment

Choose a number of varying responses from the above check-list and, from the list of facial components, make out a description of how the individual parts of the face would act together to form the particular expression for each response.

Gesture

Apart from actors, politicians and public speakers who may rehearse a telling gesture to emphasise a point, many of the gestures which people employ as they speak or listen are used unselfconsciously. When the speaker becomes excited, for example, sweeping movements of the arms or the banging of a fist into an open palm may act to reinforce what is being said. Alternatively, the propping of the head upon a cupped hand may signal that what is being said is boring and failing to interest.

Of course, some gestures are consciously and deliberately made. The car driver who points a finger to their head with a screwing motion is demonstrating what they think about the quality of someone's driving!

The range of gestures that utilise head, shoulders, arms, hands, fingers, legs and feet is indeed wide. Though frequently supporting the spoken word, gestures may either be used, consciously, to replace speech, as, for example, with the finger placed in front of the lips urging silence. Unconscious signals from the listener – the brushing of the hand across mouth and chin may be 'saying', 'I'm not sure that I go along with what is being said'. On the other hand, someone may seek to calm a meeting which is becoming heated by consciously patting down the air with both open palms which transmit the sense of, 'Steady on, let's not lose our tempers over this!'

Commonly used gestures

The following gestures are seen regularly in daily life, either reinforcing or substituting for the spoken word:

Head

nodding sideways to urge someone along
nodding up and down
shaking sideways
inclined briefly
cradled in one or both hands

Arms and hands

widely outstretched
jammed into trouser pockets
firmly folded across the chest
holding the back of the head with fingers laced
making chopping movements with the side of the hand
hands pressed together in 'praying' position'
one or both hands held over mouth
flat of hand patting desk-top
hand brushing something away in the air
both hands placed open upon the chest

Fingers

running through the hair
drumming on table-top
stroking mouth and chin
stabbing the air with forefinger
clenched into a fist
manipulated in an arm-wave
patting the fingertips together with the fingers of both hands out-stretched
rubbing the thumb and fingers together

Legs and feet

leg and foot making kicking motion
foot or toes tapping the ground
moving legs up and down while seated

Posture

The way people 'arrange their bodies' as they stand or sit may also be extremely communicative. The candidate at interview, for example, who sits hunched into a chair with arms tight, hands clenched, and legs and feet pressed and folded together is probably 'saying' very 'loudly' to the interviewers, 'I am feeling extremely nervous.' By the same token, the interviewee who lolls and sprawls in the chair may be revealing an unpleasant over-confidence and familiarity. As a general rule, the body frame is more widely spread in a relaxed position, whether seated or standing, when someone feels at ease, and is more tightly held, with arms and legs together when discomfort, nervousness or tension is being experienced.

The ability to interpret such signals and to act as necessary to disarm or reassure is invaluable in promoting good human relations.

Assignment

Add to the above examples of gesture and posture and then describe the sort of messages sent through each example and identify the contexts in which they may be seen.

Communicating face-to-face

Face-to-face communication is the oxygen in the life-blood of business and public service organisations. Despite the efficiency and speed of modern telecommunications – essential in their way – there is no totally acceptable substitute for people talking and reacting in close, direct contact. How often at work are sentiments expressed such as:

'Pop into my office and we'll talk it over.'

'I'm sure we can thrash this out round a table.'

'I'm glad I've bumped into you, Jane, I'd like your opinion on . . .'

Communicating face-to-face embraces a wide variety of situations:

private discussions in offices
encounters in corridors
conversation over lunch in staff restaurants
taking part in meetings
selling across the sales counter
explaining on the factory floor
discussing in the large open office
speaking at conferences
questioning at interviews

Also, the context of the dialogue may render it formal or informal. A 'natter' over lunch will be expressed in words very different from those used at a formal appointment interview. Also, the way in which a dialogue develops will depend entirely upon its context and the relationship of its participants, who may be conversing with the aim of directing or requesting, informing or persuading, congratulating or disciplining.

Whatever the circumstances, the reason why most people prefer most of the time to communicate face-to-face is that such a medium best provides them with 'a total impression' in a way that written communication or telephone calls do not. This impression derives not only from what is being said, but from the whole manner of a person's delivery, including non-verbal communication factors. Moreover, the medium permits instant feedback, the means of asking snap questions and of, sometimes, obtaining prompt answers!

In face-to-face contact many 'tools' of communication are working in concert: intonation of the voice, facial expression, gesture, posture and movement, all of which provide a much fuller and often more accurate indication of the import of any given message.

Talking point

The interview process is loaded against the reserved, quiet and introverted. Yet more often than not they may be better in the job than the brash, assertive or plausible candidate.

Factors affecting face-to-face communication

What, then, are the most important factors which affect and influence direct personal contact? Whether the context is formal or informal and whether there has been an opportunity to plan beforehand will clearly make a difference. The following check-list includes some of the main ingredients necessary for effective face-to-face communication:

Check before you speak

1 *Plan beforehand* – have supporting notes and documents to hand.
2 *Explore opposing points of view* – look at the situation from the other point of view and have counter-arguments ready if needed.
3 *Check out the location of the contact* – it helps to be familiar with surroundings, whether for a meeting or interview.
4 *Exclude interruptions and distractions* – frequent telephone-calls or staff interruptions prevent concentration.
5 *Consider the person or people you will be seeing* – it pays to be as well informed as possible about colleagues, associates or customers, and to know 'what makes them tick'.
6 *Select a mode of speaking appopriate to the situation* – being over-familiar and 'chatty' or reserved and formal may prove blocks to effective communication, depending upon the context of the dialogue.
7 *Check your appearance* – dress is another way of signalling what we represent, or how we wish to be accepted.

Talking point

In the interview situation, there is, inevitably, a conflict between truth and self-projection.

Tips on face-to-face oral communication

Mannerism

Avoid irritating, unpleasant or discourteous mannerisms of speech, gesture or posture.

Do not distract by 'fiddling' with a pencil, doodling or indulging in other distractions.

Thinking

It is vital to think before you speak – once a statement is uttered it may be difficult to retract.

If you agree with a point, try to develop it constructively; if you disagree do not become over-assertive. Show that you can see more than one point of view.

Remember, it is better to say a little which is considered, than a lot which is superficial.

Courtesy

The effective communicator is always courteous. Avoid:
interrupting,
contradicting,
'showing off' to impress others,
making someone 'look small',
losing your temper,
being condescending,
showing boredom or impatience.

Timing

Choose the right moment to speak; sometimes it is better to let others have their say first.

Listen for the drop in a person's voice, look for a smile or nod which may indicate that someone has finished making a point.

Be alert for the signs a person makes when he wishes to end a conversation or interview.

Know when you have won and leave promptly!

Structuring

If others are to follow your argument and value what you say, it is important that you structure your points logically, and express them in connected phrases and sentences.

It is also essential that you do not speak for too long at a time; people will quickly reject what you have to say if you deprive them of the opportunity to have their say too!

Listening

Failing to listen to someone is not only a grave discourtesy, but also may result in your looking silly or making a *faux-pas*.

Pay attention, consider the implications of what is being said. Look at the speaker, provide him with feedback to show you are following.

Reacting and contributing

One of the quickest ways of alienating others is to show no reaction to what they have said. Enthusiastic agreement or determined disagreement both indicate that there is an interest and commitment present.

Ensure you make some positive contribution to the dialogue – if you have nothing to say, people will assume that you have nothing of value to contribute and may assess you accordingly.

Styling

Strive to ensure that the manner in which you speak is appropriate to the circumstances.

Choose your words and expressions carefully, mindful of the personalities and backgrounds of others present.

It is easy to give offence but difficult to overcome its effects.

The telephone

Telecommunications systems in general, and the telephone in particular have become indispensable tools for communicating the spoken word in business today.

Indeed, the range of telecommunications services now offered to the businessman is amazingly wide and still growing fast!

People and organisations are now linked nationally and globally by networks of satellite, radio, undersea cable and land-line which provide telephone, telex, computer and video conference links. Moreover, the extensive development of computerised telephone exchanges, is resulting in the provision of a much more sophisticated telephone service, and many organisations now operate their own private network system over remote locations. The introduction of microprocessor facilities into telephone services has made possible, for example, the automatic calling of engaged numbers until a line is free, the abbreviated dialling of frequently sought telephone numbers, as well as a wide range of automatic message recording features. The near future will almost certainly bring a video-telephone service to business and domestic users.

For some time to come, however, the oral-aural telephone network will continue to be the most widely used of the telecommunications systems, and a mastery of telephone techniques is essential for those planning a career or already working in industry, commerce or government.

Talking point

The telephone is an interrupting inconvenience in organisations far more frequently than it is a time-saving helpmate.

The first, and indeed principal factor to be borne in mind by the telephone user is that the medium is oral and aural but *not* visual! As has been already discussed in the section on non-verbal communication, one of the main benefits of face-to-face communication is being able to see facial expression, gesture and posture which help enormously to convey the significance or implications of what is being said.

Telephone users, however, often refer to the 'disembodied voice' which is much more difficult to understand and which may be prone to communication breakdowns for a number of reasons including:

the spoken message is inaudible
the spoken word is misheard
the spoken message is misinterpreted because required feedback is not forthcoming

To become an effective user of the telephone,

therefore, requires the acquisition of specialist skills ranging from distinct articulation of the spoken word to expertise in handling sophisticated telephone equipment. Such skills are particularly important in view of the dehumanising effect which using the telephone may have on people who cannot see the person they are talking to!

The following check-list indicates the principal skills which using the telephone successfully involves:

Checklist of effective telephoning techniques

However sophisticated an IT-driven telephone system may be, it is only as good as its user – whether in terms of operations know-how or in developed oral communication skills. The checklist set out below will help you to use the telephone at work professionally and cost-effectively:

1 Before calling

- make sure you are **fully familiar** with the CABX/Key System your organisation has installed, so as to avoid frustration and loss of face,
- ensure you have checked that the number you will call up is the correct one; BT reckon that organisations waste millions of pounds each year on wrong number connections,
- prepare your list of points and action requirements on paper or monitor screen beforehand to avoid oversights and omissions and to emphasise deadlines,
- likewise draw up a checklist of questions (with answer spaces) so you can jot down the answers to sought-after information quickly and easily,
- 'bone up' on personal/company data about your call-taker by calling up your client/contact database; it definitely does help to be able to refer to wife/partner/children by name, or to ask after the new branch in Bournemouth just launched, and so on,
- have to hand any files, papers or screened data you may wish to refer to during your call – 'Hang on a minute while I just fetch the file' sounds unprofessional and wastes time and money,
- anticipate any tricky points, objections or snags likely to arise during the call; practise in your mind how you will handle them; jot down any prompts, etc,
- know who the decision-makers are in the organisation you are calling; avoid wasting time by allowing a hierarchy of support staff make you repeat your message before telling you that they don't deal with that aspect!
- arrange to avoid interruptions and distractions during calls – you may miss a vital word or point; ensure your confidential calls are in fact just that,

- plan your calls to take advantage of lower cost times and tariffs.

2 During your call

- always make time for suitably polite greetings and pleasantries: – 'How are you John, still surviving?' 'That new branch of yours still raking in the shekels?' which help to break the ice and re-establish rapport,
- remember always that your contact cannot see your face; so make sure you **sound** decisive, concerned, interested, confident and heed to that good advice to 'smile with your voice!'
- don't forget to check your notes from time-to-time and to supply spellings or repeats of key names, addresses, numbers and the like,
- always obtain clear feedback as to whether the heart of the message has been correctly received and noted,
- make sure that your required deadlines and actions are understood and accepted as being realistic and feasible,
- remember to note down on a message pad any information supplied to you during the call by your call-taker – especially names, dates, phone numbers or addresses,
- however sorely tried or upset, *always conduct your calls calmly* and never lose your temper over the phone – upsets on the phone are difficult to smooth over because of the nature of the medium and the time-lapse before a subsequent face-to-face meeting,
- remember to close your call courteously, thanking your contact for his time and help; try to keep your calls brief – telephoning is not cheap and someone may be trying to get hold of you.

3 After the call

- make it a habit to transcribe all scribbled notes of the call **immediately** and to route messages directly to relevant staff; call any arising meetings promptly on your LAN/messaging system – or you may forget!
- make any entries on your electronic notepad or jobs list arising from the call,
- clear your desk and re-file all the papers, etc you fetched out to do with the call – you will want them again one day,
- make time to analyse the implications of the call and how it may affect you and your work before other tasks intervene and its impact dims.

Talking point

There's far too much mystique preached about using the telephone – you just pick the thing up, make contact and talk!

As a call-taker

Keep all the above points in mind, but above all, make sure you jot down the key points of the incoming message and secure essential names, dates, numbers, addresses etc. Don't be afraid to ask two or three times for a tricky spelling or set of data. If you don't get them right, the whole point and cost of the call will be wasted anyway!

Never be an anonymous call-taker – supply your name and job title from the outset. No one likes dealing with furtive people who try to conceal their identity so as to avoid responsibility for follow-up action the in-coming call demands.

Call style

- Do sound cheerful, helpful, 'on-the-ball', competent, authoritative, in control.
- Don't sound casual, over-familiar, sarcastic, icy, condescending, abrupt, impatient or intolerant.

Talking point

The ability to use the telephone is generally taken for granted. Yet the national bill for its misuse and abuse must run into millions.

'Just a minute . . .'

A customer once telephoned the book department of a large store to enquire whether a particular text had arrived which had been on order for some weeks. A young voice answers,

'I'm afraid Miss Standshawe's at lunch.'

The caller then asked if there was any means of checking – from a goods in or order processing ledger – whether the book in question had arrived, but was met with the same response,

'Well, you see, Miss Stanshawe's at lunch.'

Whereupon the caller asked if the sales assistant would mind having a look to see if there was any sign of the book. The assistant said,

'Just a minute . . .'

After about ten minutes of waiting, the caller heard a second, young voice whisper,

'Go on. You can put the 'phone down now. He's bound to have rung off!'

What does the above situation reveal about the inadequacies of the book department's and store's management?

Example of a completed message using a pre-printed message pad

Priority status.

Essential information in case message is wrongly delivered.

| URGENT | YES ✓ | NO |

Message for __Jack Foster, Accounts Dept__

Time _____11.15_____ Date _22.5.19--_

Sometimes the dates and times of receipt of message are very important. Also provides note of time elapsed since message arrived.

When you were out

Ms __Sandra Jones, Accounts Dept__

Of __COMPUTA SOFTWARE LTD, High St, Kingston-on-Thames__

Telephone __01-632 9632   Ext 275__

Good messages always convey: who, of whom, where located, telephone nos, including STD code and extension.

- [✓] Telephoned
- [✓] Wants you to phone
- [ ] Will phone later
- [ ] Returned your call
- [ ] Wants to see you
- [ ] Came to see you
- [ ] Will come back later

Most message pads include a tick checklist of back-up information for recipient, of which this specimen shows a sample.

Message __Apparently, our payment for their integrated accounts package ACCOUNTAZED is overdue for settlement. Sum due is £895.00. We stand to lose settlement discount unless we pay within 7 days. Ms Jones can authorise discount if you contact her directly and confirm payment on way.__

The effective message is: clearly written, unambiguous, provides essential detail and indicates follow-up action needed.

Taken by __Jean Roberts__

For follow-up briefing if needed.

© Copyright 1969, 1977 Laure Office Aids Inc. V. W. Eimicke Associates Inc.

Produced by Waterlow Business Forms (A Division of Oyez Stationery Ltd.)
Oyez House, 16 Third Avenue, Denbigh West Industrial Estate, Bletchley, Milton Keynes MK1 1TE.

FORM OA1
2/87

(Reproduced by kind permission of Waterlow Business Forms)

Telephone support toolkit

- A list of names numbers, addresses and details of contacts, ideally kept in the form of a computer database so that the required information may be called up and displayed on a monitor.
- A list of national IDD prefixes for long-distance calls, ideally in the form of a computer database.
- Loaded abbreviated numbers for frequently used calls.
- Pre-printed message pad and pens.
- Up-to-date directory of internal extension numbers.
- Access to national/international telephone directories and local/national *Yellow Pages*.
- A list of local number prefixes.
- Access to LAN/WAN communications module.
- CABX operating terminal.

Telephone situations to role-play and discuss

The following telephone situations may be used as the basis for role-playing simulation exercises or developed for group discussion and analysis purposes.

It is helpful to tape-record simulations for subsequent evaluation, or to duplicate dialogue transcriptions, for members of the group.

1 Mr Jones, an impatient, but important client, calls to speak to Mrs French, Sales Manager, who is out. Her secretary takes the call.

2 An irate customer succeeds in being connected to the General Manager of Home and Leisure Departmental Stores Ltd. He proceeds to complain vehemently about a defective television set he purchased from his local branch and the company's failure to rectify matters.

3 A prospective applicant rings in response to the current advertisement for a shorthand typist in the Office Administration Department. The Personnel Manager's secretary takes the call. Her principal is at a meeting.

4 You receive an urgent 'phone-call, as Personal Assistant to the Managing Director, from the Personnel Manager wishing to inform your principal that important negotiations with trade union negotiators have just broken down. The officers of the union are about to recommend an immediate strike with official backing if their demands for a new bonus incentive scheme are not met. The Managing Director is with a client company discussing a new product.

5 The Personal Assistant of the County Treasurer receives a telephone call from one of the Treasurer's personal friends who insists on speaking to him. He is at an important meeting and has left instructions that he does not wish to be disturbed. The friend maintains that he wishes to speak to him upon a personal and confidential matter and will not, apparently, be put off.

6 The secretary of the Chief Buyer of Smartahomes Building Contractors Ltd, receives a call from a Sales Representative wishing to speak to the Chief Buyer about a new line. The Buyer tells you, the assistant, to handle the call.

7 As the Manager of a selling organisation, you are engaged upon the telephone with an important but extremely long-winded customer. What techniques could you adopt to end the call without seeming discourteous?

8 You are trying to obtain a number to make an urgent call but you keep getting a wrong number. What do you do?

Oral aspects of meetings

The way in which organisations have developed over recent years has resulted in the meeting being used much more frequently for decision-making and problem-solving. This has come about largely because of the pressures imposed upon business and government to adopt more participative and open styles of management and employee involvement.

Some managers feel that meetings are a poor way of arriving at decisions, preferring the process of consulting individuals and then making up their own minds. The opponents of 'management by meetings' would point to the extensive use of people's time – often with little to show for it, the cost in terms of the combined salary total per hour of those present, and the poor quality of decisions made, based on consensus and compromise. They would also refer to the tendencies of some meetings to deepen rifts between people and departments rather than to heal them. There is more than a little truth in such points of view.

Nevertheless, most organisations consider that the advantages outweigh the disadvantages. Meetings *do* tend to improve communication between people and departments by 'keeping people in the picture'. They also help people to feel involved, and to consider that their contributions matter. Moreover, when it comes to implementing decisions, those who have shared in the decision-making process are much more likely to use their influence and authority to help put into practice what has been decided in principle.

Talking point

Meetings are usually little more than opportunities for people to confirm their innate prejudices to each other.

Meetings, then, both formal and informal, are used as a communications medium to:

plan	future policy, strategies
design	systems, regulations, processes
analyse	past performance, activities and problem situations
develop	new products, promotions, structures
negotiate	salaries, conditions of service, work methods
persuade	motivate personnel, explain changes

Progressive organisations also use the meeting to bring together different departments and staff to solve problems in a way which serves to integrate companies or departments and to break down traditional, sectional interests. Thus meetings may take place under the group title of:

quality circle
working party
task force
study group
management committee
negotiating panel

Whether the meeting is formal and interdepartmental or informal and within a departmental section, it is likely to have aims to meet and to require the active participation of all present. In addition, although the process may not be specifically referred to, the meeting will, if it is to be successful, result in the modifying of the opinions and attitudes of at least some of those present.

Thus there is present in all types of meeting an element of persuasion or 'winning over'. This means that the participant must develop a number of skills and professional practices if he is to make a positive and effective contribution.

Talking point

Nothing is achieved through meetings that couldn't be done more quickly, cheaply and with much less fuss by a series of individual conversations.

Being informed

It is essential that all relevant 'homework' is done before the meeting – reading minutes and reports, obtaining briefings, researching files and documents, appraising situations. Appearing misinformed or 'behind the times' invalidates the force of any contribution.

Being aware of other participants

Very few people attend meetings with entirely open minds; people may have hobby-horses, pet projects, confirmed attitudes or 'axes to grind'. They may also have 'soft spots', susceptibilities. If they are to be won over, or their support gained, then consideration will need to be given to 'where they stand' and 'what they stand for'.

Being ready for opposition

For any contribution to be accepted it must be able to withstand challenge and opposition from those with conflicting points of view. Views, standpoints and positions must therefore be critically examined and the ground prepared for answering criticisms.

How to take part in meetings effectively

The ability to speak effectively is nowhere put to a more rigorous test than in a meeting. The following rules-of-thumb illustrate areas involving such skills:

Listen first Each meeting develops its own climate. Its temperature may become boiling or frosty. By listening and waiting, you will be able to assess not only the general climate, but also the moods and attitudes of individuals. Test the temperature first, before diving in!

See where the land lies Most meetings tend to comprise sub-groups or caucuses allied to achieve common objectives. While speaking or providing feedback, others may reveal where sympathies or antipathies lie.

Timing If your contribution is to be effective, then timing the moment to speak is all-important. Personal judgement is important here to perceive when a developed argument proposed by another is failing, or when the ground has been prepared and participants are sympathetic or amenable.

Succinctness More good ideas fall by the wayside by being 'oversold' in protracted explanations than are dismissed by reason of their brevity. Keep your points short and simple. Use any previous arguments to support your opening statement, justify your points with generally appreciated examples and stress your main contention when closing.

Involving others If other participants have shown a like-minded point of view, ensure you make reference to their contributions. In this way you will broaden the base of your approach and may win helpful allies.

Overcoming counter-arguments When people are behaving reasonably and rationally, the most convincing means of persuasion is the use of a superior argument. If, therefore, your approach seems more logical, rational and justifiable, then the opposing arguments must be analysed and shown to be inferior.

It is in this situation that human relations skills are at a premium. No one likes to see his own argument demolished or derided. Moreover, such an argument may well be the 'sheet anchor' of four people out of a committee of ten. The whole process requires, therefore, the capacity for 'gentle persuasion' rather than the brutality of the battering ram!

Loss of face One of the hurts which goes deepest and which people least forgive is when someone causes them to 'lose face' in the company of associates or colleagues.

It is deceptively easy to make someone 'look

small' by treating what they have said with scorn, contempt or heavy sarcasm. Additionally, the hierarchical structure of an organisation may make it difficult for them to reply in the same vein. Some actions may make an enemy, or at least an opponent, for long after the meeting – even though nothing further may be said! Consideration for others and the ability to construct 'face-saving' formulae, approaches and remarks is one of the most important skills which those who take part in meetings need to acquire.

Integrity not obduracy Holding to a point of view generally challenged by others may require a great deal of courage and integrity, and, in general, commands respect. It is important, however, that you look objectively at your attitudes in such circumstances. Stubborn resistance to persuasion may indicate a closed mind, pettiness or even spite. The mark of the mature person is that he or she has the strength of personality to defer to a superior argument – graciously!

Courtesy Each participant at a meeting is inevitably being assessed by his peers. People are quick to label behaviour as boorish, arrogant or rude. Bad habits in this regard are easy to acquire by:

- Interrupting someone by 'talking over them'.

- Exchanging leers, winks or grins with a neighbour as a means of criticising what is being said.
- Showing annoyance by 'switching off' or sulking silently.
- Showing boredom by lounging or doodling.
- Engaging in a conversation while someone else is talking.
- Losing your temper.
- Belittling others when speaking yourself.
- Failing to show the chairman due respect.
- Monopolising the proceedings by being long-winded.
- Failing to pay attention, and then showing it.
- Looking constantly at a clock or watch.

Good manners displayed by attentiveness, politeness, consideration of other points of view and respect for the rule of procedure are the hall-marks of the effective participator.

Talking point

Contributing effectively at meetings has more to do with listening than with speaking.

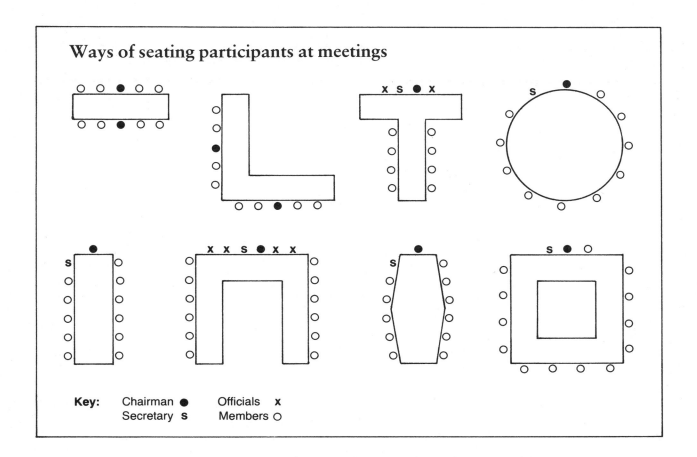

Ways of seating participants at meetings

Key: Chairman ● Officials **x**
         Secretary **s** Members ○

Being an effective note-taker and relayer of information

The business of any meeting is only partially concluded when it closes. For decisions to be effective, participants may either be expected to implement actions themselves, or to relay information back to their own sections or departments. Thus it is essential that the main points of the meeting are noted clearly. From such notes you may be required either to deliver an oral report to your superior, or to disseminate information informally to colleagues.

One attitude to guard against: participation in meetings provides automatic membership to a small, perhaps even elite group within an organisation. Such membership may also result in your acquiring information not generally known. It is a natural tendency, therefore, to keep such information to yourself or to release it in small portions, while enjoying the status which goes with having knowledge not given to others. Of course, some meetings deal with confidential matters and expect that members respect the fact. However, your membership of a meeting group may be to act as an information disseminator. Hoarding information is a common cause of communication breakdown, is resented by those around you and reflects insecurity rather than efficiency.

Talking point

Meetings are for bureaucrats. The doers are usually out of the office, busily doing!

Self assessment questions

1 Are you happy that you have eliminated all lazy speech habits and unconscious adverse speech mannerisms from your spoken word use?

2 Have your recently evaluated your oral communication characteristics by audio-visual recording and play-back?

3 Have you made a conscious effort yet to develop your listening skills?

4 How good are you at creating a register and tone in your spoken word work which meets the needs of different recipients?

5 Do you now make it part of your interpersonal communication approach to look out for NVC signals and react appropriately?

6 Have you given any thought to your own NVC traits and whether they tend to help or hinder you? Consider your posture, dress, expression and gesture habits.

7 How good are you at putting someone at ease in face-to-face situations and encouraging them to open up?

8 How effective is your telephone technique – as a call-maker and taker?

9 Could you use a CABX telephone extension confidently?

10 How do you rate yourself as a participant in meetings? Where could you improve?

Summary of main points

1   Some managers spend more than 70% of their jobs in oral communication activities spanning interviews, meetings, selling, presenting, briefing, or training etc.

2   Speaking and listening skills may be divided into those which devise and sequence logical and clear structures, those which support the message through effective speech mechanics and delivery techniques, and those which create styles, tones and registers appropriate to specific contexts.

3   The factors promoting effective delivery comprise: accent, pronunciation, enunciation/articulation, intonation, emphasis and projection.

4   Good listening skills include: concentration, correct NVC signal interpretation, ability to recall key data, ability to establish rapport and elicit information, awareness and control of own transmitted NVC signals, ability to transcribe the spoken word into clear notes.

5   Non-verbal communication is divided into kinesics, the study of expression, gesture and movements, proxemics, the study of physical contact, positioning and posture vis-à-vis others, and paralinguistics, the study of utterances which are not words.

6   IT has been radically influenced by microchip technology, which plays a major role in ISDN message distribution systems, CABX/key system private and public exchanges, mobile phones and allied telecommunications peripherals like fax, telex, Prestel and video-conferencing.

7   CABX switchboards are essentially programmable and supply a number of sophisticated features including call holding, call barring, camp-on-line, call back when busy, group hunt, call diversion, conferencing, follow-me routing, music on hold etc.

8   British Telecom market a wide range of business telephone services, including conferencing, Citicall, *Yellow Pages*, pay and credit card sales, Freefone service, mobile phone services, and radiopaging.

9   ISDN system architecture combines voice messaging, digitised computer data transmission, fax telex and viewdata transmissions and videoconferencing.

10   Guidelines exist for preparing to make calls, executing them and following up their outcomes; these centre upon prior planning of a call's points and having allied information to hand; transmitting messages clearly and unambiguously; securing positive feedback and acting promptly upon follow-up actions and briefing colleagues.

11   Specialised oral communication skills are needed for effective participation in meetings: timing contributions, confirming the lie of the land, involving and supporting others, overcoming counter-arguments, maintaining positive relationships and taking/relaying notes effectively.

12   The design of meeting tables and seating plans has a proven effect upon the success of meetings.

Activities and assignments _____

Quick review quiz

1 Draw up a list of typically occurring oral communication situations in organisations.

2 Set into an appropriate sequence the main stages of creating and structuring an oral delivery.

3 Define and describe the features which characterise the mechanics of speaking.

4 What careless speech habits should be avoided or corrected?

5 How would you define good listening skills?

6 What is meant by the non-verbal communication terms: kinesics, proxemics, paralinguistics?

7 What part do NVC signals play in the oral communication process?

8 Give examples of how effective NVC signalling can aid oral message delivery.

9 How would you detect nervousness, unease or hostility in a person? What oral communication strategies are available for dealing with these moods or responses?

10 What oral communication skills are needed for effective face-to-face interaction such as the interview or meeting?

11 Draw up three checklists of guidelines for *a*) before *b*) during and *c*) after making a telephone call.

12 What particular activities are needed in effective call-taking?

13 What constitutes a handy 'telephone toolkit' to keep by the phone in the office?

14 Why is it so important to avoid causing loss of face?

15 How does the seating plan of participants around different kinds of meetings table affect the proceedings?

16 How does taking part in a meeting differ from one-to-one oral communication? What characterises the different skills needed to communicate successfully in either situation?

Oral communication assignments

1 Make a tape-recording of members of the group discussing one of the Talking points in this Unit. Analyse the tape for evidence of irritating speech mannerisms. Consider how the manner of delivery of any points could be improved.

2 Enact the following situations in role-play simulation:

a) a door-to-door salesman selling brushes or polishes
b) a sales representative selling office stationery
c) a sales assistant selling cosmetics

First, make notes on product details, selling benefits and prices, then sell the products to a sceptical consumer. Record the transaction on tape and then analyse the language used for persuasiveness and effectiveness.

3 Deliver a short talk to the group on one of the following:

a) How to address a group
b) Taking part in meetings
c) Using the telephone effectively
d) Coping at interviews
e) The impact of information technology upon the work of the office

Two or more members of the group may deliver the same talk. Listening group members should assess each talk for subject-matter, organisation, delivery and effectiveness.

4 An employee in your company is persistently late in arriving for work. Several warnings have had little effect. Simulate the disciplinary interview between manager and employee called to resolve the matter. The employee is aware that others are also late in the mornings.

5 Morale in your organisation is low. Working conditions have deteriorated because of lack of investment. Managers are hard-pressed and irritable. Staff turnover is high. Productivity is low. A meeting of departmental heads has been called to suggest solutions. Simulate the meeting.

6 Two members of staff have been at loggerheads recently over what each considers as an intrusion of the other into his job. One supervises office purchasing, while the other supervises secretarial staff and ensures they are equipped to work efficiently.

Each accuses the other of inefficiency. Matters come to a head and the manager decides to sort the matter out. Simulate any resulting interviews and analyse your solutions.

7 Interview members of your organisation on their attitudes to taking part in meetings. (It will help to design a small questionnaire.) Collate your findings and report back orally to your group.

8 Recently you have received a number of letters from customers unhappy about the way they have been treated on the telephone when making a complaint about your firm's products. You have called a meeting of all staff to explain to them your company's new procedure for handling telephone complaints. Draft the procedure in notice form. Explain its principal points orally to assembled staff.

9 An irate customer telephones to complain about the non-delivery of goods promised faithfully two days ago. The delay has been caused by an unofficial 'go slow' in the factory. Simulate the telephone call.

10 Examine the diagrams of seating arrangements for meetings. Decide which plan would be most appropriate for which sort of meeting. Suggest any short-comings in any of the seating plans illustrated. (See p 185.)

11 Simulate a committee meeting of your student association. Discuss any of the following agenda items:

a) Increasing student participation
b) Extending the scope of activities
c) Voluntary help in the community
d) Organising a special event for charity

12 Tape-record one of the discussions from Unit 8 Discussion topics list. Analyse the progress of the discussion and its conclusions. Establish how far arguments were rationally based and how far emotionally biased. Try to establish the quality of the conclusions reached. Make notes of the proceedings. Deliver an oral report to someone who was not present; ask him or her to validate it against the taped transcript.

13 Write an article for the *Receptionists' Quarterly Journal* about non-verbal communication and how the ability to recognise and interpret NVC signals can help receptionists in their work.

14 Hold a discussion with your whole group. Seek to establish what the group considers to be the most important factors influencing the ability to use the spoken word successfully. Produce a report of the discussion.

Research and report back assignments

1 In pairs, select *one* of the BT telephone services for business listed on page 95. Having researched it thoroughly, deliver a ten minute oral presentation on it (supported by AVA) to your group and provide members with a suitable factsheet.

2 Find out what services are currently provided by UK telephone companies in *one* of the following areas:

a) mobile telephones,
b) conferencing services,
c) directories and information support,
d) international call-making.

Having assembled your material, brief your group orally and field any arising questions. Your briefing should be supported by helpful visual aids.

3 Find out how the telephone system works in your college or school and draw up an outline schedule on how to use it effectively.

4 Find out what features characterise a CABX system in use in your locality. Make an audio or video tape summarising your findings for your group to access as a study resource.

5 Arrange to interview a series of local managers and their senior support staff. Establish what they see as the most important oral communication skills. Give an account of your findings to your group as a prelude to a group discussion on most commonly instanced skills.

6 In pairs, arrange to interview three or four managers and then three or four secretaries in your area. Ask them to explain to you what they see as the important telephoning techniques they employ daily. Give your group a suitable oral briefing on your findings and distribute an appropriate handout.

7 Arrange to interview a series of local private sector managers and their public service counterparts. Your brief is to find out what they consider to be the important oral communication skills they need as participants in meetings. Display your findings in a suitable format.

Talking point

The interviewing process, since it is quite artificial, rarely arrives at any meaningful conclusions.

Work experience and simulation assignments

1 By arrangement, sit in as an observer on an attachment organisation meeting; study how contributions are made, how arguments are introduced and developed, the parts played by rational and/or emotive argument, the process of decision-making and movement to agreed outcomes and actions etc. From this experience and your own researches and reading, write an article entitled: 'How To Take Part Successfully In Meetings'.

2 Carry out a survey in your organisation of the importance managers and staff attach to interpreting and acting upon NVC signalling. With permission, report your findings back to your group.

3 Conduct a series of discussions with managers who interview staff regularly either in the job application process or as a regular staff appraisal activity. Use your findings and further reading to produce an entry for the organisation's training manual entitled:

either: 'How To Interview Job Applicants Successfully'

or: 'How To Conduct An Effective Appraisal Interview'

4 Arrange to interview recent appointees in the organisation; seek to establish what they consider to be the skills needed to do well in a selection interview. Use your notes to help you compose an article intended for your school/college magazine entitled:

'How To Interview Well For Your First Full-time Post'

5 Carry out a survey of the uses to which your attachment organisation's telephone system is put and the means by which its costs are controlled. Summarise your findings in a short informal report.

6 Investigate the features of the CABX telephone system in use in your attachment organisation and how they aid efficient and effective work. Give an AVA-supported oral report to your group on your findings.

7 Design a questionnaire for a cross-section of the staff in your attachment organisation to complete which surveys those qualities and skills which respondents consider are needed in an effective and successful oral communicator. Analyse your survey's data and present it suitably to your class, comparing your findings with those relating to other local organisations.

8 Arrange to interview sales personnel in your attachment organisation to find out what oral and non-verbal communication skills are needed to sell successfully. Summarise your findings in a 10-minute oral presentation to your class.

Case studies

Temperature soars at Freshair!

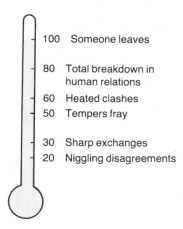

100	Someone leaves
80	Total breakdown in human relations
60	Heated clashes
50	Tempers fray
30	Sharp exchanges
20	Niggling disagreements

Friday 15th March had begun quietly for Jean French, personal assistant to Mr Trevor Jones, Managing Director of Freshair Conditioning Limited. This was just as well, since most of the senior managers were attending the one-day seminar on combatting sick office syndrome at Porchester House.

COMBATTING SICK OFFICE SYNDROME

A one-day Seminar at Porchester House, Cranbrook given by Management Consultancy Services Limited Friday 15th March 19--
PROGRAMME

0930—0945	Assembly and Coffee
0945—1000	Welcoming Address. Mr Paul Dixon, Managing Director, Management Consultancy Services Limited
1000—1100	What are sick offices? Professor Richard Mason, Faculty of Environmental Science, University of Wessex
1100—1115	Coffee
1115—1215	Introducing Effective SOS Countermeasures, Gordon Hayward, MSc, FRS, Management Consultancy Services Limited
1230—1330	Lunch
1345—1445	Seminar Study Groups
1500—1530	Open Forum
1530—1615	Plenary Session
1615	Closing Address Mr Paul Dixon

Freshair's progress in the field of air-conditioning and ventilation had been meteoric. The key to its success lay in the excellent design work of the research and development team and the aggressive marketing and selling of its products. The result was a growing demand for Freshair's systems – a demand which was daily increasing the already heavy workload of the small management team.

Temperature rises

Jean French was busy helping to prepare Freshair's Annual General Report when she was interrupted by the ringing of her telephone:

'Any chance of seeing Mr Jones, today, Jean?' The request came from Peter Simpson, a leading designer in the Research and Development Department.

'I'm afraid not. He's not due back from Porchester House until five this afternoon. Is there anything I can do to help?'

'Not really. Thanks all the same. It's just that Fred Bolton's coming the old acid again over the Metallia Engineering design. Thinks we can just wave a magic wand to suit his customers' slightest whims! I'll leave it for now – I'd forgotten the seminar.'

Jean frowned as she put down the telephone. It was common knowledge that Peter Simpson and Fred Bolton (Assistant Sales Manager) were like oil and water – their different personalities made it very difficult for them to blend or mix. Peter was conscientious and something of a perfectionist – Freshair's success owed a very great deal to his imaginative and effective design work. Fred Bolton, on the other hand, was an aggressive and dedicated salesman, whose customers always came first. He and Peter Simpson had clashed frequently.

Jean felt that the problem had been made worse in recent months because Mr Rowe, who headed the Research and Development Department had tended to ignore the growing animosity between the two. 'As if we didn't have enough to do,' he'd said to her one day. 'Why can't people just get on with the job? I mean, if Peter just got on with designing and Fred with selling, things would be fine!' Jean had wondered whether she ought to discuss the situation with Mr Jones, or whether she ought to mind her own business. In the event, she had said nothing and there had seemed to be a lull . . .

Heatwave

At 11 o'clock the phone rang again. It was Peter Simpson on the line:

'Jean? Peter. Look, Bolton has been in here again! And this time I've really had enough of his finger-stabbing and rudeness! I tell you, Jean, if somebody doesn't get him off my back — I quit! In fact, I quit anyway!'

Jean's heart sank. 'Peter, I'm sure things are not as bad as they seem to you just now. Have you spoken to Mr Rowe?'

'You're kidding! When Fred and I were having our barney just now, he bolted for his office like a frightened rabbit!'

With an effort at transmitting calmness and reassurance Jean said, 'Look, Peter, would you please just stay by your phone for a few minutes. I'm sure that matters can be resolved. I'll call you right back!' Peter reluctantly agreed.

'On Jean's desk were a copy of the Sick Office Syndrome Seminar programme and a copy of a memorandum sent by Mr Jones the previous day to senior managers. (*See below*.)

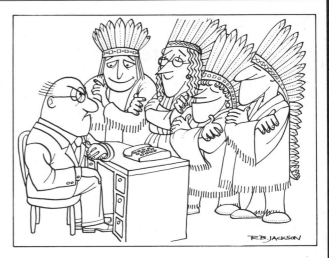

'I've called you in because I'm not too happy about the way things have been going here lately.'

Assignments

1 In a role-play sequence, resolve Jean French's dilemma.

2 In groups, consider the case study carefully and agree upon a plan of action which Jean French should initiate to try to save the situation. Make notes of your solution and compare it with those reached by other groups.

3 Write a detailed analysis of the problems facing Freshair. Give your own suggestions for resolving the immediate problem and your ideas on tackling the wider issues.

4 Should Jean have informed Mr Jones of the growing animosity between the two managers, or should she have considered it none of her business and kept quiet?

Follow-up assignments

1 Find out how a one-day seminar tends to be organised. Explore the idea of your group mounting one to involve other groups. Choose a topic related to communication studies. Invite visiting speakers, lecturing staff or students from your group to address the participants. Share the administrative arrangements among your group members.

2 Discuss the following topic in a general group session:

'One of a manager's most difficult tasks is to ensure that his staff work amicably together. If personality clashes are inevitable in organisations, it is his or her job to see that they are kept under control and not allowed to interfere with the organisation's objectives.'

Are personality clashes inevitable in organisations? What can managers do to prevent them from arising? Faced with one, what communication principles should a manager adopt in seeking to resolve it?

```
                          MEMORANDUM


    To:     All Senior Managers          Ref:   TJ/JF

    From:   T Jones, Managing Director    Date:  14th March 199-


    Subject:  SICK OFFICE SYNDROME SEMINAR
              PORCHESTER HOUSE 15th MARCH 199-


    The following staff will be attending tomorrow the one-day seminar on the subject
    of Sick Office Syndrome problems in air conditioning installations:

        Mr T Jones     Managing Director
        Mr P Knight    Accounts Manager
        Mr D Banks     Sales Manager
        Mr S Kirby     Production Manager
        Mrs W Young    Personnel Manager

    Mr Rowe will deal with any urgent business during the day.  You are requested to
    consult with your departmental head on any important matters today, so as to avoid
    problems arising during tomorrow's seminar.
```

Case study

Professor Arnold's breakdown

Today is the day of Auto Components Ltd's Annual Sales Conference, which has been organised by Mr Charles Dutton, sales director. The conference is to follow this programme:

Auto Components Limited

Annual Sales Meeting

0930—1000	Assemble in coffee lounge
1000—1015	Opening Address by Mr G. Rose, managing director
1015—1100	'Profitable Retail Marketing' Professor James Arnold
1100—1145	'Better Selling Techniques' Mr Paul Hendrix
1145—1230	Open forum
1230—1400	Lunch
1400—1530	Study groups
1530—1545	Tea
1545—1630	Plenary session

The Annual Conference is taking place in the company's Conference Room at its Head Office. The time is 0935. Mr Dutton is already in the Conference Room making final arrangements with Mr Hendrix. Professor Arnold has not yet arrived.

At this moment the telephone rings in the office of Mr Dutton's personal assistant. It is Professor Arnold, ringing from a public telephone box opposite the Hare and Hounds, Barringford, a rural village some 23 miles from Head Office. When the personal assistant takes the call, Professor Arnold explains that his car has broken down; he sounds agitated and proposes to walk down into the village to see if he can find a garage or a bus.

Assignment

Either:
Discuss what action the personal assistant should take.
Or:
Simulate the telephone conversation and any ensuing telephone calls or actions.
Auto Components has a modern, extensively installed CABX switchboard system.

Case study

'A little something I dreamed up!'

Hotex Furnishings Ltd is a company which manufactures and sells a range of furniture and fittings to hotels and restaurants. The firm was founded by Sir Alfred Gaskin, a forthright and determined person and a confirmed entrepreneur. Much of the company's success has been due to his efforts.

The personal secretary to Mr John Chesterton, managing director, has, among her responsibilities, the job of looking after bookings of the directors' dining suite, which seats 10 people, has its own drinks cabinet and is serviced by Mrs Rosina Carter, an extremely capable but rather temperamental staff restaurant manageress.

Today, Mr Chesterton has called a working lunch meeting in the dining suite for eight of the company's marketing executives at 12.45 p.m. At present he is holding an important meeting with accounts staff preparing for the annual audit.

The time is now 11.30 a.m. The telephone rings in the personal secretary's office of Mr Chesterton's suite. It is Sir Alfred on the line:

'Hello, Carol? Sir Alfred here. I'm at the Phoenix Hotel. I've been selling the directors here our new line in dining tables and chairs, and I'm pretty sure I've won them over. But it needs a few final touches. So I want you to contact Mrs Carter straight away and tell her I'm bringing six guests and myself over for drinks and lunch at about one. I shall need the dining suite, of course. You know the drill. I realise it's a bit short notice, but this could mean a really big order if they buy for their chain. See if you can get Mrs C. to pull something out of the bag. Must go now or I'll be missed!'

Assignment

Either discuss how the personal secretary should resolve the situation.
Or:
Simulate any subsequent arrangements made over the telephone.

Case study

Pulses race over communications at Pulsar!

A meeting has been called at Pulsar Electronics Ltd to discuss the proposed appointment of a Communication Officer, whose job would be to coordinate company communications. Present at the meeting are: John White, Managing Director and Chairman; Kay James, Personnel Manager; David Kesan, Sales Manager; Lawrence Carr, Marketing Manager; Caroline Brooks, Office Manager; Harry Brent, Production Manager; Jean Bates, Company Secretary and Peter Short, Accounts Manager.

Chairman:
Right. Everyone's here. I think we should start. As you know, I have called this meeting to discuss the proposed appointment of a Communication Officer. The company's growth and dispersed buildings have made internal communication more difficult. It has therefore been suggested that someone working full-time to coordinate would improve the situation. Who would like to start the ball rolling?

Harry Brent:
I'm going to lay my cards on the table. I think the idea, though fine in principle, will never work in practice. I remember when we tried employing a trouble-shooter in the Works. The thing was a flop because the operatives still went through their union channels and management went up the traditional line.

Lawrence Carr:
Just a moment, Harry, I'm not sure a Works trouble-shooter and a Communication Officer are quite the same thing. As I see it, this new post will enable someone to coordinate areas like desk-top publishing the house magazine, notices, internal and external publicity generally and to act as an advisor to senior staff – like yourself.

Peter Short:
That's all very well, Larry, but I think Harry's got a point. Without sufficient authority this new Officer will be a loose floater. Departmental heads will still keep control of any important communications.

Kay James:
Peter and Harry are both right – to a degree. As I see it, this new post is a natural for Personnel Department. After all, we already run the house magazine and are deeply committed to personnel communications.

Harry Brent:
Oho! Another lieutenant for Kay's Commandos in the pipe-line! Do I detect a take-over bid!

Chairman: (cutting in)
That was uncalled for, Harry. I wonder though whether attachment to any particular department would be appropriate in this case.

Kay James: (ruffled)
Well, so far all we've had from some quarters (looking hard at Harry) is a completely negative attitude. At least mine was a *constructive* proposal. . . .

David Kean:
In my view, I think we're all looking at this from too personal a position. Larry's right. There are a number of important functions going by the board because none of us has the time to devote to them. Obviously the job would call for tact and initiative, and clearly there would be overlap in, say, Personnel and Training and Marketing. But surely the value of a new post would be to have an expert, independent and with no departmental axe to grind. I see no reason why he or she could not report to the M.D.

Caroline Brooks:
I've been sitting here listening, because I had no fixed views when I came in. If you don't mind my saying so, everything seems to be proceeding a little too fast. Surely the best approach would be to establish whether departmental heads are for or against in principle – since their cooperation would be essential – and then to draw up a job specification and description which 'a' would work and 'b' other heads would accept.

Harry Brent:
Never underestimate a woman! If *you* don't mind my saying so, Caroline, I think you're trying to push us into a quick decision before we've even had time to have a proper exploratory discussion. How can we decide in principle before we've had a chance to examine the situation fully. It's a big decision. I don't think we should rush into it. . . .

Assignment

Assess the contribution of each member.
Comment on the Chairman's role.
Suggest how you think the meeting a) would end and b) should end.
Carry on the meeting by role-play simulation.

Multi media assignment

All out at Alumix?

Before attempting this assignment you will need to research the following: Dismissal and Grievance Procedures; Summary and Unfair Dismissal; Industrial Tribunal Procedures.

Situation

For the past three weeks, the wife of Mr Fred Jackson, a machine operator at Alumix Alloys, has been seriously ill. Fred has been very worried about her and is currently on a course of tranquillisers prescribed by his family doctor, but is still at work.

Fred operates a machine that needs constant attention, and Alumix's company regulations state that a relief operator must be summoned to take over temporarily if the machine is left for any reason. If left unminded, the machine could cause serious injury to other factory workers, and three weeks ago, Alumix had issued a works reminder about the dangers of unattended machines.

Feeling rather agitated, and in need of a smoke, Fred leaves his machine, thinking he'll only be away 'for a few minutes', and goes into the staff restroom. He has only been there a minute or two when he is startled by the appearance of Mr Alfred Parker, the foreman for his part of the factory. Fred becomes extremely upset and is unable to express himself very clearly. Mr Parker is known as a strict but fair man.

Mr Parker reports the absence of Fred from his machine to the assistant works manager. Both consider Fred to have been in breach of company regulations.

The management of Alumix take a serious view of the situation. Fred is summoned to the Works Manager's office, and following the company's procedures is summarily dismissed for culpable negligence.

Fred returns to his locker in a very upset state, claiming to his friends that he was not given a chance to state his side of the case. At this stage the shop steward of Fred's trade union, the Allied Workers' Association, arrives and asks Fred to put him in the picture. The shop steward's view is that Fred has been 'unfairly dismissed', and he determines to take the matter to his branch.

Meanwhile, word of Fred's summary dismissal has spread round the factory like wildfire! The factory staff have decided to take matters into their own hands and are threatening an unofficial walk-out, claiming that Fred is being victimised. Extremely concerned, Mr Parker tries to telephone the Works Manager, but obtains no reply. He therefore, determines to ring Mr French, the company's Personnel Manager. He is out, but his Deputy, Miss Sally Barnes takes the call.

The following day, the Works Committee, including trade union representatives, seeks and obtains a meeting with the management of Alumix to try to sort out the problem.

Several weeks pass (you may at this stage assume that the meeting between the Works Committee and management was unsuccessful). Both Alumix and the Allied Workers' Association think they have a strong case, and Fred's dismissal is taken to the local Industrial Tribunal for judgment.

Assignments

1 Face-to-face encounter
Simulate the encounter between Fred and Mr Parker. Two of Fred's friends, taking a legitimate break enter the restroom and join in.

2 Dismissal interview
Simulate the interview between Fred and the works management personnel.

3 Briefing conversation
Simulate the conversation between Fred and the shop steward, Mr Tom Harris.

4 Telephone call
Simulate the call between Mr Parker and Sally Barnes and any subsequent action taken.

5 Meeting
Simulate the meeting between the Works Committee and management.

6 Hearing
Having prepared a case, a management and union team simulate the hearing before the Industrial Tribunal panel.

9 Persuasive communication

Overview

Unit 9 provides you with information and guidelines on:

- The business and public service contexts in which persuasive communication skills are commonly employed: advertising, selling, marketing, public relations, etc.
- The components and key features which characterise persuasive and rational communication languages and styles.
- How persuasive skills are used in: advertising, selling and public relations.
- What media are currently used to advertise products and services.
- Tips on how to devise an effective display advertisement and leaflet.
- The stages which make up an effective face-to-face sales approach and what constitutes a successful sales person's profile.
- Checklists of product selling points and buyers' motivation traits.
- What public relations are and how they work; how to produce effective public relations material, and how to create press releases which will be published.
- Model display advertisements, leaflet and press release with explanatory notes.

'OK! You've convinced me!'
'Wrap it, I'll take it!'
'The feeling of the meeting is, then, that we go for the management buy-out option . . .'
'I rest my case . . .'

Unit 9 examines the persuasive communication practices and processes which precede statements like those above which signify the success of a sales pitch, convincing argument, well presented case or decision-making process. If we were all Vulcan rationalists like the imperturbable Mr Spock of Star-Trek fame, then there would be no need for persuasive communication techniques, since rational argument and logical imperatives would win hands down all the time. As it is, however, all human beings run on a kind of intellectual two-stroke mixture in which reason, logic and scientific method are blended with personal attitudes, prejudices and subjective hobby-horses!

Persuasion – a legitimate communication tool

This being the case, techniques of persuasive communication are key weapons in the effective manager's armoury, and not only effective but legitimate. If you pause to consider the nature of the business and social cultures of the developed world, where societies are founded on free trade, market economies and consumer purchasing power, techniques of persuasive communication are *essential* in:

- selling to consumers or companies,
- advertising to sell goods and services,
- public relations to maintain a positive image,
- presentations and demonstrations to win over senior managers or clients,
- public meetings to press a case or point of view,
- lobbying to influence decision makers,
- political or boardroom debating.

All these business activities play an important part in ensuring a free flow of uncensored ideas and in raising people's awareness. Without persuasive communication, the free flow of business would quickly become a trickle as demand for goods and services dried up.

Talking point

Should office managers and administrators seek to acquire advanced persuasive skills, or is there something underhand and rather dishonest about the whole business?

Persuasive communication in business and public administration

The following checklist highlights some of the areas in which persuasive commmunication is regularly employed in daily routines:

Advertising

In commercials, display advertisements, point-of-sale merchandising, hoarding posters, sales circulars, sponsorship advertising, etc.

Public Relations

In press meetings, press/news releases, company livery and corporate image designs, in-house newsletters, client communication services, etc.

Sales

Face-to-face selling, sales letter circulars, unsolicited mailshots, product promotion campaigns, sales conferences, dealership training and support services, etc.

Meetings, Presentations, Addresses

Presenting new ideas or developments for senior management acceptance, motivating/reassuring personnel, industrial relations – conveying positions, presenting annual accounts and activities to shareholders, etc.

Pressure Groups and Lobbyists

Putting cases at public meetings/enquiries, lobbying local councillors and MPs, organising protest meetings, marches or demonstrations, writing letters to the press, advertising in newspapers, leafleting households, etc.

The above checklist is by no means exhaustive, but it does illustrate how broad is the persuasive communication net cast over both private and public sectors and the range of legitimate uses of persuasive skills in organisations.

The languages of persuasive communication

Before examining typical specimens of persuasive communication it is helpful to analyse the language of persuasion and to identify those characteristics which distinguish persuasive and emotive communication from its rational and logic-driven counterpart.

The following table illustrates how these contrasting uses of language are defined and explained:

The building bricks of persuasive and rational language

Persuasive Language

Rational Language

Vocabulary Characteristics

Preference for:
- Short words – Old English, Saxon, Norse-based – which pluck on the heartstrings of home, hearth, patriotism, loved ones. etc, eg: farm, land, woods, fire, house, stream, green, wife, warm, hot, cool, love, friend.

Preference for:
- Greek/Latin/Norman French polysyllabic source words used in administration/government, eg: domicile, bureaucracy, respondent, resident, analysis, extrapolate.

Syntax and Structure Characteristics

Preference for:
- short sentences and clauses,
- use of imperatives – 'Don't delay!'
- liking for simple verbs with prepositions: 'get on with',
- simple syntax structures:
  Subject + Main Verb + Extensions
- active not passive constructions:
  'Your life *will change*.' not
  'Your life *will be changed*.'
- personal pronouns for names: you he/she they you'll,
- adjectives and adverbs liberally sprinkled in text, eg: sparkling, cosy, safe, new, fast, really, very, now, absolutely, extra.

Preference for:
- long sentences, acceptable if well punctuated and structured in clauses,
- balanced sequences, structures and logical progressions:
  'if . . . then . . .' 'because this . . . then this . . .'
  'given this . . . therefore this . . .' etc,
- structures preferred where subsidiary points lead inevitably to main points in logical sequences,
- impersonal passive structures common: 'Managers *were surveyed*',
- Objective constructions, without emotive words, colloquial forms or personal constructions, eg: 'The questionnaires were evaluated', 'The results were analysed'.

Treatment of Ideas and Material

Preference for:
- selective, not comprehensive treatment or argument,
- deliberate emphasis on chosen points,
- highlighting of consequences of *not* accepting proposed views,
- conscious demolition of perceived counter-arguments,
- objections anticipated and overridden,
- selective use of facts and figures which will bolster argument,
- willingness to play on people's emotions – desires, fears, worries, self-images, etc.

Preference for:
- rigorous research into all available data,
- willingness to acknowledge exceptions, contrary indications, etc,
- even-handed presentation of pros and cons,
- development of outcomes based on irrefutable evidence and logical progressions (QED),
- willingness to let facts speak for themselves,
- avoidance of emotive appeals and manipulations.

Style Characteristics

Preference for:
- informal, chatty, easy-going tones and registers,
- use of homespun proverbs and sayings,
- liking for familiar contractions: you'll, they'll, wouldn't, etc,
- concrete not abstract images: 'gets clothes dawn-fresh!',
- use of unfulfilled comparatives: 'Presto cleans faster!'.
- liking for fast movement, urgent tones and rapid succession of images,
- use of colours and textures to reinforce moods and atmospheres: golds, reds, greens, blues, velvets, silks, marbles.

Preference for:
- abstract verbs and nouns to convey meaning: 'evaluation, conclusion, process, consideration, experiment, select, appraise, etc,
- use of logic-based link-words: 'however, as a result of, this being the case', etc,
- preference for words with a single, non-emotive meaning: equation, ratio, percentage, optimum, etc,
- avoidance of words which can be taken ambiguously or which are used colloquially: 'lots, not too bad, OK, terrific'.

The table has set out some of the major contrasting characteristics of persuasive and rational communication so as to bring out the features which distinguish them. You should, however, keep in mind that not all persuasive communication takes the form of the brash hard sell – 'Get Some Now!', and that a great deal of persuasive communication is subtle, sophisticated and complex. This being so, it will contain many of the features which characterise rational and logical argument. Indeed, in today's business world, the effective communicator must be on constant guard in order to spot arguments which are illogical, specious or even fraudulent but which are masquerading as reasoned and rational statements.

Talking points

1 It what circumstances is the use of persuasive argument illegitimate and unacceptable?
2 How can you spot irrational arguments and statements? How should they be counteracted in, say, a meeting, discussion or during negotiations?
3 To what extent is the use of persuasive techniques in communicating consciously and unconsciously employed in situations at work?
4 How far do you agree with the characteristics identified in the above chart? Have you identified any others in your experience? Do you agree that it is possible to set out to produce a composition which successfully moulds the opinions of its readers on a given subject? Or is it successful only because its readers see through the ploys but agree to be persuaded?

Effective persuasion relies on studying your recipient

Age

People's outlooks and attitudes vary according to their age – a factor to be borne in mind when writing to an older or younger recipient.

Background

People are moulded by their experiences and lifestyles. The metropolitan city-dweller and the rural farmworker inhabit different worlds, as do the small trader and the chairman of the multinational corporation. It is important, therefore, to choose a style and approach in sympathy with the recipient's background.

Education

In our modern, high-technology society there are many different types of education – practical, technical and academic, and not all are linguistic-based. Every effort should therefore be made to express the message in terms which its recipient will understand and readily accept without being either baffled or patronised.

Interests and outlook

It is sometimes helpful to establish a common area of interest with the recipient of the message – not from any sense of seeking to flatter, but rather to establish a rapport. Similarly, knowledge of the recipient's outlook will forestall any tactless observations or remarks.

Specialisms and responsibilities

The nature and extent of the recipient's specialisms and responsibilities also have a bearing on the style with which he is addressed. Doctors, solicitors, surveyors or civil engineers writing to fellow specialists may well employ language which they would understand but which to the layman might appear to be jargon. It is essential, therefore, to use a specialist or general vocabulary with care, so as to avoid obscurity or unnecessary over-simplification.

Relationship of writer and recipient

The style of a communication's message may well be affected by the relationship of writer and recipient. What may be recognised as friendly banter between long-established business associates may be regarded as over-familiarity in another context. In addition, the special relationship, for example, between business and customer may require particular care in establishing an appropriately courteous tone, which is informal without becoming over-familiar.

Applications of persuasive communication

Advertising and sales promotion

Advertising – the art of bringing together seller and purchaser in order to conclude a bargain that suits both – is as old as exchange and barter. Vast libraries exist to impart the skills of successful advertising to successive generations of retailers, advertising agency executives, marketeers and sales managers alike. Indeed, large companies employ industrial and social psychologists to advise upon the potential effectiveness of advertising concepts and strategies, and to survey product requirements, buying trends, life-styles and culture changes, all of which have a bearing on the ways in which goods or services are advertised.

Indeed, at the centre of effective advertising in business is the ability to design an equation which matches what the producer or service provider has to offer with what the consumer wants or needs. Manufacturers of staple commodities – food, housing, clothes, heat or light cater at bottom for what people *need*. The purveyors of, say, perfume, holidays, alcoholic drinks, fashion clothes, gourmet cuisine or sun-beds provide what people *want* once having satisfied their needs: sensuality, bonhomie, escape from routines, enhanced self-image and so on.

In order to secure the sale, close the deal or effect the contract, advertisements are devised – whether by organisations in-house, or through retained advertising agencies to achieve the following goals:

● To draw the launch of a new product or service to the notice of potential customers.
● To maintain or improve a market position in face of competition.
● To lift a jaded product or service which has been improved or updated; to extend a product's life-cycle.
● To maintain a satisfactory level of awareness and acceptance of an established firm's product range.
● To support local/regional/national sales campaigns.
● To advertise customer support/ancillary services or environmental positions which improve corporate images.

In the case of newspaper or journal 'for sale' classifieds or situations vacant display advertisements, the essential aim is to convey what are the main features of the sales item – motor-cycle, hi-fi stack, job or gardening service – and to state what is required to effect the contract. This may be simply, a negotiable sum of money or an annual salary plus allied employment package. And so underpinning all effective advertising is an implied two-way contract or deal – 'supply this to obtain that' or, 'meet these stipulations and we'll deliver these benefits'. Indeed, sales forces are always being briefed in the 'unique selling benefits' of their products and how they supply customer wants or needs better than those of their competitors.

The media of advertising and sales promotion

Entrepreneurial advertisers are always finding new and stimulating ways of reaching their customers – with unsolicited fax messages, perfumed magazine inserts or unsolicited cut-down versions of software programs. The following checklist identifies some of the principal advertising media in current use:

Current advertising media

Printed/graphics media

● Colour/BW display advertisements in newspapers, magazines, trade-journals etc.
● Classified small-ads in newspapers/magazines.
● Leaflets/brochures/handouts/prospectuses/catalogues.
● Posters: A3, double-crown, roadside hoarding, etc.
● Sales/unsolicited sales letters.
● Slogans, catch-phrases, one-liners.

Visual/aural media

● Radio/television/cinema commercials: on videos, film or tape.
● Illuminations, fascia-boards, signs, placards.
● Musical call-signs, jingles, theme-music.
● Trade-marks, logos, motifs, house-styles, uniforms, livery.

Coordinated events

● Exhibitions
● Shows
● Demonstrations
● Sales
● House-parties to sell franchised products
● Festivals
● Markets
● Sponsored/charity events

These events coordinate and channel oral/aural/textual/graphics/tactile and visual advertising stimuli.

Advertising/sales promotion jargon terms

Hard sell

Approach in advertisements which lists major product/service features, reasons for buying the item, price and/or discount – essentially factual.

Soft sell

Promotes atmosphere/mood of acceptability of product – sunshine breakfasts, wicked luxury, deserved pampering, imminent seduction, etc. around the product; costs and detailed specifications omitted – essentially evocative.

Copy

The textual/graphic/visual material comprising the advertisement – hence copywriter, copy date, copy deadline.

Knocking copy

Advertising which stresses short-comings or inferiorities of competing products/services.

Caption

Short phrase which explains photos/artwork/illustrations, etc.

Headline

Shocking, witty, funny, emotive short set of words which introduces or concludes advertisement.

The media

Newspapers, journals, magazines, television companies, radio stations, street hoarding owners, etc., who publish advertisements.

Merchandising

Creating demand for products and services at their point of sale with the help of packaging, labelling, shelf placards, take-away leaflets.

Story-board

Advertising design-tool: sequenced cartoons/drawings with captions to convey intended thrust and direction of film or video commercial.

Tips on how to construct an effective display advertisement or leaflet

Clearly the art of effective copywriting is not mastered in a few hours. However, in an advertising context, most managers and administrators will be expected to produce from time to time working drafts of advertising material to meet personnel selection needs or requests from marketing colleagues for informed and accurate copy. The checklist below identifies key components of the display advertisement and leaflet and suggests tips on their design.

Visual/graphic images

Today photographs, line-drawings, patterns and pre-designed artwork can be very simply imported into display advertisements and leaflets via DTP. But take care to ensure that distortion does not arise from 'cropping' such artwork to the desired format. Make sure such illustrative material is up to date and represents the latest model or specificiation; set high standards – readers today will compare your artwork with that of *Vogue, Good Housekeeping* and newspaper colour supplements. Remember that

many DTP software packages contain pre-drawn 'clip-art' for instant inclusion in your advertisement; also that local newspapers have artwork libraries of logos and visual inserts for inclusion in the advertisements they publish for you.

Keep in mind the old proverb: a picture is worth 10,000 words!

Talking point

'A really good leaflet never ends up as junk mail!' What do you consider to be the features of a successful leaflet?

Headlines

Except where the visual material carries the message, it is the headline that opens the door to your advertisement's success, since its prime function is to gain attention and prompt the reader to make the time to absorb the overall message.

Headline styles vary considerably according to their context – in display advertisements for management recruitment they tend to be factual, sober and rather staid; in general selling situations more adventuresome and bold:

MANAGER: CUSTOMER SERVICES

Developing Total Quality Concepts in Customer Care

or

Extravagant. Exorbitant. Extortionate. Extremely Reasonable. Stella Artois. Reassuringly Expensive.

or

Do Your Sales Suffer
From Your Sales Reps' Burble Diarrhoea?
*Ease your pain – and theirs –
with an immediate dose of SDA's
sales development training,
with instant after effects!*

or

Leaking Pipes Your Problem?
Call in Homesafe Heating Engineers –
End of Problem!

Devising eye-catching headlines is not easy, but *is* worth the time and trouble. Good headlines convey the aim and thrust of the advertisement instantly, so seek to compose short phrases which run smoothly off the tongue – alliteration and assonance help here – and which create the response you want. Stella Artois, for example see their lager as the brand leader of the top-of-the-market range, while Staff Development Associates (SDA) have sought to find a headline which will compete successfully for attention in a busy sales manager's in-tray and Homesafe Heating have concentrated on imparting an image of instant and effective service. Remember that you can 'top and tail' advertisements and leaflets effectively with headlines and enlarge upon their messages with secondary streamers. Lastly, keep firmly in mind the significant effect which the choice of type or fount used and the point size of the typeface selected will have on the visual impact and acceptance of the headline. Make sure you try out several in trial goes and test them on colleagues.

Talking point

Does the soft sell advertising approach work? If so, why?

Composition and structure of the message

In display advertisements brevity and concise expression are at a premium. Their senses and interests deadened by numerous competing advertisements, most readers tend to ignore long-winded sentences condensed into minuscule print! So keep your sales points to a minimum and opt for simple sequences emphasising key factors:

- You will speak Spanish in three weeks!
- Salary not less than £15,000 p.a.
- Non-contributory pension scheme and removal assistance.

It is often helpful to use what are, in effect, emboldened section-headings to introduce grouped points:

Our Employment Package Includes:
- Six weeks paid vacation p.a. and public holidays.
- Excellent occupational pension scheme.
- Special Group BUPA medical insurance scheme.
- No cost Company leased car provision.
- Generous maternity/paternity leave and crèche facilities.

While brevity is the watchword, make sure that your condensed points still convey their meaning clearly and unambiguously. In composing your message

points ensure you opt for the short word not the long, choose the familiar not the exotic, avoid slang and over-familiarity and prefer Saxon/Old English vocabulary to its Latinate equivalents.

Before drafting your advertisement or leaflet, make sure that you have refined your facts and figures to an essential minimum and that you have double-checked that they are *up-to-date, and accurate!*

Use of white space and proportions

Given the cost of newspaper and magazine advertising, it is highly tempting to get your money's worth by cramming as much material into your display space as possible. Avoid this temptation like the plague. It is always worth investing in an area of square centimetres large enough to provide an ample frame for your message and to lend visual impact to your design by surrounding your headlines, streamers and section headings with white space which lures and seduces the tired eye!

By the same token, don't forget to utilise techniques of centering, indentation and double-spacing to lead the eye on to key topics or ensuing points.

Action statements and follow-up instructions

However successful the visual impact of your message, all will go for nothing if your reader is not given the 'shortest way home' in terms of meeting your action requirements. Therefore make it easy for him or her! Compose enthusing action prompts. Print names, phone-numbers and postal addresses boldly. Include pre-printed reply cut-outs for quick completion, supply a bonus or discount for prompt responses, etc:

Just pop in, call us or return the form below TODAY to obtain your personal shopping catalogue! And we'll mail your free Shopping Guide BY RETURN!

Our New-Start Career Hot-Line is Open 24 Hours A Day! Just dial 01-123-6000 – Now!

Lastly, make time to vet and proof-read your draft copy scrupulously. Nothing detracts from otherwise good copy more than glaring spelling, punctuation and syntax errors. And remember to number and date all working drafts in sequence and to circulate latest drafts along with instructions to destroy previous issues.

Talking point

What criticisms do you have of the way that advertising is created and communicated today? What *new* advertising standards would you introduce?

Western Riverside Waste Authority

General Manager

£35,000 package including non-contributory leased car (Pay award pending)

We are seeking a committed senior manager to lead this progressive authority now firmly established after its inception 3 years ago which has the major task of disposing of waste from the four inner London boroughs of Hammersmith & Fulham, Kensington & Chelsea, Lambeth and Wandsworth.

The Job

• To be responsible for the operation of two major refuse transfer stations and a civic amenity site located in Wandsworth.
• To provide strategic management, with particular emphasis on planning future waste disposal arrangements for the authority.
• To be responsible for the management of over 80 staff based at two stations and civic amenity site.
• Responsible for the efficient operation of budgetary and administrative systems as well as the negotiation of major contracts.
• To actively promote the running of the operations in a safety conscious and environmentally sensitive way.

The Person

The person we are seeking would ideally possess:
• An engineering background HNC/degree level.
• Significant managerial experience within the waste disposal industry or process engineering.
• Advanced negotiating skills.
• A flair for strategic thinking and priority setting in a dynamic environment.
• The ability to assume 'hands on' control when required.

Although experience in the waste industry would be an advantage, consideration will be given to candidates with other appropriate experience.

Benefits include index linked pension, generous leave entitlement and relocation package if required.

The salary and benefits package attached to this post reflects the fact that we are looking to appoint someone with outstanding qualities which are required to lead the Authority in a period of significant change and the introduction of new developments.

If you would like an informal discussion about this post please contact the Clerk to the Authority, Mr G. K. Jones on 01-871 6001, who should also be contacted for application forms and further details either by telephone or at the following address: Town Hall, Wandsworth High Street, Wandsworth SW18 2PU. Closing date for applications: 6th September 1989.

W·R·W·A

WRWA noteworthy design/display features

1 Clear, bold headline and eye-catching, enforcing streamer.
2 Succinctly written job overview paragraph –
who, to do what, where.
3 Major job requirements and expectations set out in an easy-to absorb checklist.
4 Brief but concentrated personnel specification set out to match job requirements.
5 Additional employment package benefits are detailed.
6 Informal initial contact arrangements encourage prompt follow-up.
7 Clear details of to whom, where and by when to apply are shown.
8 Organisation and logo in ample white space convey an image of substance and help to proportion a helpfully detailed advertisement.

"You're not flogging ad space! I thought you wanted a real job."

"Yes, I am and it's just the job I wanted. The career pospects are real enough."

"Don't tell me 'young dynamic company ... due to expansion you'll be a manager next week ... retire at 30...' – you've been had!"

"Well, the Company has more than doubled in size over the last 2 years, and it's been established over ten years. The average age is early 20's, five of our Publishers are under 30! By the way, they all started in ad sales."

"Got it! You fell for the line about megabuck OTE. Bet they didn't tell you about the impossible targets?"

"No, I fell for the good basic salary plus the commission opportunity to earn nearly half as much again. My first year's training programme is good news too."

"Where did you say you worked?"

CENTAUR
L I M I T E D

"Centaur Communications Ltd, 50 Poland Street, London, W1V 4AX. Write to the Personnel and Training Manager and tell her why you're right for the U.K.'s fastest growing business publishing house."

An equal opportunity employer.

Centaur Limited's innovative appeal

Given the sameness about most recruiting advertisement's layout and style, Centaur's imaginative approach and use of contrasting founts ensure it will be read and acted on.

Talking point

'Staff would work better if managers sometimes gave them the straight facts, never mind the persuasion bit!'

Persuasive communication and selling

This section surveys the particular persuasive skills which are needed to sell effectively – whether ideas, lingerie or insurance! While only some of your student group may be expected to embark upon careers in sales and sales administration, the tips and guidelines set out below will prove helpful both to you and all your fellow students, since working in organisations effectively requires that we all have to sell:

- ● ourselves ● our pet projects ● our staff ● our department's or unit's raison d'être ● our firm to clients ● and, almost, our souls

on occasion!

What makes a successful salesman?

The Hollywood stereotype of the successful salesman is usually of a genial, paunchy, flamboyant Old Stager, who's 'been around', who definitely has 'the gift of the gab' but who is not too bothered by unethical or seamy business practices.

This stereotyped caricature is unlikely to sell very well in today's business climate where the sales representative is expected to be:

- ● **smartly dressed and in good shape**
  buyers or 'prospects' invariably relate the desirability of the product (or service) with the visual appearance of its seller; an old but true proverb says that the salesman must first sell himself, and that includes personal appearance – well-groomed hair, freshly laundered shirt, polished shoes, etc.
- ● **expertly informed and up-to-date on his wares**
  buyers are always evaluating competing products in retailing or company procurement and no salesman call sell effectively if his information is sketchy, out-dated or invalidated by embarrassing gaps.
- ● **expertly informed about sales trends and the market**
  the successful salesman has to be expertly informed about local/regional/national/international sales trends and market characteristics; almost certainly buyers will advance counter-arguments, objections or ripostes during a sales pitch about costs, consumer trends, competitors' activities, etc which the successful salesman must be aware of and ready to overcome on the basis of high-quality information rather than blind assertion.
- ● **skilled and sympathetic in understanding the buyer's needs and problems**
  just as 'no one ever won an argument with a customer', so no salesmen ever built sales

without first establishing and then developing rapport with the buyer.

- **able to handle objections, complaints or 'hassles' without giving offence or upsetting the buyer**

  most sales representatives are both 'front-line troops' and ambassadors for their companies – and so to the buyer, they are the company; one reckless remark or rude response can 'blow' years of goodwill and high-volume purchasing.

- **a good listener, amateur psychologist and sincere exponent of his chosen field**

  invaluable market intelligence stems from casual conversation and gossip if the salesman has a sympathetic ear; further, abundant sales tend to follow around those sales people who have the skill of putting retailers, buyers and assistants at their ease and who are able to demonstrate a sincere enthusiasm and involvement in their sales sector and product service range.

And as if that weren't sufficient, the successful sales person will be expected by his or her employers to possess developed expertise in self-organisation, sales administration, and follow-up customer maintenance techniques.

Selling face-to-face

While there are many other successful means of selling: direct mail, telephone-selling, unsolicited mailing and faxing etc undoubtedly the most powerful is the 'flesh and blood' negotiating process where customer and sales person interact face-to-face. In some ways it may be regarded as a ritual process in which both parties are aware of the roles they are expected to play. Certainly this selling process conforms to social and cultural practices – which may vary considerably from country to country. The haggling norms of the Arab souk or bazaar would be treated very dustily in a Rolls-Royce salesroom or Paris fashion-house salon! Nevertheless, there are patterns and sequences which typify the European face-to-face selling which are listed below for you to examine:

Guidelines on face-to-face selling

A well-tried and tested formula is summarised in the acronym AIDA: Awareness—Information—Desire—Action!

Awareness: as the first step, this phase seeks to make the customer aware of a product or service; no 'hard sell' is undertaken, rather a consciousness-raising move: 'We're bringing out an improved version of the economy model next month. I'll leave you these brochures to browse through . . .'

Information: the next step (on the next visit) may be for the salesman to brief the customer on the pro-

duct's specifications and attractions, to answer any arising queries and to counter any objections or uncertainties, etc.

Desire: if phases one and two have gone according to plan, the buyer will be signalling evidence of a desire to acquire the product, evidenced by remarks like:
'Well, we might try a case or two – if the price is right!'
or:
'I might be able to shift a case if you could guarantee delivery before this week-end.'

Action: having created the desire to buy, the final phase is for the salesman to 'close the deal' by initiating actions which cause the customer to make a definite commitment to buy:
'I'll just put you down for the three cases, then, Mrs Harbold, if you could just sign here . . . Lovely!'
'I'll just pop over to the car to telephone the warehouse. I'm sure we've got a dozen gross left at the old price. I'll make sure they despatch them this minute, and you'll have 'em first thing tomorrow!'

Other sales specialists sequence the selling steps as:

1 Re-establishing rapport: an initial period of small talk about 'the car, the golf, the test match score' – whatever the conscientious rep has noted as items which interest the buyer.

2 Lead-in to the desired sales pitch: general and low-key exchanges about business trends provide a cue for the salesman to introduce his sales item: 'Funny you should say that, we've just modified ours. Look, here's a sample of the new version (*hands it to the buyer to examine*) see how the cunning devils in R & D have re-routed that circuit . . . and that alone has increased its life by 30%!'

3 Delivery of major selling points, features and benefits for the buyer and his customers: ever-watchful of the buyers' reactions, the salesman unfolds his practised sales routine, varying it according to the personality of the buyer and the overall context of the sale; depending on the product and circumstances, stress will be given to aspects such as price, performance, design features, durability (see chart below).

4 Countering/overcoming objections or buyer resistance: short of giving away money-trees, the sales person is bound to encounter some resistance to his selling efforts such as cash-flow problems, over-stocking, lulls in trade, and existing loyalty to a competing brand. These must be countered by sales tools like special offers, a one-off extended credit deal, a sale-or return deal, or an introductory extra discount.

5 Closing the sale: in all sales transactions, a psychological moment arrives when the buyer is ready to say 'yes'. The practised salesman knows how to spot the verbal/NVC signals, knows when he's said enough and which technique will work to seal the bargain. *Note:* effective sales people *never* oversell, create overstocking, over-commit their customers financially or sulk if they walk away unsuccessful that day, for 'today's browse is tomorrow's sale!'

Talking point

'Sales techniques are OK in theory, but once you're in there pitching, the moment you stop to think of what phase you're at, you've lost it!' Is there some truth in this 'old hand's' view?

Checklist of a product's selling points

- What it costs.
- What it costs to run/service/insure.
- After-sales support: guarantees, servicing, spares availability and costs.
- Design features: reliability, latest model, market-leader, wealth of extras.
- Durability: length of warranty, specification of components, tried-and-tested construction, trouble-free track-record.
- Availability: order cycle, delivery time, distribution back-up.
- Sales support: merchandising, sales literature back-up, dealer training schemes, etc.

What motivates a buyer?

The motivations underlying the desire to buy are many and varied. The psychologist in the sale person will, however, invariably spot these motivators:

- pack-leader needs
- vanity
- status perceptions
- snob-appeal
- desire to be one-of-the-boys
- exclusivity of product
- conspicuous consumption appeal
- sex-appeal
- keeping up with Jones
- last-in scramble

Talking point

Are the billions spent each year on advertising, sales promotion and public relations worthwhile, or largely wasted?

Persuasive communication and public relations

Everyone has heard of terms like, publicity, PR, 'a good or bad press' and so on, yet when put on the spot, few are actually able to provide a working definition of what public relations is and what it does. This section will provide you with a clear survey of the application of persuasive communication in the context of public relations.

As the label suggests, PR has to do with the interface between the organisation and the general public, with those people who:

- buy the firm's products or services,
- live near one of its factories or office blocks,
- hold shares in the company,
- pay community charges and local taxes to the borough, district or county if the organisation is in the public sector,
- are thinking of buying its products, working for it, moving into its domain,
- are in a position to speak of it well in influential circles.

In other words, the 'public' part of public relations includes anyone whose views or opinions matter to the organisation.

As far as the 'relations' part of the label is concerned, the organisation applying a PR function is anxious that the public maintains the following kinds of attitude to it:

- has a high regard for what the organisation does,
- considers its products: innovative, reliable, well-made and designed, value-for-money, etc,
- believes it to be well run, expertly managed, with a human side and caring approach towards its own staff as well as its customers,
- esteems its directors/officers who create expert long-term strategies which contribute to the national economy,
- is aware of its good track record in industrial relations – firm but fair, strike-free,
- sees that it cares about issues like the environment, pollution, public health, public/employee safety.

In short, the 'relations' aspect hinges upon developing and maintaining a positive and favourable image in the eyes of the public at large.

Large organisations discreetly spend hundreds of thousands of pounds annually on public relations either:

by retaining a public relations agency or consultancy to work for them (PR departments sometimes form part of larger advertising agencies) *or,*

through their own in-house PR function, which may be a unit within the marketing arm, or a function of an information or press office.

Why should such organisations expend large sums on activities which are often difficult to quantify in terms of a concrete return on the investment? Perhaps the answer is the same as that given by a successful firm which manufactures sweets. When asked why it continued to pump money into advertising sweets and snacks which were household names, the answer came back:

'We know what profit we make when we advertise; we don't want to find out what might happen to it if we stopped!'

Other reasons for promoting PR actively include:

- to possess a good track record locally when a planning application or expansion plan is submitted,
- to be able to recruit the cream of school/college/ university-leavers who want to work 'for the best',
- to maintain customers' brand loyalty and supportive shopping habits and life-styles,
- to weather localised storms and upsets by having secured a broad regional, national or global appeal,
- to add an edge to business promotions, negotiations or strategies by going in as 'Mr Good Guy'.

PR or advertising

It is important to understand the innate difference between public relations and advertising. 'Above the line' advertising seeks to sell a specific product or service openly and directly. 'Below the line' advertising (such as sport sponsorships) seeks to promote a corporate image and gain general favour. Public relations activities tend to be similar to 'soft sell, below the line' advertising, but cast a far wider net – to increase public acceptability, to influence politicians or to change public opinion and so on – than the advertisement created simply to increase sales and profits.

How public relations works

Naturally enough, if PR is to influence the public at large, then it has to be through the mass media:

- BBC/ITV newscasts
- TV documentaries and news programmes
- Radio news and magazine programmes
- National and local newspaper news items and interest features
- Informatiion points and desks at exhibitions, shows and special events
- Sponsoring of high-visibility sports people and teams – football clubs, grand prix drivers
- News items/features in targeted trade-journals, hobbyist or leisure magazines

- Unsolicited mailshots, leaflets, newsletters
- Annual shareholders' reports and staff newsletters
- Publications for general (or subsidised sale), eg *A History Of Brewing, BBC Year Book 199-.*

Talking point

'Who needs public relations?'

The media of public relations

The public relations function is usually carried out by one or more staff with either a press or broadcasting background or long-term and carefully nurtured relationships with journalists, broadcasting presenters, exhibition organisers, advertising and media people generally. PR executives have to be good at networking, able to woo and cajole newspaper or radio/TV journalists to find time or space for their story. For in essence, the job of the PR man or woman is to be on the look-out constantly for company/institution newsworthy events, products, inventions, developments, human interest angles which can be processed into:

- Press bulletins, press releases, press conference briefings
- Fax/telex releases to TV/radio stations
- Photo opportunities for local/national newspapers
- Letters to the local/national press advertising features
- Material for direct mailing and leafleting
- Handouts at annual general meetings or public meetings
- Material for sports event commentators
- Briefing packs for visiting VIPs or foreign delegations
- Free/low cost educational packs for schools and colleges
- Informational circulars to local government and charities
- Briefing notes for top managers' speaking engagements

As well as selecting communications media like those set out above, PR officers also include breakfast, luncheon or dinner meetings with decision-makers like MPs, professional association and charitable trust chief officers, senior local government officials and councillors and company directors in their PR strategies. A convivial word-of-mouth account or updating in the right ear may prove invaluable to a current PR project.

Guidelines on producing effective public relations material

Effective PR material tends to be:
- factual not emotional,
- impartial, not obviously grinding a company axe,
- newsworthy, not overblowing a trivial event,
- appealing to human interest, not totally statistical,
- appropriately channelled – to either district, national or international news media, depending on the level of newsworthiness,
- bang up-to-date – no one is interested in 'stale news',
- professionally formatted with contact names, telephone numbers, addresses and embargo dates (see model on page 209).

Note: while PR releases tend to follow the above guidelines, it goes without saying that the overall effect of the carefully sifted material of the release will be to project the organisation in a good light!

Protest groups and lobbies

While public relations tends to be identified with the juggernauts of industry, it should be remembered that, today, in virtually every locality special interest activists exist, whether civic trust, environmentalists or dog-lovers, whose entire reason for being may be to undertake an effective PR lobbying and opinion-moulding role. Such bodies will use PR tools and tactics just like those outlined above.

Model press release explanatory notes

1 **An embargo date** is the date *before which* the press release should not be printed, nor its news leaked; embargo dates are especially important with, say, the launch of a brand new motor-car at a motor show; embargo dates should always be displayed prominently at the top of press releases for instant impact.

2 **A press release headline** should be drafted like a letter's subject-heading to convey clearly and simply the theme of the press release; it is the editor's prerogative to change it into a more 'frothy' or dramatic version, etc.

3 **The opening statement** of a press release should communicate the essence of the piece factually and directly.

4 **Facts and figures** should help to provide interest and point to a press release, while adjectives like 'latest', 'state-of-the-art' and 'mammoth' legitimately convey a sense of current newsworthiness and importance.

5 **More follows** this device is added to the foot of each page preceding a continuation page so as to ensure that related text does not become separated and thus omitted in error.

6 **Continuation sheet referencing** serves the same purpose as that used in letter layout, and confirms the subject-matter, page number and date.

7 **Catch line** each continuation sheet's text is begun with three or four words, themselves a repetition of the last three of four of the previous page – here, 'a sophisticated desk-top'.

8 **Key quotations** are often used in press releases

to add variety and human interest to the piece; very often they are composed in advance by the press release writer, following the gist of what is to be said, and cleared in advance with the speaker; or they may be extracted from a circulated confidential copy of a speech to be delivered at the event covered.

Note here the tone and general direction of the quotations, which ensure that the generosity of MIS is fully publicised and acknowledged, and that the computer block development is promoted as part of the college's ongoing community service role.

9 **Closing paragraph** to make it easier to edit press releases without major features being excised, a useful convention is to close with material which is expendable and which could be omitted without impairing the piece's major news.

10 **– ends –** this device signals simply and effectively the close of the press release and that no more continuation sheets follow.

11 **Contact details** reporters who cover the event, or editors thereafter may need to follow up news items in the press release; contact details should therefore comprise named contact with delegated authority to speak, address, phone and fax numbers.

12 **Format** press releases are usually printed on A4 in a 10/12 pitch, using double-spacing and wide margins to aid sub-editing.

Note: the date of the production of the press release, 18 June 199-, reveals that it was produced several days *before* Lord Castleton's visit; newspaper editorial staff on local papers need press releases several days ahead of publication dates, so as to be able to lay out pages and photographs.

MODEL PRESS RELEASE

(1)

Embargo date: Wednesday 23 June 199–

(2)

NEW COMPUTER BLOCK AT HIGHLAND COLLEGE OPENED

BY TRADE AND INDUSTRY MINISTER

Lord Castleton, Secretary of State for the Department of
Trade and Industry, yesterday visited Highland College of
Technology during his tour of Wessex to open the new
computer block on the East Downland campus. (3)

The College's new computer block comprises three suites each
housing 20 of MIS Computing Limited's latest supermini
networked computer terminals, possessing state-of-the-art
(4) Intol 80386 microchips and OSI operating system, with a
mammoth 628 megabytes of hard-disk memory.

Each terminal user can also access the suite's local area
network system which routes electronic messages to other
suite users in seconds, or which brings software programs,
and working files to each terminal from the supermini's
vast central memory just as fast.

Further features of each suite are a sophisticated desk-top

(5)
- more follows -

⑥ Highland College   - 2 -   18 June 199-

New Computer Block

⑦ a sophisticated desk-top publishing system (the MIS DTPXL)

which supports versatile computer-designed text and graphics

production. High-resolution print-outs (over 1,000 dots per

square inch) ④ in an extensive range of print styles and sizes

is effected by an MIS Galaxy laser-printer.

Declaring the computer suites up, running and open for

business, Lord Castleton said, ⑧ "This superb provision is an

excellent example of how fruitful local collaboration with

industry can be. We are all grateful for the generosity of

MIS Computing's board of directors and shareholders in

making a donation of this magnitude to Highland College.

Indeed, Westchester's whole community - teenagers, office

workers, managers and business owners - stand to benefit

from the hightech courses these suites will provide."

Dr Joan Murray, Principal of Highland College, in proposing a

vote of thanks to MIS Computing echoed Lord Castleton's

words, stressing the impact which the installation would have

on improving the human resource skills of local businesses.

- more follows -

Highland College   - 3 -   18 June 199-
New Computer Block

"I was relieved to learn," she observed, "that our MIS
computers have an excellent cooling system, since I
am sure they are going to be working flat out for our
business community from nine in the morning to nine at
night!"

The three computer suites are expected to service the ⑨
computing and information processing needs of over 2,000
⑫students each week, and to supply more than 130,000
student terminal-contact hours each year. The three suites ⑫
will form part of the College's Computer Services Department.

⑩
- ends -

CONTACT: ⑪

Caroline Jefferies   ⑪Tel: 0795 - 567321/3
Information Officer   Fax: 0795 - 565651
Highland College
East Down Drive
Westchester Wessex WS2 3DG   ⑪18 June 199-

The press release as news item

The fact that a press release – produced by a public relations officer working to promote the interests of the organisation – looks just like another news item in a newspaper is not accidental. It is the result of carefully adopting the style features and approaches outlined above. Indeed, we all read 'news items' daily which are, in fact, press releases. At times when news is slow or dull, a hard-pressed editor may be glad of 500 words to help fill a page – provided that it is not glaringly slanted or biased, but is factual and genuinely newsworthy.

Self assessment questions

1 How do you rate your persuasive communication skills on a scale of 1-10? In what contexts and situations do you think you need more practice so as to improve?

2 With which kind of writing do you feel most at home – persuasive or rational? Why? When did you last evaluate critically a work simulating assignment to establish its effectiveness and to identify weak spots in it for correction?

3 What positive actions are you taking at present to improve your persuasive vocabulary?

4 How convinced are you about the legitimacy of persuasive communication and techniques of advertising and selling? What personal ethical standards will encompass your own approach in these areas?

5 Can you yet devise an effective display advertisement and leaflet, so as to be able to 'notch up' these important skills?

6 Are you satisfied that you have now mastered the demanding expertise of press release production?

Summary of main points _____

1 Persuasive communication comprises skills which seek to: convince, motivate, exhort and influence for a particular purpose, to lead decision-making, to support management objectives, to advertise, sell, lobby or promote. All the communication media and channels may be employed to this end.

2 Special language skills are adopted to create persuasive effects, in which emotive vocabulary, short and simple syntax/structure, selective and partial treatment and informal/familiar style and register play a central part.

3 Persuasive skills are especially needed in advertising to bring products and services to buyers' attention at various phases of the product life cycle; popular advertising media include the tv/radio commercial, display/classified newspaper or magazine insertion, roadside hoarding, mailshot, poster and point-of-sale merchandising placard.

4 The key features of effective display advertising design are: the graphic/visual image, the headline, the message text, formatting and use of space techniques and clear action statements and follow-up instructions.

5 The effective sales person is: smartly but not overdressed and groomed, expertly informed about his product or services and well informed about his commercial or industrial markets; he is skilled at establishing rapport and in eliciting information, and has a mastery of direct selling techniques and approaches.

6 The direct selling process may be divided into five distinct phases: re-establishing rapport, arousing interest in the product, promoting its major attrtactions, overcoming objections and closing the sale; this process is also encapsulated in the AIDA acronym: Awareness – Interest – Desire – Action.

7 Sales people stress some of the following principal attributes in their selling: cost, after sales service, performance, reliability, durability, up-to-date design and construction, availability/access, warranty conditions etc.

8 Public relations seeks to promote an organisation's image so that it is favourably regarded and esteemed by the public. It is felt that such esteem aids the organisation in meeting its goals and aims.

9 Public relations communications are channelled through the mass media, locally, nationally and globally as: tv news items, newspaper press or news releases, or as sponsorship activities, personal lobbying, subsidised publications or unsolicited circularising etc.

10 Effective PR messages tend to be: factual, newsworthy, not overstated, supported by human interest aspects, suitably channelled in an appropriate medium, up to date and professionally delivered.

11 Press releases features: embargo dates, simple and factual headlines, sequencing in a descending order, key direct quotes, catch lines, more follows and ends devices, continuation sheet referencing and follow-up contact details; they are set out in double spacing with wide margins in an easy-to-assimilate typescript, pitch.

Activities and assignments _____

Quick review quiz

1 Outline five different situations, common to all kinds of organisation in which persuasive skills are important.

2 Explain what is meant by the following terms:

ginger group, pressure group, lobbying.

3 Distinguish between the vocabulary characteristics of persuasive and rational language.

4 What features characterise a persuasive message's
   a) syntax and structure,
   b) treatment of material,
   c) style and tone?

5 What aspects of a recipient's profile should be considered when creating a persuasive message?

6 Draw up a checklist of words which are used to describe
   a) persuasive and
   b) rational communications.

7 Explain briefly five major reasons for advertising.

8 List the advertising media currently used which are
   a) aural/visual,
   b) textual/graphic and
   c) multimedia.

9 Explain what is meant by the following specialist terms:
   hard sell,
   soft sell,
   knocking copy,
   caption,
   merchandising,
   point-of-sale,
   story-board.

10 Draw up a set of brief guidelines on how to create a successful display advertisement.

11 List the characterisics of a successful sales person.

12 Explain what AIDA stands for.

13 Describe briefly the stages of a successful face-to-face sales pitch.

14 What are the typical features of a product or service which are highlighted in a sales approach?

15 Explain briefly five personality traits which motivate consumers.

16 Describe the role of a public relations unit in an organisation.

17 Outline the media and channels used in public relations communication.

18 What forms of communication are used in PR to disseminate news, developments and human interest stories, etc?

19 What features should a good PR message embody?

20 What are the design features of an effective recruitment advertisement?

21 Explain the conventions by which a press release is produced and the format features it should possess.

Persuasive communication assignments

1 In Unit 6 you undertook an assignment to survey the reasons why students in your Department chose to study there. Now, in pairs, design a leaflet (using DTP technology to produce it) which either publicises the course you are pursuing, or another in the Department's programme. Your leaflet should not exceed two sides of A4 or four of A5. Compare your version with others produced by your group and decide why the one you think best has excelled the others.

2 Your Departmental Head's secretary is to retire shortly after twenty years' expert and faithful service. The HOD is devastated at the thought of having to cope alone! You have therefore been asked to research into the job role of Mrs Harrison (Departmental Secretary) and then to devise a suitably worded and designed display advertisement to go into your *Middleton Weekly News* situations vacant columns. Your HOD's words echo in your mind: 'Try to produce something special which will attract a really effective organiser who isn't a dragon, and who is likely to be more interested in education than the pay-cheque − if you can!'

3 Your company, Avionic Engines Plc has just broken the world records for speed ascents to 10 000, 20 000 and 30 000 metres with its newly announced jet engine the Cougar Mark IV, fitted to a Royal Navy Dragonfly VTOL jump jet. The test pilots involved were highly complimentary about

the engine's performance and even thrust. The event was watched by Sir Harry Davidson, Chairman of Avionic, along with other board members, representatives from the Ministry of Defence and invited air and military attachés from allied countries. The engine cost some £150 million to develop and it is expected to win sales of over £2 billion in the next two years. Avionic employs some 3,000 factory and administration personnel at its Cheltenham complex, where morale has been low following problems in solving metal fatigue cracking in Avionic's commercial passenger jet engine, the AV Transglobal Mark III.

Using the above information and including additional realistic data, compose a suitable press release for distribution to the national press, TV news companies and international news agencies. Produce your press release on a word processor using accepted conventions of layout.

4 In pairs, design an advertisement for insertion in the *Sunday Reporter* Colour Supplement (a paper popular with managerial/professional people with above average incomes) which will in your view effectively promote the timeshare holiday cottages which your company, Leisure Share Limited, have just completed on three sites – in the Lake District, in North Wales and in the Scottish Highlands. Each timeshare slot is of a week's duration, but slots can be purchased in up to three-week units. It's a first come, first served situation based on completion of 30-year lease contracts. Leisure Share also include a compulsory maintenance contract at reasonable annual costs to ensure the properties are well looked after all year.

Compose a suitable draft advertisement indicating your use of colour, typographical features and artwork, etc. Your advertisement is to be a full two-page, high impact, 'we'll worry about the costs later!' affair which aims to lift a somewhat sagging level of demand so far.

5 Six months ago, you and your best friend were made redundant from H J Carter & Son, Builders and Contractors. With the help of a government grant and training, you both set up a partnership selling and installing double-glazed doors, windows and conservatories which you obtain from Warmaglow Double Glazing Plc, a manufacturer which has granted you a local exclusive dealership. Warmaglow's products are well made and provide you with a good profit margin, such that you are able to offer appealing discounts and special offers. Warmaglow give a 20-year warranty with their products and you guarantee your installations unconditionally. At present, it is early summer, and sales are flagging. You and your partner therefore decide to mount a sales campaign and set out to produce the following sales literature:

a) a two-sided A4 (or A5) leaflet to deliver to local housing estates,
b) an unsolicited sales letter and advertising material for mailing to affluent country house owners,
c) a suitable information pack for commerical property owners.

By arrangment with your teacher, undertake all or some of the a), b), c) assignments and compare your sales literature with that produced by the rest of your group, selecting the most effective for display.

6 Select *one* of the items of office equipment listed below. Then decide upon one manufacturer's model of the item you pick which is on sale locally. Collect a set of sales leaflets, brochures and information packs on it and make yourself thoroughly conversant with its major features and benefits.

a) compact photocopier
b) desk-top office dictating machine
c) desk-top calculator with print-out.

Using any of the literature you have acquired and/or devising your own to act as support material, sell the piece of equipment of your choice to one of your fellow students in a role-play sequence. (Remember to check the selling guidelines on pages 205 first.)

You may wish to video or audio-tape a series of such class role-play simulations for later analysis and discussion. As a class, decide who made the best sales approach and why.

7 Your local television company has recently introduced a 'Soapbox Session' – a ten-minute slot after the early evening news in which members of the public air their views on a matter they feel strongly about, so as to encourage public debate and influence the decision-making process. The TV company, Mercia Television, has just circularised your locality, trawling for likely 'Soapbox Session' contributors. They assure the hesitant that coaching will be given on delivery techniques, that the text will be on autocue to avoid memory lapses, etc and that hospitality cars will pick up and set down contributors on the evening when rehearsal and recording takes place.

a) As Jo(e) Richards, Assistant Producer of 'Soapbox Session' devise a suitable unsolicited circular letter to go to a selected group of reviewers which you think likely to result in your receiving applications to become a 'Soapbox Session' contributor.
b) Draw up a set of guidelines on how to write the ten-minute piece of persuasive views which will be delivered by the contributor on air, and further tips on self-presentation while on camera.
c) As a member of the public who applied and was successful, carry out the following assignments:

1 Write a piece to last ten minutes which energetically yet convincingly argues your case on *one* of the following:

● Encouraging people to work from home.
● Better facilities and opportunities for women at work.
● More effective methods for dealing with those who pollute the environment.
● The immediate creation of a United States Of Europe.
● Or a topic about which you feel strongly.

2 When you have edited and revised your presentation to your satisfaction, arrange to produce it on your college/school CCTV video system.

When a series of presentations has been recorded, arrange a screening to your own (or another) group and after a discussion on each one, decide which were the strong/weak points about the presentations and why.

8 You work for Crossroads Publishing Limited, a company which specialises in vocational education and training books and study aids. Your job title is: Commissioning Editor, Business Studies Division, and you are responsible for securing new books and material for publishing in the 16 + business education market. Recently, as a result of talking to people in the field and of surveying the current range of competing products, you become strongly convinced that Crossroads should branch out into an area of publishing new to it, namely that of travel, tourism and leisure. You know that some of the senior managers and working directors have become rather blinkered in their outlooks, given the steady but stable success of Crossroads business and secretarial publishing. But you *know* there's a market in the travel/tourism/leisure education and training field to be exploited!

Having carried out your research into the current education/training provisions in this field and their likely textbook and study material support needs, deliver an oral presentation to Crossroad's Project Development Committee (which comprises the company's decision-makers) suitably supported by AVA-presented data which you have obtained.

Research and report back assignments

1 Over some two weeks, scour newspapers, magazines and unsolicited mail you can collect so as to acquire a set of display advertisements, leaflets, unsolicited sales letters, etc. which you consider either examples of good practice, or specimens which failed to convey their messages effectively. Present your sets to your group, along with your evaluation of each set.

2 In a similar way, peruse the advertising copy of published advertisements and pick out headlines, paragraphs, captions, etc. which you think are good examples of persuasive communication at work. Arrange to display the best in your base room after a suitable discussion of the language techniques you discover.

3 Arrange to interview 3-4 sales people working in your locality. Talk to salesmen who sell into the retail, distribution, industrial/technical and export markets. Find out what they see as the techniques of direct and indirect selling and write a report of your findings for distribution to your group.

4 Arrange to visit an advertising agency in your district. Having ascertained who does what and how, provide an oral presentation to your group on your findings.

5 Arrange to interview the proprietor of a local shop or cash-and-carry warehouse. Ask what features a new product needs to possess for them to try it. Ask also what qualities they think make a good sales person.

6 Arrange to visit an organisation with a public relations function. Find out what the PR unit does, what kind of documents it produces (ask for specimens/models!) and how they seek to measure success. Relay your findings in an account to your group.

7 Arrange to sit in on one of the following meetings, and brief your group on what persuasive oral communication skills you detected:

a) a county council public meeting
b) a Crown Court case
c) a district council meeting.

Work experience and simulation assignments

1 Arrange to collect a representative sample of your attachment organisation's advertising, sales promotion and informational literature. Select what you think the most interesting and display these items as a collage in your base room.

2 Find out how your organisation organises its advertising. Draw up a clear flow-chart to illustrate each phase of the process and share it with your group.

3 Ask your organisation's senior managers what policies they have in place as to when, how and what they will advertise through which channels. Ask what they see as the most effective kind of

advertising for them. Deliver your findings to your group in a suitable form, having cleared your material with your attachment supervisor.

4 If your organisation has a public relations unit or commissions an agency to undertake a public relations service for them, interview a range of managers/directors to establish what they see PR doing for them and the organisation. Write up your findings in a short account.

5 Ask to see whether you can take part in/observe the production of an advertising sequence or PR project. Brief your group on your experiences.

Case study:

'Theme park proposals blow lid off Dimchester!'

Dimchester is situated in a delightful part of the UK, surrounded by beautiful countryside, historic buildings, quaint villages and market towns. It is, in fact a growing tourist trap, with tour operators both at home and abroad marketing the area successfully in their package holiday brochures and sales literature.

So successful, in fact, has the tourist trade become, local residents are grumbling ever more stridently about the long queues to get out of supermarkets, the congestion on the pavements and roads, the impossibility of getting served in local pubs and restaurants and the rapid increase in property prices as one-time tourists become retired local inhabitants or week-end cottage owners.

The lid on the local kettle of Dimchester, the largest market town in the area and seat of the county council, blew off last week when the *Dimchester Chronicle* plastered large banner headlines on its front page as follows:

MULTI-MILLION POUND HOLI-DAY CAMP AND THEME PARK
Proposal for Northwold!

The leading article which followed broke the news that Megallion Enterprises Plc had submitted plans to convert 60 acres of land-fill ground and adjacent disused timber mill land (owned by the county council of Woldshire) into a 500-bedroomed holiday camp with funfair, theme park amusements and speedway motor-cycling and stock-car racing tracks. Megallion propose to spend some £15 million on the venture which would create some 200 additional jobs in the area.

News of the plan spread like wildfire. Elderly residents were appalled, teen-agers excited, shopkeepers secretly gleeful and the people who lived around the Northwold suburb of Dimchester up in arms! They immediately formed a Hands Off Northwold! Association and began a heated lobbying process directed at Woldshire County and Dimchester District Councils. Sales of the *Dimchester Chronicle* shot up as both local residents and tourists alike devoured the weekly batch of readers' letters on the subject.

After several weeks of uproar, the Dimchester District Council decided to arrange a public meeting at which all interested parties would be represented. The County Council Planning committee were due to meet the following day to decide upon Megallion's planning application, and effectively thus seal the fate of the whole proposal.

Assignments

As a class, role-play the public meeting, with syndicate groups taking on the roles of:

- Megallion's MD and support staff
- The Committee of the Hands Off Northwold! Association
- Representatives of Woldshire's Planning Dept.
- The Chairman and Committee Members of the Dimchester Chamber of Commerce
- The President and Committee of the Dimchester Branch of the Association For Preserving Rural England
- The Secretary and support staff for the Woldshire/Northshire Regional Tourist Board
- The Chairman and Members of Dimchester District Council's Amenities Committee

Naturally local residents at the meeting will also make sure they have their say!

As part of the general simulation, by arrangement with your teacher, carry out one or more of the following assignments:

a) Prior to the meeting, the various interested parties devoted much energy to lobbying council members and, in particular, the Woldshire Planning Committee Members – and so did you, as a representative of a group strongly for or against the Megallion proposals. Draft your group's letter which is to be delivered to the Chairman of the Planning Committee during the morning of the day of the public meeting.

b) As one of the interested parties listed above, the Chairman of the Meeting has asked you to join a panel of speakers, each of whom will be given a five-minute slot to put their case. Prepare and deliver in the meeting your group's case.

c) Write a letter to the *Dimchester Chronicle* in the capacity of one of the leaders of the groups listed above, either applauding or deploring the outcome of last night's public meeting.

d) As the editor of the *Dimchester Chronicle* (swayed by considerations of either increased future advertising if the *Chronicle* supports the scheme, or possible falling sales as irate readers switch to the *Northshire Gazette* – also likely if the *Chronicle* supports the scheme!) compose an editorial for publication in the *Chronicle's* next edition following the outcome of the meeting and the planning decision (which went the same way).

Compare editorials to see which one steered the best course between 'the rock and the hard place' and discuss the problems and challenges which beset editors of local papers.

10

Working in organisations 2: managing, leading, evaluating

Overview

Unit 10 provides you with information and guidelines on:

- A working definition of management and its role in organisations.
- A detailed survey of important milestones in the development of management thinking and approaches and current management trends.
- Major leadership traits and characteristics.
- Current management issues and preoccupations: effective delegation, managing time, managing targets and budgets, effective decision making, managing conflict, managing stress, managing change, handling negotiations.
- Techniques of evaluation of work: work study, organisation and methods, job enrichment, job rotation, job enlargement, job analysis, the management services function.
- Design and the office: HASAW, ergonomics, systems furniture and fittings.

At the heart of the study of people, communication and organisations lies the role of managers/leaders and how they measure and evaluate the work for which they are responsible. Unit 10 provides you with an overview of the major schools of management thought, an assessment of leadership styles and approaches and an examination of work measurement and evaluation techniques.

Towards a definition of management

The moment an organisation develops beyond the initial 'one-man-band' stage and employees are hired, the need for effective management is born. Many definitions of what management is and how it is carried out have been devised by specialists and researchers. At the centre of all lies the core belief that:

'Management is the process of achieving pre-set aims and objectives through the work of others.'

Around this skeletal definition a number of management activities are built which flesh it out further:

A manager's role is to:

- devise strategies and policies which will secure future growth and development,

- control and coordinate a mix of available resources – people, money, materials – so as to earn a profit or to run the organisation cost-effectively,
- interpret and respond to changes in economic, social and technological trends, so as to keep the organisation sharp and competitive,
- develop new entrants into the organisation, so as to ensure its long-term survival and success,
- promote interpersonal communication and tele-communications systems so that the organisation benefits from an open exchange of information and ideas.

This Unit also considers the tension which can exist between the manager and the managed which may give rise to a jaundiced 'fish-eye' view of management, looking up from under:

'Managing is the art of getting other people to do the work while stealing any thunder going, yet passing the buck promptly if things so wrong!'

Since the early 1900s successive generations of management practitioners and social scientists have undertaken impressive field research involving on-the-spot observation, interviewing and surveying, in their efforts to establish what management is.

Also during this century, massive changes in society – in education, class structures, life-styles, beliefs and values – have affected how people regard work, how they behave as workers and how they expect to manage and be managed. This section briefly surveys some of the major milestones in the development of management thought and practice. Its purpose is to form a springboard for your further investigations and to aid your understanding of present-day management and leadership styles.

Milestones in management thinking

Frederick Taylor (1856-1917)
The Science of Shovelling and the Beginnings of Scientific Management.

American engineer – 'The father of modern management' – studies of methods of working used by labourers in the steel industry paved the way for work study, organisation and method analysis and work appraisal specialisms – also began a process of investigation based on the idea that 'what is good for the employee is also good for the employer'.

Max Weber (1864-1920)
Power, authority and their impact on leadership styles

German born – made study of the structure of organisations and means whereby managers are able to impose authority – identified three types of organisation: Charismatic (authority is based on a form of devoted loyalty to the leader), Rational-legal (authority is made legal because leader manages from position of respected authority and expertise), Traditional (authority stems from hallowed custom and practice) – important contribution was to show how leader's authority depends on subordinates' respect for his acknowledged expertise.

Henri Fayol (1841-1915)
The Fayol 14-point management profile
(From *General and Industrial Management* by Henri Fayol © I EEE 1984 with permission of Lake Publishing Company)

Perhaps the most important of early management thinkers – formulated a management profile consisting of 14 definitive activities: 1) Division of work, 2) Authority, 3) Discipline, 4) Unity of command, 5) Unity of direction, 6) Subordination of individual interests to the general interest, 7) Remuneration, 8) Centralisation, 9) Scalar chain (the perceived line of authority), 10) Order, 11) Equity, 12) Stability of tenure of personnel, 13) Initiative, 14) Esprit de corps. His thinking led to developments such as line-management-based organisational hierarchies, specialist departments and role of senior managers as corporate strategists and anticipated the motivation studies of the human relations management school of the 1940s and 50s.

Elton Mayo (1880-1949)
The Hawthorne Studies – group solidarity and motivation

Australian – worked mostly in the USA – carried out a series of experiments in the 1930s at Western Electric's Hawthorne works in Chicago revealing that factory operatives' output and motivation improved significantly when sympathetic interest was shown in their work and showed the power of peer group pressure (power exerted by group over its members) which meant that what the group chose to do was as important as what the management wanted them to do – studies brought into the limelight importance of a caring and supportive management approach in motivating groups with strong member-centred loyalties.

Douglas McGregor (1906-1964)
Theory X and Theory Y

American social psychologist and management consultant – identified two contrasting management styles in the running of organisations – Theory X where management relies on material incentives (rates for job, bonuses, etc) to motivate the workforce which is seen as basically lazy and needing strict supervision, and Theory Y where employees are seen as willing to work and accept responsibility given an encouraging approach is adopted by management. Studies examine conflicts and tensions arising when different levels of management do not follow same management style – his twin scenarios focused attention on what style of management was likely to succeed in what type of organisation.

Frederick Herzberg (1923–)

Herzberg's Five Major Motivators
● achievement ● recognition ● the work itself
● responsibility ● and advancement.

Carried out studies in the late 1950s in Pittsburgh into the motivation of people at work – listed a number of factors under headings of 'Motivators' (nature of task, achievement, recognition, responsibility, advancement) and 'Hygiene factors' (salary, bonuses, commission, working conditions, acceptability of supervision, pleasantness of working environment, job security) – good hygiene factors help to maintain a person's feeling about work but do not in themselves motivate (a big pay rise soon becomes accepted as the norm).

Abraham Maslow (1908-1970)
Hierarchy of needs

Maslow's hierarchy of needs

'Low' needs have over-riding force and power

Physiological
Safety
Social belonging
Esteem
Self-actualisation

'High' needs can only be satisfied once 'low' needs have been met

Published *A Theory of Human Motivation* in 1943 demonstrating his theory that man is a 'perpetually wanting animal' whose needs and expectations moved upwards in a stepped hierarchy – only when lower needs had been satisfied would the person be impelled to seek the next level of satisfaction – rated basic needs higher in motivational power than the more advanced ones (see diagram opposite).

Rensis Likert (1903–)
Principles of supportive relationships

American social scientist – research mainly concerned with manager/managed relationships and based on premise that effective manager/worker output relies on mutual respect and trust – interested in potential of interlocking work groups which he believed to be the basis of all organisational structures – task of management is to create a climate in which such groups can work harmoniously – considered that to be effective managers need to be friendly and supportive, firm but just and worthy of staff's confidence and respect, committed to employee welfare and advancement, caring of weaker personnel, able to plan and organise and expert in their fields – stressed the importance of consensus decision-making involving all working groups.

E F Schumacher (1911-1977)
'Small is beautiful'

Professor Schumacher's observation 'Small is beautiful' was used extensively in the 1970s to describe a trend in manufacturing management for small groups of workers to be engaged in the complete process of manufacturing a product (eg a motor-car) rather than each worker being employed in a repetitive job on a production line – the opportunities for workers to progress to more complex and satisfying jobs enabled problems of high absenteeism and low morale associated with a production line environment to be overcome in some companies.

Kenneth Boulding (1910–)
Systems management

Defined a management approach as early as 1956, popularly called in 1970s and 80s systems management – management scientists at the time amalgamated elements of scientific management approach widely used in engineering and computer science into a systems view in which: 1) organisations were to be seen as social systems where inputs (money, materials, etc) are processed into (value-added) outputs (goods and services) 2) such systems had to be carefully controlled to ensure a stable environment but be capable of adaptation in order to survive in a changing world, 3) health of systems had to be maintained by regular acquisition and analysis of feedback.

Organisational systems model

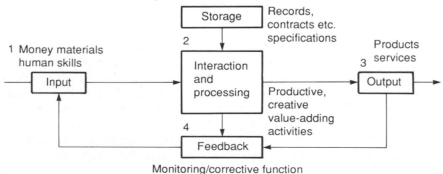

The 'pay-back' theory

The general materialistic climate of the 1980s gave rise to a management approach that acknowledged the truth of the saying 'nothing is for nothing' and that support staff required a quid pro quo – emergence of the hard-nosed political organisation man or woman with definite career goals and the confidence to drive hard bargains with their bosses to achieve them.

'Pick-n-mix' management style

No particular management approach holds sway at present – body of management research since Taylor is absorbed – present day approach is eclectic (drawn from many sources) selecting a style which best fits the situation (contingency management) – 1980s has seen a renewal of management ethics and codes of practice in the form of management charters – organisations have a more enlightened approach to the development of their managers.

Management by objectives

In the 1960s and early 1970s a swing occurred to this more task-centred approach which opened the way for an outcome-centred and task-based management style, establishment of sophisticated systems of job appraisal and performance rating, fairer salary scales and employment packages and more informed and realistic ideas of what managers could be expected to achieve. The approach is based on 1) discussion between a manager and his subordinates of proposed objectives, 2) negotiation of those objectives and agreement on means of achieving them, dead-lines, etc, 3) quantifying of targets (eg. 10% increase in turnover). A process is then set up whereby the manager can monitor progress, modify targets and take corrective action at the appropriate time.

The MCI Code of Practice

When an organisation joins the Management Charter Initiative, it makes a pledge to both current and future managers through the 10-point Code of Practice. The organisation will promise:

1 To improve leadership and management skills throughout its structure.

2 To encourage managers to continuously develop their management and leadership skills.

3 To provide a coherent framework for self-development within the context of corporate goals.

4 To ensure that the development of managerial expertise is a continuous process, fully integrated with the work flow.

5 To provide ready access to relevant learning and development opportunities – both internal and external – with requisite support and time released.

6 To encourage and help managers acquire recognised relevant qualifications.

7 To participate actively in the appropriate MCI networks.

8 Directly and through networks, to strengthen links with management education sources.

9 To contribute to closer links with educational establishments.

10 To appoint a director or equivalent to oversee the fulfilment of these undertakings.

Summary

This survey of management thinking and practice is by no means exhaustive. Yet it provides some important areas for your further study and research.

What it will have clearly shown – and the most important aspect for you to remember – is that there is no single correct or right way to manage. Effective management depends entirely on the mix of: the manager's personality and what style fits it best, the kind of people and tasks to be managed,

MANAGEMENT BY OBJECTIVES AND RESULTS PROCESS

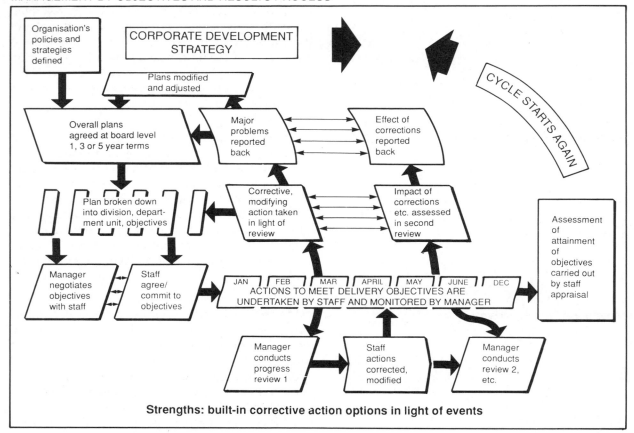

the culture and beliefs of the organisation and the social/ economic backdrop at the time.

Perhaps the simplest and best advice is that: 'Good managers sleep well at night – because they have clear consciences after the decisions of each working day.'

Talking Point

To what extent would you go along with Maslow's theory of a hierarchy of needs in people at work?

Major leadership traits and characteristics

The preceding section has surveyed some of the major milestones in management thinking, as well as establishing a working definition of management. Perhaps the single most important quality a manager possesses is his or her ability to lead the team or group over whom a line-management authority exists.

The effective manager is often deemed to be able to 'lead from the front' or to be able to get his team to carry out instructions or to follow examples readily because they respect the example the manager sets – by living up to the standards he expects from his team himself, by not shirking difficult

decisions or by putting in that little more time or effort than other team members.

The section that follows examines some of the major leadership styles and theories. Measure your own ideas and views against them and consider what leadership approaches best suit different organisations and various contexts arising within them.

The trait approach

Popular in the 1950s and 60s, the trait approach identified a series of personal qualities which leaders were supposed to possess. The following list represents those that were claimed to be most widely referred to in surveys as leadership characteristics:

- intelligence
- articulate and convincing speaking skills
- decisiveness
- drive and determination
- initiative
- cooperativeness and social skills
- ability to get things done
- insight and perception
- self-assurance and conviction

The trait approach tends to be disregarded by some management specialists and personnel recruiting managers because the list of qualities is endlessly variable and difficult to assess objectively. Nevertheless, few managers would disagree that there are personality traits in leaders which separate them from the pack – not least a stubborn determination to achieve for themselves what they set out to do.

Talking point

Dr Johnson once wrote: 'No man but a blockhead ever wrote, except for money.' How far do you go along with Herzberg's view that salaries and other monetary rewards are hygiene and not motivating factors?

The style theory

Supporters of the style theory consider that organisations possess different management systems – whether because of the nature of their work or because of an historical kind of management style. Thus various organisations will have a system which leans to being:

Dictatorial or Benevolent-Autocratic or Consultative or Democratic

The style theory – of which Rensis Likert was a leading investigator – states that leadership in such organisations will tend to reflect that of the system, either by being more task-centred or more people-centred.

Talking point

Do you see any dangers in a wholesale adoption of the MBOR management approach?

The leadership grid approach

A number of management experts – Blake, Mouton, Reddin – devised various grids or matrices as handy visual aids to support their theories of leadership, which took the 'style' view a stage further. Blake and Mouton's grid, for example plotted a leadership style which could either be high in a task or a people approach: or a mixture of the two:

The ideal leader would display a style which blended both – neither forgetting the task outcomes in

supporting his team, yet neither overlooking staff needs while securing the outcome desired. In a similar way, Reddin's grid identified leadership styles ranging from 'deserter' to 'developer', and detailed instances in which a compromising approach would be legitimate.

Fiedler's contingency theory

An American, F E Fiedler, published a theory in 1967 which he called a contingency model. This contended that a leadership style – in the same manager and organisation – could vary from being very task-centred to being very people-centred, depending on what the manager's relationship was with his staff at the time.

Funnily enough, a very task-centred approach seemed to be equally successful when the situation was very favourable or very unfavourable to the manager. When it was neither one nor the other, a people-centred arroach seemed most successful. While Fiedler claimed to have validated this theory in documented cases, other specialists remained sceptical.

The 'best fit' leadership approach

More recently, management specialists have supported an approach to leading staff called the 'best fit'. Here the leader/manager – whether consciously or unconsciously – emphasises a mix of the basic three ingredients of leadership:

The Task   The Support Staff   The Leader

Some situations – say where a fast, 'no arguments!' decision is needed may see a fit like this, where the leader and task components are high:

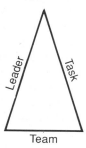

Another scenario, say where the situation is dynamic and fast-changing, may require a much more staff-leader consultative style:

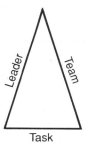

Entrepreneurs

Undoubtedly the most flamboyant and fascinating leaders in commerce and industry are its entrepreneurs – men and women possessing a prodigious amount of self-confidence and tireless energy which are harnessed to the goal of creating multinational empires within a working lifetime!

Each business generation produces its crop of high-achieving go-getters, whether a Howard Hughes, Lord Hanson, Anita Roddick or Richard Branson. Entrepreneurs are characterised by their ability to see business opportunities where others perceive problems, and by an unshakeable belief in their latest brain-child, coupled with a willingness to gamble for high stakes and to attack mountains of work like a computer game 'munch-man'. Entrepreneurs combine a love of the unconventional with boundless energy. The end products of this mix are production-line motor-car manufacture, natural body care chainstores or cut-price air travel.

While entrepreneurs may be easy to work for – in that they demand total loyalty and expect to make all the important decisions – as leaders they are a 'hard act to follow', since few of their subordinates possess the innate flair and intuition which come naturally to the builders of business empires.

Intrapreneurs

Nevertheless, top directors in multinational companies have come to recognise the importance of harnessing and directing an entrepreneurial spirit within their organisations, and have created the role of the *intra*preneur. Intrapreneurs are people who display a swashbuckling disregard for bureaucratic conventions within their organisations and who are energetic and daring enough to break out of constricting modes of business practice and company routines in order to bring to the market a new product range or service concept. As leaders, intrapreneurs tend to surround themselves with like-minded lieutenants willing to take risks in order to climb fast. Their goal-centred drive, however, sometimes carries with it seeds of destruction such as an inability to trust, delegate or consult.

Talking point

Can 'Small Is Beautiful' ever work in large-scale manufacturing enterprises employing thousands of employees in dispersed locations?

Leading by example

A more transferable kind of leadership is that which is capable of emulation, where subordinates are able to see their manager as a role-model with standards and traits which may be imitated. Such leaders tend to create patterns of set examples, whether in the form of taking unpopular decisions or of steadfast loyalty to the organisation during bad times and so on with which their teams can identify and then develop for themselves.

Talking point

Can entre- and intrapreneurs also be leaders or is the management of their empire-building ideas better left to others?

There is now a tendency towards a 'pick-n-mix' or 'best fit' style, which favours a pragmatic 'try this approach and see if it works' view of leadership. Certainly, effective leadership styles vary enormously, from the leader with personal charisma – 'I'd follow him (or her) to the ends of the earth!', to the macho man's man style, to the quietly supportive style. Perhaps it is appropriate to give an ancient Chinese philospher the last word on what makes a good leader:

'It is a wise leader who so leads his people that they themselves come to believe *they* made the decisions leading to happy outcomes.'

Needless to say, it is a rare leader who is able to put his team's esteem and 'self-actualisation' needs before his own ego-needs when it comes to the taking of credit!

Leadership talking points

1 What do you think are the qualities of leadership a good manager should possess?

2 If you were one of an interviewing team of senior managers about to select a junior manager for an important promotion, what sort of evidence of leadership would you look for in those short-listed?

3 Do you agree that an organisation's management style can be either broadly dictatorial or broadly democratic? Or is this a wild over-simplification?

4 Do you think that managers/leaders tend either to be task- or people-centred in their management styles because of deep-rooted personality traits – and there's an end of it! Or do you think that a manager could consciously mix the two to achieve a given management task?

5 Can leaders be made? If so, how?

6 'He leads from the front!' is an often quoted response about certain managers. What is meant by it?

Current management issues and preoccupations

Effective delegation

While in essence the manager's role is to 'achieve predetermined objectives through the work of others' – a process termed delegation – in reality effective delegation is not easily achieved. Many managers suffer from the 'boomerang effect', in which tasks parcelled out to subordinates have an uncanny way of winging their way back to their originator barely attempted, or not done at all! The excuses tendered are often plausible at first sight, but quickly come to smack of poor management of time, a lack of motivation, an unwillingness to take decisions or poor self-organisation.

What can the hard-pressed manager do in such circumstances? Firstly, he or she has to get well organised – to log the time, date and deadline of what jobs were delegated to what assistants. 'As soon as possible', ASAP and other polite requests for action 'sometime' are no subsitute for a clear 'by Wednesday 31 July, latest please' given deadlines. Also, it is important for the manager to agree deadlines for involved work with staff *in advance*, so that there is no ground for subsequent excuses or 'wrigglings'! Secondly, the manager needs an habitual routine of bringing forward documents and reminders well in advance of deadlines to act as memory-joggers for progress-chasing and review. Thirdly, the manager needs to grow a thicker skin so as to be able to ask firm and direct questions about work due or overdue:

'Harry, the Goodson tender specifications were due yesterday – I've set aside two hours to work on them this afternoon, so I'm assuming they'll be available . . .' Pause.

'Jean, you were committed to getting the new launch advertising campaign drafts ready a week ago. The presentation to the board is in two days' time. You've given me no intimation of any problems, so I am relying on having them by 2.00 pm this afternoon – unless you want to go over any snags with me now . . .'

In many organisations today, managers have a powerful support tool in this area in the form of the regular appraisal interview; clearly staff who are regularly failing to meet reasonable and agreed deadlines for submitting work of an acceptable quality are inviting serious criticism about their overall suitability. In short, then, effective delegation requires a maintained logging system, secured agreement and commitment to the task and its due date, sufficient progress chasing to make the proverbial 'stitch in time', and a willingness to convey to staff the consequences of slackness. The 'country club' manager unwilling to establish clear action expectations in this regard will soon find himself doing other people's work for them – after hours or at home!

Talking point

Which system do you think most likely to work effectively in organisations – Theory X, Theory Y, or a mixture of both? Can they be mixed? Is McGregor's thinking relevant to today's organisational structures?

Managing time

While trying to assist support staff to manage their time better, managers must not lose sight of the constant, pressing need to manage their time to best effect. Perhaps a cliché, but still well worth repeating is the proverbial: 'A manager's most precious resource is time!'

The development of desk-top organiser software packages has provided the busy manager with a host of handy and invaluable time and labour-saving support tools:

● electronic diary and meetings scheduler
● electronic notebook for recording aide-mémoires
● appointments scheduler
● Email messaging system
● integrated desk-top information software
● electronic database for personal information, etc.

For example, the meetings scheduler takes the strain out of finding the common denominator hour when all five section heads can attend a meeting, by interrogating their diaries and provisionally fixing the meeting – and booking the conference room – in seconds! Similarly, audio-visual signals on network software can remind the busy manager of an important job and deadline. However, all the electronic gadgetry in the world will be of little use if the manager has not internalised these regular practices:

● *daily first/last thing briefings* with secretary/PA to review commitments, update priorities, etc,
● *regular reviews of time scheduling* with secretary so as to block out in advance sessions needed for uninterrupted work to meet given deadlines,
● *setting up of routine meetings/reports* for the manager to receive status/updating/progress-chasing reports from section heads, etc,
● *development of project-management skills* in support teams, so they can get on with less supervision,
● *development of PA/secretary*: the skills and potential of secretarial staff are sadly under-utilised by many managers who thus waste the chance of delegating work and making more time for key activities,
● *periodic time-log review* to assess how much time is being spent on: phoning, dictating, meetings, report-writing, etc, and to see how costly time can be saved by changing working habits,

- *periodic audit of routine returns/form filling, etc*: some companies regularly review their routine reporting and form-based returns to see what can be discontinued because of lack of use, changed circumstances,
- *regular re-prioritising of tasks*: valuable time can be wasted on continuing detail work for a job which has acquired a low status/priority,
- *developing skim-reading techniques* and building rapid-reading skills which save on reading time; asking support staff to produce abstracts of important articles, and so on,
- *structuring interviews*: economically pre-arranged time-spans for visiting clients, salesmen, etc which are 'closed on time' by the manager or intervening secretary help to prevent the 'quick word' becoming a lengthy ramble.

The single, most important contributor to an effective management of time is the control and minimalising of unscheduled interruptions. The busy manager then wins time to think and plan ahead, and thus access the two best time-savers there are!

Open-door management

However busy the time-conscious manager is, time should still be made available to keep in touch with the busy department – through an 'open-door' approach!

Managing targets and budgets

Almost every activity in an organisation today is measured and assessed within the management function. As we have already discovered, MBOR and systems management both rely on timely feedback to ensure that aims and objectives are met. Directors and senior management have a constant need to know how the organisation is doing and to 'take its pulse' regularly. Correspondingly, divisional and departmental managers (especially in the middle ranks of organisations) find a large part of their job comprises the achievement of predetermined (and negotiated) targets, together with working within preset budgets – of money, of human resources or materials.

Common target areas:

Sales management: sales turnover to preset monthly/annual target.

Production: Output actual to output target; actual to target wastage rates, absentee rates, delivery date schedules, etc.

Computer services: target to actual downtime per month – expressed in minutes/hours when DP facilities out of action.

Accounts: Actual to target number of days of credit – length of overdue accounts.

Targets may be set on an historical basis – last year's turnover plus 15 per cent, or a profit percentage basis – net profit to be 12 per cent of sales turnover, a 'ground-zero' basis of 100 per cent waste-free production and so on. The establishment of targets is a cause for negotiation based on realism. Their delivery requires careful planning, allocation of sub-targets and team coordination. A key factor here is the availability of accurate information promptly. Today many organisations operate real-time databases which can display on demand: sales to date, gross profit margins, projected net profits, etc. Similarly, large organisations employ teams of management accountants to supply regular reports, using established accounting formulas and ratios:

- the current ratio of assets over liabilities,
- the liquidity ratio – which checks cash-flow return on capital invested, etc.

Managers achieve targets through a mixture of:

- *judiciously sub-allocating the component parts* eg by sales region, district office, sales representative, etc,
- *planning and executing*: advertising and sales campaigns, safety drives, quality circles and suggestion bonuses, creation of new markets, cost-cutting exercises, etc,
- *motivating staff* concerned through sales conferences, in-house recognition of achievement, bonuses, prizes, etc,
- *using models and forecasts* to predict buying/marketing trends and eventualities.

According to one contemporary view of the motivation process, the 'quid-pro-quo' or 'what's-in-it-for-me?' factor plays a crucial role in obtaining the most out of people working to meet targets; managers must therefore be able to offer worthwhile rewards – not just monetary ones – to achieve targets through workforces.

Keeping within budget is a common cause of restless nights among managers; today organisations exact strict penalties for failure. Overspends may be deducted from the following year's allocations, jobs may be axed to pay for the overspend, other factories within the group maybe get the work instead, and so on.

Managers, therefore, devote much energy – through spreadsheet records of reducing balances; securing best buy prices for goods and services; ongoing analysis of costs (especially in manufacturing); constant refining of production/administration methods; (eg through work study) and the monitoring of cost/profit centres set up within departments or units. Manufacturers, for example, now employ 'just-in-time' production procedures where parts arrive at the assembly-line just when needed and without costly, high volume, on-site stocks being held. While budgetary control may sound like a specialist accounting term, today *all* managers need to have acquired skills in maintaining or reducing costs while expanding turnover and profitability.

Talking point

'The systems management approach works brilliantly in textbook models, but is far too impersonal and rigid ever to work in practice!'

Effective decision-making

One of the simplest ways of distinguishing between a good and a poor manager is to vet the quality of their decison making. At the top of the managerial tree, company directors and civil servants are charged with making decisions which involve millions of pounds and the jobs of thousands; or outcomes which could affect the material wealth of the country for many years. Middle and junior managers, while limited to making sectional rather than corporate decisons, can also make a significant difference between an organisation's profit or loss. Little wonder, then, that management specialists have given so much attention to the processes of decision-making and decision management.

Most experts see decision-making as moving through five distinct phases:

Stages in the decision-making process

1 Open, free-ranging, brain-storming survey of idea
2 Detailed evaluation of aspects and options
3 Selection of most attractive/practical option
4 Implementing the decision; marking its boundaries
5 Analysing outcomes and effecting called-for follow-up.

---

1 Aims and Concepts

The first stage concerns a brainstorming survey of what the issue in question is all about: Why research a new product? Who for? To do what? What market? What's in it for the firm? Long- or short-term prospects, product life? Do we have the technology? The production capacity?

2 In-depth evaluation of strategies and options

Having undertaken a wide-ranging overview of the background, nature, scope and desired outcomes of the idea, the second phase is to quantify it, cost it, test it in models and prototypes – generally to evaluate it from all angles. From this stage will probably emerge several options. Marketeers refer to optimistic and pessimistic scenarios; R & D scientists may produce high-, middle- and low-cost research programme options and suggest alternative test designs.

3 Selecting the best available option

The third stage is usually marked by a trade-off between identified options – dearest/cheapest, fastest/slowest; needs bought-in expertise/we have in-house skills, etc. At this stage some experts refer to the common practice of 'satisficing', where managers opt for the easiest, cheapest, 'least hassle' way out that can convince a majority, even though this may not be the best solution. Important in this stage also is to consider the costs of making *no* decision.

4 Implementing the decision

Once the go-ahead in principle is made, the decision is implemented and boundary positions identified: limit of injected cash, length of trial period, amount of time available, number of employees committed, etc. Also, the required outcomes of the decision are carefully identified and circulated to all concerned.

5 Post-decision evaluation and feedback

The decision having been implemented, its outcomes (predicted and unpredicted) and its costs and benefits are analysed. In their light, follow-up activities are either reinforced and expanded, stabilised, or reduced or terminated.

Effective managers pursue this kind of decision-making process more or less strenuously depending on the importance of the decision. Ineffective ones allow emotion, prejudice, stubborness, and a failure to think things through to mar the process. They also generally fail to unearth the relevant facts and factors or to interpret them correctly.

Talking point

'The contingency – "Anything goes" model – demonstrates the lack today of any kind of business ethic or moral basis for management practice.' Fair comment? Do achieved ends justify any management means today?

Managing conflict

Even the most happy family has its rows and upsets, and organisations are no different. Few managers therefore escape an involvement in conflicts from time to time. Conflict scenarios vary enormously, yet most have their roots in human behaviour and psychology:

- X feels he/she has been slighted, put-down, shown up, made to look a fool, 'wound up', etc by Y and either reacts angrily or sulks; either way productivity falls as tensions mount until, possibly, one or two people quit.
- The working group is upset by a new policy/ standing order/working condition imposed by management and introduces an official or unspoken work-to-rule to vent anger and frustration.
- Y gets promoted; X and Z feel by-passed and start a whispering campaign that makes Y's life a misery.
- Z fails to get appointed to the restructured Project Managment Group and therefore feels humiliated, by-passed, put out to grass and overtaken by a younger whizz-kid; resentment smoulders and the working atmosphere suffers.

Such examples serve to illustrate that conflict arises mostly from interpersonal relationships, although we have already seen (Unit 1) instances of conflict caused by counter-running interests: management role *v.* union membership, or from a mismatch between a person's ethical code and actions required by management.

Resolving conflict is a highly fatiguing and demanding process. Firstly, the manager has to become skilled in identifying its early warning signs – changes in staff's behaviour patterns in small things, or huddled groups in earnest 'conflab' which dies away on approach, stress-related absenteeism, etc. Here a discreet secretary can be a great help to the preoccupied manager in alerting him to danger signs.

Having sensed a conflict situation – or having been confronted by it – the manager needs to take immediate steps to defuse it. This usually involves private, individual interviews with affected parties to hear all sides of the dispute. Having decided first upon a fair and attainable solution, the manager then needs to bring the involved parties together to deliver a solution/judgement and – what is quite essential – to secure a clearly expressed acceptance from all sides that there will be no rancour. Of course people say one thing in a manager's office and do another outside on their own patch. Thinking managers therefore make the time to monitor post-reconciliation behaviour and attitudes – and rightly come down hard on those who harbour grudges.

On occasion, a removal from the conflict situation is the only practical solution. Deep-seated personality clashes between two key personnel may require a transfer of one out of the 'aggro arena'. Again, advice may be needed for staff who are unable to square the circle of, say, young children and full-time working so that children are put first and job second, by arranging part-time work until further notice.

Key elements of successful conflict resolution by the manager are:

- strict fairness and impartiality,
- trustworthy and sensitive approach to gain confidence,
- even-handed examination of each party's position,
- identifying root causes and deciding on corrective actions,
- outcomes must be enforceable and fair,
- resolution of the conflict must be accepted – sincerely – by all parties,
- loss of face must be avoided/minimised,
- reconciliation must be monitored for sincerity/ working in practice,
- transfers/job-role changes may be necessary.

The process resolving interpersonal conflict in support staff is most stressful in the phases which bring affected parties together. Here the manager will need to have rehearsed a very clear line of argument and be prepared to pull out all his or her persuasive communication stops!

NOTE: In some conflict situations it may be helpful for a third-party counsellor to be brought in to manage the resolution process as a totally disinterested referee.

Talking point

Is conflict necessarily a 'bad thing' in organisations? Can it ever be productive?

Managing stress

Stress is a killer. Every day hundreds of people suffer heart attacks aggravated by stress, and many die. Stress also maims minds. Each year thousands of people are hospitalised in psychiatric centres suffering from mental breakdowns, nervous collapses or depression – where stress has proved a contributive factor. Happily many recover from heart attacks and bouts of mental illness to go on to realise their potential and goal aims. Yet their pain and illness could often have been foreseen and prevented.

Thus all managers have a bounden duty to prevent stress becoming a health hazard among their staff. Small amounts of stress are inescapable, and part of living. Indeed, some experts believe that people perfom better – in sport, in the theatre or at work – if 'psyched up' with the adrenalin flowing. But this is not the same as this kind of stress:

Job overload
'My work is piling up with shorter and shorter deadlines and everyone's yelling for overdue WP copy . . . and I just can't cope any more!'

Lack of proper management guidance
'No one ever tells me what I'm supposed to do and everyone snaps at me for treading on their toes. I can't seem to grasp hold of what's wanted of me and I worry that I'm not doing my job, so I'll get the bullet!'

Deliberate exclusion
'Ever since I had a row with JJ, I've been frozen out; no more informational memos, meetings called that I don't get invited to any more – although matters are raised affecting my department . . . I think somebody's trying to tell me something!'

Many causes of stress are to do with office politics and the dark side of human nature where ambition, jealousy, envy and petty spite conspire to upset and injure targeted individuals. Some employees are also their own worst enemies in that they have sensitive natures, 'thin skins' and are vulnerable to masked bullying or being 'picked on'.

Yet other causes of stress have nothing to do with having become isolated from the pack. They concern:

- *Not enough responsibility:* a job beneath someone's capabilities can soon lead to frustration and stress

- *Too much responsibility:* very conscientious employees may become worriers if promoted too high or too fast, and this may lead to stress and nervous disorders.

- *Inadequate/non-existent job description:* staff who lack a clearly stated set of responsibilities delegated from their superiors are likely to flounder, yet overwork in an effort to ensure they are doing enough. A failure ever to receive recognition, praise or at least confirmation that the work is going satisfactorily can also lead to stress.

- *Over-exposure to people and communication overload:* many managers try to maintain an overloaded interface with their staff and contacts, who are thus encouraged to check out every decision with the boss and to want his personal ear constantly. This commonly causes stress as the manager tries to keep twenty jobs, forty staff and thirty messages all spinning at once like plates on a juggler's bamboo sticks. Usually the manager's brains end up spinning fastest!

Further causes include conflict situations – between personnel or between employee and the organisa-tion, troubles at home, affairs of the heart – especially affaires within organisations, money troubles and so on.

The effective manager needs to tackle stress among his staff in a way similar to that of handling conflict. First, he must be ever-alert to symptoms and signs of stressed behaviour. Secondly, affected staff must be sensitively interviewed and section leaders questioned until the surface and then root causes of the stress are identified. With the staff member and his supervisor, the manager then needs to review work roles, responsibilities, team membership – whatever interfaces or activities are causing the stress and then to devise a programme which will alleviate the stress-causing factors. The affected person's future work and state of mind should be carefully and discreetly monitored for signs of recurrent stress. If the manager has interceded early and well, then the problem may be cured for good.

Stress signals

- Increased nervousness
- Shorter fuse – irritability
- Fall in work output
- Increase in making mistakes
- Physical disorders: nervous ticks, shortness of breath
- Absenteeism, idling, vacant moods
- Intolerance increase
- Rise in smoking, drinking, pill-taking
- Apparently unmotivated weeping
- Unwillingness to see staff

Both managers and support staff have a responsibility to counter stress symptoms by:

- engaging in 'switching off' recreations: sport, hobbies, away-days, long week-ends, etc,
- getting enough of the right food and rest,
- pacing work throughout the day – taking time out for a stroll to see a colleague,
- balancing work with social life, not taking work home every night,
- doing relaxation/meditation exercises,
- keeping a sense of humour and perspective,
- planning work and rest times in balanced mixes a week at a time and sticking to the plan.

The effective manager knows the dangers of stress for himself and his team and keeps its prevention always high on his personal agenda.

Talking point

How important are recognition and acknowledgement to you?

Managing negotiations

A crucial management skill lies in the ability to secure desired outcomes by gaining the acceptance of others for plans, proposals or policies. This objective is often secured through the process of negotiation.

Good negotiations leave both parties feeling that they have achieved most of what they hoped for. Like bazaar bartering, negotiations tend to move from established first positions to a meeting in the middle – where, say, a pay deal is offered and accepted, compromise having been made by both parties.

Like the direct sales approach, negotiation requires practised skills:

First positions: both parties prepare their ground in first positions – usually what their ideal outcome scenario is.

Preliminary skirmishing: both sides 'test the water' with their proposals. *Note*: wily negotiators generally decide in advance what their 'worst situation' acceptance point is, and also, the point at which negotiations would be called off or adjourned.

Agreeing the non-contentious parts: to build an atmosphere of goodwill and a productive working relationship, non-contentious issues and second-tier matters are often negotiated first.

Trading-off the deal: the essence of negotiation lies in trading off some aspects so as to gain others; intelligent negotiators always know what parts of their package are most readily negotiable in this sense. This stage is marked by hard and detailed bargaining; good negotiators make it their business to be expert in the other side's views, specialisms and work. Lack of inside or expert knowledge about the other side is a poor negotiating base.

Spotting the favourable balance and sealing the deal: experienced negotiators become very skilled at knowing when they have wrung as many concessions out as are forthcoming; like all good communicators, they know when to stop; at this stage it is vital to have listed mutually agreed conditions, concessions, undertakings and so on for the record and for later issue in a joint statement.

Saving the face and leaving something in the pot

Wise negotiators who emerge victorious from a negotiating sequence always ensure that the other party is not left having totally lost face – especially, as in pay-round negotiations, there is always a next time to deal with the same team of negotiators. Likewise, unless negotiating unconditional surrender, victorious negotiators 'leave something in the pot' for the other side to take back and display as their 'winnings'. In this way a little oil is left on the 'next time' negotiation wheel.

Confirming the deal

The final phase is marked by trade union members or their executive committees, or boards of directors, or HM Government, for example, accepting negotiated proposals and confirming or ratifying the agreement reached. *Note*: almost all negotiated agreements are given a limited time-span and will almost always list scenarios which could invalidate the agreement or require its modification, for example a rise in bank rate, the value of the pound, mortgage interest rates, maintenance of productivity increases, etc.

The negotiating manager therefore needs to:

- Research and prepare the topic for negotiation thoroughly.
- Anticipate the other party's proposals and have ready counter-proposals.
- Study the personalities and susceptibilities of his opponents.
- Draw up a checklist of pawns which could be sacrificed in the negotiating chess match.
- Identify clearly the back-stop position which is his sticking-point.
- Clarify regularly what precisely the other side is proposing or agreeing to and record it as the process unfolds.
- Spot when he has achieved his aims and seal the deal promptly.
- Keep superiors in continuous touch while securing ongoing approvals for concessions.

Some 'wheeler-dealer' managers love to negotiate, others find it an irksome chore. For all managers, however, developing effective negotiating skills lies at the very heart of successful trading, workforce motivation and the industrial relations which underpin the economy.

Talking point

What do you think it is today that 'legitimises' a manager's actions and authority in organisations? A mesmerising personality? Hire and fire power? Sweet reasonableness?

Talking point

What features do you think likely to characterise management styles over the next decade? Why?

Managing change

Today one of the most demanding challenges facing managers is to manage change successfully. The pace of current technological change – in computerised manufacturing, in telecommunications and in organisational information systems and so on is little short of alarming. The past ten or so years in the UK have witnessed a severe recession, economic boom and over-heating, sharp demographic downturns in the teenage population, wide-scale movements of the population, all of which betoken radical changes in how people live, work and adapt to changed circumstances.

The management of change, then, has become an ongoing preoccupation for the effective manager. It is marked above all by a flexible, almost lateral-thinking approach, allied to a willingness to think again – and yet again in the light of the un-suspected. For by definition, no one knows precisely where change leads!

Checklist of factors affecting the management of change.

- A readiness to keep abreast of developments in one's specialist field through trade journals, technical texts, etc.
- A willingness to keep an open mind in the light of new products and processes.
- An enthusiasm for experimenting and innovating – even if this means failing at times.
- A strong commitment to staff and self-development, including devoting significant investment to it.
- A preparedness to discard young – but obsolete – equipment and systems: four-year depreciation periods are a long time in IT and the electronic office machine market!
- A ruthless critical eye for the outmoded, old-hat and passé – in products, services, routines and systems.

While the manager may be a paragon of virtue where the above attitudes to change are concerned, his staff may be very comfortable in cosy routines, comfortable ruts and warmly familiar practices. Thus introducing change successfully needs first an effective campaign in consciousness-raising and attitude leading. It also requires careful planning to overcome objections and opting out. The following chart lists some of the major tools the manager can use in managing change.

Talking point

What do you think Henri Fayol meant by 'unity of command and direction'?

Tools for managing change

- Phased prior consultation and structured communication about the proposed changes with all involved parties.
- Creation of quality circles and study groups to examine proposals and suggest responses – participation in the process is essential if staff are to accept change.
- Countering of rumour and gossip by displaying frequent official communications with top management status.
- Good project management to phase-in change and leave enough time to effect staff development and training on new equipment and or systems.
- Setting up of 'grouse lines' to deal sympathetically with problems or grumbles.
- Fixing of and sticking to firm deadlines for change-overs – say to electronic mail LAN networking or a flexible hours working system.
- Ensuring that organisational 'decision-leading' staff are wooed and won over early on – the 'ripple effect'.
- Holding section-leader/team/departmental meetings to review the effects of changes openly and honestly; letting staff articulate fears, concerns or frustrations so as to maintain their goodwill and proactive involvement.

Change and organisational development

In many large organisations, the continuous process of managing change is called 'organisation development' or OD. Sometimes staff functions in posts such as industrial psychologist are created so as to install resident experts to advise senior management on how to coordinate and manage the change process.

Evaluation techniques

So far Unit 10 has concentrated on management and leadership in organisations. The processes of evaluation – of quality, effectiveness, targets, outcomes and work done – form an important part of, in fact an essential feedback role in, all organisations. Techniques of evaluation are particularly important in those organisations employing extended tiers of people in line management functions where also many hundreds or thousands of employees work. For when lines of communication become extended, the 'What did he say? Pass it On!' syndrome comes into play, and bit by bit, the organisation is in danger of losing its way.

The role of O&M and work study

In essence, the twin functions of organisation & methods and work study evolved to ensure that work carried out was not only efficient, but effective. The case history on page 236: 'Cutting through to the heart of the problem' illustrates the world of difference that exists between the two. O&M and work study embrace the following activities:

- Employing the most economical routines and processes in terms of costs, time and effort or energy.
- Coordinating routines to avoid duplication and overlap.
- Ensuring that good communication practices avoid breakdowns, ambiguities or exclusions when information is channelled around the organisation.
- Maximising productivity and minimising waste by scrutinising the ways in which jobs are undertaken and evaluating them to see how they may be done more effectively.
- Evaluating plant and equipment to ensure that it is being used to its optimum output potential.
- Appraising the ways in which factories and offices are laid out so that people, machines and materials are harmoniously grouped to minimise delays, bottlenecks or frustrations.

Such are the principal considerations of those company or public service personnel whose role is to optimise the efficiency and effectiveness of the organisation's working processes. The activities they undertake are termed 'work study' in the manufacturing side of a company's activities and 'organisation and methods' in the general area of office administration.

In organisational terms, the people engaged in such work are usually deemed to be in the 'staff' as opposed to 'line' management of the organisation and as such often report through a departmental head direct to the managing director. In larger organisations they may be grouped together as a management services department as the diagram on page 235 illustrates. As you can see, in a large organisation, the management services department encompasses the work of accounting experts, economists, systems analysts, programmers and data preparation operatives – in effect a DP unit – as well as specialists in work measurement and office ergonomics (the specialist study of people in a working environment). If the company embodies a manufacturing arm, then the management services department may also include specialist work study staff evaluating production processes.

It is not difficult to justify such an extensive management services operation in companies with multi-million pound turnovers, since a single improvement in production techniques or administrative procedures may save thousands of pounds a day.

In the context of what an organisation and methods unit or department principally undertakes, it is interesting to recall the work of a data processing team since there are a number of correspondences between an O&M evaluation of a job and the creation of a DP routine – both rely on rational thinking and sequential logic – and it is thus no accident that a DP presence is often to be found in firms within the management services department.

Perhaps the simplest and best way to examine the O&M role is in terms of having a specialist group who can examine the questions which follow (or similar ones) and then proffer answers to them aim-

The role of work study and O & M

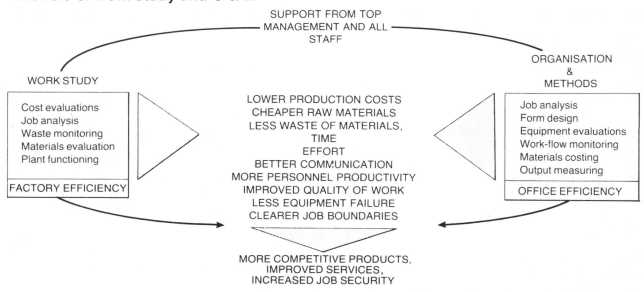

ed at improving efficiency and effectiveness:

- *Who* actually, precisely and in fine detail is doing what?
- And *what* precisely, actually and in fine detail are they doing?
- *Why* are they doing it? (In what way, following what procedures etc?)
- *When* are they doing it? (At what time intervals, according to what schedules, timetables, cycles of activity?)
- *Where* are they doing it? (Over how many locations, requiring how much movement?)
- *How* are they doing it? (In what sort of work patterns, using what type of equipment, forms, administrative procedures?)
- *To what effect* are they doing it? (Is the operation cost-effective, economical, profitable, achieving quality, worthwhile?)
- *Should it be done at all?* (Who would miss it if it were cut out of company activities?)

The continuous posing of such questions and the attainment of productive answers forms the daily bread-and-butter work of the O&M or work study specialist. Historically, the work of staff constantly probing into work routines and practices has not always been managed very well by senior organisational staff. If O&M work is to be truly effective, it has to operate in a climate which is cooperative. If line managers remain suspicious of O&M and factory operatives resentful of enforced work-rates which are imposed rather than negotiated, then the result may be that lip-service is paid to the introduction of revised work routines while, in effect, little changes.

Thus senior managment has an obligation to ensure that O&M is not seen as a form of private intelligence to which only the MD is privy and which lies at the root of the imposition of unpopular policies. At the same time, no managing director worth his salt can afford to stand idly by while parts of his or her company lurch cheerfully along,

Management services – organisation structure.
Work study related to factory-based operations may also be incorporated.

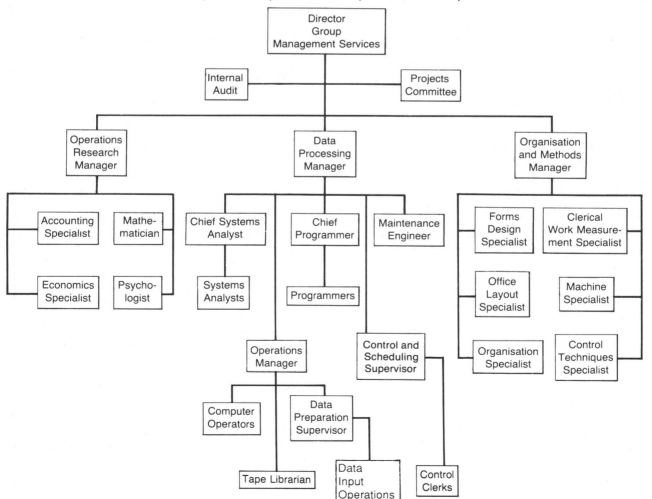

wasting money or failing to make their proper contribution to profits.

Astute senior management has managed to steer a route between these two rock-strewn shores by evolving structures and policies whereby staff at all levels benefit from the introduction of more efficient work practices. For example, part of a departmental manager's salary may be paid on a scale allied to the cost-effectiveness of his department. In production terms this could mean achieving or exceeding production targets or minimising waste and defective products. For the sales manager it may mean achieving his sales target but it might include a reward based on the number of new customers found and the turn-over they contribute. For the office administration manager it could mean the running of the administration arm within a total of given expenditure – for payroll, equipment, consumables and repairs, with a bonus relating to any further savings made.

In other words, imaginative management is able to connect all the way down the organisational hierarchy rewards – extra money, holidays, promotion, etc – with the achievement of more economic ways of running the business. In this way, the Works Manager may welcome the Work Study Officer with open arms. However, it would be oversimplifying the case if the role and functions of trade unions were not to be included in the general mix of O&M and work study activities, since the objectives of management and trade union officials may not always entirely coincide. While management may see the introduction of a particular operation as cost-cutting and labour-saving, the trade union involved may regard it as pay-reducing and redundancy-causing.

Thus in many firms the implementation of recommendations made by O&M staff may require an ongoing dialogue and the fostering of good relationships by senior managment – as much with their

---

Cutting through to the heart of the problem

There was a large company which had been in the widget manufacturing business for some years. Recently, however, sales had slumped, the percentage of defective widgets being produced had grown alarmingly and overall staff morale had plummeted.

Correspondingly, a team of outside management consultants was called in to go over the company with a fine tooth comb to find out what was going wrong. In part of the team was an Office Administration specialist and his assistant, a kind of apprentice learning the consultancy business.

One day they went into the Widget Evaluation Department, which had a high reputation for efficiency. The young apprentice was deeply impressed. Everywhere she looked she saw smartly dressed personnel beavering away with barely time to acknowledge passing colleagues. In one corner reports were being produced on expensive WP equipment at a high rate of knots, while in another several executives were dictating almost continuously into the latest audio equipment. Further along the office there were the latest filing systems and micro-fiche equipment allied to computers – it was all highly impressive in the eyes of the apprentice consultant. It was obviously impressing her boss, whose eyes roved everywhere, and who asked a series of short but practical questions.

After an hour or two of observation and interview, the consultant specialist said to his assistant:

'Right, I've seen enough. We'll come back tomorrow sharp at nine a.m., and I want you to bring with you two large plastic dustbins and a pair of large shears.'

Mystified, but not daring to question the boss, the apprentice wandered off in search of a hardware shop.

The next morning, just before nine o'clock, master and assistant walked into the Widget Evaluation Department, and to the young lady's horror, the consultant began to sweep whole desktops of paperwork and in-trays into the large dustbins. With the shears he cut extension telephone cables and dropped telephones into the bins never minding about terminating peoples' calls in mid sentence! Within minutes the whole department was in uproar and, as the consultant had anticipated, the company's top staff burst into the office, looking either angry, aghast or bewildered.

'What is the meaning of this?' thundered the Managing Director, having got the consultant into the privacy of his own office as quickly as possible.

'Simply,' replied the consultant calmly, 'that in the Widget Evaluation Department you have created an endless loop of activity in which not one sliver of useful information gets out of the office! Those gentlemen over in the far corner, they are all generating audio dictation reports for word processing across the room,' he said, referring to the WP staff whose power plugs he had de-activated. 'Which,' he continued dramatically, 'are all filed in your LAN network's file server at the far end of the office!

'In effect, nothing ever leaves this room – so what's the point? If you had introduced your own Organisation and Methods Unit some while ago, you wouldn't have needed the particular piece of showmanship I indulged in. But I think it did help me to get your undivided attention!'

With that, a duly thoughtful Managing Director and an experienced Manangement Consultant got down to discussing productively how O&M and work study techniques could pull the company round.

own trade unionist officials/employees as with company staff, ignoring the trade union dimension.

Nowhere is this need more apparent than in the manufacturing arms of companies. For very many years, in factories up and down the country, pay has been linked to productivity. The more washers or nuts and bolts an operative could make in an hour, having regard for wastage rates, the more he or she could earn.

As a consequence, factory operatives, charge-hands, foremen, shop-stewards and works managers alike became very much involved in what was termed 'the rate for the job'. In the 1930s and 1940s, the 'labour' side of the of the manufacturing industry became concerned lest the 'rate for the job' should be 'busted' by operatives demonstrating to work study staff that they could complete a process quicker or turn out products faster. 'Rate-busting' became a dirty word, since it too often came to be accompanied by short-lived increases in bonuses for increased production, while the increased rate soon became the norm.

In the 1950s and 1960s, however, management introduced more sophisticated production incentives which linked quality to ouput and placed more of the control for performance in the hands of the operatives themselves.

In the office, too, post Second World War management methods became slowly more progressive as employees' job expectations grew and trade unions blossomed in the clerical, secretarial and administrative management sectors. Thus the seemingly endless rows of copy typists which characterised some pre-war large offices gradually became transformed into smaller working units with greater consideration given to their working environment. In 1963 in the UK the Offices, Shops and Railways Act was introduced, which reformed existing legislation about statutory minimum standards for facilities at work, including:

- the minimum floorspace to be allocated to each employee,
- the standards to be followed in lighting, ventilating and heating work premises,
- the ratio of male and female toilets to the number of staff employed as well as general hygiene provisions,
- the inclusion of restrooms in places of work,
- regulations to improve working conditions with regard to noise levels, dangerous equipment, first-aid provisons and the like.

In the 1970s, as the cost of office accommodation increased, and as companies wished to become more flexible in their use of floorspace, new approaches to the office as a working environment were introduced. The open-plan office was devised, which functioned without solid partitions, but used plants, filing-cabinets and screens to break down the 'open barn' appearance of large offices.

Such developments were followed by what the Germans called 'Bürolandschaft' which translates into 'office landscaping' which was achieved through the design of fully integrated office fixtures and fittings, together with acoustic screens which broke down larger spaces into smaller ones without shutting everyone up in self-enclosed rooms. In this system equipment design was also taken into consideration so that tables, desk-tops, power connections and cables were all taken into account and delivered as a coordinated package. The widespread introduction of IT-based systems and office equipment led further to 'turn-key' systems furniture and network 'plumbing' being designed and installed.

While such developments were popular both with office architects and employers seeking to contain rental overheads, they did not always meet with the approval of the staff who had to work in them, who sometimes felt they had lost out in the areas of privacy, available floorspace and the loss of confidentiality. Some also suffered from the rise of the 'Sick Office Syndrome' where electronic smells, photocopying chemicals and inefficient air-conditioning plant caused headaches and sickness.

Talking point

Why are so many manufacturing companies still operating linear production lines, with all their accompanying people problems? Surely a better way could be found by now!

Skill-based learning and workplace assessment

An essential part of effective work study and organisation and methods lies in providing follow-up training and development for personnel whose jobs and operations have been evaluated. No savings of time or money can be made by introducing a new technique or process which has not been fully mastered by the operators involved.

Consequently, much emphasis is placed today upon skill-based training – both on and off the job. The National Council For Vocational Qualifications is currently establishing comprehensive sets of vocational qualifications based upon the acquisition of series of 'can-do' competences. These have been identified by lead-industry groups as being central to jobs in sectors as diverse as engineering, agriculture or distribution. Such qualifications are assessed partly in colleges of further education or commercial training agencies 'off the job' and partly by line managers and supervisors guiding and assessing the work of personnel in training in the course of their 'on the job' daily work.

The aim of this practical and work-relevant

scheme is to bring about a general and significant improvement in the expertise of the nation's workforce within a short time, so as to meet the increased technical efficiency of work competition.

As a result, every manager today needs to be equipped to conduct practical training and assessment at his or her place of work.

Work study and the manufacturing process

Work study tends to concentrate upon the sequence of operations and activities which make up the production process. Its aim is to maximise output while minimising waste and lost production time by monitoring and improving:

- the percentage of reduction in costs attained by the introduction of a particular process,
- the precise ratio of units produced to defective units scrapped,
- the ratio of customer complaints to sales orders processed,
- the number of hours of 'downtime' of plant and equipment to hours of continuous use,
- the amount of savings made as a proportion of total production costs by switching to an alternative source of raw materials,
- the amount of money or man-hours saved by modifying a production or clerical process,
- the amount of money saved by introducing a system which requires a lower level of stock holding,

and so on.

In this way, the work of work study and O&M practitioners became quantifiable and thus straightforward for top management to appreciate – by how much, by how many, by when, etc.

The methodology of work study and O&M

Much of the work of the management services team is achieved via the successful completion of a project. In *Organisation and Methods*, R.G. Anderson lists the following stages which go to make up an O&M project:

1 Preliminary survey of terms of reference.
2 Planning the assignment.
3 Collecting the facts.
4 Developing the ideas.
5 Recording the facts.
6 Examining the facts.
7 Developing alternative procedures or methods.
8 Comparison of costs and benefits of alternative procedures or methods.
9 Presenting and selling recommendations (to company personnel).
10 Planning and implementation of recommendations.
11 Follow up, updating and review as required.

As the checklist illustrates, O&M has everything to do with a factual and rational approach to problem-solving and is very much in tune with the concept of the systems approach to management.

The process of carrying out the O&M project relies on techniques similar to those involved in researching and writing a report, where there is also a fact-finding stage, a stage of collating and synthesising of facts in order of priority and importance, a writing stage and an implementation stage.

O&M and work study specialists tend to employ the following techniques of fact-finding:

- Observation of staff in action.
- Observation of plant and equipment in action.
- Interviews with personnel at all levels.
- Analysis of operations into each component part or step and timing or measuring its contribution.
- Checking the flow of work for hold-ups or bottle-necks.
- Measuring distances walked by staff as part of a work process.
- Analysing the relationship of the locations of personnel to tools, spares, workbench, equipment, stock etc, and producing work-flow charts for analysis.
- Comparing the rate of output, cost, reduction in time or costs etc before and after introducing a modification.

When the many facets of the work study and O&M practitioner are seen in the light of the above overview, it is not difficult to understand why the team needs to include:

- a cost accountant familiar with all aspects of production finance,
- a statistician and mathematician well versed in analytical and computational techniques,
- a group able to devise and implement data processing systems as part of the analytical process,
- staff skilled in eliciting information via interviews,
- personnel specialising in the operations and technical data of the plant and equipment in use and related to the company's sphere of interest, eg printing or injection moulding plant.

The management services function

Today many larger organisations in both private and public sectors include in their departmental structures a Managment Service Department or Unit. The function of management services is broadly to maintain a regular monitoring of work practices in factories, workrooms, offices or shops, to record systematically actual processes and then to analyse them with a view to devising improved routines, processes or operations which are more economic and cost effective. Work study and O&M, then, will often form part of the management services advisory role to senior managment.

Part of the work of management services is to advise on job enhancement and enrichment.

Talking point

Is the reason for the introduction of management services departments in organisations the failure of the line departments to do their jobs properly?

Job enhancement

In the manufacturing side of industry the problems of repetitiveness in the work routine and the associated boredom it generates, along with poor motivation causing mediocre output, were recognised in the 1960s and efforts were made to increase job satisfaction. In manufacturing industry these centred around:

job rotation,
job enlargement and,
job enrichment.

Job rotation

In this approach, operatives were trained to do several jobs within their competence. For example, the operative might spend one week as a machinist, the next as an overhead crane driver and the third as a packer. The idea was to provide more variety in the work and a change of scenery. A positive spin-off was that companies created much more versatile workforces – sick staff could be replaced quickly and easily. Attitudes changed as staff came to be involved with more of the total operation and saw more of the problems and difficulties of others.

Unexpectedly, it did not always prove a popular development as some older workers preferred to work day in and day out at the same machine since they could talk to old friends and felt part of a closely-knit team.

Job enlargement and enrichment

Here the idea was to analyse a series of connected jobs to see what skills and activities might be combined so as to create a more demanding and therefore satisfying job. For example, the copy typist might be given some word processing to do and thus extend his or her repertoire and learn fresh skills which counterbalanced longstanding and perhaps stale ones.

The advantages which ensued included not only an increase in job satisfaction, but also the creation of a better qualified workforce.

Thus in general, job rotation, job enlargement and job enrichment were all designed to:

- increase levels of job-satisfaction,
- improve employee morale,
- develop a more versatile labour force,
- improve overall staff competencies.

Within some firms, however, such practices were seen as potential job destroyers – it should be borne in mind that the affluent economy of the 1960s had led to over-manning in some organisations and so employees wished to protect their own jobs and were not keen to see other staff acquiring their own skills. Nevertheless, the process did contribute to improving employees' skills and to increasing job satisfaction.

Talking point

How important do you consider group norms, loyalties and peer group pressures to be in organisations today? Are such behaviour patterns and attitudes still a force to be reckoned with by today's managers?

Job enhancement and legislation

Just as managers were devoting more energy to improving their human relations techniques in handling staff, so in post-war Britain was Parliament, through successive governments, reforming and revising company, factory and industrial law to provide better conditions of service. Acts of particular importance were:

Office Shops and Railways Act 1963
Employers' Liability (Compulsory Insurance) Act 1969
Health and Safety at Work Act (HASAW) 1974
Fire Precautions Act 1971
Employment Protection Acts 1975 and (Consolidation) 1978
Data Protection Act 1984
Trade Union Reform and Employment Relations Act (TURER) 1993

The Health and Safety at Work Act revised and consolidated previous Factory Acts and laid down essential requirements for both employee and employer in order to secure a safe working environment. For instance, the individual employee was given a responsibility to ensure that he worked safely and with due consideration for the safety of others, and was not able to 'pass the buck' to his employer if an accident arose from his own negligence. The Employee Protection Acts gave far more security to employees and established sophisticated mechanisms for grievance dismissal procedures and recourse to Industrial Tribunals in cases of dispute over dismissal.

The Employers' Liability (Compulsory Insurance Act) 1969, obliged employers to insure all employees against possible injury.

In effect, the legal reforms of the 1960s and 1970s did much to enhance the jobs of employees across the country by giving them more job security, better access to legal redress in cases of dispute and generally improved working conditions.

Talking point

Do you identify with the human relations/ behavioural school of management's views? Do you believe in the importance of the 'principle of supportive relationships' and the central place of 'self-actualisation needs' in today's management approaches? Is the delivery of job satisfaction a central duty of managers?

Job appraisal and job evaluation

Two further aspects of administering people's jobs need to be included in this topic's survey. They are job appraisal and job evaluation.

Job appraisal

It is one thing to have designed a particular job to a careful specification and to have described its main features. It is quite another to ensure that the job is being steadfastly carried out from one year to another!

If management's interest goes no further than designing the job then there is little or nothing to prevent an employee progressively shedding those bits of his job he does not care for to concentrate upon those he enjoys. And indeed this is what often happens in organisations which fail to monitor their employees' progress and performance. Also, personnel in the private sector in particular tend to be rewarded by promotion or pay rise according to the results they achieve and so it is important to have a system in operation to measure achievement and effectiveness as objectively as possible.

To do this various methods of appraising an employee's performance have been developed. This is generally achieved by the employee and his immediate manager discussing in some detail objectives to be set and met in the coming year. These could include meeting a sales target, completing a project, re-equipping a factory, completing a course of staff development and so on. Additionally, the employee and manager will often discuss the employee's strengths and weaknesses and what actions need to be taken to improve areas of sketchy knowledge or poor communication skills and so on. As a result, a schedule or programme may be drawn up which is agreed to by both parties as a plan of action for the coming year.

At its end, the employee will be invited to an appraisal interview conducted by his immediate superior, but with the boss's own superior in attendance to see fair play and to ensure that neither favouritism nor victimisation arises. The immediate manager will review the year's progress with the employee and either by means of a form or report will make his appraisal of him or her. A copy of the appraisal will then customarily be given to the employee who will have been invited to signify his acceptance of the appraisal or to add any dissenting views.

This process is referred to as 'open appraisal' since it is achieved with the full knowledge and involvement of the employee. Other appraisal systems may be 'closed' to a greater or smaller degree in that they are produced in whole or part confidentially. Such appraisals may be linked to pay or may be carried out solely as a means of evolving an individual's development programme. Or they may form the basis of a promotion process.

Talking point

All the super efficient management theories in the world won't stop employees structuring 90 per cent of their jobs as *they* want them!

Job evaluation

Here, the range of jobs which span a company's activities are ordered into a kind of league which is then used as a basis for awarding pay and other benefits. Sometimes the ranking order is fairly arbitrary and achieved subjectively – a senior clerk's job is rated lower than a shop foreman's for example.

Alternatively, the precise nature of each job may be measured according to a series of yardsticks universally applied in an effort to be more objective. Such yardstick measurements include:

How many staff and what levels report to this post? For how much financial expenditure is the post resonsible?
For how much (and costing what) equipment is the post responsible?
For how long last the consequences of the decisions made in this post? How far-reaching is their effect?

and so on. The league of jobs thus ranked and evaluated then provides a basis for ongoing negotiations with trade unions, etc, on pay and also forms the means of sustaining differentials between jobs in areas like pay and conditions of service.

Talking point

'Human relations based managment is management gone soft!'

Design and the office

One of the major factors in creating and maintaining efficiency and effectiveness in office administration lies undoubtedly in the way in which offices are designed and laid out. It may be fairly surmised that Scrooge did not worry himself unduly about Bob Cratchit's working area and we may be quite sure that Scrooge wouldn't have regarded it as worthy of any extended planning or financial investment! Fortunately for today's millions of office workers in the UK, current employers are much more far-sighted than was Ebenezer Scrooge in creating an office environment which would promote productivity and help to minimise staff turnover.

Modern psychological research has demonstrated the effects which colours and textures have on people's moods and attitudes. Red, for example, is seen as a colour tending to agitate and disquiet while green tends to calm and reassure. Strong colours act as a visual distraction while pastel shades are easy to work near.

The study of ergonomics

Over the past twenty or so years, the study of ergonomics has come to the fore in organisations. It encompasses the relationship of the worker to his environment. It has to do with designing layouts – of factory plant or office furniture – and with movements – of people around office equipment and cabinets or factory machines – and with the design and manufacture of the furniture of the workplace, whether bench, desk, chair, stool or draughtsman's drawing board.

Essentially, the aim of ergonomics is to ensure that the components of the work place outlined above are designed in such a way that effective work can be carried out smoothly, in a user friendly and economic way. It also helps to ensure that productivity is not lost because of backstrain, eyesight problems, bottlenecks and so on.

Ergonomics is of growing importance to both managers and support personnel, especially in locations where many people work in close surroundings like open offices or factory floors.

In equipment terms the science of ergonomics has resulted in typists' and managers' chairs being better designed for their posture and so as to avoid backache and fatigue.Typewriters, computer keyboards and monitors incorporate design factors allowing them to be adjusted for different individual use.

British Standards have researched into the lighting needs of office personnel and provided manufacturers with specifications to follow, backed up by legislation.

> ## Talking point
>
> If you gave office workers the chance, they would convert every single open plan office into individualised, enclosed office rooms tomorrow! The only people who like open plan office systems are the firms that install them, and the top managers who thus keep costs down, but don't have to work in them!'

Facilities management

Of recent years a new work-place support concept has emerged termed 'facilities management'. The underlying idea is that an external company will take over the management of one or more facilities or support services which its client uses regularly. A simple example is the provision and maintenance of all indoor plants and greenery within a multi-storey office block, which saves staff the time spent in maintaining them and the wastage of neglected plants. More sophisticated facilities management may take the form of a turnkey data processing service in which entire networks and configurations of hardware are installed and maintained, applications software is provided, one-off programs designed and data – like weekly/monthly payroll – processed to predetermined deadlines. Again, facilities such as systems open-plan offices and their desk-top equipment may be provided and serviced by external agencies.

As with all services, there is a price to be paid for facilities managment, not only in increased operation costs which have to be met, but also in added potential risk to security and privacy and a reliance upon a third party for key functions.

Features of good office design

Government Acts like the HASAW Act have prompted dangerous and untidy trailing cables to be incorporated in walls, floors or furniture by office designers. Further legislation on noise levels has led to the introduction of acoustic covers on noisy printers and acoustic screens around open-plan working areas.

The components of good office design include:

- satisfying current legislation: toilets, restroom, room-space per employee, adequate heat and light, etc,
- consideration of personnel work flow associated with moving around the office area so as to avoid congestion and possible accidents,
- setting up work groups or teams in clusters; optimising access between staff who work closely,
- standardising on equipment to simplify procedures and staff training and to reduce costs,

TRADITIONAL OFFICE LAYOUT

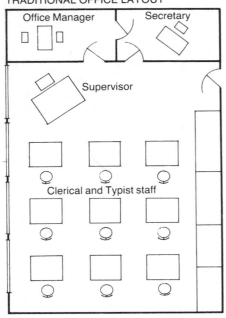

LANDSCAPED OFFICE SYSTEMS LAYOUT

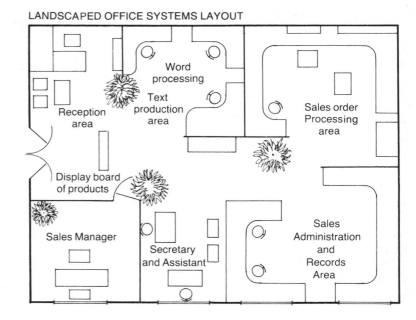

- allowing for privacy and confidentiality – enclosed interview rooms may form part of an open-plan design,
- catering for aesthetics by creating pleasing visual and tactile effects with colour, fabrics, surfaces, materials, etc,
- minimising noise problems with acoustic ceiling-hung baffle panels, acoustic screens and covers,
- ensuring that the installation is flexible – panels and screens may be re-sited to provide for a fresh layout in the light of changed needs,
- giving employees an opportunity to impose a personal identity on work areas through photographs, brought in flowers, ornaments, etc.
- avoiding health-hazarding 'sick office syndrome' conditions.

This checklist – not exhaustive – proves a tall order for employers to satisfy when the constraints are considered:

Meeting legal requirements.

Minimising costs of floor-space rental, heat, light and rates bills, etc.

Affording the 'high-tech' equipment of current electronic office technology.

Coping with the status and hierarchy structures within the company.

Avoiding customers and visitors overhearing either confidential discussions or being embarrassed by heated exchanges among staff.

In the context of office design, and the evolution of 'Bürolandschaft' and open-plan offices, the needs of the staff and the overall costs of maintaining offices are not easy to reconcile. Indeed, there is nearly always what the Americans call a trade-off to be made. For example, the traditional self-enclosed office box – four walls, a door, and a window looking out over the car-park – minimised the stress of working as part of a group since the occupant could determine whom he saw and who saw him, and could hold confidential discussions without having to use a *sotto voce* level of conversation. On the other hand, such office boxes did little to promote effective communication face-to-face among personnel, who tended – especially if managers – to become isolated from the daily doings of the work-place, i.e. the general office.

In some open-plan offices, the trade-off is reversed in that while communications and involvement may improve, the qualities of privacy, confidentiality and control of who takes up an individual's time may worsen.

Some 'total' office systems have attempted to resolve this problem by supplying both shoulder-high partitions and plastic corner windows affixed to them as well as more traditional roof-high partitions to form offices for more senior staff, training and conference rooms and so on.

Perhaps the most encouraging trend in the development of modern office layouts is that the lines of demarcation such as seniority and status which separate staff as a whole are becoming much more blurred as both senior and junior staff occupy the same open access areas within a complex, either as offices, restaurants, or social/rest areas.

Talking point

Having studied the section on Management, how would you now define the practice of management? What do you now see as its most important strands?

Talking point

Are managers a necessary evil? Could you envisage a progression of McGregor's Theory Y concept in organisations in which everyone was 'left to get on with it', and did?

Conclusion

Unit 10 has covered a lot of ground. It has surveyed the evolution of current management practices and leadership styles, surveying important milestones along the way. It has also examined the techniques and processes by which work is analysed and evaluated. Lastly, it has briefly overviewed aspects of office design and ergonomics.

As a future manager or administrator, you will need now to pause and reflect upon the many issues Unit 10 has raised. Good managers are always in short supply since the demands which managing and leading make are high. Yet the techniques and skills can be learned and polished through study, a listening ear and, above all, experience.

Your immediate steps should now be to ask the people who know – practising managers – what they see as the manager's role and how leadership is practised. Then comparing notes with fellow students will prove valuable in indentifying contrasting styles and techniques. Your work experience organisation will also help you enormously to compare the theory with the reality. Seek to listen and learn well, since you may be thrust into a supervisory management role sooner than you think, in which other people will expect *you* to 'lead from the front' and grasp the nettle of the tricky decision!

Self assessment questions

1 Having studied Unit 10's survey of management practices, review your own potential strengths and weaknesses as a future manager. Identify those areas you most need to develop further.

2 How would you assess your existing leadership qualities on a scale of 1 (low) to 10 (high)? What traits and techniques do you think you most need to strengthen?

3 Have you ever considered yourself as likely to have a career in which you will need daily to motivate people at work? How good are you at present at motivating others? Consider what opportunities exist for you to develop such skills.

4 How much thought have you given so far to the role of work study and job analysis in organisations? Have you tended to gloss over it because it 'looks a bit technical'? If so, make time to become better acquainted with the subject since it will certainly figure somewhere in your future career!

5 What thought have you given to design in office and work environments? How is an informed appreciation likely to make you a better manager of people at work?

Summary of main points

1   Essentially, management may be defined as the process of achieving predetermined goals through the effective coordination of the work of others; the management mix includes: devising strategies and policies, controlling human, financial and material resources, effective communication, responsiveness to change and self and staff development.

2   Some of the major milestones in the development of management concept and practice were: Taylor's observations of labouring operations; Weber's concept of legitimised authority in organisations, Fayol's fourteen management functions, Mayo's Hawthorne Studies on motivation and peer group pressures; Herzberg's motivator/hygiene factor theory; Maslow's hierarchy of needs, McGregor's Theory X and Theory Y, Likert's definition of the 'principle of supportive relationships'; MBOR – management by objectives and results; systems management – input, process, output, feedback, monitoring and control of the organisation's functions; 'Small Is Beautiful!' manufacturing processes; the 'pay-back' motivation theory and the 'best-fit, pick-n-mix' eclectic management approach.

3   Major leadership theories include: the Trait Theory, The Style Theory and the Leadership Grid – Task/People – Approach.

4   Current management issues and preoccupations include: how to delegate without 'the boomerang effect'; how to manage your own use of time; how to manage targets and budgets – by careful forward planning and delegated sub-division of the whole; how to make effective decisions which aren't defeatist compromises; how to manage conflict without alienating staff; how to spot the early signs of hazardous stress and how to combat it; the techniques of handling negotiations; how to manage change.

5   Evaluation techniques include: work study; the analysis of manufacturing operations, organisation and methods, the analysis of work patterns and flows; techniques of job analysis and appraisal; aspects of job enhancement and enrichment.

6   Aspects of office design and the contributory features of the Health & Safety At Work Act (HASAW) 1974, the Office, Shops & Railways Act 1963, etc, features of good office design, including ergonomics and 'total system' open office design.

Activities and assignments _____

Quick review quiz

1 Give a brief definition of management.

2 What are the ingredients of the 'management mix'?

3 What was Frederick Taylor's contribution to management practice?

4 What did Max Weber understand by his term the 'rational-legal' organisation? In Weber's view, what made a manager's authority legitimate in an organisation?

5 How many of Henri Fayol's fourteen features of management can you recall?

6 What is a scalar chain?

7 What discoveries did Elton Mayo and his associates uncover in The Hawthorne Studies?

8 Explain briefly how Maslow's 'hierarchy of needs' concept works.

9 Explain the theory behind Herzberg's motivator and hygiene factor theory. Identify the five major motivators.

10 Distinguish between Douglas McGregor's Theory X and Theory Y approaches of management in organisations.

11 What traits did Rensis Likert identify in the kind of management style which he called 'supportive'?

12 How does the Management By Objectives and Results approach work?

13 How was the 'Small Is Beautiful!' concept introduced into industrial work? What did it achieve?

14 What are the major features of a systems management approach?

15 What characterises the pay-back theory of motivation?

16 How does a 'best-fit', 'pick-n-mix' (more properly called eclectic and contingent) management style work?

17 What were the most commonly selected features of a good leader identified in the leadership traits surveys?

18 What leadership approaches did Blake and Mouton draw attention to in their 'Task/People' grid?

19 What did Fiedler's contingency model of leadership propose?

20 What are the major features of effective delegation?

21 What steps can a manger take to manage his time better?

22 What guidelines are available to assist a manager in achieving targets and managing budgets?

23 List the steps which go to make up an effective decision-making process.

24 How should a manager seek to manage conflict?

25 What kinds of stress can be dangerous hazards in organisations?

26 What are the symptoms of stress? How can stress be combated?

27 List the stages of an effective negotiation process.

28 What factors should a manager take into account in managing change?

29 Explain the techniques of evaluation called work study and organisation and methods.

30 Detail the features of good office design and explain how the science of ergonomics can help.

Research and report back assignments

1 In pairs, make arrangements to interview several local managers, ideally of varying seniority. Find out how they would define the manager's role and what they see as an overall effective approach which suits the organisation they work for. Brief your group on your findings with an oral presentation.

2 Select *one* of the 'Milestones In Management' theories of management – say, Maslow's hierarchy of needs.Then, 'bounce it off' one or two practising managers to check their reactions as to its validity – in whole or part – today. Share your findings with your group and discuss whether there are, or are not, some universal management truths in the Milestone studies surveyed in this unit.

3 In pairs, carry out a local survey into worker motivation. Your aim is to discover how today's managers motivate their support staff: on a factory shop floor, in a large office-based organisation, a retail store, a professional service business like a chartered accountants or solicitors' partnership. Write a short report to summarise your findings and distribute it to your group.

4 Arrange to interview contacts – including neighbours and social acquaintances. Ask them to explain briefly and in simple terms what they see as the characteristics of a leader in a work situation. It may help for them to describe someone they respect and admire. Then cross-check your list of features with those listed in Unit 10 and see if they tally.

5 Arrange to visit a local factory. Your aim is to find out how the management conducts:

● work study and job analysis,
● job rotation/enhancement,
● quality assurance and control,
● even-flow of production.

Find out what techniques of management underpin these functions and report back to your group in an oral presentation (with AVA support).

6 Find out if any local managers consider that they are using either the management by objectives and results or systems management approaches. Check how they have been tailored to suit particular instances. If they appear obsolete, ask why they no longer suit current management approaches.

7 See what you can discover about the work of professional institutes of management such as:

The Institute of Management
The Institute Of Training And Development
The Institute Of Administrative Managers

Find out what codes or charters of management practice they espouse. Produce you findings on a factsheet for your fellow students and the group database.

8 Managing can be a lonely job. What support systems and networks are active to support managers in your locality? Brief your group on your findings.

Work simulation and experience assignments

1 Arrange to interview heads of department in your college or school. Ask them to explain what they see as the management style of the institution and seek to establish the underlying reasons for the management style that has been adopted.

2 With the help of your teacher/lecturer, draw up the following documents:

● A personnel specification for your head of department.
● A job description for your school/college principal/head teacher.

3 In your attachment organisation, arrange to interview three or four managers and/or supervisors. Then select two of the following management activities surveyed in Unit 10, and find out how the managers approach the challenges of:

● effective delegation,
● managing their own time,
● managing allocated targets and budgets,
● making effective decisions,
● managing conflict,
● managing stress in themselves and support staff,
● carrying out negotiations.

Having secured your data, compose a suitable entry on each for inclusion in the organisation's manager's training manual. Discuss your entries with your supervisor first, then copy them to your group for evaluation.

4 Find out how your organisation is managing change – in product design, marketing, office equipment technology, etc. With your findings to hand, write a suitable article of some 500 words, entitled:

'How to manage the challenge of change!'

This article is intended for the next issue of your district's Management Association's newsletter.

5 Arrange to shadow for two or three days a Work Study or O&M unit in your organisation. Keep a diary of what took place and why. With permission, relay your experiences to your group in a short talk.

6 Ask your supervisor to help you or secure the services of a manager in *one* of the following functions to give a talk about it to your group:

● Management services
● Computer services
● Personnel and training

The theme of their talk should be:

The challenges and management demands of my department

Make sure your class has prepared some good post-talk discussion questions including one about what makes a functional department different in management terms from a line department. Also, remember to nominate a speaker to propose a vote of thanks.

7 Find out who has the responsibility in your organisation for office/factory floor design and layout. Arrange an interview to find out what factors influence his or her decisions on what to install and how to lay it out. Summarise your findings in a suitable format to share with your group.

8 With permission, ask staff for their views of working in an open office with systems fixtures as against the cubicle, boxed office alternative. Summarise the pros and cons you discover and lead a group discussion on the subject in your class, suitably framing your source data for anonymity/ confidentiality, etc.

Case studies

'You're the manager – you sort it out!'

In groups of three or four in a general class discussion, consider the following brief scenarios and decide what immediate action you, as the manager, would take.

1 Jo Stacey was appointed by you as your department's Information Processing Supervisor some four weeks ago. She is responsible for coordinating all information and text processing and maintaining your communications facilities. Reporting to her are eight employees who work on desk-top terminals and operate your fax, telex, and photocopying equipment. The longest serving member of the group is Diane Jackson, who thought that getting the supervisor's job was a foregone conclusion. Since Jo Stacey's arrival, there has been a tension in the group and you are getting vibrations that they are giving Jo a hard time, although she has said nothing. You believe Diane is 'stirring it up'.

What do you do?

2 You are the Accounts Manager of Midland Counties Transport Limited. Jack Whitley is your Senior Accounts clerk, responsible for some twelve ledger clerks and clerical assistants. Jack's section looks after the company's accounts, payroll, etc.

Jack is now 58 years old and has been with Midland for the past seventeen years. His work record is good; while not a high flier, he has proved loyal, steady and reliable – if more than a little conservative and traditionalist in his outlooks. Once Jack has devised a system to his satisfaction, it takes a lot to get him to change it. His section get on well with him, because they know where they stand with him, and have become thoroughly familiar with his accounting and book-keeping routines.

However, the advent of the EC single market has caused Midland's directors to invest heavily in an expansion programme which will take their articulated lorries from the Midlands, through the Eurotunnel and across the European Community. At the same time, you and the board have decided that the firm's accounting procedures must be completely transferred from your predominantly paper-based system to a fully networked, integrated accounts software application, in order to cope with

your growing business, and to provide the sophisticated management accounting information your board now expects.

When you first briefed Jack on this, as you had anticipated, he took the news hard: 'Waste of money if you ask me. These programs you're talking about – from what I hear, they're littered with bugs or viruses or whatever and staff spend most of their time trying to sort out, what do they call 'em – crashes! My set-up hasn't crashed once in seventeen years!'

You quickly realise you have a problem on your hands. Your board has given you the clearest of instructions.The new integrated system has to be installed, up and running with staff trained to use it competently within twelve weeks, in time for it to be operational for Midland's new financial year.

How are you going to manage this situation?

3 You are the Sales Manager of West Country Ice Cream Limited, a manufacturing company which makes and distributes a range of ice-cream based products throughout the West Country. Your firm sells mainly to retail stores, sea-front kiosks, sole-trader mobile vendors, smaller hotels and guest-houses. Jim Ackroyd is one of three of your District Managers, with a territory extending over Cornwall. He has three sales personnel reporting to him. Traditionally, West Country's management style has been aggressive and rather 'macho' – bustling in with sharper discounts to win business, and so on, pushed on relentlessly by 'Big Barnie Baggott' West Country's ambitious and hard-bitten owner.

This summer sales have been disastrous. A succession of wet depressions have hit the holiday trade hard and sales of ice-cream are down some 50 per cent. Over the past two weeks you have noticed unexpected signs of stress in Jim Ackroyd. Once or twice in afternoon phone conversations he sounded as if he'd been drinking; reports have filtered back to you of confrontations with customers – unheard of before, given Jim's easy-going nature. Yesterday by chance you overheard him relating his worries over his latest sales figures. A family man with young children, Jim's financial position, as you already know, is stretched. This morning, he looks grim and pale as you see him checking orders in an adjacent office.

You decide you must talk to Jim privately. How will you handle the situation? What options are open to you?

Case Study

'More business is a problem?'

You are the Works Manager of Zenith Engineering Limited, which manufactures a range of motor-car parts – alloy wheels, steering wheels, brake drums, shock-absorbers, etc. Until now, your entire production has been sold to three UK car makers, Brook Motor Company plc, which produces mass-market saloon cars, Wayfarer plc, which makes four-wheel drive vehicles for country and off-road use, and Leopard Sports plc, a manufacturer with an international reputation for up-market sports cars and coupé limousines.

So far, they have taken all your product. No hassles. Neat. Tidy.

Yesterday your MD briefed you on two approaches that have been made to your board to buy your products. One is from the mammoth Japanese company Tobishi Motor Company (UK) Limited, makers of very competitively priced mass-market family cars, and the other from HMF Motors (UK) Limited, a wholly owned subsidiary of one of West Germany's strongest motor-car manufacturers. Naturally enough, your MD is excited – more business, more profit, more jobs, better dividends for shareholders in the offing – no problem!

But your feet are nearer to the ground. At the moment your factory is working to 95 per cent full capacity for most of the year – although the current high interest rates are dampening demand for cars in the UK. Zenith's personnel manager is not finding it easy to recruit factory workers who will do shift work, and has to bus them to and fro within a radius of 25 miles. Producing your types of product for new models would mean expensive re-tooling and R&D work. In any case, where is your plant capacity to be found?

How are Brook, Wayfarer and Leopard going to react? Might not they take their business elsewhere if the service they have grown used to is diluted? On the other hand, what about the old saying, 'No business remains static – it grows or shrinks!' How often do these sorts of business opportunities come along? But what if you over-extend yourselves?

Your mind became 'fazed' with all these contradictory thoughts spilling over as your MD briefed you. His final words were: 'Well, it's still early days, but I have to give a presentation to the Board a week today on our essential response to the two proposals under negotiation – either one could virtually double our production over the next five years! Of course, I'd like your own suggestions before the end of this week, as to how we should proceed. Something setting out the main pros and cons as you see them would do fine to start with. Oh, and by the way, both Tobishi and HMF would want to start taking up product within six months!'

You soon realise the MD has given you the toughest decision-making process you've ever had to face! You immediately make it your first priority and set to work . . .

Assignments

In groups of three or four, carry out the following assignments:

1 Re-read the case study and then set out a clear schedule of the factors involved in reaching what you consider to be the best decison. Study the section in Unit 10 on decision-making (page 229) before your start.

2 Compose a two A4-page preliminary report for the MD on what you see as the opportunities and the problems. Identify what additional information you will need in order to present a detailed response to the two proposals on the table.

3 Take a copy of the case study to a local works manager and ask him or her to go through the kinds of issue the case study presents and what factors he or she would consider as central to effective decision making in the given scenario.

4 Lastly, make a summarising checklist of the factors and features you discovered from working on the case study which had a bearing on the decison-making process. Compare yours with those produced by other class syndicate groups.

11

Information technology 2: software and applications

Overview

Unit 11 provides you with information and guidelines on:

- The various ways in which documents may be processed: batch, real-time, on-line, and stand-alone methods.
- The major applications for which software programs are employed in business departments.
- An overview of the main types of software used in large-scale operations: project planning, modelling, database and spreadsheet systems, graphics and image processing, etc.
- The impact of applications software on manual paper-based document cycles, including fully integrated accounts packages.
- How the following software applications work: desk-top integrated information management packages including electronic diary and notebook, spreadsheets, databases, word processing packages, computerised graphics applications.

In Unit 5, we examined the systems and hardware currently used in organisations to process information. Unit 11 surveys the software packages which complement the computing hardware and office equipment machines; the various ways – applications – in which the software is used by different parts of the organisation are also explained.

Unit 11 is divided into three main sections.The first part details the ways in which data is processed and the spread of applications in various user departments and contexts. The second part explores in more detail how the most widely used software

applications packages work and what features are important for you to know about. Finally, Unit 11 provides an overiew of computerised graphics applications.

An applications overview

The current 'state of the art' of computer applications may be summarised as a 'rich picture'. On the one hand, large organisations enjoy long-established centralised provisions run by able computer services personnel. Such departments employ data processing techniques such as batch, real-time and on-line processing (see below), and may maintain vast storehouses of data in a single database. On the other hand there are many users who rely mainly on stand-alone, desk-top PCs to run shops, partnerships and small businesses. In between are units and departments within large organisations – and medium-sized firms – that employ small to medium-sized LAN/WAN networks and which download software from file servers or super-mini computers.

Applications software use varies considerably in such contrasting organisations. While the sole trader is happy with a rudimentary spreadsheet and database, multinational directors will not be content with less than the most sophisticated CMIS system in place.

In order to gain an appreciation of software applications, it is helpful to start with an examination of five different ways of processing data.

Documents and data processing

Batch processing

Information recorded on paper originals has been transferred on to computerised files ever since the early 1960s, when punched tape coded data was converted into binary digit sequences and then into computer print-outs. Since then, information needed on a regular cyclical basis – payroll data, monthly accounts statements, rate demands, electricity or gas bills, etc, has been produced and printed out in what are called batch printing runs. This system enables, say, the A-H, I-N and O-Z account customers' statements to be run off on separate days by large firms. Batch processing is used very extensively today by banks, public utilities, large distributors and retailers. A distinct advantage is that batch processing may also be undertaken at low-traffic, low-cost times, say at week-ends or overnight.

Real-time data processing

By contrast, real-time data processing relies upon a database which is being constantly updated. For example, each year in the UK millions of people book foreign holidays with package tour operators. In order to ensure a trouble-free holiday, such operators need to ensure – *at the time the booking is made* – that:

- seats on the plane are available at the requested time and date,
- the hotel still has the type of accommodation requested,
- special needs – dietary, disabled facilities, etc – can be provided.

Real-time data processing provides the solution, by maintaining databases which, at any time of enquiry, display on the travel agent's monitor the actual state of the bookings in 'real time', eg at 11.46 a.m. on Saturday 15 January 199-!

On-line data processing

Today, many multinational organisations employ on-line data processing techniques with their single, unified information database which all employees can access, subject to the level of their clearance. Such databases are usually held in a central location and employ extremely powerful mainframe computers. For example, the clearing banks in the UK make extensive use of such mainframes to obtain current details of a customer's account, credit status, standing order/direct debit instructions and so on.

By the same token, credit card companies and credit status organisations can confirm directly to retailers whether a requested credit purchase may go ahead because the customer, in the shop, is creditworthy at that moment.

Time shared data processing

Small companies may decide to lease access to a computer bureau's large computer facilities as a means of processing data. The development of long-distance package switching of digitised data and general telecommunictions support has made this option very attractive. Large companies also rent private lines to exchange computerised data across countries and continents.

Stand-alone data processing

Maybe the humblest, but undoubtedly still the most widely used form of processing information, is through the direct interaction between computer user, computer system, and applications software.

What characterises this kind of data processing is the freedom and flexibility of the process, in which creativity and output are limited only by the user's imagination, the computer's power and the software's design features. Naturally such a mix is widely adopted by authors, small business users, and hobbyists.

Nevertheless, it is interesting that even in large organisations management teams still like to interact independently with their own personal terminal.

The processing mix

A major advantage of the development of open systems integration (OSI), by which computers of different manufacture may be interconnected and networked, is that the individual employee and home-based user can use their terminals at times independently, yet, linked through modems and ISDN, access central databanks instantaneously.

Major software applications in user departments

The following section identifies some of the most widely used applications of computer software programs. Nevertheless, it is important that you keep in mind the ability of larger organisations to commission and instal purpose-designed software – indeed many employ skilled systems analysts and programmers just for this purpose:

Sales Department

Handling sales enquiries.

Production of annual sales forecasts broken down into regions, districts and branches.

Sales analysis on a weekly/monthly basis identifying product breakdown, profit leaders, slow-moving items, etc.

Results of sales promotions and special offers.

Monitoring of sales representatives' calls, new business, expenses, etc.

Monitoring of general sales performance daily, weekly, monthly and comparing actual performance to forecast performance – 'sales to budget'.

Accounts Department

Maintenance of an integrated accounts system: sales ledger, purchase ledger, nominal ledger, payroll, etc.

Maintenance of credit control system and recovery of bad debts.

Supply to senior managment of one-off or regular status reports on, for example, cash-flow, profits, expenses, days of credit of account customers, etc.

Supply to company's chartered accountants of details of the company's books to facilitate the annual presentation and auditing of the accounts.

Production Department

Maintenance of purchasing records and status of stocks.

Quality control systems for minimising defective production.

Production planning – matching output capacity to forecast and actual demand.

Calculating operatives' hours of work, bonuses, etc – see links with Accounts Department and payroll.

Monitoring the manufacturing process to control machining, drilling, assembly, paint-spraying, etc.

Control of goods moving out of the factory – see also links with Despatch Department.

Research and Development

Producing designs, computer models and three-dimensional projections of potential products.

Storing informational databases and approved designs for future reference.

Facilitating access to the databases (at a fee) of other research establishments – for example foreign universitites and research institutes.

Testing product performance via computer simulation to check design and performance features.

Analysing and evaluating product tests.

Providing production specialists with programs which control the machines to manufacture the product or to reprogram existing robotic (CAM) plant.

Personnel Department

Maintaining personnel records on computer.

Establishing databases of personnel data from which to design staff development programmes, retirement preparation courses, manpower needs, etc.

Producing and storing job specification and job description records for review and redevelopment.

Maintaining job appraisal and salary review records.

Office Administration Department

Maintaining records on company equipment and servicing dates.

Ordering office stationery and general supplies.

Monitoring administative costs, human resources, materials.

Marketing Department

Analysis of market research surveys and questionnaires, etc.

Simulation of markets and of product design, performance and packaging.

Maintenance of advertising campaign schedules, space orders with newspapers and magazines, etc.

Maintenance of database on market statistics by segment, by product, etc.

Though this list is by no means exhaustive, it does emphasise the all-embracing nature of software applications which are employed in the various departments of a large national company. Correspondingly, it is not difficult to imagine the amount of staff training and development which companies have had to undertake during recent years in order to ensure that competitors did not overtake them by becoming more adept at using IT systems and software profitably, whether in the making, selling or distribution of products.

Types of applications software for large-scale use

The following types of applications software tend to be commonly employed in large-scale operations:

Project Planning For many years organisations have used a system called PERT (Programme Evaluation & Review Technique) to coordinate complex projects. PERT systems are now supported by versatile project planners, well able to allow for many variables and 'what-ifs'.

Modelling & Forecasting Computer models are nowadays used a great deal in: R&D, scientific programmes, marketing and advertising to mimic different sets of conditions, trends, markets or patterns. Central government also uses them extensively to interpret and predict economic trends.

Relational Databases Powerful software now exists in database form which can embrace many thousands of records and millions of fields. Such databases are used to store data in national databanks like DSS, Health, Inland Revenue,

The information flow handled by software applications

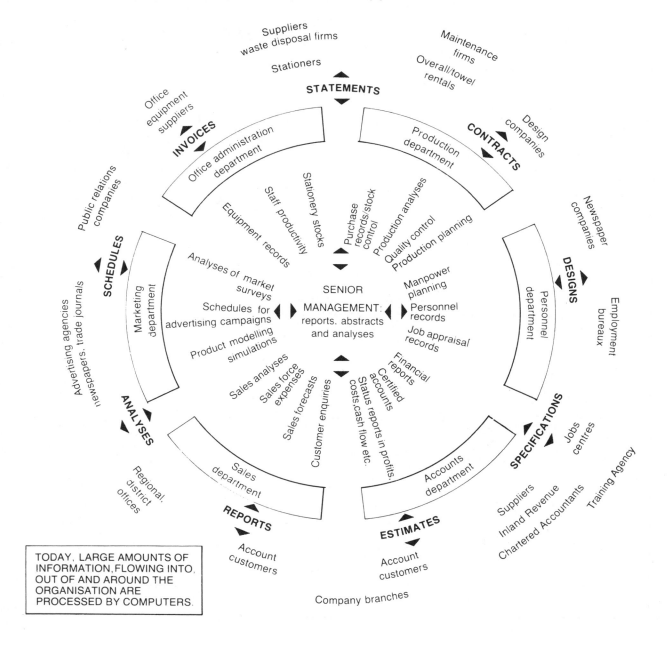

TODAY, LARGE AMOUNTS OF INFORMATION, FLOWING INTO, OUT OF AND AROUND THE ORGANISATION ARE PROCESSED BY COMPUTERS.

motor-vehicle or criminal records. Large companies also use them to store information like design data, product specifications, personnel records or customer data.

Powerful spreadsheets Technical and accounts departments can now install powerful spreadsheets which combine a three-dimensional 'number-crunching' effect – by cross-referencing and accessing data from hundreds of poster-sized electronic sheets – with the facility to import or export data from other centrally stored software files and pro-grams, so as to compile integrated reports and so on.

Graphics & Image Processing Marketing, repro-graphics and training departments can now produce highly appealing and sophisticated charts, slides, OHP foils and allied presentation material from software which processes data first produced on computer and then enhanced through the overlaying of visual and graphics effects. Such software is a boon to managers and trainers needing to present information effectively.

Sales documentation: manual system – monthly cycle

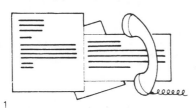

1
SALES ORDER RECEIVED
by letter, telex, telephone sales rep's order book etc.

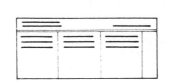

2
REQUISITION NOTE RAISED IN STORES
to authorise the movement of the goods to the Despatch Dept.

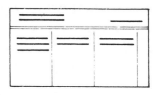

3
STOCK CARD AMENDED
the card relating to the bin or shelves where the goods are kept is amended and a reduce balance shown.

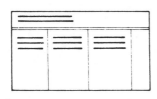

6
TRANSACTION ENTERED ON CUSTOMER'S SALES LEDGER CARD

the total of the invoice will be added to the current month's sales to the customer's account and a cumulative total brought forward.

6A
CREDIT NOTE RAISED
if the goods prove faulty or damaged on arrival, then a Credit Note may be raised to refund the amount charged.

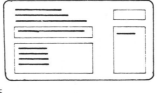

5
DELIVERY/ADVICE NOTE
this note (often an unpriced NCR copy of the invoice) is taken by the goods deliveryman to the purchaser as proof of delivery and a signature obtained.

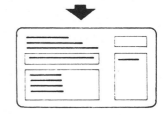

4
SALES INVOICE IS RAISED
this will include quantity, description, price and customer's account number and VAT due on the sale.

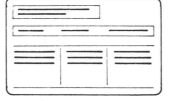

7
STATEMENT OF ACCOUNT DESPATCHED AT END OF TRADING PERIOD (e.g. MONTHLY)

this will itemise the invoices raised during the month and present a total amount due, together with any settlement discount terms which may' apply. VAT will also be included with the listed invoice transactions.

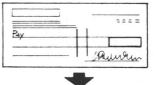

8
THE CUSTOMER WILL DESPATCH A CHEQUE IN PAYMENT WITH A REMITTANCE ADVICE NOTE

this payment is recorded within the sales ledger and the amount taken from customer's account ledger card, thus reducing the balance owing — remember that subsequent invoices will have been raised before the statement in 7 is due for payment.

PROCESS STARTS AGAIN

Computerising manual paper systems

Almost certainly the most radical information processing change in organisations over the past ten or so years has been the computerising of manual, paper-based information processing and storage systems. Where previously purchase and sales sequences were structured in carbon-coated or chemically treated copy sets – three advice note copies, three invoice copies, etc – the introduction of computerised accounts and sales administration software has enabled businesses to keep paper to a minimum and to retain in-house records electronically. This change has done away with countless filing cabinets and racks as data on disk is infinitely more space-saving. Moreover, accessing such data is far quicker and simpler (and less hazardous) than straining for top-shelf files!

The chart on page 254 illustrates a conventional paper-based sales documentation cycle and how computer software has improved it:

Computerised improvements of the paper-based sales documentation monthly cycle

1   Increasingly, large purchasers – motor-car makers, electrical white goods manufacturers – are ordering their requirements on direct 'hot-line' private computer lease-lines. Many firms leave purchase order forms with customers which are designed as data entry forms for faxing direct to the order section's data entry clerk, who then starts off the computer-based sales order sequence, which is linked into the company's integrated accounts software (see pages 256 and 257 Fretwell Downing diagram).

2 and 3   The seller's warehouse or stores holding stocks for release against purchase order will electronically adjust its stock holding database and print out collection and delivery advice notes for delivery personnel.

4 and 6   The accounts department will enter the sales transaction on the account customer's computerised file, make the necessary adjustment to its in-house sales ledger, print out an invoice for posting and add the purchase to the customer's computerised monthly statement for later batch printing and despatch.

5   Note that companies still require a customer's signature on a piece of paper – the retained delivery or advice note.

6A   Credits raised because of accounting errors or goods returned, etc. will be despatched in paper form, but electronic adjustments will be made to the customer's statement file and the firm's sales ledger.

7   The customer's monthly statement of account is produced from existing computer records and batch-printed for posting.

8   Payment may be made by cheque or bank giro credit transfer – again by computer!

Talking point

To what extent do you think the widespread use of applications software in both private and public sectors should be reflected in 11-18 plus education?

Fully integrated accounts packages

One of the far-reaching results in the design and development of computer software has been the introduction of 'turnkey' computer programs which are capable of masterminding virtually the entire accounting function within a company.

Not only will such programs process the data relating to the various accounts ledgers – sales, purchase, nominal etc, and produce trial balances and profit and loss accounts, they will also make available various financial reports to meet management accounting demands such as: what is the current average credit period in days, or what is the current cash flow situation?

The diagram of Fretwell-Downing Data Systems Limited's integrated Business Management System on pages 256–7 illustrates in helpful detail how a software program can be designed to integrate certain finanical operations – here the maintenance of a sales order processing, stock control and accounts system.

Notice that the program is able to provide a number of different ways of accessing the stored information:

1   via on-line review
2   via printed report
3   via outputs specifically stipulated by the user

In order to satisfy chartered accountants and the Inland Revenue, such sophisticated electronic accounting systems need to be able to demonstrate what is termed an audit trail. This is a system which can prove the integrity of the accounting effected electronically by tracing a process step-by-step from the original document (say a customer's printed order), to the payment of the arising invoice forming part of a given printed statement.

Other checking processes are maintained by the users of such programs including a system called 'check digit' verification, which is the addition of a specially calculated number on the end of, say,

Fretwell-Downing Data Systems Ltd

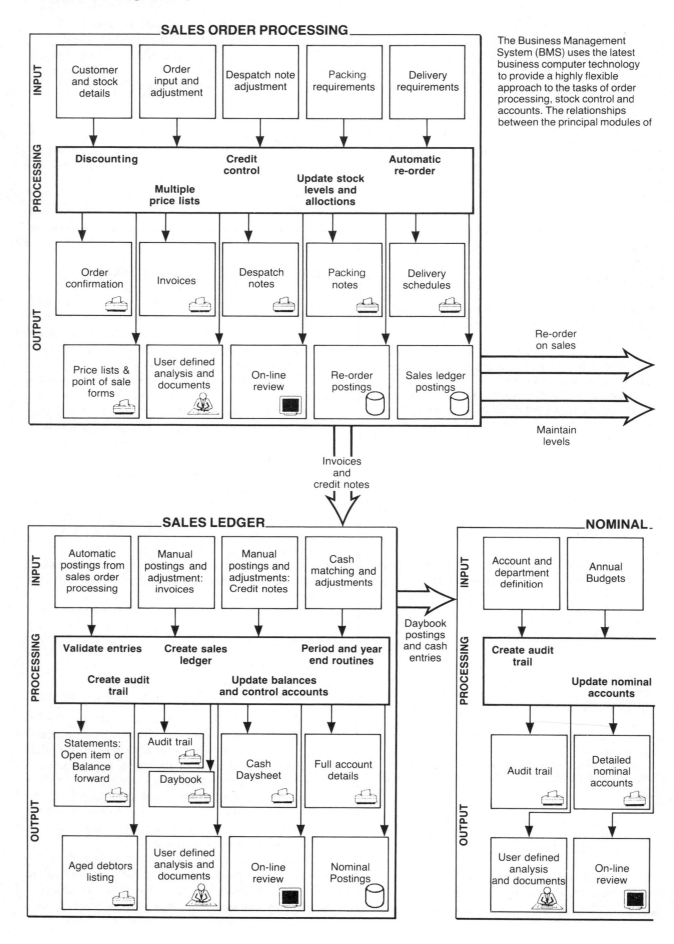

The Business Management System (BMS) uses the latest business computer technology to provide a highly flexible approach to the tasks of order processing, stock control and accounts. The relationships between the principal modules of

Sales Order Processing with Invoicing, Purchase Order Processing, Stock Control, Sales Ledger, Purchase Ledger and Nominal Ledger are illustrated here. The choice of modules and their specific components within the BMS framework can be geared to precise user requirements.

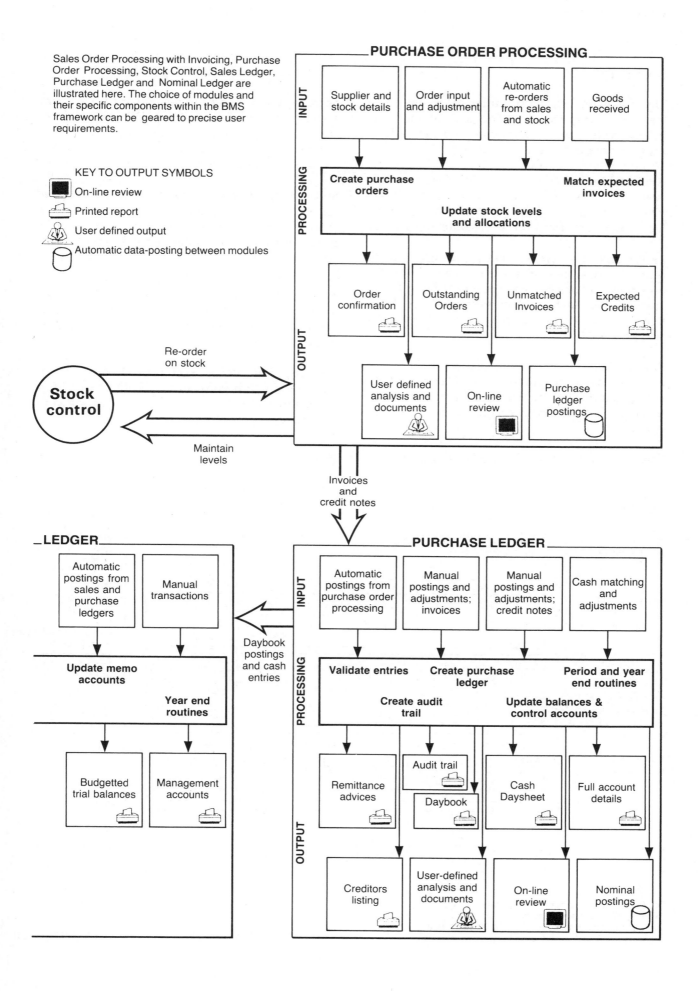

KEY TO OUTPUT SYMBOLS

On-line review

Printed report

User defined output

Automatic data-posting between modules

PURCHASE ORDER PROCESSING

INPUT

| Supplier and stock details | Order input and adjustment | Automatic re-orders from sales and stock | Goods received |

PROCESSING

Create purchase orders   **Match expected invoices**

Update stock levels and allocations

OUTPUT

| Order confirmation | Outstanding Orders | Unmatched Invoices | Expected Credits |

| User defined analysis and documents | On-line review | Purchase ledger postings |

Stock control

Re-order on stock

Maintain levels

Invoices and credit notes

LEDGER

| Automatic postings from sales and purchase ledgers | Manual transactions |

Update memo accounts

Year end routines

| Budgetted trial balances | Management accounts |

Daybook postings and cash entries

PURCHASE LEDGER

INPUT

| Automatic postings from purchase order processing | Manual postings and adjustments; invoices | Manual postings and adjustments; credit notes | Cash matching and adjustments |

PROCESSING

Validate entries   Create purchase ledger   Period and year end routines

Create audit trail   Update balances & control accounts

OUTPUT

| Remittance advices | Audit trail / Daybook | Cash Daysheet | Full account details |

| Creditors listing | User-defined analysis and documents | On-line review | Nominal postings |

an account number or payroll number as a means of ensuring regularly that the system is functioning correctly.

Summary

The following checklist summarises the main features of large-scale software applications which interact with systems hardware and networks to provide organisation-wide support:

Availability: systems running 24 hours a day, all year long, provide round-the-clock access to key files and programs, whether accessed from the office after hours, from home or commercial hotel.

Power and capacity: resident in mammoth mainframe CPUs, large-scale software is, by virtue of its own powerful design, extremely fast, sophisticated and versatile; the files it creates may likewise be extensive; they can also be accessed and interrogated at high speed.

Shareability: centrally located files and software can easily be shared by multi-users and teams and files exchanged through networks at the press of a key; inter-group communications are therefore enhanced.

Single, unified database: the maintenance of a single, real-time updated database helps to prevent the use of outmoded or corrupt data and ensures that all personnel are making decisions based on the same shared information.

Security: the creation and maintenance of a central system, supported by dedicated DP personnel aids security; key files and data are copied hourly/daily to remote locations to avoid accidental loss of part or all of the database.

Software/application upgrades: in-house designed software may be upgraded at will, in the light of changing circumstances; large users of commercial packages get 'first bite of the cherry' when upgrades are announced.

Innovation: when unified software systems are in place, managment can ensure that all selected personnel are given access to the same changes and introductions simultaneously, thus securing a cost-efficient process.

Training and staff development: the use of organisation-wide software applications simplifies and standardises the training of staff in software operations.

Specimen computer-produced sales invoice

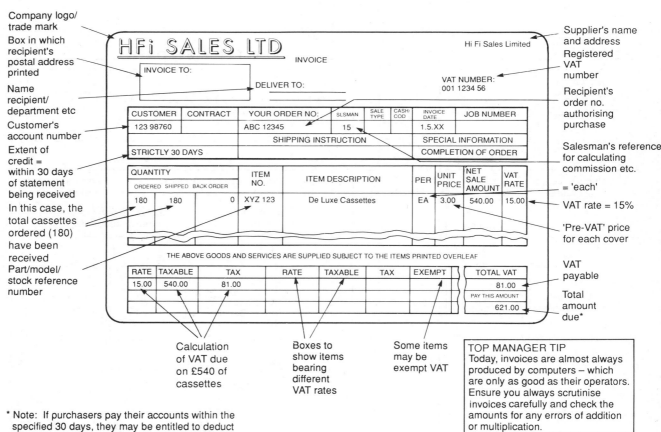

*Note: If purchasers pay their accounts within the specified 30 days, they may be entitled to deduct a 'settlement discount' (say 3.75%) off the total due.

Based upon the invoice of MAR-COM SYSTEMS LTD

Talking point

Given the need of virtually all office workers from now on to be proficient in spreadsheeet, WP and database operations, how would you modify (if at all!) your current course of study, so as to ensure their mastery before its completion?

Software applications and the individual user

This section examines the current range of software applications which are in general administrative use. Wherever your future career leads, it is virtually certain that you will need to be not only familiar with, but proficient in the use of the applications software outlined below.

Desk-top information management: LAN-based or stand-alone.

Currently there are two extremely useful software applications systems or packages available to the busy office worker. They share many similarities but are intended for different kinds of user. Firstly, there is the range of applications which come with the installation of a LAN network, and secondly there is the 'integrated desk-top information managment package' which usually arrives as a set of floppies for installing into a stand-alone PC. (Note: such packages may also be installed in LAN systems).

(1) LAN-based desk-top information management

The following section details the major features of most LAN software applications.

LAN software application packages

The following software applications are frequently offered by data processing management to LAN users:

- **Electronic mail** with in-tray and out-tray features for holding messages, a means of attracting users' attention to the arrival of important messages, and a system for sending a message to designated groups – say an office team or a group of sales representatives.

- **Word processing packages** In addition to a simple WP facility built into the LAN system, users can be given access to any one of the major word processing packages – provided it is installed into the LAN.

- **Database package** The same goes for major database packages; the LAN offers its own means of storing data in shared or personal

'cabinets', but equally, the user can readily access any highly sophisticated database on to which to insert records of information.

- **Spreadsheet** Again, the DP Department will almost certainly offer a major spreadsheet facility for accounts, marketing and production users.

- **Integrated management information package** This particular application software is likely to be frequently used by all office administrators, since it joins together electronic diary appointments scheduling, notepad, meetings scheduling, etc – with straightforward, easy to use WP, spreadsheet, database, graphics and communications components and allows the user to transfer data from one package feature to another quickly and easily: calculations made on the spreadsheet can be swiftly incorporated into a word processed report.

- **Graphics package** Many managers are frequently required to communicate statistics and data in chart, graph or other visual form. Thus most LANs will include a package capable of converting data from one format to another – for example, a manager is able to see whether his information communicates more readily and effectively as a pie-chart, bar-chart, histogram or line-graph, etc. Similarly he can select those colour combinations which give his graphic data eye-catching appeal or increased ease of understanding.

- **A.N. Other package** The LAN can deliver whatever application package has been designed for networked use and so this checklist could carry on indefinitely!

LAN communications and services

In addition to the above application software features, LANs offer through modems and gateways a means of accessing these communications facilities:

- **Telephone-call making** Quick access to personal telephone directory with display of associated notes.

- **Automatic call dialling** This facility built into the LAN enables workstation users to dial calls automatically by providing, through a communications facility, direct access to the telephone network.

- **External communications services** By means of electronic routing and interconnection systems, LAN users can access:

National/international BT telephone services,

International fax, telex, and teletex systems via British Telecom services,

LAN Email 'Tapestry'

'Send mail' ikon menu and sample message

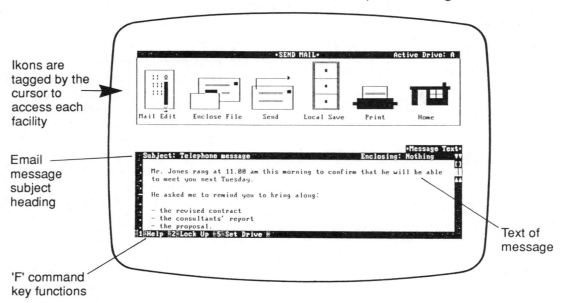

Ikons are tagged by the cursor to access each facility

Email message subject heading

'F' command key functions

Text of message

Prestel viewdata system and other European counterparts,

Other organisations' computer databanks and databases of information via Prestel gateways services.

National/international electronic mail services like BT Gold, Datacom, and Prestel Mailbox.

● **Internal Communications Services** Email: electronic mail systems commonly include these features:

In-coming Email
Flagging up the arrival of an incoming message, construction of a directory of incoming mail by date/time of arrival.

Indication of what mail has/has not been read by user,

Facility to store or discard incoming mail,

Facility for reading mail on a monitor and sending it on to any additional LAN user, making a hard copy of message for reference outside LAN, displaying on a monitor screen a 'flag' to indicate that an urgent Email message has arrived, while user is operating, say, spreadsheet package.

Outgoing Email
Ability to set up predetermined groups of message recipients and to send the same Email messages simultaneously to all − say, an Accounts Department Credit Control group of five staff, or all Heads of Department, or all staff working in Personnel.

Facility to check whether the recipents of despatched mail have/have not yet read it.

Ability to set up a 'bring forward' system for Emailed messages with action requests

All outgoing mail is electronically filed for user reference

Facility to send a created file with an Email message to another LAN user.

Ability to put a 'destroy' message deadline into outgoing mail; this is a valuable feature which erases messages directly their relevance has expired (eg information about new product launch) and prevents LAN memory being wasted.

(2) Stand-alone integrated desk-top information managers

While the above range of software applications are available to LAN/WAN network users who benefit from the extra power/capacity of their mini/mainframe CPU's, ingenious software designers have managed to cram a wide range of features and facilities into floppy disk packs for more modest single PC user work. These packages are called 'integrated', since they allow the various programs they embody to intercommunicate. For instance, text, numerical tables, charts and specifications can all be produced independently on internal 'stand-alone' components − WP, spreadsheet, graphics and database programs and then edited together into a single report document.

A typical integrated information management package will include these features:

LAN network 'Tapestry' – sample ikon menu

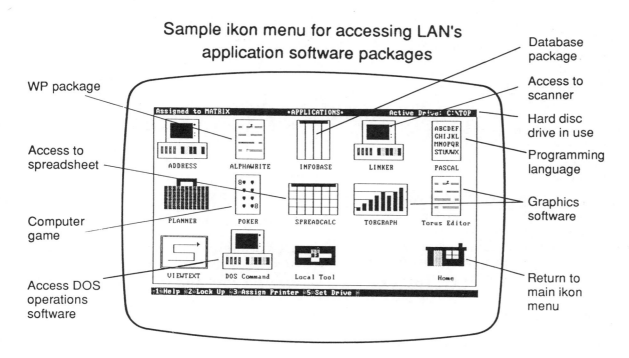

The application menu acts like the index of a software library, providing access by means of cursor tagging to any package installed in the network.

Email in-tray list of arrived messages

```
┌─IN TRAY──────────────────────────────────────────────────────────────┐
│ Mary King                    Number of messages =      9              │
├──────────────────────────────────────────────────────────────────────┤
│ Please could you.....         *24Aug88 10:55        P.Piper           │
│ Please can you make.....      *19Aug88 15:30        P.Piper           │
│ Do not forget...               19Aug88 15:28        B.Whiffin         │
│ Marketing Meeting             *19Aug88 15:26 .DOC   J.Campbell        │
│ Sales Review Meeting          *19Aug88 15:25        J.Campbell        │
│ Please send ..                 21Jan88 10:20        N.Hooper          │
│ 1988 Plan Review              *08Jan88 17:26        C.Allen           │
│ Holidays                      *08Jan88 17:13        C.Allen           │
│ PC User Group Seminar         *08Jan88 17:10        C.Allen           │
├──────────────────────────────────────────────────────────────────────┤
│ View Msg.   Distrbn.   Get file   Forward    Tag Delete  Archive      │
└──────────────────────────────────────────────────────────────────────┘

 * indicates unread mail
 .DOC indicates that a file is attached to the message
```

(Reproduced by kind permission of IBM (UK) Ltd)

- Spreadsheet
- Business Graphics
- Database Manager
- Word Processor
- Calculator
- Communications
- Business Functions
- Five-Year Calendar
- Diary
- Appointments/Meetings Scheduler
- Notebook/Jotter
- Task Prioritiser
- Report Planner

Naturally enough, such facilities tend not to have the sophistication or power of much larger applications programs, but they do provide a very flexible and often user-friendly 'electronic office' which the small-scale user can very quickly install at his workplace, or carry with him in a lap-top computer kit.

Specimen electronic diary – a week on display

The electronic diary

A great boon to both manager and secretary, the electronic diary can be scrolled forwards or backwards in daily, weekly, monthly or annual modes for up to five years; it can accept appointments both provisional and confirmed, block out private work periods, flag up reminders for days/weeks/months ahead, supply room for out of office hours appointments and cross-reference appointments or tasks to more detailed notes and reminders entered into the resident electronic notepad.

The meetings scheduler

Note: LAN diaries can be interconnected with other network users' diaries and thus team meetings can be readily scheduled at 'next earliest all-team

```
                    Appointment Schedule
                         A. George
                     04/04/   - 08/04/

           March              April              May
        S  M  T  W  T  F  S   S  M  T  W  T  F  S   S  M  T  W  T  F  S     Weeks and
              1  2  3  4  5               1  2   1  2  3  4  5  6  7        months
        6  7  8  9 10 11 12   3  4  5  6  7  8  9   8  9 10 11 12 13 14     may be
       13 14 15 16 17 18 19  10 11 12 13 14 15 16  15 16 17 18 19 20 21    scanned
       20 21 22 23 24 25 26  17 18 19 20 21 22 23  22 23 24 25 26 27 28    at will
       27 28 29 30 31        24 25 26 27 28 29 30  29 30 31


  Monday        04/04/
    08:00    18:30     V ALISON - 1 DAY VACATION
    NOTES:             V JAN JONES - VACATION 4TH - 8TH INCL.

  Tuesday       05/04/
    00:00    00:01     i NEW STUDENT STARTS TODAY
    09:00    10:30     m MONDAY REVIEW - PQ AG
    14:00    16:00     m MANAGEMENT SUPPORT MEETING - CONF ROOM 2
    NOTES:             V JAN JONES - VACATION 4TH - 8TH INCL.

  Wednesday     06/04/
    10:00    11:00     M NEW STUDENT- EMMA JONES - INDUCTION
    11:00    12:00     M DEPARTMENT REVIEW - CONF ROOM 4
    I4:00    16:00     I MEETING PREPARATION TIME
    16:00    17:30     M COMMUNICATIONS STATUS - AG OFFICE
    NOTES:             V JAN JONES - VACATION 4TH - 8TH INCL.

  Thursday      07/04/
    09:00    09:05     i REMINDER - AG TO TELEPHONE BOROUGH COUNCIL
    10:00    12:30     i PRESENTATION PREPARATION FOR 16TH
    14:00    14:30     M ARTICLE REVIEW - D EVANS CHICHESTER COLLEGE / AG
    NOTES:             V JAN JONES - VACATION 4TH - 8TH INCL.

  Friday        08/04/
    08:00    17:00     i KEEP FREE - POSSIBLE VISIT- time to be confirmed
    NOTES:             V JAN JONES - VACATION 4TH - 8TH INCL.
```

Key:
I = information
M = meeting
V = vacation

Notes may
be keyed
in as
required

*Professional Office System: IBM's Information Management System

(Reproduced by kind permission of IBM (UK) Ltd)

availability'; some LAN software also enables rooms and AVA equipment to be booked at the same time!

The electronic notepad

An invaluable tool, the electronic notepad enables the busy office worker to jot down immediately – reminders, follow-up tasks, details or particulars, etc – in either a rapid note or structured way. Moreover, such notes can be cross-filed to the diary or database to ensure they are signalled up at the right moment!

The indispensable trio: spreadsheet, database and word processing packages

The Spreadsheet

Originally used for scientific and accounts applications, the spreadsheet also now supports a multitude of calculation-based activities in production, marketing, sales, R&D and public administration. The following section outlines how 'Multiplan', a popular spreadsheet works. A spreadsheet's major attractions lie in its ability to:

- use pre-installed formulae to effect the same calculation on data entered periodically into columns, say, the reducing balance resulting from purchases charged to a budget allocation,
- make the same amendment, say, a change in buying terms or discounts to be awarded, throughout a series of existing entries, without having to change each one individually,
- interconnect and import/export calculations from one display sheet to any other one of 50-100 others,
- (in networked facilities or integrated packages) import data from files created by other software applications or likewise export for synthesis into reports, etc.

How a spreadsheet works

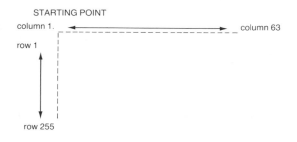

Imagine a rectangle of space which is some 63 columns wide and 255 rows deep as a large sheet of paper, which is made up of a grid of smaller rec-

tangles, each one consisting of a single column width and row depth, as follows.

Thus a 'window' of the spreadsheet which can be displayed on a VDU screen would look as follows:

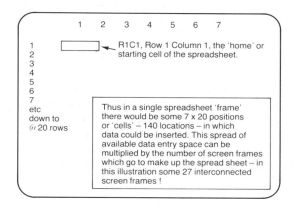

As well as the spaces in which to enter data or text, the screen frame of the spreadsheet – the normal 'screen of information which is displayed' at any given time – will show additional information to assist the user in operating it. The diagram on page 264 illustrates a typical spreadsheet window layout.

Screen layout display of the 'Multiplan' spreadsheet software package

As the diagram below indicates, in addition to the set of grids or cells for holding data, the monitor will display the following information customarily to assist the spread-sheet user.

1 Numbers or letters to indicate each column, for example, 1, 2, 3 or A, B, C as far as 63 numerically or as AB, BB, CB etc, to signify columns beyond 26 (A-Z) etc.

2 Numbers to indicate rows going down the grid vertically indicating the location of each row of cells (say, 1-255).

3 An illuminated box or pointer to show which particular cell or grid is in use – that is, where any data will be positioned within the displayed frame.

4 A selection of commands set out as a 'menu' which the user can activate and employ upon demand, for example, to edit or amend a screenful of data, to delete an entry, to move instantly to another screen frame of data altogether – say columns 36 to 42 and rows 24 to 44, to change a formula, to print a screen and so on. Such a set of commands would

be referred to as a menu selection or command line. When a particular command is activated – say to edit a piece of text on screen, then a space or additional command line may be used to show the line of text or data being edited before it is transferred into the displayed screen frame.

5   Additionally the spreadsheet – usually at its foot – will display information on a message line. This line will remind the user of what he or she can do as a next step – it will act as a reminder or 'prompt' line, or may advise the user of an error in the operation of the spreadsheet.

6   A further line at the bottom of the screen frame is the 'status line'. This line is used to show the user where he or she is in terms of the spreadsheet – that is, in which row/cell the pointer or illuminated cursor is located; what information the pointer is highlighting, and sometimes further helpful information such as the amount of available unused space on the spreadsheet; the title of the file being created or edited; or what formula is being constructed to manipulate rows of figures.

7   In addition, the screen can, in a sense, be 'overprinted' at any time to introduce a detailed page of HELP prompts or to subdivide the screen frame into a series of 'windows' which display on screen data temporarily borrowed from other screen frames some distance from the one in use. While the 'overprinting' window command is in use, the original screen frame remains on screen partially visible. Some spreadsheets provide a number of windows of information taken from different parts of the package to be displayed simultaneously – either to act as a visible reminder of stored data for cross-reference, or to indicate how certain spreadsheet commands could assist the user.

Spreadsheets now play a central role in the financial, statistical, buying, selling, designing and marketing functions of business; in the public sector, they are also extensively used in treasury, planning, surveying and management services functions. It is therefore important that you learn how to drive one well!

Example of the screen layout of a spreadsheet

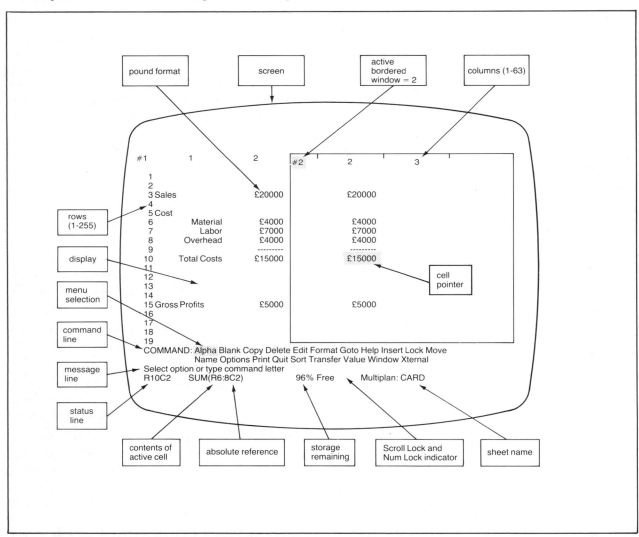

Reproduced by permission of IBM (UK) Ltd and Microsoft Corporation USA

The Database

The term database simply stands for an assembled collection of information or data, parts of which may be sorted or classified into desired lists and sequences. For example, an employment agency may have at any one time 200-300 temps on its books available for either top-flight PA, junior secretarial, WP operations or clerical assistant work. By entering key particulars about each one – name, address, phone number, skills, qualifications, foreign language proficiency, competence in which WP software package, etc, the agency manager can – extremely quickly – interrogate the company's database of registered personnel so as to extract and match a short-list to an employer's requested job needs or particular specification.

How a database works

A database package contains a program which enables its user to design a kind of electronic card-index system which may be illustrated as follows:

A database consists of three major components:

The file: which represents the collection of records (like the set of cards in the boxed card index). To be of any use in the orderly world of the database, a file must comprise records of the same design and type, say, all head office personnel, all items in the export product range, all examination records of the 1990-1991 full-time enrolled students.

The record: which sets out the recorded data about one of the persons or items which go to make up the file. In the case of the above employment agency's temps, the record may contain all the recorded information on Angela Gibbons, bilingual secretary.

The field: at the heart of the way a database works are its fields. Each file is the sum of a number of records where each and every one has been designed upon an identical template. This electronic master form is itself made up of a series of fields. Again, using the temps file example, Angela Gibbon's record – and everyone else's – will have been compiled by filling in preconstructed blank boxes which are the record's fields. For instance, Angela's record will comprise in part her full name, correct postal address, telephone number, nationality, date of birth and sex. In addition, it will include field boxes to list skills, equipment experience and so on.

The great value of the database lies in its ability to locate, in a twinkling, information which lies waiting in each record's filled-out fields. Thus the employment agency is able to scan its temps file and extract from its 346 records the particulars, say, of

Components of a database

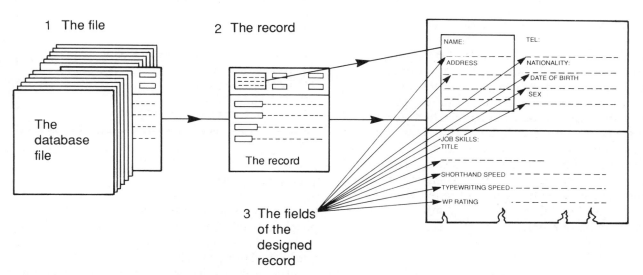

A database comprises: a file of records of a standardised design divided into fields for specified searches

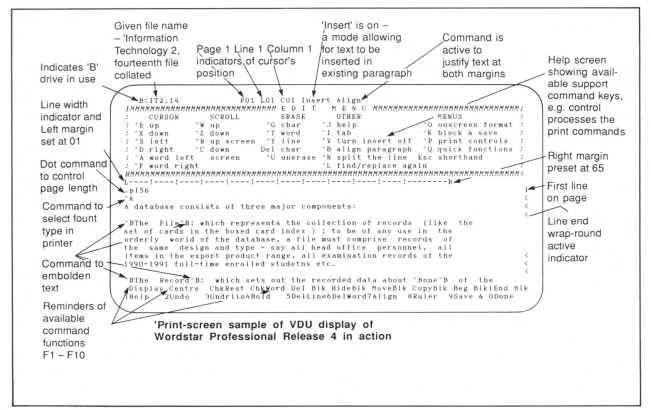

Indicates 'B' drive in use

Line width indicator and Left margin set at 01

Dot command to control page length

Command to select fount type in printer

Command to embolden text

Reminders of available command functions F1 – F10

Given file name – 'Information Technology 2, fourteenth file collated

Page 1 Line 1 Column 1 indicators of cursor's position

'Insert' is on – a mode allowing for text to be inserted in existing paragraph

Command is active to justify text at both margins

Help screen showing available support command keys, e.g. control processes the print commands

Right margin preset at 65

First line on page

Line end wrap-round active indicator

'Print-screen sample of VDU display of Wordstar Professional Release 4 in action

Reproduced by kind permission of WordStar International Inc.

each of five registered temps whose fields reveal that:

1 they are postgraduates,
2 they are currently available,
3 they speak fluent German and Spanish,
4 they can handle competently the WP package the prospective employer uses,
5 their remuneration requirements are in line with what the employer will pay, and so on.

In this way, a properly compiled database can save hours of searching for specific sets of data on what could be thousands of records. But, it is important to note that, while individualised information can be entered on each record, only the information which has been entered into the predesigned fields in a standardised way can be searched, sorted and displayed as indicated above. Thus it is crucial in designing an effective database for the user to have tested it out in pilot form first, so as to ensure that the fields as set up will be able to deliver the desired data across the entry range of predetermined sorts and searches. Otherwise a painful and time-consuming reorganisation of assembled data is unavoidable.

Talking point

How do you see software applications developing in businesses during the coming decade?

Some major applications of databases

- personnel training/pay/promotion/disciplinary etc records
- account customer particulars
- staff specialisms/qualifications
- fleet servicing records
- product specifications and standards
- insurance and pension records
- mailing lists
- price lists
- product design records
- branch/property maintenance data
- patient records
- sales call records
- training materials
- scientific research abstracts, etc.

The word processor

Just as every office worker used to wonder how ever people coped before the advent of the photocopier, so text processing staff nowadays ask the same question about pre-WP times!

Certainly WP software, perhaps more than any other, has changed the way in which information, primarily text, is processed. At the heart of every WP package is the ability afforded to the user to create, move, add, delete, insert, embolden, edit, underscore or capitalise text while it is still in electronic form displayed on the monitor screen.

As a result, WP has raised onto a higher plane the practice of text creation at the keyboard. Instead of managers or executives having to dictate items for subsequent shorthand or audio transcription, they now can, however modest their two-fingered keyboarding skills, compose and Email messages for themselves.

Moreover, the expert text processor, whether secretary or WP operator, now has a highly sophisticated 'toolkit' including many time and labour-saving devices, with which, through an on-line printer, to produce extemely attractive, crisp documents.

How word processing works

The components of word processing are: the monitor screen (computer being taken for granted), keyboard, on-line printer, floppy or hard disk storage media, and of course installed software package.

The user calls up the WP software from either loaded floppy or resident hard disk and then either inserts a work disk into the computer's right-hand disk drive on which to write files, or creates one directly on the hard disk. WP programs are always installed in drive A left-hand disk drives. Each newly created work file is given a logical and easy-to-recall file name.

At the outset a home screen will be displayed on which (see illustration on page 266) a help screen may be displayed at the top of the screen, and a function or F key listing at the foot. Practised users can switch these off at will and use all the screen.

The monitor screen is mainly taken up with a simulation of the eventual printed page (in whole or part) so the operator may design the text as it will appear in print (more or less) depending on the type of WP program used. The WP package incorporates many features of its typewriter precursor, including line-width margin settings, page-length settings, line spacings and so on. Additionally, it can justify both margins, so that text display is clean and attractive. Automatically, when the text reaches the right-hand margin, it is 'wrapped around' to start neatly at the next line's left-hand margin.

Errors and omissions or second/third etc modifications of words, phrases or lines may be simply entered either between existing words or by keying-in over them (which erases them). In this way, a passage can be honed and polished many times before printing if need be.

Also as the text unfolds, it can be given format features such as:

- double spacing,
- expanded height and width,
- emboldening and underscoring,
- reverse printing,
- alternative fount and pitch.

These features are secured by the 'topping and tailing' of selected text with specific function commands which instruct the printer.

Entire paragraphs and pages can be re-sequenced by 'block and move' commands, and pages can be numbered and provided with header and footer information automatically.

Pre-produced standard paragraphs can be called up and inserted at will in a process called 'boiler-plating' and indexes of specified words or entries can be composed for every created file.

Also, standard letters or schedules can be produced and then linked to lists of named recipients with their postal addresses which are stored on what are called non-document files. The two files, one of standard text (with blank spaces for personalised additions to be taken from the non-document file), and the other of listings on the non-document file, may then be merged by the printer to produce, say, circular sales letters with individualised, personal entries.

In essence, the word processing package's marvellous features are accessed and controlled by a mix of:

- QWERTY keyboard text production input (just like using a typewriter keyboard),
- the use of FUNCTION KEYS F1-F10, which have been pre-programmed to activate specific instructions like: 'Help', Delete Line, Save & Continue, etc,
- the use of QWERTY keys with the CONTROL or ALT command keys, which allow further access to a wide range of commands,
- the selection of number codes preceded by a full-stop, called DOT COMMANDS, which are mainly used to set print formats and styles.

Once created, WP files may be stored safely on floppy or hard disk for future reference and access. They may also be copied to other disks or Emailed around a network etc.

With the development of integrated information management packages and LAN software cross-links, information produced on other types of software may be imported and included in a harmonised WP document for high quality presentation.

Summary

Whether in stand-alone, integrated or networked form, the trio of spreadsheet, database and word processing applications packages form an essential set of communication tools for business and public service administrators and support staff. This section has provided you with an overview of their main features and uses, but you must now acquire competent operating skills for each, which will later enable you to adapt to those versions your organisation employs.

Simply put, these skills will be as important to

your future as reading, writing and 'rithmetic have been to your past and present!

Computer-designed graphics

The production of tables, graphs, charts, diagrams and pictograms as a means of communicating number-based information is not new, but creating graphics by means of software application packages for delivery to slide or view-foil making, or large-screen transmission via computerised systems is.

The development of versatile software which offers the user contrasting display options, whether pie-chart or stacked bar-chart, table or line-graph, and which also supplies extensive colour mixes and fount styles to support the graphic data has revolutionised visual communications and presentations.

In a very short time, senior managers have come to expect highly professional presentations and conference AVA/graphics support. Indeed, the design and production of graphic display material is nowadays an important string to every repro-graphics department's bow.

Graphics media available in a graphics package

Table
Sets of figures in columns for analysis and comparison

Pie chart
Parts of a total arranged in pie 'wedges'.

Line graph
Display of joined points plotted against vertical and horizontal scales

Bar chart (clustered, stacked or 3-D)
Amounts depicted as 'slabs of area' set against each other for comparison

Histogram
A means of displaying a total which is distributed into component parts according to, age, size, etc

Map/contour diagram
Geographic maps, contours and shapes (say of car body designs) which may be shown on the VDU in 3-D and rotated

Symbol chart pictogram
Eye-catching symbols are used to show comparative volumes or sizes in order to make statistics more interesting and memorable.

Talking point

Do you anticipate the spread of any interpersonal relations difficulties or health problems as a result of software systems being widely used at work?

Application of graphics software in the office

Naturally, graphics software may be used for any number of communication purposes, depending on the topic and the user's imagination. However, set out here are some of the major uses which are made of graphics in business and public service activities.

Graphics applications

Accounts	To show profits by product, breakdowns of costs, money owed by account customers, salary costs, etc.
Production	To show percentage of rejects in output, to monitor loss of production times, to show operator costs per unit of production, to display computerised designs, etc.
Sales	To compare sales turnover by region or shop, to compare sales to target, to monitor new calls made by sales reps, to show sales by product, etc.
Marketing	To compare shares of the known market, to indicate competing prices, to provide statistics on consumer demand and product specifications, etc.
Personnel	To show the age of the workforce, to illustrate pensions investments, to indicate labour turnover rates and trends, etc.
Project management	To monitor the progress of large-scale projects visually – like building a shopping precinct.
Presentations	To provide (either from monitor screen or colour printout) paper sheet or transparency presentation material for top management perusal.

Computerised graphics

Production

It is no idle boast of major graphics software houses that their packages provide an 'in-house art studio' for users. In fact, many companies are now producing their own colour brochures and informational literature to high standards, having developed a staff member into a graphics technician, able to operate both graphics and DTP software expertly. Thus colour tones, half-tones, cross-hatching and shading as well as multiple founts and images accessed from scanners, now form the components of an exciting 'graphics palette' from which to create arresting and appealing documents.

Driving the software

Data in graphics packages may be manipulated in a variety of ways. The points, for instance, which go to make up the line graph for a given subject may be inputted by means of keying them as separate numbers – 2345, 6543, 5678, etc. The software does the rest and positions each point correctly on the X-Y axis of the graph. Alternatively, a set of figures may be produced on a spreadsheet and, thanks to the foresight of the programmers, be converted into the components of, say, a pie chart by means of a simple function command! Again, charts may be plotted by the use of a mouse to draw lines or bar chart slabs onto a pre-installed scale. The use of windows software may also be brought into play to overlay different graphics material for visual effect.

Most graphics packages contain resident graphs and charts – line graph, stacked or clustered bar chart, 3-D contouring, etc – which are readily summoned up as 'frames' in which to insert data. Moreover, some graphics packages enable the user to switch installed data from, for example, a line graph to a bar chart to assess which medium offers the better means of communication. Also, colours, tones, shading, hatching, etc, can be tried out and altered at will on any given graphic display until the most appropriate is devised. Then it may be printed on to paper or OHP transparency.

One of the most useful features of an integrated information management package from the secretary's point of view lies in the facility to design a graph or chart with the graphics software and then to 'swap' it directly on to, say, a report which is being word processed. And, correspondingly, to install a set of calculations using the spreadsheet software, and to convert, say, the resultant costs of various aspects of a project into an instant pie chart by 'swapping' the calculations into the graphics software.

Colour and resolution

Today monitor screens are produced with a high number of pixels per square centimetre with VGA colour monitors fast becoming the industry standard. Pixels are a measurement of colour density and resolution. For instance, it is now possible to display Old Master paintings on computer monitor screens with a faithful reproduction of the original's colours! By the same token, high-quality colour printers are able to print out graphics displays with anything from 8 to 156 (or more) colours and tones available.

The media for graphics number display

The 'exploded' pie chart

Pie charts are made up of a set of data which goes to form a *known* total. Here, the known total is 12.5% or £62.5 m for Comfort; 23% or £115 m for Melia; and £322.5m has been identified as the market taken by other manufacturers. The technique of showing the wedge of pie in 'exploded' form helps to emphasise it.

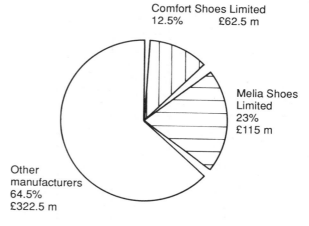

Total market value = £500 m

The bar chart

The bar chart supplies a means of comparing several items which are common to a number of subjects. Here, the different products of the company are being compared in terms of the number of each which has been sold in the month of August. Note the need for a key to explain the shaded items. Sometimes bars in such charts are 'stacked' to include several items within each bar.

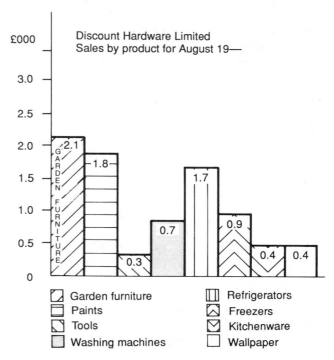

Clustered 3-D bar chart

The bar chart is very much like the line graph — it is used to compare items — but instead of displaying connected points as lines, it sets blocks of area (the 'bars') side-by-side for prompt comparison. The bars are usually coloured differently or given varying cross-hatching to make them stand out from each other.

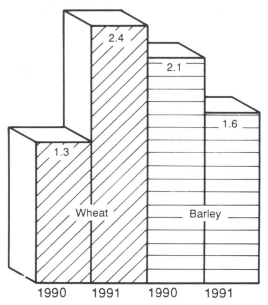

Production of wheat and barley in millions of tonnes

The X-Y axis line graph

Here, amounts are plotted against two known variables. The vertical X axis often provides a scale for amounts and the Y horizontal axis for time — in this case, showing the comparison between thousands of pounds worth of products sold in years A and B, plotted against each month of a year. Line graphs may display four or five items being compared in this way, each being easily distinguished with the aid of colour.

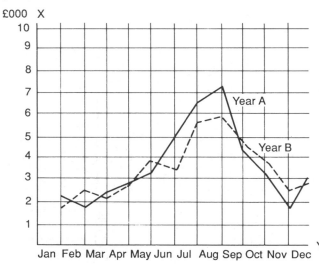

Symbol, chart or pictogram

Graphics packages and DTP software usually include pre-drawn objects (called clip art) which may be used to aid graphic communication, eg cars, houses, wheatsheaves. Or the user may draw them freehand with a mouse. Such symbols are used to help give a set of figures or statistics more impact and appeal, as a symbol, chart or pictogram.

3-D contour map

This technique is particularly useful for the designer, draughtsman and scientist, since it enables items to be viewed as if in three dimensions. Uses include the design of products like aeroplanes, cars and buildings.

Map

Many graphics packages include sets of maps as outlines which may be coloured and annotated according to the user's requirements.

Examples of how charts, graphs, etc, can be displayed on screen using graphics software are shown below:

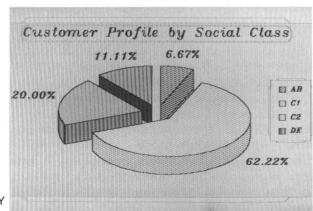

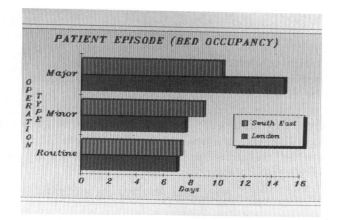

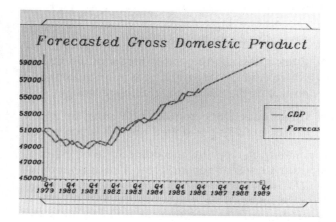

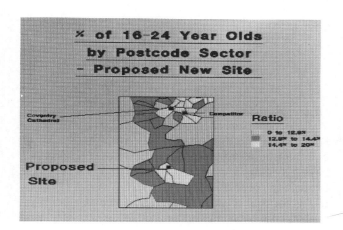

(Photographs by Mike Taylor) Reproduced by kind permission of SPSS (UK) Ltd.

Charts and diagrams are also used extensively outside of computer-driven presentations as training and work analysis tools.

Specimen block diagram in a feasibility report

A specimen block diagram showing the main features of a computerised system for handling customers' orders is shown below. This kind of diagram is frequently included in a feasibility report.

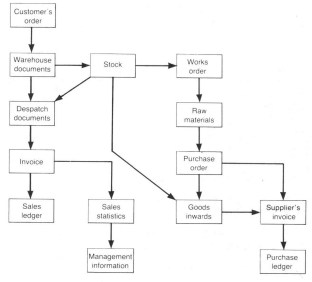

Notice in the above diagram how a visual representation makes each stage of this feasibility study of computerising customers' orders much easier to follow.

Bar chart: time schedule for building

The use of bar charts (see example below) to represent activities which overlap helps to identify potential bottlenecks and to establish priority areas.

	J	F	M	A	M	J	J	A	S	O	N	D
Foundations												
Walls and floors												
Roof												
Electric wiring												
Plumbing												
Gas piping												
Windows and doors												
Glazing												
Plastering												
Decorating, tiling, etc.												

Example of a flow process chart

A procedure analysis chart consists of a list of written descriptions of all the operations in a procedure, with a symbol at the side of each operation indicating its type. The standard BSS work symbols shown on page 272 are used. The descriptions on the chart are very brief. There may be an additional column indicating the forms used for each operation.

The purpose of a procedure chart is to aid the study and analysis of the procedure so that the steps involved and their sequence can be seen at a glance. After this comes the difficult task of analysis of faults and making improvements.

The procedure is analysed in vertical columns for the purpose of diagnosing and assessing faults. In such a chart, the distance travelled by documents and the time taken are recorded by subsequent study.

EXAMPLE OF A FLOW PROCESS CHART

SCRAP NOTE REFERENCE	DISTANCE-METRES
1 ⟩ TO COST OFFICE – RECEIVED FROM FACTORY VIA INSPECTION DEPARTMENT	300
1 ◯ PLACE IN "IN" TRAY	
1 ◯ SORT IN PRODUCT NUMBER SEQUENCE	
2 ◯ SORT IN PART NUMBER SEQUENCE BY PRODUCT	6
2 ⟩ TO COST RECORDS FILE	
3 ◯ SELECT APPROPRIATE COST RECORD SHEET ⎤ REPEAT FOR EACH SCRAP NOTE	
4 ◯ RECORD STANDARD COST DATA ⎦	
3 ⟩ TO 1ST COMPTOMETER OPERATOR	9
2 ◯ PLACE IN "IN" TRAY	
5 ◯ CALCULATE COST OF SCRAP ⎤ REPEAT FOR EACH SCRAP NOTE	
4 ⟩ TO 2ND COMPTOMETER OPERATOR	3
3 ◯ PLACE IN "IN" TRAY	
1 ▢ CHECK CALCULATIONS ⎤ REPEAT FOR EACH SCRAP NOTE	
5 ⟩ TO COST CLERK	12
4 ◯ PLACE IN "IN" TRAY	
6 ◯ SUMMARISE COST OF SCRAP BY PRODUCT	
7 ◯ RECORD COST OF SCRAP ON SCRAP REPORT	
6 ⟩ TO FILE	3
▽ FILE SCRAP NOTES	
SUMMARY	
◯ OPERATION	7
▢ INSPECTION	1
⟩ TRANSPORT	6
◗ DELAY	4
▽ STORAGE	1
TOTAL DISTANCE –	METRES 333

Desk-top publishing (DTP)

Desk-top publishing (sometimes referred to as electronic publishing) has been one of the fastest growing IT developments of the 1980s. Its rapid uptake was the result of a number of factors and influences, principal among which was that the equipment was already in existence – PC desk-top computer with hard disk, laser printer, scanner and mouse. What was the vital additional ingredient was of course the software to do the creative job.

In a nutshell, a desk-top publishing system provides its user with the means of producing page-by-page and document-by-document highly attractive and well printed copy – that is a mix of:

- **text** in a wide variety of typefaces and sizes,

- **photographs, drawings, graphs and charts** all capable of being enlarged or reduced to fit a predetermined space,

- **lines, rules, shading, cross-hatching and frames** which either make reading easier or create visual appeal as part of the overall page design,

- **imported artwork from the DTP software** which can be quickly positioned on to a given page.

Previously, such printed matter had to be given to a printing house to set and print. The development of DTP, however, has had a profound effect upon the production of organisational documents and the presentation of information, as it has brought the printing house – with many of its visual and graphics devices and effects – right into the heart of office information processing.

How desk-top publishing works

It is, perhaps, simplest to envisage DTP as a kind of enhanced word processing and visual image combining system. Desk-top publishing creates an electronic page of text on the PC's visual display screen using aspects of the mix outlined above. The text for this mix is usually originated by means of a current commercial word processing package and, in a similar way, previously devised charts and graphs, etc, may be installed into the DTP system from a graphics software package. Photographic or drawn images are installed by means of a scanner. Once all the desired ingredients have been 'loaded' into the DTP system, the process of designing each page of the document may commence.

The screen on this desk-top publishing unit shows graphics and text combined on the Aldus Pagemaker system, with the mouse cursor control in the foreground.

Desk-top publishing: step-by-step

1   The mock-up phase

A mock-up of the desired page or document is created which provides the DTP editor with a clear idea of such aspects as the nature and required size of illustrations – quarter page, 3 cm x single column etc, and the way in which text is to be displayed – in simple paragraphs, in columns divided by rules, with emboldened paragraph titles, or with a reversed white text in a black box, etc. The mock-up will also show the size of any required headline for eye-catching effect.

In organisations where DTP is established,the mock-up phase will also include a choice of typefaces (technically known as founts) and the respective sizes of typefaces for use in different areas of the page. The sizes of different founts varies considerably – just think of the size of some newspaper headlines and the small print of some books and documents – and is measured in points (a printer's term).

2   The text/graphics installing phase

The text (often called 'copy' for desk-top publishing) is usually produced in organisations by departmental secretaries – as the wording for an advertisement, a handbook to set out a product's specifications, items for the organisation's house journal or as a sales brochure, etc. This copy may be produced via hard or floppy disk.

Where the text producer is familiar with the organisation's DTP system and its software is compatible with the WP package in departmental use, the WP copy may be given format/editing instructions to assist the subsequent DTP editing process, but it usually falls to the DTP operator to work on the word-processed text in order to make it suitable for DTP editing (this may involve taking out underscoring or emboldening instructions etc if the DTP page is to be reformatted from scratch).

3   The editing phase

The text and graphics having been installed into the DTP system, the editing process may begin. In order to design each page – using the mix of typefaces and graphics outlined above a mouse is used as the DTP's control mechanism to move the cursor rapidly around the screen. It can pull down (bring into play or activate) various DTP menus of instructions – such as the shading of a space, the reversing of black on white, the 'cropping' or cutting to a required size of a picture or the enlargement of the page on the VDU either to see it as a whole or to see a magnified portion of it. In addition to the mouse, the PC keyboard is used with its command keys in the editing process.

At the outset of the editing process , the DTP operator will check the mock-ups and, to save time, will select a style sheet (sometimes called a template) from the DTP's memory which most closely resembles the desired page design. Such a sheet is a kind of skeletal blank page with, for example, the rules and columns already set, and margins already specified etc.

The operator may then 'pull down' the various menus which contain the instructions which he wishes to use to design the required page. These menus include:

File for leading data on to the page and subsequently storing it – simply the setting up of a file in the normal way,

View to provide enlarged or reduced displays and to check illustrative material,

Page to add page sequencing and numbering features, to set up right-hand and left-hand page alignments and to set the ongoing page structure, etc.

Frame to insert lines, rules, boxes to a desired size.

Graphic to add illustrations on to page designs,

Type to enable the operator to select the chosen fount or typeface and its size.

Note: Various DTP software applications have similar functions grouped in similar menus, and provide an extended range of instructions which the operator can select or 'tag' in order to build up the page with the desired typeface, graphics and layout. Also, for ease of use, ikon 'tool kits' are available for selection by mouse to draw lines, circles and move items around the page, etc.

4 The printing phase

When the editing phase is completed, the printing process via laser printer is begun. The laser printer with its high quality end product and ability to print in an extensive range of typefaces (founts) and type sizes (points) is what makes DTP so incredibly versatile and useful in larger organisations. Even so, it should be kept in mind that a laser printer with a resolution of at least 300 dots per inch cannot compare for print quality with professional printing by the phototypesetting process in which a resolution of some 1100 dpsi is used. However, if need be, the DTP print command sequence can be relayed on to a phototypesetter.

Note: In order to achieve the best results, it is important that a high resolution monitor screen is used, together with a laser printer which is fully compatible with the DTP software – changing laser printers will change the format of the designed page.

Proofreading

At each stage of the DTP process it is essential to proofread copy carefully. The nearer one approaches the end product, the more difficult and time-consuming it is to correct errors of spelling or layout.

Founts and presentation

While individual secretaries (say in an advertising department or working for a senior manager) may become expert regular users of a DTP system, it is more likely that they will originate text on their own desk-top PCs for installation into the DTP unit which will be operated by a specialist member of staff working full-time in the organisation's reprographics centre. Nevertheless, it is very important today to become more informed and aware than ever before of elements of page design and the visual impact of different kinds of typeface and type size. For example, a Roman fount conveys a sense of respectability stemming from the length of time it has existed and been absorbed in serious publications. Alternatively, the Courier type style communicates clean, crisp modernity and Script imparts a friendly, informal message, while Old English would look quite out of place save on a fascia for Ye Olde Englishe Tea Shoppe! Given that DTP has put a wide range of founts and printing techniques

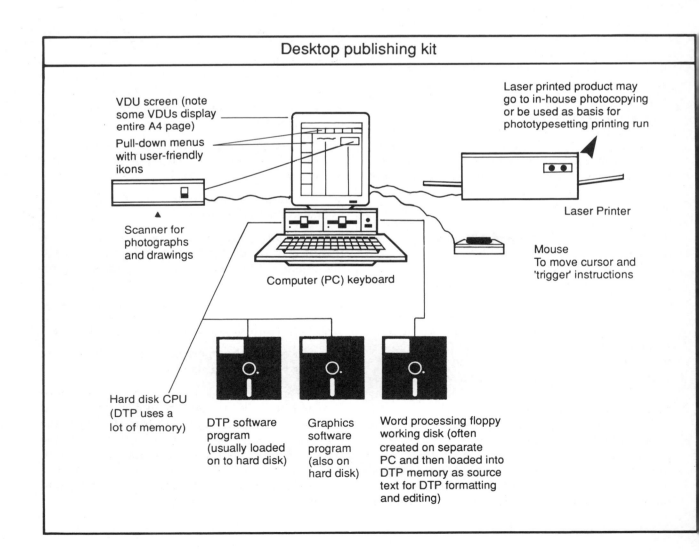

Desktop publishing kit

VDU screen (note some VDUs display entire A4 page)

Pull-down menus with user-friendly ikons

Scanner for photographs and drawings

Laser printed product may go to in-house photocopying or be used as basis for phototypesetting printing run

Laser Printer

Mouse
To move cursor and 'trigger' instructions

Computer (PC) keyboard

Hard disk CPU (DTP uses a lot of memory)

DTP software program (usually loaded on to hard disk)

Graphics software program (also on hard disk)

Word processing floppy working disk (often created on separate PC and then loaded into DTP memory as source text for DTP formatting and editing)

at the disposal of in-house publishing, secretaries and their managers are bound to find that more is expected of them in terms of the quality and standards of the documents they produce for certain purposes, such as reports to the board of directors, circular sales leaflets and brochures to clients and AVA presentation materials for senior management, etc.

Aldus Pagemaker in action

Examples of Aldus pagemaker screen layouts

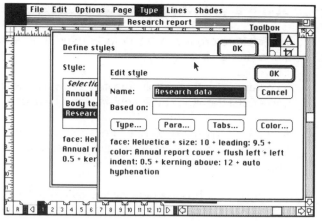

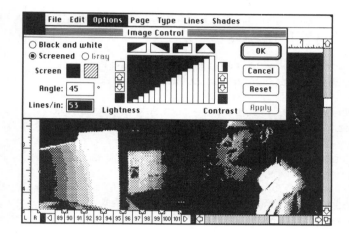

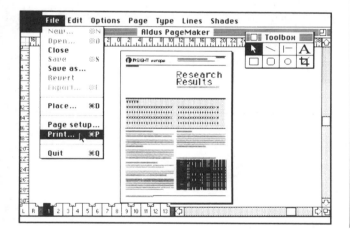

Summary of main points

1 Software-produced documents may be printed/distributed by: batch, real-time, on-line or stand-alone processing methods.

2 Standardised, centrally located software available to all personnel and giving access to a single, unified databank is revolutionising organisational communications.

3 Large-scale uses of software applications include: company-wide accounts, project planning, modelling and forecasting, relational database and spreadsheet use, graphics and image processing.

4 Paper-based document cycles such as the sales cycle or requisition/purchase order cycle have been revolutionised by computerised documentation systems.

5 Networked software, standardised and available to all personnel has the advantages of being: always available, shareable, secure, readily upgradeable, more powerful and more accessible.

6 LAN and desk-top integrated information mangement software includes: electronic diary, notebook, WP, spreadsheet, database, communications, graphics and calculations features.

7 Spreadsheets work by providing formula-creating devices which enable complex calculations to be undertaken, modified at will and imported/exported to further sheets or files.

8 Databases are made up of files, records and fields. They are used to store data in classified arrangements which may be accessed and searched in specific patterns.

9 Word processing software is used to create, edit, format and process text electronically before printing/distributing a final draft; it is controlled by a mix of qwerty keyboard, function command keys and dot command instructions.

10 Tables, charts, graphs, diagrams, pictograms and maps, etc can now be produced by graphics/image processing software to be used in presentation, conferences, training or promotional contexts.

11 Desk-top publishing revolutionised the quality and design of all kinds of document – newsletters, sales leaflets, price-lists, reports, prospectuses, etc which could be created and printed at modest cost in house by organisations.

Activities and assignments

Quick review quiz

1 Explain briefly the difference between: batch, real-time, on-line and stand-alone data processing.

2 List some of the major software applications commonly used in the following private sector departments:

Sales,
Marketing,
Accounts,
Personnel,
Production.

3 What typical large-scale applications software uses can you indentify?

4 Explain how computerisation has improved the sales document cycle.

5 What information would you expect to find on a computer-produced sales invoice?

6 How does an integrated accounts package work in broad terms?

7 What are the advantages to an organisation of installing centralised, standardised software which is networked to personnel?

8 What are the major features of a LAN software system?

9 What typical components would you expect to find in an integrated desk-top information management package?

10 Explain the major features of an electronic diary.

11 Explain briefly how each of the following software packages work:

spreadsheet,
database,
word processing,
graphics.

12 Distinguish between a file, record and field of a database.

13 List some major applications of:

a spreadsheet,
a database,
a WP package.

14 What sort of information is best suited to graphics software processing for presentation use?

15 Explain what the following are:

a pixel,
a VGA monitor,
a 3-D contour map.

16 Describe what each of the following are and in what kind of context they would be used:

a stacked bar chart,
an exploded pie chart,
a flow process chart,
a bar time chart.

Assignments using applications software

1 Your manager, in the District Council's Community Charge Department has produced the latest breakdown of where the money goes:

For every £100 of income, the following is expended:

Council housing	£52.49
Private housing	£ 8.66
Leisure services	£ 6.17
Refuse collection	£ 5.24
Planning	£ 4.76
Environmental health	£ 4.54
Financial assistance	£ 8.32
Other services	£ 9.82

She has asked you to use your department's graphics software to produce a suitable pie-chart as a basis for a colour slide/view-foil.

2 Design a series of bar charts which may be constructed from information gained from students in your group on attitudes to national daily newpapers based on the following questions:

a) Which national newspaper do you prefer to read?

b) Which national daily newspaper provides:

  i) the best news/information coverage?
  ii) the best sports coverage?
  iii) the best coverage of political affairs?
  iv) the best coverage of women's interest items?

Produce your bar-charts on a graphics software application.

When you have completed your research, write a short article on what you think you have discovered about your group's attitudes to the daily press.

3 Assume that you work in the training department of International Shipping Limited. As part of a programme to improve the visual communication skills of its supervisors and junior managers, the company is in the process of producing a training manual of 'Effective Visual Communication'. You have been asked to research and to compile a part of the manual which deals with one of the following: *a*) the bar chart, *b*) the line graph, *c*) the pie chart and how to produce them using a graphics software package. Devise a suitable structure, content and layout which you think will most readily assist the staff identified to produce and to interpret bar charts, line graphs or pie charts. Compare your effort with those produced by other members of your group and comment upon their likely effectiveness. Illustrate your briefing with suitable print-out illustrations.

4 You have been called in as business adviser to Mr Jack Green who owns a large discount electrical goods retail store in the centre of a large conurbation. In the year ended last December, the sales of his principal four products – hi-fi, home computers, televisions and washing machines was as follows:

	Hi-Fi £	Home computers £	Tele-visions £	Washing machines £
Jan	9400	7480	8890	7960
Feb	6750	6760	7760	6740
Mar	7230	5370	7430	6390
Apr	6180	5450	6590	6420
May	5400	6790	4320	5430
June	4950	3860	4160	4330
July	8840	5930	5430	6980
Aug	3790	3220	4380	3140
Sept	5860	4630	4760	4140
Oct	6940	5750	5420	5120
Nov	7880	6890	6130	4980
Dec	10530	12430	7130	3760

a) Use a graphics package to display your line graph illustrating the sales of the above four products for last year.
b) What does your line graph tell you about the nature of Mr Green's business? Write a brief interpretation to accompany your line graph.
c) Assuming that each of the four main products enjoys the same profit margin, what advice would you give Mr Green regarding his buying and trading plans for next year? (You should base your advice on the information you have plotted on your line graph.)
d) What advice could you give Mr Green (based on your graph) about advertising and sales promotion of his four main products for next year?
e) In view of the nature of the sales of the four main products over the last year, what additional electrical products can you suggest Mr Green should stock to help improve annual sales performance? When would you suggest they be marketed most strongly? Why?

5 Your head of department is being pressed by his secretary to 'deliver the spreadsheet program you keep promising to record my petty cash imprest system!' A flash of inspiration reminds him that your group is currently studying spreadsheets! You know the rest: . . .'jolly grateful if you could. . . spare time. . . talk to Betty. . . find out what she wants. . . jolly good experience' and so on.

Out of the kindness of your hearts, you design and deliver the application!

6 Your head of department has recently been approached by a local employment agency which specialises (among other things) in supplying students for vacation and part-time jobs in the locality. Ever since the local economy began to boom, demand has been high for all sorts of temporary jobs, including shiftwork and unsocial hours working. As a result, in groups of three to four, you have been asked to design a database of appropriate particulars which could be used to shortlist suitable students for interview.

Note: Your HOD will counsel all intending students before any particulars are forwarded with their and their parents' permissions.

Design a suitable database.

7 Each day, each month and each academic year, the department in which you are studying is spending money – either on consumable materials such as stationery or on equipment and repairs.

In pairs, explore what services a spreadsheet can provide, and having learned how to operate a spreadsheet, design a system using the spreadsheet to show how a budget of money can be monitored as it is expended – for example for your department's outgoings – so as to provide an up-to-date record at any time of outstanding balances and in what areas the income was spent.

8 Assume that you work as assistant to the Sales Manager of a national company selling a range of office equipment to high street stores and in some cases direct to firms and educational insititutions.

Today your boss greets you with these words:

You know, I'm just not satisfied that we are managing to communicate our sales statistics and analyses to our sales representatives in the field. I've just looked again at my monthly report to the sales reps, and it just looks too wordy and dull. What we could do with is one of those graphics software packages I've just been reading about in this month's 'Business Computer News'! Apparently they can transfer numbers and columns of figures into coloured pie-charts, graphs and what have you – now that's just the thing I need to give my reports some visual impact and appeal!

Needless to say, you are delegated to find out about the kind of services a graphics software package can provide. Your Sales Manager has asked you to devise a factsheet and to obtain any relevant catalogues or brochures which he can digest prior to raising the prospect of acquiring such a package at the next meeting with his regional managers.

Produce the appropriate factsheet in not more than 300 words and submit it with any suitable leaflets or brochures you are able to locate.

9 Your Principal/Head teacher is short of the cash to purchase urgently needed replacement computers in the Information Processing Suite. He/she decides to lay on a 'soft sell' evening with refreshments and a tour of the college/school's facilities in order to promote a sponsorship campaign among the local larger companies. Firms which sponsor (buy) a PC terminal or contribute to the LAN network to link them will have their names inscribed in gold leaf in an illuminated address for display in the Main Foyer. They will also receive VIP treatment in the Training Restaurant and Drama Theatre etc.

You have been asked to identify 20 likely local firms and to devise a suitable circular letter and non-document mailing list to promote the evening to local chairmen, chief executives, managing directors and general managers. Use a WP package to produce a suitable merged mailshot.

10 Your school/college has decided to computerise its record-keeping across the board. One important set of statistics and data needed concerns all full-time leavers — whether they leave during or after the completion of the course. Essentially what is needed is:

A means of checking who left courses early and why.
What happened to students after they left — university? polytechnic? full-time work? VSO? part-time work? or what?
What qualifications did they obtain?
When did they join? Finish? What course?
What percentage went into employment related to their studies?

Design a suitable database record to meet this specification and pilot it with the help of your teacher.

11 In groups of three or four, first design a questionnaire with the aim of discovering the reading habits of your own (or a similar) class. You essentially want to know how long students read each day/week; what they read — for study, for recreation expressed in genres like — fiction, biography, travel, etc; what newspaper they read daily/Sundays; what kind of articles they prefer — news, feature, etc. You also want to know if they have had their eyes tested in the last two years and how long and for what purposes they may read the text on a monitor screen each day/week. You really mean to find out what makes them tick — in reading terms!

When you have assembled all your raw data, use an integrated management information package (sometimes called a desk-top organiser) to integrate the text, tables and graphics of a report to your class entitled:

'You And Your Reading: Characteristics, Trends and Implications'

Note: you should seek to display your information and statistics as appealingly and strikingly as the package will allow.

12 You work as Assistant Personnel Manager in the head office of Autorent Limited, a company specialising in all kinds of motor-vehicle rental. At present you are reviewing your personnel recruitment documentation and systems. Currently secretarial support staff are wasting a lot of time producing one-off letters which could be standardised. Stored paragraphs could be inserted by the boilerplating method to take care of recurring eventualities. You have been asked to design a letter for WP production which is to be sent to all applicants whose applications are unsuccessful. The letter is to cover two separate situations:

a) To advise those applicants who, it has been decided, will not be called for interview, following upon the receipt of their application particulars for a given job
b) to inform those shortlisted applicants who attended for interview that they were unsuccessful

Your manager wants to add a piece to thank them and to encourage them to apply for any other similar post arising in the future. Adding any further features you think appropriate, compose a suitable letter using WP, create the standard paragraphs for boilerplating in a non-document file and then test out your version, supplying print-outs for group comparison. In a discussion, examine the range of applications to which this kind of word processing could be put in organisations.

Research and report back assignments

1 By arrangement, visit the local branch of a national travel agency at an off-peak time. Ask to be shown how one of their real-time computer programs, such as Travicom, operates. Find out what data is available and how the booking process is carried out. Report back to your group on your findings.

2 In pairs, make contact with the manager of one of the following departments in a company or public service organisation in your locality:

- Production
- Sales
- Marketing
- Personnel
- Accounts
- Treasury
- Social Services
- Surveying
- Highways

Arrange to be shown the kind of applications software currently in use and the purposes to which it is put. Summarise your findings in an illustrated oral report to your group.

3 Select one of the following software applications and carry out a fact-finding survey of what is currently on the market and what the typical range of its features is:

- A project managment package (for office use)
- An integrated information management package
- A LAN software system
- A WP package for high-level/high volume work
- A graphics package for presentation work
- A middle-of-the-range spreadsheet or database

Select the version you think − from the sales literature − most likely to give value for money for a medium-sized office administration department, and try to secure a demonstration disk of your chosen package. Then, having fully briefed yourself, produce in a suitable format an analysis of your findings as though for the office administration manager.

4 In pairs, arrange to visit a local company which has computerised its sales or purchasing transactions; seek to acquire an informed understanding of either process and secure any sample forms or print-outs available. Brief your group on your findings and display your samples in your base room.

5 As a class, undertake a survey, through established contacts and networks, of what various uses are being made locally of database packages. Set out your findings in an eye-catching wall display, and show which type of package is being employed for what application.

6 In small groups, arrange to visit a local organisation that has set up a text/information processing service centre to meet the needs of a series of managers and executives. Find out what WP applications software is in use and what features the WP operators (sometimes called correspondence secretaries) find particularly helpful. Brief your class with an AVA-supported account on how such a unit

runs and what contribution the software makes to its effectiveness.

7 Arrange to visit a local computer bureau and find out about the range of services available to local organisations which the bureau markets. Convey your findings to your group in the form of a sales brochure for the bureau.

Work experience assignments

1 Find out which kinds of data processing are used in your attachment organisation. Obtain permission to see them in progress and then write a short, factual account of your observations to display in your base room.

2 With permission, talk to one or more user teams which are employing a particular software application on a large scale. Find out what features of it help them to achieve their objectives. Summarise your findings in a short account to copy to your class.

3 If your organisation has a LAN installed, seek authority to survey the users (or a cross-section) to establish which features are most frequently used and why; also seek to establish what features are regarded as most useful and why. Report your findings (with permission) to your group.

4 Find out what software applications are used for what purposes in PCs working in a stand-alone, intelligent terminal mode in the department in which you are attached. Brief your group on your findings.

5 Ask to see an electronic diary and meetings scheduler in action if possible and try to have a 'practice go' on them; produce a factsheet summarising the major features of both and how they aid organisational communication.

6 With permission, carry out a survey of what tasks the organisation's large-scale applications spreadsheet (or relational database) carries out; arrange if possible to see it in action. With permission report back to your group on what you discovered.

7 Ask to be taken through the main features of the organisation's integrated accounts package, so as to gain an insight into the way each ledger and transaction is interconnected and recorded. With authorisation, report back to your group and illustrate your account suitably.

8 Find out what graphics software is available to support what kind of needs in your organisation; ask to see samples of what it can produce. Keep some copies for your file if possible.

Case study

The Henry Perkins Legacy

Henry Perkins (Builders) Limited was a private building company which was established in 1932 in Dilchester, a thriving market town in the middle of a rural area. The district was much favoured by wealthy couples buying retirement properties, London commuters looking for week-end cottages to acquire cheaply and renovate, and, because of its proximity to ports and the motorway network, young industrial companies in the field of electronics and light engineering.

Until recently, the company had been controlled by the iron grip of the 'Old Man', Henry Perkins, a staunch traditionalist who believed that 'the old, tried and tested ways are best', disliked things he called 'newfangled' and stood no nonsense from his family or employees.

The workforce currently numbers 52 site employees, with some 30-40 self-employed sub-contractors, depending on the number of contracts with work in progress, and an office staff of 13, which is organised as shown in the diagram below.

Three months ago Henry Perkins died peacefully in his sleep at the age of 72, leaving his two sons, David and Andrew and his daughter Julie as directors of a prosperous business run on distinctly old-fashioned lines. At a recent meeting of directors, David, eldest son and now managing director gave this report:

'As we agreed, I've spent the past week reviewing our administrative procedures and, broadly speaking, this is the picture. We have at any given time about 100 active account customers, 30 or so large concerns and 70 small works customers. We're kept busy on the accounts side, which is virtually a paper-based system, because we have to maintain careful costing records of jobs over several months or more and because a lot of our purchase ledger work is involved in keeping track of frequent orders, even though some are quite modest.

'Our accountants do our payroll every week, but I can't say they're as cheap as they were. And we're getting more complaints from the site men about mistakes in their payslips and their bonuses and what have you.

'On the stock control side, we still seem to be losing money on materials which just seem to disappear. We need a better system for controlling what leaves here and what unused materials ought to be coming back! And our filing system could do with a complete overhaul. I spent half an hour yesterday looking for the Robertson contract, and eventually found it in the Robinson and Parker file. There must be some better way of handling contracts we are regularly referring to while they're active.

'Then there's our company image. If you look at our letterheads and stationery, we look as if we're still in the "jobbing builder pulling handcart" age, instead of doing most of our work for the council and the business park. And don't forget that a lot of the people moving into the area have worked for big outfits. I don't think our existing electronic typewriters and vintage copier can deliver the quality of text processing we need now, never mind the time taken to get a mailshot out.

'Lastly, there's what I think the experts call our "informational database". We're always getting in each other's way, or kicking our heels to get at our reference files, suppliers' price lists, contract stipulations, stock sheets and so on. We ought to take a fresh look at how we could organise this aspect better – we're not only wasting time and money, but getting under each others' skin at times.

Henry Perkins (Builders) Limited organisation chart

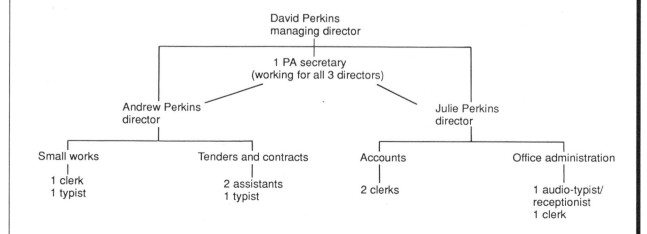

'Well, that must be enough for starters. Dad did us proud in his way and we've him to thank for seeing us through some sticky times. But time doesn't stand still. If we're to remain competitive, we must undertake a root and branch overhaul of our administration, and be prepared to take a few chances with computers and information technology before our competitors steal a march on us – especially with our tendered contract work increasing.'

Assignments

Talking points

1 What do you see as the Perkins board's most pressing problems?

2 How could the board reorganise existing staff to meet the need for the changes David Jenkins has identified?

3 What new information mangement systems and applications software do you think would be most likely to meet the current (and future expansion) needs of Henry Perkins (Builders) Limited?

Activity

In groups of three or four, re-read the case study carefully and make any reference notes. Then produce the following;

a) A fresh organisational chart showing any proposed staff/management restructuring; include a written commentary for your chart.
b) A rationale – in appropriate form – for the acquistion of any new equipment, systems and applications software you think needed; your rationale should include current cost estimates for each major item and a prioritised plan for what should be introduced first.
c) An evaluation of what future administrative developments are likely to be needed – and planned for – during the next three years, given that the company is well-placed to double its business in a thriving locality, with a young and innovative board of directors.

12

Meetings, conferences and presentations

Overview

Unit 12 provides you with information and guidelines on:

- The features common to all types of meeting; goals, objectives, outcomes etc.
- An overview of different types of meeting: statutory, executive, managerial, brainstorming, etc.
- The structures of committees and their procedures: executive, advisory, ad hoc, standing, etc.
- A survey of committee officers' roles and duties: chairman, vice-chairman, secretary, treasurer, member.
- An explanation of how the cycle of monthly committee meetings is administered and what documents service such meetings: notice, agenda, chairman's agenda, minutes, etc.
- How to produce meetings documentation in currently accepted styles and formats.
- Models and specimens of: notices, agendas, resolution, narrative and action minutes, proposals and resolutions.
- Guidelines on how to write in reported speech.
- How to organise a conference.
- How to give an oral presentation supported by audio-visual aids.

Introduction

The term, 'meeting' is used so widely nowadays, and given so many different interpretations that it has come to mean almost all things to all people. At one end of the meetings' spectrum are those which are formally conducted and governed by rules of procedure as laid down by a company's Memorandum and Articles of Association or the Standing Orders of a county council. At the other end are the easy, informal types of meetings such as the managerial brain-storming meeting at which executives keep making suggestions about, say, product development, in the hope of crystallising a totally new idea or approach.

Some types of limited company and various local government councils are required to hold certain meetings by statute, as a result of government legislation. A company's Articles or a council's Standing Orders will prescribe rules about giving adequate notice of a meeting, what constitutes a quorum (the minimum number of members needed to be present for a meeting to be held), what sort of business a meeting should conduct, and when and where certain types of meeting, such as board meetings, or Annual Meetings of a council, should be held. In addition, such rules will indicate what rights the shareholder or member of the public possesses in areas such as voting or admission.

Common factors of meetings

Goals:
Goals or aims have been identified which the meeting elects to achieve

Outcome:
The members of the meeting have an interest in the outcome of its business

Interests:
Participants represent sectional or official points of view

Action or information:
A problem situation, plans or attitudes need to be resolved or crystallised; information needs to be imparted and disseminated

Deadlines:
The business of the meeting takes place within a limited time-scale which affects the potential effectiveness of decisions or the relevance of information

Leadership:
Someone has assumed or been assigned the leadership of the meeting

---

Meetings are held by people from all walks of life and in countless company, public service or sports and leisure contexts. At the top of an organisational pyramid company directors may meet to evolve company policy and decide future strategies. Members of trade unions may meet to hammer out an approach to imminent pay negotiations. Alternatively, members of an angling club committee may meet to discuss the dates and locations of the following season's fishing matches.

Indeed, whether as a tool of management, instruction of local or central government, or forum of the voluntary club, the meeting has, for many years, been employed as a means of making decisions – usually binding, upon those participating in the meeting, of spreading information or a means of resolving a particular problem. Through the medium of the meeting, people are able to make suggestions, voice criticisms and express opinions. Moreover, the physical promixity of people seated round a table to 'thrash things out,' creates a special type of relationship among those present which no form of written exchange or electronic substitutes is able to produce.

Like most communciations channels, however, the meeting is also a potential source of communication failure or break-down. It may become sterile and unproductive, costly to call and a source of time-wasting. Much depends upon the qualities of the members attending and their respective skills in communicating effectively through the constraints imposed by rules, procedures or conventions. Certainly all types of meetings share certain common factors which serve to unite those attending and to direct their thoughts and actions.

Different types of meeting

Since meetings take place within such a diversity of organisations and are used for so many different purposes, to arrive at a definition true for all types of meeting is virtually impossible, save in the broadest of terms.

Yet, the hostility which the calling of some meetings produces in those required or invited to attend often derives from an inadequate understanding of basics. If the meetings are poorly organised they quickly become 'a waste of time'; if they fail to result in action they are deemed 'pointless'; if the participants bring with them misconceptions about the 'terms of reference' which limit the powers of those attending a meeting, they are likely to become disappointed or embittered about the value or effectiveness of meetings.

It is therefore important to define the nature of certain types of meeting, to appreciate the procedures and conventions which govern their conduct and then to evaluate their effectiveness in contributing to sound decision-making and good administration.

Definitions of meetings

Statutory

A legal definition of a meeting based on case law precedent is:

'the coming together of at least two persons for any lawful purpose'.

To embrace statutory meetings of companies and public institutions, this definition may be enlarged:

an assembly of persons meeting in accordance with legally defined rules and procedures to discharge business as required by law.

Executive

In the on-going administration of companies or local and central government many meetings take place which are participative – all present share in the making of decisions which leads to action being taken:

an assembly of people with common interests arriving at decisions and instituting actions through the process of an exchange of relevant views and information which leads to an agreement favoured by the majority of those present and subsequently supported by all.

Briefing

Some meetings are called, however, within organisations to relay decisions or information from a more senior level:

an assembly of people in a 'reporting to' position within an organisational hierarchy who are summoned to receive, accept and comply with the requirements of formulated decisions or to retain information for use relayed to them by a person in authority over them.

Advisory

In some organisations people meet to generate advice or to make suggestions for submission to a higher authority:

an assembly of people meeting to formulate advice, suggestions or proposals for submission to a higher executive body for ratification.

Managerial

Many informal meetings occur (some arising spontaneously) between a manager and his subordinates or counterparts to exchange opinions, give advice or supply information as part of the managerial decision-making process:

a gathering of people within an organisation (but not necessarily restricted to the organisation) with clearly defined inter-personal relationships, meeting to exchange views, attitudes, or information with a view to making decisions and instituting actions.

Task force, working-party, quality circle

A modern approach to solving an organisation's problems has been to bring together a group of people with varying responsibilities and from different departments to pursue a particular task or to resolve a specific problem:

an assembly of people drawn from various levels and sectors of an organisation, embodying different specialisms, brought together to find the solution to a problem by working outside the normal administrative structure.

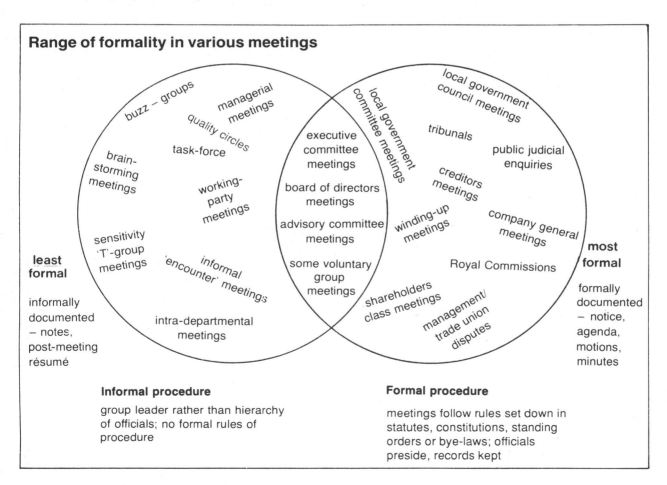

Range of formality in various meetings

buzz – groups
managerial meetings
quality circles
task-force
brain-storming meetings
working-party meetings
sensitivity 'T'-group meetings
'encounter' meetings
informal meetings
intra-departmental meetings

executive committee meetings
board of directors meetings
advisory committee meetings
some voluntary group meetings

local government committee meetings

local government council meetings
tribunals
public judicial enquiries
creditors meetings
winding-up meetings
company general meetings
Royal Commissions
shareholders class meetings
management/ trade union disputes

least formal

informally documented – notes, post-meeting résumé

most formal

formally documented – notice, agenda, motions, minutes

Informal procedure

group leader rather than hierarchy of officials; no formal rules of procedure

Formal procedure

meetings follow rules set down in statutes, constitutions, standing orders or bye-laws; officials preside, records kept

Brain-storming, buzz-groups

Some informal meetings are called with the aim of generating a fresh approach or new ideas relating to organisational activities:

an informal assembly of people who aim to generate ideas, suggestions or approaches to organisational activities from an unrestricted interchange of views, opinions and attitudes.

Formal structures and procedures

The preceding definitions and 'range of formality' diagram should be taken as guide-lines since the degree of formality with which a meeting is conducted depends not only upon the existence of a constitution, standing orders or rules, but also upon the climate or atmosphere generated within any organisation.

However, many formal meetings, especially those run by committees, follow broadly similar lines and share equivalent structures and procedures. Generally speaking there is a correlation between the degree of formality of a meeting and the importance of its decisions:

Policy-making executive
Affects entire organisation, usually made by a meeting of the board of directors or made by senior or middle management probably affecting departments or divisions.

Implementive, routine, administrative
Day-to-day decisions made within departments.

Executive committee
One which has the power to act upon decisions.

Advisory committee, consultative committee
One which refers advice to a main, executive committee.

Standing committee
One which meets during an indefinite period.

Ad hoc committee
A committee constituted to carry out a particular task (from the Latin *ad hoc*: 'for this purpose').

Sub-committee
One performing for and reporting to a main committee.

Policy committee
In large organisations, one which takes major decisions affecting future activities.

Management committee
A form of executive committee which manages the important affairs of an organisation.

Membership committee
Clubs, such as golf clubs, use such committees to vet and control membership.

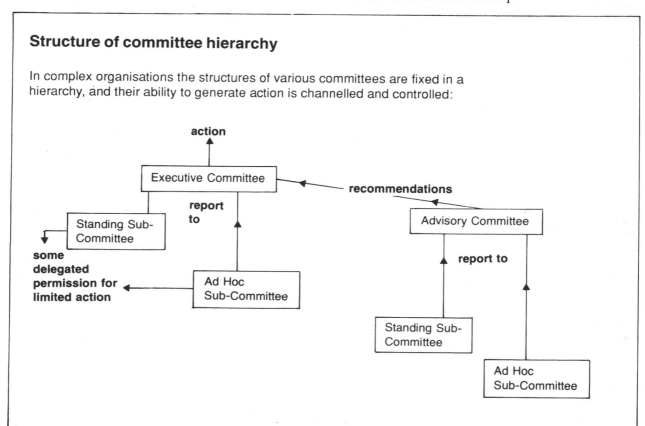

Structure of committee hierarchy

In complex organisations the structures of various committees are fixed in a hierarchy, and their ability to generate action is channelled and controlled:

Composition of an executive committee

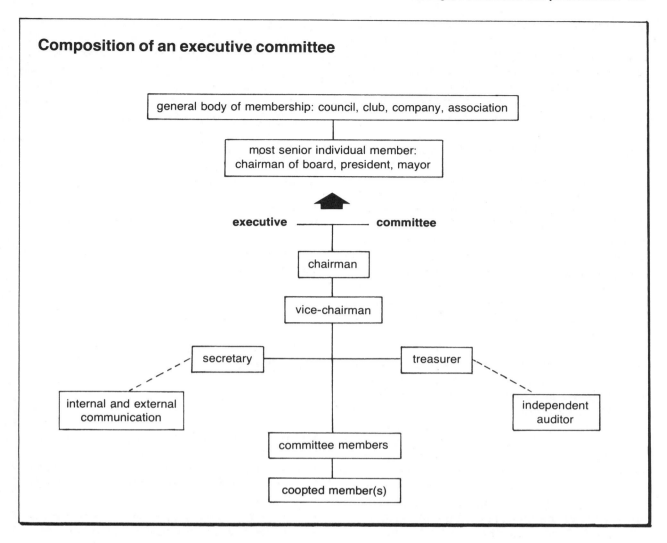

| general body of membership: council, club, company, association |

| most senior individual member: chairman of board, president, mayor |

executive ———— **committee**

chairman

vice-chairman

secretary — treasurer

internal and external communication

independent auditor

committee members

coopted member(s)

The composition and functions of an executive committee naturally vary according to the type of organisation it is serving. The diagram above broadly represents a popular type of executive committee to be found in commerce, the public service or voluntary clubs. In large organisations the financial function may be integrated into an accounting department; the committee may be responsible through a board of directors to shareholders, or through a local government council to rate-payers.

In voluntary clubs particularly, a president or captain may act as a figure-head positioned between the executive committee and the club members, although the chairman of the executive committee is responsible for directing its activities and for presiding at its meetings. Some executive committees include a vice-chairman, usually a senior, experienced member, able to stand in for the chairman if need be. The secretary has a close relationship with the chairman in planning the business of meetings and generally administering the committee's work, while the treasurer keeps a watching brief and record of the committee's finances for an annual audit. The members of the committee may

be elected or appointed by the general membership, serving for a pre-established term of office. Sometimes committees ask an expert or specialist to join them as a 'coopted member'; he or she may, or may not, be given the right to vote at committee meetings.

In the case of voluntary clubs and associations, the annual financial records, expressed by the treasurer in balance sheet form, are checked against receipts by an independently appointed auditor. In this way the general membership is reassured of the integrity of its committee.

The rules of the game

All meetings, whether statutorily called, run by company departments, or organised by local voluntary clubs, are governed by rules. Sometimes the rules take the form of laws decreed by Act of Parliament, sometimes the form of company regulations lodged with the Registrar of Companies, and sometimes, in the case of a voluntary society, the form of a constitution. Even when no written rules exist – as may be the case in, for example, inter-departmental company meetings – there nevertheless exists a set of 'unspoken rules or conventions' which participants will have learned and which are just as effective in regulating activities.

The best piece of advice for those whose work or whose leisure interests involve them in taking part in meetings, therefore, is:

It pays to know the rules of the game!

An inexperienced company director or county councillor may find him or herself outmanoeuvred or reduced to helpless silence by someone better versed in procedural technicalities – points of order or information – sometimes introduced to win a point or demolish opposition! Even in leisure or voluntary association committee meetings passions have been known to run high over the venue of the annual outing, and even here, it pays to know exactly what the club's constitution has to say on any particular point or procedure.

In the case of those meetings called within the confines of an organisation – a company or local government department – there may be no specific rules to guide procedure at a meeting, although it is held beneath the 'general umbrella' of local government or company law. Here it is much more difficult to grasp the rules of the game, since they are sometimes obscure and capable of change. Such meetings are largely controlled by those members possessing either status or assertive personalities.

In this type of meeting much will depend upon the quality of the chairman, who will need to be a leader, persuader, diplomat, tactician and healer rolled into one!

The inexperienced participator in meetings should, then, take the trouble to learn the rules, written or unspoken, and should 'play himself in' by listening to and observing his fellow-participants in action. Gradually he will perceive the responses and attitudes which motivate his peers, may discern where he will gain a sympathetic ear, and where a rebuff. He should also ensure that he has 'done his homework' before speaking, since if he is to sway his audience, he must first gain their respect. He should also bear in mind that *he* has to become acceptable to his peers before his ideas or suggestions are accepted.

Written rules affecting meetings

Companies

Memorandum and Articles of Association:

Required by Company Law, the Memorandum and Articles define aims, activities and procedure of a company and are lodged with a Registrar of Companies.

Councils

Acts of Parliament and Standing Orders:

Much council procedure is governed either by Act of Parliament – Local Government Act 1972, Public Bodies (Admission to Meetings) Act 1960 and approved rules in Standing Orders.

Voluntary bodies

Written constitutions:

Voluntary clubs, associations and societies adhere to rules and bye-laws set down in a 'constitution', usually drawn up by founder-members: its rules also govern the composition of committees and meetings procedures.

Extract from an angling club's constitution

CONSTITUTION

9. THE COMMITTEE   The Committee shall meet at least once in each calendar month to examine the accounts and to arrange the affairs of the Society in accordance with Committee Standing Orders.

The Committee shall promote the interests of the Society and shall have the power to take and defend legal proceedings. Such power may only be exercised after a resolution has been duly proposed, seconded and carried in Committee by a majority vote of those present and voting. Any expenditure of funds for the purpose of litigation must be shown in the Society's accounts and be ratified by a simple majority of members in general meeting not later than the next Annual General Meeting after the termination of such litigation.

THE CHAIRMAN – shall have the power of vote in committee if he wishes to exercise it, but shall have a further and casting vote in the event of equal votes of those present and voting.

THE VICE CHAIRMAN – shall serve as a Committee Member and take the place of the Chairman at a Committee Meeting in the absence of the elected Chairman.

THE HON TREASURER – shall deal with all financial matters of the Society, keeping an orderly record of income and expenditure and prepare the books for audit at the end of each financial year, being March 31st. He shall receive annually an honorarium which shall be decided by calculation at 6½p per Society member.

Extract from a county council's standing orders

STANDING ORDERS

(3) These Standing Orders shall take effect subject to any statutory provision for the time being in force affecting local authorities.

N.B. The main Standing Orders applying to Committees and Sub-Committees have been indicated by sidelines.

MEETINGS OF THE COUNCIL

Annual Meeting

2. (1) Each Annual Meeting of the Council shall be combined with an Ordinary Meeting and shall be held at the County Hall, Chichester, commencing at ten thirty o'clock in the forenoon, unless the Council or the Chairman shall otherwise direct.

Ordinary Meetings

(2) Ordinary Meetings shall be held at the County Hall, Chichester, at ten thirty o'clock in the forenoon, unless the Council or the Chairman shall otherwise direct.

Minutes

9. (1) The Minutes of the business done at each meeting of the Council shall be printed and a copy sent to each member with the summons to attend the next meeting of the Council.

(2) As soon as the Minutes have been read, or if they are taken as read under Standing Order 10(3), the Chairman shall put the question "That the minutes of the meeting of the Council held on the   day of   be signed as a true record".

(3) No motion or discussion shall take place upon the Minutes, except upon their accuracy and any question of their accuracy shall be raised by motion. If no such question is raised, or if it is raised then as soon as it has been disposed of, the Chairman shall sign the minutes.

Document sequence

1 Minutes:
Agreed written record of business of a meeting

2 Notice:
Written 'invitation' to meeting's participants

3 Proposals, agenda items:
Business proposed for debate at meeting

4 Committee agenda:
List of items of business for discussion

5 Chairman's agenda:
Similar to committee agenda, but includes helpful background or briefing notes prepared by the Secretary

Note: **Advance notice:**
Some organisations require notices, proposals and agendas to be sent out and received by a fixed number of days in advance of the meeting to which they refer.

Talking point

'Decisions take too long to reach in committees and when they are arrived at invariably they take the form of harmless compromises.'

Meetings: document cycle for monthly meetings

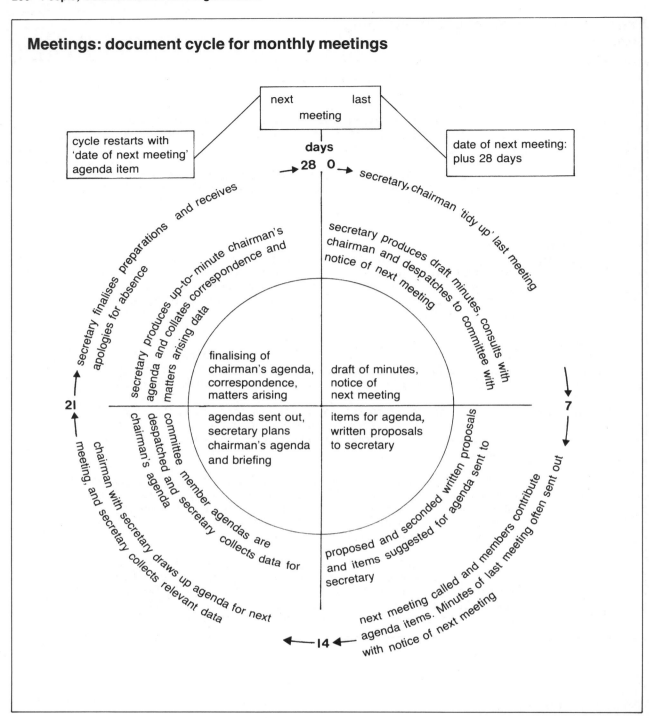

next   last
meeting

days

cycle restarts with
'date of next meeting'
agenda item

date of next meeting:
plus 28 days

28   0

secretary, chairman 'tidy up' last meeting

secretary finalises preparations and receives
apologies for absence

secretary produces up-to-minute chairman's
agenda and collates correspondence and
matters arising data

secretary produces draft minutes, consults with
chairman and despatches to committee with
notice of next meeting

finalising of
chairman's agenda,
correspondence,
matters arising

draft of minutes,
notice of
next meeting

21

7

agendas sent out,
secretary plans
chairman's agenda
and briefing

items for agenda,
written proposals
to secretary

committee member agendas are
despatched and secretary
chairman's agenda   collects data for

proposed and seconded written proposals
and items suggested for agenda sent to
secretary

chairman with secretary draws up agenda for next
meeting, and secretary collects relevant data

next meeting called and members contribute
agenda items. Minutes of last meeting often sent out
with notice of next meeting

14

The participants

Profile of the chairman

There are as many different types of style of chairmanship as there are meetings. Where meetings are held without formal procedures or written rules, the chairman's role is often very loosely interpreted. He or she may do no more than provide the impetus for discussion and the interchange of ideas.

In formally structured meetings, however, the chairman's responsibilites become much more com-

plex, requiring him to implement a code of written rules, adhere to long-established procedures and exercise sometimes discrete and sometimes explicit control over the participants at a meeting.

The following guide-lines indicate the broad areas of responsibility of the chairman presiding over meetings of the executive committee kind.

Authority

The chairman (or chairwoman) at meetings governed by the rules of Articles, Standing Orders or a

Constitution has many responsibilities to discharge, all of which depend upon his (or her) authority, which will have been prescribed and written down. As the leader of a committee or working party, the chairman will have as a principal duty the responsibility to ensure that all business is conducted fairly, according to the rules which obtain. For example, he or she may have to decide whether a speaker is 'out of order', or whether an item has been fairly introduced under 'Matters Arising'. In addition, the chairman will, at times, need to use initiative to solve problems not covered by precedent or covered in the written rules. Many aspects of procedure in formal meetings, such as addressing remarks to the chair, exist to reinforce the chairman's authority and ability more readily to control the meeting.

Social skills

Though many chairmen possess different styles in the chair, they all need to be skilled in handling people. Not only must meetings proceed according to rules, they must also generate a cooperative atmosphere or climate so that decisions of a good quality may be made from the active participation of all present. It is therefore the chairman's responsibility to see that all members are given a chance to speak or to reply, that no one speaker dominates, that private conversations or quarrels do not develop and that no one 'switches off' out of boredom or frustration. Similarly, the chairman must ensure that the discussion remains relevant to the business in hand and that members do not meander down unproductive byways or parade their pet arguments. Equally, he or she may at times need to supply a résumé of the argument to help members crystallise their thoughts as they near the point of decision. And, while using such social skills, the chairman must avoid seeming to favour any particular group or party within the committee. Qualities of tact and diplomacy are therefore essential in exercising the duties of a chairman.

Administration

Although the secretary attends to much of a committee's administration, it is the chairman who has overall responsibility to ensure that work of a committee proceeds smoothly. With the active support and assistance of the secretary, the chairman must ensure that accurate records in the form of minutes are kept, that committee members are kept fully informed of developments, that all financial matters are conscientiously attended to. In order to monitor delegated duties, the chairman will very often ask for reports to be made as a means of disseminating information and providing progress or status checks. Sometimes the chairman may decide to set up a sub-committee to deal with a particular problem or to organise an event.

Policy and direction

By adopting an impartial approach in meetings the chairman is able to keep in mind the wider objectives and perspectives of the committee, in order to be able to dissuade members from making commitments to untenable positions, or from taking extreme actions without heeding the wider issues or implications. Like the good manager, the good chairman achieves the committee's objectives through the active cooperation of other people – the committee members attending the meetings.

Profile of the secretary

The secretary is, perhaps, best regarded as the hub of the committee around whom its work revolves. The conscientious secretary undertakes much detailed work, frequently behind the scenes, to ensure that lines of communication between committee members and the organisation as a whole are kept open. In addition, the secretary has a duty to perform administrative tasks punctually and efficiently.

The chairman's 'right hand'

In terms of the seating arrangements of many a committee or working party, the secretary is to be found, quite literally, at the right hand of the chairman. Indeed, this physical proximity is symbolic of the full cooperation and rapport which must exist between chairman and secretary if the work of a committee is to be productive.

Very often, the other duties a chairman may undertake, either at work or in his or her local community, will mean that much of the routine and detailed work of the committee is left to the secretary. Nevertheless the considerate secretary takes pains to ensure that the chairman is kept fully briefed at all times by means of the chairman's agenda, written briefings, or copies of documents and liaison between meetings. The chairman and the secretary will usually consult over the drafting of minutes, the compilation of an agenda and the calling of meetings.

During the meeting itself, the secretary will keep alert to come to the aid of the chairman, if need be with detailed information, a helpful up-dating or confirmation of any late developments. Moreover, the secretary must be careful to see that such supportive action does not detract in any way from the chairman's control or authority in the meeting but is proffered unobtrusively. Thus the relationship of the secretary to the chairman is largely supportive and it is not always easy for the secretary to accept the constraints which the role imposes. However, the good chairman and secretary realise that they are very much a team and the secretary generally derives much personal satisfaction from being at the centre of the committee's activities.

Administration

Though often enjoying much freedom of action, it is important to remember that the secretary's administrative duties are delegated to him or her and usually set out, for example, in a society's constitution or in the case of a County Secretary, the council's Standing Orders.

In broad terms, the secretary administers the committee's business. The responsibility includes keeping and distributing records of meetings in the form of minutes and keeping the regular cycle of meetings running smoothly. In this context, the secretary is responsible for producing the minutes of the last meeting to despatch to committee members often with notice of the next. In the case of formal meetings the secretary will accept written proposals from members of the committee to incorporate in a committee agenda, which members must also receive in good time before a meeting. The secretary must also compile a chairman's agenda and attend to any correspondence, written reports or briefings which the committee may need to receive. Before a subsequent meeting, the secretary very often needs to follow up any task delegated to him or her which may be referred to under 'Matters Arising' and will also need to collect any apologies for absence to pass on to the chairman.

In addition, it usually falls to the secretary to ensure that the venue of the meeting has been booked and that the meeting or conference room itself is fully prepared with a suitable seating arrangement, notepaper, and any further requirements or refreshments which may be needed. The thoughtful secretary also brings copies of relevant documents to the meeting in case committee members arrive without them.

A further duty of the secretary is to see that any absent committee member is kept informed of the business of a meeting and that that member receives copies of the appropriate minutes and other documents. As well as servicing the committee in this way, the secretary is also responsible for circulating papers or reports upon request to the organisation's membership and for maintaining any noticeboard which may display committee notices.

Lastly, the secretary has a duty to ensure that the chairman is supported in the sometimes demanding task of conducting a meeting's business in such a way that neither rancour, hostility nor boredom interfere with its work, and that attendance at meetings does not fall off as a result of low morale.

Note: The marketing of home computers and software at modest prices has provided busy secretaries of voluntary sector committees with an invaluable administration tool.

Profile of the treasurer

The treasurer has a crucial part to play in the work of any committee responsible for managing an organisation's funds. The treasurer not only keeps careful account of all income and expenditure during a financial year, but also acts as 'watch-dog', monitoring the financial implications of projects and activities, so that the enthusiasm of committee members does not outrun the organisation's financial resources.

Financial administration

The treasurer is expected to keep careful records of all financial transactions which a committee may make on behalf of its members, so that at the end of each year he or she is able to present a treasurer's report and balance sheet at an Annual General Meeting. Such a duty involves the keeping of all receipts, bills, cheque stubs, bank statements and petty cash records so that the accounts may be substantiated.

In time for the Annual General Meeting, the treasurer of a society will pass the accounts and records to an independent auditor who checks and verifies them, so that the integrity both of the treasurer and the committee is preserved when the accounts are presented for the scrutiny of the membership. This function is mirrored in company practice in the work of the accounts or financial director and the company's chartered accountants.

Advisory role

In many situations, the decisions of a committee or working party may involve the spending of money. The treasurer is not only responsible for keeping an up-to-date record of the organisation's financial status − often to be found as an item on the committee agenda − but also to advise the committee on the financial aspects of proposed ventures, even though this may mean 'pouring cold water' on someone's cherished scheme! In this way, the treasurer maintains the solvency of the organisation − essential to almost every undertaking.

Talking point

Of what use is the meeting in all its various forms as a means of democratic decision-making? Where, for example, lies the accountability for decisions made in an organisation by a committee drawn from various departments and levels in the hierarchy? Are effective decisions inevitably 'one man' (or woman) decisions?

Written documentation

If any committee, working party or convened meeting is to function effectively, it will need to pay careful attention to the range of written documentation it produces, whether a letter, report, agenda or minutes. Where meetings are concerned, written communications either prepare members for business, record business transacted or implement business decided upon. Broadly, the range of written documentation through which a committee will transmit much of its activities is:

1 Notice of meeting
2 Minutes of the last meeting
3 Committee members' agenda
4 Chairman's agenda
5 Chairman's additional briefing
6 Formal, written proposals; motions
7 Correspondence
8 Financial reports
9 Written reports

The secretary produces the first five items, and may ensure that members' proposals are framed appropriately. He or she will also attend to any necessary correspondence, while the treasurer is responsible for financial reports and statements, and the chairman of the committee may oversee the production of any committee report.

Note: There is sometimes confusion over the use of the terms Proposal, Motion and Resolution. It is perhaps helpful to regard the written submission of an item for discussion, before a meeting is held, as a 'proposal'. During the meeting, when the item is brought up for discussion, it is generally referred to as a 'motion'. Whether as a proposal or a motion the item will, in formal meetings, need to be sponsored by a proposer and seconder. If the motion is carried it thereafter becomes a 'resolution' which has been passed by a majority of voters.

The notice

Notices of meetings, despatched in advance according to standing regulations, may be written in one of several formats:

1 A form postcard Such postcards are pre-printed and used to call routine, perhaps monthly, meetings. Spaces are left for the secretary to enter the committee member's name, and the day, date, time and venue of the meeting. Though there is less of a personal touch, they save the secretary valuable time and effort.

2 Centred notification Some notices are produced on sheets of A5 landscape headed notepaper. The essential information is imparted in a centred paragraph.

3 Letter format Sometimes formal meetings are called by means of a personally written letter from the secretary to each committee member on the organisation's headed notepaper.

4 Memorandum In the case of meetings called by a company or public-service department, the format used is frequently the memorandum.

Talking point

'The most important decisions are usually made before the meeting starts.' Is the practice of lobbying fair? Should it be stopped? Could it be? Does it matter?

Agendas

As well as providing a kind of 'early warning system' to help meeting participants to prepare themselves for the topics to be covered, the committee members' agenda acts both as a 'running-order' schedule and time-table during a meeting. The adroit chairman will ensure that agendas are not allowed to become too long or ponderous. Similarly, careful thought may also be given to the position of an item of business on an agenda, where either 'the decks may be cleared' of less important items before a thorny problem is tackled, or where an important item of business is dealt with first, while members are fresh. It is in such instances that the acumen and experience of the chairman is invaluable.

The committee members' agenda

As has already been outlined, committee meetings in particular subscribe to certain formalities. Thus the first three items on a routine agenda tend to be set out as follows:

1 Apologies for absence Having declared the meeting open (while the secretary records the time) the chairman will announce the 'apologies', sent in advance to the secretary, of any member unable to attend the meeting.

2 Minutes of the last meeting Here, the chairman will ask members, who generally will have received a copy of the minutes beforehand, whether they represent a true record of the previous meeting which he or she may sign. Discussion of this item will be limited to the actual wording of the minutes which must be accurate in fact and fair in implication.

3 Matters arising Some chairmen tend to dislike this item on the grounds that it provides an opportunity for controversial topics to be re-opened for discussion. There are numerous instances, however, when a situation may have developed, or where the secretary or a committee member may have pursued a particular item which arose directly from the last meeting and which should be reported.

Additionally, some committee agendas include as a fourth item, 'Correspondence'. Its inclusion as a regular feature of an agenda depends upon the frequency and extent of any exchange of letters between the committee and third parties.

These three (or four) items on the committee members' agenda represent a kind of ritual opening of the meeting, preserving the integrity and continuity of completed and on-going business before the fresh business which the meeting was primarily called to discharge, commences.

The new business is set out as a number of items in the middle of the agenda. At a meeting of a local branch of a professional institute they might appear as follows:

4 Publicity for new season's programme of events

5 Topic and speaker for meeting: 4 March 19—

6 Visit to PC User exhibition, Olympia

7 Proposal to levy an admission charge at meetings: That an admission charge of £1 per head be levied by the Branch to cover the cost of coffee and biscuits and to contribute towards Branch funds.
   Proposer: Mr J Pearson
   Seconder: Mrs M Jenkins

Having debated and decided upon action for items 4–7 (for an explanation of proposals, motions and resolutions see above), the new business of the meeting will have been virtually concluded and the chairman will have delegated the actions to be implemented to members. There remain two items on the agenda to be dealt with:

8 Any other business

9 Date of next meeting Some chairmen do not like to include item **8**, since it allows members to introduce items without prior notice, may test the patience of members at the end of a meeting or may enable pet schemes and hobby-horses to be paraded for the 'umpteenth' time. On the other hand, such an item does allow a member to introduce a topic which he or she may feel has not been given sufficient attention, or which may have been overlooked entirely. If such a topic is sufficiently important, it may well appear as an item on the agenda of the committee's next meeting. The last duty of the chairman is to decide upon a date for the next committee meeting in consultation with the members. Thereafter the meeting is formally closed, and the secretary records the time.

'I didn't bother with an agenda this time — you know how awkward they get when they come prepared.'

Note: on some agendas 'Any Other Business' appears as the final item. The ordering of agenda items in this respect seems to be a matter of committee preference.

The chairman's agenda

The chairman's agenda is, essentially, an annotated version of the committee member's agenda. Both will carry identical agenda items in the same sequence. The chairman's agenda, however, will include after each item sufficient space for the secretary to insert background, briefing notes such as updating information, explanations of newly-developed situations, diplomatic reminders of past personality clashes and so on, to help the chairman to conduct the meeting both authoritatively and tactfully.

The chairman's agenda is particularly valuable for the chairman or chairwoman whose prestige or status lends respect to the position they occupy, but whose other commitments may prevent them from retaining the detailed knowledge which the secretary readily absorbs from dealing with the committee's administration.

In this respect the attentive secretary may make an important contribution to the smooth progress of the meeting, although it is only the chairman or chairwoman who will fully appreciate such indispensable 'behind-the-scenes' work.

Talking point

'Too much store is set by the traditional formal procedures by which some meetings are conducted. All too often they become the means by which the expert "bam-boozles" the layman.'

Specimen committee agenda

The National Institute of Computer Services Managers

NEWTOWN BRANCH

The next Committee Meeting of the Branch will take place on Wednesday 5th June 199- in the Shelley Room of the White Unicorn Hotel, 7.30 p.m. for 8.00 p.m.

Agenda

1. Apologies for absence

2. Minutes of the last meeting

3. Matters arising from the minutes

4. Publicity for new season's programme of events

5. Topic and speaker for meeting: Wednesday 4th March 199-

6. Visit to PC User Exhibition

7. Proposal to levy an admission charge at meetings:

    That an admission charge of £1.00 per head be levied by the Branch as an admission charge to meetings to cover the cost of coffee and biscuits and to contribute towards branch funds

    > Proposer: Mr J Pearson
    > Seconder: Mrs M Jenkins

8. Any other business

9. Date of next meeting

Chairman: A J Lucas   Vice-Chairman: R T Nicholas
Honorary Secretary: M T Wilkins
Honorary Treasurer: H Jones
Committee Members: E W Booth, F C Carpenter, M Jenkins,
                   G O F Nelson, J Pearson, K D Williams
Honorary Secretary's Address:
  'Appletree', Buxton Avenue, Newtown, Surrey, NE12 5AI
  Telephone: 'Business – Newtown 45712 Home – Newtown 46783

Specimen chairman's agenda

THE NATIONAL INSTITUTE OF COMPUTER SERVICES MANAGERS

Newtown Branch

CHAIRMAN'S AGENDA

For the Branch Committee Meeting of Wednesday
5 June, to be held in the Shelley Room of the
White Unicorn Hotel at 8.00 pm.   CHAIRMAN'S NOTES

1   Apologies For Absence:
      Mr Booth will be visiting his wife in hospital.
      Mr Williams hopes to come but will be late –
      visit to London.

2   Minutes Of The Last Meeting:
      Mr Carpenter has intimated that he was not
      categorically against the change of venue for
      Branch Committee Meetings, and that his remarks
      as they appear in the Minutes of the Last Meeting
      have been misconstrued.

3   Matters Arising:
      Item 6: The manager of the Blue Boar has con-
      firmed that the Committee Room of the Hotel
      will be available on the third Wednesday of each
      month from 1 August onwards.

      Excelsior Printing Ltd. have promised the New
      Season's programmes by Friday 26 June at the
      latest.

4   Publicity For New Season's Programme Of Events:
      There does not appear to be any likelihood of the
      Newtown Chronicle repeating last year's price for
      the display advertisement. I spoke to the adver-
      tising manager on the 'phone last Thursday.

5   Topic And Speaker For Meeting: Wednesday 4 March 199–
      Lord Grenville has written respectfully to decline
      our invitation to speak. Copy of letter attached.

6   Visit To PC User Exhibition, Olympia:
      The Olympia management have confirmed that they
      still have vacancies for parties on Saturday
      25 September. 15% discount on admission
      charges for parties over 25.

7   Proposal To Levy Admission Charge At Meetings:
      As you will recall, John Pearson proposed a
      similar motion at last year's June meeting.
      His motion was defeated last year 6:2.

      I understand Harold Jones is concerned about the
      Branch's ability to fund its activities in the
      programme for the New Season.

Special kinds of meetings

In addition to the regular and routine meetings, often held at monthly intervals, through which companies, public service departments and associations carry out their business, circumstances may arise which make it necessary to hold general or 'out-of-the-ordinary', termed 'extraordinary', meetings:

Annual General Meetings

Once a year all the members of an organisation meet to receive activity and financial reports and proposals for future developments and to elect or re-appoint officers.

Extraordinary General Meetings

Sometimes events occur which are sufficiently important and urgent to require the calling of a meeting of all members of an organisation, who may be asked to vote upon a particular matter or to grant special powers to an executive committee or board of directors to enable them to meet a specific contingency.

Creditors' meetings

When companies are unable to continue to trade by reason of insolvency, the official receiver will call a meeting of creditors to appoint a liquidator and arrange for the 'winding-up' of its activities.

Other types of special meeting include Shareholders' Class Meetings, Public Enquiries or occasional *ad hoc* meetings called to conduct business lying outside the normal routines and terms of reference of organisations.

Talking point

'If the cost of holding meetings was calculated more frequently, there would soon be fewer of them – and better ones at that!'

Examples of notices calling meetings

Postcard

Wessex Association Of Licensed Victuallers

NOTICE OF COMMITTEE MEETING

The next Committee Meeting will be held on:

Day: Wednesday   Date: 16th March 19 - -

Time: 8.00 p.m.   Venue: Dog and Duck, Hately.

I hope you will be able to attend.

signed:

Joe Kemp

Honorary Secretary

Electronic mail

```
Unclassified                    Page 1
          NOTICE OF MEETING

To:  All Section Heads
From:  Office Admin Manager

PURPOSE OF MEETING
Review budget allocations

Date 12 May 199- Venue - Conf Room
Start time: 1400
Finish: 1600
PLEASE BRING ALL BACK-UP DOCUMENTATION
```

A typical agenda for an Annual General Meeting of a voluntary society

1 Apologies for absence
2 Minutes of the last meeting
3 Matters arising
4 Chairman's report
5 Treasurer's report and presentation of accounts
6 Election of officers
7 (See note below)

Note: There are various ways in which an agenda for an Annual General Meeting may be concluded. For example, item 7 may take the form of, 'Revision of the constitution', or 'Vote of thanks to the president', who may be retiring. In other words, there may be specific business to conduct at any particular Annual General Meeting after more routine matters have been carried.

Some AGM agendas include items such as, 'Any other business' and 'Date of next meeting' to form the conclusion of the meeting. At other Annual General Meetings, however, 'Any other business' may be omitted and discussion and reporting limited to specific items such as those indicated above. Much depends upon the climate, precedents and the composition of the constitution in the case of voluntary organisations. The nature of the Articles of Association of a particular company will also influence items of business other than those required by its Articles or by statute.

In the case of Annual General Meetings of the companies governed by the Companies Acts, the usual business conducted includes the receiving of reports upon company progress and performance, the presentation of the company's accounts and dividends (if any are distributed) and the election or appointment of any directors if these are due.

Minutes

Producing the minutes of a meeting is probably the most demanding task assigned to the secretary or counterpart. In the course of their production, the secretary needs to bear in mind not only that they should be a scrupulous record of the meeting's business, but he or she should also remember that members will be scrutinising them for any potential slights or reported inaccuracies. In addition, the secretary must appreciate the possible future importance of any set of minutes which may be used as a reference or source of precedent, and also that, while members may exchange mutual insults in the heat of the moment, neither they nor the chairman will thank the secretary for a verbatim report transcribed into reported speech for successive generations of committee members to wonder at!

Why minutes are so important is not difficult to appreciate. They incorporate a number of important functions, essential to the effective working of any meeting or committee. Firstly, the work of a committee or working party is largely evolutionary. Principles are progressively established; rules made and later modified; procedures and attitudes are developed and precedents formed. An ongoing set of minutes, therefore, provides both a source of reference and authority for chairman and members alike. A half-forgotten change made to a constitution which is recorded in the minutes may become crucial at a future date. Without such a source of reference, the work of any committee would be grossly impeded by a return to first principles whenever controversial business arose.

Closely allied to the reference aspect of minutes is their value in other ways as a written record. Human nature being what it is, orally communicated decisions have a way of being 'misremembered' when the occasion suits. The written record ensures, however, that democratically made decisions cannot be 'overlooked' or unilaterally abrogated by either chairman or caucus. When changes to the rules are sought, the minutes ensure that they are made through established procedures.

The minutes also render each participant at a meeting accountable for his or her utterances. The sure knowledge that an outrageous attitude, surly obstructiveness or domineering interjections are likely to find their way into distributed minutes frequently serves to hold less considerate committee members in check. On the other hand, dissenting members are able to insist on having a particular point minuted either as a source for future reference or to indicate a strong disapproval of a matter at issue.

In some organisations the minutes record only the decision reached, and a veil is drawn over the preceding debate. Such minutes are 'resolution minutes', since a motion which is successfully carried in a meeting is thereafter referred to as a 'Resolution'. Such minutes may be variously expressed:

Resolution minutes:

```
RESOLVED: That the company's Eastbrook
branch be closed with immediate effect.
```

or

```
It was resolved that the company's
Eastbrook branch be closed with
immediate effect.
```

Alternatively, the chairman of a committee may prefer to have the interplay of various attitudes leading up to a decision included in the minutes. When the principal viewpoints of members are summarised in this way, the minutes are referred to as 'narrative minutes'.

Narrative minutes:

```
The chairman invited comment upon the
steep decline in the Eastbrook branch's
turnover during the past nine months.
Mr Weston felt that the branch had
always suffered a lack of sufficient
advertising support.  Mr Hopkins drew
attention to the parlous state of the
district as a result of urban renewal
work.
        While generally sympathetic, Mrs
Peters alluded to the rapid turnover
of staff - six sales assistants in
three months.  In citing the tendered
resignation of the branch manager, Mr
Watkins emphasised the gravity of the
situation.  In summarising, the chair-
man referred the meeting to company
policy, which clearly stated that
branch closure was an inevitable con-
sequence of continued trading losses.

By a majority of 7-3, it was decided
to close the Eastbrook branch with
immediate effect.
```

The reasons for preferring either resolution or narrative minutes may be briefly summarised as follows:

Resolution minutes

In meetings where it is important for participants to maintain a united front and accept collective responsibility (for example boards of directors or senior officers in public service) then a preference is understandable for a minutes' format which publishes decisions reached, while concealing from junior levels of the organisation strong disagreements or conflicts. In addition, the minutes of formal meetings required by statute may be more appropriately recorded by means of a brief 'resolution statement'. There are also convincing arguments for employing a format which is, above all, succinct and which relates only that information which is necessary to enable decisions to be implemented.

Narrative minutes

On the other hand, there are many types of meeting for which it would be both more appropriate and, indeed useful, to have a summary of the main points of a discussion which precedes the reaching of a decision. For example, when management decisions are being debated, a managing director may well prefer to have the approaches, attitudes and judgements of his or her executives set down in detail, so that individual accountability is recorded for given commitments or objections. In this way,

a 'profile' of reliability and soundness of judgement may be identified, even when a single dissenter is in a minority at a meeting but subsequently proved right by a future turn of events. Thus managers, through narrative minutes, are persuaded to make responsible utterances and considered judgements.

Where voluntary bodies are concerned, narrative minutes provide a valuable psychological boost. When committee members give up their spare time to attend meetings, the extent of their motivation and the degree of their commitment may be enhanced by seeing *their* names and synopses of *their* contributions to the work of the club or association and to the decision-making process.

It is much more difficult, of course, for a secretary to write narrative minutes which achieve a successful compromise between terseness and long-windedness, and which report accurately without giving offence or glossing over points of conflict or deep-rooted disagreement.

In some organisations a compromise is achieved between the brevity of resolution minutes and the detail of narrative minutes. Where it is particularly important for executive decisions to be implemented swiftly, and where there is infrequent contact among participants between meetings, then the format sometimes referred to as action minutes may be employed. Here the proceedings are reported briefly and the name of the person delegated to act upon a particular item is entered in a column, usually on the right-hand side of the minutes page, opposite the reference to the item.

Specimen minutes relayed to participants by a LAN office system (IBM's PROFS)

```
Unclassified                    Page 1

CHAIRMAN:              A GEORGE

SECRETARY:            J STREET

PURPOSE OF MEETING:   MANAGEMENT SUPPORT MEETING
                      - MINUTES

DATE OF MEETING:      5 APRIL 19XX

ATTENDEES:            A GEORGE
                      J STREET
                      M R SMITH

ABSENTEES:            NIL

Further actions were agreed as follows :

1. AREA 1

It was decided to  further explore the suggestion of
upgrading section 2.

              ACTION : M R SMITH

2. AREA 2

No actions to be taken required this month.


ALISON GEORGE
D.220  26/32
Personnel Dept
721-4943
HVTVM2 (AGEORGE)
```

Reproduced by kind permission of IBM (UK) Ltd

```
                    MINUTES:                              ACTION BY:




   5    MEMBERSHIP DRIVE

        The Chairman referred to the decline in branch
        membership during the past six months and asked
        the Membership Secretary for a report.  In view
        of the gravity of the situation, it was decided       John Watkins,
        to institute an intensive recruiting campaign         Membership
        including an open meeting and visits to local         Secretary
        companies.  The Membership Secretary, John
        Watkins, was asked to submit a detailed strategy
        and programme for the next meeting.
```

Action minutes

The advantage of such a format is that it is very clear who has undertaken or been asked to do what. When minutes are circulated, it is immediately clear to a participant whether he or she has been required to act in any way, or may read and file the minutes on an 'information only' basis. As the minutes format is overtly directional, however, its use is, perhaps, better restricted to those meetings within organisations where there is an obvious 'line authority'. If used in the context of voluntary organisations, there is a possibility of members feeling that they are being coerced and 'driven' rather than wooed and 'led' by the chairman.

> **Talking point**
>
> LAN calls meetings 'at the drop of a hat' — boon or plague?

Format

There are a number of different ways in which minutes are set out on paper. In some instances, the minutes are numbered and given headings which reproduce exactly the sequence and numbering of the items as they appear on the agenda. In some organisations, however, each minute is numbered consecutively from the very beginning of the first numbered minute of the first meeting onwards. Thus the thirteenth committee meeting may discuss items 261 to 268 on the agenda. In some institutions, particularly in local government, a system is adopted frequently which gives an item on the agenda a number such as, 3.0 or 4.0 or 5.0, followed by its title or heading. Points which are minuted under such headings are then referenced 3.1, 3.2, 3.3 etc.

In the absence of any single, universally adopted format, the following points should be borne in mind:

1 The sequence of items on the agenda should be followed.
2 There should be an intelligent use made of spacing and indentation to help the reader to identify item headings and follow referencing systems.
3 Reported statements should be clearly attributable to identified speakers.
4 Care should be taken to use the correct names of speakers or to identify speakers by their designations — chairman, treasurer, etc.
5 Where names are recorded in lists (for example, of those present) the precedence of officers should be followed by an alphabetical list of members.

> **Talking point**
>
> In meetings chairmen and members tend to deserve each other.

Specimen resolution minutes

MINUTES OF THE BOARD OF DIRECTORS MEETING

Held at the Registered Offices of Delta
Business Systems Ltd on Thursday 16th
July 199– at 10.30 a.m.

PRESENT: R K Baldwin (in the chair); P J Lewis, T A R Sheldon,
J T Talbot, H C Wilkinson, directors: N Cartwright,
Company Secretary

Apologies for absence were received from K T Frewin.

261 MINUTES OF THE LAST MEETING

The minutes of the last meeting, previously circulated, were
taken as read and signed as a true record.

262 MATTERS ARISING

There were no matters arising.

263 COMPANY LOGO, LIVERY AND CORPORATE IMAGE

It was resolved that the R P Silverton advertising agency be
appointed to develop new company logo and livery designs as
part of the company's policy to revitalise its corporate
image.

264 INTRODUCTION OF LAN/WAN SYSTEM AT HEAD OFFICE

It was resloved that a Local/Wide Area Network System be
introduced in the company's head office with effect from
1st September 199–.

265 RELOCATION OF SOUTH WEST REGIONAL OFFICE

It was resolved that the company's South West Regional Office
be relocated at 46–52 Tamar Road, Plymouth, Devon. The office
to be fully operational by 15th August 199–.

266 DATE OF NEXT MEETING

The date of the next meeting of the Board of Directors was
scheduled for Thursday 13th August 199–.

signed:

R K Baldwin

R K Baldwin
Managing Director

13th August 199–

Specimen narrative minutes

THE NATIONAL INSTITUTE OF COMPUTER SERVICE MANAGERS   NEWTOWN BRANCH

MINUTES

Committee Meeting of The National Institute
of Computer Services Managers, Newtown Branch,
held on Wednesday 5th June 199- in the Shelley
Room of the White Lion Hotel at 8.00 p.m.

PRESENT   A.J. Lucas, Chairman; M.T. Wilkins, Hon. Secretary; H. Jones
Hon. Treasurer; F.C. Carpenter; M. Jenkins; G.O.F. Nelson;
J. Pearson; K.D. Williams.

1. APOLOGIES FOR ABSENCE

Apologies for absence were received from R.T. Nicholas, Vice-Chairman, and
E.W. Booth.

2. MINUTES OF THE LAST MEETING

Mr. Carpenter drew attention to item 6 of the minutes of the last meeting,
Branch Committee Meetings – Change of Venue. He affirmed that his remarks
had been misinterpreted and that he was not categorically against the
proposed change of venue. By general consent it was agreed to substitute
'had strong reservations about' for 'was categorically against' in Item 6.

3. MATTERS ARISING

The Secretary reported that in connection with Item 6, the manager of the
Blue Boar was able to offer his hotel's committee room on the third Wednesday of each month from 1st August onwards. The chairman then requested
the Secretary to confirm acceptance of the offer by letter.

According to the latest information, the Secretary informed the meeting that
Excelsior Printing Ltd. had promised the new season's programmes by Friday
26th June. Mr. Nelson pointed out that it was essential for the programmes
to be available by that date for distribution purposes. The Chairman asked
Mr. Nelson to liaise with the Secretary to ensure that the promised delivery
date was met.

4. PUBLICITY FOR THE NEW SEASON'S PROGRAMME OF EVENTS

THe Chairman, in referring to the branch's advertisements placed with the
Newtown Chronicle, confirmed that the cost of such advertising was certain
to increase. The Treasurer expressed his concern at any prospective increase
in advertising expenditure in view of the agreed increases for speakers'
expenses and mail-shots to members. After a wide-ranging discussion of the
branch's expenditure on publicity, it was decided to place an order for six
advertisements with the Newtown Chronicle instead of the customary seven to
offset the anticipated increase in charges.

5. TOPIC AND SPEAKER FOR MEETING: WEDNESDAY 4th MARCH 199-

The Chairman asked the Secretary to read to the meeting the letter received from Lord Grenville, who tendered his apologies for having to decline the invitation to speak on 4th March. Suggestions were then requested for possible alternative speakers. Mrs Jenkins proposed that the Rt. Hon. Charles Hawkins, M.P. for Newtown East be approached, but it was generally agreed that M.P.s were subject to last-minute, unavoidable commitments in Westminster. Mr. Williams suggested Mr. John Farnham, Computer Services Manager for Global Computers, an acknowledged expert in developments in computer language. In the absence of any further suggestions, the Chairman requested the Secretary to write to Mr. Farnham inviting him to speak at the 4th March Meeting.

6. VISIT TO PC USER EXHIBITION, OLYMPIA

The Secretary relayed to the meeting the confirmation from the Olympia management regarding existing vacancies for parties on 25th September 199-. A discount of 15% was offered on admission charges for parties over 25 in number. Strong interest was expressed by all present, and the Chairman asked the Secretary to order 30 tickets at the party rate. Mr. Williams offered to arrange the hiring of a motor-coach and was requested to report progress at the next meeting.

7. PROPOSAL TO LEVY AN ADMISSION CHARGE AT MEETINGS

The Chairman referred the meeting to Mr. Pearson's proposal on the agenda for the meeting. Before asking Mr. Pearson to speak on his motion, the Chairman reminded the meeting that the subject of admission charges to branch meetings had arisen during the previous season. It was a difficult matter and the financial status of the branch merited that it be re-examined. Mr. Pearson emphasised the rise in the cost of meetings and referred to the minutes of the meeting of Wednesday 17th October 199-, which recorded his prediction that events would prove him right about the need for an admission charge. He was advocating a levy of £1:00, which he did not think would prove financially embarrassing to members and would not, in his opinion, result in falling attendances. Opposing the motion, Mr. Nelson felt strongly that members already paid a sufficiently large sum in annual membership fees to the Institute and that branch meetings should be funded from the allocation made to Institute Branches from Computer House. Mrs. Jenkins reminded the meeting that she had opposed the introduction of the charge when it was last debated, but felt that such a levy was the only fair way of keeping the branch solvent during the coming season. The Treasurer echoed Mrs. Jenkins' concern and stated that he was in favour of the motion. In view of the expression of conflicting views, the Chairman asked for a vote on the motion before the meeting. The motion was carried by 5 votes to 3.

8. ANY OTHER BUSINESS

Mr. Carpenter raised the matter of branch reports submitted to the Institute Journal. He had noted that for the past two quarters, no mention had been made of Newtown branch activities. The Chairman promised to look into the matter and to report back.

Mrs. Jenkins drew the meeting's attention to the new magazine, 'Computer Monthly'. She was personally acquainted with the editor and was able to recommend it to members without reservation.

9. DATE OF NEXT MEETING

The next Committee Meeting was scheduled for Wednesday 3rd July 199-.

Using reported speech

Reported speech, sometimes called indirect speech, is the name given to the kind of writing that reports what someone else has said. It is essential to master the rules of reported speech in order to compose correct narrative minutes.

'I am sorry to arrive late for the meeting, my shuttle flight was delayed', said the Sales Manager (Scotland). DIRECT SPEECH

The Sales Manager (Scotland) said that he was sorry to arrive late for the meeting. His shuttle flight had been delayed. CLOSE RENDERING IN REPORTED SPEECH

The Sales Manager (Scotland) apologised for his late arrival due to his shuttle flight's delay. ABBREVIATED REPORTED SPEECH FORM

Rule one: changing personal pronouns
'I, we, you' become 'he, she, they'.
'I am . . .' becomes 'He said he was . . .'
'was delayed . . .' becomes 'had been delayed . . .'

Just as first and second persons are transposed to the third person, so tenses of verbs shift back into the past, because by the time the minutes are being composed the meeting has become a past event.

Rule two: the tenses of verbs

The tense of the verb in direct speech goes 'one further back' in reported speech:

I write	he/she wrote
I am writing...	he/she was writing
I wrote...	he/she had written/wrote
I was writing	he/she had been writing
I have written...	he/she had written
I have been writing	he/she had been writing
I had written...	he/she had written (cannot go further back)

Notice that future tenses become conditional:

I shall write	he/she would write
I shall be writing...	he/she would be writing
I shall have written...	he/she would have written

The conditional is needed because it is an intention to write and we don't know whether 'he' actually did!

Rule three: the distancing effect

When people use direct speech – say in a meeting – the event is happening 'here and now'. When the meeting is reported at a later date, however, the discussion is in the past and took place 'there and then'. For this reason, a number of words and expressions need to be adjusted:

today ... that day, now ... then, here ... there, this ... that, these ... those, tomorrow ... the next/following day, yesterday ... the previous day

Rule four: conveying the tone of the direct speech

If the reported speech writer is not very careful, the reporting may easily slip into a dull 'he said, she said, he said, she said', so it is important to vary the words that introduce the reported speech:

urged that, asked whether, insisted that, suggested that etc.

Talking point

A good meetings secretary is often measured by the quality and fluency of his or her minute writing.

Terminology of meetings

The following list includes some of the principal terms used in meetings. This list is by no means exhaustive, however, and you should use it as a basis for your own, more extensive check-list of important technical terms relating to meetings.

Ad hoc   from Latin, meaning 'for the purpose of', as for example, when a sub-committee is set up to organise a works outing

Adjourn   to hold a meeting over until a later date

Advisory   providing advice or suggestion, not taking action

Agenda   a schedule of items drawn up for discussion at a meeting

AGM   Annual General Meeting; all members are usually eligible to attend

Apologies   excuses given in advance for inability to attend a meeting

Articles of Association   rules required by Company Law which govern a company's activities

Bye-laws   rules regulating an organisation's activities

Chairman   leader or person given authority to conduct a meeting

Chairman's Agenda   based upon the committee agenda, but containing explanatory notes

Collective responsibility   a convention by which all committee members agree to abide by a majority decision

Committee   a group of people usually elected or appointed who meet to conduct agreed business and report to a senior body

Consensus   agreement by general consent, no formal vote being taken

Constitution   set of rules governing activities of voluntary bodies

Convene   to call a meeting

Executive having the power to act upon taken decisions

Extraordinary meeting a meeting called for all members to discuss a serious issue affecting all is called an Extraordinary General Meeting; otherwise a non-routine meeting called for a specific purpose

Ex officio given powers or rights by reason of office. For example a trades union convenor may be an ex officio member of a works council

Honorary post a duty performed without payment – Honorary Secretary

Information, point of the drawing of attention in a meeting to a relevant item of fact

Lobbying a practice of seeking members' support before a meeting

Minutes the written record of a meeting; resolution minutes record only decisions reached, while narrative minutes provide a record of the decision-making process

Motion the name given to a 'proposal' when it is being discussed at a meeting

Mover one who speaks on behalf of a motion

Nem. con. from Latin, literally, 'no one speaking against'

Opposer one who speaks against a motion

Order, point of the drawing of attention to a breach of rules or procedures

Other business either items left over from a previous meeting, or items discussed after the main business of a meeting

Proposal the name given to a submitted item for discussion (usually written) before a meeting takes place

Proxy literally, 'on behalf of another person' – 'a proxy vote'

Resolution the name given to a 'motion' which has been passed or carried; used after the decision has been reached

Secretary committee official responsible for the internal and external administration of a committee

Secret ballot a system of voting in secret

Sine die from Latin, literally, 'without a day', that is to say indefinitely, e.g. 'adjourned sine die'

Standing committee a committee which has an indefinite term of office

Seconder one who supports the 'proposer' of a motion or proposal by 'seconding' it

Treasurer committee official responsible for its financial records and transactions

Unanimous all being in favour

Vote, casting when two sides are deadlocked a chairman may record a second or 'casting vote' to ensure a decision is made

---

Talking point

'The best committee is a committee of one!'

Organising a conference

Helping with the planning and organisation of a conference is undoubtedly one of the most challenging yet rewarding roles you can undertake, since it will almost certainly require all your accumulated skill and expertise!

Both private and public sector organisations mount conferences, on a local, regional, national or international basis, for a variety of reasons:

● To share knowledge and attitudes about a newly emerged topic – like information technology in the office.
● To be given an expert updating on a given theme by national/international experts.
● To evolve a response to a particular topic as a group of specialists.

Indeed, the reasons for mounting conferences are many and varied, but all involve bringing together a large group of people – as delegates – to listen to expert speakers and to take part in arising discussions and forums.

Increasingly, conferences are taking place, both nationally and internationally, by means of telecommunications links or hookups. The following systems are now available to conference organisers:

Audio telephone conferencing National and international telephone systems are able to interlink say, 20 executives of a multinational company so that each can hear the others clearly and converse with them, as if in the same room. Such a facility can make extensive savings in the costs of bringing such executives physically together.

Audio-visual teleconferencing Sight is added to sound by transmitting television signals (via landline, submarine cable, or satellite) so that while conversing, executives can also see each other, and any item or visual material being presented or examined. Moreover, video tapes and clips may be introduced for all to view and comment upon. Telecommunications companies are now able to set up conference studios on employers' premises for such national or international teleconferences.

Computer workstation conferencing The technology which enables digitised signals to be transmitted through telephone lines has made possible the interlinking of remotely located computer workstations. Here, a PC user may interact with a central coordinator who sends out information to a 'circle' of users – for example displayed screens of written data. Each circle member may key in comments and responses viewable by all, or may 'converse' with an individual participant of the conference circle in privacy.

This particular conferencing/communications system is proving a popular means of supplying open learning and training, while hobbyists use it as a means of keeping in touch and accessing a central bulletin board of information.

Interactive software conferencing A leading computer manufacturer has recently launched a system through which a PC user can dial up a colleague (or colleagues) across the world and, with contact established, transmit a screen-displayed, software application – say a graph, chart or document – which may be updated, modified or altered by any of the participants, as they converse over the phone! This particular break-through is proving a boon to designers, engineers and scientists all over the world.

The main stages of organising a conference

The chart on page 307 illustrates the main stages of conference organisation and provides a series of checklists which the team of organisers will draw up and action during each phase.

The 'Go' decision

Deciding to mount a conference is no light matter and the decision-makers will need to ensure they have the commitment and the financial and administrative resources to make it a success. A poorly organised conference will mar an organisation's corporate image.

Usually, organisations mounting conferences hope for a return on the investment made, such as making a profit, but the return is often less tangible though equally important – improved awareness of the firm's activities and products, enhanced public relations, acceptance as a leader in a specialist field, etc.

Whatever the motivation to undertake the highly complex and demanding task of planning and running a successful conference, the essential ingredients from the outset are:

● Creating a skilled, communicative team.
● Devising and keeping to a conference project plan.
● Assigning clearly understood and accepted responsibilities to team members.

Strategic planning

At the beginning of the planning period, the team must make a series of important decisions which will affect the eventual success of the conference:

Theme What will the conference be about? Are its topics likely to attract sufficient delegates by being topical and interesting?

Venue When, where and for how long will the conference take place? How long is too long? Is the proposed venue (location) easy to reach, regionally, nationally or internationally?

Clientele What kinds of delegate will the conference attract? Will the conference's proposed topics and speakers prove sufficiently appealing?

Speakers What sorts of speaker can the team interest? What fees might they require? Can they be afforded?

Extra features What supportive features should be included? A lavish evening social programme? Tours and shopping trips for delegates' spouses? Exhibitions and displays?

Costing and budgeting

Crucial to the success of the conference is the creation of an effective budget. Organisers usually approach this aspect by designing a break-even chart. Such a chart indicates:

The amount of money which will be spent on fixed costs: hire of conference suite, speakers' fees, early advertising, hire of AVA, etc.

The amount of money which will be spent on variable costs: additional hotel accommodation, additional covers ordered for delegates' meals, extra delegates' packs and printed conference papers, etc.

The amount of income which each confirmed booking generates.

On the basis of charting such financial information, it is possible to project accurately how many conference places at, say, £200 per day (fully residential) and how many places at £120 per day (conference only) need to be sold in order to recover outgoings. Where income and outgoings meet is called the 'break-even point'. As sales climb beyond it, a profit is made.

Here it is also worth noting that conference organisers frequently seek commercial sponsors – say, equipment manufacturers, publishers or government agencies – to sponsor the conference by donating significant sums to offset costs. They, too, expect a return on their investment in terms of

Organising a national/international conference

A checklist of major items and their place in the Conference Project Plan

Major decisions:
When? Where? What?
Who speaks? Who comes?
What will it cost?

Vital deadlines to be met
Speakers secured programme designed and mailed bookings secured: budget finalised

Attention to detail counts!
Meeting speakers' needs ensuring delegates comfort anticipating wants and needs providing good communications

Week: 0 — 1 — 5 — 8 — 25 — 48 — 51 — 52 — 55

'Go' Decision	Strategic Planning	Costing and conference budget	Promotion and sales drive — Finalising speakers and programme	Promotion and sales drive — Services to organise	Detail work run-up	Conference takes place	Post-conference
Form conference planning team and identify roles: • Chairman • Marketing • Delegates coordinator • Hotel and catering, etc	Decide: • Theme • Dates • Duration • Venue • Clientele/target delegates Map out: • Target speakers • Topics • Supportive provisions • Exhibition • Book/equipment display • Social programme	Identify cost centres and set fees for delegates • Fees of speakers • Cost of hotel accommodation • Hire of suite(s) • Catering Specialist services: • AVA/communications • Decor • Transport • Reprography Marketing and publicity: • Advertising • Programme printing • Delegates' packs Construct a break-even chart	Produce and mail first programme Obtain confirmations from invited speakers and: • Photographs • Talk synopses • Curriculum vitaes Market conference: • Advertisements • Mailshots • Press releases • Articles • Letters to VIPs • Phone calls • Free entries in specialist journals Set up conference administration unit and coordinator Devise systems to process bookings	Produce and mail final programme Confirm provisional venue and hotel bookings Hire: • AVA specialists • Transport – coaches/minibuses • Catering specialists • Decor/signs/logos/backdrops specialists Design and print day-programmes and delegate packs Checks arrival times of speakers and VIPs	Prepare venue: Registration/enquiry desk • Seating • Podium • AVA equipment • Cloaks • Press room • Speakers' quiet room • Car parking • Dining facilities Finalise: • Reception • Procedures • Name badges • Parking vouchers • Seating plans • Social programme for spouses • Escorts for VIPs • Mobile phones for organisers • Rehearsals for speakers (identify internal 'stand-by' speakers)	'Think!' • Patrol • Monitor • Observe • Anticipate • Back-up • Maintain PR profile Look after: • Speakers • VIPs • Delegates	Produce: • Conference accounts • Pay bills • Write thank you letters • Hold team debriefing meeting • Produce conference report and mail/publish it

publicity and advertising of their sponsorship.

The principal costs centres to be considered are displayed on the chart on page 307 and include: Speakers' fees, hotel accommodation, catering, advertising and publicity costs, hiring of venue and transport, paper and printing and conference staffing costs.

Break-even chart

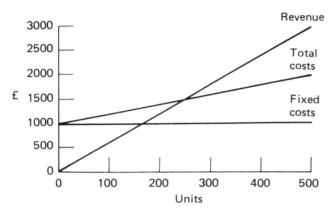

Profit at 500 units of output £1000.
Break-even point 250 units.

Promotion and sales drive

Often the fine tuning of the conference programme is taking place during the early stages of the sales drive. Thus a first draft programme will sometimes include the phrase 'speaker to be announced' against a particular day and time. Needless to say, it is crucial to secure top-quality speakers early to ensure a successful sales drive.

Typically, conferences are advertised in specialist magazines and journals which the targeted delegates are likely to see. In addition, mailshots of publicity literature and proposed programmes are sent to likely participants. Frequently large volume mailshots are needed as a response rate of three per cent is typical, of whom half may actually take part. Additionally, certain potential delegates may receive personal letters of invitation, especially if they are VIPs and/or important decision-makers. The advertising account for an international conference will often amount to several thousand pounds.

Once the conference begins to be marketed and applications invited, a central unit needs to be set up to handle bookings and to act as a communications centre. At this stage, ensuring that hotel accommodation can be extended as demand grows is essential, since it is imprudent to book too many rooms too early. Many hotels operate a flexible system, provided that bookings are made sufficiently early – a central factor in conference planning.

A typical conference application form for day delegates to an international conference will communicate clear indications of days to be attended, whether or not social events are desired and the name, address and job designation of the applicant, with home and office telephone numbers. Note too the provision of a special conference telephone number (so as not to overburden normal incoming CABX lines) and the conference fax number – essential for international conferences.

Hiring of conference services

Provisional bookings will have been made early in the conference planning sequence and need to be confirmed some twelve to eight weeks before the start date. These include:

● The specialist company which will provide the conference audio-visual aids, such as back-projection, TV, lighting and sound, OHP slide projection and screen, microphones – lapel, multi-directional and roving. Such companies also stage-manage the speakers' presentations.

Videoconferencing

- The firm which will provide drapes, flowers and decorations for conference foyer, suite and reception areas.

- The catering company which will provide refreshments, lunches, post-conference cocktail receptions and banquets, etc. They will need updating on confirmed numbers of covers and any special dietary requirements as the conference nears.

- Printers may need to be supplied with detailed day programmes which include photographs and biographies of speakers as well as synopses of their lectures.

- Transport and drivers may need to be hired to convey delegates between hotels and the conference venue.

- The conference venue for approximate numbers, facilities and equipment needed, notices and signs required, fire regulations, etc.

The run-up to the conference

As the first day of the conference draws near, the pace quickens. During the last two preceding weeks, many practical tasks need to be carried out. Some may seem small but all are crucial. For instance, ensuring that staff running exhibitions have sufficient power points, and have not been forgotten in catering arrangements. Similarly, cloakroom facilities need to be considered and sufficient provided to avoid bottlenecks and late starts to lunches and so on. A good conference team tends to coordinate the final stages in terms of:

- Attending to speakers' needs

- Ensuring delegates' comfort and enjoyment

- Looking after VIPs

- Ensuring good press coverage

- Planning for easy access and smooth movement around the conference venue

- Ensuring the registration system will work effectively so that delegates are 'processed' quickly and numbers checked for lunches, etc. Here a computerised database system is extremely helpful, which is used from initial booking onwards. Also, different coloured day lapel stickers or badges are invaluable in helping organisers to identify speakers, VIPs, residential delegates, etc.

Post-conference tasks

Clearly there is important work to do in dismantling equipment and in tidying the venue. Also, once all bills are received and paid, a set of accounts needs to be produced which details sources and totals of income and also the various expenditure headings. Thus a residual profit (or loss) will be calculated.

In addition, it is important to ensure that visiting speakers are hospitably seen to their departure points and that they promptly receive fees and letters of thanks.

Finally, it is important to hold a conference debriefing meeting to analyse outcomes and to learn from experience.

Conference administrative documents

Set out below is a checklist of the typical documents and administrative schedules which are used in administering a conference. Make sure you know the key features of content and format for each:

- Conference planning schedules

- Draft budgets, interim reports and final conference accounts

- Accounts rendered for goods and services supplied

- Invitation letters to speakers and follow-up correspondence or faxed documents

- Form letter to speakers requesting: photograph, biographic notes and synopsis of talk

- Form mailshot letter to advertise conference

- Display advertisement copy and publicity material

- Conference draft programme, final programme and day programmes

- Delegates' application forms, maps and factsheets

- Letters/forms to book hotel accommodation

- Computer printouts of confirmed delegates (regularly updated)

- Hiring contracts/agreements for conference services (book photographer if required)

- Draft menus, seating plans, layouts

- Listing of confirmed VIPs

- Draft/final press releases, articles, features

- Delegates' wallet documents – day programmes, talk summaries, handouts, notepads and any promotional items as 'giveaways'

- Social programme itineraries and details

- Written briefings to conference organising staff

- Name badges, car parking tickets, place cards

- Conference reports: draft and final

- Post-conference letters of thanks

How to give an effective oral presentation

A significant trend in the use of IT-centred systems and software of recent years has been the attention given to the delivery of both text-based and orally transmitted messages.

We have already examined the immense impact of DTP, graphics software and laser printers on the production and presentation of printed documents.

It is now equally important to study and acquire the techniques of giving an effective oral presentation. The following section will provide you with a series of essential tips and guidelines to develop and expand.

Guidelines on effective oral presentation supported by audio visual aids

Simply, there are three distinct phases to any successful oral presentation:

1 Preparation → 2 Delivery → 3 Follow-up

1 Preparation

Clarifying: aims, outcomes and the audience profile

Clarify your brief – what, exactly, are you supposed to be achieving through the presentation – informing, persuading, enthusing, analysing, influencing – or a mixture of these?

Who will be present at the presentation? Senior decision-makers? Peer-group colleagues? Support staff? Clients? Members of the public?

Will they be: technical experts, know the jargon, be fully familiar with in-house procedures and acronyms, etc? Or will they be from outside, laymen, unfamiliar with your organisation's operations?

So, how will you structure and pitch your presentation, so as to carry your audience with you at all times and to keep their interest and attention?

Fail to consider these vital aspects and your presentation is likely to flop even before you start to plan it in detail!

Gathering the raw material

At the very outset, decide upon – and stick to – a clear title for your presentation, eg 'The Impact of the 1992 EEC Single Market On Company Exports'

This title must be explicit, short and precise, for you will use it as a yardstick to measure the priority and relevance of the data you collect for your presentation.

The next stage is to collect the raw material of the presentation: existing documents – reports, memos, charts, statistics, photographs, cuttings, video-tape sequences as well as personal notes, ideas, jottings, etc, on the given subject.

Imposing The Structure

Now you are ready to impose your own structure and sequence of points on your chosen theme. This will entail your perusing all your data and sub-dividing it into related groupings. These groupings will then need to be placed into a running order – usually on the tried and tested sequence:

INTRODUCTION → DEVELOPMENT AND EXAMPLE (OR ARGUMENT/COUNTER ARGUMENT) → SUMMARY → CONCLUSION → (RECOMMENDATIONS)

It helps to detail the main points of each of these phases on draft paper (or on WP software which is more flexible) so as to reduce them to the main factors and to arrow in where an AVA illustration will be used.

In fact, a major reason for carrying out this stage systematically is so that you absorb the data you will deliver largely from memory!

Selecting the AVA illustrations

You now need to decide upon the AVA items you will employ and to ensure you have their design and production well in hand in good time. Good AVA support material is:

'bang up-to-date'; eye-catching, completely relevant, brief in display, quick, simple and easy to absorb – in fact, memorable!

AVA media

AVA media commonly employed are: overhead projection view foils with coloured contents; 35mm colour slides used with a carousel and advance button (sometimes also with an audio-taped commentary); large TV-monitor- screened data from linked computer or video-recorder; paper flip-charts and coloured pens (for use during delivery) audio-taped sequences; whiteboard/colour pen use (now with electronic print-out facility!); printed hand-outs, models, samples, exhibits etc. for handing round and keeping.

Always remember: a single effective visual aid is worth hundreds of droning, repetitive spoken words!

2 Delivery

'Sussing Out' The Location

It is crucial to inspect the venue of the presentation a day or so beforehand in order to check out: Seating: will everyone be able to see you and your AVAs? Lighting and AVA- delivery equipment: is it properly installed? Is it working properly? Can people at the back see your OHPs and TV screens clearly and easily? Are your handouts already on seats or in wallets or ready to give out? Is the public address/microphone system working properly? Is there suitable ventilation and temperature to stop people going to sleep? Are refreshments to hand?

Careful attention to such points marks the difference between a professional and embarrassingly amateurish performance

Cue – cards and prompts

At the heart of all successful deliveries lies the ability of the speaker to talk fluently (and not to read a prepared text) with only occasional reference to notes. Eye-contact with the audience and NVC gesture unrestricted by constant reference to pages of text etc are vital ingredients of an effective oral presentation. Presenters therefore assemble their main points on sets of small cards on which are printed in large bold capitals cue words or phrases only, which trigger a sequence of points in the presenter's mind, like:

> EEC EXISTING TARIFFS

or, CURRENT COMPANY TURNOVER BY COUNTRY:

> WEST GERMANY: £3.5 MILLION P.A. etc

AVA prompts are also included on such cards:

> SHOW OHP 9: PIE CHART OF COMPANY EEC EXPORTS

(*Note*: some speakers prefer to use sequenced points on A4 sheets and employ different colours and highlighters, while top presenters have access to text charts, diagrams rolled forward on autocue equipment invisible to the audience.)

Pace, pitch and time

Many presentations suffer from poor pacing, pitch and timing. Rehearsal and experience help. Basically, the speaker must keep watching for audience reaction. Leaning forward with interest, good eye-contact, yawning, fidgeting and so on are typical signs to look out for and to react to. The presenter should respond promptly by changing pace, voice-pitch and emphasis, or by telling a joke or whatever **other** device to regain interest and attention.

The presenter's 'third eye' is constantly checking the clock! In fact many good presenters mark scheduled time lapses on their cue cards or sheets to aid them in keeping to a delivery schedule. It is always better to cut a presentation back 'on the hoof' in order to finish promptly.

Questions and answers

No audience likes the presentation experience to be entirely passive where they are concerned. And so a period for taking and answering questions is essential to an effective presentation. Good speakers anticipate likely 'hot potato' questions and have prepared their ground well in advance.

Follow-up activities

Some speakers deliberately withhold their handouts and summaries, etc until after their presentation. It can be self-defeating to start to address an audience which is busy perusing the handouts you have just distributed!

Notes, cards, AVA material and equipment should all be safely collected and filed away – for the next time; the dais and location must always be left tidy as a courtesy to the next speaker or user. Sales circulars, questionnaires or other follow-up communications must be despatched promptly, as well as any 'thank you' notes to those who have assisted you.

Self-assessment questions

1 Are you clear about the different types of meeting currently called and the distinctions between the various types of procedures and structures which they feature?

2 Are you sure you know what types of meeting are suited to what sorts of organisational contexts and desired outcomes?

3 If you had to chair a meeting or act as a committee's secretary or treasurer, would you now know what would be expected of you?

4 If required, could you now produce meetings documentation according to established conventions and layouts? If not, which documents do you need to revise?

5 If asked, could you now make an effective contribution to organising a conference?

6 Are you now confident in your ability to design and deliver an AVA-supported oral presentation?

If you are still unsure about any of the above questions, make time now to revise and strengthen your weak points!

Summary of main points

1 All types of meeting share common features: goals, outcomes, interests, deadlines.

2 Various types of meeting take place across a spectrum of formality-informality including statutory, executive, briefing, advisory, managerial, shareholders, task-force, brainstorming.

3 Meetings are called to: create policy, devise strategies, make decisions; to approve actions, to give advice, to consult, to carry out tasks requested from above.

4 Committees are structured in ways reflecting their roles: executive, advisory, standing, membership, *ad hoc*, sub- and so on.

5 A committee's officers normally comprise: chairman, vice-chairman, secretary, treasurer, full member, coopted member with any other specified posts such as 'membership secretary', social secretary.

6 The procedure governing the conduct of meetings may derive from: company law, local government regulations, written voluntary constitutions, in-house company procedures, custom and practice.

7 Many meetings are called on a regular basis, say, monthly, and follow a cycle of administration: notice of meeting, agenda setting and despatch, devising of chairman's agenda, collating of correspondence, holding of meeting, production and distribution of minutes.

8 The functions of the officer roles of a committee are: chairman to supervise and lead; secretary to administer and service; treasurer to maintain financial records and reports; vice-chairman to deputise as required.

9 The documentation of meetings follows established formats and conventions: notices formally call meetings, agendas prompt and brief the committee and chairman, minutes faithfully record the business and decisions reached, proposals formally word an item to be discussed.

10 Minutes are set down in a variety of forms according to convention: resolution record only decisions reached; narrative summarise all debate; action identify tasks and 'doers' of tasks.

11 Reported speech sets out narrative minutes in third person and distanced past tenses.

12 A terminology of meetings exists which includes many Latinate abbreviations: *ad hoc, sine die, nem con,* etc which must be memorised.

13 Organising a conference requires intensive planning in these stages: go decision, strategic planning, costing and budgeting, promoting and speaker-finding, programme design, delegate services, delivery supervision, post-conference debriefing.

14 Effective oral presentations with AVA support requires detailed preparation and profiling of audience's expectations, pre-delivery checks of venue, cue-based 'natural' delivery: pace, pitch and time, judicious insertion of AVA illustrations, timely closure and prompt follow-ups.

Activities and assignments _____

Quick review quiz

1 What factors are common to all meetings?

2 How many different types of meeting can you recall?

3 Explain the difference between executive and advisory committees.

4 List the most common reasons for calling a meeting.

5 Define the following terms: *ad hoc*, standing, sub-, auditor, constitution, bye-law, standing orders, coopted, quorate.

6 List the activities a secretary undertakes during the administrative cycle of monthly committee meetings.

7 Define briefly the responsibilities of the:

chairman,
secretary,
treasurer.

8 List the set of documents which are normally involved in meetings' administration.

9 Explain the difference between a member's and chairman's agenda. How does the agenda for an Annual General Meeting differ from others?

10 List the items which go to make up a conventional agenda.

11 What ways exist for referencing agenda items?

12 Explain the conventions for setting out:

narrative,
resolution,
action minutes.

Describe the types of meeting each best suits.

13 What is

a) a proposal,
b) a resolution,
c) a point of order,
d) a point of information?

What characterises their formats?

14 What are the main rules for writing in reported speech?

15 Explain what the following terms mean:

collective responsibility,
ex officio,
nem con,
sine die,
casting vote,
proxy,
ultra vires.

16 How has IT extended the facilities of international conferences?

17 List the major phases of organising a successful conference.

18 What documents can you recall which are commonly produced in the process of organising a conference?

19 Explain the main stages of giving an effective oral presentation.

20 Describe briefly the AVA resources commonly available to support an oral presentation and what each supplies.

21 What sort of checks would you make of your venue prior to delivering your presentation?

Meetings: simulation assignments

Notice

1 The chairman of the Middletown Traders' Association has recently expressed to you his dissatisfaction with the format of notices sent to committee members to call regular monthly meetings. Several members of the committee have expressed their concern at taking no part in the compilation of committee meeting agendas, despite their attempts to submit agenda items. The chairman has therefore asked you to design a suitable notice format for discussion at the next meeting. The committee has met for some years in the Small Committee Room of the Middletown Town Hall, High Street, Middletown, Midshire ML13 2AC.

Agendas

2 'Ah, Jim, come on in. I've been trying to sort out the items for inclusion in the agenda for the next committee meeting. I saw that written proposal

from Jack Burton about changing the date for the Christmas Dance from Saturday 14th December to the 21st. Jack reckons there'll be more of a Christmas spirit nearer the day. You'd better put his proposal into the appropriate format. The seconder is Mrs Bignall. Then there's the complaints about the club-room bar prices. We must deal with that. Oh, and while I remember, I believe you said we've had a number of letters from fixture secretaries asking for dates for next summer's first team cricket fixtures. We ought to settle that one. As you know, I couldn't persuade Ken Palmer not to resign as Hon. Treasurer. You've had four nominations? Yes, well, it's most unfortunate but we can't afford to let the situation drag on. I'll ask Ken meanwhile to act as a caretaker. I think that's about it. Could you draft a committee members' agenda? You'd better give some thought to the running order. I'd help out but I'm late for a section meeting. Thanks a lot!'

As Honorary Secretary of the Lifelong Insurance Co. Ltd Sports & Social Club, Ashburnley Crescent, Richmond, Surrey SU16 4TJ, draft the agenda asked for. The meeting is on Thursday 18 September 199- at 8.00 pm in the Clubhouse Committee Room.

3 The chairman, Mr Peter Turner of the Lifelong Insurance Co. Ltd Sports and Social Club has just telephoned you to say that he won't be able to take the chair at tomorrow's committee meeting. He has asked Mrs Kean, vice-chairman, to take the chair in his absence. As Mrs Kean is not as familiar with the background to the items on the agenda as he is, Mr Turner has asked you to prepare a chairman's agenda for her. The following are the points for her to keep in mind which Mr Turner has suggested:

J Burton proposal – problem of changing band booking – has Gordon Wilson already booked the Post House Hotel ballroom? Jack tends to go on at length when he warms to his theme.
    Upset Miss Grainger at the last meeting – her suggestions to form Ladies' Soccer Team.
    Bar prices – main source of funds to run club-house – recent poor attendance by members mid-week – charges up by brewery – check Ken Palmer.
    Letters from cricket clubs – who is hon. sec. of cricket team? Harry Fielding will know – job needs delegating.
    Ken Palmer – resignation – tricky – have been criticisms of Ken's record-keeping – Harry Fielding keen to have office – not nominated – Ken fed up with sniping.

Correspondence

4 At the Lifelong Sports and Social Club committee meeting it was decided not to offer Albion Engineering Sports Club a cricket fixture next summer. After last season's match your clubhouse was left in a damaged state; repairs cost £365.00. Several ladies also complained of the language which was used during the evening at the bar.
As Honorary Secretary, you have been asked to write to the Cricket Club Secretary, declining their offer of a fixture. Coincidentally, Albion Engineering Ltd is a client of Lifelong Insurance!

Report

5 As a development of the Lifelong committee meeting's discussion of the Christmas Dance, it was decided to form an *ad hoc* sub-committee to arrange it under the chairmanship of Jack Burton. As the sub-committeee's secretary, you have been asked to draft a report on the arrangements for submission at the next meeting.

Public address, narrative minutes, meeting simulation

6 As Chairman of the Laystone College Students' Association, you are currently preparing your Chairman's Report for the forthcoming Annual General Meeting. The following are some of the events and topics you have to report upon. You may add others if you wish:

The number of active members has declined during the year – attendance at social events has generally declined.

Criticisms have been levelled at the committee – lack of decent events – programme curtailed – too autocratic.

But – members do not offer help or services – all is left to committee – Social Secretary – organised three discos singlehanded. Three resignations from committee during year – pressure of work – personality clashes.

Liaison with students' associations of neighbouring colleges – three meetings – little progress on joint approach to local accommodation problems – joint social committee formed to plan inter-college social events – starts next session.

Events: Christmas Dance – great success – thanks to Principal and staff for support; Sport – Ladies' Basketball Team won District League – Men came second in Regional Cup – Soccer Team hampered by lack of practice – won 5, lost 6, drew 2; Pram Race – collected £137.00 for charity – winners – Chris Parker and Susan Curtis; Summer Leavers' Ball – hope as good turnout as for Christmas – tickets still available from Social Secretary.

Financial situation – leave to Treasurer but say balance of £434.28 – thanks to Treasurer and Committee's good management.

Future – emphasise unless better support many facilities and events will die – which now take for granted – questionnaire being sent out to ask for suggestions for preferred future programme.

Thanks – thank all college staff and committee for help during year – too many to name – wish success to successor.

a) Tape-record or write out in direct speech the chairman's report based on the above topics. Your aims should be to structure the speech logically and to place suitable emphasis on important points.

b) Write out in narrative minutes from the Annual General Meeting's agenda item: Chairman's Report, using the direct speech report in Assignment *a*.

c) Compose a suitable AGM agenda for the meeting of the Laystone College Students' Association and then role-play the meeting. Assume that relations between the committee and the general membership have deteriorated and that some noisy dissatisfaction is voiced from the floor.

d) Write the minutes of your simulated Annual General Meeting in narrative minutes form.

Resolution minutes

7 Write in resolution minutes form minutes appropriate for a board of directors' meeting for the following:

a decision to introduce the post of Information Officer into the management structure,

the decision to terminate the company's laundering contract with Speedy Cleaning Services Ltd currently due for renewal.

8 Organise a brain-storming meeting aimed at establishing a methodical approach to studying. Produce a study guide for distribution to new students.

Email meetings messaging

9 You work as assistant to the Works Manager. An emergency has arisen over the break-down of the No. 4 kiln in your pottery works. You have a Deputy Works Manager, four foremen and a Plant Computer Supervisor. Compose a suitable notice and agenda to send directly over your LAN network for an urgent meeting this afternoon to reschedule production operations. Use a LAN network to devise and route your Email message.

10 Use a LAN network meetings scheduler to call a meeting of the above personnel, using their electronic diaries as an information base. Your meeting is scheduled for a week's time, and is to review matters following the repair of No 4 kiln. It will take place in the Works Manager's office and last 45 minutes.

Research and report back assignments

1 In pairs, arrange to interview a local county council officer responsible for servicing a committee meeting; ask him/her what is involved and what procedures govern the process. Report back to your group on your findings.

2 Research into the company law underpinning the following:

directors' meetings,
shareholders' AGMs,
creditors' meetings.

Brief your group with a summary factsheet.

3 Find out how a local organisation uses quality circle or task-force group meetings to aid decision-making and development. Give an oral account of your findings to your group.

4 Collect a set comprising: notice, agenda, minutes relating to a recent meeting of a local club, society or voluntary committee. With permission, display these – and any other samples you can secure legitimately – on your base-room wall.

5 Arrange to sit in on a local public council meeting; take notes and brief your group on what took place, how, and to what effect.

6 Interview a local company secretary; ask him or her to explain to you how his company's board of directors' meetings are conducted, and what conventions are applied. With permission, report back to your group orally.

7 Interview two or three managers and establish what procedures they adopt in order to hold effective departmental and section meetings. Brief your group orally on what you ascertain.

8 Interview a local senior secretary who services high-level meetings in a local firm. Find out what techniques and procedures are adopted to ensure their effective administration. Brief your group with a flow-chart and notes.

9 Seek to acquire – with permission – a copy of a local honorary treasurer's annual financial report submitted to an AGM.

10 Collect samples of different types of minutes from various local organisations. Mount a display of a 'best selection' in your base-room, having discussed their style and format.

11 In pairs, interview a local group of managers and support staff who have recently mounted a conference; from your findings, prepare an oral presentation (with AVA!) of the tips you learned from your investigations.

12 Arrange to interview members of your school/college staff who regularly give talks. Find out what their techniques comprise and set them out in a suitable format as a group handout.

13 Interview a local manager whose job involves him or her in giving top-level presentations; find out how the challenge is approached and effected. If possible, ask the manager to come and talk about his presenter role to your group.

Work experience and simulation assignments

1 Seek to sit in on a meeting in your attachment organisation as an observer. You may need to give an undertaking to respect confidential information. For your own development, watch closely how the meeting is chaired, structured and decisions reached. See how given and accepted roles are played.

2 Ask for permission to view some non-confidential notices, agendas, minutes and other support documents. Study their layout and composition carefully and check against this Unit's guidelines. Ask to copy some for models, if permitted.

3 Secure authorisation to look through some of the major documents relating to the mounting of a conference such as: invitations to speakers, programmes, speakers' biographies, speech summaries and other conference handouts. Your task is to find out how they are composed and why. With permission, brief your group on your attachment organisation's approach.

4 Ask your supervisor to facilitate your interviewing a manager as for Research And Report Back Assignment 13 above.

5 Find out what systems and equipment your organisation uses to support AVA oral presentations. Brief your group on your findings.

6 Carry out a survey in your attachment organisation aimed at establishing what types of meetings are held, by whom, under what procedures and for what purposes. Deliver your findings in a written report to your supervisor and, with permission, copy it to your group.

Case studies

Mending the cracks in Plastimould

Plastimould Ltd is a company manufacturing a range of household utensils from a chemical base – bowls, buckets, pipes, brushes etc. For the past six weeks it has had a serious industrial dispute on its hands. One of the stages in the production process has been declared 'unsafe' by the unionised factory staff.

This stage concerns the cleaning out of vats which have contained the material for moulding into the various products in the company's range. It is accepted by both management and union representatives that it is possible during the cleaning process for fumes to be generated which are dangerous to the skin and which under no circumstances should be inhaled.

Recently three men have collapsed not long after working on the cleansing of the vats and they are still off work sick. After the third man had fallen ill, the union decided after a full meeting of the factory union membership to ban any of the union's members from working on the vat cleansing process. The effect of this ban was to halt production completely.

The union want an independent enquiry into the dangers and effects to health stemming from the cleansing process. For their part, management have declared that the cleansing process is perfectly safe, provided that the protective clothing and equipment provided is worn and used as specified in company regulations.

The union's position is that the clothing is old-fashioned, having been designed more than ten years previously, and that no one to their knowledge had carried out any recent tests to confirm the effectiveness of its protection. The men have complained that it is too hot to wear, and that its bulkiness makes it impossible to work in the more inaccessible parts of the vats. The respirators are also, according to the men, inefficient, especially when any physical exertion is required.

Management has pointed out that the protective clothing and equipment conforms to the safety specifications laid down for such work in the relevant section of the industrial safety legislation. The men, says management, have been cutting safety corners to boost bonus earnings by not wearing all the equipment and clothing when there is a clear need to. If there have been instances of men becoming sick, which management will not accept as being a direct consequence of the cleansing process, then it must be the result of contributory negligence.

The union regards this last attitude of management as totally hypocritical. It claims that in the past management has turned 'a blind eye' to total adherence to factory safety regulations. Only now that the company is faced with a law-suit for damages arising from the medical condition of the three workers currently sick in hospital has the accusation of 'contributory negligence' arisen. In any case, the company has failed in its obligation to inform its factory staff adequately of the potential dangers involved in the cleansing process, and now, 'caught red-handed', was trying to prevent an independent enquiry from being set up.

The latest rejoinder from management is that unless a formula can be decided to re-start production with immediate effect, there may well be a possibility that the parent company of Plastimould will divert its production to another factory in another country, thus causing wide-spread redundancy. The union is inclined to see this as bluff, although some members concede that the six-week lay-off must have had crippling effect on the company's financial position.

Assignments

1 Form the management or union team, prepare your case for a 'return-to-work' negotiating meeting and then simulate the meeting. Observers or a team member should take notes and produce narrative minutes.

2 Depending upon the outcome of the meeting draft either a 'joint communiqué' or separate statements for circulation to Plastimould staff.

3 As an individual student write an essay on the problems implicit in the case study and suggest how you think the management and the union would resolve their differences.

Frosty climate at Arctura

Recently, your company, Arctura Refrigeration Ltd has been experiencing a serious problem affecting both its export sales and production departments. The company manufactures a range of refrigerators and freezers, many of which are sold abroad. Of recent months relations have deteriorated between the Export Sales Department and the Production Department. The root of the problem lies in the failure of the company's production department to meet production targets and deadlines for refrigerators and freezers ordered by customers in Middle and Far Eastern markets.

The Export Sales Manager, Mr K D Mears, is receiving letters daily from customers and agents complaining bitterly about broken promises over delivery dates and emphasising the danger of loss of business and the closing of accounts. Until some three months ago, the company's overseas order book had been full, but as a result of the recent poor performance in production, there has been a decline in repeat orders. This situation has been reported by the Export Sales Manager, who drew the Managing Director's attention to the fact that competitors were exploiting the situation to the full.

The Production Manager, Mr J D P Jones, has recently been critical of the poor communications existing between the Export Sales and Production Departments. Orders have been taken, he affirmed, which did not take into account the company's overall production capacity and the production commitment to a more profitable home market. There had also been a spate of late modifications to individual product specifications which had made it impossible to plan an efficient production schedule. Batches of both refrigerators and freezers were being stored because they had not met a modified order requirement.

A further complication lies in the current 'work to rule' being followed by the factory's operatives, members of the Metal Workers' Union, in pursuit of an improved bonus scheme. Talks with the company's management team, headed by the Personnel Manager, Mrs K Wheatley, have broken down over agreement on a revised basic rate of pay and hourly output targets upon which bonus rates are based.

The following are the company's personnel involved principally in the problem:

Mr A Hartley, Managing Director
A N Other, Personal Assistant to the M.D.

Mr K D Mears, Export Sales Manager
Miss A Jameson, Assistant Export Sales Manager
Mrs P Nielson, Export Sales Order Co-ordinator

Mr J D P Jones, Production Manager
Mr R V Kershaw, Assistant Production Manager
Mr N P Oliver, Work Progress Officer

Mrs K Wheatley, Personnel Manager
Miss K Bright, Personal Assistant to the Personnel Manager

Mr P R Grimshaw, Works Convener, Metal Workers' Union
Mr J K Briggs, Shop Steward
Mrs R Roberts, Shop Steward

Assignments

1 As Personal Assistant to the Managing Director, you have been asked to draft a memorandum report for Mr Hartley, outlining an approach aimed at solving the problem by 'getting people round a table'. You have been asked to specify the type and number of meetings you would suggest, who should take part and what procedures should be followed in any given meeting.

2 In order to develop this case study further, it is possible to provide additional background and briefing notes for each interested group and then to proceed to a role-playing simulation of one or more meetings. Secretaries may be appointed to *each group* to take minutes of any meeting. Each set of minutes may be produced and circulated to all participants. It may well be instructive to compare the various sets of minutes of the same meeting drawn up by groups with different aims and outlooks. Remember, however, that it is customary to produce only one set of minutes in normal circumstances.

The Henry Perkins Legacy – Take 2!

Re-read The Henry Perkins Legacy Case Study at the end of Unit 11. Refresh your memory on the Discussion Topics and review your assignment work on the case study. Then, in groups of three to five, simulate a board meeting called to examine the options and proposals open to the company in installing an up-to-date CMIS system. Your teacher will help you to allocate roles; suitable agendas and minutes of your meeting are to be composed.

Multi-media assignment

Newbourne Knights – rescued from distress!

Background

The Newbourne Knights is a voluntary charitable society of Newbourne citizens, whose charitable activities are mainly concerned with raising money to provide outings, entertainment and treats for local underprivileged old people and children. Its committee meets monthly in the Committee Room of the Old Town Hall, High Street, Newbourne at 7.30 pm. As a member of the committee, you receive the following telephone call from Mrs Jean Carson, Chairman:

'Sorry to trouble you, but Harold Johnson (Hon. Sec.) has just gone down with 'flu. Do you think you could take over as Acting Honorary Secretary to organise the next committee meeting on the 21st? You'll need to get a notice out as soon as possible – and ask for any agenda items as well, to be sent to you by – well, you fix a deadline.'

A week later, you have a discussion with Jean Carson about the items to be included on the committee agenda. The following points emerge from your conversation:

'It's time we made a date for the annual senior citizens' outing – and I think we'd better set up a sub-committee again to organise it.

'Jack Peters says he'd like to make a Treasurer's Report and also provide a breakdown on the cost of the children's Christmas party – I gather he's a bit fed up because some committee members haven't yet given him their raffle ticket money.

'Mrs Simpson rang to say she's annoyed because her suggestion for holding an Easter Bonnet competition was omitted from Item 6 in last meeting's minutes – Future Programme. Don't forget that we need her support in laying on the refreshments for the Spring Holiday Fete, which we ought to start discussing now.

'Oh, and I mustn't forget to thank Mrs Hargreaves for her recent donation under AOB.

'By the way, here's a letter from the vicar of St Peter's offering his garden for the Spring Bank Holiday Fete again.'

Assume that the committee meeting duly takes place and that its items of business are as indicated on the committee agenda above. Unfortunately, the day before the meeting, Mrs Carson rang you to say she couldn't attend as a relative was seriously ill and she had to visit her. She asked you to prepare a chairman's agenda for Mr John Dickinson, Vice-Chairman, based on the committee agenda, to enable him to chair the meeting.

With Mr Dickinson in the chair, with you as Acting Secretary, and with eight other committee members attending, the meeting proceeds. Amongst other matters agreed, a sub-committee is formed to organise the annual senior citizens' outing.

The selected sub-committee, formed to plan the senior citizens' outing, has been asked to investigate suitable ideas for it, locations, costs, transport, refreshments etc.

Assignments

1 Notice
Draft a suitable notice to call the next committee meeting.

2 Committee agenda
As she was in a hurry to visit the matron of the Newbourne Nursing Home, Mrs Carson has asked you to draw up a committee agenda based on the points raised above, and has asked you to use your discretion in forming a running order of items.

3 Chairman's agenda
Prepare the chairman's agenda requested by Mrs Carson for Mr Dickinson, based on the above committee agenda produced.

4 Meeting simulation
Simulate the committee meeting, having produced and circulated the relevant documents and prepared notes etc.

5 Minutes
Produce narrative minutes of the meeting.

6 Report
Draft a report of the sub-committee's outing plans to submit to the next committee meeting.

13

Aspects of personnel

Photo Sally & Richard Greenhill

Overview

Unit 13 provides you with information and guidelines on:

- Recruitment/selection procedures from both the employer's and applicant's viewpoint.
- How to draw up personnel/job applications and job descriptions.
- How to devise display recruitment advertisements.
- Model letter of application, job description and personnel specification.
- How to take part in interviews successfully.
- Guidelines on designing application forms, curricula vitae, personnel requisitions, interview and disciplinary reports.
- Major services of a personnel department: recruitment, training, employee appraisal and review, industrial relations, welfare and social aspects, pensions and retirement.

The job application process

The process of obtaining a worthwhile job − as a rung on a career ladder − forms an important part of your studies at this stage of your course. You may of course, already be in full-time employment, but it will do you no harm to review that part of the recruitment or selection process which considers the applicant's viewpoint and needs as a preparation for your next job application. For this reason, the survey of personnel aspects in Unit 13 begins with the job application process. Unit 13 also examines

the major activities of the personnel department and the way it administers the affairs of the organisation's employees.

The applicant's viewpoint

1 The career exploration and counselling phase

A period of careful consideration should first be given to the sort of sector or field in which the applicant has a genuine interest and to which he or she could dedicate most of his or her waking hours.

This process may take some time to unfold and it is sensible for young adults to obtain expert careers advice and to take the trouble to research various sectors personally. It can be equally fatal either to drift into a particular area of commerce, industry or public service or to 'follow in father's footsteps' just because that's what is expected.

2 The finding out where jobs are phase

Once the particular sector in which to find a good job has been identified – say publishing, personnel management, accounting, selling, manufacturing or the like – the next step is to discover how available jobs in such a particular sector are advertised or publicised.

The following checklist provides an overview of likely sources of information about available posts.

In a national context

Some jobs are advertised nationally, especially if a large organisation is looking to recruit a number of trainees at one time. Therefore jobs are likely to be found advertised in:

National daily press *The Times, The Independent, The Daily Telegraph*, etc. (Some national dailies advertise certain sectors on particular days – *The Times*: secretarial posts, 'Crème de la crème' on Wednesdays; *Guardian*: teaching posts on Tuesdays. So it pays to check out when likely advertisements appear.)

Sunday newspapers *The Sunday Times, The Observer, The Sunday Telegraph*, etc. Currently some of the Sunday newspapers produce as many as 10–15 pages of job advertisements. Many are for senior positions, but some do ask for trainees or advertise junior posts.

Professional and trade journals and newspapers In the UK there are literally hundreds of specialist journals and magazines published weekly or monthly for various specialist workforces, from doctors to plumbers, nurses to chemical engineers, lawyers to public health officers. Almost certainly there will be one for the area in which you are interested. It therefore pays either to become a regular subscriber of such a journal or to see whether it is taken by your local municipal, college or school library.

Television and radio Occasionally organisations will take out commercials for jobs to be broadcast on the national broadcasting media; these are not very extensively used for advertising jobs but sometimes a worthwhile opening – especially in the public sector – may be spotted. Most local radio stations adopt regular job advertising spots, however.

In a local context

The local daily and weekly press The local equivalent of the national daily newspaper is often the weekly paper serving a district and concentrating on local news. Some larger towns do support evening dailies and occasionally a morning local paper. These newspapers provide a fruitful source of local job opportunities, although, each opening must be evaluated on its merits in terms of opportunities to progress and conditions of service, when smaller, local firms are set against larger, national ones.

Free newspaper Increasingly weekly newspapers are springing up which depend upon their advertising revenue for their income and are thus delivered free to householders. Again local jobs are advertised in free newspapers, whose display advertising rates are often cheaper than those of the established local press.

Careers Centre For young people up to the age of 18, the local Careers Centre provides not only expert advice, but also a job finding service, since local employers often send to the Centres copies of job advertisements, job specifications and details, or just simply telephone to provide information about a current opening.

Job Centres Local Job Centres operate in a similar way, and advertise available jobs on window and reception display boards. Job Centre staff become very knowledgeable about local conditions and openings and their advice is worth obtaining.

In addition, Job Centres act as information agencies for details about Youth Training and Employment Training Schemes for mature students, which are offered by the Training Agency.

Private Employment Bureaux Increasingly, privately owned employment bureau are opening not only in London but in provincial towns and cities. They act as a kind of broker between the employer and the applicant, and often work closely with local personnel officers. Theirs is a highly competitive world and they have to maintain high standards in order to survive. Usually they earn a fee from the employer if someone registered with them is appointed by a firm. But it always pays to be absolutely clear about any financial commitments being accepted whenever a job applicant registers with a private employment bureau, and to scrutinise fully any document requiring a signature.

Word of mouth In many organisations the fastest route that confidential communication takes is the company grapevine!

It may well be worth while in this respect for the job hunter to alert suitable friends and relatives and ask them to keep eyes and ears open for an opportunity to be quickly followed up even before it appears in the national or local press.

Self advertisement An additional and very productive strategy for the job applicant to adopt while examining the national and local media for job advertisements is to devise a suitable personal letter of 'unsolicited application' and to send it with a current curriculum vitae to a whole range of national and local employers. It turns out sometimes that the arrival of such a letter coincides with the decision to create a new post or look for a replacement for a member of staff who has been promoted or who has retired or resigned. Such actions also demonstrate the applicant's initiative to a potential employer.

3 Responding to an advertisement phase

Sooner or later, an advertisement is spotted which excites the individual who decides to apply for the advertised post.

Even at this early stage, some essential questions need to be posed and answered by the applicant:

- Am I ready to apply?
  Nowadays employers can afford to set high demands for their job applicants to meet and many will expect a curriculum vitae – a schematic checklist of education, examination successes, experience etc (*see* page 332) – to accompany the written application. So ideally, the CV should have been designed, vetted and flawlessly duplicated before the first advertisement is responded to.
- What do I know about this employing organisation? Does it enjoy a good reputation for the way it treats its staff?
- Does the job appear to give scope for personal development and prospects for advancement? Or does it seem a dead-end post?
- What clues does the advertisement provide about conditions of service – pension scheme, holidays, pay, hours of work, personal development, etc?
- Do I know to whom I shall be applying or am I expected to reply to a box number? It is generally preferable to know who you are dealing with when offering your services.
- Am I expected in the first instance merely to send off for an application form and further details of the post? If so, only a short, polite letter asking for them is needed initially. An official letter of application is expected to accompany the completed application form.
- Do I really want this job? Or shall I be wasting everybody's time by turning it down if it is offered to me?

4 The detailed application phase

This phase will involve three major tasks:

- completing the application form effectively,
- composing a letter of application,
- doing further fact-finding research about the firm and the advertised job.

Here, the following tips may prove useful:

Look up the company in *Who Owns Whom* and its directors or main board directors in *Who's Who*. This can forestall any faux pas about certain countries or pastimes which are close to the corporate heart or form the interviewer's pet hobbies!

Look the firm up in *Kompass* to see what they make if they are in manufacturing. Check their position on the stock market if they are a public company – are their shares rising? Or falling?

Ask friends and relatives what they know or can find out about the company and its trading record. Will it still be about in two years' time or will you have been made redundant and have to start all over again?

5 The preparation for interview phase

All being well, you will have been shortlisted for an interview and advised so by letter specifying a given date and time.

A short and courteous letter of acceptance should be directly despatched and then preparations begin in earnest! Your application documents have worked and you are almost certainly one of the last five applicants selected for interview.

The conscientious candidate will have kept photocopies of all the application documents to refresh his or her mind and will be drafting the sort of questions expected to come up at interview and deciding upon the answers to be given.

Careful thought will be given to what constitutes the appropriate outfit or suit to wear to the interview and timetables will have been double checked to ensure arrival at the interview location in good time. In this regard, the crafty candidate arrives early and, if possible, tours the company areas which are accessible to 'get the feel' of the place. Noticeboards, foyer areas and offices visible through glass partitions may reveal a great deal about the quality and image an organisation projects and maintains. If everything looks sloppy and disorganised then the chances of acquiring useful career skills may be slim. However, the organised firm will almost certainly lay on a tour in any case, and in such a firm the applicant is unlikely to get past the reception area without an escort!

6 The interview phase

This is the crucial part of job application, since all

is either won or lost at the interview. To perform well, the applicant must:

- master nerves and shyness,
- listen carefully to the questions posed,
- respond fluently but without gabbling endlessly nor by uttering monotones,
- avoid irritating speech mannerisms and physical movements like playing with a ring or scratching an ear.

In fact, the interview phase requires careful preparation and practice and is dealt with in detail on pages 328–31.

7 The acceptance phase

If the interview has gone well, the applicant is offered the post – either immediately at the interview or within a day or so by letter. The offer will be confirmed by letter in any case and by law has to be followed up within 13 weeks of employment commencing with a detailed contract of employment. The prudent interviewee therefore does not wait until it is too late to check up on salary, terms of notice on either side etc, but clarifies such central matters at the interview phase. It then remains for the applicant to respond with a formal letter of acceptance and to provide his existing employer with the required written notice – again usually by letter. Subject to the recruiting company obtaining acceptable references from the applicant's employer, the process is complete.

Except that the shrewd applicant does not spend the time left working out his notice by running down his present employer or giving voice to thoughtless criticisms of the firm and the people who run it. No company or manager is perfect, and who knows, perhaps the wheel will one day turn full circle, and the applicant wish to apply for a more senior post at his old company! As is usually the case, 'a still tongue makes a wise head' in such matters.

The employer's viewpoint

Just as the job applicant has his own set of activities to mastermind during the job application process, so indeed has the employer. As the chart on page 329 illustrates, the employing organisation – if it is a thorough and conscientious one – has to carry out a good deal of preliminary work before the advertisement for a particular post can be published.

The following sections outline the work carried out by the recruiting organisation:

1 The job creation phase

Long before a post can be brought to the attention of would-be applicants a decision has to be taken on whether and when to create it if it is an entirely new one, for example arising from the redeployment of staff, or on how it should be revised, modified and updated if it is an existing one just vacated. Interestingly, it is often at this stage that senior managers come to realise how much 'Old Jonesy' quietly got on with it, or how different his job has become from the one they thought he was doing! And this is one good reason among many for regular reviews of job specifications and job descriptions (see below). The reasons for jobs arising in a firm are many – a new store may be opened, someone retires, an employee's spouse is promoted to another part of the country and so on.

2 Job analysis: the job specification and job description

To avoid the chaos which ensues, not to mention the toes that get trodden on without their implementation, progressive organisations have for many years maintained careful records or statements about the jobs their staff do.

This process forms part of what is termed job analysis. This function is usually carried out either by an organisation and methods unit which forms part of a management services department, or is undertaken by the personnel department.

Briefly, each job is carefully monitored to establish in detail its component parts and also to determine the skills, qualifications and personal attributes which a person needs to enable them to do the job competently.

The job specification

It is the job specification (sometimes called 'personnel specification') which sets out as a schedule the skills, technical competencies, knowledge and experience which are needed to carry out the job. For example, a word processing operator would be 'profiled' in the specification as needing, among other attributes:

- twenty-twenty or corrected vision (the job entails a great deal of visual work),
- the ability to use a computer efficiently (indeed, the job centres upon manipulating text via a keyboard and VDU),
- a thorough knowledge of the word processing package being used in both theory and practice;
- a creative and imaginative flair (sometimes WP operators solve textual and display problems by manipulating the software in ways not mentioned in the manual),
- a methodical and conscientious approach to work (editing the MD's Annual Report is not a job for a 'slapdash artist'!),
- the ability to spell correctly and to proof-read well and so on.

There is no single, approved way in which to set

out a job specification, but as you will have noticed from the examples given above, the specification identifies a number of factors needed which can be classified as follows:

1 Physical attributes or proficiencies
2 Manual skills
3 Knowledge skills
4 Personality and social skills.

Many job specifications are, appropriately, drawn up therefore according to the headings of the NIP Seven Point Plan (see page 332), specifying requirements in the areas of physical make-up, attainments, general intelligence, special aptitudes, disposition, etc.

The job description

The function of the job description is to set down clearly what a **particular job** consists of and to set it in a context. For example, a sales representative's job will customarily be set out according to sections such as:

1 The job's title.
2 If appropriate, its coded position on a league table ranging from the most junior to the most senior posts, so staff can place it promptly in the hierarchy.
3 A brief outline of its major role.
4 The identity of the person who supervises the work, ie the job holder's immediate superior in a 'reports to' function.
5 The identity of anyone reporting to the job holder, ie any subordinate staff.
6 The job description then proceeds to catalogue the major responsibilities involved.

For example the job description of the sales representative may include descriptions such as:

● follow a schedule of visits (to existing customers) on a monthly cycle to obtain sales orders;
● submit weekly (for receipt at District Office by Mondays) a sales report using the relevant report forms – or Email messaging procedures.
● keep proper records, supported by receipts of expenses arising solely and entirely from the requirements of the post. Submit such expenses records weekly;

and so on.

Of course, it is much easier to compile a job description for someone with an orderly and structured job than it is for an employee like an advertising copywriter who is expected to be creative every day and whose job is often self-directed.

3 Details for the applicants phase

Once the job specification and description have been designed or revised, the schedule detailing the main

features of the organisation along with the principal benefits and requirements of the job may be drawn up and duplicated in anticipation of applications.

4 The advertising phase

How this is approached depends on a number of factors, including the seniority of the post, whether the organisation is large enough to support a personnel department to design advertisements and so on. For some managerial posts, large firms employ specialist consultancy firms which place the advertisement while not revealing the company's identity and which undertake the initial screening and interviewing to save the hiring company time.

However managed, someone has to assume responsibility for placing advertisements in what is potentially the most effective newspaper or journal (or mix of both).

The specimen advertisement on page 325 illustrates some of the major aspects of display advertising. But bear in mind that different posts require different approaches and different organisations have evolved preferred ways of advertising.

5 The shortlisting phase

The existence of a job specification does much to aid the sifting of applications, since it specifies what skills, attainments, knowledge, etc are deemed necessary. Some personnel staff draw up schedules to assist in the selection process by listing requirements under such headings as:

VITAL
  IMPORTANT
    USEFUL
      NON-ESSENTIAL

They then measure applications against such a yardstick.

It is important for the applicant to bear in mind that he or she is often competing in this phase with as many as 100 fellow applicants and that sometimes pressure of work may cause the barely legible or long-winded application to be instantly discarded. In the same way, the 'tatty' or casual-looking application may be given short shrift!

Once a shortlist (or sometimes an initial 'long shortlist' if there are to be two sets of interviews) has been established, then the given referees will be contacted to provide a confidential reference about the applicant. As this takes time and effort, it is crucial for applicants to approach referees to ask for their support and willingness to act as referees *before* they receive reference requests out of the blue!

Components of the recruitment display advertisement

1 Display advertisements need bold eye-catching headlines, allied to a visually interesting

2 logo or piece of artwork. Notice that this artwork sets a mood of upward success which is not daunting. The company knows that it is highly regarded so it displays its name prominently to attract high-calibre applicants.

4 The advertisement's job title also needs to be displayed prominently.

5 This advertisement seizes upon four main 'carrots' to interest the applicant without becoming too detailed or involved. Notice that in this advertisement no 'hard' details are given about pay, hours of work etc.

6 Having conveyed what is on offer, the advertisement briefly sets out the salient features (which are looked for) in an applicant.

7 The name and address of the person to write to are clearly and fully displayed.

8 Note that Sparks & Muncer PLC pride themselves on providing equal career opportunities for men and women. The inclusion of this slogan is good public relations as well as an attraction to female applicants.

EXCELLENT OPENING FOR HIGH FLYERS!

SPARKS & MUNCER PLC
require
TRAINEE BRANCH MANAGERS

- Excellent Prospects
- First Class Training
- Highly Regarded
  Salary and Conditions of Service Schemes
- Non Contributory Pension Schemes

If you are a good team-member, able to work hard on your own initiative, like meeting and beating challenges, are aged between 16–19 and possess at least 3 GCSEs then write for further details and an application form to:

Mrs Jean Macdonald,
Personnel Manager,
Sparks & Muncer PLC,
Brompton Road,
London WC1 6AJ

and quote ref. JM/TBN

SPARKS & MUNCER PLC ARE AN EQUAL
OPPORTUNITY EMPLOYER!

A DISPLAY ADVERTISEMENT
should be
- VISUALLY ARRESTING
- SHORT ON TEXT
- APPEALING IN TONE
- EASY TO GRASP

6 The interview phase

Prior to holding the interviews, the organisation will arrange final discussions to establish in fine detail exactly the kind of person they are seeking and to structure the interviewing process. Sometimes four or five managers may interview candidates in a sequence and compare notes. Sometimes they may act together as a panel. Nowadays employment law has resulted in (quite properly) a lengthy and sometimes costly procedure being needed before an employee may be dismissed. As a result, the applicant can be sure that the interviewing staff will have done their homework and be ready to ensure that the selection process provides a truly testing dialogue so that selection mistakes are minimised!

7 The job offer phase

Sometimes an interviewing panel will recall an applicant from a waiting room and make an orally delivered job offer at the close of the interview. Some firms, however, may prefer interviewing staff to 'sleep on it' and write to all candidates the next day offering the post to one of them. Yet others may wait to see if the first preference applicant accepts or rejects the post before contacting the second choice.

However tackled, the job offer will be made within a day or so of interview. It may be that the official contract for the job is enclosed with the letter offering the post. Applicants should always keep in mind that this is a binding document on both sides.

8 Approaching the applicant's current employer phase

It is a long established code of professional practice that recruiting companies will not approach an applicant's current employers without his or her permission. Nevertheless, oral or written job offers are often qualified by the phrases:

. . . subject to the receipt of suitable references from your current employer.

This phase is almost always perfunctory in that candidates are rarely rejected after the job offer has been made, but it does illustrate the thoroughness of the job selection process from the employer's viewpoint.

Tips on writing a letter of application

We first saw Jane Simmond's letter of application for the post of Private Secretary to the Export Sales Manager of Finosa Fabrics Limited in the Topic on letter writing as an example of letter structuring. It is also a useful model to study in the context of applying for a job.

A letter which supports a completed application form and accompanies a curriculum vitae has a different job to do from the letter which is the only submitted application document. The latter is sometimes requested as the sole means of written application and has to do the job all by itself:

'Interested applicants are invited to apply by letter to . . .'

In the former case, the main functions of the letter of application are:

- To formalise the act of application. Jane Simmond's opening paragraph does that and gets it out of the way. Note the need always to refer to any enclosed documents – the application form and CV – to ensure they are not overlooked or misplaced.

- To act as a summary of what are considered the major strengths of the application. Bear in mind it does no harm to repeat them as a way of imprinting them on an employer's mind. He or she may be sifting through several dozen applications.
- To emphasise the applicant's suitability to *this particular advertised post*. Consider that the application form will have gathered the information the *employer* seeks and that the CV must of necessity be an all-purpose document to support an application for different types of job. The specific advertisement will have asked for particular qualities or abilities and the written letter

provides a chance to demonstrate their possession – as far as the applicant is genuinely able to do so.

- Good letters of application convey a sense of enthusiasm for gaining the advertised post without being either 'gushy' or 'swollen-headed' in reciting accomplishments. The tone of Jane's letter seeks to meet this requirement:

'the advertised post particularly appeals to me since . . .'
'I gained a valuable insight into German business methods . . .'
'If called, I should be pleased to attend for an interview at any time . . .'

- The accompanying letter of application should be kept fairly short – the equivalent of one side of A4 is suggested – and should be written by hand. Firstly since this is still established etiquette, and secondly because employers like to get the feel of the application in personal terms. A few even submit handwriting for analysis, so this should sharpen up the scribblers and microscopic hieroglyphics writers among us!

- The tone of the letter is properly formal and so the Dear Sir or Dear Madam . . . Yours faithfully salutation and subscription are appropriate.

While it is not always easy, avoid including too many 'I's in sentence constructions and particularly as the opening words of paragraphs. The British are a funny lot and the ability to blow one's trumpet discreetly is expected in job applications!

FINOSA FABRICS LTD require a PERSONAL ASSISTANT to the EXPORT SALES MANAGER (EUROPE)

A knowledge of two EEC foreign languages is required and experience of export sales procedures is an advantage. The successful candidate will work on his or her own initiative and be able to handle incoming telephone, fax and telex messages and documentation from French or German agents. He or she must also be prepared to travel abroad.

The company provides excellent conditions of service, including five weeks paid holiday per annum subsidised insurance and restaurant facilities. Salary negotiable according to age and experience.
Apply in writing to: The Personnel Manager, Finosa Fabrics Ltd, 4 York Way, London WC2B 6AK

Applications to be received by 30 May 19—

Dear Sir,

I should like to apply for the post of personal assistant to your Export Sales Director recently advertised in 'The Daily Sentinel', and have pleasure in enclosing my completed application form and copy of my curriculum vitae.

The advertised post particularly appeals to me, since my own career aspirations and education have been specifically directed for the last two years towards an administrative career in the field of export sales.

In the sixth form at Redbrook High School I specialised in Advanced-level German, French and English and proceeded in September 199- to Reabrook College of Technology, where I embarked upon a bi-lingual Euro-administrator course leading to the Institute of Export's Diploma in Export Studies.

The course includes intensive commercial language studies (I am specialising in German), communication, office administration and export studies with particular emphasis on E.E.C. procedures and documentation. In addition I am studying shorthand, word processing and typewriting, including work in the special foreign language.

I anticipate achieving a good pass in the June Diploma examination and attaining shorthand, typewriting and word processing Advanced Certificates.

During my full-time education, I have travelled extensively in the Federal Republic of Germany and in France, and have become familiar with the customs and outlooks of both countries. In August 199- I gained a valuable insight into German business methods during a month's exchange visit to a Berufsschule in Frankfurt-am-Main.

Assisting my father for the past two years in his own company has afforded me an opportunity to use my own initiative and to obtain helpful work experience in areas such as sales documentation, customer relations and the use of data processing in the sales context.

If called, I should be pleased to attend for an interview at any time convenient to you.

My course at Redbrook College of Technology finishes on 30th June 199- and I should be available to commence a full-time appointment from the beginning of July onwards.

yours faithfully

Jane Simmonds (Miss)

Note: It is still usual for letters of application such as the one above to be handwritten.

- Make sure you convey a sense of being readily available both for interview and to start the job if successful. It does not pay to suggest a starting date between the holiday needed after the stress of examinations and one's customary winter break!

- ALWAYS take photocopies of ALL the documents despatched in support of a job application. If you are making these thick and fast, you will find it otherwise impossible to recall what you wrote – and that is precisely what the interviewers will be scrutinising in front of them when you are being interviewed!

- NEVER send originals of examination certificates etc with job applications. If employers are insistent, say you will bring them with you to any interview. Once lost, some may never be replaced in the same way, and their loss will cause much irritation.

Interviews: general introduction

The interview is used in organisations to meet the needs of many, quite different, situations. Some interviews are extremely formal affairs, where a candidate for a post may be examined and evaluated by a board or panel of interviewers. Others are conducted in a much more relaxed atmosphere, in a 'one-to-one' relationship, between, say, a manager and a subordinate.

In point of fact, it is very difficult to establish where conversation ends and the interviewing process begins in the work situation. A working definition of an interview may follow these lines:

Working definition

An interview takes place when two parties meet to satisfy pre-determined objectives by mutual interrogation.

The process is characterised by the posing and answering of questions, or by the giving and receiving of directions, instructions or advice.

In particular, both parties have specific aims to achieve by directing questions and answers to an end known usually to both interviewer and interviewee.

According to the above definition, an interview may, in effect, be taking place far more frequently than we may realise. When, for example, a manager calls a subordinate into his office, invites him to sit down and then says,

'How have things been going, lately, Jim? You've been looking rather unsettled . . .'

a counselling interview is probably about to take place to enable the manager to get to the root of a problem.

So it is that the interview process is employed to obtain information and responses in a wide variety of areas, from sales performance to accounts collection, from disciplinary proceedings to promotion selection, from counselling on personal problems to personnel appointments. The following table indicates some of the principal areas in which the interview is commonly used.

It is therefore important for the members of any organisation to regard the interview not as an intimidating process to be endured, but rather as a tool of communication from the use of which the interviewee has as much to gain as the interviewer. The truth of this observation becomes much more apparent if the interviewee in particular stops to consider that the process *is* two-way.

The following section examines the job application interview process. Careful preparation and probing questions on the part of the interviewee may result in his declining an offered post with a company which is performing poorly and where job prospects exist in theory rather than in practice. It is important, therefore, at the outset to interpret the term, 'interrogation' as 'a two-way channel for finding out'.

Main applications of the interview

Job application
Resignation – debriefing
Performance assessment
Counselling
Disciplining
Promoting
Information seeking
Instruction giving

The Interview

When interview techniques are being discussed, it is usually the formal interview which is considered. It is important to remember, however, that even in informal interview situations the guide-lines which follow will still hold true in principle, if not in detail.

In any interview, the interviewee will be assessed, either directly or indirectly in these areas:

- appearance
- deportment
- manners
- speech
- intelligence
- judgment
- values
- commonsense
- initiative
- resourcefulness
- assurance

The Job Selection Process

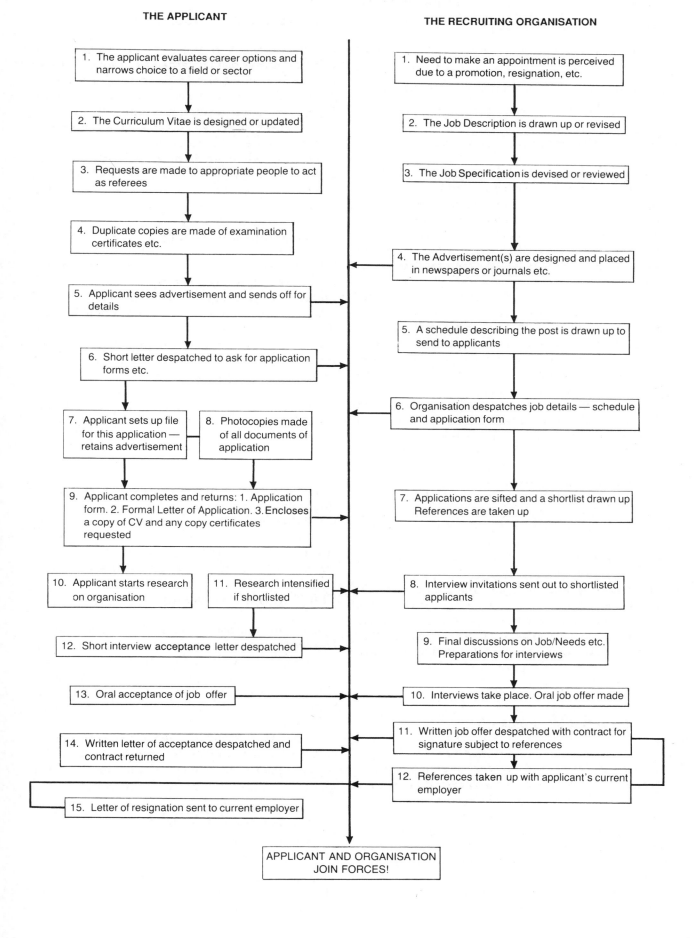

THE APPLICANT

1. The applicant evaluates career options and narrows choice to a field or sector

2. The Curriculum Vitae is designed or updated

3. Requests are made to appropriate people to act as referees

4. Duplicate copies are made of examination certificates etc.

5. Applicant sees advertisement and sends off for details

6. Short letter despatched to ask for application forms etc.

7. Applicant sets up file for this application — retains advertisement

8. Photocopies made of all documents of application

9. Applicant completes and returns: 1. Application form. 2. Formal Letter of Application. 3. Encloses a copy of CV and any copy certificates requested

10. Applicant starts research on organisation

11. Research intensified if shortlisted

12. Short interview acceptance letter despatched

13. Oral acceptance of job offer

14. Written letter of acceptance despatched and contract returned

15. Letter of resignation sent to current employer

THE RECRUITING ORGANISATION

1. Need to make an appointment is perceived due to a promotion, resignation, etc.

2. The Job Description is drawn up or revised

3. The Job Specification is devised or reviewed

4. The Advertisement(s) are designed and placed in newspapers or journals etc.

5. A schedule describing the post is drawn up to send to applicants

6. Organisation despatches job details — schedule and application form

7. Applications are sifted and a shortlist drawn up References are taken up

8. Interview invitations sent out to shortlisted applicants

9. Final discussions on Job/Needs etc. Preparations for interviews

10. Interviews take place. Oral job offer made

11. Written job offer despatched with contract for signature subject to references

12. References taken up with applicant's current employer

APPLICANT AND ORGANISATION JOIN FORCES!

Basically, the interviewer will be seeking re-assurance or information in line with the questions:

How does the interviewee project himself?

What has he to offer in terms of specialist skills or knowledge?

What has he to offer in terms of personality?

What potential to develop does he display?

Appearance, manners, deportment

As an interviewee, whether making a first job application or an employee before a promotion panel, your personal appearance matters! Rightly or wrongly other people will make judgements about you which will be influenced by your appearance. Looking smart and well-groomed is an asset in any situation and is nowhere more important than at an interview.

The way you hold yourself, move and gesticulate will also affect the way people regard you. In professional and business life attractive people are those who temper assurance with modesty, and who behave calmly, with due consideration for others. On entering the interview room, for example, take care to do so politely but not over-hesitantly, and wait to be proferred a hand to shake or to be invited to take a seat. Once seated, avoid the tendency to slouch or lounge and assume a posture which is comfortable, but alert. Also, it is sensible to hold the hands in the lap, and to return them to this position between any gestures.

It is also important to master any feelings of nervousness. Feeling nervous is natural during an interview and you may be sure that the interviewer is aware of this fact and that he or she will go to some trouble to set you at your ease. Nevertheless, allowing nerves to take over, and displaying signs of tension by hunching into the chair, wringing hands, twisting rings or biting lips not only impairs your performance, but transmits a sense of unease to the interviewer as well. The result may be that you do not do justice to yourself and that you leave doubts about your capacities in the mind of the interviewer.

Listening before speaking

Once the interview is under way, perhaps the best advice is to *listen*! It is all too easy as an interviewee to attend with only half an ear to what is being said or asked. Moreover, you will need to employ all your faculties and to keep extremely alert to ensure that you anticipate, for example, where a sequence of questions is leading you, or to see the probing which may be going on beneath an apparently harmless question!

Listening attentively will also help you to prepare your answer while a question is being framed. It is

amazing how fast the brain works in such situations.

Looking at the questioner

Rightly, the ability to 'look someone squarely in the eye' has always been regarded as a sign of honesty and assurance. It helps in any case, during an interview to look at a speaker posing a question since facial expression, gesture or posture often provide valuable insights into what is an interviewer's mind, and shows that you are paying attention.

Similarly, when providing an answer you should make eye-contact with the questioner, but not to the extent of boring into him or her with a transfixing stare!

Think before you speak!

This well-worn truism is still excellent advice to the interviewee. Blurting out a nonsense or 'gabbling' on because of nerves are traps into which the unwary often fall. Moreover, it is not possible in an interview to escape from being assessed and both the words you utter and the way in which you express yourself will reveal much about your intelligence, judgment, common sense and *nous*.

In order to answer questions successfully and in so doing to create a favourable impression, you should ask yourself these questions both before and during your answer:

Have I understood the question?
Do I appreciate what it is driving at?
Are there any traps or pitfalls present in the question?
Can I draw on my own experience to illustrate my answer?
Am I speaking clearly and convincingly?
Have I covered the ground and said enough?

Thinking *while* speaking

Just as the practised reader's eye travels ahead before reading a phrase aloud, so the practised interviewee's mind will be thinking ahead and monitoring what is being said. Additionally, the interviewee's eyes will be looking hard at the interviewer for signs of a favourable response to what is being said.

Sometimes the way in which the spoken word is constructed into phrases or sentences allows for 'rest' or 'pause' expressions to be uttered while the brain composes the next important point:

. . . as a matter of fact I . . .
. . . I accept the truth of that but . . .
. . . although my initial response might be to . . . in this case I would . . .

Also, there are means of delaying arrival at the explicit answer point of a difficult question by means of a sort of delaying tactic:

I suppose it depends to a large degree upon how the term X is interpreted . . .

I don't have an easy or quick answer to that question, but on reflection I . . .

It should be noted that interviewers are only too aware of how much easier it is to pose questions than to answer them, and make natural allowances for initial hesitancy. A word of caution, however: if an interviewee displays a frequent inability to answer questions directly, they are bound to sow in the interviewer's mind seeds of doubt regarding integrity, honesty or, quite simply, lack of knowledge.

Measure what you say

Interviewers are skilled at posing questions which cannot be answered by a simple 'yes' or 'no'. For example, a question would not be phrased:

'Did you enjoy your previous job'

but rather,

'What did you find most satisfying about your previous job?'

In this way the interviewee is invited to expand a reply rather than to offer monosyllabic answers, which inevitably cast doubts upon fluency, knowledge and assurance. It is common, however, for inexperienced interviewees to speak rapidly at great length, as if the assessment were based on words spoken per minute and the range of unrelated topics covered! You must therefore ensure that what you are saying is relevant to the question and forms a summary of the main issues as you see them. It is good practice to pause after having made what you consider an adequate number of points

'I was rather hoping you would ask me that. Yes . . . and no. I think it really depends on how one views the broader implications. Looking at it objectively, what was the question again?'

to allow the interviewer either to ask you to continue or to ask another question. Try to strike a happy medium. Saying too little prevents you from demonstrating your knowledge and ability. Saying too much reveals a disorganised and 'butterfly' mind.

Ask *your* questions

Whatever the interviewing situation, the interviewer largely has control of the interview. Nevertheless you should ensure that you make an opportunity to ask the questions *you* have framed. In the context of an application for a job, you wish to establish whether you want the organisation equally as much as it may wish to decide whether it wants you! Such opportunities tend to occur at the end of the interview but clarifying questions may be put throughout. And note: it always sounds lame and lack-lustre to say, in response to an invitation to ask your own questions: 'No, actually, you seem to have answered all of my questions already'.

A golden rule for interviewees

Be yourself!
Pretence or affectation may land you in a job, or with responsibilities which may hang, like the proverbial albatross, around your neck! Hold to what you believe in – it will almost certainly give you a happier and more fulfilled working life.

Useful information for the interviewee

The application form

The following information is generally required on an application form for a job:

Name
Address
Telephone no.
Age: date of birth
Status: married/single
Maiden name if married woman
Education
Qualifications
Current/previous experience
Present designation or title
Name and address of employers
Details, with dates, of employment since leaving full-time education
Details of salaries in each appointment
Outline of hobbies, interests
Names, addresses and occupations of referees
Date of availability
Signature and acknowledgement of accuracy of data provided

The NIP Seven Point Plan

The following headings summarise an assessment system used in selection processes by interviewers and as a basis for personnel specifications:

Physical make-up
Attainments
General intelligence
Special aptitudes
Interests
Disposition
Circumstances

The curriculum vitae

A *curriculum vitae* may be composed by using the following framework:

Personal details
Full name and current address
Telephone number
Age, status – married/single
Nationality
Dependents – wife, husband, children

Education
Secondary school(s)
College(s) ⎱ with
University ⎰ dates
Post-graduate institution
Main subjects taken
Activities, interests
Post(s) of responsibility

Qualifications
Examination passes indicating grades, dates and examining boards.

Work experience
Usually expressed by starting from immediate past and working backwards.
   Name of organisation, location, job designation, range of duties, extent of responsibilities, reasons for leaving.

Interests
Leisure activities, hobbies, indicating posts of responsibility – e.g. Honorary Secretary of Drama Club – where appropriate.

Circumstances
Period of notice required to be given.
   Mobility – car-ownership, any limiting commitments.

A *curriculum vitae* is usually set out schematically, with appropriate dates and chronological structures.

Specimen job description

JOB DESCRIPTION

Date: 12 January 199–

Previous Review Date: 15 June 199–

Job Title: Personal Secretary to
                    Deputy Sales Manager

Department: Home Sales Department

Location: Company Head Office

Responsible To: Deputy Sales Manager

Responsible For: Work of WP Assistant
                 and
                 Office Information
                 Assistant

Scope of Post: To provide secretarial
                 services and inform-
                 ational support to the
                 Deputy Sales Manager
                 and to assist in
                 administering the
                 activitites of the
                 home sales force;
                 to coordinate and
                 supervise the work of
                 the DSM's word process-
                 ing and office inform-
                 ation staff; to liaise
                 with field sales
                 personnel according to
                 DSM's briefings and
                 requests.

(Note: Job descriptions are normally set out schematically on A4 paper.)

Major Responsibilities

1 To supervise the opening of correspondence and to ensure its prompt distribution according to house practices.

2 To transcribe and deliver as appropriate incoming fax, telex and Email messages.

3 To accept, transcribe (using appropriate media) and despatch DSM's correspondence, reports, memoranda and textual messages.

4 To maintain the DSM's electronic appointments and scheduling diaries efficiently.

5 To administer the DSM's paper and electronic filing systems effectively, and to ensure the security of all computer-stored data.

6 To supervise the operation of office equipment so as to maintain efficient, cost-effective and safe practices.

7 To make travel/accomodation arrangements for DSM and designated staff as required.

8 To administer the sales force expenses payment system and to maintain the DSM's office petty cash and purchases systems.

9 To maintain a cost-effective office stationery provision in liaison with the company's administration manager.

10 To receive visitors and look after their comfort and hospitality needs.

11 To supervise the work of the DSM's office personnel so as to maintain good standards and timely completion of delegated tasks.

12 To monitor office practices and procedures and to advise the DSM on possible improvements and modifications in the light of changing office technology and information systems.

13 To ensure that office security is maintained and that confidences are not breached.

14 To promote an alert approach to HASAW matters at all times.

15 To undertake any reasonable task from time to time at the DSM's request as may be deemed appropriate within the scope of the post.

Equipment/Systems Responsibilities

Office Computer Terminals for safe operations and malfunction reporting.

Office fax, CABX extensions, photocopying and printing equipment for cost-effective and safe operations and malfunction reporting.

Office-held computer files for safe-keeping and prompt accessing and liaison with company DP manager for defect/malfunctioning reporting.

Education and Qualifications

General education to GCSE standard and vocational secretarial education to LCCI Private Secretarial Certificate/NVQ Level 3.

Previous office information processing and secretarial experience essential; the post also requires developed interpersonal/communication skills and developed office applications software and telecommunications expertise as well as word processing proficiency.

SPECIMEN PERSONNEL SPECIFICATION FOR A PERSONAL SECRETARY

Personnel Specification

Date:
Job title: Personal secretary
Reporting to: Middle tier manager

Date of previous review:

Characteristics

	Necessary	Helpful	Optional
Physical:			
20-20/Corrected vision	✓		
Good hearing	✓		
Manual dexterity for keyboarding	✓		
Good carriage and well-groomed appearance	✓		
Qualifications:			
RSA/LCC Secretarial Diploma/Certificate		✓	
Shorthand to 100 wpm	✓		
Typewriting to 40 wpm	✓		
Word processing to NVQ Level 2	✓		
Information processing to NVQ Level 2		✓	
English to GCSE A–C	✓		
French to GCSE A–C		✓	
Experience:			
Previous personal secretarial post		✓	
Coordination of overseas travel arrangements		✓	
Working under pressure to tight deadlines	✓		
Personality:			
Tact/discretion/confidentiality	✓		
Self-starter	✓		
Sense of humour		✓	
Interest/hobbies:			
Foreign languages		✓	
European culture			✓
Fashionwear/clothes sense		✓	
Circumstances:			
Able to start work 1.5.19—	✓		
Clean driving licence			✓
Willing to travel abroad		✓	
Willing to work late at times	✓		

Drawn up by: _____
Approved by: _____
Issue Date: _____

Major services of a personnel department

So far, Unit 13 has concentrated on the job application process – in no small part to aid your own personal 'job hunt', as well as to survey the general recruitment and personnel selection process.

The rest of Unit 13 provides you with an overview of the major services of a typical personnel department – from the acquisition of employees to managing their retirement pensions.

Recruitment

Managers in various departments will give their requirements for a new post to Personnel, who will draw up the documents which are needed to process a recruitment (see p. 326). New staff may be needed as a result of company expansion, an employee gaining promotion to another post, a resignation, and so on. The department may also conduct initial interviews, to produce a shortlist of candidates for the manager to see.

Induction

Once appointed, new staff need to be given an initial period (a day, a week, depending on the post) of training aimed at familiarising them with: company policies, company rules and procedures, an overview of the company's activities, its range of products or services, its structure and organisational systems and introductions to the new employee's immediate colleagues.

Training

A personnel department will coordinate and deliver a wide range of training courses for all employees, from instruction in operating a new piece of equipment, to techniques of supervision for new supervisors, to devising strategies for future company development for senior managers. Many personnel departments employ a training manager and assistants to perform this important role.

Career development and employee records

A personnel department will maintain and update detailed records for each employee which log his or her career development, any changes in duties and the sequence of job moves and/or promotions, as well as any training given. Such records are usually kept on computerised databases, which are invaluable when vetting an employee's application for a more senior post. They also help in assessing a job rating, which in some companies is directly related to pay scales – the more demanding the job, the more the pay. Thus all posts in a firm may be listed and given a reference, where the most junior job may be rated as 1, and managing director's as 35, along a continuous scale.

Employee appraisal and review

A personnel department, in liaison with respective departments, will devise, operate and update the organisation's personnel appraisal and review procedures. In brief, these usually take the form of an annual negotiation with each employee (where the job includes a degree of freedom of action and decision) to agree a set of objectives – to increase sales, efficiency or profit, or to reduce waste or employee turnover, etc – which are to be achieved within the next twelve months. At the same time, accepted changes in the employee's job tasks (job description, see page 324) may be made. During the year (at each quarter) a review interview is likely to be conducted to measure progress. Such appraisal and review procedures are linked to promotion, pay and bonuses in many firms.

Disciplinary and grievance procedures

The Employment Protection (Consolidation) Act of 1978 sets out a wide range of legal obligations an employer has to meet in order to provide employees with fair and just conditions of employment and safeguards against unfair dismissal and discrimination. As a result, it falls to a personnel department to administer the organisation's procedures for disciplining employees who have broken company and/or legal rules and instructions.

For example, an employee who smokes in a no smoking area of a petrol refinery is subject to instant dismissal for obvious reasons. On the other hand, an employee who arrives intermittently late for work because his wife is ill and there are small children at home may be justified in claiming unfair dismissal were he to be summarily dismissed. Because of the many grey areas in cases of disciplining staff, the law provides for a set machinery, known as a grievance procedure, to come into play which ensures a fair hearing, and ultimately, access to an industrial tribunal, a kind of employer/employee court, if matters have not been settled in the work place. Similarly, employees are entitled to oral and written warnings in any disciplinary process prior to being dismissed.

Relationships with trade unions and associations

Many organisations employ people who have joined trade unions or associations. They do so to have access to experts who negotiate their salaries and conditions of employment and who protect their interests in the event of a new technology or working practice being introduced by management, or when companies wish to cut back their workforces, and so on. Personnel departments employ staff who are expert in industrial relations and in negotiating with trade union officers. In this capacity, such staff act as spokespersons for the management viewpoint, but also relay the trade union's views to top management. While occasional strikes make the national headlines, it is the expert behind-the-scenes work of such personnel staff and their trade union counterparts which keeps the wheels of industry turning amicably.

Staff welfare and social activities

In a very different capacity the personnel department often supports and promotes the various clubs, recreational activities and social events which the employees of large organisations take part in. Enlightened companies regard this work as very important, since a workforce with a high morale works better, wastes and breaks less, and achieves higher output. In this context, a personnel department may also produce and distribute company newspapers and bulletins to keep employees up to date with company and staff activities.

Confidential counselling service

Many personnel departments also provide a confidential counselling service. For example, an attractive young woman working as a secretary might find herself subject to sexual harassment during the course of her work for a particular executive. In such stressful cases – and these may also include unfair and vindictive treatment of an employee by a superior, the personnel department can provide the means of offering unbiased and expert advice and of resolving the problem by prompt behind-the-scenes action, such as transferring the manager or secretary and thereby avoiding the loss (by resignation) of a valuable employee.

Pensions and retirement

Today, most large organisations operate pensions funds for their employees. Some firms offer non-contributory pensions where the employer funds the whole pension. Most operate a scheme which requires the employee to make a contribution with the employer. The Government operates a State Earnings Related Pension Scheme (SERPS) and this is very often consolidated into the overall pensions package which the organisation administers via a specialist pensions assurance company. Multinationals like Shell, ICI or IBM may have thousands of former employees enjoying pensions funded by the company pension scheme and so the coordination of company pensions may be very demanding. Lastly the personnel department will often have responsibility for a company policy of preparing staff for retirement by reducing their workload and stress in a period of some three to five years preceding retirement. This may involve reducing the working week by a day a week for the five years prior to retirement and encouraging the development of hobbies and community activities.

Summary

As you can see, the work of a personnel department is varied and challenging. Its staff need interpersonal and communication skills of a high standard as well as expertise in negotiating and in long-term records administration. The effective manager needs to possess an intelligent appreciation of the services offered by personnel. Access to personnel's non-confidential records may save you much time and effort, and you will gain expert support in areas such as recruitment, training and advice on handling staff problems.

Moreover, if you should join a small firm, you may well find yourself carrying out a number of the activities outlined above, if on a smaller scale.

Talking point

Would you like to work in a company/organisation in which pay and 'perks' were linked to performance, and measured by job appraisal? If so, why? If not, why not?

Checklists of major sections of personnel forms and schedules

Reproduced by kind permission of Waterlow Business Supplies.

Personnel requisition

Description of need	date needed: job title and category: recruitment salary range: permanent/temporary: full/part-time:
Reason for need	replacement or addition: if replacement, give reasons:
Requirements	education: qualifications: experience: other please specify:
Approval:	
Date vacancy filled:	Name:

Short application form for employment

Surname   Forenames
Address   Telephone Nos –
                     private/business
Date of birth   Nationality

Detail of any physical disabilities
Current clean driving licence?

Any criminal convictions other than a spent
conviction under the Rehabilitation of Offenders Act
1974?

Employment:
  Position applied for:
  Pay expected:
  Would you work full-time? part-time? – state
    hours/week
  If offered this post would you work in any other
capacity? – please detail
  Have you previously worked for us?
  On what date would you be available?

Note: An extended application form also asks for details of education, employment history, and personal/professional references.

Interview report (extract)

Candidates are rated in this way:

Poise

| Ill at ease, jumpy and nervous | Some-what tense, easily irritated | Reason-ably at ease | Self-ass-ured | Extremely self-assured |

☐ ☐ ☐ ☐ ☐

(Interviewers tick an appropriate box)

The areas so rated are: appearance, poise, friendliness, personality, conversational ability, alertness, knowledge of field of work, qualifications, skill, experience, drive and intiative, overall.

Disciplinary warning record (checklist of contents)

Name/job/title/department/date of warning/expires
  on:
Date/time/reference of offence:
Classification of offence: eg incompetence/bad
work/abuse/lateness/insubordination/other

Details of offence:

Previous Warnings Not Expired Details:

Note: Such careful records need to be kept by a personnel department to satisfy the requirements of the Employment Protection (Consolidation) Act.

Contents of a contract of employment

By law, a new employee must receive a written contract of employment within thirteen weeks of starting in the job. The contract represents both the rights and obligations of the employer and employee. For the employee to work conscientiously, safely and loyally, and for the employer to pay salary/wages when due, to insure the employee and provide a safe working environment. Specifically, the contract of employment sets out the agreed hours of the working day and week, the amount of paid holiday entitlement, the intervals between pay days and the salary/pay structure agreed, as well as any arrangements for paid commission, bonuses or overtime worked. In addition, the contract will clearly set out the arrangements for pension payments and the extent and duration of sick pay. Also, agreed notice of termination of the contract on either side will be included.

The contract 'package' additionally includes clear details of the job which is to be done and any organisational rules and procedures which the employee must follow.

Note: As an employee's job and duties change, for example upon promotion or transfer, a revised job description or even a revised contract of employment should be given.

Self assessment questions

1 How well prepared are you to apply for a full-time post? Are you confident you can design a good curriculum vitae and compose a personal letter aimed at getting you on to the shortlist?

2 How do you rate – for the present – your ability to be interviewed? Have you organised any trial goes yet?

3 If in an employer role, could you now confidently design from scratch a personnel specification and a job description? Could you draw up a useful interview assessment form? Could you design an effective recruiting display advertisement now?

4 Are you now fully conversant with the range of services provided by a personnel department?

If you are still unsure of your own competence in any of the above areas, make sure you make time now to revise and strengthen them!

Summary of main points

1   Recruiting employees is a vital personnel function and comprises, from the employer's view: definition of post to be advertised, drawing up of personnel specification and job description, advertising, short-listing, interviewing and offering a post, taking up references and appointing. From the job applicant's view, the process involves: career/job development decisions, scanning national/local/trade press advertisements, etc, submitting completed application forms, CV and personal letter, being interviewed and accepting/confirming job offer, resigning from current post.

2   A personnel specification itemises the physical, intellectual skills and personality characteristics a post requires; a job description details the responsibilities and tasks making up a post and the chain of command relating to it.

3   Personal letters of application are customarily hand-written and are structured so as to bring out 'plus-points' which particularly relate to the specific post being applied for; such letters normally refer to enclosed curricula vitae and application forms.

4   Success in the job application interview requires careful attention to: dress and appearance, listening skills, atttention to NVC signals, thinking on one's feet, pacing and measuring what is said, asking pertinent questions.

5   A curriculum vitae is usually sequenced as follows: personal data, education, qualifications, work experience, interests, circumstances/availability.

6   The services a personnel department provides vary according to the work of the organisation but usually span: personnel recruitment; induction, training and development; personnel records; employee appraisal and review coordination; industrial relations; disciplinary and grievance procedures; social, welfare and counselling services; pensions and retirement aspects.

7   The documentation employed in personnel departments includes: personnel specifications, job descriptions, recruitment advertisements, personnel requisitions, job application forms, personnel records, databases, standardised WP disciplinary letters and contracts of employment, etc.

Activities and assignments

Quick review quiz

1 What sources of job advertisement can you recall to which the applicant may refer?

2 What contents and features of design go to make up an effective job application form?

3 Put into a running order the tasks of the job application process which:

a) the applicant, and
b) the employer carry out.

4 What sources of information can you recall which provide information on private and public sector organisations and which would aid you in preparing for a job interview?

5 How would you prepare yourself for a job interview once you received the invitation to attend?

6 Explain what the following are used for and what information they embody:

a) a personnel/job specification,
b) a job description,
c) a personnel requisition.

7 What in your view are the features of an effective display recruitment advertisement?

8 What tips could you give to the writer of a personal letter of application for a post?

9 What guidelines can you offer a school/college leaver about the job application interview and how to succeed in it?

10 What should an interviewer be looking for in the job applicant at interview and what sort of questions should he ask?

11 What information is normally imparted in a curriculum vitae? In What sequence should the information be presented?

12 What is meant by each of the following terms:

induction,
grievance procedure,
employee appraisal,
merit-rating,
employee welfare?

13 What essential information is included in a contract of employment?

14 What sort of information would go to make up a typical personnel record in, say, the head office of an insurance company?

Research and report back assignments

1 In pairs, research the services available in your locality to aid the job applicant; compose a short account of your findings and circulate it to your group.

2 In groups of three or four, select a job sector, such as publishing, sales management, local government or computer services, and survey the kind of posts currently being advertised both locally and nationally. Design a collage of the cuttings you collect which best represent the range of opportunities; draw up a factsheet which synthesises the advertised job specifications relating to a typical post, say, personal assistant or computer programmer.

3 Arrange to interview a local personnel manager. Find out what he or she sees as the major challenges (and headaches!) of the role. Ask about the legal aspects of personnel management and how effective lines of communication are maintained.

4 Ask a local personnel manager (or general manager) to list what he sees as the most important features of an effective curriculum vitae; then, armed with your notes from your study of Unit 13, compose and duplicate your own real CV for your first or next job application.

5 Find out what sort of job three or four of your fellow students hope to obtain at the end of your course. Select a panel of students to act as prospective employers in appropriate organisations. First draw up simulated letters and forms of application, CVs and particulars of appropriate posts and then role-play the three or four interviews, video-recording them if possible for later evaluation.

6 Find out what aspects are customarily included in the induction process of new employees (of trainee manager status) in a local firm. Report back to your group on your findings.

7 In pairs, check back over the list of typical personnel department documents and forms and then see how many blanks or specimens you can collect from your network of local contacts to distribute and display in your base-room.

8 Find out how industrial relations are handled in a private and public sector local organisation and report back to your group.

9 Arrange to interview the managers of a local Job Centre and Employment Bureau and then give an oral presentation on how they interact with personnel departments.

10 Assume that you work as the secretary of the board of trustees which is responsible for a series of sheltered home complexes. These homes are sold to retired people and are built in a kind of courtyard and comprise relatively small flats in a three storey building. Part of the attraction of such sheltered homes is that there is a qualified nurse/warden on duty (shift work is involved) who is on hand in case of need or emergency. Residents can call up the warden by pressing a button – one is located in each room of each flat.

First research this kind of provision in your locality to find out about conditions of service and the scope of a typical warden's job. Then use this information with that outlined above to:

a) Devise a suitable job specification for a warden to run a new sheltered home about to open in your locality.
(Note: three wardens will be appointed to work a 24-hour shift system).

b) Design a suitable job description for the post of the senior warden, who will report to the Board of Trustees.

c) Design a display job advertisement for your local weekly newspaper advertising the posts of the three wardens to work in a new sheltered home complex about to open.

Work experience and simulation assignments

1 Ask your supervisor to see if it can be arranged for you to look at some sample personnel/job specifications and job descriptions and to take copies for your file of typical examples.

2 Interview a senior member of your attachment organisation's personnel department and find out what the major roles of the department are and how

they are discharged. Brief your group orally on what you discover.

3 Find out how your organisation handles disciplinary and grievance procedures; draw up a flow-chart to explain the process.

4 With permission, arrange to collect a 'portfolio' of specimen personnel forms, standard letters and documents which your organisation currently uses.

5 Interview the personnel manager to find out how his or her department interacts with and services other departments.

6 Survey what staff development and training programmes are undertaken and brief your group in a short written account.

7 Find out how employment and industrial law impact today upon the work of your organisation's personnel department. Summarise your findings in an article entitled:

'Personnel services and legal requirements'

8 Find out how the organisation obtains the data for its personnel records and what sort of data is held on file or database. Ask how the Data Protection Act is involved here.

9 Ask your supervisor to help you obtain information on your organisation's policy and procedures for interviewing job applicants. Give an oral presentation to your group on what you discover.

10 Find out what social, welfare and sports facilities are available to staff and how these aspects relate to their working life and morale.

11 Ask a senior member of the personnel department to explain to you how they carry out manpower planning and ensure that the organisation is equipped to cope with people moving on or retiring, and how they respond to the needs of departments for people to fill newly developing jobs and roles. Write a short report for your group to receive – with, of course, your supervisor's permission.

Case study

Wanted! Trainee Sales Manager for EXCEL COMPUTERS LTD

The company

Excel Computers Limited manufactures, markets and retails an extensive range of computers and ancillary equipment, selling to both public and private industry.

Among its other duties, Excel's Sales Department provides an administrative and information service to its 75 sales representatives. The service helps them to perform effectively in what is a highly sophisticated market – both in terms of advanced product technology and the presentation of technical information.

Excel has established a policy of appointing each year, as trainee managers, a number of school and college leavers. They are provided with excellent in-service training opportunities, including day-release to higher education courses. In addition, their training programmes include experience periods in all departments before taking on specific departmental responsibilities.

The vacancy

Personnel Manager: 'I see young Sara Maxwell has just got the job she's been hoping for in Marketing. I suppose you'll be asking me to find her replacement!'
Sales Manager: 'You're absolutely right! I'll miss Sara, of course, but I suppose Sales' loss is Marketing's gain! At all events, we ought to press on directly with the selection process in order to beat the rush at the end of June. Good college-leavers are at a premium these days! I'd better revise the personnel specification and job descriptions straight away! The following was Sara's job description:

```
                         JOB DESCRIPTION

    TITLE:           TRAINEE SALES ADMINISTRATION MANAGER

    DEPARTMENT:      SALES DEPARTMENT

    HOURS OF WORK:   37½ hour week.  Flexible Working Hours:
                     Monday - Friday Core Time: 1000 - 1600

    RESPONSIBLE TO:  The Assistant Sales Manager

    RESPONSIBLE FOR: Designated junior clerical and secretarial staff.

    AUTHORITY OVER:  Designated junior clerical and secretarial staff.

    GENERAL DESCRIPTION

    To become proficient in performing duties related to sales administration, with particular
    regard to providing a supportive service to company sales representatives.  To undertake
    work delegated by senior Sales Department personnel.  To attend in-service training courses
    as required.  To direct the work of assigned junior clerical and secretarial staff as
    requested.

    DUTIES AND RESPONSIBILITIES

    1  To work within established company regulations and to support determined company
       policies.

    2  To develop sales managerial skills, with particular reference to: sales administration
       procedures, product knowledge, marketing activities and sales information systems.

    3  To assist in the provision of administration and information services provided to the
       company's sales representative force.

    4  To liaise with Marketing Department in communicating sales promotion and advertising
       programmes to company sales representatives.

    5  To deal with arising correspondence, memoranda, reports, meetings, documentation etc.

    6  To assist the Assistant Sales Manager generally, or any other senior Sales Department
       staff as directed by the Assistant Sales Manager.

    7  To assist as required with the data processing of sales documentation and sales
       statistics.

    8  To supervise the work of junior staff members as required.

    9  To attend courses of training as required.
```

EXCEL COMPUTERS LIMITED

ORGANISATIONAL INFORMATION

HEAD OFFICE: Excel House, Guildford Road, Kingston-upon-Thames,
Surrey KT12 6GR
Telegrams: Excel, Kingston-upon-Thames
Telephone: Kingston 88000
Fax: 01-639 6848

FACTORIES: Bristol, Liverpool, Leicester

RESEARCH AND
DEVELOPMENT: Excel Laboratories, Harlow New Town

Training
Headquarters: Moorbridge Manor, Dorchester, Dorset

PERSONNEL: 16,479 Head Office: 643

DEPARTMENTS: Research and Development, Production, Marketing, Sales, Accounts, Office Administration, Personnel, Distribution and Transport, Training, Communication Services

CONDITIONS OF SERVICE (Head Office Staff)

The company's head office operates a flexible working hours system; staff work in accordance with a job appraisal scheme - all jobs are graded and promotion/remuneration is based upon performance assessed at regular intervals.
Company subsidised meals are available in the staff restaurant. Sports and social club facilities are well catered for in the company's leisure complex adjoining head office premises.
Paid Leave: junior - training management grades: 3 weeks per annum plus usual bank holidays.
Company house mortgage loans available at preferential terms.

CAREER OPPORTUNITIES:

The company's employees are encouraged to develop a knowledge of company activities as a whole and opportunities exist for careers to progress via a number of departments. The company promotes from within whenever possible.

TRAINING:

Excel Computers Limited maintains an ideally situated Training Centre at Moorbridge Manor, Dorchester. Residential courses form a central part of management development.
Applications to attend day-release higher education courses are reviewed by a standing review committee.

SALARIES

Management salaries are reviewed annually and paid monthly in arrears. Each management post follows an incremental scale, and annual increases are zoned within defined upper and lower limits according to performance.
Example: Trainee Manager Grade 6
        Entering salary: £12,500 p.a.
        First increment: £750-1500 p.a.
        Second increment: £900-1700 p.a.
All incremental scales are reviewed annually.

SALES INFORMATION

Total sales turnover last year exceeded £420 million. A new national LAN/WAN system was introduced recently. Business Computer Systems sales rose by 19% last year. Major customers included the Bestbuy Supermarket chain, Sentinel Insurance Limited, Vesco Automotive Products Limited and Harridges Stores.

FUTURE DEVELOPMENTS:

In March of this year, Sir Peter Henryson, Chairman, announced that Excel was strengthening its EEC exporting position: 'The time has come for Excel, secure in its very firm UK market, to go on to the export offensive. We have the people, the products, the marketing and the sales expertise. We intend to "excel" in a number of European and transatlantic markets. Our plans are well advanced. You are all familiar with the advertisements placed in the national press reporting the recent Annual General Meeting. Well, I strongly recommend you to "Watch This Space!"'

Assignments

1 Compose a personnel specification for the Excel Trainee Sales Administration Manager post, shortly to be advertised.

2 Devise an application form suitable for use in Excel's appointment of the Trainee Sales Administration Manager.

3 Draft an information sheet suitable for sending to candidates who have applied for the Trainee Sales Administration Manager post, outlining the scope of the job and the main features of Excel's business and organisation.

4 Design a display advertisement for the Trainee Manager post and devise an advertising strategy based on your own locality, identifying which newspapers and other media you would use to advertise the post.

5 Make a checklist of questions as follows:

a) questions which Excel interviewers would wish to ask applicants for the Trainee Manager post
b) questions which applicants would wish to ask Excel interviewers

6 Complete the application form devised in 2 above as an applicant for the post. Compose an appropriate curriculum vitae. Write a suitable letter of application to:

The Personnel Manager,
Excel Computers Limited,
Excel House,
Guildford Road,
KINGSTON-UPON-THAMES
Surrey
KT12 6GR

7 Set up Excel interviewing panels to evaluate applications received from members of the group. Discuss constructively the strengths and weaknesses of applications.

8 Simulate the interviews for the post of Trainee Sales Administration Manager. Group members should role-play the Excel panel, comprising: the Personnel Manager, the Sales Manager and the Assistant Sales Manager. Other members of the group should role-play successive applicants. Panel interviewers should have time to study applicants' letters and forms. Applicants should also digest the information in the information sheet devised in 3. Observer-role group members should assess the performances of interviewers and interviewees. Simulations may be tape- or video-recorded for subsequent evaluation.

Interview simulation

Assistant required for office administration manager . . .

The simulation is designed to involve the whole group. The interviewing panel may comprise up to three members. Authentic roles would be: managing director, personnel manager, office administration manager. Three candidate profiles are outlined below, but more candidate roles may be devised to provide a larger short-list if required. Other members of the group should be divided into two sections – observers of the interviewers and observers of the interviewees. They should meet to decide upon what they will assess and design a check-list to note performances. Each group of observers should report its assessments after the interview simulations have taken place. Interviewers and interviewees should then be asked for their reactions and impressions.

The situation

A post has recently been advertised for an assistant to the Office Administration Manager of Persona Employment Bureau Ltd. The company has 30 branches throughout the country placing secretarial, clerical and junior management personnel both in full-time and temporary positions.

The job

The duties of the assistant will mainly involve relieving the Office Administration Manager of some of his work-load. Specifically the post will include:

responsibility for the company's stationery supplies, maintenance of existing administration processes, management of computerised records systems, drafting of correspondence, memoranda, reports, composing advertisements, taking part in meetings, telephone reception. Commercial experience is not essential as training will be given. Text and data processing experience would be advantageous.

	Candidate A	Candidate B	Candidate C
Age:	18	27	38
Status:	Single	Married (no children)	Divorced (boy 15, girl 10)
Education:	Park View Comprehensive and West Park College of Further Education	Westerham Grammar School	Hightown College and Cumbria University (left after one year to get married)
Qualifications:	4 GCSEs BTEC National Award in Business and Finance Studies; including Secretarial Services option	6 'O'-levels 2 'A'-levels Shorthand/Typewriting speeds: 90/40 WP short course	5 'O'-levels 3 'A'-levels Read English at University in first year
Commercial:	Part-time Holiday Jobs One job as 'Temp' in busy office	4 years in local tax office 2 years as cabin crew member in airline: grounded with blood-pressure: later joined engineering company – made redundant	Housewife until 25 divorced at 30 succession of part-time jobs; refresher office update cours at local College just completed
Physical Appearance Interests, Circumstances:	Candidates should decide upon these factors and play a role. For example, hesitant or assured, social or solitary, flat renter or mortgagee etc.		

Note for candidates

Use the above information to provide the basic framework for your 'personality', background and career. Ensure that you have prepared your ground sufficiently.

Note for observers

Every observer should have a full brief of each candidate's background, including any 'skeletons in cupboards' deliberately 'planted' by candidates for interviewers to discover!

Role-play simulations

1 A long-service storeman in your manufacturing organisation is steadfastly refusing to implement a new set of company policies on using a recently installed computerised stock-control system which he sees as 'a waste of time – nothing wrong with our existing set up!'

As personnel manager and storeman, role-play an initial disciplinary meeting

2 Your company is 'top-heavy' with aging personnel. You have therefore – as its personnel manager – the task of addressing a group of 15 employees in the 55-plus age group on the merits of your firm's early retirement package, in order to encourage some uptake.

Research retirement and pensions and then deliver a suitable talk to your 'aging' class group!

3 Your organisation has been making some costly mistakes in employing 'round pegs in square holes' and low performers recently. As its personnel manager, you have been asked to hold a meeting with the departmental managers who do much of the interviewing in order to emphasise what steps they must take to maximise their chances of 'hiring the right person for the job.'

First prepare your ground, then simulate the meeting in which you deliver your corrective presentation. Be ready for some hard-hitting answers – your own department has not been perfect either recently!

In a post-role-play wash-up, discuss generally the difficulties which surround the interview process and how they may be minimised by sound selection techniques.

Integrated assignments

Case study

The Midstead Chronicle

Gartholme – Sir Christopher condemns the 'cosy conservationists'

The controversial industrial development project centred at Gartholme Meadows on the western approaches to Midstead last night had a noisy public airing.

As this newspaper last week predicted, the Town Hall was packed to capacity for a public meeting chaired by Lord Forderdale. Over 450 local residents arrived anxious to listen to both sides of the argument over the proposed building of an industrial estate on Gartholme Meadows.

Ardent conservationists have been locked in combat with local businessmen during the past three months. The nub of the controversy – which has divided local families – centres upon the proposed demolition of Garth Cottage, which dates back to the 17th century, and the adjacent blacksmith's forge, last used in 1948.

Hard-hitting speech

Development plans also include the construction of

a bypass running south and west of Midstead, passing through Denholme Park, a favourite Sunday strolling spot for local residents. Denholme Park was formerly the home of the dukes of Midshire.

One of last night's principal speakers was Sir Christopher Crawshaw, local businessman and chairman of the Gartholme Development Consortium. He concluded a hard-hitting and controversial speech with these words:

'And so, ladies and gentlemen, I would put the following alternatives to you. The conservationists may win. A single period cottage may remain as a silent reminder of the blinkered forces of reaction and stagnation. The six hundred unemployed people in this town may feel reassured, as they continue to search for non-existent jobs, that the honeysuckle still entwines Garth Cottage, and that the disused blacksmith's forge remains preserved for a car-owning posterity. It may be that the backward-looking forces of the cosy conservationists may triumph.'

Employment for all

'Alternatively, the proposed industrial estate at Gartholme Meadows may receive planning permission, in which case, Midstead will once again enjoy full employment and the exciting prospect of affluence and expansion. The proposed tannery alone will employ at least fifty people. Moreover, the access route to the Estate, running off the bypass in Denholme Park will relieve congestion around the Market Cross in the town centre. The entire construction of this much-needed bypass will only affect a very few old, decaying properties. The industrial estate and bypass will supply a very much needed 'shot in the arm' for Midstead, which every sensible resident will agree is at present suffering from a severe shortage of jobs and a hardening of its road arteries!

Noisy heckling

'What Midstead needs, then, is not some form of "mothballing" to preserve a few unremarkable examples of an indifferent architectural heritage, but the provision of industrial and communication amenities which will give local working people and their children the means of securing a happy and prosperous future!'

Sir Christopher's speech was punctuated with noisy heckling and has certainly added more fuel to the fire of controversy raging over Gartholme Meadows. Next week's council elections will give Midstead voters a chance to have *their* say and to tell the Town Hall in no uncertain terms what *they* want!

Main assignments

1 In groups, study the extract of Sir Christopher's speech and discuss its potential effectiveness upon the Midstead audience. Your examination of the extract should pay particular attention to:

a) appeals to the audience's emotions,
b) tricks of public address rhetoric,
c) examples of 'loaded' vocabulary,
d) the overall tone of the speech.

Discuss your findings in a general group session.

2 Draft the opposing main speech given by Miss Penelope Carstairs, President of the Midstead Conservation Society after Sir Christopher had spoken.

Simulate the Midstead Public Meeting, starting at the stage where Sir Christopher has spoken, and Miss Carstairs delivers her opposing speech. Group students should prepare questions to ask 'from the floor' to a panel comprising: Lord Forderdale (chairman), Sir Christopher Crawshaw, Miss Penelope Carstairs and Mr F Shaw, District Surveyor

3 Successive students should record a version of Miss Carstairs' speech either on video or audio-

tape for the general group to assess in the context of influencing the Midstead audience.

4 Either as a supporter of Sir Christopher or Miss Carstairs, write a letter to: The Editor, *The Midstead Chronicle*, 6 St Peter's Road, Midstead, Midshire MS14 3PR. Your letter should aim to reinforce the developers' or conservationists' viewpoint and you should bear in mind that, if printed, your letter will appear in the edition of the newspaper which is sold on the day before the local elections.

5 As a retired householder living in one of the 'old, decaying properties' referred to by Sir Christopher, write a letter to *The Midstead Chronicle* expressing *your* views on the proposed development scheme.

6 As Mr Fred Parker, independent candidate in the forthcoming council elections, write a letter to *The Midstead Chronicle* outlining your own position on the Gartholme Meadows project.

7 Form groups, each one representing the committee of the Midstead Conservation Society. In an effort to influence matters in the run-up to the local council elections, you have decided to produce a leaflet for distribution to all local residents, putting the conservationist viewpoint as forcefully as possible. Design a suitable leaflet and then compare it with those produced by other groups in a general group session.

8 Assume that the local council election has been held and that councillors sympathetic to the development of Gartholme Meadows have won the day. As editor of *The Midstead Chronicle*, draft an editorial commenting on the effect of the elections upon the development plans. Research editorials in your own local weekly papers before attempting this assignment. Compare the use of language of your editorial with that of other versions in your group.

Talking points

1 Discuss the following topics in a general group session:

One of the benefits of our local government democracy is the freedom given to local interest and pressure groups to put forward their opinions in the forum of local debate.

2 How can local media resources help to publicise the views of public pressure groups? How may they be used to best effect?

3 How effective are public meetings in influencing local politics?

Case study

The Harris Case

On Tuesday 1st February 199-, Jack Harris, a machine operator at Advance Engineering Company Limited, was summarily dismissed. . . .

'D' Machines — Extract of company regulations

Extract from the Company Regulations of Advance Engineering Company Limited:

VI SAFETY PROCEDURES

. . .3 <u>Operation of Classified Machinery</u>

Certain production processes (specified below) are effected by machines having a 'D' (Danger) classification. <u>Under no circumstances</u> may such machines be left unattended by operatives while assembly-line work is in progress.

(a) Relief Summoning Procedures

Operatives working 'D' classified machines are required to summon a relief operator before leaving the machine <u>for any reason</u> while work is in progress.

(b) <u>Summary Dismissal</u>

In view of the danger to personnel working in the vicinity of 'D' classified machines, operatives who leave them negligently unattended render themselves liable to summary dismissal.

Revised: 1st January 199—

'Try not to worry . . .'

An extract from a conversation which took place in the surgery of Jack Harris's family doctor on Wednesday 19th January 199-:

Doctor Grant:
'Well, Mr Harris, I think I'd better put you on a course of anti-depressants. I don't think you need to stay at home — especially while your wife is in hospital — but you must take things steadily. The pills I am prescribing will help you to do just that. And don't worry about Mrs Harris — she's going to be all right. . . .'

Jack Harris:
'Thank you, Doctor, I'm very grateful. It's been a worrying time ever since the wife was taken ill. Still, they told me this morning she could be out of the intensive care unit in a few days' time, if all goes well. . . .'

'Give us a break!'

An extract from a conversation between Alec Baker, Supervisor, and Jack Harris in the works staff restroom, Tuesday 1st February 19-- at 15.35 hours:

Alec Baker:
'Right, Harris, you've had it this time! This time I'm going to have to report you to Mr Watkins! You'd better put that fag out and come with me to his office — straightaway!'

Jack Harris:
'Aw, give us a break, Mr Baker, I've only just. . . . You see, I've had a lot. . . . Well, I've not been. . . .'

Alec Baker:
'Save it for Mr Watkins! Come on. It's not as if you haven't been warned about leaving a 'D' classified machine unattended. The line was clearly working when I spotted you missing! Total disregard for your workmates — that's what beats me!'

Summary dismissal

Mr Watkins' reaction on hearing of the incident from Alec Baker in the Works Manager's Office. Tuesday 1st February 19-- at 1555 hours:

'Found smoking you say. In the restroom. Well, it all seems pretty clear-cut to me! Left his 'D' machine unattended and the line in progress when you spotted his absence. You'd think they'd have more sense! Especially after my recent reminder. You'd better wheel him in, Mr Baker! . . .'

The EWA steps in

Extract of a conversation between Jack Harris and Vic Cooper, Convenor of the Engineering Workers' Association at Advance Engineering, Tuesday 1st February 19-- at 1635 hours:

Jack Harris:
'He never gave me a chance, Vic, nor did Watkins! I dunno, I just came over sort of shaky. There was

a stoppage further up the line, so I thought I'd just have a quick sit-down in the restroom. I never meant to be away more than a minute or two. . .'

'D' Machines – Notice to all works personnel

Notice to all Advance Engineering Works Personnel posted on general works noticeboard 24th January 0900 hours (see below).

MEMORANDUM

To: ALL WORKS PERSONNEL   Ref: JK/RG HSAW 24

From: WORKS MANAGER'S OFFICE   Date: 24 January 199—

OPERATION OF 'D' CLASSIFIED
MACHINES

All Works Personnel are reminded of Section VI, Para 3, Sub-sections (a) and (b) of the revised Company Regulations issued earlier this month.

Recently, instances have occurred when 'D' classified machines have been left unattended. Such acts of negligence on the part of machine operative staff could well lead to serious injury or even fatality.

All works personnel are therefore reminded that failure to comply with the above regulations will render them liable to summary dismissal.

JK Watkins

J. K. Watkins
Works Manager

Vic Cooper:
'Absent only a minute or two you say. Line stopped – again! Didn't you tell 'em you weren't feeling well? Anyway, anyone can see you're not right – not by a long chalk. Didn't give you a chance? Jack, you should have spoken up! Well, I think it's a clear case of victimisation! You'd best go home now. Charlie'll go with you. But don't you worry, you'll keep your job – or my name's not Vic Cooper! Now, I've got some telephoning to do to District Office! . . .'

'. . . on the grounds of unfair dismissal . . .'

Conversation between John Watkins, Works Manager, and Dennis Brooke, Managing Director of Advance Engineering in his office, Friday 4th February 19-- at 1015 hours:

John Watkins:
'Bad business. Not made any easier by Peter Taylor's absence (Advance's Personnel Manager, absent since Christmas because of illness). We could have done with his expertise. Of course, we had to take a firm line. If company regulations are seen to be openly flouted. . . . Open and shut case I'd say.'

Dennis Brooke:
'I'm not so sure. I know things have been too lax in the Works, but by all accounts. Jack Harris was regarded as being conscientious. I hope we haven't acted hastily over this. . . . I've a letter here from the EWA informing me of their intention to advise Mr Harris to take his case to the Industrial Tribunal and to claim unfair dismissal.
According to them, Harris was unwell at the time of the incident. Your "open and shut case" had better be as good as you think it is!'

Prior to the Industrial Tribunal's hearing, the EWA secured a written statement from Jack Harris's doctor, to the effect that Jack had been prescribed medication to alleviate anxiety caused by his wife's ill-health.

Assignments

Preliminary assignments

1 Research the following Acts of Parliament from the point of view of dismissal:

a) Trade Union and Labour Relations Act 1974
b) Employment Protection Acts 1975 and 1978 (Section 54)

c) Health and Safety at Work Act 1974, Sections 7 and 8.

d) Employment Acts 1980, 1982

2 Find out about current practices regarding industrial grievance and dismissal procedures. Give an oral report of your findings to the group.

3 Find out about the role of a works committee in a large, manufacturing company.

4 Find out how an Industrial Tribunal works, and how cases of unfair dismissal are heard and adjudicated.

5 By arrangement, visit a factory in your locality to see production processes in action. Talk to the management and works staff about potential dangers and the measures taken to prevent accidents.

Either: Write a report on your findings

Or: Give an oral account of your visit to your group.

Main assignments

1 In groups, study, from both the management and trade union point of view, the background and events leading to Jack Harris's summary dismissal. Consider, also, the dismissal from Jack Harris's personal point of view. Make notes of your conclusions for a general group discussion.

2 Form groups to represent:

a) the management of Advance Engineering
b) the District Officers and Advance shop stewards of the EWA.

Assuming that Jack Harris's case is shortly to be heard by an Industrial Tribunal, prepare either the management or the trade union case to put to the hearing. Base your case on the information given and on any additional relevant information you research.

3 Simulate the Industrial Tribunal hearing. Students should prepare to role-play the various participants. Note that the tribunal panel comprises three members and that its chairman will be qualified in law. Organisations or individuals appearing may be legally represented and advised by appropriate associations. Participants in the simulation should include:

a) the Industrial Tribunal Panel
b) representatives for Advance Engineering
c) representatives for the Engineering Workers' Association
d) Jack Harris
e) witnesses.

Other students should assume observer roles to evaluate the effectiveness of presentation of cases and judgements by the participants. The simulation should subsequently be evaluated by the general group, when observers should present their opinions.

4 Assume that you are chairman of the Industrial Tribunal. 'Write a summary of your Tribunal's findings and its judgement. Base your summary upon the evidence given in the simulation role-play in 3.

5 Design a poster for display in a factory working area emphasising the need for safety consciousness and the possible consequences of carelessness.

6 Study carefully the wording of the notice to all works personnel written by John Watkins and consider any shortcomings it might embody. Re-write the notice in a style you think would be more effective in the situation.

7 Role-play the interview between Jack Harris and the District Officer of the EWA prior to the tribunal hearing.

8 Role-play the interview between Alec Baker and John Watkins before Jack Harris is brought in.

9 Write Alec Baker's report, which John Watkins has requested, of the incident involving Jack Harris.

Follow-up assignments

1 Write an essay entitled:

Current dismissal procedures and their implications for industrial managers and trade unionists.

2 Discuss the following topics in a general group session:

a) What are the likely effects of poor communication on the shop floor.
b) Could 'The Harris Case' have been avoided? If so, how?
c) Assuming that the Industrial Tribunal recommended Jack Harris's reinstatement, what problems might ensue?

3 Write an article for the Engineering Workers' Association journal entitled:

'Unfair Dismissal – How to Prepare for an Industrial Tribunal Hearing'

4 Write an article for the Society of Works Managers' quarterly journal entitled:

'Grounds for Summary Dismissal'

Case study

Flair Heating (Nottingham) Limited

The success of Flair Heating (Nottingham) Limited really stemmed from a decision to diversify the range of its products. The company had for many years concentrated on manufacturing industrial gas-burning heating appliances used in factorles, armed forces workshops with hangars and various construction sites. The advent of North Sea gas had been accompanied by an increase in demand for gas-burning appliances both in the home and in the growing leisure industry of camping and caravanning. Consequently, Flair Heating set out to design and manufacture a range of gas-fires, heaters, lamps and other gas-burning appliances to meet this demand – a demand which had benefited both the employees and shareholders of Flair Heating alike.

Recently, Flair Heating, upon the advice of the Financial Director, introduced Value Added into its accounting procedures. One of the newer accounting concepts, Value Added indicates how the difference between sales and *direct costs* (other than wages) is shared out among the various interested parties, as the following table shows:

Flair Heating (Nottingham) Limited Statement of value added

	This Year £ million	Last Year £ million
Sales	877	700
less cost of materials and services	417	300
Value Added	460	400
Disbursed as follows:		
To employees	358	312
To Government (taxation)	32	30
To providers of loans	12	10
To shareholders	18	15
And retained in the business:		
As depreciation/replacements	20	18
As reserves	20	15
	460	400

Abridged Profit and Loss Account for this year and last year

	This Year £ million	Last Year £ million
Turnover	877	700
Surplus from trading	82	70
Interest paid	12	10
Profit before tax	70	60
Taxation	32	30
Profit after tax – attributable to shareholders	38	30
Dividends paid or recommended		
Preference	1	1
Ordinary – interim paid (3.122p)	6	5
proposed final (5.8923p)	11	9
Transfer to reserve	20	15
Capital employed financed by:	£ million	£ million
Shareholders' funds	330	270
Debentures	110	90
	440	360

How the £460 million value added was allocated this year:

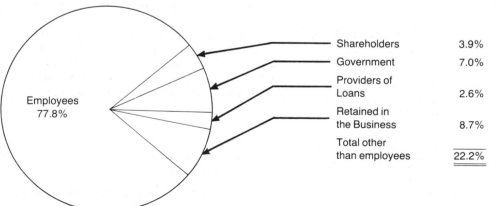

Employees	77.8%
Shareholders	3.9%
Government	7.0%
Providers of Loans	2.6%
Retained in the Business	8.7%
Total other than employees	22.2%

Flair Heating (Nottingham) Limited: the annual general meeting

At this year's Annual General Meeting, Captain Richard Kirkwright, Flair's newly appointed Chairman, made reference, not only to the large increase in turnover and the increased number of personnel employed, coupled with improved investment, but also to the increase in profit before tax of 16.7% and the substantial payments made in dividends and wages.

As he sat down, he privately congratulated himself on having delivered a particularly fine speech. He was consequently somewhat taken aback when addressed by a shareholder from the back of the hall:

'Mr Chairman, in spite of your glowing report of the past year's activities, would you mind explaining to me why the profitability of the company has fallen? According to my calculations, based on the Published Profit and Loss Account sent to me before this meeting, the company's profitability seems to have fallen by almost one per cent!'

During the commotion which followed the delivery of this 'bombshell', Dr Grimshaw, Flair Heating's Finance Director, managed to pass a note to the Chairman (to save his embarrassment) which contained several important facts.

Summoning the meeting to order, Captain Kirkwright rose, composed himself, and delivered the new facts to the complete satisfaction of all present.

After the annual general meeting

After the AGM a top management meeting was called at Flair's Head Office to investigate the causes of the fall in profitability. Although Dr Grimshaw's accounting information was correct, the Board of Directors had indicated that they were not satisfied, especially since the Annual General Meeting had been given some unwelcome publicity in the financial press.

The following points emerged:

1 There had been a rise in absenteeism and a fall in voluntary overtime.

2 The number of industrial accidents, although of a minor nature, had risen from 20 last year to 60 this year and particularly involved the much-used new welding equipment.

3 The Works Manager complained that there had been frequent delays in receiving materials, as well as technical information about newer products.

4 The Cost Control Manager reported that, due to a shortage of staff, Variance Analysis reports* had been subject to considerable delay and the reports which had been completed showed an increasing proportion of Adverse Material variances.

Assignments

Preliminary assignments

1 Find out how companies conduct the business of their Annual General Meetings. Report your findings orally to your group.

2 Research the usefulness of employing the Value Added accounting approach. Make notes of your findings to distribute to your group.

(*Note: A Variance Analysis Report indicates the difference between forecast costs and actual costs incurred.)

Main assignments

1 Flair Heating publishes a monthly house magazine, *Flair-Up* which is given to all company employees throughout the country.

Write a short article for inclusion in next month's issue to explain the usefulness of a Value Added Statement and include a pie-chart to illustrate Flair Heating's figures for last year.

As your article will be read by non-accountants, you should take care to ensure that its language is appropriately clear and simple.

2 Having studied carefully the accounting information reproduced in the case study, draft the note which you think Dr Grimshaw would have passed to Captain Kirkwright.

Compare your draft with those produced by the rest of your group, and discuss what information the note ought to convey.

3 Discuss the items referred to in the Chairman's report and the probable contents of Dr Grimshaw's note. Draft that part of the Chairman's Report which refers to the figures given and include the calculation of relevant ratios, stressing those omitted originally and making comparison with last year's figures.

4 In groups, discuss the possible underlying reasons for deficiencies recorded in the four points which emerged from the top management meeting.

Compare your findings in a general group session.

5 Assume that Flair Heating's Managing Director is anxious to get to the root of the problems which came to light after the AGM and that he has asked you to devise a questionnaire to be completed by departmental managers under the following headings:

1 Absenteeism
2 Accident rate
3 Material/information delays
4 Variance analysis reports

Provide suggested answers to the questionnaires.

6 Draft a questionnaire aimed at obtaining background information relevant to **5** above. It will be sent to Flair Heating's production workers. Bear in mind that their goodwill needs to be retained if your questionnaires are to be completed!

7 Compose a circular letter which will be sent to all production personnel to accompany the questionnaire in **6**. Your letter should explain the need for collecting the information and the use to which it will be put.

8 Assume that the Engineering Workers' Association Shop Stewards' Committee has been passed a copy of the questionnaire referred to in **6**. The Committee is concerned about the nature and intent of the questions and decides to hold a meeting to discuss the implications for their members.

Using a selected questionnaire, simulate the meeting.

9 Draft minutes of the meeting (see **8** above) to be sent to District Office.

Follow-up assignments

1 Collect a number of company Annual General Reports. (Extracts are frequently published in the national press and your library will be able to help). Analyse the type of information presented and the styles of English employed. Consider the reasons for the conclusions you draw.

2 Discuss the following topics in a general group session:

a) What factors are likely to inhibit a free exchange of information between management and workers in a large manufacturing company?
b) How important to large organisations are house magazines and journals?

Case study

Intercontel

Containerisation. An ugly word, but a streamlined concept for moving goods quickly and easily around the world's crowded roads and shipping lanes. The idea of transporting goods in sealed containers, from manufacturer to destination has aroused a good deal of controversy, yet the firms constructing the containers have somehow managed to avoid the headlines. Such a firm is Intercontel Containers Limited, based in Northampton. Intercontel's containers are used by all kinds of manufacturers and distributors both in the UK and overseas. Indeed, the initial export of containers had proved so successful for Intercontel, that the board of Directors was convinced of the advisability of expanding this area of Intercontel's sales.

Recently, for example, Intercontel received a substantial order from a company in Holland for the manufacture and delivery to Rotterdam of 200 of its 'Jumbo' containers. After securing this order, Mr Colin Cantell, Intercontel's chief salesman, visited other European industrial cities and ports and, having made contact with a number of potential customers, foresaw the enormous export potential for Intercontel containers. His subsequent report to the Managing Director, Mr David Taylor, included estimates of demand over the next three years from firms in West Germany, Holland, France, Belgium, Denmark and Spain. The projected estimates were, respectively, for next year: 1000, 300, 600, 400, 200 and 350.

Intercontel's Board soon realised that their manufacturing capacity at Northampton, already working at almost maximum levels of output, would not be able to cope with any significantly increased demand – especially when delivery dates would have to be guaranteed. Moreover, the Board felt that Intercontel would be at a cost disadvantage if containers destined for Europe had to be manufactured at a site, as far inland as Northampton especially with the prospect of the Eurotunnel being open by 1993.

Accordingly, a search was started for a suitable site for a new factory from which to mount an export drive into Europe. After careful enquiries, the most appropriate location appeared to be in Valengate, a small seaside town, only ten miles from Newhampton on the south east coast, a large industrial town with excellent port facilities and established shipping routes to a number of European ports, not to mention easy access to the Channel Tunnel.

Valengate

Valengate (population 32 000) had been a fashionable resort in Edwardian days, but a lack of investment in hotels and leisure facilities had caused a slow but sure decline in the town's tourist trade. For the past ten years it has increasingly become a favourite place for people to retire to. Valengate has some light industry – boat-building and electronic engineering – but is currently something of a business backwater.

Valengate: Distribution of Population

Ages	Number	Percentage Unemployed (16–65)
0–15	5 000	–
16–21	4 000	6
22–45	7 000	4
46–65	8 000	3
over 65	10 000	–

Many young people are currently leaving the district, to work in the more prosperous area of Dover. Some school-leavers are pursuing courses at Valengate College of Further Education, which has, among others, a competent Engineering Department, concentrating on marine engineering.

The map (*see* page 355) illustrates the physical characteristics of Valengate and indicates the two possible sites where Intercontel might be able to construct their new factory.

The sites: Park Rise and Valen Flats

On a fact-finding visit to Valengate, Mr Taylor was briefed on the two sites. Park Rise and Valen Flats by Mr Grimwade, of Grimwade and Shankley, Estate Agents:

'What I have termed "Site 1", the Park Rise site, lies at the, ah, "better" end of Valengate. It's a plot of rising ground, situated between the western end of town and Valen Park – a rather plush development, the sort of place where your senior managers might wish to reside. As a matter of fact, we have some very desirable properties on our books right now . . . But where was I? Well, land values to the west *are* rather more expensive, but the site is handy for the inner distribution road, lying between it and the B3534, which runs round Valen Head to Sunnydays Holiday Camp – about the only real tourist attraction left in Valengate of any consequence, I'm sad to say. Then there's the railway line to the north – runs across to Westquay, but it's not much used – probably only a matter of time before some Whitehall bureaucrat gets his axe into it! . . . Valengate Bus Company provides quite a good service up to Valen Park – shopping and schoolchildren, the usual sort of thing. There's just one, ah, consideration . . . the Park Rise site is, what shall I say . . . rather prominent, overlooking the town as it does. The Council might think your buildings would be a little "obvious", if you see what I mean. Still, with the development situation being what it is, I don't suppose they'd be too fussy . . .

'Now, "Site 2", Valen Flats, lies at the other end of town, or rather somewhat beyond it, just west of the river Valen, and on the other side of the gasworks. The land is flat – lowish really – but I'm reliably informed that there'd be no problems a good construction engineer couldn't sort out. And of course, there's almost twice the acreage. Unlike Site 1, which is privately owned, Site 2 currently belongs to the Council. At one time, when it looked as though Valengate might expand, there were plans to site a new, ah, sewage farm there . . . but that came to nothing. . . . In my estimation, the land might well be obtained at a cheaper price per acre than that of Site 1.

'In the last analysis, it's really up to *you*. Each site has its pros and cons, and you know the needs of your business better than I do, I feel sure. Perhaps the best next step would be to seek outline planning permission in respect of both sites, while you consider each in more detail.'

Mr Taylor thought that Mr Grimshaw's advice seemed sound and instructions were issued by Intercontel for the planning applications to be made.

The sequence of events

1 The notices of application duly appeared in the *Valengate Gazette* and the *Newhampton Times* carried a story at the same time about the interest Intercontel was showing in the area. The report was generally favourable and the venture was seen as a potential injection of new industrial life into Valengate. A further article, based upon an Intercontel press-release, revealed that the factory anticipated employing some 50 skilled and 250 semi-skilled workers (with job-training provided if required). In addition there would be about 20 administrative staff.

2 The majority of the Valengate District Councillors were in favour of Intercontel moving into the area – especially those with wards on the eastern side of Valengate. Some, however, expressed reservations about the siting of the proposed factory.

3 The application notices were read by Major James Hammersley (Ret'd), Chairman of the Valen Park Residents' Association, who snorted his disapproval over breakfast to Mrs Hammersley, and decided to call a meeting of the Residents' Committee without delay. The outcome of the meeting was a letter, written to the Chairman of the District Council, making strenuous objections to the proposed building of a factory on Park Rise (Site 1). It complained about the locally reported favourable responses made by councillors before any public meeting had been called to allow residents to voice their own opinions. The letter also drew attention to possible pollution problems and the likely noise levels which might continue by day and by night. In addition, the letter alluded to the probability of traffic congestion, especially during the summer months.

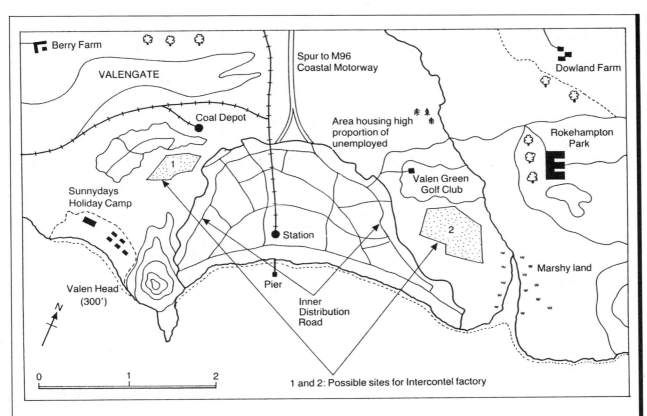

1 and 2: Possible sites for Intercontel factory

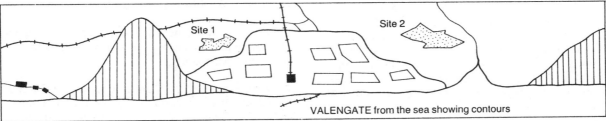

VALENGATE from the sea showing contours

4 At the next District Council meeting, it was decided to call a public meeting in Valengate Town Hall in three weeks' time at 7.30 p.m. on Friday 17th April. The Chairman was asked to arrange for suitable speakers to be invited. There was little doubt that the forthcoming public meeting would be well-attended, since public opinion in Valengate was sharply divided and in many of the town's public houses, the social, commercial and (local) political implications of Intercontel's proposals were being hotly debated.

Assignments

Preliminary assignments

1 Find out how planning applications are made to construct industrial premises on urban land. report your findings orally to your group.

2 Find out what legislation exists to protect inhabitants and surroundings from pollution of the environment. Compose a hand-out of your findings for distribution to your group.

3 Find out what 'action groups' exist in your locality to protect sectional and local interests. Make a checklist of the scope of their activities aimed at influencing public opinion.

Main assignments

1 Design a bar chart to display the information of the Valengate Distribution of Population table. Discuss the advantages and disadvantages of presenting the information either in table or bar chart form and in what circumstances you would opt for the one or the other format.

2 Draft Mr Cantell's report for Mr Taylor. It should be based on the figures given, which project an increase in container exports to the European countries specified of approximately 25% per annum for the next three years. Your report's statistics should be set out in tabular and graph formats.

3 Compose one of the notices publishing the outline planning application for Park Rise (Site 1) or Valen Flats (Site 2). Consult your local weekly paper before attempting this assignment.

4 Compose the letter which was sent by the Valen Park Residents' Association to the Chairman, Mr Richard Jackson, of the Valengate District Council.

5 Draft the notice of the forthcoming public meeting:

a) as it would appear in the *Valengate Gazette*
b) as a poster for display in Valengate libraries, on public billboards and in municipal offices.

6 Either individually or in groups, consider carefully the potential advantages and disadvantages to Intercontel of Sites 1 and 2. Draft a report (which has been commissioned by Mr Taylor) for submission to Intercontel's Board of Directors. Examine the options in detail, relay the relevant information about both sites and make recommendations.

7 As the senior officer handling Intercontel's detailed planning application (either for Site 1 or Site 2), draft a confidential memorandum to your principal indicating your views and suggesting any special conditions which the Council may wish to impose.

8 Simulate the public meeting called for Friday 17th April. The meeting is to be chaired by Lord Rokehampton. Before embarking upon the simulation, decide who the main speakers are to be. Allow the role-playing students time to prepare their speeches. Local, sectional interests should also be represented with prepared questions from the floor.

9 As a reporter for the *Valengate Gazette* attending the public meeting, simulated in Assignment **8**, take down detailed notes of the main points and compose a report for the next edition.

10 Assuming that Intercontel have constructed a factory on one of the sites, design a display advertisement for insertion in the *Valengate Gazette* to recruit staff for the factory.

11 Study carefully the words of Mr Grimwade to Mr Taylor, outlining the nature of both sites. Consider his observations from the point of view of:

a) Salesmanship
b) Objectivity
c) Helpfulness
d) Clarity and comprehensiveness

Assume that Grimwade and Shankley have been retained as estate agents for both sites.

Talking points

Discuss the following topics in a general group session:

1 What public relations exercises might Intercontel undertake in the Valengate district to help them to succeed in establishing their proposed factory?

2 What are the economic advantages to Valengate of Intercontel building a new factory there? Are there any disadvantages?

3 What part could the Valengate College of Further Education, the Training Agency and the Training Enterprise Council (TEC) play in the development of Intercontel's operation in Valengate?

Index